Power, Politics and the People

Studies in British Imperialism
and Indian Nationalism

Power, Politics and the People

Studies in British Imperialism
and Indian Nationalism

Partha Sarathi Gupta

Anthem Press
London

Anthem Press is an imprint of
Wimbledon Publishing Company
PO Box 9779
London SW19 7QA

This edition first published by Wimbledon Publishing Company 2002

British Library Cataloguing in Publication Data
Data available
Library of Congress in Publication Data
A catalogue record has been applied for

ISBN
1 84331 066 X (hbk)
1 84331 067 8 (pbk)

1 3 5 7 9 10 8 6 4 2

Printed by Newton Printing Ltd, London, UK.   www.newtonprinting.com

CONTENTS

ABBREVIATIONS

AICC	All India Congress Committee
AITUC	All India Trade Union Congress
ANZAM	Defence Agreement Between Australia, New Zealand, Malaya and Britain
ANZUS	Security Agreement between Australia, New Zealand and the USA
ASRS	Amalgamated Society of Railway Servants
CA	Constituent Assembly
CAB	Cabinet Papers, PRO, London
CENTO	Central Treaty Organization
CIGS	Chief of Imperial General Staff
CM	Cabinet Minutes
CO	Colonial Office
CR	Commonwealth Relations
CRO	Commonwealth Relations Office
DO	Dominions Office
FO	Foreign Office
GOI	Government of India
IOL	India Office Library
IOR	India Office Records
ITUF	Indian Trade Union Federation
L/P andJ/O	Political Department, Transfer of Power Papers
NAI	National Archives of India
NATO	North Atlantic Treaty Organization
PREM	Prime Minister's Files, PRO

PRO	Public Records Office
PUS	Permanent Under-Secretary
SEATO	South East Asia Treaty Organization
UNCIP	United Nations Commission for India and Pakistan

INTRODUCTION

I saw Partha Sarathi Gupta for the first time in 1949. He was made to stand up on a bench in the assembly hall of the school in which both of us happened to be pupils. Partha was asked to stand up on the bench so that he could be seen by the junior students like myself who were not tall enough to take a good look at the headboy. The headboy had come first in the state of West Bengal in the final school examinations. It was Partha Sarathi, and not, say, Satyajit Ray or any other distinguished alumnus who was held up to us as the model student of our school. Despite this unfortunate introduction—being held up as a model student is not guaranteed to endear one to one's peers—we became friends later in life. He made it a habit to come first in all examinations and had just Left Presidency College in a halo of glory when I entered it.

It is not, however, because Partha Sarathi made it a habit to come first in examinations that he will be remembered. That would be to diminish his intellectual achievement. His research into the history of the trade union movement and the railway labour force in England, his writings on the Labour Party and the process of decolonisation, his most recent work documenting a phase of the nationalist movement, and above all his meticulous teaching at Delhi University, put him in the front rank, among the best in his profession. He made professional excellence itself, so to speak, an ideology. A refusal to be swayed by passing intellectual fashions, an unhurried and steady pursuit of authenticity in the sources, an unwavering gaze at both sides of debated issues to reach a balanced judgement—these appeared to be part of his habitual intellectual stance. These were also values which were embedded in his efforts to build resources in the university library, to promote research by his students, to keep the syllabi of studies and agenda of research updated.

But again, I ask myself, is it for professional excellence that he will be remembered? Perhaps, but not entirely. Consider the moral core of a life like his. He chose his profession at a time, the early 1960s, when it was far from being attractive to the worldly-wise. Staying with Indian students and the university he served was also a deliberate choice in the decades which saw a steady flow of job-seekers leaving here for greener pastures abroad. In a city where proximity to the seat of power influences intellectuals in a variety of ways, Partha Sarathi neither identified himself with the Establishment, nor pretended to be a radical. It was a rare instance of congruence of public attitudes and personal behaviour in the milieu of intellectuals who engaged in controversies by tacit collusion and revelled in attitudinisation. Partha Sarathi also eschewed those factions in the academic community which the hegemonised join for self-protection and the hegemons create for self-promotion. For this he had to pay a price. The price was isolation. It was isolation, to some extent incapacitating, from the groups which coalesce on the patron–client axis, and from those who abuse ideological platforms for the promotion of particular interest groups—a characteristic of the universities. At the same time, this self-imposed insulation (if you prefer that softer term) from the conduits of power in academic politics brought him an uncommon degree of respect. One could have expected this respect to be translated into concrete action: for example, a festschrift in his honour would have been appropriate, but it did not materialise. Recognition from his peers came late in life. But that in a sense was trivial, because what his life demands of us is not merely professional recognition but the recognition of the values which were inscribed in his life. I recall his favourite poet W.H. Auden:

'Of whom shall we speak? For every day they die
      among us, those who were doing us some good,
And knew it was never enough but
Hoped to improve a little by living

The essays selected for this volume represent the wide range of research interests displayed in Partha Sarathi Gupta's writings between 1966 and 1998. These are some of the research papers which have remained uncollected or are not easily accessible today. In putting them together there was a choice between two organising principles: one could arrange them chronologically according to the year of publication, or on thematic lines. The first plan would have the merit of indicating the evolution of the author's interest in and approach to issues in history. On the other hand, a thematic arrangement is more reader friendly and allows us to focus on the continuities in Gupta's thinking on specific research problems. Of these options I chose the second and thus the essays in this volume are organised into five sets of general themes or areas of research addressed by him. On the whole the principle followed has been to limit editorial intervention to the minimum. In a few instances some brief passages have been omitted from texts reproduced here (e.g., passages expressing thanks to organisers of conference and the like).

The first set of essays is on the historiography of imperialism and nationalism. Of these the first essay is the last major piece of writing by Gupta, his presidential address at the Indian History Congress in its 59th session in 1998. While his usual practice was to write heavily documented papers based on archival sources and deliberately limited in scope, this essay and the next (again a presidential address, as the president of one of the sections of the Indian History Congress in 1976), offer a survey of research trends and the changing conceptual framework in the study of imperialism and nationalism. The essay of 1976 was written soon after the publication of Gupta's monograph *Imperialism and the British Labour Movement, 1914–1964* (Macmillan, London, 1975), and marks a transition from the period in Gupta's professional life when his interest was centred on the issues addressed in his doctoral thesis, to another phase when his interests broadened to include decolonisation as a long-term and many-faceted process. This extension of his research interests ultimately led him towards enquiries into some aspects of the interface between imperialism and the nationalist movement. The first essay here reflects this aspect of Gupta's latest research; it was written soon after his perspicacious 'Introduction' to the massive three-volume collection of documents on the Indian nationalist movement in 1943 and 1944 (commissioned by the Indian Council of Historical Research [ICHR]). The distinctive mark of Gupta's scholarship is evident in the comparative analysis he makes, projecting the

European historical pattern—the subject he taught at his university for over three decades—along with the South Asian identity-formation process.

The third essay in this collection, written in 1978, is a very important one. Gupta takes into account the recent trend in historiography in England and North America, represented in the writing of J. Gallagher and R. Robinson (*Africa and the Victorians*, London, 1961), D. Landes, F.S. Hinsley, R. Hyam and G. Martin, O.J. Hale *et al.* and compares that with the theory of economic imperialism since Lenin. Gupta examines the characteristics of British imperialism at the turn of the century (1895–1914) in South Africa, Latin America, West Africa and the erstwhile Ottoman Empire and offers his judgement:

Many Western historians have argued that their researches into the archival records . . . have demolished the theory of economic imperialism; therefore to explain the remarkable expansion of the British empire in this period and the involvement of Britain in an European alliance network one needed hypotheses based on the quest for power as an independent variable, and not the needs of British capitalism. This view can be shown to be quite inadequate . . .

At the same time, he argues that the Leninist formulation on the connection between capitalism and empire building, hypothesising the supersession of 'old capitalism' and a disjuncture at the turn of the century, needed to be revised or interpreted flexibly to accommodate diversities in global patterns of imperialist expansion.

The second group of essays relates to the constitutional and political processes of decolonisation—his major interest in the last two decades of his life. The essays collected here under the title 'The End-game of the Empire' explore the operation of the federalisation scheme in India in the 1930s, the changing Indo-British economic relationship and the evolution of discriminating protectionism in tariff policy in 1916–39, the relatively autonomous operation of the legal system during and immediately after the Quit India Movement of 1942 and, finally, the policy thinking in the Labour Party regime in England during 1945–51 on imperial questions. (These essays were published in 1989, 1987, 1996 and 1983 respectively.) The special characteristic of these essays is the fact that Gupta brought to bear on Indian issues his very detailed knowledge of the relevant papers in archival depositories in England.

The third major theme in this collection is 'The Army in the Imperial System'. Warren Hastings knew what he was talking about when he said in 1772 that the sword which gave the British dominion must be the instrument of its preservation. Although this tone of *ultima ratio regum* was muffled in later times, except perhaps in regimental toasts, the army remained a vitally important imperial institution. Yet there was virtually no attention paid to the history of the army till recently—and Gupta was one of the historians who pioneered academic research in this area. The four essays printed here (written in 1982, 1987 and 1992) look at the army in relation to constitutional changes in India in 1919–39, the overall strategic perspective that influenced the transfer of power arrangements from 1939, and how the British perceived the Indian National Army poised as a potential threat during the Second World War; there follows an essay on India in the commonwealth defence system in the post-1947 decade. Gupta's interest in the history of the army led to a collection of essays edited by him.

Dr Gupta's first research output was in the area of British labour history; he was exceptional among Indian historians to work on British history at Oxford. His D. Phil. thesis was on the 'History of the Amalgamated Society of Railway Servants, 1871–1915' (unpublished, Oxford, 1960). At the time he was at Oxford, British labour history was a fast-developing field of research. Exciting things were happening in that area when he chose his research topic in 1956. Henry Pelling, Gupta's research supervisor, who was publishing essays on the history of the British Communist Party, published his comprehensive book on the subject in 1958. B.C. Roberts's magisterial survey of the history of the British Trade Union Congress, 1868–1922, was also published in 1958. Research under way included those of C. Tsuzuki, A.M. Macbriar and L.J. Macfarlane whose books came out in 1961, 1962 and 1966. These ongoing research efforts directly related to Gupta's topic of research but in a more general way studies in labour history were enriched beyond measure in the 1960s by the publication of E.P. Thompson's *The Making of the English Working Class* (1963), Eric J. Hobsbawm's *Labouring Men* (1964), and Asa Briggs's *Chartist Studies* (1967). Gupta's early research formed a part of this development and till the mid-1970s this was his chief preoccupation. His essay (1976) on Indian labour history first published in a festschrift for D.D. Kosambi, was a path-breaking attempt; its substantive research may be dated now, but the agenda of research in India pointed out by him is of historiographic interest. The next essay is a spin-off from his doctoral research and offers the reader a sample of the kind of detailed empirical study that went into the making of his thesis. The third, published in 1971, anticipated in part his 1975 monograph, *Imperialism and the British Labour Movement, 1914–1964*. This was acclaimed as a definitive work in reviews by V.G. Kiernan, A.J.P. Taylor, Lord Gordon-Walker and others. It is possible that some of those who acclaimed it were doing so for the wrong reasons. Many of them saw the book as a refutation of Lenin's critique of socialists of Western Europe as lackeys of imperialism who partook of crumbs from the table of capitalist imperialism. Today the book seems valuable for the way it reveals the complexity of interaction between material interests and ideological stances, the subtle process of negotiation between political elements which are simultaneously contestants and collaborators in the system. Be that as it may, the essay in this volume on the British Labour Party and the Indian Left in 1919–39 is an important and thoroughly documented extension of the work on British politics in that monograph, into the area of Indian history.

The last three essays grouped under the title 'Culture and the Raj' are on a theme to which Gupta returned time and again. He had a keen interest in all the audio-visual media. Radio enthusiasts are a rare species these days but, like many others of his generation, he was an avid listener. One outcome of this interest was his study entitled 'Radio and the Raj'. Besides, he was deeply interested in cinema and I recall that in 1970 in Oxford he kept my wife and me enthralled for hours, describing frame by frame films he had seen. His early interest in music finds expression in 'Music and Communalism in Bengal' (1996). The earliest of his writings reproduced here is 'The Quality of Life and Indian Scholarship', a lecture he gave in 1966 in Delhi. Here he attempts an evaluation of the institutional and human resource base of the Indian universities in the previous few decades—surprisingly, this was written at the beginning of his career. The more significant thing in this essay however is probably Partha Sarathi Gupta's perception of his own location in the intellectual scene in India in the 1960s.

* * *

Writers of an introduction to a collection of essays such as this often perform an act of redundancy in restating what the author has already said. While I have taken the liberty of organising the essays into connected thematic segments, I think it is best to allow Partha Sarathi Gupta to speak for himself. It may, however, be useful to try and locate these writings in their historiographic tradition and to capture, to the extent possible, the academic and intellectual environment in which they were produced.

When he was about seventeen years of age Partha Sarathi, an undergraduate in Presidency College in Calcutta, wrote a short piece for the students' magazine in which he talked about his perception of the world around him:

We are living in the middle of the twentieth century a time when the world is passing through a crisis. . . . Before our own eyes we have seen the devastating effects of modern warfare, the monstrous exploitation of people by alien rulers, the end results of racial discrimination, and last, but not least, the abysmal gap between rich and poor. In such a situation the intelligent and imaginative young man cannot but ask himself the question why this is so . . . he cannot help being deflected from the secluded life of a disinterested scholar—aloof and remote from all directions. But the conventional idea of a good student is that he should not concern himself with problems that are outside the syllabus prescribed by his tutors (a syllabus that is often antiquated and sometimes reactionary) and never ask embarrassing, impertinent questions that may threaten the basis of the status quo. Politics, above everything, is marked taboo. For the intelligent youth of today, therefore, this idea of being a good student is not attractive. His life is intimately bound up with the changing world around him and neutrality in the face of the great ideological clashes of today cannot be imagined.

These words reflect in some measure the intellectual ambience in Calcutta in the years immediately following independence, and, of course, young Partha's cast of mind. From the turmoil that echoes in those words of 1951 the transition to the cloisters of Queen's College, Oxford, in 1953 must have been a great change. When the time came for Partha Sarathi to choose his research topic in 1956 some of the concerns expressed in that essay he wrote in 1951 might have influenced him to choose labour history. It is not merely fortuitous that Partha Sarathi became the secretary of the Oxford University Socialist Club, and later a member of the Labour Party. British labour history was at that time a newly developing area and attracted some of the best minds in England. In the event, Partha Sarathi's D. Phil. thesis was narrowly focused—like most doctoral dissertations—upon railway workers' trade unionism. But in the next fifteen years he worked his way to the broader theme of the socialist strand in the labour movement in its interface with imperialism—the subject of his major monograph in 1975. An affiliation with the British empirical tradition, a certain distaste for historical work not based on sound documentation and archival evidence, and a comparative historical perspective juxtaposing European with Indian historical experience—these were some of his intellectual traits that he might have acquired in Oxford.

When Dr Gupta returned to India he found it easy to secure a position as Reader in the University of Burdwan in Bengal (1961). After a brief stint there he joined the University of Delhi as a Reader in Economic History at the Delhi School of Economics (1961–2) and in 1962 was appointed a Reader in the Department of History at Delhi University. After five years of teaching at the University he wrote in 1966: 'As long as there are not developed genuinely strong centres of learning by fighting whatever vested interests stand in the way, Indian intellectuals will include a few brilliant scholars, a large number of dilettantes and far too many charlatans'. From a man who was not given to talking in the shrill tone of polemicists, these were strong words. Why was he so sceptical of the academic environment?

In the first place, Gupta looked upon the vast expansion of university education in the 1960s as a curse in disguise. The expansion was on account of political pressures; whatever human resource planning might have gone into organising science and technology growth, in the humanities there was no planned expansion to meet identified needs. In addition to the metropolitan universities of earlier days, a great many universities were set up (or older institutions came to be recognised as universities) to satisfy the aspirations of the states. The old 'central' or federally funded universities—in Varanasi, Aligarh, Delhi and Santiniketan—began to feel a resource constraint, since the central government was continually under pressure from the states either to channellise part of the funds to state institutions or to set up in some privileged states new central universities. Gupta, at Delhi University, reflected upon this rapid expansion and particularly the consequent difficulty in recruiting academic staff worthy of being university teachers:

[The] rapid political changes after 1945 played havoc with the development of academic disciplines. Unplanned uncoordinated quantitative inflation of centres of higher education led to a general lowering of standards all round.

Public resources were dissipated. Salaries that could be paid to university faculty, despite upgradation in 1960, compared unfavourably with jobs in the administrative services where employment increased with the 'expansion of governmental functions'. Except for a few who were 'highly idealistic', many preferred job opportunities in the government or abroad; in the universities 'good men felt pushed into a corner'; the insistence on teachers acquiring doctoral degrees led to a qualitative decline in the standard of research. On the whole, Gupta felt, 'looking at the Indian academic standards and scholarly values today [that is, in 1966] we have to confess that to a large extent quality has been sacrificed to quantitative inflation and non-academic pressures'.

These were not opinions which were likely to make a man terribly popular in academic circles (including the 'Left' establishment), or in the political coteries among townsmen in New Delhi who decide the fate of gownsmen. Gupta paid a price in terms of access to power in the decision-making bodies or positions. He chaired the Department of History at Delhi University for two years (1978–80). But he held no other academic office though many academic honours came his way such as the UGC National Lecturership (1976), the Nuffield Foundation Fellowship in Oxford (1969–71), the Smuts Fellowship at Cambridge (1980–1) and, in the last year of his life, the presidentship of the Indian History Congress (1998). Despite a hemiplegic stroke in 1989 Gupta went on teaching with undiminished commitment and his research output since then included the S.G. Deuskar Lectures at the Centre for Studies in Social Sciences in Calcutta (1993) and the editorial work for the three volumes of documents on the nationalist movement in India in 1943–4 which he completed in 1993, and which was published by the ICHR in 1997. His devotion to teaching—in particular his ability to access sources, primary and secondary, from his formidable memory-bank—became legendary. However, he never had the opportunity to play the role of an institution-builder on a scale proportionate to his calibre, to work upon the agenda of building centres of excellence, to 'fight the vested interests'—the agenda he outlined in 1966 at the beginning of his professional career. Why this was so is one of those questions which merit attention if one seriously engages with the academic environment today.

* * *

Partha Sarathi Gupta, with his highly empirical bent of mind, rarely indulged in philosophical statements about writing history. But it is interesting to pose the question: what were his philosophical postulates in the study of history?

In the last major essay he wrote, reflecting on historiography, Dr Gupta stated a basic methodological position: 'In my historical investigations I prefer enquiry and generalizations based on empirical research rather than generalizations founded on metaphysical concepts, or the manipulation of a set of abstract organized concepts'. Thirty years earlier he had written admiringly of 'the standards of scrupulous analysis of evidence and objectivity' set by R.G. Bhandarkar and Sir Jadunath Sarkar; he also believed that 'the more rigorous aspects of the discipline of British historical scholarship . . . in the field of constitutional and administrative history' had not been sufficiently imbibed by Indian historians of modern India. In his own research Gupta rigorously cited evidence. His documentation in the monograph on the British Labour Party and the imperial question attracted effusively favourable comments from almost all reviewers. Likewise his essays on Indian themes were invariably based on thorough archival research. And he was critical of authors who failed the 'archives test'. For example, although his own research findings were no different from A.K. Bagchi's, he censured Bagchi for 'not delving into the archives'; having consulted a 'wider range of sources' Gupta eventually concluded his long essay with the observation that Bagchi's view 'though written without access to archival material, is substantially correct'. Or again, he went on occasion to the length of re-examining documents cited by another author to check whether that author's conclusions indeed tallied with the evidence. In course of another exercise, he went back to the subject of imperialism and the Labour government to revise his own earlier conclusions in the light of archival material released later; his own statements were not to remain unexamined if they 'lacked the basis of archival sources'. The outcome of such exercises was not always startlingly new, but the rigorous application of the principle was of importance to him. His critics might say it is a kind of fetishism. I have heard him remark, in his usual cool and balanced manner, that strict professional standards must be maintained particularly at a time when some others in the profession wrote in a polemical vein.

Moreover, he evidently believed that historical judgements based on archival documents would ensure objectivity. He attached immense importance to the need to correct bias. V.G. Kiernan, while reviewing Gupta's book, remarked, 'Professor Gupta's aim has evidently been impartiality in particular over questions affecting his own country, India; he has achieved it remarkably well, occasionally it may be felt at the expense of some softening of discords, or blunting of sharp edges'. This criticism notwithstanding, Gupta did not try to play the role of the historian as a judge. Sometimes this led him to go against the received wisdom. A remarkable statement in this regard was his exhortation to historians in a presentation he made at the Indian History Congress (1961). He was asked to speak at a symposium on the 'contribution by Indian historians' to national integration. After outlining a research agenda for historians of the modern period, Gupta said he was not sure whether research along those lines would be regarded 'as satisfactory from an integrationist point of view'—that remained to be seen, he said. 'If it does not, we will have to state that equally plainly, for above all our first loyalty must be to the maintenance of academic integrity'. Another example: contrary to the commonly depicted picture of unrestrained governmental repression during and after the Quit India Movement, Gupta argued that the documents he collected (as part of the ICHR project on the freedom movement in India) suggested that British Indian authoritarianism was qualified by regard for law, it was a 'legal authoritarianism'. Again, on the question of 'economic imperialism', Gupta, after surveying the evidence, carefully distanced himself from the establishment view of the specialists in the area of 'Imperial and Commonwealth History' in England. His essay on this question is a fine example of his effort to cleave a middle path between, on the one hand, the prevalent fashion among the Western specialists on the subject to reject the theory of economic imperialism, and on the other hand the pristine Leninist notion directly connecting European finance capitalism with the acquisition of colonies. He quotes Frederick Engels against the mechanical application of formulae in the writing of history: 'Our conception of history is above all a guide to study, not a lever for construction a la Hegelianism.' He goes on to argue that recent research (he wrote the essay in 1978) showed

that certain reformulations were necessary in establishing the connection between British capitalism, the decision-making process in the British government, and the actual process of expansion. We see that there was far more continuity in the nature of British capitalist colonialism than has been allowed by Lenin who saw a decisive break at the turn of the century.

At the same time Gupta firmly rejected, as 'quite inadequate', the dominant view in Western historiography which suggested that imperial expansion had nothing to do with capitalism. Such positions between two barricades, and sometimes in the crossfire, was not a comfortable one to be in. One must surmise that he regarded that as the price one has to pay to be an impartial historian true to his sources and evidence.

Gupta allowed his neutral empiricism to be qualified only by the idea of 'Progress'. For some reason he thought it necessary to preface his last major essay (1998) with a declaration of 'basic ethical postulates':

I do not have a teleological view of history—such views have done a lot of harm to historical studies—but I do believe that the survival of humanity on this planet and the retention of the mastery over the natural environment by human beings are a desideratum. In that sense I am a believer in the idea of Progress.

This idea of progress is at the same time classical and contemporary—classical in that its genealogy can be traced to the Enlightenment era and contemporary in that it reflects the concerns of this day and age about human survival on planet Earth—but it is neither progress in the Whig view of history, nor progress as the Left ideologies have conceived of it. It was progress neutral in terms of either of these value systems.

Perhaps in the course of his development as a professional historian

Gupta evolved a neutrality which according to his own lights was not only ethically viable but also an academic obligation. Perhaps again, this is not wholly correct. The same man when he was seventeen years of age had written: 'Neutrality in the face of the great ideological clashes cannot be imagined' and quoting Cecil Day Lewis, 'Only ghosts can live/Between two fires.'

Sabyasachi Bhattacharya

The Historiography of Imperialism and Nationalism

SECTION I

IDENTITY FORMATION AND NATION-STATES: SOME REFLECTIONS*

All history, said Benedetto Croce, is contemporary history. By that he meant that the contemporary situation influences a historian in the choice of his subject and its treatment. I would submit that, after the fiftieth anniversary of independence, with the partition of the subcontinent, my discussion of this theme has a message for today. I end my survey with a plea for a federal polity and a confederal association among the countries of South Asia. In one's discussion one should declare one's bias, or rather, one's basic ethical postulates. I do not have a teleological view of history—such views have done a lot of harm to historical studies—but I do believe that the survival of humanity on this planet and the retention of the mastery over the natural environment by human beings are a desideratum. In that sense I am a believer in the idea of Progress. Second, I have no fascination for the gigantic or the big; this stems from an anti-authoritarian streak in me. Far too many historians, regardless of their period or area of specialisation, have equated the spatial or demographic increase of states or the proliferation of institutions within them, with progress: it is probably the legacy of centuries of historical study focused on kings, emperors, bureaucracies, military expansion. As a result the 'great tradition' gets overemphasised, and many 'little traditions' get ignored. Finally, in my historical investigations I prefer enquiry and generalisations based on empirical research rather than generalisations founded on metaphysical concepts, or the manipulation of a set of abstract oversized concepts.

Issues discussed by historians and issues about which historians remain silent, often create well-worn grooves of historiography. They cast the

*General President's address, Indian History Congress, 59th Session, Patiala 1998.

thought processes of members of the profession in the mould of certain stereotyped concepts and categories.

History is about people—not kings, rulers, nations, or states. It is about humanity as a whole in relation to efforts to improve our environment. The life experience of myriads of human collectivities through the centuries can be perceived and analysed from different angles. The theme on which I hope to provoke some thought has been also examined by scholars in sister disciplines like geography, anthropology, sociology and political science. I shall have occasion to comment on their views.

A hundred years ago, one part of Europe, the Balkan peninsula, appeared to be politically undisturbed, especially as, in the previous year (in May 1897) the rival emperors of Russia and Austria–Hungary had decided to put 'on ice' their claims and counter-claims over spheres of influence among the ethnic groups under Ottoman rule. Ninety years ago the pattern was disturbed by the annexation of Bosnia by Austria. Within six years, more political crises in that peninsula, involving interstate terrorism and localised warfare brought in their train general war on a scale unprecedented in human history. Since then the century has witnessed global wars, genocide and the invention of weapons of mass destruction. Efforts towards eliminating warfare and the arms race as a means of solving disputes between human groups have taken place over three generations, with very limited success.

Open the newspapers of any day in the last few years, and you would still be reading about Bosnia, Albania and other areas, about transborder terrorism and frontier skirmishes. The year that is about to end has seen our country and its neighbour conduct nuclear experiments, each justifying its action in the name of national security. A hundred years from today, will there be any history to write about? Or, to adapt a phrase of Marx and Engels, will the 'common ruin of the contending peoples'[1] be writ large in radioactive characters on the face of this earth?

TERMINOLOGY

'Nation', 'state', 'ethnic identity' are concepts that are often conflated when describing the social and political behaviour of human collectivities.[2] We talk about the League of Nations and the United Nations Organisation, and describe international law as the regulatory guideline for members of the aforesaid organisation, when what we are really talking about are sovereign states, whose territorial extent may or may not be coterminous with an ethnically and/or linguistically distinct group, or having a cultural compositeness, despite ethnic and linguistic diversity. Would it not be more meaningful to talk about interstate law, and a United States Organisation? Here, I shall not use the phrase 'International Affairs', because that begs the question about the nation-state, but simply refer to the same topic as a 'states-system' or a 'world-system'.[3]

This conflation of concepts is noticed in historical surveys which make no distinction between absolute monarchies or dynastycentric kingdoms; empires claiming to rule over different territories with pre-capitalist social formations; and modern states. What these traditional political structures have in common with what is called a nation-state is territory, a geographically limited space—a space within which the ruling group has a monopoly of legitimate violence. Since a territory with fixed limits is the feature common to both a state and a nation-state, we have to examine from history, how a state gets established in a geographically identifiable area, and how a human collectivity associates itself with a particular territory, sometimes with that territory only. A little later, I shall draw on the wisdom of the geographers to understand the shaping of frontiers and boundaries.

The formation of new states in Europe by the argument of national identity—like the unification of Italy in the nineteenth century—excited the imagination of the Indian intelligentsia, and the lives of Mazzini and Garibaldi were held up as ideals. A Bengali writer, Jogendranath, Vidyabhushan (1845–1904), wrote their biographies in Bengali.[4] Mahatma Gandhi in *Hind Swaraj* (1909) referred to them (especially Mazzini) as nation-building heroes.[5] Yet in European history the word 'nation' makes a hesitant entry into the political vocabulary towards the end of the eighteenth century. It had not occurred in the writings of Machiavelli,[6] nor in those of Jean Bodin, the political theorist who provided the justification for absolute monarchy. At the Peace of Westphalia (1648) which reorganised the European states-system, the word 'nation-state' did not occur in any of the treaties. The Dutch scholar

Hugo Grotius, who during the Thirty Years War wrote about the legal regulation of the conduct of warfare (*De jure belli ac pacis* [1625]) did not use the term. The justification for the existence of a monarchical state was legitimate dynastic authority, not any principle of nationhood.

To avoid confusion a distinction must be made between 'patriotism' and nationalism. The former concept is very specific to territory, the land of one's birth, and the emotion of affection and loyalty to that territory. The size of that territory and the nature of its polity is immaterial—it can be a rural locality, an urban conglomeration, or a larger area. Nation and nationalism refer to a human collectivity, not a territory.

There are four markers to identify a human collectivity and its bonding agents within a given territory. Before talking about a nation in any historical situation we have to remember these four aspects. First is the primary collectivity, what sociologists call the *Gemeinschaft,* where unity is based on fairly intimate personal contact, either centred on familial and kinship ties, or the obligations and ties of living in a rural agrarian society in a specific locality. The locality might be a fixed area of settled agriculture, or, as in the case of the nomadic tribes of Central Asia, where 'the right to move prevailed over the right to camp', a wider expanse where the tribes had 'the title to a cycle of migration'.[7] Second, a point often overlooked when talking about premodern political structures, the exact nature of transport and communication obtaining at that time. Historians of this century have got accustomed to increasingly faster modes of transport (from railways to airways) and in recent decades, the younger generation is getting used to the internet and the web. When studying history we have to forget all that. Research needs to be undertaken on the concept of time, the rhythm of work, and the pattern of communications in earlier social formations. I do not think we have done enough of that for our country. Third, it is important to know the level of literacy and its distribution within the social hierarchy. (In societies with low literacy we should also consider the effectiveness of alternative forms of learning and communication, including oral traditions.) Fourth, through what sorts of moral codes and symbols do the people in the primary collectivity identify themselves with a supra-local larger political unit, that is, a kingdom or some other form of a territorial state?

In this larger unit, which German sociologists would call the *Gesellschaft* in contradistinction to the *Gemeinschaft,* the individual's involvement is contractual, and from his or her point of view, it is an impersonal association compared to the local community. The transition from the *Gemeinschaft* to the *Gesellschaft* is not simply an interplay of variables like literacy, transport and communications, and the sacrality of certain codes and symbols; it is mediated by military power elites and/or a clerisy, with wide variations in the relative weight of all these factors.

THEORIES AND PERSPECTIVES

We can distinguish two approaches in the discussion of national identity—the primordialist (alternatively called perennialist) and the modernist. My own inclination is to support the modernist approach. The primordialist case has been argued by Anthony D. Smith. The following statement, developed over many chapters of his book gives his position:

. . . given the characteristic of human beings, their propensity to kinship and group belonging and their need for cultural symbolism for communication and meaning we should expect nations and nationalism to be perennial and, perhaps, universal.[8]

The eighteenth-century German scholar Johann Gottfried Herder (1744–1803) also wrote in a similar vein. I quote from a recent English translation.

Nature nurtures (*erzieht*) in families, the most natural state is therefore our nation, with one national character. This it retains through the ages and it is most naturally formed when it is the object of its native Princes: for a nation is as much a natural plant as a family, only with more branches. Nothing therefore appears so directly opposite to the end of government as the unnatural enlargement of states, the wild mixture of various races and nations under one crown.[9]

The modernist point of view, in various ways, is presented by Ernest Gellner, Anthony Giddens, Eric Hobsbawm, Michael Mann, and Benedict Anderson. They would all agree that, in a global historical perspective, the development of a sense of national identity and the creation of a nation-state is closely associated with the development of capitalism in the Western world and the 'dual revolution' at the end of the eighteenth century—the industrial revolution in Britain and the political revolution in France.[10] As the dates of publication of these books show, they have mostly influenced each other, despite areas of disagreement on the nuances of the problem. One other hypothesis is implicit in the modernist's position *vis-à-vis* the primordialists: nationalism is not natural but contingent. As Gellner puts it:

> The political and the cultural unit only coalesce in cases . . . when the geographical limits to which an empire can expand are at the same time the limits of a culture; but more frequently, the two frontiers diverge. Moreover, there is nothing to indicate that men have found the divergence either inconvenient or unnatural.[11]

To this I shall add a caveat. This divergence between the imperial frontiers and cultural zones will not be found inconvenient or unnatural provided the distribution of productive resources within the empire and among the social hierarchy is adequate or equitable in terms of contemporary value systems. Once an imbalance or an asymmetry is noticed in this sphere, a contingency will arise calling for modification in the nature and extent of the state.

Ernest Gellner, with his considerable experience in the sociology of North African Arabic-speaking communities, used that knowledge to suggest that national identity and the desire for a nation-state are unlikely to be discernible in pre-industrial, predominantly agrarian, societies with a low level of literacy.[12] This fits in with what we know of the medieval feudal kingdoms of Europe, where literacy was confined to a small elite (and the language used for administration and diplomacy—Latin—was not the common speech of the people), and the basis of securing the loyalty of the inhabitants to the ruling class was to socialise them as subjects. The concept of a participatory citizen body was absent. A French political scientist has objected to the binary opposition between industrial and agrarian communities and stated that the industrial bourgeoisie did not push state authorities towards standardising education and spreading literacy. Hermet argues that industrial society in the West is a nineteenth-century phenomenon and Gellner's model does not take into account the development of vernacular languages and the spread of literacy by the intermediate classes in the period between the sixteenth and eighteenth centuries.[13] This is a valid point, but it had been anticipated by Benedict Anderson. He emphasised the revolutionary impact of one development—printing—that accompanied the beginnings of mercantile capitalism from the fifteenth century.[14] Michael Mann starts from that step in the argument but points out that the position around 1700 created at the most the preconditions of the modern state:

Contracts, government records, army drill manuals, coffee-house business discussions, academies of notable officials—all these institutions secularised and spread slightly downward the shared literate culture of dominant classes … yet under capitalism, the discursive literacy of dominant classes and churches remained somewhat transnational and 'naturalization' remained limited. Anderson's 'print-capitalism' could as easily generate a transnational West as a community of nations. The nation still did not mobilize society. The transformation of such proto-nations into cross-class, state-linked and finally aggressive communities happened by [1840].[15]

In a brilliant analysis of social, economic and political developments of the late eighteenth and the first half of the nineteenth century, Mann has interwoven the roles of different strata of the capitalist classes, the traditional ruling aristocracy and military, the peasantry and the labouring poor. He has shown how the particularist segmental networks based on localities and regions (not classes) got metamorphosed into nation-states.[16] This book, and its preceding volume, deserves to be widely read and reflected upon.

I shall now comment on the primordialist approach to the interpretation of national political identity, before examining some other issues from a modernist standpoint. The primordialists confuse symptoms with structures, and encourage mystification of historical inquiry. One quotation from Anthony D. Smith would suffice. He has detected echoes of modern national conflicts in the wars between the Greeks and the Persians in the fifth century BC:

… in the realm of political culture, the Persian threat had galvanised a sense of Hellenic unity into a cultural efflorescence which only reinforced the sense of Greek superiority and uniqueness over Persian 'servitude' and 'barbarian illiteracy'.[17]

When two human collectivities are in armed conflict with each other, there is a pattern of bellicose propaganda which is repeated through the centuries, regardless of the social formation to which they belong. One cannot use that type of evidence to assert the existence of a Hellenic nation in antagonism to a Persian nation.

FRONTIERS AND BOUNDARIES

Do territorial states create nations, or pre-existing collective identities seek and eventually acquire statehood? This is an important question, but before trying to answer that I wish to explain the historical evolution of boundaries and frontiers.

This is the area where interdisciplinary cooperation between historians and geographers has been fruitful and, at all times, is most desirable. Since political and military history have been studied for a longer time than economic and social history, there is abundant evidence on the claims and counter-claims of rulers over bits of the surface of the earth. Social and economic historians studying the evolving land-use patterns of people close to the soil can suggest hypotheses about changes in an ecosystem over a period, but no hypothesis remains sustainable unless it is related to the power politics of a social stratum which exercised administrative and military control over the area, or claimed suzerainty over it. As the empires of the ancient world gave place to the feudal monarchies of medieval times, and they in turn were replaced by the sovereign states of the capitalist world-system, and as in the present century, many new states have emerged after people fought against colonial rule, a variety of theories and hypotheses have been given to explain the geographical limits of a human collectivity, and the conflicts arising from them.

The question has two aspects. First, the material basis of geographical limits, second, the perception of those limits by different human groups. The latter will vary according to age-group, occupation, and access to political power. Both aspects are relevant in explaining boundary changes, but the second is of special importance in the analysis of identity formation, in the expansionist aims of medieval monarchs and colonial rulers, and—very relevant for the discussion of nationalism and post-colonial states—in the ideology of nation-state building and national chauvinism.

In the ancient world, difficulties of communication as well as the costs of maintaining military garrisons along the periphery of an empire (be it Roman, or Chinese, or West Asian) revealed two alternative frontier policies—of strict integration, or laxity and concession.[18] The Romans sought to demarcate imperial frontiers by following, wherever possible, natural boundaries like rivers, mountain tops, watersheds. They also tried to cut military costs by means of self-sustaining border forces. From this we get the hypothesis about the frontier being a zone of contact, not a definite line of separation.[19]

By interacting with the culture of the people on the other side, the frontier often became the nucleus of the development of a distinct new collective identity. We all recognise Ukraine as a founder member of the UN. The literal meaning of the word Ukraine is 'borderland'. The word was originally a general description of lands on the periphery of Russia.[20]

During the Middle Ages, the development of clear-cut concepts of political entities and boundaries was hampered by the hierarchical system of feudal authorities with its overlapping, divided and often conflicting loyalties. The boundary between the domain of the Holy Roman Empire of Germany and that of the French king varied from time to time according to the versions of different chroniclers—in the north the variation was between the river Meuse and the Rhine and in the south between the river Saone and the Rhine. As an authority on the subject has commented,

The frontier between France and the Empire held little meaning, and it would have been a wise king or Emperor who knew where it ran. There were times, however, when a greater precision was necessary, and then the king held an inquest. . . . The local inhabitants were required to declare whose subjects they were.[21]

The concept of a fluid, permeable frontier yielded place to the idea of a clearly defined boundary as the absolute monarchies established themselves in Europe from the early sixteenth century. It is from then on that we get in diplomatic and political vocabulary the notion of a 'natural frontier'. A French writer on geography invoked Divinity in his support, writing:

It would seem that God has placed barriers which he did not wish to be easily crossed; to Spain, the Pyrenees and the sea; to France, the sea, the Pyrenees, the Rhine and the Alps of Switzerland and Piedmont, to Italy, the sea and the Alps.[22]

A number of German humanists countered such arguments based on geography and divinity with another set, based on language and history. Their objection was to the Rhine being the eastern border of France, and they wrote that Alsace (Elsass, according to German spelling) was German, that it had been thoroughly Germanised by the invasion of the Germanic tribes after the fall of the Roman Empire. The last important booklet in this vein on the German side was published in 1653. It is interesting to note that this Franco-German pamphleteering did not influence the French monarchy, although throughout the seventeenth century it was making many territorial advances towards the east. Cardinal Richelieu's approach was pragmatic, unaffected by any doctrine, and in the diplomacy of the Thirty Years War he avoided any claims on Alsace/Elsass, which remained within the Holy Roman Empire at the Peace of Westphalia (1648).[23]

After a lull of about hundred years the doctrine of 'natural frontiers' reappeared during the Enlightenment—John Locke, Montesquieu and Rousseau all wrote on it. The justification was not by history but by appeal to 'natural law'—an authority higher than history. Earlier writers were concerned about a specific area—France's eastern border. The eighteenth-century writers never defined a 'natural frontier' on the map. Rousseau put the argument more elaborately in the *Contrat Social* and some other writings, but the only topographical reference is the following:

The lie of the mountains, seas and rivers which serve as frontiers for the various nations who people it (i.e. Europe) seems to have fixed forever their number and their size. We may fairly say that the political order of the continent is, in some sense, the work of nature.[24]

A qualitative change occurred in the use of this concept when revolutionary France used it to justify warfare and the annexation of Savoy, Luxembourg and modern Belgium in terms of the Alps and the Rhine. That brings me back to the question I had posed earlier. Do nations emerge from within earlier political structures, or do pre-existing collective identities acquire a territory and become a nation-state?

I am inclined to think that it is the former rather than the latter. The case for the latter—which is in effect a variant of the primordialist approach—is weakened by the difficulties of empirically verifying a pre-existing collective identity and the trajectory of its political orientation. Some nineteenth-century European writers—liberals and socialists alike—relapsed into metaphysical idealist phrase-mongering in trying to answer this question. Friedrich Meinecke defined the nation as 'a singular and meaningful mental community'.[25] Otto Bauer, the Austrian socialist, tried to find in all members of a nation, a 'community of fate' which tied together the members of a nation into a 'community of character'.[26]

There are, however, in the existing canon (from Herder to Renan) references to more specific bonding agents of human collectivities that contribute towards creating a sense of national identity by themselves. I shall take up some of them, show their limitations and then argue that the nation-state emerges by the mutation of various elements within a state or an empire. I shall consider four aspects, religion, language, historic memories, and specific economic functions in a territorial context.

RELIGION

In the transition from the medieval to the modern in the European states-system, religious loyalties were a contested area between two feudal overlordships—the papacy and the territorially based feudal monarchies. The Roman Catholic Church claimed supra-local allegiance and thus it had little to do with territorial nationalism. On the contrary, some feudal monarchs—France and England are exemplars— managed to extract from the Church tangible and symbolic concessions which strengthened the monarchy. Not only did the French king get the unique special appellation of 'rex christianismus' (the most Christian king), he also got control over appointments in the ecclesiastical hierarchy.[27] In a similar way, long before the English Reformation initiated by Henry VIII, by the Statutes of Provisors and Praemunire during the fourteenth century, the English kings got the Pope to admit that the initiative in ecclesiastical appointments rested with the king.[28]

From the Reformation to the Enlightenment the religious issue played a role as a forcing-house of consciousness (national or class, according to the situation) within the states of pre-revolutionary Europe. The main areas were popular education, the spread of literacy and the translation of the Bible in the vernacular, all of which were facilitated by the invention of printing. In Bohemia in the fifteenth century, the reform movement initiated by John Hus was both social and literary. It was a response of the Czech middle gentry to the massive settlement of German landowning magnates during the reign of Wenceslas IV (1378–1419). Hus combined his heretical preaching with a reform of the orthography of the Czech language.[29]

The Hussite movement in Bohemia, the Lutheran Reformation in Germany, the breach with Rome by Henry VIII, the ascendancy of the Calvinist sect in Scotland, and the revolt of the Netherlands all show the part played by dissenting religious movements in providing the mass base for new political structures to emerge out of the medieval world. It also shows, however, that by themselves these movements would not have grown and cemented cohesive territorial polities; they needed the patronage and support of political elites interested in the power game. Where they did not get this support they failed, as in Bohemia, or the movement became the ideology of deprived social orders, as in mid-seventeenth-century England.[30]

Religious differences did not stand in the way of wider political integration, where other factors pointed to it. The union of Scotland and England has proved durable to this day, despite differences between two modes of worship within the Christian faith—the Presbyterian and the Anglican. It can delay the process, however. A contributing factor behind the hesitation of the southern German states (Bavaria, Baden, Wurttemberg, and the Palatinate) about joining the Prussia-dominated North German Confederation between 1866 and 1871 was the concern felt by Catholics about the safeguarding of their religious and educational entitlements.[31]

LANGUAGE

A common speech, from which a written language has evolved, is in my opinion a much more powerful bonding agent than a common faith. This had been recognised in the pre-modern period as well as by theoreticians of national identity in the age of capitalism. In medieval Europe, where the literate wrote and thought in Latin, the importance of language was recognised by secular and ecclesiastical authorities as new areas were conquered; there are interesting examples from the British Isles themselves, arising out of the English conquest of Wales, and Ireland, and their cross-border contacts with the neighbouring kingdom of Scotland.[32] In Wales a twelfth-century English archbishop needed interpreters during his tour, and in Ireland representatives of the clergy and nobility sent from England reported that 'those of Irish speech are enemies of the King and his subjects'.[33] Scotland was a linguistic melting pot with varieties of Celtic and Scandinavian dialects in the thirteenth century, but by the end of the fourteenth century, as a result of commercial intercourse, a form of the English language was widely used in the Scottish lowlands (the valley of the river Forth). In the early seventeenth century when James VI of Scotland ascended the throne of England as the first king of the Stuart dynasty, he Left on record his views that because there was 'a communitie of language, the principall means of Civil Societie . . .', a perfect union of the two parts as Great Britain should be possible under his 'benevolent' autocracy.[34]

Similarly, in France in 1539, the absolute monarch Francis I decreed that French should be used officially for legal and administrative purposes all over the kingdom.[35] Another French king reiterated that it was advisable to have the linguistic frontier coincide with the political while referring to the partition of the fiefdom of Cerdagne (a valley in the Pyrenees) between France and the Catalonia region of Spain. Henri IV told the noblemen of Lyons, 'It is apposite that because you speak French naturally you are the subjects of the King of France. I very much wish that Spanish speakers remain in Spain, Germans in Germany, but the French must be with me.'[36] It is somewhat ironic that the noblemen of Lyons were then actually using (and went on using till the eighteenth century) Provençal, a dialect of French, with a local literary form. This raises the question of identity and linguistic standardisation.

French linguistic historians distinguish between three varieties of French—the 'patois' (the regional spoken variety limited to informal occasions), regional dialects like Provençal, Bearnais, Gascon and Breton (which had, till the revolution, a complete literary culture), and the written literary standard (Francien), emanating from Paris. The French revolutionaries passed a resolution condemning the dialects as a remnant of feudal society.[37] Forty-three years later, in 1832, a young Italian, inspired by the same democratic ideals, would write, 'The nation is the universality of the citizens speaking the same tongue.'[38]

The facts cited so far show that from the age of the Renaissance and the Reformation (which is also the age of overseas expansion and commercial capitalism), the ruling elite increasingly used, for religious and secular purposes, the written form of common speech within the state. This is true of France, Britain, and Spain (the first grammar of any modern European language was published in Spain in 1492).[39] However, Italy showed a different trajectory of the development of dialect, language and territorial national identity, in the same period, in sharp contrast to France. Mazzini's words, quoted above, were very much influenced by the French Revolution and marked a departure from the Italian tradition.

Italian history is not a good example of a neat correlation between linguistic evolution, the development of the capitalist market economy, and national unification. The fourteenth-century scholar Dante Aligheri had developed the Italian language; from amongst the various dialects of the peninsula he identified the dialect of his native Tuscany and improved it to create a standardised Italian, though his main works were in Latin. In his book on the vernacular language he argued that Italian poets should use the 'pure' Tuscan form of the language for literary purposes.[40] Dante's concern for linguistic standardisation did not affect his political thinking, in which he was very much of a medieval cast of mind. His book *On the Monarchy* was a plea for a universal emperor in a kingdom where the role of the subordinate authorities was simply to act as his peace-keeping agents. He is a clear proof of the lack of any correlation between linguistic and cultural pride and territorial political loyalties.[41] Two centuries later, Machiavelli and the historian Guicciardini, show similar indifference. Machiavelli's patriotism was limited to his native Florence, capital of Tuscany.[42]

However persistent might be the sense of particularism of the different regions of Italy before the French Revolution and however different might be the socio-economic evolution of northern Italy (industrial) and southern Italy (Naples and Sicily—agricultural, with a peasantry dominated by big landowners), in one respect, at the level of the upper classes, unification had been achieved by the literate classes through linguistic standardisation. Ironically, the kingdom which played the dominant role in the unification process—Piedmont-Sardinia—did impose its own constitution on the rest of Italy and give it a unitary instead of a federal polity, but it could not impose its own language on the peninsula. The Tuscan variant of Italian, as developed since Dante and Petrarch, remained the standard. Piedmontese which 'is from every linguistic point of view, a language distinct from Italian on the one hand and French on the other, with a long tradition of writing and grammatical study' had to yield place to Tuscan.[43]

However, did this unite the people of all parts of Italy? The answer is in the negative, as Antonio Gramsci wrote, in a prison in fascist Italy, sixty years after Italian unification:

The Action Party, [i.e. the followers of Mazzini] confused the cultural unity which existed in the peninsula . . . with the political and territorial unity of the great popular masses, who were foreign to that cultural tradition and who, even supposing that they knew of its existence, couldn't care less about it.[44]

This reveals the limitations of language as a binding agent, and what I will call 'philological nationalism', that is, the self-conscious improvement of a dialect into a written language with the enlargement of its vocabulary and the preparation of standard rules of grammar and lexicology. By its very nature, the initiators of this process come from a privileged class. Their success in disseminating an alternative 'pure' vocabulary would depend on control over the educational institutions and support from the ruling dynasty or ruling coterie, which would be available if the latter could protect their vested interests by this process. If the 'pure' language fails to replace the written prose of the people (the prose of commercial transaction and litigation) it will show the resilience of the language of the masses, however hybrid or rustic it may sound to the upper strata of society. A situation can arise when there are two parallel languages existing in one territory, corresponding to social divisions, but both capable of expressing basic human emotions. Perhaps even in such situations the 'U' (upper class) language is more capable of dealing with abstract concepts and being the vehicle of scientific and technical progress, but it can do so only if it is willing to co-opt parts of the non-U vocabulary, and does not remain a prisoner of the grammarians.

The Anglo-Norman elite did not, which is why from the end of the fourteenth century Norman-French fell into disuse;[45] in a legal case of 1426 it was stated that words were pronounced differently in different parts of England, 'and one is as good as the other'.[46]

HISTORIC MEMORIES IN THE COLLECTIVE CONSCIOUSNESS

Many distinguished theoreticians of national identity have mentioned this as a factor behind the growth of national identity and the eventual formation of a nationalist ideology. I am somewhat sceptical about using this as a reliable guide. What passes off as 'collective memory' could have been manufactured or invented in the interests of a ruling group, or a political party aspiring after political power. But some oral traditions can be authentic. Although the Serbians and their neighbouring peoples (like the Bulgars) come from the same ethnic stem (Slav) and belong to the same faith (the Orthodox Church) the memory of an old kingdom of Serbia defeated by the Ottoman Turks 'was preserved in song and heroic story, and, perhaps more to the point, in the daily liturgy of the Serbian Church which had canonized most of its Kings'.[47] R.R. Davies, who has carefully studied the historical mythology of the Celtic fringe in the British Isles admits that 'we shall never know . . . how deeply rooted in popular consciousness' it is. He adds, 'What we know of popular social memory in more recent times should make us chary of believing that some of the complex historical mythology which we find recorded in the books of the literate could ever have been digested and remembered at a popular level.'[48] Oral tradition of a kinship group is useful for the social history of a locality, but to extend it to a larger territorial state seems to me to cross the border between history and the romantic novel.

That mystification of the past has contributed to the creation of a nationalist ideology was recognised by the French scholar Ernest Renan, who said, in his lecture 'What is a Nation?' (1882):

To forget and—I will venture to say—to get one's history wrong, are essential features in the making of a nation; and thus the advance of historical studies is often a danger to nationality.[49]

ECONOMIC FUNCTIONS IN A
GEOGRAPHICAL SETTING

We thus see that attempts to argue the existence for a collectivity with a specific territorial location, in terms of religion, or language, or collective historical memory does not stand up to critical examination, so far as Europe is concerned. However, when measured in terms of geographically conditioned economic functions, some areas were nation-states in embryo. These are the Netherlands, Norway, and Switzerland. Although the Dutch language is very close to the German as spoken in northern Germany, the peculiar geography of the Netherlands—low lying, necessitating a seafaring way of life and mastery over techniques of reclaiming land by dikes—fostered a separate pattern of existence among the Dutch. The Norwegian adoption of the 'Viking' way of life was related to the growth of skilled ship-building technology which was facilitated by local factor endowments (timber, iron, and iron tools). Thirteenth-century improvements in overland transport and bridge-building to help the south–north trade between the Mediterranean and the Baltic made the St Gotthard Pass in the Alps vitally important, and laid the economic basis for an independent 'pass state' in the region, that is, Switzerland or, rather, the confederation of Swiss cantons.[50] In the Netherlands and Switzerland (very little studied, unfortunately, in our European history courses) we see a special type of nation-state— the 'consociational nation'—in which 'the political elites of distinct social groups succeed in establishing a viable pluralistic state by a process of mutual forbearance and accommodation'.[51]

NATIONS EMERGE FROM WITHIN
STATES AND EMPIRES

I shall now argue the case that West and Central European history shows that the sense of national identity among dispersed local communities emerges from the experience of living under a specific political authority, and that all the bonding agents which I have taken up so far acquire their effectiveness only because they get linked with political elites who were ruling or were aspirants to political power.

The Norwegian-born scholar Stein Rokkan, in two masterly studies of the interplay of ethno-linguistic and geo-economic factors in Central and Western Europe between the fall of the Roman Empire and the mid-seventeenth century, has shown that 'although the empire broke up as a political system of territorial control, much of the economic as well as the cultural infrastructure of long-distance communication [i.e. the Catholic Church hierarchy] was Left intact'. He also shows how core areas developed at the edges of the city-studded territories of the old empire, mainly on the coastal plains west and north of the empire, in France, England, Scandinavia, and later in Spain; how the monarchs in these areas were able to generate resources within concentrated agrarian structures and develop a functional network of relationships with the urban bourgeoisie and with the military and bureaucratic-cum-ecclesiastical agencies for state building.[52]

The medieval king was the focus of popular loyalty, and the idea of his semi-spiritual qualities is inherent in the widespread belief that the royal touch could cure the disease scrofula.[53] In England the phrase 'community of the realm', used in medieval documents on the judicial ratification by parliament of royal decisions on taxation and legal pronouncements, anticipated the idea of a nation.[54] The monarch was regularly on the move, and coronations, royal processions and the formal entries of kings into the medieval royal boroughs through the gates of the walled towns, were used for projecting the royal authority. Such rituals used mythology, Christianity and patriotic symbols. The increasing use of the English language in parliamentary proceedings and in royal proclamations sent to every country reporting the success of Henry V in his campaigns in France in the early fifteenth century helped a sense of nationhood to grow. As one historian comments, Henry V 'may have claimed the French Crown, but in England he discouraged the use of the French language in government and literate society'.[55]

Thus in England, through the economic tribulations of the Later Middle Ages, the emergence of a national identity was assisted by a political process in which the monarch, in association with the estates of the realm, developed institutions and a network of communications based on a common language and legal system. However, if the English 'had attained a match between their perceived identity as a people and the regnal authority, political structures and state institutions which served, upheld and fostered that identity',[56] a British nation had a long gestation period. In the fourteenth century when the English monarchy had failed militarily in its efforts to assert overlordship in Scotland (the Battle of Bannockburn, 1314, and the victory of Robert Bruce) a sense of a national unity emerged in Scotland, the contemporary testimony of which was the Declaration of Arbroath (1320) acknowledging Robert Bruce (Robert I) as the Scottish King.[57] Like the English the Scots had also achieved a match between perceived identity and regnal authority.

England treated Ireland as a colony and could not incorporate Wales within its feudal monarchical polity. The ethnic, linguistic, cultural and political distinctiveness of the chiefdoms in the mountainous valleys of Wales were resistant to it. The centralising tendencies of the early Tudors (at one stroke of the pen Henry VIII replaced Welsh customary laws by English legislation) led the Welsh educated classes to react by taking greater interest in their history, mythology and language.[58] In succeeding centuries, even after the industrial revolution, this distinctiveness was seen in the weakness of the Anglican Church in Wales (the Welsh people were non-conformist chapel-goers), and the continued vitality of the Welsh language (kept alive through annual festivals like the Eisteddfod), and the propensity of the electorate in Wales to vote against the Conservative Party.[59] Even the unitary administration of Britain has had in recent years come to appreciate the need for devolution so far as Wales is concerned.

The historical experience of the United Kingdom shows that a national identity can emerge even out of medieval political structures when the political elite makes use of administrative and legal instruments to create a network linking local communities. When such instruments are applied too crudely (as in Wales or in Ireland), it sets off a reaction for regional self-assertion by language, dissenting religion, and the self-conscious preservation of the poetry and myths of a medieval past. Collective memory is not a primordial instinct. It is very much an instrument, used for modern purposes.

I have spent some time examining one small insular part of Europe as a case study, primarily because the transition from feudalism to capitalism occurred there earliest, along with the emergence of modern representative government. The continent of Europe, from the Atlantic to the Vistula, the Baltic to the Mediterranean, made the transition at the end of the eighteenth century. When medieval estates-based polities were overthrown by revolution and warfare (1789–1815), the emerging polities of the continent contained potential fault-lines. These could be along class divisions, or cultural (linguistic/ethnic/religious) divisions. Both were noticed in the 'long' nineteenth century and provoked a large corpus of liberal, democratic and socialist speculation.

After two centuries of political experimentation involving massive human cost in wars and revolution, the European Union of today probably approximates the ideal political arrangement for an area highly interdependent economically, but diverse in terms of language and culture. Let us note the mistakes they made on the way, since the French Revolution, and the spread of popular sovereignty, so that the people of our subcontinent (which is the same size as Europe without Russia) can avoid them. One major mistake was the belief in revolutionary France that the 'general will' required the elimination of all particularist institutions, that the best way to create a state of equal citizens was to insist on uniformity, condemn the regional dialects and impose a uniform linguistic standard for all.[60] The result, ironically, increased 'the political relevance of . . . clerics, still providing the most education, and of obscure philologists'[61]—not a consequence intended by the secular revolutionaries wedded to the ideal of a 'republic of virtue'.

Another mistake was the transformation of the revolutionary principle of fraternity into an ideology of annexationist foreign policy.[62] The academic doctrine of 'natural frontiers' was now used in a doctrinaire manner to extend the boundaries of France, without seriously considering the will of the local population, appealing to the law of nature.[63] Predictably, in the nineteenth century German publicists emphasised the linguistic frontier; songs and ballads denying the French any claim to the Rhine frontier multiplied and one stanza in a song that later became the German national anthem (Deutschland uber Alles) had lines which laid claim to the whole of Central Europe— from the Meuse in the west to Memel (in Lithuania) in the east, and the Adige (a valley in the southern Alps) in the south to the Baltic Sea in the north.[64] These became all part of Hitler's Germany in the mid-twentieth century. It is not surprising why one historian should have commented

Nationalism by 1944 had come a long way since the French Revolution. Europeans could see it as a Janus; one face showed the venerable features of Garibaldi, the other the grinning mask of the death-camp commandant.[65]

THE ABUSE OF HISTORY

For these unlovely features of nationalism—illiberal, exclusivist, anti-humanist—teachers, historians and the governmental education departments in some countries bear some responsibility. Since there is a real danger of this abuse infecting our country, I wish to give some examples from what happened in Europe, mainly as a warning.

History had been made a compulsory subject by official decree in Prussian elementary schools in October 1872. A speech of Kaiser William II in December 1890 set the tone for all the guidelines for teachers issued after that; he had said, 'We must bring up nationalistic young Germans, and not young Greeks and Romans.'[66] One of the most popular textbooks emphasised militarism and the continuity in German history from the time of the Roman Empire. Most lesson plans and history outlines spewed hatred of France.[67] Senior historians like Heinrich von Treitschke became in effect propagandists for a teleological interpretation which saw the Bismarckian unification and the semi-authoritarian state under Prussian domination as the ultimate destiny of the German people. However, some spoke against this dominant intellectual fashion and drew attention to alternative possibilities. Friedrich Meinecke was one such. In his *Age of German Liberalism (1795–1815)* he emphasised the liberal political reforms in Prussia (the work of Stein, Boyne, Humboldt and others) and his writings 'marked the beginning of a critical revision of the period of the establishment of the Reich'.[68] Like Germany, both Italian nationalists and, later, Italian Fascists, drew their inspiration from a mystified perception of the Italian past, and during the Fascist period systematically indoctrinated school children with that politically slanted viewpoint. We expect this from Fascists, but we also have to admit that much-admired cult figures like Mazzini developed propaganda for political mobilisation on the basis of an uncritically glorified view of history. He valorised the Roman imperial conquests which to him had been a civilising mission, and added that later the genius of Italy 'incarnated itself in the papacy'.[69] Even the moderate leader Gioberti, who opposed Mazzini's republicanism and his unitary political solution with his own programme of a federation of the Italian states presided over by the papacy, displayed a similar mystification. He 'outdid Mazzini in denigration of French civilisation and in elaborate demonstration that Italy had been chosen by God to be the depository of his work'.[70]

It is now generally agreed among scholars that the way Italy was unified by the military and diplomatic manoeuvres of the Piedmontese statesman Cavour was tantamount to the annexation by industrially advanced northern Italy of the less developed southern Italy (Naples and Sicily) and that a potential agrarian revolution in south Italy (especially Sicily) was aborted as a result. The imposition of the unitary Piedmontese constitution over the whole peninsula Left no openings for the solution of the socio-economic problems specific to the south.[71]

When that constitution failed to solve Italy's problems after the First World War and Fascism made its appearance, honest historical research was one of the victims. Certain editions of printed historical documents of the Risorgimento period aimed to play down divisions among Italians (especially class divisions) altogether.[72] The romanticised version of Italian history was used by the fascist educational policy-makers. An analysis of school textbooks has shown that children were to be Left with one overriding impression: the world revolved around Italy, and Italy in turn revolved around Mussolini and the Fascist Party. In 1935 the education minister wrote in the ministry yearbook that 'the destiny of Rome is a perennially imperial destiny'.[73]

We should remember these examples as a warning, for similar tendencies are lurking beneath the surface in India. Thirty-three years ago, at the session of this Congress in Allahabad in December 1965 we all applauded D.D. Kosambi, when in the evening symposium, he held up to ridicule the claims made by some Indians that civilisation spread from India—that Buda-Pest (in Hungary) was a corruption of Buddha-Prastha, and that Guatemala was a corruption of Gautamalaya. There have been reports recently that similar unscientific historical hypotheses are part of the curriculum of a chain of schools run by a private organisation in our country.[74]

SOUTH ASIA—PARALLELS AND PARADOXES

This survey of political structures and ideologies in European civilisation has highlighted some points around which we can examine the South Asian past. Like Europe, this subcontinent saw the formation of states once settled agriculture emerged. Kinship networks based on lineage gradually gave way to states, in the two north Indian river systems.[75] The research in recent years on the spread of the 'high culture' of the Brahminical tradition in the first millennium BC and on the boundaries and cohesiveness of the early Indian empires gives some territorial precision to the political structures of northern India in the pre-Christian era.[76]

I mentioned earlier that physical geography often determined the area within which a territorial state can function in pre-capitalist societies.[77] For South Asia the study of the political history and geography of the earliest centuries has for a long time been characterised by treating either of the two northern river systems (and some towns within them) as the core areas. A Tamil scholar quoted by Vincent Smith (whose textbook showed a similar northern bias) wrote in 1908,

The scientific historian of India ought to begin his study with the basin of the Krishna, of the Cauvery, of the Vaigai, rather than with the Gangetic plain, as it has been now long, too long, the fashion.[78]

Research on peninsular India and the societies and states originating there has made considerable strides since the days of Vincent Smith. It can no longer be viewed as the periphery of a process of 'Aryanisation', or as areas geographically destined to be brought under the paramountcy of an imperial polity based on north India. The work on historical geography by Subbarayalu, followed by that of other scholars, some of whom have engaged in controversy with the late Burton Stein over his theory of the 'segmentary state' have provided food for thought on the political geography of state formation in the period during the first millennium AD.[79]

We can now speculate on the early medieval polities becoming 'nations-in-embryo' as happened in Europe between the High Middle Ages and the Reformation. If we were seriously to undertake interdisciplinary workshops on historical geography, with the participation of scholars of Indian languages and literature, anthropologists who have studied kinship patterns and lineages, as well as students of modes of production, we should be able to advance the understanding of the nature of civil society in relation to the state in diverse parts of the subcontinent. We can then evaluate the differential effects of British commercial penetration, direct political domination and indirect rule (through the princely states) in different parts of South Asia.

The contrast between the European and the South Asian experience lies in the following. In Europe, techno-economic changes since 1500 accelerated around 1800, and were accompanied by political and social restructuring, as a result of which the peoples of Europe were regrouped into new social and political units which were called nation-states. These have recently been reorganised as a supranational European Union. In South Asia, on the other hand, a comprehensive subcontinental political unity, under the aegis of some imperium or other, remained elusive till the British paramountcy. The same differentiation between regional vernaculars as occurred in Europe happened here, at about the same time. The same cosmopolitanism of a literary elite using a classical language (Sanskrit or Persian) which transcended the regions was noticeable here. In between phases of imperial unity, region-based kingdoms with their distinct local cultures established themselves, some-times in the provinces of the previous empires, as in Awadh and Hyderabad in the eighteenth century, or sometimes united by a vibrant faith, as in the Punjab.

What did the British Raj do? It established a modern network of communications, permitted a dependent capitalism to grow, and created a reasonably efficient administrative unity through the codification of laws.[80] From the time of Lord Wellesley provincial boundaries were drawn and redrawn to meet the financial and military needs of imperial expansion, regardless of linguistic or cultural cohesiveness, with an intervening mosaic of princely states.[81]

The British unification of the subcontinent cannot be likened to the reorganisation of Western and Central Europe which happened during the Napoleonic empire and which was partially retained even at the Congress of Vienna.[82] Just as Napoleon's defeat and the Vienna settle-ment Left a legacy of unresolved problems mainly connected with the Habsburg dominions (Central Europe, Italy and the Balkans), which have taken 180 years to be sorted out, at tremendous human and material cost, so has the decline of the Raj between 1919 and 1947 Left a legacy of irrational boundaries and uneven regional imbalances in the political and economic development of the subcontinent as a whole.

One underresearched aspect of identity formation in this subconti-nent, beyond the local community, is the geographical knowledge that the educated classes acquired during colonial rule, and their degree of identification with the artificially created provinces of the Raj. It is important to analyse the geographical understanding of India among the first generation of Congress delegates. An analysis of those resolutions of the Congress in its first fifteen years where the government was regularly criticised for spending Indian revenues for military expansion *outside India* show that the areas 'outside' included Afghanistan, Baluchistan, Chitral, Gilgit and Upper Burma. Evidently, to these leaders, 'historic memories' of the empires of Ashoka and Kanishka had no contemporary relevance. So much for the 'primordialist' theorists. Ironically it was the imperialist historian Vincent Smith who lauded the Mauryas for having achieved the 'scientific frontier' which the Mughals held only intermittently, and the English could never attain.[83] When E.V. Ramaswamy Naicker (Periyar) gave political expression to his anti-Brahmin movement and defined his 'Dravidisthan', he claimed the whole of the Madras Presidency, although the presidency was not a historic kingdom, but an administrative construct of the British. By contrast the Dravida Munnetra Kazhagam (DMK) leader C.M. Annadurai located his Tamil territorial identity in Tamilaham—the area between Kanyakumari and the Tirupati temple.[84]

If we do not want the twenty-first century to be wasted in dissipating human resources for a self-destructive armaments race, and avoid the tragedies that Europe went through in the present century, we should critically approach the history of South Asia for the last hundred years with an agenda for research which also asks some fresh questions. These questions should probe the configuration of the 'fragments' that lay below the highly visible history of the parties of the elite, understand the motive forces behind popular movements, not equate the history of one all-India party with the history of a nation, explain (without explaining away) the divisions which the Raj exploited by analysing their local specificities, analyse whether the perception by many political figures of the whole of South Asia as a single successor state to the British Indian empire was conducive to securing the greatest measure of anti-imperial consensus. It was clear from the reform of 1909 and the subsequent reforms that the communal card would be played for the containment of anti-imperialism on an all-India scale. In the last thirty years of the Raj when a Britain weakened by the Great War (1914–18) conceded some very limited space to the principle of representative government, the Montford reforms of 1919, and the Government of India Act (1935), the underlying strategy was to have an overarching monetary and geopolitical military control while conceding provincial autonomy and federating the princely states.[85]

Scholars have been so preoccupied with examining the all-India struggle between the Raj, the Congress and the Muslim League, that enough attention has not been paid to the records of the Reforms Office (in the National Archives) between the Simon Commission and the Cripps Mission, which have data on how the introduction of 'provincial autonomy' kindled the desire to establish localised political identities in some provinces, and for redrawing the boundaries on a linguistic basis; there are not enough monographs on that period.[86]

In the late 1930s 'federation' had become a distasteful word to Indian nationalists because it got associated with the scheme of the Raj (Constitution Act of 1935) to counterpoise their electoral strength with a phalanx of feudal supporters—to use a European analogy, to balance the 'Third Estate' by the other Estates. Considering that civil society in the subcontinent is fascinatingly rich in its diversity, it was most unfortunate that Indian leaders had a mental block on the general concept of federation and opposed giving residuary powers to the provinces. The mindset that produced the report of the Nehru Committee (1928) was very Jacobin/Mazzinian in outlook, and repeated all the mistakes of the French revolutionaries (which I have earlier alluded to) in its stern plea for a unitary constitution. By the end of the 1930s many Congress leaders (including Gandhi) were throwing out feelers to Liberal British politicians that they should persuade the British government to accept the Congress as representing the entire nation.[87] This was the nationalist variant of the much-criticised (in my opinion, justifiably) Leninist assumption that a vanguard party represented the working class.[88] However, Maulana Abul Kalam Azad, in his presidential address at the Ramgarh session of the Congress in 1940 did not reveal any allergy to the federal concept.

In Europe the old multi-ethnic multilingual empires collapsed in the First World War. Within twenty months after Armistice Day (11 November 1918) new states were carved out of the old empires.[89] Subsequent history has shown that viable nation-states cannot be forced out of old structures in a matter of months. Another traumatic world war and a transitory 'revolution from above' claiming to bring socialism and people's democracy have still Left parts of south-eastern Europe in a state of disequilibrium.

In South Asia the carving-up process took fifteen months (16 May 1946 Cabinet Mission Plan to 14/15 August 1947 transfer of power, with partition) and the new governments 'inherited (and chose to retain) [the] apparatus of the colonial state largely unaltered, including that of the police, army, judiciary, legal system as well as the much-vaunted civil service . . .'[90]

Indian history did not end on 15 August 1947.[91] Over the past fifty years India, Pakistan, and (since 1971) Bangladesh have seen many sporadic incidents of violence but also a fair degree of determination and success in trying to make up for the lag in development created by two centuries of colonialism. In our own country, if we were to shed some of the centralist features of the Government of India Act (1935) which we carried over to the Indian Constitution,[92] and make India a genuine federation of states, we will set an example to our immediate neighbours and be in a position to make the states of SAARC a genuine confederation of peoples of a common civilisation, partners in development.

NOTES

1. K. Marx and F. Engels, *The Communist Manifesto* (1848). In the original text the authors refer to 'the common ruin of the contending classes'.
2. T.J. Oommen (ed.), *Citizenship and National Identity* (New Delhi, 1997) p. 13.
3. P.J. Taylor, *Political Geography: World System, Nation State and Locality* (New York, 1994), pp. 4–11.
4. T. Raychaudhuri, *Europe Reconsidered* (Delhi, 1988), p. 14.
5. M.K. Gandhi, 'Hind Swaraj', in *Collected Works of Mahatma Gandhi*, vol. 10 (Ahmedabad, 1963), pp. 40ff.
6. J. Hale, *Machiavelli and Renaissance Italy* (London, 1961), pp. 20–2 and pp. 144f.
7. Owen Lattimore, *Inner Asian Frontier of China* (Oxford, 1988 reprint of 1940 edn), p. 66.
8. Anthony David Smith, *Ethnic Origins of Nations* (London, 1986), p. 12.
9. Quoted in A.W. Orridge, 'Uneven Development and Nationalism', *Political Studies*, vol. 29, 1981, p. 2, n. 3.
10. E.J. Hobsbawm, *Nations and Nationalism Since 1780* (Cambridge, 1992 edn); Ernest Gellner, *Nations and Nationalism* (London, 1983); Anthony

Giddens, *Nation-State and Violence* (Cambridge, 1985), especially ch. 8 entitled 'Class, Sovereignty and Citizenship'; Michael Mann, *The Sources of Social Power*, vol. 2, *Rise of Classes and Nation-States 1760–1914* (Cambridge 1993), especially ch. 7; Benedict Anderson, *Imagined Communities* (London, 1983; revised edn 1992).

11. E. Gellner, *Thought and Change* (London, 1964), p. 152.

12. The argument has been developed at various places in Gellner's *Nations and Nationalism,* especially pp. 14–17, 72–8.

13. Guy Hermet, *Histoire des nations et du nationalisme en Europe* (Paris, 1996), pp. 68–70, 72–6.

14. Anderson, *op.cit,* ch. 3 and also pp. 78ff; also see Stein Rokkan, 'Territories, Centres and Peripheries', in Jean Gottman (ed.), *Centre and Periphery* (London, 1981), p. 173, where he writes 'Gutenberg created an essential technology for the building of nations.'

15. Mann, *op.cit.,* pp. 217f.

16. Ibid., pp. 218–52.

17. Smith, *op.cit.,* p. 63.

18. For the Roman Empire, see S.B. Jones, 'Boundary Concepts in the Setting of Place and Time' *Annals of the American Association of Geographers,* (hereafter *AAAG*), vol. XLIX, 1959, pp. 246f; for China, the classic work of Lattimore, *op.cit.,* pp. 77, 495–510.

19. L.K.D. Kristof, 'The Nature of Frontiers and Boundaries', *AAAG,* vol. XLIX, 1959, pp. 269–90; also S.B. Jones, *op.cit.,* p. 246.

20. Kristof, *op.cit.,* p. 269, n. 7.

21. N.G. Pounds, 'Origin of the Idea of Natural Frontiers in France', *AAAG,* vol. XLI, 1951, pp. 149–50.

22. Quoted in ibid., p. 154.

23. Ibid., p. 156, n. 56.

24. N.G. Pounds, 'France and 'Les Limites naturelles' from the seventeenth to the twentieth centuries' *AAAG,* XLIV, 1954, pp. 51–3.

25. In the original it reads 'eine eigenartige und inhaltsreiche geistige Gemeinschaft', in F. Meinecke, *Weltburgertum und National Staat* (Munich, 1962 edn of 1907 text), p. 9. Translation mine. The American translation of this work, entitled *Cosmopolitanism and the Nation-State,* is not available in India.

26. Karl W. Deutsch, *Nationalism and Social Communication* (New York, 1953), p. 5.

27. James B. Holt, *The State in Early Modern France* (Cambridge, 1995), ch. 1.

28. R.A. Griffith, 'The Later Middle Ages, 1290–1485', in Kenneth O. Morgan (ed.), *Oxford Illustrated History of Britain* (Oxford, 1984), p. 212.

29. Hermet, *op.cit.*, p. 59.
30. Christopher Hill, *The World Turned Upside Down* (London, 1972).
31. C.G. Windell, *The Catholics and German Unity, 1866–71* (Minneapolis, 1954).
32. Unless otherwise stated, the details in this paragraph are based on R.R. Davies, 'The Peoples of Britain and Ireland, 1100–1400: Language and Historical Mythology', *Transactions of the Royal Historical Society*, (hereafter *TRHS*) 6s, vol. VII, 1997, pp. 1–24.
33. Ibid., p. 13.
34. Jenny Wormald, 'The Creation of Britain: Multiple Kingdoms or Core and Colonies?' *TRHS*, 6s, vol. II, 1992, pp. 177f. The spelling in the seventeenth-century original has not been changed.
35. Anderson, *op.cit.*, p. 42.
36. Hermet, *op.cit.*, p. 58.
37. Einer Haugen, 'Dialect, Languages, Nation', *American Anthropologist*, vol. 68, 1966, pp. 922–8; also see Deutsch, *op.cit.*, p. 26, linguistic map of France.
38. Mazzini as quoted in L. Namier, *Vanished Supremacies* (London, 1958), p. 46.
39. Charles G. Nauert, Jr., *Humanism and the Culture of Renaissance Europe* (Cambridge, 1995), p. 179; also see ibid., pp. 173–95 for development of vernacular literature.
40. John Breuilly, *Nationalism and the State* (Manchester, 1982), pp. 4f. Dante's lead was followed. The humanist poet Pietro Bembo, though himself a Venetian, wrote a treatise 'Della Volgar Lingua' in 1525, justifying why he used Tuscan for his literary works (Nauert, *op.cit.*, p. 174).
41. Breuilly, *op.cit.*, p. 5.
42. Hale, *op.cit.*, pp. 20–2.
43. Haugen, *op.cit.*, p. 925.
44. Q. Hoare and G.N. Smith (eds) *Selections from the Prison Notebooks of Antonio Gramsci* (London, 1971), p. 63. The date when Gramsci wrote this in his 'Notes on Italian History' is given on p. 90.
45. A very good book on this subject is Thorlac Turville-Petre, *England the Nation: Language, Literature and National Identity, 1280–1340* (Oxford, 1996).
46. Griffith, *loc.cit.*, p. 216. A similar tolerance has not been shown in India with regard to the listing of national languages (Oommen, *op.cit.*, p. 161).
47. Hobsbawm, *op.cit.*, p. 76.
48. Davies, *loc.cit.*, p. 21.
49. Ernest Renan, 'What is a Nation?' (1882), reprinted in Alfred Zimmern (ed.), *Modern Political Doctrines* (London, 1939), p. 190.

50. Karl W. Deutsch, *Nationalism and Social Communication—An Enquiry into the Foundations of Nationality* (New York, 1953), p. 16; Charlotte Muret, 'The Swiss Pattern for a Federated Europe', in E.M. Earle (ed.), *Nationalism and Internationalism* (New York, 1950).

51. Hans Daalder, 'On Building Consociational Nations: The cases of the Netherlands and Switzerland', *International Social Science Journal,* vol. XXIII, 1971, pp. 355–70; also see Muret, *op.cit.* David O. Moberg 'Social Differentiation in the Netherlands', *Social Forces*, vol. IV, 1961, pp. 333–7. One suspects that if earlier generations of South Asian historians and political scientists had not been hypnotised by the political and constitutional experiences of countries like Britain, France, Germany and Italy, they coud have drawn valuable inputs from the histories of smaller European countries.

52. Rokkan, *loc.cit.,* p. 171; S. Rokkan, 'Dimensions of State Formation', in C. Tilly (ed.), *Formation of National States in Western Europe* (Princeton, 1974), pp. 574–89.

53. Marc Bloch, *The Royal Touch* (London, 1973; first published Paris 1924).

54. Susan Reynolds, *Kingdoms and Communities in Western Europe, 900–1300* (Oxford, 1984), ch. 8.

55. Griffith, *loc.cit.,* p. 222.

56. R.R. Davies, 'The Peoples of Britain and Ireland—Identities, 1100–1400' *TRHS,* 6s, vol. IV, 1994, p. 18.

57. A.A.M. Duncan, *The Nation of Scots and the Declaration of Arbroath* (London, 1970).

58. Morgan, *op.cit.,* pp. 252–3. Professor Oommen is incorrect in saying (*op.cit.,* p. 15) that Wales was not annexed.

59. Kenneth O. Morgan, *Wales in British Politics, 1868–1922* (Cardiff, 1980).

60. See n. 37 above. Abbe Gregoire's linguistic survey of 1790 shows that three-quarters of the population knew some French, but only 10 per cent could speak it properly (Mann, *op.cit.,* p. 240).

61. Mann, ibid.

62. Mann, ibid., ch. 7, section 4, 'Post-1792 Militarism', has a good discussion of this.

63. Pounds, as in n. 24 above, pp. 54–6.

64. Ibid., pp. 58–9. Because of its pan-German overtones, this stanza remains excluded from the present-day national anthem.

65. Hugh Seton-Watson, *Nationalism and Communism* (London, 1964), p. 31.

66. Walter C. Langsam, 'Nationalism and History in the Prussian Elementary Schools Under William II', in Earle (ed.), *op.cit.,* pp. 241–60. The quotation is at p. 243.

67. Ibid., p. 259.
68. Carlo Antoni, *From History to Sociology: The Transition in German Historical Thinking* (London, 1959), p. 87. Chapter 3 of this book is devoted entirely to Meinecke.
69. G. Mazzini, *Duties of Man* (London, 1907 edn), p. 58.
70. W.L. Langer, *Political and Social Upheaval, 1837–1852* (New York, 1969), p. 253.
71. As Gramsci put it, '... unity had not taken place on a basis of equality, but as hegemony of the North over the Mezzogiorno in a territorial version of the town–country relationship—in other words, that the North concretely was an 'octopus' which enriched itself at the expense of the South, and that its economic-industrial increment was in direct proportion to the impoverishment of the economy and the agriculture of the South' *(op.cit.* pp. 70f). Also see C. Seton-Watson, *Italy, from Liberation to Fascism, 1870–1928* (Oxford, 1967).
72. Carroll Quigley, 'Falsification of a Source in Risorgimento History', *Journal of Modern History,* XX (1948), pp. 223–6.
73. Tracy H. Koon, 'Fascist Mythmaking: The Italian Regime's Appeal to Youth', in Ivo Banac *et al.* (ed.), *Nation and Ideology: Essays in Honour of Wayne S. Vucinich* (New York, 1981), pp. 387–407. The following typical quotation in a training manual for ten-year-olds is self-explanatory: 'If you listen carefully you may still hear the terrible tread of the Roman legions.... Caesar has come to life again in the Duce ... step into the ranks of the army and be the best soldiers' (ibid., p. 396).
74. I am referring to the history curriculum of the network of schools run by the Vidya Bharati, which was reported in the national press between 23 and 25 October 1998.
75. Romila Thapar, *From Lineage to State* (Bombay, 1984).
76. Romila Thapar, *The Mauryas Revisited* (Calcutta, 1987); Kumkum Roy, 'In Which Part of South Asia did the Early Brahminical Tradition (1st millennium BC) Take its Form?' *Studies in History,* IX (n.s.) (1993), pp. 1–32. Gouri Lad, Mahabharata *and Archaeological Evidence* (Poona, 1983). The standard work of Professor Dinesh C. Sircar is of course a basic work of reference on which later scholars have built (D.C. Sircar, *Cosmography and Geography in Early Indian Literature* [Calcutta 1967].
77. See nn. 56–8 above, for reference to Wales. Also, for the ancient Greek city states, P. Anderson, *Passages from Antiquity to Feudalism* (London, 1978 edn), pp. 20–2.
78. V.A. Smith, *Early History of India* (Oxford, 1924 edn) p. 8.
79. Y. Subbarayalu, *Political Geography of the Chola Country* (Madras, 1973); B. Stein, *Peasant, State and Society in Medieval South India* (Delhi, 1980);

B.D. Chattopadhyaya, *The Making of Early Medieval India* (Delhi, 1994), ch. 8. In the light of what I said earlier at p. 6 about communications, I find the following observation of Burton Stein, in the context of his controversial thesis, to be plain commonsense; about the centralised unitary state he writes: 'Such a state [did not] exist in most of the world prior to the industrial revolution which provided the technology and mobile force required to sustain unitary states as we know them' (*op.cit.*, p. 264).

80. On the administrative and legal side, see B.B. Misra, *The Administrative History of India, 1834–1947* (Delhi, 1970), chs V–VII.

81. Ibid., ch. IV.

82. Even though many old dynasties got their thrones back, the abolition of serfdom in the Rhineland and Prussia was not reversed nor was the abolition of the temporal power of the papacy outside Italy, or the accretion in the size of individual German states like Bavaria and Baden.

83. Smith, *op.cit.*, p. 126.

84. E.S. Viswanathan, *Political Career of E. V. Ramaswamy Naicker* (Madras, 1983); P.N.S. Mansergh and P. Moon (eds), *Transfer of Power*, vol. I (1970). doc. no 446 at p. 555. On Tamilaham, see Stein, *op.cit*, p. 107. I am grateful to Dr Sumathi Ramaswamy for enlightening me on this issue.

85. I have been examining the British Public Records and private papers along with Indian archival sources over the past two decades and some of my findings on these points are available in the following: P.S. Gupta, 'Federalism and Provincial Autonomy as Devices of Imperial Control'. 'State and Business in the Age of Discriminating Protection', 'Imperial Strategy and the Transfer of Power, 1939–1951', 'Radio and the Raj, 1921–1947', all in this volume.

86. Rani D. Shankardass, *The First Congress Raj: Provincial Autonomy in Bombay* (Delhi, 1982); David Baker, *Changing Political Leadership in an Indian Province: The C.P. and Berar 1919–39* (Delhi, 1980); Ian Talbot, *Khizi Tiwana, the Punjab Unionist Party and the Partition of India* (Richmond, 1996); Vinita Damodaran, *Broken Promises* (Delhi, 1992), dealing with Bihar; Amalendu Guha, *From Planter Raj to Swaraj* (Delhi, 1977) and his sectional presidential address at the 44th session of the Indian History Congress (1983).

87. Lord Lothian's correspondence with Gandhiji shows this (Scottish Record Office, Edinburgh).

88. For criticism of the theory of the Vanguard Party within the socialist tradition, see the writings of Rosa Luxembourg.

89. The Treaty of Trianon which fixed the boundaries of a shrunken Hungary, enlarging Yugoslavia, Romania and even Czechoslovakia in the process, was signed on 4 June 1920.

90. I am quoting from Pranab Bardhan's essay 'The State Against Society', in S. Bose and A. Jalal (eds), *Nationalism, Democracy and Development: State and Politics in India* (Delhi, 1997). There are many thought-provoking essays in this volume, especially Amartya Sen's 'On Interpreting India's Past'.

91. A recently published textbook has the history of all the South Asian countries up to the 1990s and is therefore a welcome supplement to the textbooks commonly used, which stop the story short at August 1947 (S. Bose and A. Jalal, *Modern South Asia: History, Culture, Political Economy* [Delhi, 1998].

92. For example, Article 356, which is an echo of Section 93 of the Government of India Act, 1935. A distinguished senior advocate of the Supreme Court has recently written, 'An Imperial Provision, Article 356 is a Political Nuisance' (Rajeev Dhavan, 'The BJP or the Constitution', *The Hindu*, 25 September 1998, p. 10). In this connection I wish to draw attention to the following publication, the proceedings of a seminar held in New Delhi a little over a decade ago, which showed that people who had been close to the corridors of power realised the importance of the federal idea, and that India could not be a monolith; see, in particular, the presentation of the late Rasheeduddin Khan (at pp. 40–50), and the observations of Shri N.K. Mukherji and the late P.N. Haksar at pp. 63–4. (R.C. Dutt (ed.), *Nation-Building in India* [Delhi, 1987].

THE DECLINE AND FALL OF
THE BRITISH EMPIRE*

I have very close personal ties with Kerala,[1] and Calicut has historic associations with the theme on which I wish to speak today. It was in this city that Vasco da Gama's arrival started the process of European colonialism in Asia—the after-effects of which are still with us. This worldwide phenomenon needs to be looked at afresh from the perspective of the colonial peoples, as a distinguished Indian historian reminded us fifteen years ago at a previous session of this Congress.[2]

There is now enough original material in India on microfilm to make possible research on aspects of British imperial policy.[3] I shall limit myself to surveying the state of the question in the historiography of British imperialism in the twentieth century, and indicate areas where research is desirable.

I

The term 'imperialism' in general and British imperialism in particular have been subject to a fairly continuous onslaught from a number of Western historians for some time past. There are some, like Keith Hancock, or Kitson Clark, who objected to the use of the term altogether;[4] others, while using it, give it the specific connotation of the establishment of direct colonial rule. Most of them are convinced that imperialism was the result not so much of economic impulses or of the humanitarian desire to bring civilisation and good government to non-European peoples as of the urge to dominate.

A recent volume in the Cambridge Commonwealth Series opens

* Presidential Address, Indian History Congress, Section IV ('Countries Other than India'), Calicut/Kozhikode, 1976.

with the sentence, 'Let it be agreed then that the theory of "economic imperialism" is dead, and that there is no further point in trying to discuss British imperial history within the framework it has created'.[5] Landes makes some pertinent criticisms of oversimplified versions of the Marxist explanation, and sees the persistence of European expansionism in the nineteenth century as born of the desire of stronger peoples to dominate the weaker.[6] Benjamin Cohen has devoted a book to doing the same,[7] and Hinsley has argued that, 'imperialism in the nineteenth century was not the necessary outcome of capitalism but the natural expression of power in the conditions of the time'.[8]

Hale in his textbook in the highly reputed 'Harper' series argued that 'considerations of native welfare under trusteeship began to replace colonial exploitation', and approvingly quoted Fieldhouse's negative verdict on what he called 'the Hobson–Leninist dogma'.[9] Corelli Barnett in a provocative study entitled *The Collapse of British Power*, regards British interwar colonial policy as 'an essay in altruism', and the place of India in the British mind as being 'in the last resort . . . founded not upon calculation but upon love'.[10] Since Britain doggedly adhered to appeasement in the 1920s and the 1930s, so much so that she was barely prepared militarily in 1939, he argues that her foreign and imperial policy was based on lofty ethical values inappropriate in the realm of international relations. Ever since the Congress of Vienna, apparently, 'moral principle and moral purpose rather than strategy or mere interest' was the 'inspiration of English policy'. Evidence of late nineteenth-century jingoism is slurred over by painting the imperialists as being 'often idealists of the true moralising and romantic Victorian model'. The creation of the League of Nations is used to support the hypothesis that the 'moralists and internationalists [had] set the tone of British war-making and mythmaking'.[11] A reviewer has praised Barnett for 'his integration of foreign and defence policy with financial, industrial and many other questions'.[12] Barnett does try to do this but finally produces an erudite piece of special pleading.

II

Academic studies of British imperialism, whether in Britain, Canada, the US, or Australia have for a long time been unable to shake off the straitjacket of the narrow constitutional framework. The formal assumption of sovereignty or paramountcy is regarded as the beginning of empire, and all types of informal control ignored. British economic or strategic penetration in China, Argentina, and various parts of west and central Asia is thus by and large ignored by specialists in 'imperial and commonwealth history'. Controversies about the periodisation of British imperialism show this constitutional bias by highlighting years when government policy or public opinion debated the question of the devolution or demission of imperial authority, without considering whether the network of economic interests binding Britain and the colonies was influenced thereby in any significant way.[13] Research has also concentrated on studying colonial constitutions, the pattern of colonial administration, and the degree of autonomy and initiative enjoyed by colonial governors or legislators.[14] From such studies some modern historians have sought to develop the 'peripheral' theory of imperial expansion—that if the impulse towards expansion stems from an autonomous authority such imperialism should be considered not as *British* imperialism, but as that of the New Zealanders, the British settlers in the Cape Colony, or the East India Company.[15] This line of argumentation as well as the general preoccupation with constitutional history have led to an undue emphasis on the history of the white dominions or of the settler colonies in Africa and the West Indies. As more and more evidence of colonial autonomy in such areas is piled up the revisionists are inclined to ask, 'Was there a British Empire?'[16]

Some distinguished historians consciously tried to overcome the limitations of their earlier training by deliberately bringing the concept of 'informal' empire into British historiography and underplaying the importance of constitutional issues. Robinson and Gallagher's classic article (1953) was a path-breaker in this respect,[17] but they themselves have not consistently used this broader definition of imperialism in their later work. Thus, in *Africa and the Victorians* they write, 'If by imperialism is meant the growth of metropolitan control, imperialism in South Africa between 1881 and 1895 declined.'[18] Even more recently, Hyam and Martin have criticised the constitutional bias but their own writings do not break fresh ground.[19] Political, as opposed to legal–constitutional, factors are stressed, but their self-imposed ban on economic factors limits them from probing further.

Because of this constitutional bias, the raw material is limited to the records of those departments directly dealing with the formal empire—the Colonial Office, the India Office, and (since 1925) the Dominions Office. These records deal with particular problems faced by administrators in specific areas of the empire. Using only these records leads even historians who profess to abjure a constitutional or administrative approach to emphasise unduly the technical problems of colonial administration, paternalistic efforts at colonial reform, and intra-departmental squabbles between Whitehall and the colonial rulers. Such records seldom provide any insight into wider economic, diplomatic, and strategic imperatives. The study of imperialism thus gets divorced from the study of the dynamics of British capitalism, which after all has been the main driving force behind the rise of Britain to the status of a great power since the seventeenth century.[20] To redress the balance we need to look at government departments of greater prestige, and, in some cases, of longer ancestry—the Treasury, the Foreign Office, the Board of Trade, the War Office, and the Admiralty. Questions should be framed in such a way as to enable us not simply to show how decisions were arrived at by interdepartmental discussions, but also how these discussions reveal the ruling classes' explicit or implicit assumptions about the national interest. Once this approach is accepted, we are likely to find that the maintenance and furtherance of British capitalism lay behind most of the widely varied manifestations of imperial policy. In concrete terms a study of the Foreign Office records relating to southern Persia is as much a study in imperialism as a study based on the Colonial Office records relating to New Zealand.

To discuss British imperialism by merging the formal and informal empire together and placing it in the context of British capitalism raises one difficulty. In the 1860s a large part of the globe (including Western Europe and America) had accepted free trade or very low tariffs.[21] Would all countries which then had a high turnover of trade with Britain and imported large quantities of British capital count as part of the British empire? Evidently not. In the case of Western Europe or the US the bargaining power of the political and economic elites of these countries was sufficiently strong to ensure that the gains of such trade were reciprocal. In the case of Turkey and Latin America, Britain had superior bargaining power and these countries can be classified as part of the British informal empire.[22] The historian who first used the concept of 'informal empire' in the context of Argentina was H.S. Ferns.[23] Subsequently he was dissatisfied with his own use of the term. His detailed researches showed how important Britain was as an exporter of capital and goods to Argentina and as a customer for Argentine primary produce, and how, over a period of time Argentina possessed a weak industrial structure compared to Britain. Yet Ferns argues that British imperialism in Argentina was a myth, first because there was no occasion to use overt political power, and second because certain sections of Argentine farmers prospered at the expense of the British farmer.[24] This is irrelevant. The Marxist case for capitalist imperialism is proved by the prosperity of the industrial and financial bourgeoisie in Britain and their ability to exercise dominant influence on Argentine economic life.

We can therefore include parts of Latin America within the British informal empire. We must remember however that the ease with which Palmerstonian gunboat diplomacy could be used to chastise a semi-colony in Asia or Africa (China, Turkey, Egypt) was less easy in South America because of the Monroe Doctrine. During the Venezuela crisis of 1902–3 Britain realised this and trimmed her policy so as not to offend the US.[25]

A similar difficulty faces us in the case of the self-governing colonies—in short, the 'peripheral' theory of imperialism. The problem cannot be dismissed because after the white dominions became *de facto* sovereign states their imperial sins in the economic and military spheres were wrongly visited on Britain, sometimes by Marxist scholars. R. Palme Dutt in 1953, in describing the sterling area dollar pool after 1945, suggested that the British balance of payments was being sustained by the dollar surpluses of Malaya and the Gold Coast, but in the years 1947–9 the real culprits were later shown to have been the white dominions.[26] Anti-Marxist scholars pointed to such mistakes as examples of the alleged superficiality of Marxism.

The problem of the white colonies can be solved by defining the British capitalist class not as a homogeneous group necessarily located in Britain, bur as a series of interlocking interests, located in different parts of the empire, collaborating with each other and united by the sense of being all-British communities. Indeed, in the 1830s and 1840s, with the acceptance of free trade, mercantilist theories of colonies lost their justification and instead an empire of settlement and investment was visualised.[27] The British politicians who conceded responsible self-government to British colonies did so expecting that this would promote the prosperity of British capitalism and stimulate the flow of investment and trade further. Neither the British rulers nor the colonial leaders who wanted self-government questioned the retention of commercial, foreign, and defence policy in the hands of Whitehall.[28]

Given this, it is not so very important that over the question of the annexation of certain islands in the Pacific there were differences between London and New Zealand.[29] What is important is that the New Zealand economy was in effect an agrarian sector of the British economy. It was heavily dependent on Britain for capital and markets, and its agricultural trade cycle closely followed the industrial trade cycle in Britain.[30] Similarly, the empire-building efforts of Cecil Rhodes in Cape Colony cannot be delinked from British capitalism. There may have been occasional differences between Lord Salisbury and Cecil Rhodes, just as there were differences between Warren Hastings and the Court of Directors of the East India Company, but the interests of London and Cape Town were very close. As Trevor Lloyd has put it, 'The more capital the mine owners needed, the more permanent their position in Africa became, which meant that they had to take an interest in the political situation, and at the same time the closer their links with the London capital market became.'[31]

The peripheral explanation of imperialism as a separate form of imperialism—distinct from British—is applicable only when the colony becomes not only a self-governing dominion but chooses to pursue economic and foreign policies different from those of Britain. In the nineteenth century very few did so. The interests of these collaborating communities of British settlers all merge in the promotion of British trade and investment throughout the world. As Robinson has put it, the white settler was 'the ideal, prefabricated collaborator'.[32]

III

The concept of 'collaborators' was initially popularised by Robinson and Gallagher. Although the term has been cynically misapplied by some younger Cambridge historians in the course of writing about nationalism, we still need to use it in a specific and unambiguous sense if we wish to explain the mechanics of British expansionism. The vast, thickly populated empire was run in Britain's commercial interests with a relatively small number of British imperial personnel located in the outposts. In such a situation, British settlers in Canada and Australia, rich *taluqdars* and princes in parts of India, and tribal chiefs in Africa, all were useful to British capitalism in its worldwide quest for markets, investment outlets and raw material supplies, with the minimum expenditure on administrative overheads. Hobsbawm has shown how, in the nineteenth century, in order to avoid a social revolution from below, the British industrial bourgeoisie compromised with the landed interests, and as a result was obliged to tolerate a fair degree of institutional inefficiency. In the very long run this was bad for the British economy, but in the mid-nineteenth century 'the cost of institutional inefficiency . . . was little more than petty cash to the most dynamic industrial economy of the world'.[33] Similarly, the cost of sharing some of the gains of colonial exploitation with local collaborators was considered negligible. The really interesting situation arose when, in course of time, new social groups emerged overseas, or some British settlers themselves became capitalists competing with the metropolis. If then the British ruling class, under the influence of past experience, still tried to buy them off, they sometimes found that the cost was prohibitive.

So far as the dominions are concerned, for our purposes they ceased to be part of the British empire when they developed a local capitalist industry which significantly competed with Britain, and when the city of London and the Bank of England ceased to influence their monetary policies. Judged by these criteria Canada was outside the British empire and close to the US during the period of the Canada–US reciprocity treaty (1854–66), developed a local economic nationalism between 1878 and 1897, and came again within the economic zone of Britain between 1897 and 1914, when both preference for British trade and imports of British capital made the links stronger. After 1919, and especially after Britain abandoned the gold standard in 1931, Canada moved out of the imperial economic network, with her industry increasingly protected by tariffs and her currency managed with an eye on maintaining its value at par with the US dollar.[34] For the 1930s we can say that the territories of the dependent empire and ex-mandates

like Iraq which eventually formed the Sterling Area constituted an empire
the rationale of which was economic and Britain hoped that it would
provide some security in a period of worldwide contraction of markets.

Before developing an explanatory model for British imperial decline
in the interwar years, it has to be recognised that British imperialism
before 1914 does not fit Lenin's formula: that the last stage of capitalism is characterised by the growth of cartels, export of capital to the
newly annexed colonial territories and finance capital. There is a complete lack of correlation between the territories formally annexed by
Britain and the flow of British foreign investment between 1870 and
1914; nor was British capitalism at that time characterised either by
large combines or the interlocking of banks and industry.[35] As the
Marxist historian Michael Barratt-Brown has shown, Lenin had drawn
a composite picture of imperialism, taking in features from France,
Britain and Germany, which gave a false coherence to the doctrine.[36]
The purpose of historical materialism being to give specific causal
connections between a capitalist class and their state policy, in studying
Britain there is no point in trying to establish a link between capital
exports and cartels and colonial policy. We should concentrate on
how far policy was guided by the quest for markets, raw materials,
and concern to protect existing investments.

Second, a dogmatic adherence to the doctrine that this period marked
the highest stage of capitalism makes one see the connection between
imperialism and economic necessity too narrowly, to imply that the
acquisition of each colonial territory or the extension of each zone of
informal empire was so crucial that without it British capitalism would
have collapsed. Such a rigid stand will make the whole Marxist explanation vulnerable to such obvious facts as that between 1901 and 1910
the dependent African colonies took only 2.5 per cent of British
investments,[37] or that only four per cent of British capital export was
involved in the hectic diplomatic activity of British consuls in China
in the late nineteenth century.[38]

A better way of establishing the connection between capitalism and
empire is to show that more often than not the ruling group sought
territory not for prestige or for spreading the gospel but for keeping it
free for British trade or for protecting a trade route. Till 1932 Britain
did not need a protected market, but wanted to ensure that other

protectionist powers did not divide up the rest of the world among themselves.[39] It is irrelevant to argue against the economic interpretation that in the period between 1932 and 1939 the colonial territories took only between 22 and 25 per cent of British exports. One measures the utility of a colony not by the percentage of actual trade but by the general importance that a protected market has in a period of competition and shrinking world trade.[40] Nor is it relevant to argue, as Corelli Barnett does, that the absence of economic motives is borne out by the fact that these colonial territories did not have their resources fully exploited.[41] No Marxist historian ever argued that there would be instant correlation in the changes occurring at the base and at the superstructure, least of all in the superstructure of ideas influencing policy. A generation of Treasury officials trained to think that government expenditure could not stimulate investment and economic activity continued to pour cold water on schemes to develop the colonies.[42] As a result Britain did not get as much as she could have out of her African colonies in the interwar years.

Besides, investment opportunities continued to flourish in traditional areas—Latin America continued to be attractive to British capital till 1928.[43] Therefore African territory, acquired in a pre-emptive manner during the late-nineteenth-century scramble, could well be left to the last in the queue for investments. Pressure from the electorate at home for unemployment relief could—and did—lead to more industrial schemes (for the relief of unemployment) being located in Britain than in the colonies.[44] The colonies still remained reliable areas because they permitted protection against Japanese competition and because Britain had a decisive say in prohibiting them industrialising in a manner competitive to Britain.[45]

Another rigid formulation that is not a necessary part of the theory of capitalist imperialism is the view that capitalism and militarism are invariably linked, that capitalist nations are bound to go to war with each other. To maintain the validity of such a hypothesis is to ignore the evidence of the scaling down of armaments between 1922 and 1932. It can also boomerang against its proponents, as for example when Corelli Barnett argues that Britain's demobilisation and her adherence to a policy of arms limitations till 1937 is proof that she was not in the empire-building business for capitalist reasons.[46] Without going to the extent of Schumpeter or Hicks, who believed that pure capitalism is a guarantee of peace, and that wars occur because of the atavistic impulses of pre-capitalist social groups,[47] one can say that there can be situations when the ruling class of a capitalist nation would avoid going to war with another capitalist nation. Historically the capitalist class has gone to war against their own workers or against colonial peoples, or against capitalists of different nationalities, provided that the losses incurred in battle had a reasonable prospect of being more than made up by business profits afterwards. But if technological developments in a war between capitalist countries bring unprecedented devastation and carry off among its millions dead many members of the ruling classes, then it is perfectly understandable that for some time thereafter a capitalist nation—especially one heavily dependent on international trade— would try to avoid war with technologically developed nations. It may turn violent in breaking strikes at home and suppressing national movements abroad, but it would avoid a general war.

Such indeed were the specific effects of the First World War on Britain. Out of 488,000 troops killed in France or Flanders 37,452 were officers; out of 14,561 members of the Oxford Union who enlisted 2680 were killed, a heavy toll from among members of the ruling class. With 57 aerial raids causing 2907 casualties, 1413 among civilians, the traditional sense of security provided by the English Channel was gone.[48] Until the radar and the Spitfire were invented in the late 1930s there was always the fear, as expressed in Baldwin's tell-tale phrase, that 'the bomber will always get through'.[49]

British capitalism was thus constrained in its imperialist capabilities by certain specific limits—a hangover of old-fashioned economic thought at the Treasury, a desire to avoid continental land warfare; and also because of the commitment of the ruling classes to the form of parliamentary democracy. Fascist ideologies made little headway.[50] It meant that public opinion as reflected in the results of by-elections and elections and in opinion polls, could not be ignored by decision-makers. On some issues opinion could be manipulated; on others, especially on those affecting war and peace, it was less easy.[51]

IV

The decline of the British empire after the First World War can now be understood not in terms of national psychology but in terms of the dialectical interaction between economic ambitions and political realities, military goals and financial constraints.

On the eve of the war the serious capitalist rivals of Britain were Germany, the US, and Japan, but for well-known historic reasons it was Germany which posed a threat to Britain, while Japan was an ally, and the US a potential ally. As long as London remained the world's financial centre, free-trading Britain did not really think in terms of territory. She already had plenty; Germany had the maximum motive for redividing the globe,[52] and faced with German ambitions British strategists had a very difficult task in allocating the relative shares of resources for military operations in Britain, on the continent, and in the far corners of the empire.[53] When war came, all energies were focused on defeating Germany, whatever the area of fighting—the Middle East or Flanders—but from 1916 the imperial appetite was growing. For strategic and economic reasons Mesopotamia and Palestine in West Asia and Nauru in the Pacific were acquired, and any justification in terms of trusteeship and the civilising mission was very much an afterthought.[54] As Cabinet Secretary Sir Maurice Hankey put it,

. . . . I had suggested that the acquisition, or British control in some form or another, of the oil deposits in Mesopotamia was almost a vital consideration to us, as oil in the future would be as important as coal is now. Your comment on this had been that this was a purely Imperialistic War Aim.

I suppose that, if the matter is put as crudely as I put it, it is imperialistic, and though this does not shock me, I suppose it would shock President Wilson and some of our Allies. Nevertheless, it appears to me, even viewed from the point of view of the idealist, that it is almost unavoidable that we should acquire the Northern regions of Mesopotamia. . . . I presume . . . that neither President Wilson nor anyone else will wish to place the vast regions of Mesopotamia bordering the Tigris and Euphrates again under Turkish control. . . . If these regions are not to be under the control of the Turk, under whose control are they to be? I submit there is only one possible answer, and that is that, in some form or another, they will come under British control.[55]

The war, while increasing the British lion's appetite, had weakened its digestive capacity. Collaborators who helped win the war also limited British capitalism's opportunities to make the most of her gains. Organised labour at home, having improved its bargaining position, prevented wage reductions on any significant scale, and put paid in 1923 to Conservative efforts to persuade the electorate to accept imperial preference and tariff reform.[56] With the sale of British capital assets in the US, Wall Street emerged as a rival centre of international finance to London, thus making nonsense of all British plans to restore the pound sterling to its pre-war role—attempts which the British Treasury nevertheless continued to make.[57] American and Canadian pressure made it impossible for Britain to renew the Anglo-Japanese alliance,[58] and many a time in the next two decades British ministers were to regret it.[59] Finally, because of the strength of nationalist opinion in India, it was less easy to treat India as 'an English barrack in the Oriental Seas', not costing the British taxpayer anything. However, while the Government of India's refusal to bear the cost of defending Mesopotamia points to these difficulties, it was still possible to use India and Indian troops to defend British interests on the Arab coast and the Persian Gulf—a subject which has not been studied in depth for the interwar years.[60]

The social background of successive British prime ministers now was more obviously bourgeois and less aristocratic:[61] Bonar Law, an iron-merchant from Glasgow, Baldwin, proprietor of an iron and steel firm, and Neville Chamberlain, son of a Birmingham ironmonger, were all able businessmen. It was their misfortune that the economic advice available to them made them pursue a deflationary monetary policy which, while forcing cuts in government expenditure, did not ultimately increase British exports.[62] These cuts affected the armed forces, who were told to proceed on the assumption that there would be no major war for ten years. British imperial defence capabilities were further reduced when financial necessity in 1928 made Winston Churchill introduce the moving ten-year rule.[63]

The ten-year rule was prompted, however misguidedly, by concern for economic recovery, and was not a sign of pacifism or unwillingness to defend the empire. Cheaper ways of defending and policing the empire by air attack had meanwhile been developed and were being applied in west Asia and India—a striking contrast to official nervousness about the vulnerability of Britain to aerial bombing.[64] Corelli Barnett misses the point about imperialism when he comments sadly on the small proportion of Indian manpower used for imperial defence.[65]

Until 1931 imperial defence proceeded on the racialist assumption that sophisticated weapons would not be given to coloured troops.[66] Even after the principle had been abandoned, the actual process of Indianisation was slow.[67]

Meanwhile, even though tariff reform and imperial preference had been ruled out by the election of 1923, colonial economic policy remained preoccupied with reaping benefits for Britain alone. Throughout the 1920s Leopold Amery and W. Ormsby-Gore tried to coax money out of the Treasury for colonial development in order to provide fresh markets for British goods, culminating in the Colonial Development Act of 1929.[68] Both in its inception and in its operation the act was expected to help the British economy.[69] American competition in the field of Rhodesian copper or colonial rubber resources was sought to be fought by all available diplomatic weapons.[70] Where, as in the case of west Asian oil, Britain was militarily and economically not strong enough to maintain the undoubted supremacy which she had had in 1919, she took care that her vital strategic interests were preserved by rights of pre-emption in time of war.[71] Four years before Britain went protectionist, neo-mercantilist pressures were brought on the Crown agents for the colonies, asking them invariably to make store purchases from Britain.[72] And in 1930 the Federation of British Industries made proposals for the reallocation of industrial production within the empire—proposals which made partial concessions to colonial industrialists but were essentially blueprints to freeze the industrial development of the colonies at a certain stage to the advantage of Britain.[73] A subject as yet unexplored is what follow-up was taken on the proposals of the government's Ottawa Economic Committee, which was considering such suggestions of the Federation of British Industries.[74] Also inadequately developed is the issue of the central banks which were set up in the sterling bloc countries under the guiding hand of the Bank of England.[75]

Throughout the 1930s the Colonial Office was concerned to protect British trade in the colonial markets against Japanese competition.[76] Where, as in Malaya, Chinese merchants posed a potential threat to the British trading community, a measure of administrative decentralisation, by which the Malayan sultans were to be used as a counterpoise, was adopted.[77] Concessions to Indian capitalists (in cotton textiles and iron and steel) were expected to facilitate British trade in other commodities.

Lancashire's relative decline in India is not to be equated with the decline of British capitalist interests in India. It was in the 1930s, after all, that enterprises like the Imperial Chemical Industries established their foothold in India.[78] The private correspondence of Finance Member Sir James Grigg shows that he was not only hostile to Indian capitalist interests but wished to take advantage of disunities in the Congress ranks to weaken them.[79]

Against these developments Drummond's findings in *Imperial Economic Policy* do not add up to much.[80] He has simply documented from archival sources that the self-governing dominions were able to protect their interests better than Britain could in the bargaining over tariff schedules for commodities in inter-commonwealth trade. This is not surprising, but not very relevant to the study of the penetration of British capitalism in territories which were in a weaker bargaining position, the colonial empire and other less developed areas. What little he has to say on the colonial territories and their prospects for industrialisation is ill-documented.[81] In arguing that the government permitted the colonies to industrialise he has ignored the evidence of the report of an interdepartmental committee which definitely shows a bias against the colonies competing industrially with Britain.[82]

Important areas for research can be the patterns of investment and trade among the sterling bloc countries after 1932, and the nature of Anglo-American economic relations during and after the World Economic Conference. We know that Roosevelt's preoccupation with domestic economic affairs made him oppose permanent currency stabilisation, and that the conference ended in failure.[83] What has not been worked on is the massive material pertaining to the conference among the British cabinet papers, which should provide some clue to the foreign economic policy of the British government and which should be studied with papers relating to the Ottawa agreements.[84] While the Conservative government had not understood or adopted Keynesian remedies to solve the unemployment problem, they were seriously concerned to carry through the rationalisation and reorganisation of British industry in order to enlarge the volume of exports.[85] Indeed, preoccupation with economic stability for the sake of commercial recovery was Neville Chamberlain's justification for a slower rate of investment in the rearmament drive than that demanded by the chiefs of staff.[86]

The policy of appeasement is thus ultimately meaningful and justi-fiable only in imperial terms. It is superficial to explain it in terms of the wickedness of individuals who departed from a glorious British tradition of protecting the weaker party in a European squabble.[87] The policy pursued at Munich was very much in the tradition of nineteenth-century British diplomacy in Central and Eastern Europe.[88] An over-extended empire, whose defences were run on a shoe-string budget, could not possibly fight Japan, Italy, and Germany simultaneously. The Low Countries and the western frontier might be secure if Germany's desire for *lebensraum* in the east was not interfered with. In any case it would not affect 'the thin red line of oil and trade' down the Mediterra-nean and the Red Sea with which British imperialists were primarily concerned.[89] (In this indirect way Britain may have connived at a poten-tial threat to Russia although Stalin turned the tables very effectively.[90])

The British did not oppose Japan during the Manchurian crisis till the undeclared Sino-Japanese war because that seemed the only way to safeguard existing and potential business interests. With America offering no firm promise of military cooperation,[91] with the construc-tion of the Singapore base delayed because Labour opposed it in 1924,[92] and with US–British commercial interests occasionally diverging,[93] it was understandable that the Federation of British Industries would try to come to terms with the Japanese in Manchuria, and that links with Chiang Kai-shek would be sustained by getting Leith-Ross to help stabilise Chinese currency.[94] Ultimately, however, Japan proved more intractable and the British considered that their interests would be better served by supporting Chiang.[95]

The uncertain situation in Japan and the possibility that Anglo-Japanese trade rivalry could lead to military rivalry explain why Italy's Abyssinia policy was condoned, culminating in the Hoare–Laval Pact.[96] From the standpoint of British imperial interests it was a disaster to defer to public opinion and repudiate it. As late as 1934 the Defence Appreciation of the chiefs of staff excluded Italy from the list of potential enemies.[97] During the crisis Admiral Chatfield pointed out that to ensure the safe movement of the Fleet to East Asia, Britain needed a friendly Italy and a peaceful Mediterranean.[98] Since these considerations persisted till 1940, Britain continued to woo Italy, risking a cabinet crisis in February 1938.[99] It is significant that the triumvirate of cabinet ministers who supported Chamberlain strongly against Eden on this occasion were persons with Indian experience—Halifax, Simon and Hoare—who had just built a constitutional system to prop up the empire in South Asia and who knew that peace was needed for the new collaborators of the Raj to consolidate their position.[100]

Thanks to Grandi, and, on occasion, Ciano, the policy of appeasement of Italy paid off in Italy's neutrality in 1939[101]—a fact which both Chamberlain and Churchill set great store by.[102] But they had of course reckoned without the unpredictable nature of Mussolini's impulses.[103]

The anti-appeasers in the Conservative Party were few and mustered their largest strength only during the Munich crisis.[104] Had Hitler not marched into Prague on 15 March 1939 Chamberlain would have been able to avoid giving the guarantees to Poland and Romania, for it was only after that that public opinion became a factor to be reckoned with by party managers.[105] It was only then that the chiefs of staff were able to persuade a reluctant Chamberlain to open talks with Russia which, as we know, foundered on Poland's refusal to allow Russian troop movements through their country.[106]

Thus it is apparent that not only is appeasement best understood in imperial terms, but imperialism itself is best understood in capitalist terms. Those who had to decide on defending the empire calculated carefully the financial costs and commercial benefits likely to arise from an aggressive posture. They acted like businessmen, and not like power-hungry pro-consuls simply wishing to paint the map red.

V

One of the great strengths of the Marxist approach is its ability to distinguish between subjective intention and objective results. The desperate and, in some respects, heroic war effort of the British people under Churchill succeeded where it deserved to succeed—in the task of national defence in the battle of Britain. It failed, where it deserved to fail, in the protection of the empire in South Asia. Notwithstanding Churchill's repeated statements to the contrary, the hope of restoring the empire in Asia went up in smoke along with the *Prince of Wales* and the *Repulse*. Hoping against hope, nevertheless, attempts were made to restore the empire everywhere except in South Asia, and it was only three years after the shock of the Suez crisis (1956) that Harold Macmillan's 'wind of change' speech heralded the final winding up of the formal empire.

It is in this post-war period, when British capitalism was gradually allowing itself to be subordinated to American and European multi-national corporations, that the persistence of formal imperialism can be sometimes explained by hypotheses based on 'power-hunger' or the 'sacred trust'. And it was probably because such motives were found to involve more outlay than profit that the formal empire was dissolved rapidly, leaving the task of exploiting the less developed world to the well-tried technique of informal control—this time by gigantic multi-national corporations using the black or the brown sahib as the collaborator, rather than the white settler.[107]

In 1959, when Central Africa was seething with protests against the settler-dominated federation, a European champion of African rights—Guy Clutton-Brock—was jailed by Sir Roy Welensky. Vicky, the brilliant cartoonist of the *New Statesman*, drew a sketch showing Sir Roy in clerical dress, pointing to Clutton-Brock behind bars and speaking to the British colonial secretary (similarly attired): 'He is there for heresy; been practising what we preach.'[108] This recalls the old adage that 'hypocrisy is the tribute which vice pays to virtue', a proverb worth remembering in any study of British colonial policy.

Few systems of exploitation can survive for long if they starkly expose their character for all to see. The heart of the heartless world is to be found in a set of values that give legitimacy and respectability to the system, and give an illusion—to exploiter and exploited alike—that the system was for the common good and not private profit.

All along, British colonial administrators have justified themselves in the name of trusteeship, but there were some radicals who were sceptical of this and wanted to expose the reality of exploitation. Among their successes should be counted the *Memorandum on Native Policy in East Africa* (1930), the Colonial Development and Welfare Act (1940), and the four-year tenure of Creech-Jones as the Labour Secretary of State for Colonies (1946–50).[109] It was in this last period that, against heavy odds, some efforts were made to evolve a positive colonial policy in the interests of the indigenous population, and such radicals felt that they should not leave the colonies to the tender mercies of international capital until the positive policy had shown some chance of success.

Similarly, it is in this period, when all commonsense considerations of financial solvency, economic recovery, and the balance of payments required that Britain should cut her overseas commitments to the minimum (especially as the US had taken over the role of world policeman on behalf of capitalism) the British attempts to be an independent nuclear power, their retention of bases east of Suez and, above all, the disastrous Suez adventure, indicated that the quest for power and prestige can play its part, in the short run, in determining the life span of an empire.

Nevertheless, the main driving force of formal empire building and decolonisation remained what it had always been—the protection of British overseas economic interests. Of the colonial wars fought in this last period only two—Cyprus and Suez—could be characterised as being inspired by the illusion of power. The wars in Malaya and Kenya had the defence of economic privileges behind them.

I said earlier that British imperial historiography needs to be rescued from the narrow limits imposed by constitutional historians and by the records of departments of state dealing directly with the formal empire. As the formal empire ended but British capitalism and its overseas interests survived, this point was underlined by the recommendations of the Duncan Committee which led to the merger of the foreign, commonwealth, and colonial offices.[110] The emphasis that this report put on trade expansion made a disillusioned radical of the Overseas Development Institute complain, '[according to the Duncan Committee] a diplomat is a man who goes abroad to sell washing machines, vacuum cleaners and guns for his country.'[111] The critic was wrong, and the Duncan report right. The overseas policy of Britain, inside or outside the empire, had mainly been the promotion of British trade. The rise and the decline of the empire is best understood in these terms.

NOTES

1. My wife belongs to Kerala.
2. S. Gopal, 'Presidential Address, Section III', *Proceedings of the 24th Session of the Indian History Congress, 1961* (Calcutta, 1963), p. 202.
3. In Delhi University we have obtained on microfilm a range of material from the Public Record Office, London, relating to this. In this lecture unpublished Crown copyright material in the Public Record Office appears by permission of the Controller of Her Majesty's Stationary Office.

4. G.R. Kitson Clark, *An Expanding Society* (Cambridge, 1967), p. 85.
5. Ronald Hyam and Ged Martin, *Reappraisals in British Imperial History* (London, 1975), p. 1.
6. D. Landes, 'Some Thoughts on the Nature of Economic Imperialism', *Journal of Economic History*, XXI (1961).
7. Benjamin J. Cohen, *The Question of Imperialism* (London, 1974), p. 234ff.
8. F.H. Hinsley, *Power and the Pursuit of Peace: Theory and Practice in the History of Relations Between States* (Cambridge, 1963), p. 348.
9. Oron J. Hale, *The Great Illusion, 1900–1914* (New York, 1971), pp. 6–13.
10. Corelli Barnett, *The Collapse of British Power* (London, 1972), pp. 125–33.
11. Ibid., pp. 21, 54, 58. The point about the League of Nations has since been demolished in G.W. Egerton, 'The Lloyd George Government and the Creation of the League of Nations', *American Historical Review*, LXXIX (1974), pp. 435–41.
12. *History*, October 1973, p. 477.
13. C.A. Bodelsen, *Studies in Mid-Victorian Imperialism* (London, 1960 reprint of 1924 edn), pp. 79, 83–5, 89–94; C.C. Eldridge, *England's Mission: The Imperial Idea in the Age of Gladstone and Disraeli, 1868–1880* (London, 1973), chs 3–5; Hyam and Martin, *Reappraisals*, ch. 5; W.L. Langer, *Diplomacy of Imperialism* (New York, 1951 edn), p. 70.
14. D.B. Swinfen, *Imperial Control of Colonial Legislation, 1813–1856* (Oxford, 1970), especially ch. 8: J.W. Cell, *British Colonial Administration in the Mid-nineteenth Century: The Policy-making Process* (New Haven, 1970); W.P. Morrell, *British Colonial Policy in the Mid-Victorian Age* (Oxford, 1969).
15. For New Zealand, D.K. Fieldhouse, *Economics and Empire, 1830–1914* (London, 1973), pp. 76ff; for the Cape Colony, R. Robinson and J. Gallagher, *Africa and the Victorians* (London, 1961), chs 6, 7, 14; for the East India Company, Sir Cyril Philip's extraordinary statement that the brevity of British rule in India is indicated by the fact that the Crown took control of administration in 1858 and that with the Montford Reforms steps were taken to wind up the empire. (Preface to H.L. Singh's *Problems and Policies of the British in India* [Bombay, 1962].
16. Ged Martin, 'Was there a British Empire?' *Historical Journal*, XV (1972), pp. 582–69.
17. R. Robinson and J. Gallagher, 'The Imperialism of Free Trade', *Economic History Review*, 2s, VI (1953).
18. R. Robinson and J. Gallagher, *Africa and the Victorians*, p. 212.

19. Hyam and Martin, *op.cit.*, pp. 17–18. Readers should not be put off by the opening sentence of this book. Some of the essays are good.

20. Even Robinson and Gallagher admit it, for example, Robinson, in the course of discussion on his paper at an Oxford seminar in 1970 (R. Owen and B. Sutcliffe eds, *Studies in the Theory of Imperialism* [London, 1972], p. 141). Elsewhere the same point has been grudgingly conceded: 'On an Olympian view, the taking of Egypt might seem to have been the logical outcome of two great movements of European expansion since the end of the eighteenth century. One was the long build-up of British trade and power in the east . . .' Robinson and Gallagher, 'The Partition of Africa', in *New Cambridge Modern History*, XI (Cambridge, 1962), p. 601.

21. *Cambridge Economic History of Europe*, vol. IV, part I (Cambridge, 1965), p. 428.

22. F.E. Bailey, *British Policy and the Turkish Reform Movement, 1826–1856* (Cambridge, Mass., 1942); Charles Webster, *Foreign Policy of Palmerston* (London, 1951); D.C.M. Platt, *Latin America and British Trade, 1806–1914* (London, 1972), ch. 10.

23. H.S. Ferns, 'Britain's Informal Empire in Argentina, 1806–1914', *Past and Present*, no. 4 (November 1953), pp. 60–74.

24. H.S. Ferns, *Britain and Argentina in the Nineteenth Century* (Oxford, 1960), pp. 488–9.

25. Miriam Hood, *Gunboat Diplomacy, 1895–1905: Great Power Pressure in Venezuela* (London, 1975), pp. 165–7, 169f.

26. R. Palme Dutt, *The Crisis of Britain and the British Empire* (Bombay, 1953), p. 323; E. Zupnick, *Britain's Post-War Dollar Problem* (New York, 1957), pp. 129–31.

27. J.M. Ward, *Colonial Self-Government: The British Experience, 1759–1856* (London, 1976), pp. 240–2.

28. Ibid., pp. 174, 210, 218–36.

29. Fieldhouse, *op.cit.*, pp. 237–9.

30. C.G.F. Simkin, *The Instability of a Dependent Economy: Economic Fluctuations in New Zealand, 1840–1914* (Oxford, 1951), pp. 194–8; also chs 10, 11.

31. T.O. Lloyd, 'Africa and Hobson's Imperialism', *Past and Present*, no. 55 (May 1972), p. 124.

32. Owen and Sutcliffe, *op.cit.*, p. 124.

33. E.J. Hobsbawm, *Industry and Empire* (Harmondsworth, 1968), p. 238.

34. L.C.A. Knowles and C.M. Knowles, *The Economic Development of the British Overseas Empire*, vol. II, Canada (London, 1930), ch. 13; A.K. Cairncross, 'Investment in Canada, 1900–1913', in A.R. Hall (ed.), *Export of Capital from Britain, 1870–1914* (London, 1968); Ian M. Drummond, *Imperial Economic Policy, 1917–1939* (London, 1974), p. 228.

35. The facts are available in D.K. Fieldhouse, 'Imperialism: An Historiographical Revision', *Economic History Review*, 2 s, XIV (1961); the Marxist historian V.G. Kiernan has also commented that the 'capital-export theory … in a good many ways hampered rather than assisted Lenin', V.G. Kiernan, *Marxism and Imperialism* (London, 1974), p. 463.
36. M. Barratt-Brown, *After Imperialism* (London, 1970 edn), p. 97.
37. Ibid., p. 110.
38. David Mclean, 'Finance and Informal Empire, Before the First World War', *Economic History Review*, 25, XXIX (May 1976), p. 304.
39. Fieldhouse, *Economics and Empire*, documents this quite well. Although he led the attack on the capital export theory, his detailed researches have made him realise the importance of the imperialism of trade (*op.cit.*, p. xvi).
40. The theoretical point has been well argued in Prabhat Patnaik, 'External Markets and Capitalist Development', *Economic Journal*, LXXXII (1972), pp. 1320–1.
41. Barnett, *op.cit.*, pp. 124–33.
42. Donald Winch, *Economics and Policy: A Historical Survey* (London, 1972), chs 4, 6, 10; P.S. Gupta, *Imperialism and the British Labour Movement, 1914–1964* (London, 1975), p. 85, for a typical quotation from Hopkins.
43. J.F. Rippy, *British Investments in Latin America, 1822–1939* (Minneapolis, 1959), pp. 84ff.
44. In the Public Record Office (hereafter PRO), Cab 27/114 and Cab 27/191 contain the proceedings of all the meetings of the Cabinet Committee on Unemployment in the interwar years, and the bulk of them deal with domestic development schemes. Another volume (Cab 27/490) dealing with the worst period of the slump (September–November 1932) is preoccupied with domestic issues, except for a couple of papers on trade with Russia, and does not refer to the empire.
45. On Japanese competition, Gupta *op.cit.*, p. 249; on the question of colonial industrialisation, the report of an interdepartmental committee later issued as a confidential print (CO 885/40 Misc. no. 445 'Report of the Interdepartmental Committee on the Industrial Development of the Colonial Empire, March 1934).
46. Barnett, *passim*.
47. For a summary of their views, see M. Barratt-Brown, *Economics of Imperialism* (Harmondsworth, 1974), pp. 30–9.
48. A. Marwick, *The Deluge: British Society and the First World War* (London, 1965), pp. 198, 290; C.E. Carrington, *Soldiers from the War Returning* (London, 1965), p. 274.
49. K. Middlemas and J. Barnes, *Baldwin* (London, 1969), pp. 735–6.
50. Robert Skidelsky, *Oswald Mosley* (New York, 1975), pp. 368–72, 378.

51. cf Baldwin's contemporary assessment of by-election trends as given in Middlemas and Barnes, *op.cit.*, pp. 805–6.
52. Fritz Fischer, *Germany's Aims in the First World War* (London, 1966).
53. The details are discussed fully in John Gooch, *The Plans of War: The General Staff and British Military Strategy, c. 1900–1916* (London, 1974). A useful summary is provided in Michael Howard, *The Continental Commitment* (Harmondsworth, 1974), chs 1, 2.
54. V.H. Rothwell, *British War Aims and Peace Diplomacy* (Oxford, 1971), pp. 282f, 286–7, 289–90; also see Max Beloff, *Imperial Sunset*, vol. 1 (London, 1969), pp. 239–73.
55. M.P.A. Hankey to A.J. Balfour, 12 August 1918, personal and secret (PRO, Cab 21/119, War Cabinet: Petroleum Situation in British Empire and Mesopotamian and Persian Oil Fields, August 1916).
56. Chris Cook, *The Age of Alignment: Electoral Politics in Britain, 1922–1929* (London, 1975), pp. 113, 138–9, 176; Middlemas and Barnes, *op.cit.*, pp. 218–49; Gupta, *op.cit.*, pp. 59–61.
57. Winch, *op.cit.*, ch. 5; D.E. Moggridge, *British Monetary Policy, 1924–31* (Cambridge, 1972), pp. 2–36, 232–4.
58. I.H. Nish, 'Japan and the Ending of the Anglo-Japanese Alliance', in K. Bourne and D.C. Watt (eds) *Studies in International History* (London, 1967), pp. 378–82; also see Beloff, *op.cit.*, pp. 336–44, and Howard, *op.cit.*, p. 88.
59. See Churchill's remark at a cabinet meeting on 22 July 1926, Cab 2/4, Committee of Imperial Defence, minutes of 215th meeting, p 11; for Neville Chamberlain's similar views in November 1933, see W. Roger Louis, *British Strategy in the Far East* (Oxford, 1971), p. 207.
60. I have touched on some of the lines of inquiry in *Imperialism and the British Labour Movement*, pp. 96, 166ff.
61. E.J. Hobsbawm first drew attention to the novelty of having a man of Bonar Law's background elevated to the leadership of the Conservative party, E.J. Hobsbawm, 'Twentieth Century British Politics', *Past and Present*, no. 11 (April 1957) p. 102. The point can be developed to include Law's successors till 1940.
62. S. Pollard, *Gold Standard and Employment Policies between the Wars* (London, 1970).
63. Corelli Barnett, *Britain and Her Army, 1509–1970* (London, 1970), p. 410; Howard, *op.cit.*, pp. 89–90.
64. H.R. Allen, *The Legacy of Lord Trenchard* (London, 1972), p. 39. Cab 16/87 shows that air power was proposed to be used more extensively after 1930 for these purposes.
65. Barnett, *op.cit.*, p. 79.
66. Gupta, *op.cit.*, pp. 171–2.

67. Philip Mason's *Matter of Honour* (New York, 1974) is based not on contemporary records but on personal recollections, and probably over-estimates the smoothness of the transition to a non-racist army.
68. E.A. Brett, *Colonialism and Underdevelopment in East Africa: The Politics of Economic Change, 1919–39* (London, 1973), chs 3, 4; Gupta, *op.cit.*, pp. 71–9.
69. On the inception of the act see Gupta, *op.cit.*, pp. 135–42; on its operation, see Brett, *op.cit.*, ch. 4.
70. On copper, see Gupta, *op.cit.*, pp. 147–8; on rubber, see Joseph Brandes, *Herbert Hoover and Economic Diplomacy* (Pittsburgh, 1962), ch. 5.
71. D.J. Payton-Smith, *Oil: Study of War-time Policy and Administration* (London, 1971), pp. 13, 16, 43.
72. PRO, CO 323/1064/61509.
73. Gupta, *op.cit.*, pp. 148–9.
74. Drummond does not appear to have looked at these files.
75. There are some suggestions for lines of inquiry in Susan Strange, *Sterling and British Policy* (Oxford, 1971), pp. 55ff.
76. Gupta, *op.cit.*, p. 249.
77. Ibid., pp. 262–3 and the references cited therein.
78. Amiya K. Bagchi, *Private Investment in India, 1900–1939* (Cambridge, 1972), p. 442.
79. P.J. Grigg to Lord Lothian, 16 April 1938 (Lothian Papers, Scottish Record Office, Edinburgh, GD 40 17/362ff 353 59).
80. Ian M. Drummond, *Imperial Economic Policy, 1917–1939* (London, 1974).
81. Ibid., pp. 427–46.
82. See note 45 above.
83. Robert H. Ferrell, *American Diplomacy in the Great Depression* (New Haven, 1957), pp. 261–72.
84. For example Sir Maurice Hankey's private file on the World Economic Conference, kept as Cab 21/374–7.
85. Winch, *op.cit.*, pp. 215–27.
86. Letter of Chamberlain (9 February 1936) quoted in Keith Feiling, *Life of Neville Chamberlain* (London 1970 edn), p. 314.
87. A fairly up-to-date survey of the literature on this controversy is to be found in Keith Robbins, 'Appeasement: New Tasks for the Historian', *International Affairs*, XLVIII (1972), pp. 625–30, and in Maurice Cowling, *Impact of Hitler* (Cambridge, 1975).
88. Paul Schroeder, 'Munich and the British Tradition', *Historical Journal* XIX (1976), p. 225.
89. Cowling, *op.cit.*, pp. 7–8, 396–7; Howard, *op.cit.*, p. 120.

90. Sidney Aster, *1939: Making of the Second World War* (London, 1973) is the most exhaustive study of the subject so far.

91. Dorothy Borg, *The United States and the Far Eastern Crisis, 1933–38* (Cambridge, Mass., 1964), pp. 272–3, 376, 489–90.

92. Gupta, *op.cit.*, p. 95.

93. Borg, *op.cit.*, pp. 132–7.

94. Anne Trotter, *Britain and East Asia, 1933–37* (Cambridge, 1975), chs 7–9.

95. Bradford A. Lee, *Britain and the Sino-Japanese War, 1937–39* (Stanford, 1973), pp. 210–12, 219.

96. C.J. Lowe and F. Marzari, *Italian Foreign Policy, 1870–1940* (London, 1975), pp. 253–270.

97. Cowling, *op.cit.*, p. 70; for the public uproar over the Hoare–Laval Pact as seen by Conservative backbenchers, Neville Thompson, *The Anti-Appeasers* (Oxford, 1971), pp. 87–9.

98. Quoted in Arthur J. Marder, *From the Dardanelles to the Oran* (Oxford, 1974), p. 99.

99. The best strategic appreciation is in Lawrence R. Pratt, *East of Malta, West of Suez: Britain's Mediterranean Crisis, 1936–39* (Cambridge, 1975), especially chs 1–4.

100. All contemporary accounts agree on the role of this triumvirate.

101. Lowe and Marzari, *op.cit.*, pp. 328–30, 359–82: Aster, *op.cit.*, pp. 128–37: Feiling, *op.cit.*, p. 422.

102. Cowling, *op.cit.*, p. 369.

103. Lowe and Marzari, *op.cit.*, p. 363.

104. Thompson, *op.cit.*, pp. 42–3.

105. Cowling, *op.cit.*, p. 394.

106. Feiling, *op.cit.*, p. 403; Aster, *op.cit.*, pp. 174–7; and chs 10, 11.

107. Cf. Samir Amin, *Neo-Colonialism in West Africa* (Harmondsworth, 1973).

108. *New Statesman*, 21 March 1959, p. 388.

109. Gupta, *op.cit.*, pp. 179–87, 247–8, 309–35.

110. Andrew Shonfield, 'The Duncan Report and its Critics', *International Affairs*, XLVI (1970), pp. 261–3.

111. Comment by Martin Stainland, ibid., p. 912.

ECONOMIC IMPERIALISM: THE CASE OF THE BRITISH EMPIRE, 1895–1914*

In this essay I shall examine certain peculiarities of British capitalism and their manifestations in varied types of colonialism and imperialism in the period after 1895. After a preliminary theoretical statement I proceed to delineate those characteristics, and I focus, so far as colonialism and imperialism are concerned, on the British role in South Africa, Latin America, West Africa, and parts of the Ottoman Empire. The time period covered is short, roughly from the early 1890s to 1914. The choice of these different regions is dictated by the need to bring out the contrasting pattern that is central to my argument.

Many Western historians have argued that their researches into the archival records over the last twenty years have demolished the theory of economic imperialism; therefore to explain the remarkable expansion of the British empire in this period and the involvement of Britain in a European alliance network one needed hypotheses based on 'the quest for power' as an independent variable, and not the needs of British capitalism.[1] This view can be shown to be quite inadequate but, so far as Britain is concerned, we can do so honestly and without suppression of evidence only if we accept a more flexible formulation of the connection between capitalism and empire building at the turn of the century than that given in the following quotation from Lenin's *Imperialism*:

For Europe, the time when the new capitalism *definitely* superseded the old can be established with fair precision: it was the beginning of the twentieth century.[2]

As we shall see, there was more continuity than discontinuity in the nature of British capitalism and its extraterritorial expansionist urges;

*Unpublished paper, Indo-GDR Seminar, Berlin, 1978.

the late 1890s mark a break in some sectors of the economy and some parts of the globe, but not elsewhere.

A second point needs to be made. In his polemic against Kautsky, in course of dismissing the latter's suggestion that the 'internationalisation of capital [sc. gave] the hope of peace among nations under capitalism', Lenin argued that it was irrelevant 'to obscure the *substance* of the present economic struggle (the division of the world) and to emphasize now this and now another *form* of the struggle'.[3] I submit that the historian of the diplomacy of imperialism cannot afford to neglect either the *form* (the decision-making process) or the *substance* (the issues at stake). In history, cause and consequence can be studied only in chronological sequence and in doing so we see that form and substance interact dialectically and each influences the other. The specific character of the capitalist expansionism of a particular country (e.g., whether it is 'old' colonialism or 'new' imperialism) would be very much influenced by whether it was the outcome of actual war or threat of war, or of secret diplomatic bargains between diplomats and the commercial lobbies interested in that area. The stakes involved in these bargains (markets, investment outlets, or monopsonistic purchases of raw materials) would also vary because not all European countries were at the same level of development at the turn of the century.

Three features of the British economy at this time distinguish it from Germany and America: (1) a much lower degree of concentration in industrial organisation (i.e., the absence of cartels etc.), (2) a high degree of cosmopolitanism on the part of the financiers of the City of London, and the absence of 'investment banks' of the type described by Rudolf Hilferding in *Das Finanz-kapital*, (3) export of capital, measured in terms of its share in the gross national product, tending to be sometimes more and sometimes less than the level of domestic investment, depending on market conditions.[4] Incidentally, the export of capital was not a new but a continuous feature of the British economy throughout the nineteenth century and was designed to assist in the export of commodities.[5] Whether in the beginning of the century its direction shifted to the colonial world and its purpose became not the export of commodities but the earning of super-profits has been much debated and needs to be carefully looked into.

The relatively low level of concentration in industry is illustrated by the fact that in 1905, the number of industrial groups with a capital of more than £5 million were only 12 in Britain but 35 in the US, and while those having more than £10 million were only three, the equivalent figure was 15 in the US. The biggest British group was Imperial Tobacco with a capital of only £17 million, whereas the biggest US group (United States Steel) and the second biggest (American Tobacco) had investments of £282 and £103 million respectively.[6] Even if one defines a large industrial group in Britain to include a minimum investment of only about £2 million, the British list comes to 52, and the American to 48, but the Americans have more high-value investments than the British. Within the British list of 52, 25 are in the producers' goods sector and 27 in the consumer goods sector, although strictly speaking, of the 25, eight were textile industries involved in processing and finishing thread and cloth (dyeing, bleaching, sewing, thread making), and so the heavy capital goods sector really can claim to have only 17. This suggests that the quest for mass markets at home and abroad rather than the export of capital goods was the driving force behind British imperialism. Export of commodities did not get replaced by the export of capital.

In spite of world competition the staple export trades of cotton textiles, coal, and shipbuilding were doing well out of free trade at the turn of the century. There was an active but a minority group in iron and steel for protectionist imperialism, but shipbuilders found their costs lowered by dumped German steel. This made the shipbuilding interest remain aloof from protectionist movements. Similarly, as Semmel and Rempel have shown, the City of London and British banking houses and most Conservative and Unionist members of parliament involved in international finance and in cotton, coal and shipping stood apart from Joseph Chamberlain's campaign for protectionist imperialism and tariff reform. In any assessment of British imperial diplomacy and its character, it has to be remembered that at this time British 'invisible' exports were growing faster than her commodity exports.[8]

Finally, as regards the volume of net investment and the proportions devoted to home and to foreign investment we note the following. The proportion of the net national product devoted to home investment (measured as a percentage of the net national product) was more or less higher than that of foreign investment in the decade before the Boer War, and it was only after 1908 that there was a shift in favour of foreign investments.[9]

Apart from these characteristics of the British economy, there is one feature of the decision-making structure of the late-nineteenth-century Foreign Office that is relevant to our discussion. Engels had noted in 1892:

In England, the bourgeoisie never held undivided sway. Even the victory of 1832 Left the landed aristocracy in almost exclusive possession of all the leading Government offices. . . . The English bourgeoisie are, up to the present day, so deeply penetrated by a sense of their social inferiority that they keep up, at their own expense and that of the nation, an ornamental cast of drones to represent the nation worthily at all State function[s]. . . .'[10]

In the British diplomatic service a slightly patronising attitude towards the commercial attache was always noticeable, and the consular service, which did the bulk of the work of supplying commercial intelligence, was given a lower status.[11] From the 1880s there was an increasing awareness of the need to reform this situation and to attract more persons with a business background into the consular service (with Lord Lansdowne as foreign secretary playing an important role), but the net result was not as much of an improvement as hoped for.[12]

We have now sketched the peculiar divisions within the British ruling classes which are necessary to remember while examining the link between capitalism and empire in South Africa; the extent to which commerce and politics got intertwined in the partition of West Africa; whether any part of Latin America could be called a part of the British informal empire; and finally, the imperialism of railway building and oil exploration in Mesopotamia and the Persian Gulf.

SOUTH AFRICA

The historiography of British expansion in southern Africa and the consequent Boer War at the turn of the century used to be dominated in the West before 1939 by the contemporary writings of the English radical economist J.A. Hobson.[13] Hobson's data, fitted within Lenin's theoretical framework, give the impression that big companies like Cecil Rhodes' Consolidated Goldfields or Alfred Beit's Wernher, Beit & Company (operating through Rand Mines) moved into the Transvaal goldfields at a time when investment opportunities were low in Britain, and were attracted not only by gold but also by the prospects of super-profits from the exploitation of cheap native labour. The German Kaiser's telegram to President Kruger as well as the pro-Boer sentiments expressed in the German press suggested that this was one of the first signs of 'redivision and repartition of the globe'. The facts which non-Marxist political diplomatic historians like J.S. Galbraith, R. Robinson, J. Gallagher, and Ronald Hyam have discovered and used to counter this interpretation are given below. As we shall argue, their data does not succeed in delinking the connection between British capitalism and the South African crisis because further researches of G. Blainey, Trevor Lloyd and J.S. Marais have shown that there were strong economic factors. The upshot of these researches however is not to restate the old theory but to seek a new formulation.

The Robinson–Gallagher explanation centred on characterising the self-governing Cape Colony as capable of pursuing an independent expansionist policy at variance with the needs of the metropolitan country. With an electorate composed of British-born merchants and mining prospectors and local Afrikaner merchants and farmers (although most such farmers had Left in the Great Trek), with income from gold speculation strengthening the wealth and importance of the ruling class and, finally, the specific ambitions of Cecil Rhodes, British metropolitan control was diminishing.[14] Rhodes and Salisbury, the British prime minister, repeatedly differed over political plans.[15] Colonial Secretary Joseph Chamberlain's support to the Jameson Raid (in which the initiative had come from Cecil Rhodes and some of his mining colleagues) was guided by the fear that 'the substitution of an entirely independent Republic governed by or for the capitalists of the Rand would be very much worse for British interests in the Transvaal itself and for British influence in South Africa'.[16] And this 'British interest' was throughout interpreted purely in strategic terms, that is, to ensure the security of the Cape route to the east for the British navy.

In one sense of course the capitalists of South Africa had some independence and the crisis that forced Rhodes to take the desperate step of the Jameson Raid and the subsequent diplomatic manoeuvring to provoke the Boer War was not a general crisis of metropolitan capital but a specific crisis of certain deep-level gold-mining concerns. However in the process new links were forged between the City of London and the 'deep-level' mines in which Rhodes, Beit and others. had an interest.

Initially neither Rhodes' nor Beit's concerns, big as they were, were floated as trusts with direct involvement of metropolitan finance capital. Rhodes and Beit had made their fortune in South Africa, and Beit's firm (Wernher, Beit & Company) was a partnership, which, via its subsidiary H. Eckstein & Company of South Africa, owned almost half the shares in the Rand mines. Dr Blainey's researches into the technology and economics of gold-mining operations in the Transvaal by the 'Uitlanders' have shown that there were two types of gold-mining undertakings in the Rand—the less capital-intensive 'outcrop' mines, and the more capital-intensive deep-level mines. While the former were doing well out of ploughed-back profits within the framework of the fiscal policies pursued by the Boer republic, the deep-level mine owners (Rhodes, Beit, and Farrar) were facing a crisis. Without raising additional capital on the London money market their undertakings coud not penetrate the deep levels where rich veins of gold were known to exist; at the same time without breaking the Boer republic's dynamite monopoly and changing its structure of taxation these mine owners' future prospects of handsome profits were uncertain.[17] The City of London was unlikely to lend them money until their political position in the Transvaal became strong. They were already pressing them to reduce costs, especially in the direction of native wages.[18] The plotters in the Jameson Raid were virtually all deep-level mine owners. Thus developed an alliance between metropolitan finance and certain British-born South African gold miners, about which Trevor Lloyd has aptly commented:

The more capital the mine owners needed, the more permanent their position in Africa became, which meant that they had to take an interest in the political situation, and the same time the closer their links with the London capital market became.[19]

The evidence of the British government's surreptitious involvement in the Jameson Raid in December 1895 and its willing partnership in the Boer War in 1899 is now overwhelming, and if one is less hypnotised by the Salisbury Papers (as Robinson and Gallagher were) and examines the evidence of the Balfour Papers and the Chamberlain Papers one notices that the British government were fully aware of the economic (and not just the strategic) stake involved.[20] We also know that the British strategy after the end of hostilities was to design such a constitution as would ensure a numerical majority of a loyal and English population so that the political and economic links were retained.[21]

The Boer War should not be regarded as an imperialist war between Britain and Germany by proxy but rather a colonialist war by an advanced industrial capitalist group against a farmer oligarchy of Dutch settlers. Most international capitalists had opposed Kruger, whatever might have been the state of public opinion against Britain on the continent. Of the gold miners in South Africa who operated with German capital, A. Goerz and G. Albu supported Kruger, but Alfred Beit, a loyal German national, was very much involved in the plotting of the Jameson Raid (because his was a deep-level mine). He also agreed, along with Lord Rothschild, to the British government's suggestion to frustrate Kruger's efforts to raise a loan in Europe.[22] (The French and German governments had also made representations to Kruger against the opposition by the *Volkard* [Transvaal legislature] to reducing the railway rates and ending the dynamite monopoly.)[23] We know from the Holstein Papers that the German chancellor, von Bulow, wished for an indecisive outcome for the Boer War and did not want the English to 'lose their position as a Great Power',[24] which suggests that there was no firm prospect of an alliance between German finance capital and President Kruger.

Britain won the Boer War but partially lost the peace. In spite of elaborate efforts to design a constitution and an electoral system which they hoped would bring to power a loyal Briton, Sir Richard Solomon, as prime minister, the election results showed a victory for the Afrikaner *Het Volk,* and the emergence of General Botha as the prime minister of South Africa. As Joseph Chamberlain had apprehended (see note 16) not all Rand capitalists (including even some of British origin like J.A. Robinson) could be completely trusted to vote for the British party. This was the outcome of contradictions and conflicts among the social classes comprising the small white electorate in South Africa. From this date the South African ruling class was not wholly subordinate to and part of the metropolitan ruling class but allied to it. Its viability in its own right increased in proportion as Britain became weakened by the First World War and the Depression.

WEST AFRICA

Robinson and Gallagher explained the British acquisition of Nigeria and the Gold Coast and their willingness to concede by treaty large areas of West Africa to the French purely in military diplomatic terms—they gave a free hand to the French in West Africa in order to keep control over the Nile valley and the Suez route to India.[25] This argument is buttressed with statistics showing the decline in the volume of the palm oil trade between Nigeria and Liverpool,[26] and by the fact that, even as late as 1913, West Africa's share of British capital exports was a mere £37.3 million out of a total £1780 million invested within the empire and a grand total of £3763.3 million invested abroad (empire and non-empire countries taken together).[27] A new angle into the subject is provided by the researches of A.G. Hopkins and others, which shows that while finance capitalist expansionism for the export of capital might not have been a driving force, the mercantile colonialism of British business houses certainly was. Till the 1880s the pattern of colonial exchange had been the production of palm oil or cocoa by African peasants in the interior, the merchandising of these to the coast by African peasants or middlemen, the final export business being in the hands of British merchants. Imports of European manufactured goods were also controlled by the British. From the 1870s some indigenous Africans succeeded in breaking into the import trade of the coast. The technical revolution in transport—the coming of the steamship—cheapened costs of imports and shifted the terms of trade against the primary producers of the interior. At the same time in the neighbouring areas French and German colonialists were putting up tariff walls. In such a situation the British coastal traders attempted to pass on their reduced profit margins to the African middlemen and the African peasant; the Africans sometimes retaliated by holding up produce.[28]

It is against this background that the merchants lobbied for and succeeded in getting government action for a military expedition into the interior which resulted in the conquest of Nigeria.[29] Once again the connection between capitalism and colonialism is established, but once again it is markets rather than the export of capital which is the motive power. To be sure, some degree of concentration is noticeable in the British sector of the West African economy from the turn of the century. Small- and medium-sized mercantile houses—European or African—declined in numbers and large-scale limited liability companies emerge. There was a monopoly in shipping, and the shipping magnate helped to found a commercial bank which had no competitor till 1926. While the government built the railways (a total mileage of 711 only, mainly to serve the export trade) the rest of the economy remained relatively untouched by the 'new' trends in capitalism. Competition persisted among four or five big firms, and palm oil production remained peasant based rather than plantation based.[30] None of these incipient features of monopoly (shipping) and state capitalism (railways) really warrant the British venture into West Africa being described as marking a qualitative change in the nature of British colonialism. The pattern of international exchange was still between primary producing peasants and a British manufacturing economy characterised by, as we have seen, the absence of combinations and cartels. Only in the post-1920 era, when the gigantic United Africa Company was formed,[31] did something approximating the Leninist model become a reality.

LATIN AMERICA

'Economic annexation is fully achievable without political annomation, and is widely practiced', wrote Lenin.[32] In this section on British economic involvement in Latin America, as also in the final study on Mesopotamia, I would like to see how far, given the structure of British capitalism as outlined above, it succeeded in carving out an 'informal' empire. In the South and Central American continent one should also draw a threefold distinction—Central America and the states in the neighbourhood of Venezuela, where the British were feeling the pinch of severe US and German competition; Brazil, Peru, Uruguay where British traditional exports were able to hold their own; and Argentina where the British stake was the greatest.

The Venezuelan crisis of 1902–3 had shown that Britain feared the wrath of America more than the disappointment of Germany when she backed out of an adventure in 'gunboat diplomacy' in the interests of British and German bondholders.[33] By 1906–11, on an average the US was providing 49.2 per cent of Central American imports and

Britain was still managing to hold on to 21.7 per cent with Germany trailing behind with 13.4 per cent; this abstention was therefore probably wise from the point of view of British imperialism.[34] What is more significant, and what tends to confirm part of Lenin's argument about the profitability of the export of capital and its usefulness in the export of commodities, is the tie-up between British capital exports, higher rates of British dividends, and the export of British commodities in Latin America in the period 1900–10. Despite foreign competition, the export drive of traditional British goods (coal and cotton) was maintained, and was certainly assisted by the propensity of those who imported British capital to buy British manufactures. There was no formal 'tying of loans' but the correlation between export of capital and export of commodities is striking.[35] And in the first decade of the century the rates of return on Latin American investments were higher by between 2 and $1^1/_2$ per cent than fixed interest home investments and by $1^1/_2$ to 2 per cent from investments in the colonial empire.[36] The crucial part played by Argentina in this (mentioned by Lenin) cannot be denied. Elsewhere, as in Brazil and Mexico, and even Peru and Colombia, an indigenous cotton textile industry had grown under the shelter of protective tariffs, and so exports of British cotton piece-goods to Argentina 'enabled Lancashire to fill the gap created by import substitution in Brazil, Mexico, and Peru'.[37]

Yet there are difficulties in regarding Argentina as an informal empire of Britain, the economic policy of which could be easily manipulated by the British government and British financiers.[38] First, British commercial banks in Latin America, while being vigorously active in traditional discounting business and exchange operations and attracting one-quarter of Argentine bank deposits, did not involve themselves in 'promoting, exploiting, or underwriting purposes'. Second, the 'Calve clause', by which foreign contractors renounced any recourse to diplomatic intervention and agreed to abide by the decision of the municipal lawcourts ensured a greater degree of control over British business than existed in China. The Baring crisis was, after all, weathered without any British gunboat diplomacy, and with British bondholders accepting debt settlement below par. When after a decade's interval a railway investment boom in Argentina again took place, it was found that the Argentine government had stopped the practice of guaranteeing the interest on the railways, and was encouraging French and other companies to compete with British railway promoters.[39] Third, some sections of the Argentine ruling oligarchy—like the owners of the big ranches producing beef—were in a position to resist getting totally dependent on British packaging and exporting firms, unlike the dependence of the Gold Coast cocoa farmer on the export houses.[40] Argentina had a complementary and in many respects a dependent economy in relation to Britain, but was it a colonial or a semi-colonial economy?

PERSIAN GULF AND MESOPOTAMIA

A more valid example of imperialist tendencies without direct annexation is seen in British policy regarding that part of the Ottoman Empire lying around the Persian Gulf. The literature on the Berlin–Baghdad railway, British policy towards Kuwait, and the British stake in Mesopotamian oil is vast, and one Indian scholar has investigated the extent to which the locus of decision-making was with the British bureaucracy in India rather than with metropolitan pressure groups.[41]

Three questions relevant to the theory of economic imperialism are illustrated by the tangled diplomacy of the period 1899 to 1909. In so far as the British bureaucracy in India decisively influenced policy-makers in London, how far was it guided by considerations of power unrelated to economic needs? Did the efforts made by Lord Lansdowne in 1903 to internationalise the Baghdad railway fail because they were doomed to failure? The point is of some importance because of the Lenin–Kautsky controversy on whether international cartels could be a factor in favour of peace between capitalist nations or not. Third, how does the freedom of manoeuvre of British capitalist interest get restricted, after 1903, by the compulsions of diplomatic and strategic alliances with France?

At first sight Lord Curzon's Russophobia with regard to Persia, his passionate determination not to let any foreign power have access to the Persian Gulf, and his initiative in declaring Kuwait a protectorate, suggest that he was thinking mainly of power and glory.[42] David Dilks has further asserted that although Curzon was a director of W. D'Arcy's company (the precursor of Anglo-Persian Oil), oil prospects did not figure at all in his calculations when formulating policy.[43] A closer probe into the available evidence suggests that this is not so. As Parliamentary Under-Secretary for Foreign Affairs Curzon had taken steps to improve commercial reporting,[44] and so was aware that Germany was a bigger commercial threat than Russia. In scorning the idea of an Anglo-German understanding on the Baghdad railway to stall a Russian advance, he wrote, 'In international politics the Germans seem to be very undesirable bedfellows.'[45] A few years later, in 1906 when the Anglo-German negotiations about the Baghdad railway were about to be resumed, Percy Cox, the consular representative at Basrah, gave a report on the problem which shows very clearly the preoccupation of the official with British trade prospects in that area.[46]

I am inclined to believe that the failure of Lord Lansdowne's proposals to internationalise the Baghdad railway was not due to the inherent incompatibility of British and German capitalism but to lack of good political management.[47] Joseph Chamberlain, deeply concerned about German competition, undoubtedly played an important behind-the-scenes role in thwarting these proposals.[48] But, as we have seen, and as the tariff reform campaign (1903–6) showed, he did not have support from the majority of the British business elite.[49] The press campaign was probably Russian inspired (via Paris) and its anti-Semitic undertones appealed to the prejudices of the British petty bourgeoisie.[50] The lobby of the Euphrates Steam Navigation Company (which plied only two steamers)[51] could not have been an important factor. The lobby of the P and O and the British bondholders were certainly more important but whether of decisive importance is debatable. The matter warrants further investigation.

As regards D'Arcy's oil concessions, the records of the Government of India show that when D'Arcy had struck oil in some promising wells he asked for help from the British government. This was refused, after which his request was transferred to India and involved both direct financial support and also assistance in establishing contacts with British financiers in India. There was a hint that if he failed to get such support he would be obliged to seek it from non-British sources. The files of the Government of India do indicate that the bureaucracy used to make a distinction between support given for diplomatic reasons and support for economic reasons, and only a viable commercial blueprint would be acceptable for pecuniary support. Since the foreign department wanted to give him some encouragement and the finance department was reluctant to get too involved, the final decision was as follows:

The conclusion is that the Government of India should have nothing to do with the business as a business; and as to in any way recommending it to the Chambers of Commerce, we should certainly do nothing of the sort. Mr D'Arcy is personally in touch with leading financiers and capitalists and does not require our intervention with private firms or individuals. He does want some such form of government recognition as would assist him not only with the Persian government, but also with capitalists, by assuring the latter that they would receive adequate protection in their dealing with the Persian government. On political grounds I would gladly see such recognition given, but to be useful it must be clear, tangible and visible to the naked eye. . . . It seems to me that the most we can say is that we have full sympathy with Mr D'Arcy's enterprise, and if he could show how we could assist him without incurring pecuniary liabilities . . . we should be willing to consider his proposals.[52]

This approach was very typical of the extent to which in 1904 the Indian government or for that matter the British government would support an individual entrepreneur. When after the Morocco crisis (1905–6) the increasing naval cooperation between France and Britain and the diminishing prospects of an Anglo-German naval agreement ensured the success of Admiral Fisher's policy of substituting petroleum for coal for the British navy, government involvement in D'Arcy's enterprise became considerable, culminating in the purchase of the majority of shares in it in 1913.[53] At the same time, since this was occurring within the framework of the Anglo-French entente, British government support to Sir Ernest Cassels' National Bank of Turkey was given only to the extent that it did not offend the French government and its concern for the interests of the Ottoman Bank.[54]

Engels wrote, 'Our conception of history is above all a guide to study, not a lever for construction a la Hegelianism.'[55] The above case studies were attempted to show that certain reformulations were necessary in establishing the connection between British capitalism, the decision-making process in the British government, and the actual process of expansion. We see that there was far more continuity in the nature of British capitalist colonialism than had been allowed by Lenin who saw a decisive break at the turn of the century. In places like Latin America the rivalries of the capitalists of other countries and certain inherent strengths of the local ruling classes could sometimes limit the capacity of the British to dominate the economy completely. Since the British government had to recoup its losses in the Boer War and could not afford to pursue another expensive bellicose policy immediately after, it was but logical that Balfour and Lansdowne would try to seek an agreement with Germany over the Baghdad railway. Once that failed, however, and the Entente Cordiale emerged, the necessities of the entente drove Britain more and more into joint action with France and prevented it from coming to a naval agreement with Germany. Navalism and militarism—secondary derivatives of imperialism—in turn started influencing the British economy marginally. The government share-holding in the Anglo-Persian Oil Company symbolised one *new* trend. Similarly in 1905 among the lists of big British business houses which we had described at the outset, the one most vertically integrated was the armaments industry—Vickers, Son & Maxim and Armstrong Whitworth—and their success was due to the regularisation of government orders.[56] On the eve of the war the physiognomy as well as the face of British capitalism remained the same, only its fangs were new.

NOTES

1. R. Robinson and J. Gallagher, *Africa and the Victorians* (London, 1961); D. Landes, 'Some Thoughts on the Nature of Economic Imperialism', *Journal of Economic History*, XXI (1961); F.H. Hinsley, *Power and the Pursuit of Peace* (Cambridge, 1963), p. 348; R. Hyam and G. Martin, *Reappraisals in British Imperial History* (London, 1975); D.J. Hale, *The Great Illusion, 1900–1914* (New York, 1971), pp. 6, 13.

2. Lenin, *Collected Works*, XXII, p. 200; also see his periodisation of the transition, ibid., p. 202.

3. Ibid., pp. 252–3.

4. M. Barratt-Brown, *After Imperialism* (London, 1970 edn), pp. 91–111; also see Table X, National Income and Investment, Annually at Current Prices, 1870–1913, in W. Ashworth, *Economic History of England, 1870–1939* (London, 1960).

5. Barratt-Brown, *op.cit.;* L.H. Jenks, *The Migration of British Capital to 1875* (New York, 1927).

6. P.L. Payne, 'The Emergence of the Large-scale Company in Great Britain, 1870–1914', *Economic History Review*, 2s, XX (1967), p. 533 and Table I on pp. 539–41.

7. B. Semmel, *Imperialism and Social Reform* (London, 1960), pp. 145–7; Richard A. Rempel, *Unionists Divided: Arthur Balfour, Joseph Chamberlain and the Unionist Free Traders* (London, 1977), pp. 97–104.

8. Ashworth, *op.cit.*, p. 153.

9. Ibid., p. 188.

10. Marx–Engels, *Selected Works,* vol. II (Moscow, 1951), p. 102.

11. D.C.M. Platt, 'The Role of the Consular Service in Overseas Trade, 1825–1914', *Economic History Review,* 2s, XV (1962–3), *passim.*

12. Zara A. Steiner, *The Foreign Office and Foreign Policy, 1891–1914* (Cambridge, 1969), pp. 56–7, 168.

13. J.A. Hobson, *Imperialism* (London, 1902).

14. Robinson and Gallagher, *op.cit.*, pp. 212–15, 234–53.

15. Ibid., pp. 295–6 (on the Cape-to-Cairo route).

16. Ibid., pp. 428f.; also see J.S. Marais, *The Fall of Kruger's Republic* (Oxford, 1961), p. 88.

17. On this, see G. Blainey, 'Lost Causes of the Jameson Raid', *Economic History Review,* 2s, XVII (1964–5), *passim,* in particular pp. 354–61.

18. Marais, *op.cit.*, p. 187.

19. Trevor Lloyd, 'Africa and Hobson's Imperialism', *Past and Present* (May 1972), p. 151.

20. Marais, chs IV–XII; also see D. Judd, *Balfour and the British Empire* (London, 1968), ch. X.

21. Ronald Hyam, 'The Myth of the Magnanimous Gesture: The Liberal Government, Smuts and Conciliation, 1906', in Hyam and Martin, *Reappraisals in British Imperial History,* pp. 175–7.

22. Marais, *op.cit.*, pp. 212, 229–30.

23. Ibid., pp. 192–4.

24. Bulow's marginal notes on Eckardstein to Holstein, 21 December 1899, printed in N. Rich and M.H. Fisher (eds), *The Holstein Papers,* vol. IV (Cambridge, 1963), pp. 171–4.

25. Gallagher and Robinson, *op.cit.*, p. 379.

26. Ibid., p. 384, n. 1.

27. H. Feis, *Europe, the World's Banker* (New York, 1964 edn), p. 23.

28. A.G. Hopkins, *An Economic History of West Africa* (London, 1973), pp. 151–62.

29. A.G. Hopkins, 'Economic Imperialism in West Africa: Lagos, 1880–92', *Economic History Review* 2s, XXI (1968), pp. 599–603.

30. Hopkins, *Economic History of West Africa,* pp. 199–204.

31. Ibid., p. 199.

32. Lenin, *Collected Works,* XXIII, p. 44.

33. Miriam Hood, *Gunboat Diplomacy, 1895–1905: Great Power Pressure in Venezuela* (London, 1975), pp. 165–7, 169f; G.W. Monger, *End of Isolation* (London, 1963), p. 106.

34. D.C.M. Platt, *Latin America and British Trade 1806–1914* (London, 1972), p. 302.

35. Ibid., pp. 176–82, 279–81 and Fig. V on p. 281.

36. Ibid., p. 286.

37. Ibid., p. 183; also see Table XIII on p. 187 and Table XIV on p. 183.

38. D.C.M. Platt, 'Economic Imperialism and the Businessman: Britain and Latin America Before 1914', in R. Owen and B. Sutcliffe, *Studies in the Theory of Imperialism* (London, 1972), *passim.*

39. Ibid., p. 301; H.S. Ferns, *Britain and Argentina in the Nineteenth Century* (Oxford, 1960), pp. 477–8.

40. Platt, *loc.cit.,* p. 304.

41. Ravinder Kumar, *India and the Persian Gulf Region, 1859–1907* (Bombay, 1965).

42. Cf. account of S. Gopal, *British Policy in India* (Cambridge, 1965).

43. David Dilks, *Curzon in India,* vol. I (London, 1969), p. 158.

44. Platt, 'The Consular Service', *Economic History Review,* 2s XV (1962–3), p. 501; Steiner, *op.cit.,* p. 31.

45. Curzon to Hamilton, 9 August 1899 (Curzon Papers microfilm, NAI Reel 1); also see his memo of November 1898 complaining that the Germans are 'making a determined bid to get hold of the Bussorah trade', quoted in Briton C. Busch, *Britain and the Persian Gulf, 1894–1914* (Berkeley, 1967), p. 106.

46. Busch, *op.cit.,* pp. 307–8.

47. Kumar, *op.cit.,* pp. 171–8.

48. Ibid., p. 175. The role of Chamberlain has since been further emphasised by Monger who had access to papers which Kumar could not see. Monger, *End of Isolation,* p. 122.

49. See note 7 above.

50. On the Russian inspiration, see source cited by Dilks, *Curzon in India,* vol. II (London, 1970), p. 57; on anti-semitism, see speech quoted in Kumar, *op.cit.,* p. 174.

51. See 'Commercial Report on the Baghdad Railway Scheme', NAI Foreign-Secret E. Prog. May 1901, nos. 5–7. The data on the steamships are at p. 25.

52. Note by E. Fg. Law, 12 June 1904, in keep-withs (hereafter kw) to NAI Foreign, Secret, E. Prog. August 1904, 454–62 ('Mr D'Arcy's Oil Concessions in Persia').

53. Marian Jack, 'The Purchase of the British Government's Shares in the British Petroleum Company, 1912–1914', *Past and Present,* April 1968.
54. Marian Kent, 'Agent of Empire? The National Bank of Turkey and British Foreign Policy', *Historical Journal*, XVIII (1975).
55. Engels to Schmidt, 5 August 1890, in Marx–Engels *Selected Works,* vol. II (Moscow, 1951), p. 442.
56. P.L. Payne, *op.cit.,* p. 534.

The End-game of Empire

SECTION II

FEDERALISM AND PROVINCIAL AUTONOMY AS DEVICES OF IMPERIAL CONTROL*

B y the time Britain had effectively established its paramountcy in India, ruling about one-third of the subcontinent directly, and influencing, in imperial interests, the policies of the remaining two-thirds (the princely states), imperial necessity had established certain minimum levels of administrative and economic unification of India. To give but a few examples, the civil and criminal codes, railway policy, and the free movement of trade within British India were testimonies to that. The great vested British interests which together comprised the authority that felt vulnerable to opposition from Indians were the British expatriate businessmen in India, the British exporters to India, the City of London which was concerned about the servicing of the Indian debt, the British bureaucracy in India, and the British army in India.[1] Opposition to British domination could come from social groups with a limited local perspective or from groups which, for reasons of ideology or self-interest, developed an all-India nationalist perspective. For the British Raj, political success lay in defeating the latter. At the local or at the all-India level, such opposition reflected social forces some of which could be accommodated within the framework of colonialism by modification of priorities within the British

*Paper read at a seminar organised by Delhi University and Shastri Indo-Canadian Institute in 1983. Published in Aparna Basu (ed.), *Imperialism, Nationalism and Regionalism in Canadian and Modern Indian History* (Delhi, 1989).

(Unpublished Crown copyright records are quoted by permission of the Controllers of H.M. Stationery Office. Thanks are due to the Scottish Record Office for permission to use the Lothian Papers, the Cambridge South Asia Centre for the Benthall Papers, Churchill College archives for the papers of Sir James Grigg, the Cambridge University Library for the Baldwin Papers, the Liverpool City Library for the papers of Lord Derby, and the Bodleian Library for the papers of the Conservative Party.)

interests mentioned above, and some which were far too hostile to be so accommodated. These latter were either direct challenges to a whole group of British interests or subversive of the social order which permitted the operation of colonialism.

It is by now a truism that after 1917 the imperial power was more vulnerable than before and that, to maintain authority, constitutional adjustments had to be made along with a reshuffling of priorities. Among these we notice administrative devolution, provincial autonomy, and the federation of component units. These are themselves politically neutral. They can often help to strengthen the sense of national feeling in a geographically large or culturally pluralist state, as in Canada, Switzerland, or Belgium. In the context of colonial rule, however, they were conceived of as an attempt to deflect all-India challenges to British authority. Many Conservative British officials who heartily disliked even the small concessions to the principle of responsible government and elected assemblies made in 1919, were persuaded to accept the reforms because they made them relatively free to develop their own techniques of encouraging loyalist elements in their own localities. 'Provincial autonomy', liberal as it was, smacked of divide and rule.[2] Yet imperial dominance had derived its maximum economic and political advantage from the unification of the subcontinent. As these new techniques were used there were frequent queries from British interests about their relative fortunes in the new dispensation. Would the constitution be able to keep out of the corridors of power any all-India party which did not recognise the legitimacy of British rule or the imperial claim to decide when, how and if at all power should be totally transferred?

This essay will examine the approach to provincial autonomy in the years after 1927, till the outbreak of war brought in a new situation. It will analyse two of the contradictions within colonial interests that were revealed in some detail, the problem of transferring the law and order portfolio and the distribution of the income tax between the centre and the provinces. After a brief account of the period till 1931, I shall concentrate on the four years when the Government of India Act (1935) was in the making, and conclude with some observations on how far the calculations of the Conservative imperial power had been successful. The eight years between the appointment of the Indian

Statutory Commission (the 'Simon Commission') and the passage of the Act of 1935 were characterised by the world economic crisis, political and agrarian agitation in India, three changes of government in Britain (1929, 1931, and the defections of the free trade Liberals in 1932), and the end of free trade and international gold standard in Britain. The constitution was put into effect in British India against the background of threats of war in both Europe and Asia. So, in the last resort, protecting the constitution could only be done by political goodwill. Military force was limited. As Lord Reading, former viceroy and Liberal politician, put it to J.R. MacDonald, urging him to make a success of the Second Round Table Conference, 'If we fail, then it will be a case of troops and money from here, when we can spare neither and when we shall be preoccupied with our own financial and economic troubles.'[3]

I

The Government of India Act (1919) had transferred only three departments—education, local self-government, and health—to elected ministers, and had Left other crucial portfolios like finance and home to the imperial bureaucracy. At the centre there was a legislative assembly entitled to vote on the budget but the viceroy could restore any cuts imposed by it. At both the centre and the provinces a group of officials sat in the assemblies with the right to vote and support the government's side. Many officials did not like this role, this being not part of their training, but in terms of imperial requirements there was no alternative.

When the Indian Statutory Commission was appointed in anticipation of the decennium of the Act of 1919, a cross-section of Indian political opinion, ranging from the Indian Liberals, to some groups of Muslims and the Congress, boycotted it, and set about drafting an alternative constitution. This constitution, known as the Nehru report (after Motilal Nehru, its chairman), preferred a unitary constitution for the whole of British India. On the other hand Muslim politicians preferred to have a federal constitution with residual power to the provinces. The pros and cons of federal and unitary systems in India in the colonial period have as a result been analysed as if it was essentially a difference between politicians with different religious affiliations. How much of federalism and how much of central control suited the imperial authorities has not been subjected to critical scrutiny.

The extensive boycott of the Simon Commission ensured that it heard evidence only from regional and minority groups. Its report also took no notice of all-India political nationalism. By recommending no change at the centre it followed the tradition of 1919, but it conceded provincial autonomy subject to special powers for the governors. By the time the report was published in June 1930, the advent of the Labour government in Britain and the heightened tempo of Gandhi's Civil Disobedience Movement had made Viceroy Irwin realise that only by sharing some powers at the centre with business groups and moderate politicians (involving a few concessions at the expense of specific British interests) could the Civil Disobedience Movement be controlled.[4]

The First Round Table Conference accepted the principle of a federation of autonomous British provinces and princely India, leaving details of the federal structure to be worked out by subcommittees. There was unanimity on some major issues, like the rapid Indianisation of the Indian army and the federal assembly's freedom to decide the customs revenue. Before the second session, the Labour government had fallen, to be succeeded by the National Government. It was this second session that Gandhi attended, but was unable to make any headway against the combined opposition of the European expatriates and Muslim leaders like the Aga Khan.

In the National Government the Conservatives were in the majority. The coalition character of the government was carefully maintained by both MacDonald and Baldwin, and cabinet discussions were often very prolonged as a result, but the general election in the autumn of 1931 gave the Conservatives such a massive majority that henceforth their point of view on India and the empire prevailed over the more liberal approaches of the previous government. The Tory Secretary of State for India Sir Samuel Hoare argued the case for provincial autonomy and the postponement of constitutional advance at the centre with the following points:

... it has the strong support of the Minorities. The most significant feature of this autumn's discussions has been the consolidation of a single front by the Moslems, the depressed classes, the Christians, and the Anglo-Indians.

There is a grave risk of our having no friends in India at all if we disregard the representatives of the 120 million Indians who have hitherto refused to take part in civil disobedience.[5]

This remained a dominant theme in Conservative thinking. It was also supported by the European expatriate interests. Their representative Sir Edward Benthall, who had teamed up with the Muslim communalist delegates at both round table conferences felt reassured by Lothian's view that the relations between the provinces and the centre would be limited.[6] Pressure on MacDonald from the Indian Liberals, Lord Reading and others ensured that the notion of a simultaneous advance at the centre was not abandoned officially; but as late as May 1932 Hoare was keen on going ahead with a bill in favour of provincial autonomy only, until finally dissuaded by Viceroy Willingdon.[7]

The concern for some advance at the centre as sketched out at the First Round Table Conference was expressed by Willingdon and British Liberals because, while putting down Gandhi's movement with a firm hand, they valued the support of the Indian Liberals. If the Conservatives were happily contemplating the support of the minority groups, the Liberals were aware that without some advance at the centre, no cooperation would be forthcoming from business groups and from Indian Liberals associated with them. The Liberal Lord Lothian, undersecretary of state for India, visiting India as chairman of the franchise committee, concluded that while civil disobedience had suffered a severe drubbing the 1919 constitution had 'been under sentence of death for two or three years' and could not be revived. It was 'really weakening everywhere'. Only a firm promise of a new constitutional settlement which did not go back on the promise of a federal centre was likely to ensure support from the moderates.[8] Sykes, the governor of Bombay, argued, 'Ordinance basis of our rule in India cannot be continued indefinitely,' and added a plea for a federal centre where Britain would exercise strong financial control.[9]

On the other hand there was little sympathy with the idea of central control by the federal government from Hoare and Simon. In August 1932 MacDonald had been persuaded to give the Communal Award on the Franchise Question to satisfy the demands of influential Muslim groups in Punjab and Bengal, whose case had been pleaded by Viceroy Willingdon.[10] To clinch the political advantage from this, Hoare and

Simon, on the eve of the Second Round Table Conference, took a strong line in favour of minimal central control on provinces. While discussing the draft constitution prepared for the cabinet committee in September 1932, Hoare argued that 'the general conception of the constitution ought to be that the centre of gravity should henceforth shift from the centre to the Provinces'.[11] Apart from administrative reasons,

there were more serious reasons in favour of the change. Considerations of imperial safety demanded a greater variety in the Indian picture than it now presented. When a solid mass of Indian interests was too often to be found in opposition to a solid mass of British interests; and it had become clear that the Moslem population of India would never accept the Reforms scheme if steps were not taken to ensure the reality of Provincial Autonomy. The unitary idea must be regarded as dead, although it was not always recognised by Indian opinion. . . .

Simon added that he hoped to see the extent of Provincial Autonomy so complete that the Federal Government would be denied 'all power of interference in provincial subjects.'[12] When the reforms commissioner J. Dunnett mildly suggested that there should be some proviso to secure uniformity of the great Indian legal codes like the penal code, Hoare, while not objecting to such technical details, reiterated that he 'strongly opposed . . . any arrangement which perpetuated the present all-pervading influence of the Centre—that was a conception from which it was essential that the new Constitution should get completely away'.[13] The official mind visualised that the special powers given to the governor within the framework of responsible government and provincial autonomy, would enable imperial interests to be safeguarded:

The absence of organised parties, of vitality in the electorate, of homogeneity in the legislature and in the Cabinet, and of experience in the political executive accordingly suggest conditions favourable to the effective association of the Governor as an imperial partner in the work of government.[14]

During the preparation of the despatch setting forth the views of the Government of India during Lord Irwin's viceroyalty (the drafting committee sat from 25 June to 20 September 1930) the Punjabi Muslim leader Sir Fazl-i-Husain repeatedly clashed with some British officials (like Dunnett) who had pleaded, on administrative grounds, for some central control over provinces. Fazl-i-Husain also supported leaving of residuary powers to the units.[15] The Government of India now began to reveal an inner contradiction: how were regional or communal anti-Congress groups to be placated while safeguarding imperial interests. This is discussed in the next two sections, where the questions of the devolution of law and order, and centre–province financial relations are discussed. As we shall see, the decisive factor in the centralist thrust was the cluster of imperial interests mentioned earlier; the opposition of Indians was brushed aside. There was no question of abandoning the reforms altogether though that would have pleased Winston Churchill and the Conservative die-hards. Answering a query of Stanley Baldwin about the draft constitutional proposals published in March 1933, Lord Brabourne, governor of Bombay, wrote:

I have taken great pains to find out what the ICS and Police officers in the Presidency really think of the White Paper proposals and in nearly every case their attitude can be summed up as a dislike of the whole thing but a firm conviction that it is much too late to go back now. Some of the younger Policemen are strongly against the whole policy but their line is that 'given enough police we can control any trouble in India'—which may or may not be the case but is hardly what we want.[16]

II

During the discussion in the summer of 1930, in course of arguing against extreme provincialism, James Dunnett had pleaded for some superintendence, direction and control by the central government of the provinces. In some federal states, as in the US and Switzerland, there were federal agencies to execute federal laws, whereas in British India the practice so far had been to supplement the all-India services by using the provincial police force and similar bodies as agents of the central government. Expense alone ruled out the creation of mutually exclusive and completely self-sufficient federal and provincial bureaucracies. Against this Sir Fazl-i-Husain, apprehensive that a party might be in power at the centre which had a different outlook from that in a province, argued that such supervisory powers over the provinces should be at the personal discretion of the governor-general, without any reference to the central legislature or the central government.

Since all parties present at the First Round Table Conference were agreed on making 'law and order' a provincial subject under a responsible minister, the imperial authorities were concerned about how to control classes of offences like terrorism and communism which could not be done without some control from the centre. Under the existing constitution, controlled by the bureaucracy, police administration in the provinces was divided between a political branch (which dealt with these issues) and a criminal branch which dealt with ordinary crime. The deputy inspector-general of police in charge of these usually dealt directly with the chief secretary of the provincial government. The existing Police Acts, passed long before there was any question of Indian participation in the legislative process, put the inspector-general of police under the control of the provincial government. 'A local government without any alteration of law, could, by unwise interference, reduce the discipline of the police.' Attempts to prevent this and develop some concurrent jurisdiction over the police between the centre and the provinces placed the British Home Member Sir Harry Haig and Sir Fazl-i-Husain once again on opposite sides. Haig did not like the supervisory powers over law and order to be vested in the person of the governor-general rather than the central government because then the latter might adopt 'a merely critical attitude towards a policy for which they were relieved of all responsibility'. (What worried Sir Harry was a recurrence of a situation like 1930 when, with only dominion status defined as a far-off goal, people could be mobilised for complete independence and the moderate nationalists would tend to sit on the fence.) Sir Fazl-i-Husain put in a strongly worded caveat at the end of this despatch:

It appears to me that there is greater need for laying down in the constitution that the centre shall not interfere with the provinces than of inserting a provision that the province shall obey the order of the centre. . . . We cannot have provincial autonomy, and at the same time a centralised administration of law and order.

In October 1931, at the Second Round Table Conference where, as we have seen, Hoare had started to support minority groups against the Congress, he asked Haig if it was not possible to eliminate the federal government altogether from the picture in the administration of law and order, giving the governor-general personal powers like the US president. Haig did not consider it practicable, and stuck to his original position. Loose supervisory powers 'might have very far-reaching effects and would lead to centrifugal tendencies'.[17]

In Bengal, the European expatriate businessmen were in a quandary over their general support to specific Muslim elite groups and their demand for the maximum measure of provincial autonomy, and their concern for their own safety from revolutionary violent groups. To the suggestion that complete provincial autonomy combined with no change at the centre would suit Britain best, Benthall countered that the 'great majority of the security services in Bengal would forthwith resign and in six months the province would be lost. For twenty years Bengal had been run only with the aid of the CID which could not be maintained under the conditions visualised. . . .'[18] Both Lothian and Benthall about this time advised the Reforms Office to emulate the US in developing self-sufficient federal bureaucracies for federal functions, especially taxation and police.[19]

Nearly two years passed before the Conservative government in Britain, anxious to consolidate its support among the anti-Congress groups, took note of these fears of European expatriates and bureaucrats. Following the tradition of Fazl-i-Husain, his successor, Zafrullah Khan, had added a note of dissent to a Reforms Office despatch of 15 July 1932 which suggested that the federal government and the provincial governments should have some concurrent administrative jurisdiction over the maintenance of peace and over criminal legislation, control of arms and the press. Hoare supported Zafrullah Khan's alternative view that governors-general and governors, under the their personal direction should do the task of coordination.[20] The Conservative politician remained far apart from the Conservative bureaucrat. Haig sourly noted,

I feel the Secretary of State has formed a picture of the Governor-General of the future as a Great Mogul, maintaining order throughout the country by his personal authority. . . . Unless we are going to allow the disintegration of India, there must be certain points with which both centralised and provincial legislature will be concerned.[21]

Hoare ignored this.

The initial balance struck between imperial interests and the conciliation of the autonomists was weighted on the side of the latter. The White Paper on Indian constitutional reform published in March 1933 made police and law and order a provincial subject (no. 50 in list II), but not to the point wanted by Dunnett and Hague in putting criminal law and the code of criminal procedure in the concurrent list (nos. 9 and 10). It was silent on the issue of the central coordination of intelligence on subversive activities and follow-up action. As Hoare put it, to avoid appearing 'provocative to provincial governments' the White Paper had avoided specific constitutional provisions requiring the provincial government to supply information to the federal government.[22]

London was aware that European expatriates, especially in Bengal, were worried about revolutionary violence, but much ingenuity would be needed to provide a constitutional basis for controlling criminal intelligence behind the back of responsible ministers. A cabinet paper put it lucidly:

It is no exaggeration to say that most of the extreme politicians in Bengal are themselves connected with terrorist associations, and their news figure in the dossiers of the Intelligence Branch of the Presidency. (If ministers were) *constitutionally* . . . able to demand access to all their secret reports and to their dossiers. . . . the advent of a Congress ministry in Bengal would necessarily entail the immediate destruction of existing dossiers; for otherwise the source of information would be disclosed. . . . The very lives of the Agents depend on the safeguarding of their reports and of their identity. . . .[23]

The Government of India and the provincial governments were prepared to let the provincial intelligence agencies come under the control of responsible ministers. The existing Central Intelligence Bureau was to be detached from the home department, attached to defence or external affairs (where funds were not votable by the assembly) and have a few liaison officials in each province. From the imperial point of view, its weakness was that a nationalist ministry could legitimately so starve the provincial CID of funds that it would be unable to follow up the centre's suggestions; or could deem it just prudent not to cooperate with central IB officials. The London officials' alternative scheme which they had not succeeded in incorporating into the White Paper, was embodied in the Government of India Act, thanks to the persistent lobbying of European interests in Britain, and Conservative constituency party organs.[24] Under this scheme, in each province the regular police and the criminal branch of the CID were transferred to the ministers but that part of the staff which did intelligence work on 'All-India subversive movements' was to function as a direct agent of the governor-general and have special liaison with the governor.[25] The ideas were embodied in paragraphs 94–97 of the Joint Select Committee of the British Parliament and enacted in sections 57 and 58 of the Government of India Act.[26] Imperial misgivings expressed earlier about the inspector-general of police being placed under ministerial control[27] were allayed by requiring the governor's prior consent before rules governing the Police Acts were amended.[28] The Central Intelligence Bureau was specifically mentioned in the federal legislative list under 'defence'.[29]

The period between the publication of the White Paper and the Government of India Act, when a centralising thrust took place in European and imperial interests, did not produce any noticeable backlash from politicians like Sir Fazl-i-Husain and Sir Zafrullah Khan who had earlier been quick with their notes of dissent. The India Office also does appear to have taken for granted their continued support for even the modified constitutional proposals (in contrast to the Congress). This office had always felt that these politicians were exaggerating when they said that their safety depended on the lowest form of federal control because the Indian army had and was likely to continue to have a majority of Muslims. An India Office note for the Third Round Table Conference on centre–province relations had concluded by saying:

Moreover, it seems likely that by the time the Governor-General falls completely under the domination of his ministers, the Indian Army, as distinct from British troops, is likely to have passed under Indian control. So far as one can foresee, the Army will be predominantly Muslim, and is likely to be quite as powerful a factor in the Federation as any Hindu Executive and Legislature.[30]

III

Provincial autonomy could be either a device for deflecting all-India nationalism in imperial interests or alternatively a training ground for self-government. In either case it involved different financial priorities. Between 1927 and 1935 the British government at first went a long way to provide elastic sources of revenue for its provincially oriented allies but then found that imperial interests (defence budget, home charges) required that these sources of revenue should be outside the control of self-governing provinces.

The Government of India Act (1919) left income tax, an important elastic source of revenue, to the central government. There were repeated criticisms of this throughout the decade even from political groups that were not close to the Congress. Since these groups had given evidence before the Simon Commission, the latter felt obliged to state their point of view. Sir Walter Layton, the economist who advised the commission, recommended that 50 per cent of the income tax should be available for distribution.

From the First Round Table Conference in November 1930 till almost two years after, the distribution of income tax was hotly debated, revealing a significant cleavage between imperial and local perspectives. The first draft of the constitution prepared by Lord Sankey towards the end of the Labour government had only done an outline financial chapter. At the Second Round Table Conference in September–December 1931, the financial subcommittee of the Federal Structures Committee, whose chairman was the Conservative Lord Peel, decided, under pressure from the Indians, in favour of provincialising income tax and making the central government dependent on provincial contributions. Peel described the work of the committee at a cabinet meeting which met to discuss the protests of the Government of India:

... speaking privately, there had been a tendency throughout its deliberations to remove any and every source of revenue from the centre, for the benefit of the provinces. It had needed all his own efforts to retain for the centre what few sources of revenue he had in fact been able to save.[32]

Another committee under the Conservative statesman Lord Eustace Percy went into the details of the scheme, and recommended a modified form of provincialisation of income tax. Both these were political proposals designed to isolate radical nationalists and so they Left some parts of imperial finances uncovered. The only way to convince London that the centre should have the bulk of the finances (or at least a decisive say in its allocation) was to point to the danger to imperial interests: as the new reforms commissioner W.H. Lewis wrote, 'When financial safeguards are discussed, the point is fully emphasised that 80 per cent of the federal revenues are required for the military budget, debt, and pension charges, etc., for which parliament must take responsibility.

The same emphasis is required when federal finance is under consideration.'[33]

This argument was embodied in a long despatch (36 pages, 96 paras) in which the key sentence ran, '*The Federal Budget is therefore essentially a defence and credit budget, and thus must not be tampered with*' (italics in the original).[34] Probably because Sir Fazl-i-Husain had given a note of dissent to the government despatch, Hoare's initial reaction was to comment that there might be more to be said for Peel's scheme.[35] However, by the middle of November 1932 Hoare had been won over by the financial interests in Britain. Peel pleaded for avoiding the mistakes of the 1919 reforms and giving the provinces elastic sources of revenue. Lord Percy added that 'he was more inclined to trust Indians on finance than on any other subjects'. Hoare replied that 'this was far from being the view held in the House of Commons and the City of London, and the serious apprehension felt in these quarters would have to be taken into account'.[36] Many British Indian delegates at the federal finance committee of this round table conference argued that a reduction of military expenditure would enable the federal government to be solvent without income tax, and reiterated that their claim for the right of provinces to levy a surcharge was not palatable to the Government of India; Hoare was unwilling to lose the political support of the Indians who would cooperate. He kept the provincial surcharge.

The Act of 1935 Left it all to an arbitral award by someone appointed by the British government to decide how much initial grant the provinces should receive on the eve of autonomy and how much would be the share of provinces in income tax.

Sir Otto Niemeyer's award arranged for a deferred payment of 50 per cent to the provinces, apart from providing minimum and fixed resources to each province to bear the expenses of the new constitution.[37] (The Government of India had wanted a permanent share of 60 per cent for the centre.) Its effect was to limit the scope for expansion in army expenditure. It was a contradiction between the needs of imperial defence and the needs of imperial credit. Within an imperial framework no constitutional change could solve it.

The possibility of cuts in army expenditure had been noted earlier in the civilian wing of the British administration—by Parsons in June

1932,[38] and J.B. Taylor (the future governor of the Reserve Bank of India) in April 1933.[39] The commander-in-chief had warned against a cut of Rs 15 crore because then the frontiers would be Left defenceless, the princely states could not be helped, and the defence of the 3400 miles of railway security would be weakened. The 'only sanction of law and order would be the goodwill of the people',[40] and an imperial power could not afford to depend entirely on that. By Niemeyer's award the existing level of army expenditure was saved but the military authorities were ill-equipped to face imperial problems.

IV

During the debate on the report of the Simon Commission in July 1930 the reforms commissioner James Dunnett had noted, while making some calculations about the relative advantages of direct or indirect elections to the central legislative assembly, 'There is something disquieting in the thought of a single all-India Party controlling the centre as well as the majority of the provincial governments in India.'[41] Unfortunately for the future of the Raj the first general elections under the new constitution returned the Congress to power in five of the eleven provinces, and in Bombay also the Congress formed a stable ministry. In the North-West Frontier Province its allies, the 'Red Shirts', were in power. The bureaucracy now had limited options. If they succeeded in getting the princely states to federate and send their nominees to the federal assembly, a much-hoped-for counterweight to the nationalists might emerge. If the provincial Congress ministers became preoccupied with local problems and acquired a mind of their own it was even better. Lothian hoped for this.[42] If on the other hand, before these had materialised, fresh burdens were imposed on imperial interests, then a breach between the government and the nationalists appeared very likely.

Assumption of office by the Congress had not resulted in any significant relaxation either by its rank and file or by its local leaders in their opposition to that part of the federal constitution whereby princes were to nominate the representatives. As the agitation against the princely states mounted in 1938 the commander-in-chief noted that the question of internal security was 'likely to be just as serious if not more so than in the past'.[43] The home minister added that there was always the risk of simultaneous resignation of Congress governments and the inevitable use of emergency powers of direct administration laid down in the constitution. If such a thing happened it 'would almost certainly be followed by some kind of civil disobedience on a much larger scale than has been experienced before' and would this time cover not only towns, but rural India. For this the British army was necessary.[44]

Faced with the difficulties of recruiting British soldiers, the British war minister proposed the reduction of four British battalions from those stationed in India. He also suggested that India maintain and pay for an imperial reserve division for operation east of Suez. The Government of India was concerned that the 'British element will be reduced by 30 per cent at a time when the political situation in India is far more threatening than it has ever been since 1857'.[45]

Privately, and in official despatches, all authorities, including the die-hard finance member Sir James Grigg, gave reasons explaining why they could neither dispense with British troops nor afford to increase the army budget. In any case even without the costs of the Imperial Reserve Division, Hoare–Belisha's pay hike for British soldiers was going to add to Indian defence expenditure for that part of the British army that was borne on the Indian list. The imperial authorities in India could just about manage that out of the existing budget but no more. If the government wished its constitution to find fruition not only at the provinces but also at the centre, then, in the transitional period, with a Congress-dominated central legislative assembly, the safest thing was to transfer the burden of the imperial reserve defence to Britain.

The result of this deadlock was the appointment of the Chatfield Committee to consider whether the British government would contribute towards the cost of Indian manpower in imperial defence. The very fact that such a situation could arise was symptomatic of the failure to carry through the principle of federation and devolution before the nationalist party got bogged down with the details of provincial administration and lost its nationalist urge. Desperate efforts by Linlithgow on the eve of the Second World War to get the princes to accede did not succeed. The timing of the end of the British Raj in India, the nature of the elite groups who would be ruling the centre, the whole question of partition, were now to depend on the worldwide social and economic upheavals caused by the Second World War.

NOTES

1. B.R. Tomlinson *Political Economy of the Raj*, (London, 1979), p. 27, mentions only three of these—the British exporter, the 'Home charges' and the use of Indian troops at Indian expense overseas.
2. R. Danzig. 'The Many layered Cake', *Modern Asian Studies*, VIII (1974), p. 64.
3. Reading to MacDonald, 28 November 1931, f. 6 (Macd. Papers 30/69/ 698).
4. Irwin's remarks at the proceedings of the informal meeting of the Executive Council, 26 June 1930 (NAI—Reforms—Reforms—1939— file 67/V).
5. Note by Secretary of State for India for the Cabinet, 9 November 1931 (Cab 27/41 RTC [31] 11).
6. Benthall to P.H. Browne, 23 October 1931 (Benthall Papers, Box II, File 1931–2).
7. Cab 27/521 CI (32), nos. 5, 7, 8 and 11 for all the correspondence on this.
8. Lothian to Reading, 25 February 1932 (GD 40/17/159, ff. 21–2). In another letter of the same date to his cabinet colleague Sir John Simon, Lothian said that the report of the Simon Commission itself had passed the death sentence on the Montford scheme (ibid., ff 23–5).
9. Sykes to Willingdon, 11 April 1932 (Cab 27/521 CI [32] 9).
10. On this, see David Page, *Prelude to Partition* (Delhi, 1982) and Robin Moore, *Crisis of Indian Unity* (Oxford, 1974).
11. The provincial part of the draft constitution had been prepared by Lord Sankey (who had been Lord Chancellor both in the Labour government and the National government) as early as 13 May 1932 (Cab 27/521 CI [32] 6). It was a slightly modified version of the one prepared on 27 July 1931 during the tenure of the Labour government (Cab 27.470 BDG [31] 8).
12. Cab 27/520 CI (32), 12th Meeting of the Cabinet Committee on India, 18 October 1932.
13. Ibid., 13th Meeting, 20 October 1932.
14. Cab 27/521 CI (32) 21, 'Scheme of Safeguards Proposed and Method of its Operation', para 21.
15. NAI—Reforms—Reforms—1930—file 67/V/30. Proc. of 12th Meeting, 19 July 1930; Sir Fazl-i-Husain's note, 3 September 1930 (ibid., file 67/ X/30).
16. Brabourne to Baldwin (Baldwin Papers, vol. 106, f. 348).

17. NAI—Reforms—Reforms—1930—file 67/VI.

18. Memo. of discussion at 37 Ballygunge Park, 18 February 1932 (Benthall Papers, Box II, File 1931–2, item 26). Those present were Lord Lothian, Sir John Kerr, Edward Benthall, H. Carey Morgan, W.W.K. Page, E. Villiers and 'T.C.M.'

19. Lothian to Dunnett, 9 February 1932; Benthall to Dunnett, 2 May 1932 (kept in NAI—Reforms—Reforms—1932—file 85/32).

20. Cab 27/521 CI (32) 29, Appendix, Secretary of State to Viceroy, 30 September 1932.

21. Haig's Minute, 3 October 1932 (NAI—Reforms—Reforms—1932, file 014/32 kw, p. 15).

22. *Proposals for Indian Constitutional Reforms* (Delhi, 1953), para 114.

23. Cab 27/521 CI (32) 59, 'Defence Security Intelligence', paras 2 and 4.

24. The papers of Lord Derby, a member of the Joint Select Committee, and the resolutions of British Conservative party branches testify to this.

25. As in n. 23.

26. Government of India Act, 1935, clauses 57 and 58.

27. See notes 19 and 20 above.

28. See relevant clause of the Act.

29. NAI—Reforms—General—1935—file 6/I/35, GIA, Secretary of State to Government of India P & J (c) 4775, 25 January 1935, para 28.

30. Cab 27/469 RTC (31) 4, India Office departmental note on communal and minority problems, 25 September 1931, para 8.

31. P.J. Thomas, *The Growth of Federal Finance in India* (Madras, 1939), ch. xxx, *passim*.

32. Cab 27/520 CI (32), 27th meeting, 16 November 1932.

33. Lewis to Schuster, 12 May 1932, kept in NAI—Reforms—Reforms—1932—file 125/32 kw, p. 4.

34. Despatch to Secretary of State, 13 June 1932, para 6 (NAI—Reforms—Reforms—1932—file 123–32).

35. Cab 27/520, 27th Meeting, 16 November 1932.

36. Indian Round Table Conference (2nd session), *Proceedings of Federal Structures Committee and Minorities Committee*, vol. I (Calcutta, 1932) paras 4, 5 and 6.

37. Niemeyer to Grigg, 23 October 1935 (PJGG 3/113 [d] 29).

38. Note by Parsons, 2 June 1932 in NAI—Reforms—Reforms—1932—file 123 kw, pp. 4f.

39. Note by J.B. Taylor, 7 April 1933 in Finance—Finance—1933—file 17 (23)-F.

40. GCI to Secretary of State, 15 May 1933, Appendix VII in ibid.

41. NAI—Reforms—Reforms—Secret Notes 1930, no. 31.
42. Lothian to Halifax, 3 May 1937 (GD 40/17/37, f. 439–40).
43. IOR L/WS/1/153, file WS, 1931, f. 23–4.
44. Ibid., f. 26.
45. Cab. 6/6 198–D, para 10.

STATE AND BUSINESS IN INDIA IN THE AGE OF DISCRIMINATORY PROTECTION, 1916–1939*

I t is a truism to say that there is a sharp contrast between the predominantly interventionist attitude of Indian governments since 1947 and the predominantly *laissez-faire* approach of the British Raj before 1914.[1] The years between 1916 and 1939, with which we are concerned in this essay, are more complex. In 1916 the Indian Industrial Commission was appointed, and three years later were enacted the Montagu–Chelmsford (Montford) Reforms. In 1939 the Second World War broke out, the Congress ministries resigned in the provinces where they had formed the government, and wartime controls were

*Paper read at IIMA Seminar, Series in Business History, Ahmedabad, 1984, and published in Dwijendra Tripathi (ed.), *State and Business in India: A Historical Perspective* (Delhi, 1987).

The material from British records was collected when the author was Smuts Visiting Fellow in Commonwealth Studies at Cambridge in 1980–1. Unpublished Crown copyright records at the Public Record Office and the India Office Records are reproduced by permission from H.M. Stationery Office. These also include the private papers of Brabourne, Irwin, Mac Donald and Reading. Other collections which have been used are listed below with acknowledgement to custodians of the papers and the owners of copyright as indicated:

National Archives of India	Government of India
Benthall Papers	Cambridge South Asia Archives and Sir Paul Benthall
Federation of British Industries	Modern Records Centre, University of Warwick
Earl of Derby Papers	Liverpool City Library
James Grigg Papers	Churchill College Archives and Lady Grigg
Walter Runciman Papers	University of Newcastle-on-Tyne
Neville Chamberlain Papers	University of Birmingham Library
Austen Chamberlain Papers	
Wedgwood Benn Papers	Stansgate Collection, House of Lords Record Office
Arthur Steel-Maitland Papers	Scottish Record Office, Edinburgh

gradually imposed. In between, there were periods of turbulence and quiescence in the political economy of India and Britain which I shall be analysing in the course of this essay. Before doing so, however, let us look at the areas of agreement and disagreement among scholars who have contributed to the study of the subject in recent years.

There is agreement among writers as diverse as Bagchi, Dewey, and Tomlinson that the overall assistance given by government for industrial development was very limited. The debate has centred on which areas government helped in but could have helped more, what the main limitations of government were, and why this was so. Bagchi castigated the British Indian government for a half-hearted attitude to protectionism, deplored the absence of all-India coordination, and pointed to the racial bias against Indian entrants to areas of activity hitherto occupied by Europeans. According to him, because successive governments pursued a deflationary policy, government demand was limited and this hampered the development of heavy industry in particular.[2]

Bagchi's formidable list of indictments has naturally evoked a reaction from scholars, some of whom have been quick to point out that he had not consulted any archival sources, whereas they had.[3] On the issue of a half-hearted attitude to protectionism, Clive Dewey countered by saying that the acceptance by the Government of India of the majority report of the Indian Fiscal Commission (September 1922), which had recommended discriminatory protection, transferred an important element of sovereignty from Britain to India. Henceforth it was not any British influence but rather bargains between different Indian pressure groups and the Indian government which decided the level of tariffs.[4] The second volume of the *Cambridge Economic History of India* has supported the position taken by Dewey.[5] Tomlinson while not so categorical, argued that the central legislative assembly set up under the reforms of 1919 acted as a restraining factor on the government when British and Indian interests were opposed to each other.[6] Ray, following Bagchi and like him without examining the archives on this particular issue, restated the old nationalist argument that nothing really changed after 1922. An essentially bureaucratic government kept the initiative to itself; it was neither bound to refer all applications to the proposed Tariff Board nor to accept its recommendations.[7] Another scholar, Chatterji, attempted to strengthen this line of argument by research into the India Office Records but left out a great many other sources which are crucial for clinching the issue.[8] My examination of a wider range of sources (both in Britain and India) leads me broadly to support the position taken by Bagchi, Ray, and Chatterji and challenge the position taken in the *Cambridge Economic History of India* and two recent articles of Dewey on free trade and industrial policy.[9]

On the absence of all-India coordination on industrial policy (Bagchi's second indictment), Dewey argued that the transition from a war economy to a peacetime economy coincided with the Montford Reforms which made industry a provincial subject and thus hindered an effective implementation of the report of the Industrial Commission.[10] He was on reasonably firm ground where he wrote that the Industrial Commission was set up at the height of the war when economic controls and state assistance had acquired some respectability in Britain, but that after the war orthodox economic liberalism reasserted itself, and exchange stability took precedence over public expenditure. In such circumstances interventionist arguments did not appeal to the official mind. Dewey, however, is less convincing when he attributes the lack of coordination mainly to the Montford Reforms. Such provincial autonomy as was given under these reforms (in which industry was made first a provincial and later a concurrent subject) did not rule out some degree of all-India coordination and pooling of experiences.[11] An even more serious methodological criticism of Dewey on industrial policy is that there is insufficient analysis in his work of the way commercial policy and industrial policy interacted during the war and its aftermath. The archival sources for the two overlap a great deal, and the same officials were involved in drafting despatches on both subjects. Dewey put his treatment of the 'imperialism of free trade' almost in a separate compartment from his treatment of industrial policy, and in each article looked back and forward within the confines of his self-limited topic. This might explain his inability to see the interactions in government policy as between two branches of the Department of Commerce and Industry. He succumbs to the pitfalls of writing what J.H. Hexter has called 'tunnel history'.[12]

Whether overt racial bias in favour of British expatriate firms and against indigenous firms seriously influenced the Government of India is more difficult to substantiate. Bagchi considered it an important factor, but the type of evidence he produced was not convincing.[13] The allegation of racial prejudice made before a government inquiry commission, unless substantiated by other testimony, would be tantamount to mere advocacy. The hypothesis can be better tested by examining the industries that the government favoured with tariff protection, or the firms which managed to get contracts for the purchase of government stores.

There is general agreement between Bagchi, Ray, and Tomlinson that the deflationary monetary policy of the government (designed to keep the rupee–sterling ratio stable) acted as a damper to the expansion of government demand both in the 1920s and the 1930s.[14] Behind this was the long-standing assumption of the imperial subsystem in India that, since it was expected to pay for its upkeep, it could only follow a financial policy that satisfied current orthodoxies in Britain. I would agree with Dewey when, criticising the oversimplified nationalist allegations of British commercial lobbying behind every decision taken in India, he states that the Government of India and the India Office were guided by financial imperatives.[15] I would, however, add a necessary caveat that deviations from orthodox finance were ruled out as much to protect the imperial administrative apparatus as to protect any specific Indian interest group.

Bagchi, Ray, and Tomlinson have all tended to treat the period 1914–39 as one unit, and discuss different subthemes in that time period. This blurs the discontinuities in the political economy of the Raj, discontinuities caused by a number of factors: the exigencies of war and post-war Depression; the world crisis of 1929–31; the Civil Disobedience Movement, the emergence of the sterling area bloc and the system of imperial preferences; and finally the constitutional settlement of 1935. For my analysis, I have taken shorter time periods, 1916–22, 1923–9, 1929–35, and 1935–40. Before describing some basic features of these periods as they affected Britain and India, I would like to point out that this approach enables me to test, while reading the evidence, how far a useful distinction can be drawn between the Government of India as representing Indian interests (and educated Indian opinion) and Whitehall as representing imperial interests (with the India Office acting as an agent). Imperial interests should not be narrowly defined simply in terms of India as a market for British exports, India as a source of remittances to maintain the 'home charges', and the use of the Indian army at India's cost to cover the overseas commitments of

Britain. These, located outside India, are stressed by Tomlinson, but one must add aspects of the imperial 'subsystem' in India, which consisted of British expatriate businessmen, British members of the Indian services (whose numbers were declining slowly in this period) and the British element in the Indian army.[16]

In the years 1916–22, a coalition government under Asquith, which had been ruling Britain since May 1915, was replaced by another under Lloyd George in December 1916. Both coalitions included a strong ginger-group of Conservative and Unionist supporters of protection (tariff reform, as they liked to call it) and imperial preference. Prominent among them were Austen Chamberlain, secretary of state for India till 14 July 1917, A. Bonar Law, secretary of state for colonies till December 1916 and chancellor of the exchequer, and Walter Long, president of the Board of Trade till December 1916 and afterwards in charge of the Colonial Office. Arthur Steel-Maitland, another tariff reformer, who was a member of Parliament from Austen Chamberlain's neighbouring constituency in Birmingham, served as under-Secretary of colonies under both Bonar Law and Long.[17] Proposals for constitutional reform designed to win the support of the political and economic elites of India had been formulated by Lord Hardinge in 1915. These were gradually processed by Chamberlain, modified by his successor Edwin Montagu, and eventually emerged as the Montford Reforms of 1919. There was, in the four years just after the armistice of November 1918, increasing unemployment in Britain and widespread social and political unrest in India. Moderate Indian political leaders accepted the Montford Reforms and broke away from the Congress calling themselves Liberals, while the Congress started the Non-Cooperation Movement. That in turn was called off by Gandhi in February 1922.

A new phase started the following month, with the forced exit of Edwin Montagu from the coalition government of Lloyd George. For about seven years, successive British cabinets and viceroys refused to modify the structure of government and endeavoured to boost the morale of the civil and military services in India. Britain was ruled by a Conservative government, except for nine months in 1924 when a minority Labour government held office.

The period 1929–35 saw very rapid economic and political change, with world Depression and the breakdown of international trade. These affected the imperial relationship, and, along with the effects of the Civil

Disobedience Movement, influenced the political framework. Britain experienced three changes of government and one change of prime minister. In the final period 1935–40, decisions of the government appeared to be taken within the framework of provincial autonomy but many vital powers remained concentrated in the hands of the governor-general and his bureaucracy.

I

Early in May 1915 Sir W.H. Clark, commerce member in the Viceroy's Council, considered it politically important to deflect the attention of India's political and business groups from protectionist nationalism. At his suggestion, Ernest Low, secretary to the commerce department, wrote a long note in which the key sentences towards the end were the following:

The public . . . have a policy [of protectionism] on the theoretical advantages of which a large section of them are unanimously agreed: which has been tried in many countries and can point to a considerable measure of success. . . . It is incumbent on government to show that this policy is . . . unnecessary, by being able to point to other lines of action which have been tried. . . . As a first step towards this end, it is necessary to appoint a committee of enquiry. . . . From the scope of such an enquiry all questions relating to protection will *ex hypothesi* be excluded. Government starts with the fundamental assumption that this policy is dangerous in India, and the enquiry will concern itself only with the examination of the alternative policies.'[18]

Clark added: 'I have asked Secretary to prepare this note. . . . The proposals in the latter part of it are the outcome of frequent discussions between us.'[19]

In the Viceroy's Council only two members (C.H.A. Hill and R.H. Craddock) opposed the exclusion of the 'fiscal question', Craddock pointing to the danger of 'subsidised Japanese manufactures' capturing the Indian market while Europe was at war.[20] Lord Hardinge and the Indian member Sir Sankaran Nair sought to let the proposed commission consider protective tariffs in exceptional cases, but gave up when Clarke vehemently objected, arguing that it was vitally important that the government have 'an alternative policy to Indian protectionist propaganda.'[21] In November the Indian government proposed to the secretary of state that an industrial commission, with these restricted terms of reference, should start work as soon as circumstances permitted after the war ended.[22]

As always, the government did not wish to be seen as acting under pressure. A cable was sent to London on 26 January 1916 for a reply to the despatch when it turned out that Sir Ibrahim Rahimatullah had given notice of a motion on industrial policy in the central legislature. London had already made up its mind by 14 January, and so the reply came promptly on 1 February, surprising the Government of India by its wanting the commission to be appointed straightway without waiting for the end of the war.[23] London was apprehensive that Britain's wartime ally Japan would otherwise establish a firm control over the markets for the goods hitherto imported from Germany and Austria.[24] However, like the Government of India, on the issue of including or excluding tariff policy the officials as well as the ministers were divided. Lord Islington, the under-secretary of state for India, had been most vehement about the need to forestall Japan by rapid industrial development but, being a Liberal, did not react the way Craddock had done in the Viceroy's Council. To him the exclusion of tariffs 'seem[ed] necessary if controversy [was] to be avoided . . ., not necessarily controversy in India but controversy between India and other parts of the Empire, especially the UK'.[25] The Permanent Under-Secretary of State Sir T.W. Holderness was a doctrinaire free trader.[26] His junior civil servant L.J. Kershaw made a very sensible point:

in view of the fact that we are here concerned not with established industries like cotton or jute, but with small nascent industries, a suggestion might perhaps be made that the terms of reference might be drafted in less uncompromising terms than the Government of India contemplate.[27]

Austen Chamberlain allowed Islington and Holderness to have their way. (Later, during the debate in the Indian legislature the official spokesman attributed the exclusion of the tariff issue to Chamberlain's parliamentary speech on the cotton duties delivered on 1 February. He was quite irritated: 'They [the Government of India] had decided not to extend the enquiry into fiscal policy before the orders of H.M. Government were issued on these cotton duties, and they ought not now to have laid the exclusion to the door of the Home government.'[28])

However, he was not a person to ignore an opportunity to utilise the protectionist lobby in India to the advantage of the tariff reform group in the wider imperial context. Historians have taken insufficient notice of how the tariff reform circles, led by Chamberlain, attempted a flanking movement against the position officially approved both by the India Office and the Government of India.[29] From the middle of February till the middle of August they dropped hints to the Indian government about how to widen the terms of reference of the Industrial Commission so as to include the tariff issue to the advantage of Britain. This was done by using a development in wartime economic diplomacy to bargain for protective tariffs in India in return for preference for Britain as against other countries, especially Japan.

About the same time as the Indian government was working out details about a post-war industrial commission, there germinated, in some commercial and political circles in France and Britain, the idea of institutionalising a permanent international economic system. In this system Germany would be excluded from inter-allied trade by high tariffs. Differential rates of tariffs and preferences among the allies and their colonies would ensure that the metropolis of an empire would have the maximum degree of preference in trade with its colonies, followed by its allied countries. The French initiators of this policy had kept the British Foreign Office informed of every step unofficially. Therefore when in January 1916 some British commercial circles responded to it and came out with an 'After-war Customs Union' with a four-tier tariff, the French government proposed an inter-allied conference on wartime and post-war economic arrangements later in the year. They invited not only Britain, but Russia, Italy, and Japan as well. In mid-February Japan's acceptance had not yet been received, but the British Foreign Office was well aware that the Japanese press was clamouring for 'revision of the Anglo-Japanese alliance, preferential rights in China, reversal of anti-Japanese policy in Canada and Australia, improved facilities of trade with India and so on'.[30]

This was used by Chamberlain to persuade Holderness of the need to study the possible impact of the Japanese threat to India.[31] Under Chamberlain's direction, Kershaw wrote to Ernest Low demi-officially, giving details of the proposed conference and providing two hints about possible tariff changes in Britain after the war and about the advantages of differential duties to India. The wording of both was Chamberlain's, inserted by him in the draft. The last paragraph (written by Chamberlain) read:

His Majesty's Government have already decided that it will be necessary to review the fiscal policy of India in connection with that of the Empire at the close of the war, but they have not so far laid down the principles by which they would be guided when considering it.

The ministers's corrections in earlier parts of the draft strengthened the plea for having differential tariffs in India by adding that any consequent retaliatory action would 'not be serious except in cases where the importing country could render itself independent of India'.[32]

With fellow tariff reformers at the Colonial Office (Bonar Law and Steel-Maitland), the Board of Trade (Walter Long as president) and at the India Office (L.J. Kershaw) very critical of the restricted terms of reference of the proposed industrial commission,[33] Chamberlain continued his private lobbying of the Indian government. The agenda of the Paris conference gave an opening to discuss intra-imperial co-operation with discriminatory tariffs, officially should the need arise.[34] On 8 May 1916, as a preparatory move for that, the Secretary of State for Colonies Bonar Law sent a circular to the colonies and dominions suggesting the agenda for a conference of Britain, the dominions and India on post-war commercial policy: what industries were essential for military security, what steps were needed to recover trade lost during the war and to find new markets, how far the development of the empire's resources could make it self-sufficient, and how improved sources of supply could be prevented from falling under foreign control.[35] Two days before that, Chamberlain, ascertaining that such a circular would be sent, coordinated his efforts with Steel-Maitland, and sent one copy privately to the viceroy.[36] The Paris conference led to the formation of the 'Committee on Industry and Trade after the War' under Lord Balfour of Burleigh.

The setting up of this committee gladdened the tariff reformers because its terms of reference included the prevention of imperial sources of supply falling under foreign control, as well as the development of imperial resources. At its first meeting on 25 July the chairman, explaining what 'empire development' meant, said that the intention was imperial self-sufficiency, although that phrase had been omitted from the published terms of reference so as to prevent unnecessary anxiety on the part of Britain's wartime allies.[37] On the other hand, at the India Office Sir T.W. Holderness was so critical of what he called 'this discredited expedient of the colonial policy of the eighteenth century' that in the same month he had stalled a specific move by leather manufacturers to divert the trade of Indian hides and skins exclusively into the empire.[38] He had also held back any decision by the India Office on the relevance of Lord Balfour's inquiry so far as India was concerned.[39] Chamberlain, however, 'heartily approve[d] the proposed enquiry', and asserted that the British government would ratify or approve the conclusions of the conference proposed by the French government. So the Government of India was to 'take these conclusions in their consideration at once in their bearing on Indian policy'. In order that 'India may move as far as possible on the same lines' as Britain and the dominions, he would ask the Board of Trade and the Colonial Office 'to keep [his department] fully informed'.[40]

To persuade senior Indian officials in advance that the work of the Industrial Commission should parallel that of the committee under Lord Balfour, Chamberlain made Kershaw send them advance copies of a draft despatch (from the revenue department) which had two significant clauses reflecting the mood of the tariff reformers. Paragraph 4 concluded thus:

... the broad question of fiscal policy ... generally and in detail, should be considered by Your Excellency's government in preparation for the Imperial Conference. I leave it to you to decide whether you should carry out the necessary enquiries departmentally or through the Commission on Indian industries which you have already appointed. In the latter case it might be necessary to enlarge the Commission's terms of reference so as to include in them the recommendations of the Paris Conference and the specific question on which Lord Balfour's Committee have been required to advise His Majesty's Government. ...

A later paragraph (no. 5) referred to 'the probability that the future fiscal policy of India, in the largest sense, [would] have to conform to the policy which Parliament [might] see fit to approve for this country'. In the light of that, the Indian government was to decide whether by enlarging the terms of reference it was giving the fiscal question undue 'publicity and importance', and if so, it should informally consult the Industrial Commission 'on the subjects referred to Lord Balfour's Committee'.[41]

Finance Member William Meyer was very angry. The previous March he had taken great care to see that the terms of reference of the Industrial Commission were so worded that the question of tariffs against Britain and the dominions could never arise.[42] On receiving this draft he commented:

I am most strongly against converting the Industries Commission into an agency for dealing with fiscal problems. The Commission was not constituted with reference to that object, and taken as a whole its *personnel* would not be the best people to deal with it. It includes, for instance, a rabid protectionist in the shape of Pandit Madan Mohan Malaviya. . . . The expansion of the scope of the Commission to include 'tariff reform' would be regarded as yielding to the claim that has been raised on this subject by a number of Indian politicians.[43]

Even before Meyer expressed these views to Sir George Barnes (who had succeeded Clark as commerce member), Chamberlain had been obliged, doubtlessly under pressure from the free trade and finance lobby, to agree to a watered-down version of the despatch quoted above. The official despatch on how India should respond to the plans of empire development eliminated paragraph 5, and modified a portion of paragraph 4 which now ended thus:

I leave it to you to decide in what manner the necessary enquiries should be carried out, but as at present advised, I am of opinion that the most convenient course would be to supplement departmental enquiries by informal consultation with the Commission on Indian industries which you have already appointed.[44]

To follow up these instructions the Indian government started a series of departmental surveys of raw material resources unutilised or only partly utilised in India, passing on the information to the Industrial Commission, but the latter remained precluded altogether from considering whether some of them could not be developed by protecting infant industries.[45]

The preceding account shows that Dewey's observation is wide off the mark: 'Commonplaces which served as substitutes for economic thought in official circles shifted towards protection.'[46] Protectionist tariff reformers were a minority in official circles in London and even more in India. Equally misleading is his statement that although Lord Hardinge came out with instructions to keep India 'straight' on free trade, he demanded 'fiscal autonomy'.[47] In the last month of his governor-generalship (March 1916) demands for greater freedom for Indian officials in fiscal policy were frequent. But these arose simply from a desire to ensure that the existing system in India (free trade, financial orthodoxy) was not compromised by bargains struck at international conferences like the proposed Paris conference where British tariff reformers might have had an edge, and no Government of India official would be present. J.B. Brunayte, secretary of the finance department, was worried that the currency and revenue requirements of the government would be disturbed 'under a scheme such as the Allies appear[ed] to have vaguely in mind'. Finance Member William Meyer agreed with him and wanted 'larger fiscal powers generally' as a *quid pro quo*.[48] Without this relative autonomy, influenced neither by Britain's short-term diplomatic preoccupations nor by Indian political views, the British subsystem in India would not be able to support itself out of India's revenues.[49] Privately even Meyer acknowledged:

Politically India will not be satisfied unless she gets the right, which the dominions enjoy, of buttressing her revenues and industries by putting duties for these purposes upon imports from the United Kingdom and other parts of the Empire but, if this were conceded, she would be quite willing to put larger duties on imports from foreign countries and to discriminate in other respects between Allied nations and others.

He, therefore, warned that the effects of Indian revenues must be the paramount consideration.[50]

Thus, the demand for fiscal autonomy voiced in governmental circles and conveyed to the India Office did not synchronise with Indian political opinion, although in the letter of the viceroy to London the protectionist sentiment in India was mentioned as one of the factors which required that a Government of India official represent India at the Paris conference. The main thrust of the letter was on the advantages of upholding the *status quo*.[51] Yet the demand for fiscal autonomy was disturbing, especially at a time when the new viceroy, Chelmsford, was suggesting that at the end of the war a statement be made of the ultimate goals of British rule in India.[52] Austen Chamberlain had lost out to the Liberals in his first bid to make the industrial inquiry in India serve the same purpose as the Committee on Industry and Trade. He evidently believed that unless another attempt was made to commit India explicitly to a system of preferential trade within the empire, economic nationalism in India in the post-war world would not distinguish between Britain and Japan. All the efforts towards an industrial inquiry in anticipation of the Japanese threat would have been a waste. A terse telegram he sent in September 1916 regarding representation at international economic conferences asked the viceroy to remember that this would 'raise difficult constitutional questions requiring very careful examination'.[53] The changeover from the Asquith government to the war cabinet of Lloyd George strengthened the tariff reform lobby, with Bonar Law now at the Treasury and Walter Long at the Colonial Office. There were no further demands from Indian officials about fiscal powers, but they were aware that a change in Britain's traditional free trade policy was not entirely out of question. The circular sent by the commerce and industry department to the provinces asking for data on how Indian industrial resources could help the empire mentioned that a change in Britain's fiscal policy could not be ruled out, although the existing system had served Britain and India well in the past.[54]

Precisely at this time, the political temperature in India rose with the Congress and the Muslim League signing the Lucknow Pact in December 1916. This was followed by a joint demand for self-government at an early date. The far more modest constitutional proposals of Chelmsford and his council had been sent the previous month and there was initially no question of any announcement on them before the end of the war. But the new situation made Chamberlain agree on 23 January 1917 to let the viceroy declare that the government would make an announcement in due course.[55]

It became necessary to get Indian external economic policy in line with Britain and the rest of the empire without delay. By coincidence, on 23 January the Federation of British Industries had sent a memorandum to Steel-Maitland at the Colonial Office, anticipating likely fiscal changes after the war. Except for the Manchester Chamber of Commerce, all other chambers of commerce seemed to think that a new international economic arraignment, not based on free trade, might become necessary.[56] Shortly before this, Walter Long at the Colonial Office had agreed that nominees of the Government of India could represent India at the imperial conference in March 1917, thinking this would prevent renewed pressure for India's self-government.[57] After perusing extensive material sent from India regarding India's resources, Chamberlain sent the viceroy an advance copy of the interim report of the Balfour Committee, even before it had been considered in the cabinet.[58] This report, prepared in anticipation of the imperial conference, had suggested that Britain declare that henceforth preference should be given to the products and manufactures of the overseas dominions 'in respect of any custom duties now or hereafter to be imposed on imports into the United Kingdom'.[59] This rather obvious attempt to work towards reciprocal preferences from India encouraged the officials, now aware of the increased political expectations in India, to make a modest bid for fiscal autonomy. The underlying considerations were still financial—Commerce Member Barnes found a four-decker tariff (as proposed in the report) cumbersome, and Finance Member Meyers would give the dominions preference only if there was reciprocity.[60] The Government of India accepted the Balfour Committee's suggestions about the development of raw materials and foodstuff, and the exclusion of persons who were not British subjects from the development of minerals vital to national security. There were two sentences which introduced a new element:

. . . we regard the development of Indian industries as essential and our commercial policy should be framed with this object primarily in view. . . . We also consider that for the above purposes it is essential that subject to due regard for imperial interests, we should have a free hand in framing India's fiscal policy.

Preferences to the dominions would depend on the treatment of Indians by individual dominions.[61]

The reaction in London was not favourable except from Kershaw who pointed out that India's future industrialisation might involve 'stiff protection against commonwealth products' and that until the empire could absorb the surplus product of India, it was 'of vital importance that foreign markets should remain open'. Holderness bluntly stated that India's political position did not justify the claim to fiscal freedom. As he put it:

If India is not ripe for self-government in the political sense or for responsible institutions, her government must remain largely a government of officials. . . . A government of this kind derives its authority from this country and its claim to freedom in fiscal matters, as enjoyed by a dominion government, is as gross a violation of political laws as the claim of a human being to fly in the air without wings or machinery would be of the laws of gravity.

He proposed to make this clear to the Indian invitees to the imperial conference, Sir James Meston, Sir S.P. Sinha, and the Maharaja of Bikaner.[62] That India was a dependency could not be more clearly stated.

Austen Chamberlain made it clear that unless India fell in line with the idea of imperial preference, he would not exert himself to get excise duty on Indian cotton goods removed. For,

whilst I have been glad to fight the battle of India against a particular impost forced upon her in spite of the universal discontent which it created in India and British Indian circles, I should not be prepared to back India in a policy of selfish isolation which disregarded her Imperial obligations and was not founded upon the principle that the property and the trade of each part of the Empire is the common stock of the Empire as a whole, and that we cannot weaken each other without weakening ourselves.[63]

Under the frontal attack most of the bureaucracy started having second thoughts, and some revealed their concern for the state of British industry. One junior official argued that his calculations showed that India would not gain much from imperial preference, unless India also got the power to adopt protection.[64] Others senior to him were more pliant. A.H. Ley was 'personally in favour of now definitely stating' that the Indian government would accept the principle of imperial preference. He was anxious about the prospects of the British car industry and dyestuff industry, not to mention a number of others, which in his opinion stood to gain a great deal from preference given in India.

Ernest Low, who as we have seen had started the process that led to the appointment of the Indian Industrial Commission, stressed the importance of retaining the sympathy of Austen Chamberlain.[65]

The final reply of the Indian government reached London after Edwin Montagu had succeeded Chamberlain as secretary of state. In this despatch the government was willing to accept a moderate preference which was to be achieved by increasing duties on goods from other countries and retaining the existing revenue tariffs on British goods. This was coupled with a request for a 'freer hand . . . in . . . fiscal policy', some protection for infant industries and the repeal of the cotton excise duty.[66] At the India Office almost everyone was agreed that there could be no *quid pro quo*. Holderness argued at the imperial conference that the Indian representatives had pledged themselves to preference, and now there could be no bargaining over it.[67] In the following year Montagu, Islington, and Holderness were all urging that preference for British goods should be given as soon as possible.[68] The record of the imperial government from 1915 to the end of the war on the question of formulating an industrial policy, thus, has to be seen as an attempt to preclude a balanced discussion on the place of tariffs in any scheme of industrial development, followed by an attempt from the centre to ensure that India as a market for British goods remained unscathed after the war.

The Industrial Commission published its report in 1918, without any reference to the fiscal question, but the minority report of Malaviya showed that the original purpose of deflecting Indian attention away from protection had not succeeded. It was not going to succeed because as long as a weakened British economy demanded preference for British goods, a strengthened political opinion in India held on to its point of view. In July 1919 Montagu asked that before a decision on imperial preference was taken 'the views of all sections of the public who [were] interested [be] obtained'.[69] The Indian government responded by appointing a committee of the (still unreformed) Imperial Legislative Council, with Commerce Member Sir George Barnes as a member, to discuss whether imperial preference could be given on the existing Indian tariffs, and also to recommend the future fiscal policy of India.[70] Within two months this committee produced a unanimous report saying that 'moderate preference' on import duties would neither appreciably benefit nor significantly harm India. But on the second question it refused to commit itself. Pointedly drawing attention to the exclusion of the fiscal question from the Industrial Commission, it demanded 'an equally strong and representative commission to examine the whole question of the future fiscal policy of India'.[71] C.A. Innes was reluctant to appoint a commission, regretting that the Industrial Commission was expressly debarred from raising the tariff question in any way', unlike the Balfour Committee. The latter, unhampered by such restriction, 'dealt with fiscal policy in its true proportion, that is, as one but not necessarily the only way of helping home industries'.[72] Like A.H. Ley, he was also concerned about the condition of Britain: 'It is known that Indians generally are strongly in favour of protection against England, and the effect of the proposal might be to embarrass the Home Government which already is having a very difficult time.'[73]

This reluctance to appoint a commission was shared by many others. G.W. Lowndes did not like the idea because it would delay a decision on 'the question of Imperial Preference for years, and this may become an urgent question for the Empire as a whole at any moment'. Malcolm Hailey doubted its utility, Finance Secretary Gubbay wished to restrict its terms of reference, and the home secretary wrote that since 'the atmosphere of Indian political life [was] now filled with racial feeling to saturation point' a commission on a subject 'in which racial prejudices [were] likely to receive more public attention than . . . the interest of the Indian masses' was most undesirable.[74] Nevertheless, T.H. Holland, fresh from his experience of being chairman of the Industrial Commission, carried the day with two incisive comments: '. . . all considerations are swamped by the fact that Indian leaders will not be happy till they get it . . . institute an enquiry if only to demonstrate to the public the danger of tampering with a purely revenue-earning tariff'. Three weeks later he added that 'the question of Imperial Preference [would] not be treated patiently by Indian leaders, and they have some justification for suspecting concessions to other imperial constituents'.[75]

The majority and minority reports of the Fiscal Commission were published in September 1922, when a purely Conservative cabinet was very likely because the Chanak crisis made the fall of Lloyd George imminent. Lord Peel, a Conservative secretary of state, had already been in charge of the India Office, having succeeded Montagu five months earlier. The change of mood in British government circles was made known to Sir Malcolm Hailey some time after Montagu's fall when he met Austen Chamberlain, at the suggestion of Viceroy Lord Reading, to explain the Indian situation and to sound him out on the approach of on the Conservatives. In Chamberlain's own words:

We mean to play our own part loyally, but of course we expect an equally loyal acceptance of the reforms on the other side—and not only of the reforms but of the conditions attaching to them, so that we cannot go further until the time fixed for a review of the progress made has arrived. . . . The conviction is borne in upon me that Montagu was not always discreet in conversation. . . . He certainly seemed to have produced in the minds of some responsible Anglo-Indians an impression that the government was ready—or nearly ready—to clear out from India, and if this impression was at all widespread it could not be otherwise than wholly mischievous.[76]

It is necessary to appreciate the political backdrop in Britain in order to understand the way the Indian government reacted to the two reports that emerged from the Indian Fiscal Commission. The minority report, with its thoroughgoing protectionist slant, was of course anathema to the Raj, but the recommendations of the majority report were subjected to further modification. Transferring any important element of sovereignty was not contemplated. The fiscal autonomy demanded by the bureaucracy in 1917 was different from the fiscal autonomy that might have emerged from a statutory tariff board as recommended by the commission. The argument of Chatterji against Dewey becomes stronger when we note the divisions within the Viceroy's Council on how to present the report of the Fiscal Commission to the Indian legislature, and also the interpretation by Lord Peel of the fiscal autonomy convention.

A young civil servant Harry Haig, who had worked out a detailed analysis of the two reports, asserted that 'the first test of the principle of fiscal autonomy' was not to approach the India Office until the government had made up its mind on what resolution to put to the central legislature. In this he was supported by Innes who felt that otherwise, 'the pronouncement [on fiscal autonomy] will become a mockery, a sham and a delusion. . . . In this matter we are being watched very narrowly.'[77] Naturally the Indian members of the council like Sapru and Shafi supported him; but the formidable Malcolm Hailey wrote that the Indian government was ultimately dependent on the British Parliament:

> It is necessary to speak somewhat frankly on this question. In Mr Montagu we had a politician absolutely devoted to what he believed to be the good of India and capable of sacrificing not only himself but, if I may say so, the Indian government in the pursuit of his ideals. In Lord Peel we have a statesman who is less idealistic but has a very high sense of duty towards the Government of India and is the trustee for its interests. I am not sure that in the long run Lord Peel may not carry greater weight in the Cabinet, because he is not idealistic, than did Mr Montagu. . . . It is also necessary to remember that the Cabinet at present has one outstanding preoccupation, namely the unemployment position in England. There are over a million men now unemployed and some of them have been unemployed for two years. . . . Any pronouncement of policy on our part will be viewed first and foremost in the light of the outstanding problem of Great Britain. That may be right or wrong, but we must look facts in the face.[78]

The matter was controversial enough to be referred to the Viceroy's Council, where the compromise reached was to record that 'when a decision [was] arrived at on any important recommendation of the Fiscal Commission, such decision should be reported to the Secretary of State for information'.[79]

The unanimous view of the Indian government took two more months to be formulated, causing anxious inquiries from Lancashire, to which the secretary of state invited *special* attention.[80] Lord Peel then decided to state categorically that the convention needed to be interpreted restrictively. Writing 'in the unrestricted freedom of a letter as [he was] not writing a despatch', he argued that the officials of the Government of India were expected to make up their mind about any fiscal question on its merits; they were expected to have prior discussions with the secretary of state 'as representing parliament in this country'. Whatever the views of the Indian legislature, if the Government of India, after having made up its mind, changed its opinion to defer to the wishes of the legislature, then the secretary of state would regard the unanimity between the government and the legislature as spurious and feel entitled to refuse consent.[81] Reading agreed that 'a mere surrender by the Government of India of its opinion to those of the Legislature would not do at all'.[82] Only three weeks before writing this, Reading had met the British-dominated Associated Chamber of Commerce to discuss the proposals of the Fiscal Commission. He reported that 'the best of these view with some apprehension the imposition of tariffs for protective purposes'. He added that relations between the mercantile community and the government were far better than they were two years before, and hoped that prominent members from it should take part in politics and become leaders of non-official opinion in the central legislature.[83] Instead of accepting the majority report of the Indian Fiscal Commission in its entirety, and deliberately to avoid being stampeded into protectionism, the government managed to get past the legislature the proposal that the tariff board should have a government nominee and that its two other members would be appointed for one year in the first instance.[84]

The preceding account has been given to question the validity of Clive Dewey's judgement that 'an important attribute of sovereignty had passed from England to India twenty-five years before independence', and that on the fiscal question the government was henceforth expected to decide its policy only with reference to different lobbies in India.[85] Had that been the intention, then, considering that the central legislature represented not just the millowners but also agrarian and labour interests, the tariff boards could have been constituted on a less *ad hoc* basis, their composition carefully balanced, and their recommendations made mandatory. Discriminatory protection then would have secured the purpose of protecting infant industry, the encouragement of improvements in productivity, as well as the safeguarding of the non-industrial sector. Pressure from Britain, and from expatriate merchant-importers in India, played not an inconsiderable role in undermining the convention even before it got started.

Expatriate merchant-importers who benefited from free trade or imperial preference were not the only British interest in India. The British expatriate firms which dominated the engineering sector would have been the immediate gainers of the recommendation of the Industrial Commission that government orders for stores purchases should not be made in London 'until the manufacturing capabilities of India had first been exhausted'.[86] Some of the policy-makers thought that this would also encourage the setting up of branch manufacturing plants by British firms in India 'as adjuncts to home manufacture'.[87]

Had fiscal autonomy and control over stores purchases really materialised at that time, they would have helped industrial development in India indirectly, even if British expatriate firms had a share in it. The Montford Reforms were, however, not very much of a watershed in the economic sphere, as has often been claimed, and true to Hailey's remarks, the British economic crisis took precedence in London in imperial decision-making. The high commissioner of India in Britain, Sir William Meyer, whose biases we have noted earlier, gave a 10 per cent preference to British manufactures when purchasing stores in 1920–1 to help out British industry suffering from German and Belgian competition due to depreciated exchanges.[88] Criticism in the Indian press led to clear instructions about purchasing in the cheapest market. This in turn disturbed the Federation of British Industries.[89] Various strategies were tried by the federation, from anonymous press campaigns to a proposal for getting all Government of India loans tied to the purchase of British goods. Financial circles in Britain, which were anxious to return to multilateralism on the gold standard at the earliest opportunity, advised the federation against the idea of tied loans, while the secretary of state assured manufacturers in Sheffield that even while placing orders under open competition the high commissioner had discretion about the quality and durability of goods![90] He also declined to delegate powers of control over stores purchase policy, arguing that as he was responsible for raising sterling loans in Britain he could not do anything to weaken the confidence of British investors.[91] At a time when, as we have seen, the Government of India had postponed the question of imperial preference until the report of the Fiscal Commission was available, the remarks of Sir A.C. Chatterjee, the first Indian member in charge of industries in the Viceroy's Council, were appropriate:

If the slate is wiped clean and if India feels that it is for herself to decide what her stores policy should be, it is quite possible that she will take a magnanimous line towards British manufactures. She will never do so as long as she feels that her policy is dictated from Whitehall.[92]

Contrary to the impression given in official retrospects of industrial policy in the early 1920s, on which Clive Dewey relied,[93] the designation of industrial development as a provincial transferred subject under the

devolution rules did not eliminate all possibilities of central coordination, or at least guidance. What really reduced the effectiveness of
the Department of Industry at the centre and disrupted the practice
of holding annual conferences of the directors of industries of different
provinces was the Retrenchment Committee.[94] Retrenchment was
symptomatic of the deflationary policy pursued both in Britain and
India to stabilise the exchange, and so it was not provincial autonomy
but imperial policy which we have to hold responsible.

II

The six relatively trouble-free years from June 1923 to mid-1929 witnessed
in Britain the political unpopularity of an electoral programme based
on tariffs and imperial preference[95] and, afterwards, a consensus within
the political elite that Britain's overseas economic relations should continue
to be guided by multilateral trading and a return to the gold standard.
In India the central government was faced with nothing more serious
than criticism in the central legislature, and occasional, but essentially
uncoordinated, labour troubles in different parts of the country until
the beginning of 1928. Except for a nine-month interlude, the British
government remained a Conservative one, with Lord Birkenhead, deeply
hostile to the Montford Reforms, as the secretary of state from December
1924 to 1928.[96] Reading's successor in 1926 was the Conservative Lord
Irwin who shifted towards a more liberal posture only at the end of this
period.

There was no change in the tariff policy as reinterpreted by Lord Peel
in the letter to Reading quoted earlier. Though a document I have quoted
has been cited as evidence in a recent work to argue that the fiscal
autonomy convention had been fully established by 1924,[97] that documents is not only inconclusive but should be read in the context of
other documents I have mentioned in the same book.[98] The evidence is
a letter from the Labour Secretary of State Lord Olivier to the British
Indian-born communist Saklatvala, upholding the fiscal autonomy convention in the way Montagu would have done. Saklatvala had opposed
the grant of protection to TISCO (Tata Iron & Steel Company) lest it
should jeopardise his plan for left wing unity between British workers
and Indian workers; he had instead suggested a policy of government

bounties, and in general a more interventionist policy in India by a Labour government, even if it went against the bourgeois nationalists.[99]

For a Labour government, which was anxious to steer clear of communists and also unable to agree to the Indian demand for an immediate round table conference for constitutional talks (because of the opposition of the viceroy and his officials), an economic concession to TISCO, strongly recommended by the viceroy as a gesture to nationalist opinion, was advisable.[100] However, the official memorandum prepared by the India Office, which Olivier asked the cabinet to endorse after the Steel Protection Bill had been agreed to, made no departure from Lord Peel's interpretation. Two significant paragraphs, which are self-explanatory, are quoted below:[101]

Para 12. He [the secretary of state] has, however, thought it desirable to point out to the Government of India that this does not mean that they should discontinue the established practice of consulting him on important questions of tariff policy before formulating their views upon them.

Para 13. He also regards the convention, in so far as it has been established, as necessarily subject to the following qualification. By rule under Section 19-A of the Government of India Act, the powers of superintendence, direction, and control vested in the Secretary of State and in the Secretary of State in Council may in relation to transferred subjects be exercised among other things—

(1) to safeguard imperial interests, and

(2) to determine the position of the Government of India in respect of questions arising between India and other parts of the British Empire.

It is the view of the Secretary of State and of the Government that this provision represents a fundamental principle which applies to all cases of devolution of control by the Secretary of State; and although no similar provision was included in the recommendations of the Joint Select Committee of 1919 about fiscal policy, they hold that this omission cannot in practice limit the responsibility of the Secretary of State for doing what is necessary to safeguard Imperial interests. . . .

Only on iron and steel, paper, and matches was protection given in this period. When the revenue tariff on sugar was fixed on a specific rather than an *ad valorem* basis in 1924, the aim was only to stabilise revenue receipts, although the government was aware that in the uncertain state of the world sugar market capital for investment in the industry was not forthcoming, and that the 'Agrarian Party' in the legislature would welcome a protective duty on sugar.[102] The inner history of why the Tariff Board took no action to protect the magnesium chloride or the cement industry has not survived.[103] On the other hand, in a situation where Indo-British rivalry did not figure—the protection to the bamboo paper industry—official assumptions about the greater virtue of a discriminating tariff over a government bounty are clearly revealed.[104] In this case, a literal interpretation of the Tariff Board's recommendation of a five-year protective duty as well as a bounty would have benefited only one British firm, managed by Andrew Yule, to try out a particular patent. In rejecting bounties but lengthening the period of protective tariff to seven years, the secretary of the commerce department wrote:

I submit that all that a policy of discriminating protection demands is to arrange the tariffs or bounties to allow a fair chance to make good to an industry which satisfies the conditions laid down by the Fiscal Commission and has a fair prospect of success, but cannot develop owing to foreign competition. It is no part of such policy to decide the relative value of partially tried patent processes or to offer government financial aid indiscriminately to different patent processes.[105]

Finance Member Blackett and Commerce Member Innes, while rejecting bounties, thought that as a matter of policy, wherever the Tariff Board put forward a reasoned case for a tariff, the government should accept its recommendations.[106] In 1923, on grounds of economy the government had rejected the plea from the paper manufacturers (mainly British owned) that it should buy all its paper requirements from them.[107] However, when a case for protection to the paper industry had been made out, it was willing to concede it. Given the orthodox financial policy of the government, the question of government bounties was much more objectionable.

Tariffs apart, there were alternative ways in which the government could have extended its assistance to industrial development in this period, either by expanding the production potential of the ordnance factories under the army department, or by continuing to press for the liberalisation of stores rules or by encouraging the provinces which had enacted or were desirous of enacting legislation on state aid to industries. Except for the stores rules, in all other areas, either because of pressure from vested interests or for doctrinaire reasons, the government would not or could not make any headway.

Pressure from both India and Britain prevented the ordnance factories from branching out into related areas. In 1923 a paternalist director-general of ordnance proudly noted that the ordnance factories, when inspected by a group of British investors, elicited the comment: 'You are the first people we have met out here who have told us and shown us that first-class work can be done by Indian workmen.' His own involvement in his work was strong enough for him to write:

The following arguments were used to me recently on this matter of not making stores in India (i) that there was severe unemployment in England just now, (ii) that if manufactured goods were not produced in England and exported England could not pay her way. Both statements are, of course, true but hardly sufficient to justify discouragement of manufacturing in India.[108]

At the higher level of policy-making this degree of identification with India faded away. Pressure groups took over. Annoyed that without having consulted the Bengal Chamber of Commerce but having consulted the Marwari Association of Calcutta and the Bengal National Chamber of Commerce early in 1923, the director-general of ordnance had utilised excess capacity to produce brass utensils under contract with a Marwari businessman, and also made fishplates for a railway company, the Associated Chambers of Commerce (Assocham) launched a campaign that ordnance factories should not compete with private enterprise. It quoted the report of the Retrenchment Committee and the Indian Stores Committee in support.[109] Three months later, almost similar resolutions were sent to the India Office by the Overseas Committee of the Federation of British Industries.[110] Although some British officials and A.C. Chatterjee (the Indian member for industries in the Viceroy's Council) were impressed by the argument of the director-general of ordnance that his factories could and should act as demonstration factories, and another British official was happy that these machine-made utensils were actually competing not with British goods but with cheap brass goods of Italian manufacture,[111] the last word lay with Innes. He wrote that 'taking the broad view' the Assocham was 'right to keep a jealous eye on competition by government with private enterprise in commerce and industry'. He added:

Ordinarily such competition is unfair. It is inevitable in that it has behind it all the resources of government. Moreover, government as manufacturer has special advantages. It pays no income-tax and in India it pays no customs duty on imported material. In the long run, too, it pays government rather to encourage private manufacturing than to go for manufacturing itself. I have much sympathy therefore with the businessman's point of view in this matter.[112]

The viceroy's order-in-council said that the production in 'ordnance factories of articles required by other government departments or by the private consumer should be confined, as far as possible, to articles ... not manufactured by private enterprise in India'.[113] The Federation of British Industries found the reply from the India Office 'eminently satisfactory' but decided to keep a vigilant eye.[114] Not only did the episode show the leverage of the Assocham with the government, but also its links with manufacturers in Britain who had taken up its case.

There was no contradiction, as regards the amendment of the stores rules, between the claims of the Indian and the British sectors of private enterprise in India, nor any between the merchant-importer and the manufacturer based in India over the question of tenders being asked for in rupees. (Indeed, Colonel Paddon, director-general of the London stores department, was apprehensive in 1930 that with the coming of rupee tenders, high-cost British manufacturers with contacts in India might get a differential price advantage over cheaper continental ex-porters.)[115] So in this field the persistence of the Indian government to have the purchase of stores delegated to it bore fruit. From April 1925 it separated the establishment costs of the high commission in London from its expenditure on stores, putting the latter on departmen-tal budget heads so that, in case cheaper goods were available in India, the money could be reappropriated.[116] The same year the Reforms Inquiry Committee under Sir Alexander Muddiman recommended the delegation of stores purchasing powers by a convention. The new rules which were drafted after this decided, at the suggestion of Sir George Rainy, to give the Indian manufacturer a price preference, though the amount was not stated. Indian civil and military authorities were both agreed on this.[117] The Federation of British Industries complained about it in 1928 and 1929,[118] but they were unable to prevent the new rules from coming into effect.[119]

This was the farthest that the government went to help industry, apart from tariffs on steel, paper, and matches. The idea of state aid and bounties provoked strong reactions. The root cause lay in a commitment to orthodox financial policy to maintain imperial liabilities, although the constitutional argument that industrial development was a provincial subject was publicly used to justify the inaction of the central government on this question. Finance Member Sir Basil Blackett disliked the State Aid to Industries Bill proposed by Madras and advised the viceroy to withhold his consent. Reading, who shared the dislike, granted his consent because he was unsure of the constitutional position in a situation where the Madras governor and his council were also supporting the bill.[120] The Bihar and Orissa Act was given consent to only because of the Madras precedent, but Blackett gave a note expressing his doubts as to whether the Bihar and Orissa government would use the taxpayers' money judiciously.[121] When the chief commissioner of Delhi wanted to extend the Punjab Industrial Act (1923) to the Delhi province, the secretary of the industries department said that in this case the constitutional arguments did not apply (Delhi was centrally administered and the centre could keep a watchful eye over how the money was spent). However, Blackett won his point by a terse note: 'We should refuse unhesitatingly.'[122] As it turned out, the Punjab Act was, by 1930, a success story.[123]

For similar reasons, during the discussion on a bounty to the bamboo paper industry, as recommended by the Tariff Board, Blackett noted: 'I regard the whole recent tendency towards government loans and guarantees to Indian manufacturing concerns as thoroughly objectionable and extremely dangerous.'[124] In vain did Sir B.N. Mitra quote the Montagu despatch of 25 September 1919 in which the idea of government aid to pioneering factories had been approved.[125] The secretary to the commerce department wrote: 'It is not for the Government of India to build pioneer factories. A new 5000-ton mill in Cuttack would cost at least Rs 40 lakhs besides any loss in running. Then there would be the question of government competition in trade and still more the question of getting out of it.'[126] His opposite number in the industries department, A.H. Ley, did not contest it; only Mitra, the Indian member of the Viceroy's Council did.

In reply to a resolution in the Council of State by Seth Govind Das on 5 September 1927 that the central government should set aside

Rs 50 lakh for industrial development, the government spokesman, Sir Alan McWatters, pleaded both constitutional inability and financial stringency. With some casuistry, he quoted the documents precedent to the Montford act to argue that under the act the right of the central government to declare an industry to be of all-India importance, after consulting the provinces concerned, referred only to *existing* industries. 'There was no intention of making the starting of new industries a central subject,' he declared. He had no effective reply to Sir Manmohandas Ramji, who regretted the evaporation of the spirit of the Indian Industrial Commission, and argued that a dozen industries (shipbuilding, dyeing, chemicals among them) could be taken up as central subjects requiring the full attention of the government.[127] Shipbuilding, of course, was out of the question in the colonial situation because of the power of Lord Inchcape in the British India Steam Navigation Company. Efforts to reserve coastal shipping for the Indian firms (which in practice meant the Scindia Steam Navigation Company) did not succeed.[128] The Federation of British Industries, which lobbied against the Indian Coastal Reservation Bill, was reassured by Birkenhead, but it also wrote to the secretary of the Simon Commission that in any future constitution for India there should be a clause against 'any measure involving the expropriation of British interest and British capital from Indian trade and commerce'.[129]

To sum up: on the eve of the onset of the world Depression and political unrest, the government had given protective tariffs to very few industries, only one of which could be considered basic, but shown some success in disentangling itself from pressures in Britain and giving preference to Indian manufactures in its stores purchase policy. If we leave out the limited assistance given to TISCO, there is nothing in the evidence to suggest that since the end of the war, the Government of India had been tilting in favour of Indian entrepreneurs and against British firms in India. Sir Edward Benthall argued the other way in a talk with Gandhi in 1931, but this cannot be used as evidence, as the scholar who has cited it, himself admits.[130] The problems of many expatriate firms came not from government policy but from the superior ingenuity of new Indian entrants in the field, like the Marwaris in the Calcutta jute industry.[131]

III

The main contrast between the Labour government (1929–31) and the Conservative-dominated national government (1931–35) lay in the greater degree of accommodation with Indian business interests the former was willing to encourage. The global economic scenario also rapidly changed with the onset of the Depression in 1929, the futile attempts to keep Britain wedded to free trade and the gold standard in 1930–1, the abandonment of the gold standard by Britain in September 1931 and its acceptance of protective tariffs and imperial preference a year later. In a world market where the Depression was leading to a rapid shrinking of international trade, Indian capitalists wanted to get control of economic policy in India and government assistance for further development, while British expatriates wished to maintain their existing position. The views of British exporters ranged from a desire to end the fiscal autonomy convention to arrangements that would ensure preferential treatment for British goods being linked with any upward revision of the tariff in India. In a rapidly changing political and economic scenario each of these groups raised and lowered their sights according to the economic circumstances and the political colour of the government in Britain.

Increasingly aware by 1928 that the support given by the Labour Party to the all-white Simon Commission had alienated the Indian Liberals,[132] and with this conviction strengthened by a conversation with Lord Irwin in the summer of 1929,[133] the Labour government had allowed the viceroy to announce that dominion status was the goal of constitutional development in India. Though Indian Liberals accepted the invitation to a round table conference, the widespread Congress-initiated Civil Disobedience Movement with the goal of immediate independence made most Liberals and many business groups either support boycott or sit on the fence unless control of finance and commerce at the centre passed from the bureaucracy to Indians.[134] Finance Member Sir George Schuster impressed on Lord Reading, former viceroy and a member of the British Liberal Party delegation to the round table conference, how widespread was the hostility felt by Indian business circles to the recommendation of the Simon Commission of no change at the centre.[135] The result was the federal scheme, where the finance portfolio at the centre was to be transferred to an Indian responsible to the legislature (subject to safeguards on currency management because of India's indebtedness), and MacDonald's wish, in February 1931, to send a peacemaking Cabinet Mission to India to detach moderate Congressmen and business groups from the radical nationalists.[136] In the last week of his viceroyalty Lord Irwin also promised Lala Sri Ram that the Federation of Indian Chambers of Commerce and Industry (FICCI) would be represented at the Second Round Table Conference by G.D. Birla, Jamal Hasan, and Purushottamdas Thakurdas.[137] European expatriate interests were uneasy in mid-1930 about Schuster's apparent willingness to negotiate even with Birla, and noted regretfully that the only two persons in the Labour government who could be trusted to look after British business interests were J.H. Thomas and Vernon Hartshorn, of whom only Thomas was a member of the cabinet.[138] They were also dissatisfied with what they considered pressure from the government to make the Muslim delegates accept the idea of joint electorates.[139]

During the tenure of the next government (September 1931–5), when the future Indian constitution was being hammered out, British metropolitan and expatriate interests got a much more sympathetic hearing. The first success of the latter, even before the fall of the Labour government, was to get the new viceroy, Willingdon to drop Birla and Jamal Hasan from the official delegation with the argument that the Indian economic nationalist point of view was in any case represented by the Liberals.[140] Willingdon further obliged by refusing to agree to the suggestion of the Secretary of State Wedgwood Benn, a Labourite, to include the Bengali businessman N.R. Sarkar who held strong pro-Congress views.[141]

The dominant Conservative view in the new national government, explicitly stated in the cabinet committee by the Secretary of State Samuel Hoare and endorsed by Sir John Simon and Neville Chamberlain, was to encourage provincial autonomy and minimal central government control in the new constitution so as to prevent the consolidation of all-India anti-imperial fronts.[142] The only Conservative cabinet member to suggest that it would be more far-sighted to divide anti-British movement not along communal and provincial lines but along bourgeois *vs.* radical lines by conceding financial control was Lord Irwin. In his memorandum to the cabinet committee over financial safeguards on 3 October 1932 he wrote:

Experience . . . teaches us that one of our principal strategic purposes must always be to drive a wedge between the financial and commercial classes in India on the one hand, and political extremists on the other. This question of reservation of finance may easily bring them very close together.[143]

In the attempt to encourage provincial autonomy, the devolution of taxation to the provinces went pretty far with the two committees successively appointed with Conservative chairmen, Lord Peel and Lord Percy. It pleased moderate Indians anxious for resources for developmental work.[144] Only when the Government of India warned that the needs of the army and the home charges were likely to be jeopardised by the action proposed by these reports, did the British government reconsider the point.[145] The Act of 1935 centralised the collection of income tax and left the share of the provinces to be decided by arbitration.[146]

The relative gains and losses of expatriate business, Indian business, and British exporters in the period of constitution-making can now be indicated in areas like tariffs, bounties for key industries under Indian entrepreneurship, and the prospects of central coordination of developmental assistance. How far the British bureaucracy in India differed in its approach from pressure groups in London will also become evident from this narrative. To clear the ground, one question which worried them both before and after the change of government in Britain must be disposed of—the question of the management of India's currency and the rupee–sterling ratio.

Even before the First Round Table Conference, while the despatch of the Government of India on the Simon Commission was being drafted, a senior home department official, H. W. Emerson had noted that over pensions, provident fund and fair play, the 'anxiety of the services [was] very real, because the Congress Party was pledged to the repudiation of debts'.[147] Sir Alan McWatters had added that the anxiety of the services '[was] not so much the likelihood of deliberate repudiation' but of changes of Indian policy with regard to ratio, and the actual hesitation of a popular government to maintain financial stability 'involving, in certain circumstances as it must do, contraction of currency and high bank rates'.[148] Sections of the bureaucracy were anxious to cut military expenditure on European troops, as we shall see later, but it was a minority opinion. Generally, in the years 1932–3, British officials suffered from a paralysis of initiative on the question of industrial development, being preoccupied with deflationary measures. Such initiative as there was came from Indian officials.[149]

When the views of the Government of India on the report of the Simon Commission were being drafted (and the Civil Disobedience Movement was at its peak), Lord Irwin and his council agreed that complete fiscal autonomy on tariff questions had to be granted[150] and also noted that the Simon Commission had said that it was not possible to draft a statutory safeguard against discriminatory legislation on British investment.[151] Sir George Schuster, finance member, remained worried about India's monetary situation but was anxious for a political truce so that businessmen and government could do something about it.[152] At the First Round Table Conference on 19 January 1931 he said,

The principle was generally agreed [at the instance of the British commercial community] that there should be no discrimination between the rights of the British mercantile community, firms and companies trading in India and the rights of Indian-born subjects, and that an appropriate Convention based on reciprocity should be entered into for the purpose of regulating these rights.[153]

After the Gandhi–Irwin Pact, Schuster was personally prepared to maximise the element of financial responsibility that could be given at the centre and minimise the 'extra-constitutional aspects of safeguards', though his proposal did not meet with the support of some other members. His idea of creating a standing financial council composed of a leading public member, an ex-finance minister, a leading businessman, and one ex-officio member from the proposed Reserve Bank of India was for a macro-examination of the annual budget so that financial stability was not endangered.[154] He remained a persistent advocate for an early transfer of the finance portfolio to an Indian member despite the opposition of the British Treasury and the India Office officials.[155]

Although one British delegate to the First Round Table Conference, Sir Edward Benthall, was prepared to abandon racial exclusiveness and enter into a working arrangement with Indian businessmen with similar interests,[156] as a group the British associations refused to accept the principle of equal citizenship as enunciated by Sir Tej Bahadur Sapru in the Nehru report, and wanted provisions to safeguard British commerce.[157] The India Office recognised that in view of changed circumstances, 'no safeguards, however carefully devised, could in practice prevent the Federal and Provincial governments of the future from favouring Indians and Indian firms in such matters as contracts or concessions. Executive acts involving flagrant injustice . . . could perhaps be prevented, but favouritism will have to be faced.'[158] It went on to argue that while the government's right to impose conditions on a firm getting concessions could be conceded because it was the practice, the British government should resist demands made by Congress and like-minded organisations to exclude British firms with sterling capital and London registration, or to limit equality of treatment to existing British firms and not future ones, or to reserve 'national' or key industries for Indian entrepreneurs. It regarded, in the context of the last point, the Coastal Reservation Bill as 'expropriation thinly disguised'.[159] On the last point officials in India objected. Noting that many enterprises which Indians regarded as national were in British hands, they wrote that 'it is idle to expect that Indians will be content to remain excluded indefinitely from the conduct of such enterprises, and the British commercial community will be well advised to offer their cooperation in seeking a solution which will afford to Indians the opportunity to obtain a reasonable share in undertakings of this nature'.[160]

On these issues British expatriates and Indian businessmen with Congress links negotiated during the Second Round Table Conference. Benthall talked to Gandhi on 29 September 1931 and to Birla on 4 October; Benthall and Sir Hubert Carr met Gandhi, Birla, and Sir Purushottamdas Thakurdas on 14 October and drew up what Benthall called 'a formula of sorts'.[161] It was clear to the British side that apart from reasserting autonomy in tariff policy the Indians wished to retain the major part of profits from business in India, to enact legislation to help Indian coastal shipping, and generally use government machinery to promote Indian entrepreneurship. The expatriates avoided having to make a bargain with this group in the shape of supporting central responsibility in exchange for commercial safeguards.[162] Meanwhile, they were in close touch with Muslim representatives, (who had refused to commit themselves on any question until the communal franchise was settled satisfactorily), and supported their resolve not to reach an agreement with Gandhi.[163]

Twelve months later, with Viceroy Willingdon's ordinance having suppressed the Civil Disobedience Movement, expatriate interests and the shipping monopoly closed the loopholes in the draft constitution in such a manner that a federal minister would be able to use political power to advance Indian interests in business. Existing or future British investments in India were put on a par with Indian enterprise for assistance by bounties or tariffs. Sir Joseph Bhore, a moderate nationalist and commerce member of the Viceroy's Council had pleaded for a distinction between existing British firms, who were to get equal treatment, and future entrants who might invest after the constitution was enacted. As regards the latter, he thought that the Government of India should have the right to insist that, in key heavy industries, at least 50 per cent of its directorate and capital should be Indian. He added:

If H.M.G. were definitely to lay down the proposition that a National government in India is precluded from helping Indians to overcome the handicap which their late entry into the industrial field imposes on them, then I feel perfectly sure that the position of all British undertakings in this country would become impossible in a short space of time. . . . Weapons both fair and foul would be employed and . . . boycott in many shapes and forms and fomented labour troubles would soon render their position extremely precarious.[164]

This valedictory note of Bhore as commerce member was later endorsed by his successor, C.P. Ramaswamy Iyer.[165]

When the secretary of state ignored these points and inserted a clause in the White Paper on the Indian Constitution (1933), making all companies (British or Indian) unconditionally eligible for grants, all officials in India, British and Indian, supported Bhore. They pointed out that the India Office version, 'in the case of Indian shipping . . . would be the *reductio ad absurdum* of state aid, the benefits of which might pass directly to those against whose competition the grant of aid was itself designed'.[166] The secretary of state remained unmoved because of the likely reaction in parliament which led Bhore to comment: 'It is a policy like this that will make peace and cooperation difficult in the future.'[167] In a final telegram, the Government of India wrote:

We recognise [the] pressure of British commercial opinion but on merits adhere to our view that Indians are justified in claiming that when assistance is given at the expense of [the] Indian taxpayer, compliance with conditions of [the] type recommended by [the] External Capital Committee should not be treated as racial discrimination.'[168]

One other effect of this pressure from British manufacturing interests was that the freedom of provincial legislatures to insert clauses in favour of Indian capital or ownership, which they had been exercising under the Montford Reforms and which were features of the Madras and the Bihar and Orissa Aid to Industries Acts, was taken away. Under clause 124 of the White Paper proposals, reinforced by the secretary of state's memorandum no. A-68 to the joint select committee of parliament, provincial governments' powers to impose 'Indianising' clauses were restricted to the future entrants to industrial activity. In other words, political powers would not be allowed to disburse government aid to Indian as opposed to existing British firms. This was turning the clock backward, as was pointed out by Lewis:

... it will always remain a matter of regret that in so important a question of state assistance to industrial development a scheme intended to extend responsible government in India should impose restrictions on the powers of the future legislatures from which the present legislatures are free.'[169]

Apart from this specific question of bounties to Indian enterprises, the other three areas where British pressure groups were able, in descending order of success, to get their aims embodied in the Constitution Act itself, were shipping, iron and steel, and cotton textiles. The British India Steam Navigation Company had enlisted the support of the Federation of British Industries.[170] The secretary of state had rejected the Indian government's suggestion of dropping clause 123 (dealing with shipping).[171] Attempts to establish a *modus vivendi* between the Scindia Steam Navigation group and the British India Steam Navigation Company did not satisfy either party, and the British side expressed disquiet as to whether Commerce Member Sir Joseph Bhore could really be relied on to look after British interests. Bhore along with Sir Homi Mody had negotiated an understanding, and in course of negotiations had told Walchand Hirachand of Scindia Steam that his company could 'not reach their goal in one stride, but ... only reach it by gradual stages extending over a period of time'.[172] This view, expressed in a private correspondence between Bhore and an India Office official, was duly passed on to Alexander Shaw of the British company and set alarm bells ringing. Shaw directly lobbied W. Runciman, the minister concerned, writing that Scindia Steam had never concealed that its goal was 'the elimination of British shipping from the coastal trade, and probably as far as possible from trade with India at all'. If the Government of India was supporting this 'by gradual stages' it was acquiescing in 'a policy of slow death for the British India Company'.[173] This probably explains why the shipping interests got their hopes enshrined in a specific clause (no. 115) of the Government of India Act while the cotton interests had to be satisfied with general clauses (122–4) on commercial discrimination, despite intensive lobbying by the Manchester Chamber of Commerce, Lancashire MPs like Sir Joseph Nall, and the doyen of Lancashire Conservative politicians, Lord Derby.

Chatterjee's work on the Lancashire lobby and Indian cotton industry is relatively weak on the period from 1931 to 1935, when the constitutional safeguards were being discussed and drafted.[174] There is a lot of evidence in the papers of Lord Derby, which, when read with the archives of the Manchester Chamber of Commerce, show that even after the failure of the Second Round Table Conference and growth of the 'ordinance regime' in India, the cotton interests were not as confident of pushing their aims through the India Office, let alone the Indian government, as the shipping interests or the expatriate firms in India.

In the immediate aftermath of the victory of the national government, the Lancashire MPs' made efforts to to remove the fiscal autonomy convention but, notwithstanding the preponderance of Conservative MPs in Lancashire, it had been considered politically unwise to concede to their demands.[175] During the two years—characterised by fierce Japanese competition—that followed, the authors of a Tariff Board report on cotton totally unacceptable to Lancashire and the British government had to calculate the political costs of pleasing either Lancashire or Indian business at the risk of alienating Lancashire. The Mody–Lees pact of October 1933 was one form of compromise; another was the deletion of parts of the Manchester Chamber's evidence before the parliamentary joint select committee.[176] At the end of this period, when the joint select committee produced its report and the draft bill was before Parliament, the Lancashire lobby was made to behave far more circumspectly than it would have wished.

On 3 November 1933 M.R. Jayakar and Pheroze Sethna emphasised that the governor-general's right of veto was for reserved subjects and not transferred subjects, and since commerce was to be a transferred subject there could be no question of interference with fiscal autonomy. The Indian government supported them.[177] In view of this, Lord Derby talked the Lancashire lobby out of insisting on a clause banning tariffs except for revenue purposes as that 'would be very provocative and not very effective'.[178] Lancashire spokesmen, not satisfied with a clause merely opposing discriminatory tariffs,[179] wanted it to be spelt out. They submitted an elaborate memorandum to the joint select committee. The political pundits in the India Office and the Conservative party (Samuel Hoare, Lord Eustace Percy, and Lord Derby) worked out a procedure by which the memorandum would be withdrawn after an alternative draft by Lord Percy (expressing the same intentions in more polite language) was put forward, although Lancashire would have preferred stronger terms.[180] As a result, neither in the report of the joint select committee nor in the Government of India Act were there any clauses safeguarding British cotton interests as such (unlike shipping) or questioning the fiscal autonomy of the federal government.[181]

This did not mean that the British government had willingly conceded fiscal autonomy, as seen by the discussions in the cabinet committee, during the introduction of the Government of India Bill, the instructions for the governor-general. Of two alternative drafts, one which judged a bill in India as hostile to UK interests by the test of its intentions, and the other by the test of its harmful effects on British trade, Hoare preferred the former. He was supported by Irwin, Runciman, and Hailsham. Hoare argued that 'a course of action which might incidentally only work some damage to this country was not in question; the governor-general would have to intervene only in the event of action being taken on a scale which threatened to take India out of the Empire orbit in trade matters'. Sir John Simon and Sir Thomas Inskip argued that Indians could produce bills which, while appearing to promote the interests of India, could effectively injure the interests of UK trade given that they were trade rivals in some areas. Clearer and stronger words in the relevant paragraphs were recommended.[182]

While on paper the British government refused to yield to Lancashire in 1934, it took care to send out, as successor to Sir George Schuster, a die-hard Conservative, Sir James Grigg (a senior civil servant at the Treasury). The secretary of the Manchester Chamber of Commerce found him a sympathetic listener to their problems, when he met him on the eve of his departure to India.[183] Benthall's impression of him at their first meeting was that of an 'anti protectionist. . . . desire[ing] to cut away all revenue tariffs which gave only a poor yield', someone who did not want protected industries (in particular sugar) to profiteer. He 'is out to lose no opportunity of helping the agriculturalist and the British exporter'.[184] Grigg's private papers reveal a deep hostility to Indian economic nationalism. In one of his earlier letters to Findlater Stewart at the India Office, he had criticised Bhore and wanted his successor (as commerce member) not to be a protectionist.[185] He was a great admirer of Churchill and Montagu Norman, and hostile to the idea of public expenditure as a means to stimulate development.[186]

This brings us to the question whether there was in this period any initiative taken either to coordinate all-India industrial policy, or to encourage, at least through military expenditure, some government-assisted industrial development. As to the latter point, defence expenditure had been cut (Schuster was keen on that)[187] from Rs 55.10 crore in 1928–9 to Rs 44.34 crore in 1934–5, but the cuts were not in the number of European troops in India.[188] An expert committee of service chiefs was set up after Indian delegates at the First Round Table Conference had questioned the necessity of a large number of European troops, a charge on the Indian revenues. They had been against any reduction in view of the needs of frontier defence and internal security. Differences within the Viceroy's Council had been put aside because of the insistence of the commander-in-chief.[189] Eight years later, when the Chatfield Committee recommended that European troops be reduced and the armed forces consist of more mechanised and mobile units, General Muspratt at the India Office noted that a pertinent Indian criticism could be that surplus units had been maintained in India all through the 1930s for imperial purposes. He added that having been appointed by the round table conference, 'the experts not unnaturally wished to avoid having to make reductions under pressure from Indian opinion, a position which may have tended towards some special pleading in their report.'[190] This was an acute observation, but it also showed that an opportunity to encourage industrial development by a mechanisation of the armed forced had been lost in 1931.

As regards interprovincial coordination of industrial policy, suspended since 1922, the initiative was taken by an Indian member of the civil service, H. Husain, in September 1930 supported by another, B.K. Gokhale (from Bihar). With the uncertain economic situation of 1931 Sir Joseph Bhore, 'with a certain amount of reluctance', let the matter drop.[191] The matter was revived by Husain in May 1932 in the light of the recommendations of the Indian Central Banking Enquiry Committee regarding state aid to industries. The opinion in this committee was divided three ways, with the majority report of Manu Subedar urging the creation of a centrally administered industrial banking structure, and the foreign experts urging caution. Denning, speaking for the finance department, supported the foreign experts. Secretary of Industries A.G. Clow conceded that there was 'considerable force in Mr Subedar's remark regarding the essential economic unity of India', but political development since the Montford Reforms, and the existing constitutional position showed that the current was moving the other way. The member for industries, F. Noyce, agreed.[192] (We must remember that this was the period when the government in Britain was most anxious to get provincial autonomy started without any change at the centre.) However, it would be a mistake to assume that non-Congress politicians were so provincial in their outlook that they shied away from the advantages of central services. The source cited by Tomlinson to argue that provincial jealousy prevented the creation of a central statistical department does not really bear out that contention.[193] Apart from showing that in 1935 many provinces evinced interest in industrial development, but also doubts about the availability of funds for new services like a statistical unit, the file in question ends with a note by that great provincial politician, Sir Fazl-i-Husain, in favour of creating a bureau of industrial intelligence and research. 'It is all too painfully obvious', he wrote, 'that local governments . . . will continue to do nothing but potter about . . . unless they are provided with the structure of a central coordinating . . . body.'[194] The detailed report shows that provinces were so starved of funds that they were not sure how to expand this branch of activity, and expected central assistance. Considering that at this time the Niemeyer enquiry was pending, and it was not clear whether the award would presume that each province would maintain its existing standard of administration (however high or low it might be) or that the richer would transfer funds to the poorer provinces,[195] the hesitation of the provincial governments was perfectly understandable.

The experience of these six years, marked by economic crisis, political unrest and constitution-making shows the basic validity of criticisms of government policy on grounds of financial orthodoxy, a propensity to favour the British expatriate or the British exporter, and to grant material concessions to Indians only under pressure. The decision-making process does, however, support the point made by both Judith Brown and Tomlinson: 'British imperialism' was not a monolith. That was not all. Within the imperial 'subsystem' of India, the concern of the British bureaucracy, when driven to a corner, was to fight for financial policies that would maintain the home charges rather than anything else. There was a difference of perspective depending on whether one was a boxwallah or a competition-wallah. Concern for the home charges led to a cautious financial policy, leading in turn to a lack of enthusiasm for government involvement in the financing or management of industry.

IV

As the federal constitution did not come into effect before the war it is not possible to assess how far the constitutional structure would have permitted an Indian federal government to increase protective tariffs, give government grants to Indian entrepreneurs, and make some departures from the orthodox financial policy pursued so far. I shall now examine briefly how far, with provincial autonomy operating all over India for two years but with the central government remaining under the Montford constitution, any change took place on these questions.

Indian capitalists supporting the Congress were anxiously waiting for, and were overjoyed at, the final acceptance of office by the Congress. G.D. Birla, writing to Gandhi's son who edited the *Hindustan Times* (owned by Birla), commended him for 'really statesmanlike' editorials which influenced the decision and added: 'I hope that our politicians will learn that they must not fear taking somersaults even if that be necessary.'[196] The British government, to whom all such letters were common knowledge because they were usually intercepted, was not sure of how far it could expect cooperation from this class in running the new constitution. James Grigg was deeply suspicious. He regarded the Congress right wing as the real threat to British interests, as the following passage clearly brings out:

What you call the right wing means Gandhi plus the Gujerati-cum-Marwari interests, in other words, the combination of xenophobic Hinduism with the autarchic industrialists. These are far more dangerous to British interests than the millions of peasants whose grievances are entirely economic and who have been exploited by socialists and communists who are important only so long as they can command support and financial help from the Congress organization. At the moment Birla and Co. can control Congress policy by withholding money and nobody can exist outside the Congress otherwise than as an unattached and therefore unimportant stirrer-up of agrarian unrest. Indeed I feel certain that this money question will ensure that even Nehru will go right rather than go out into the wilderness. And I feel even more certain that big business will keep Congress right for as long as we need to calculate. On the other hand Gandhi and big business are at one in wishing to undermine ultimate British control. . . .'[197]

If Grigg were a maverick his views could be dismissed as of no historical significance. He was, however, finance member, and all his budgets had to be passed by the viceroy's certification.[198] Linlithgow discussed many matters with him which had 'nothing whatever to do with him either as a member of council or a Finance Member'.[199] Because of his earlier Treasury links he had a private channel of communication with Neville Chamberlain's adviser Sir Horace Wilson. As early as September 1938, during the preparation of his budget for the ensuing financial year 1939–40, he ruled out deficit financing (because he was anticipating a deficit), so as not 'to provide the provinces with the excuse for doing what most of them [were] already itching to do'.[200] Instead, he had proposed an excise duty on cotton, which 'would be very embarrassing for the Congress High Command for they would have to choose between the interests of the handloom weavers, for whom they express such affection and the wishes of Ahmedabad whence they derived a large part of the party funds'.[201] When Zetland, the secretary of state, queried whether a cotton excise 'with all the horrid history that it [had] behind it' might not have the effect of driving the right wing of the Congress into the arms of the left wing, Grigg made the statement about the Congress right which I have quoted above.[202] Though the excise duty was not pressed by Grigg, partly because the Indo-Lancashire trade talks were in progress, Grigg's general policy remained unchanged.

One comment of Grigg about Benthall has been used by historians to suggest that there was a convergence of interest between those represented by the expatriate firms and those by Birla.[203] More reliable evidence surely would be not what Grigg thought about Benthall, but what Benthall and his fellow expatriates felt about the Congress and about the safeguards they enjoyed under the Act of 1935. In a note written after an extensive tour of India in March 1940 (after the Congress ministries had resigned), he concluded that the general line for the Europeans should be to support the Government of India Act.[204] The Congress demand for a constituent assembly elected on adult suffrage after the war spelt 'dangers for Europeans in India'.[205]

Thus, till right up to 1940 the British government in India had not worked out any long-term operational plan for the development of industry, not even for creating an industrial base for strategic purposes. Its choices were influenced by alternative types of political bargains between the claims of British exporters, British expatriates, British bureaucrats, and Indian businessmen. The assessment of the relative weights of different pressure groups that I have done suggests that Bagchi's general thesis on the role of government in industry, though written without access to archival material, is substantially correct.

NOTES

1. B.R. Tomlinson, *Political Economy of the Raj* (London, 1979), p. 57.
2. A.K. Bagchi, *Private Investment in India, 1900–1939* (Cambridge, 1972); Clive Dewey, 'The Government of India's New Industrial Policy, 1900–25', in *Economy and Society: Essays in Indian Economic and Social History*, ed. by K.N. Chaudhuri and C.J. Dewey (Delhi, 1979), pp. 233–48; Tomlinson, *Political Economy*.

3. Dewey, 'The Government of India's New Industrial Policy', p. 257, n. 73.
4. C. Dewey, 'The End of the Imperialism of Free Trade: The Eclipse of the Lancashire Lobby and the Concession of Fiscal Autonomy to India', in *The Imperial Impact: Studies in the Economic History of Africa and India*, ed. by C.J. Dewey and A.J. Hopkins (London, 1978), p. 67.
5. Dharma Kumar (ed.), *Cambridge Economic History of India*, vol. II, henceforth *CEHI-2* (Cambridge, 1983), p. 922.
6. B.R. Tomlinson, *The Indian National Congress and the Raj, 1926–42* (London, 1976), p. 14.
7. R. Ray, *Industrialization in India* (Delhi, 1979), *passim*.
8. B. Chatterji, 'The Political Economy of "Discriminating Protection": The Case of Textiles in the 1920s', *Indian Economic and Social History Review*, vol. XX (1983), pp. 239–76.
9. Since I will have occasion to refer critically to Dewey's writings in course of this chapter, I should make it clear that both papers have made contributions to knowledge for the pre-1914 period. My criticism is primarily on his handling of the evidence and his interpretation for the period after that. I am almost in agreement with Claude Markovitz's observation on Dewey: 'Solidement documentée mais peut-être pas suffisamment critique sur la politique industrielle des autorités coloniales. Les problèmes d'industrialization sont analyse en dehors de leur conteste politique, et, en particuliere, de pressions exercês par les intérèts privés brittaniques', *Annales* (1983), part I, p. 282. For the period after 1914 Dewey is not 'solidement documentée'.
10. Dewey, 'The Government of India's New Industrial Policy', pp. 240–45.
11. Ibid., p. 240, where he says, 'The chief culprit was constitutional reform'.
12. See J.H. Hexter, *Reappraisals in History* (Chicago, 1961), where he writes: 'What mainly determined the way historians split up history during the past century was a ridiculously adventitious set of circumstances: the way in which public authorities and private persons tended to order the documents which it suited their purposes to preserve.' (p. 194). Further on, his remarks are apposite: '. . . historians following the tunnel method often produced solid results . . . frequently of course the limitations that the tunnel historian imposed on himself concealed from him and from his readers as well many of the insights that might have been theirs, had he undertaken his work with a somewhat broader view of its scope and a fuller sense of what it impinged on. But such limitation was usually the consequence of lack of imagination . . .' (p. 195).

I have re-examined the Government of India files cited by Dewey, and all the surviving connected files which may or may not have been seen by him. I collated these data with corresponding India Office files and relevant private British sources. This led me to a substantially different conclusion from what is derived by readers of Dewey's articles.

13. The author admits that on this point he overpraised Bagchi when reviewing his book in the *Indian Economic and Social History Review*, vol. XII (1975), p. 327.
14. Bagchi, *Private Investment*, pp. 58–67. Ray, *Industrialization*, pp. 245–50; Tomlinson, *Political Economy*, pp. 70–92.
15. Dewey, 'End of the Imperialism', p. 39.
16. Tomlinson, *Political Economy* (n. 2), p. 27; also see Judith Brown, 'Imperial Facade: Some Constraints upon and Contradictions in the British Position in India, 1919–35', *Transactions of the Royal Historical Society*, 5s, vol. XXVI; also see P.S. Gupta, 'Imperial Strategy and the Transfer of Power, 1939–51', in this volume which has data on the army. For the civil service, see D. Potter, 'Manpower Shortage and the End of Colonialism: The Case of the Indian Civil Service', *Modern Asian Studies*, vol. VII (1973), pp. 48–73; T.H. Beaglehole, 'Rulers to Servants', ibid., XI (1977).
17. For Bonar Law, see R. Blake, *The Unknown Prime Minister* (London, 1955); for Hewins, W.A.S Hewins, *Apologia of an Imperialist* (London, 1929); for Steel-Maitland's involvement, along with Chamberlain's, in Birmingham politics, K.W.D. Rolf, 'Tories, Tariffs, and Elections: The West Midlands in British Politics' (Cambridge University, Ph.D. dissertation, 1974).
18. Note by Low, 3 May 1914, National Archives of India (NAI)—Commerce & Industry—Industry—May 1917, A1-31 kw, p. 7, para 17.
19. Note by Clark, 10 May 1915, ibid., p. 8.
20. Note by Craddock, 9 October 1915, ibid., p. 17.
21. Note by Clark, 2 November 1915, ibid., p. 19.
22. Governor-General-in-Council to Secy. of State, 26 November 1915, Progs. no. 1, ibid.
23. Viceroy to Secy. of State, 26 January 1916, India Office Records (IOR), L/E/7/855 R & S file 816 of 1916 annexed to 8417 of 1915; Secy. of State to Viceroy, 1 February 1916, and notes by Low, Clark, and Sir William Meyer (Finance Member), NAI—same files as note 18, Progs. no. 3 and kw, pp. 23–6.
24. IOR, L/E/7/855 R & S 8417 of 1915, notes by Kershaw, Islington, and Holderness.
25. Islington's notes of 28 December 1915, 12 January 1916, ibid.
26. See his views cited at n. 38 below.
27. Kershaw's note, 3 January 1916, same file as note 24.

28. On receiving the viceroy's telegram (Commerce & Industry dated 17-3-16) which mentioned the announcement to the legislature of the setting up of the Industrial Commission, Chamberlain wanted to know the respective dates of the despatch from India asking permission for an industrial inquiry and the parliamentary speech on cotton duties where he had suggested postponement of controversial questions on fiscal relations until after the war. On learning that the dates were 26 November 1915 and 1 February 1916 he irritably noted: 'These dates confirm my recollection that the marked passage of the telegram of the Government of India is an afterthought.' Then comes the passage quoted in the text. Chamberlain's notes, 21 and 22 March 1916, in IOR, L/E/7/855 R & S (WT) file 1716 of 1916 annexed to file 8417 of 1915.

29. Dewey, 'End of the Imperialism', pp. 46–8, does refer to the tariff reform bias of Austen Chamberlain but does so very sketchily without any mention of the efforts of the tariff reformers to convert the Industrial Commission into something resembling the Balfour Committee in 1916. From Dewey, 'The Government of India's New Industrial Policy', p. 255 note 54, it is clear that for the article on industrial policy he used the file I have cited in note 18 above, and from Dewey, p. 33, note 30, it is clear he had looked at one particular minute of W.H. Clark in another file, but because of the 'tunnel history' approach he completely missed the significance of the role Clark was playing, that is, to keep India tied to free trade and the traditional methods.

30. See official French government proposals dated 10 February 1916 enclosed with cabinet papers circulated by Sir Edward Grey, 21 June 1916, along with its enclosures which give details of unofficial feelers dating back to 14 September 1915; also telegram to the Foreign Office from Japan, 14 February 1916, IOR, L/E/10/5 R & S (WT) file 476 of 1916.

31. Austen Chamberlain's note, 17 February 1916, ibid.

32. Insertions made by Chamberlain in the draft of Kershaw's letter to C.E. Low, 7 March 1916 (very confidential, by secret mail), kept in same file as note 30. The text of the letter is also available in NAI—Commerce & Industry—Trade with Foreigners—March 1917, Progs. A-25 kw, p. 3.

33. Kershaw had minuted on 20 March 1916: 'At the risk of seeming obstinate I feel bound to say that I think the Govt. of India have laid unnecessary stress on the exclusion of any matters affecting the present fiscal policy and I would not be surprised to find that this emphasis may prove embarrassing.' IOR, L/E/7/855 R & S (WT) file 1716 of 1916 annexed to file 8417 of 1915. Kershaw was proved right.

34. J.D. Tomlinson, *Problems of British Economic Policy, 1870–1945* (London, 1981), p. 108.

35. NAI—Commerce & Industry—Trade with Foreigners—March 1917, Progs. A 1–25 kw, pp. 13, 34.

36. An official minute sheet kept in Chamberlain's private papers gives details of this effort by the minister. It is brief and conspiratorial enough to be quoted: 'Mr. Kershaw—Please ascertain unofficially 1. Whether the CO proposes to communicate this document to the dominion governments, 2. Whether, in any case the F.O. has any objection to my sending a copy confidentially to the Viceroy. If not, please get a copy for this purpose. A C. 6/5. Sir E. Grey—I presume there is no objection to 2. P.D. 8/5/16. [initialled] E.G.' (Chamberlain's marginal note on reverse of the sheet refers to his talking to Steel-Maitland and ascertaining that the CO would send the agenda to the dominions and colonies, and deciding to send one copy to the viceroy.) AC 20/1/2 'Paris Conference', in the Austen Chamberlain Papers.

37. BT 55/8 C & IP. Ist meeting 25/7/16 (PRO): the tussle between the tariff reformers and others is described, with special reference to the Labour members, in P.S. Gupta, *Imperialism and the British Labour Movement, 1914–1964* (London, 1975), pp. 18–21.

38. UK leather manufacturers were involved with the Imperial Institute in a committee on 'Diversion of the Hides Trade from Germany to the UK.' After Holderness attended a meeting on 3 July 1916 he reacted sharply, and minuted: 'It looks as though any committee of traders or manufacturers in this country when asked to propose a means of transferring an industry from the enemy to the U.K. will invariably fall back on the expedient of restricting export of raw material from the dependency to within Empire. It may be that this discredited expedient of the colonial policy of the 18th century will be the only weapon at our command in the changed conditions of the world after the war. But until its aggregate economical and political bearings has [*sic*] been examined by H.M.G. and until it has been deliberately approved by them as a temporary or a permanent policy pursuant on the resolutions of the Paris Conference, no suggestion that it commends itself to the S/S in Council should, I submit, be made to the Government of India.' IOR, L/E/10/12, R & S (WT) file 782 of 1917.

39. IOR, L/E/10/7, R & S (WT) file 3946 of 1916 annexed to file 3745/16. Holderness's note of 27 July 1916 for Chamberlain said that he was not clear about the character of the inquiries that the Reconstruction Committee expected the Indian government to undertake, nor was he sure that the government would ratify the Paris Conference decisions or set up a committee.

40. Chamberlain's minute, 23 July 1916 in same file as in the previous note.

41. The NAI proceedings contain the covering letters sent to Sir George Barnes and Sir William Meyer, but not the first draft of the despatch (Revenue no. 68 dated 31 July 1916). The letter can be seen in the IOR. The respective references are: NAI—Commerce & Industry—Trade with Foreigners—March 1917, Progs. A 1–25 kw, p. 24; IOR, L/E/10/7 R & S (WT) 3745 of 1916.

42. NAI—Commerce & Industry—Industry—May 1917, Progs. A 1–31, kw p. 27, note by Meyer on how the exclusion of protective tariffs could be best worded in the terms of reference of the commission so that free trade remained sacrosanct. He wrote, 'The Indian protectionist wants to "protect" against Great Britain and the dominions as well as against foreign countries. I think the passage [defining the point excluded from the terms of reference] would run better thus: 'a policy which would very directly affect the fiscal relations of India with the outside world.' (Meyer, 2 March 1916). Clark commented (3 March 1916), 'Yes, Finance member's alteration is an improvement.'

43. Meyer to Barnes, 25 August 1916, NAI—Commerce & Industry—TF—March 1917, Progs. A 1–24 kw, p. 25. The question may arise that if the exclusion of the tariff question was an avowed purpose, why was Malaviya chosen? This was because Clark wanted 'a man representing advanced moderate party who [was] also of high and recognised standing', so that the commission could appeal to Indian educated classes. Clark to Sir James Meston, 24 March 1916, 1916, at kw, p. 39 of the file cited in note 42. Meston's reply was not encouraging about Malaviya but since he would not recommend Sir Tej Bahadur Sapru or Motilal Nehru, Malaviya was almost chosen by default. In their quest for a political figure that would give them credibility, they had prepared a shortlist of Malaviya, Madhusudan Das, B.N. Sarma, and Ramachandra Rao, but some member or other of the Viceroy's Council would object to some names in the panel, kw, pp. 34ff of the file cited at note 42.

44. Secy. of State to the Govt. of India (Revenue no. 68), 18 August 1916, IOR, L/E/10/5 R & S (WT) file 3848 of 1916 annexed to F. 476/16.

45. IOR, L/E/10/7 R & S (WT) file 3745 of 1916, and connected papers, especially F. 6852/16 and 6180/16.

46. Dewey 'End of the Imperialism', p. 36.

47. Ibid., p. 45.

48. Note by J.B. Brunayte, 30 April 1916 and William Meyer's marginal notes on them, NAI—Commerce & Industry TF—March 1917, Progs. 1–25 kw, p. 9.

49. S. Bhattacharya, *Financial Foundations of the British Raj* (Simla, 1979), pp. 1–98; also see R.W. Goldsmith, *Financial Development of India, 1860–1970* (London, 1983), *passim*.

50. Meyer's observations, 1 May 1916 in same file as note 48 above.

51. Viceroy to Sec. of State, 30 May 1916, IOR, L/E/10/5 R & S (WT) file 2495/16, annexed to file 476 of 1916. Also see Low to Kershaw, 27 May 1961 in same volume (file 3160/16, annexed to 476/16). The NAI reference is as in note 48 kw, p. 11.

52. A. Rumbold, *Watershed in India, 1914–1922* (London, 1979), pp. 54–5.

53. Secy. of State to Viceroy, 1 September 1916, NAI—Commerce & Industry—TF—March 1917, A 1–25, Progs. no. 13.

54. Circular of A.H. Ley to the provincial government, 5 December 1916, IOR, L/E/10/7 R & S (WT) file 158 of 1917 annexed to f 3745/16.

55. Rumbold, *Watershed in India*, p. 63.

56. A. Steel-Maitland to R.T. Nugent (FBI), 23 January 1917, acknowledging copies of a memorandum sent to Lloyd George and the enclosures giving details of the swing in business opinion. Scottish Record Office, GD 113/5/46–55 'Trade after the War' in the Steel-Maitland collection.

57. Walter Long to Chamberlain, 30 December 1916, quoted in M. Beloff, *Imperial Sunset*, vol. I: *Britain: A Liberal Empire, 1897–1921* (London, 1969), p. 200.

58. Secy. of State to Viceroy, 15 February 1917, NAI—Commerce & Industry—TF—April 1917, Progs. A11–14, no. 12.

59. W.K. Hancock, *Survey of British Commonwealth Affairs, 1918–39*, vol. II; *Problems of Economic Policy*, part I (London, 1942), p. 97.

60. Minutes by Barnes, 23 February and by Meyer, 26 February 1917 at kw, p. 3 of file cited at note 58.

61. Progs. no. 13 in file cited at note 58.

62. Minutes by Kershaw (6 March 1917) and Holderness (7 March 1917), IOR, L/E/10/11 R & S (WT) file 1618/17 annexed to 6983 of 1916.

63. Secy. of State to Viceroy (tele. no. 834), 15 March 1917, NAI—Finance Dept—Accounts & Finance—Part C—June 1917, kw, p. 1.

64. Note by S.H. Slater, 21 March 1917, NAI—Commerce & Industry—TF—November 1917, Pt. A 6 & 7, kw, p. 12.

65. The views of A.H. Ley are to be seen in two different files of different departments. See note (25/5/17) at p. 11 of kw of file cited in note 63; another note dated 14 June 1917, prepared at Sir George Barnes's request, is Left in kw, p. 15 of file cited in note 64. C.E. Low's views are in the file cited in note 63.

66. Governor-General-in-Council to Sec. of State, 5 October 1917, Progs. no. 6 in file cited at note 64.

67. IOR, L/E/10/11 R & S (WT) file 6983 of 1916, Holderness's minute dated 26 November 1917.

68. IOR, file 6010 of 1918 annexed to the file in the previous note.

69. Secy. of State to Viceroy, 24 July 1919, NAI—Commerce—Foreign Trade—February 1923, A 1–2. The India Office Records show that he was prompted to do so because two Indians associated with the secretary of state at the India Office submitted divergent notes on Indian fiscal policy. L/E/10/20 R & S (WT) file 1555 of 1919 annexed to 5896 of 1918, contains copies of notes by S. Aftab, 30 May 1919 and P.D. Pattani, 3 June 1919; for the original holographs, see L/E/10/21 file 1587 of 1919 annexed to 1069 of 1919.

70. Note by G.B. Barnes, 20 September 1919, NAI—Commerce—Foreign Trade—February 1923, Progs. A 1–2 kw, p. 3f; also see the resolution in the Imperial Legislative Council, 19 February 1920 (NAI—Commerce—T.A. W.I.P.—April 1920, A 1–2, no. 1.)

71. Paragraph 5 of the Report. (NAI—Commerce—T.A. W.I.P.,—February 1921, A 1 & 2.) The British members of the committee were G.S. Barnes, W.E. Crum, Claude Hill, A.H. Ley, R.A. Mant, and Nigel F. Paton. Hill, the member of the Viceroy's Council for Revenue and Agriculture, had wanted the terms of reference of the Industrial Commission to be not restrictive and had suggested an alternative draft in 1915. Barnes was a free trader but knew, like Kershaw, that W.H. Clark's strategy had misfired, and A.H. Ley (whose concern for the state of British industry and exports we have already noted—see note 65 above) evidently realised that if he wished Indian businessmen and politicians to give preference to British goods against Japan, he had to agree with them for a review of fiscal policy. The non-official British members evidently decided to go along with them.

72. Note by C.A. Innes, 11 May 1920, at p. 3 of the kw of the files in the previous note.

73. Ibid., p. 5, para 5.

74. Lowndes, 26 November 1920, Hailey, 9 August 1920, Gubbay, 31 July 1920, McPherson, 28 July 1920, ibid., pp. 6, 11, 15.

75. Holland's two notes (11 November and 2 December 1920) are in ibid., pp. 13, 15f.

76. Austen Chamberlain to Lord Reading, 29 May 1922, reporting his discussions with Hailey. Austen Chamberlain Papers, AC 23/7/74.

77. Haig's note, 21 August 1922, and Innes' note, 11 October 1922 (NAI—Commerce—Tariff branch—July 1923, Pt A, no. 1, kw, pp. 6, 8).

78. Sapru and Shafi, 11 & 12 October respectively, ibid., kw, p. 8, Hailey's note, 13 October 1922, ibid., p. 9.

79. Council met on 17 October 1922, Ibid., p. 10.
80. E.J. Turner (India Office) to Govt. of India, 7 December 1922, and Innes' note, 29 December 1922, ibid., Progs. 1 and kw, p. 12.
81. Peel to Reading, 3 January 1923, Reading Papers.
82. Reading to Peel, 25 January 1923, ibid.
83. Reading to Peel, 4 January 1923, ibid.
84. Reading to Peel, 22 February 1923, ibid.
85. Dewey, 'End of the Imperialism', p. 67.
86. *Report of the Indian Industrial Commission: Summary*, p. 243, Parliamentary Papers, XVII, 1919.
87. A.C. Coubrough to T.M. Ainscough, 28 November 1918, and Ainscough to Coubrough, 1 January 1919, NAI—Indian Munitions Board—Stores branch—June 1919, A 1–3; kw, pp. 12–13.
88. The whole story and the relevant document are in NAI—Industries—Stores branch—September 1922, A 1, F, S-444(1).
89. FBI/C/27/65, Federation of British Industries, Overseas Committee Minutes, October 1921–March 1926, minute no. 538, 27 March 1922.
90. FBI/C/27/65, Overseas Committee Minutes, no. 545, 27 April 1922; also file referred to in n. 88, f 3; Peel to Reading, 25 May 1922, Reading Papers.
91. NAI—Industry & Labour—Stores—February 1923, A1–4. F, S—240 (1).
92. NAI—Industries-Stores branch—September 1922, A1, F, S—444(i), kw, p. 8.
93. Dewey relied on A.G. Clow's work written at the end of the 1920s.
94. Note prepared by Hafizullah Husain, 4 September 1930, asking for a revival of the industrial conference and giving the history, NAI—Industries & Labour—1932—Industries—I-321 (2) ff-1–3.
95. Baldwin lost the election of November–December 1923 because of this.
96. Birkenhead to Reading, 4 December 1924, proudly stating that he had given a note of dissent to the Montford Reforms.
97. *CEHI-2*, p. 922.
98. Gupta, *Imperialism and the British Labour Movement*, pp. 61–63.
99. Ibid., pp. 63–4, 109.
100. Ibid., p. 61f.
101. Cab 24/166 CP 299 (24) enclosure (PRO).
102. NAI—Legis—A & C–1924, File 61—II/24. See, in particular, note by G.L. Corbett, 4 April 1924: 'Mr Sayer tells me that in the present state of uncertainty, capital for the further development of the Indian sugar industry is not forthcoming.' Also note by McWatters, 21 June

1924, who commented on its political aspects, but rejected a protective tariff on sugar in case it ultimately reduced revenues.

103. NAI—Industries & Labour—Industries—1925, F. 216 (5) and 276 (4), deal with it but are marked 'not transferred', which in most cases means the file has been destroyed.

104. Bagchi, *Private Investment*, pp. 396ff, for an account based on published reports: the archival source is NAI—Legis—A & C-1925, F. 127 I/25.

105. Note by Chadwick, 23 August 1925, in file cited in the previous note, kw, p. 26.

106. Notes by Blackett, 6 August 1925 and Innes, 17 August 1925, ibid.

107. Controller of Printing to A.H. Ley, 20 November 1923, in NAI—Industries & Labour—Stationery & Printing—1924, File A 336 (6).

108. Note by Major-General Kenyon, 26 March 1923, in NAI—Industries & Labour—Stores—19 File S-366 (7), kw, p. 4.

109. The following files of the Industries & Labour Dept. (Stores branch) have all the information: August 1923, F. S-366 (6), 366 (8).

110. FBI/C/27/65, Overseas Committee Minutes no. 627 dated 26 April 1923.

111. The interventionist, anti-private sector minutes were from Rudman, 23 May 1923, Industries Dept. Secretary Drake (after he had read Kenyon's note cited in note 108 above), 18 April 1923, and Assistant Secretary J. Ganguly, 13 March 1925. The political argument about Italian competition from Under-Secretary Robert Smith, 16 March 1923.

112. NAI—Industries & labour—Stores—August 1923, F. 466 (7) kw, p. 9.

113. Ibid., p. 11.

114. FBI/C/27/65 minute no. 666, 6 September 1923.

115. Col. Paddon's note, 18 July 1930, at kw, p. 7 in NAI—Industries & Labour—Stores—1931, A-S-217 (98). The Assocham had pleaded for rupee tenders as early as 22 October 1923, NAI—Industries & Labour—Stores—February 1924, 183 (42)/serial no. 393.

116. Govt. of India (Finance) to High Commr. for India, 10 February 1925, NAI—Industries & Labour—Stores—General—1923, File G-13 (124).

117. NAI—Industries & Labour—Stores—1929, S-217 (67). See in particular notes by Sir G. Rainy, 11 April 1928, and Lt.-General Atkinson (Army Debt), 16 January 1928. The representations of the Federation of British Industries have Left no trace in this file, and were therefore ignored at an earlier stage.

118. FBI/C/28/66 minute no. 973, dated 5 July 1928; FBI/C/4/17, Minutes of Executive Committee, 10 April 1929, f. 163.

119. The British exporters' loss was the British expatriates' gain, and only further research into the tenders called for by government departments

and the orders given (if the material has survived) will enable us to test the hypothesis as to whether there remained an imputed racial bias in favour of British firms in India.

120. See note by H. Hussain, 8 November 1930 at f. 32 in Industries & Labour—Industries—1931, F. I-237 (3).

121. NAI—Industries & Labour—Industries—1924, F.I.-256 (4).

122. File as in note 120 above, f. 3.

123. Ibid., ff. 16–28.

124. Note dated 24 July 1924, Legis—A & C—1925, F. 127, I-27 kw, p. 15.

125. Ibid.

126. Ibid., kw, p. 13. Chadwick's note, 18 July 1925.

127. *Council of States Debates*, vol. II (1927), pp. 982, 999.

128. Ray, *Industrialization*, pp. 95–115.

129. FBI/C/28/66, Overseas Committee Minutes no. 992, 13 September 1928 and no. 997, 4 October 1928.

130. B.R. Tomlinson, 'Colonial Firms and the Decline of Colonialism in Eastern India, 1914–1947', *Modern Asian Studies*, vol. XI (1981), p. 483, n. 90.

131. O. Goswami, 'Collaboration and Conflict: European and Indian Capitalists and the Indian Jute Economy of Bengal, 1919–39', *Indian Economic and Social History Review*, vol. XIX (1982), pp. 141–80.

132. MacDonald marked the following passage in a letter to him from G.T. Garratt, who had visited India in the winter of 1927–8: 'My impression is that we have, as a party, rather let down the moderate Liberal politicians, men of the type of Jayakar and Jinnah in Bombay, who are definitely not of the Congress Party, and would be prepared to work with any Commission so long as they can get this question of status satisfactorily settled.' (G.T. Garratt to J.R. MacDonald, 17 July 1928, MacDonald Papers, 5/39. This reference number refers to the number given when it was in the care of the official biographer, David Marquand; the numbering may have been changed after the papers were transferred to the PRO).

133. Gupta, *Imperialism and the British Labour Movement*, p. 202.

134. Ibid., p. 206–7, 209–11.

135. Schuster to Irwin, 24 October 1930, reporting conversation with Lord Reading, Halifax Papers in microfilm, reel no. 9.

136. Gupta, *Imperialism and the British Labour Movement*, pp. 214–15.

137. Note by G. Cunningham, Pte. Secy. to Viceroy, 5 April 1931, NAI—Reforms—Reforms—1931, F. 35/31 pt I kw, f. 20.

138. Benthall Papers, Box VIII, Diary, 1929–33, ff 47–8 (diary entries of 7 June and 8 June 1930); Box VII f 66 (copy of letter of Sir G. Godfrey, 6 November 1930).

139. Benthall Papers, Box VII, Diaries, 1929–33 f. 101 (Benthall to Godfrey, 17 December 1930).

140. Benthall Papers, Box VII, Diaries 1929–33 f 165 (entry of 17 April H.E. the Viceroy, 5 June 1931), ff 187–94; also see NAI—Reforms—Reforms—1931-F. 35/31 part VI kw which has Secy., Bengal Chamber of Commerce to E.C. Mieville, 2 May 1931.

141. Secy. of State to Viceroy, 27 July 1931, Viceroy to Secy of State, 12 August 1931, Secy. of State to Viceroy, 13 August 1931, Stansgate Papers, 223/12.

142. Sir Samuel Hoare and Sir John Simon's observations at the cabinet committee meeting on 18 October 1932, Cab 27/520, CI (32), 12th meeting; Neville Chamberlain to Hilda Chamberlain, 6 December 1932, NC 18/1/764. This point of view was also supported by the expatriate firms' representative, Benthall Papers, Box II, item 44, ff 134, 139 containing Benthall to Browne, 30 September 1931 and 15 October 1931. This point has been fully developed in P.S. Gupta, 'Federalism and Provincial Autonomy as Devices of Imperial Control' in this book.

143. Cab 27/521 CI (52), memo, no. 25 by Irwin.

144. R. Rama Rau to W.H. Lewis, noted by the author but the reference is missing.

145. '*The federal budget is therefore essentially a defence and credit budget and these must not be tampered with.*' Despatch to the Secy. of State, 13 June 1932, para 6, italics in the original, NAI—Reforms—Reforms—1932, File 123/32.

146. The full story is told in the article cited in note 142; also, see P.J. Thomas, *Federal Finance in India* (Madras, 1939), ch. 30.

147. NAI—Reforms—Reforms—1930, F. 67/IX/30, ff 10–11.

148. Ibid., appx. II, 28 August 1930 (para 4).

149. See pp. 148–9.

150. Para 183 of Government of India despatch on the Simon Commission, 20 September 1930, *Parliamentary Papers*, XXIII, 1930–1.

151. The minutes of these three-month long discussions are in NAI—Reforms—Reforms—1930, F. 67/V/30. The point about safeguards by statute being considered not practicable by the Simon Commission was made by Sir Joseph Bhore, who had been associated with the work of the commission, on 27 June 1930.

152. Note by Schuster, entitled 'possible addition' to last para of Chapter VIII, 9 September 1930, sent at enclosure to letter to Lord Irwin of the same date, NAI—Reforms—Reforms—F. 67/X/30-R.

153. Proceedings of the RTC.

154. Schuster's memo. on financial safeguards, 17 July 1931; also his letters

to Dawson, 21 July 1931 and 17 August 1931 in NAI—Reforms—Reforms—1931, F. 85/X/31.

155. Cab 27/500 CI (32), 20th meeting, 3 November 1932.
156. Benthall Papers, Box VII, ff 52, 55 (Diary entry of 25 September 1930).
157. 'Indian Constitutional Reforms: Memorandum on Policy by the Council of the European Association', NAI—Reforms—Reforms—1931, F 154/31.
158. India Office memo, 14 May 1931, NAI—Reforms—Reforms—1931, 85/VII/31 and kw.
159. Ibid., p. 4.
160. Woodhead's note, 2 July 1931, in ibid., pp. 11–14.
161. The next sentences are based on the account given of these meetings in the following documents in the Benthall Papers, Box II, file 'Ghandi' item 14, ff 31–7, and file 1931–2, items 31 and 46.
162. Benthall Papers, Box II, item 47, f 146 (Benthall to Browne, 5 October 1931, reporting conversation with Birla).
163. Ibid., item 44, f 134 (Benthall to Brone, 15 October 1931), and item 48, f 149 (same to same 30 September 1931). Also see David Page, *Prelude to Partition* (Delhi, 1982), pp. 233–45. Page's account would have been enriched and more definitive had he consulted the Benthall Papers.
164. Note by Sir Joseph Bhore on the eve of handing over charge to C.P. Ramaswamy Iyer, 10 June 1932, NAI—Reforms—Reforms—1932, File 77/32.
165. Ibid., CPR's notes, 23 June 1932 and 7 July 1932.
166. W.H. Lewis's note 16 June 1933, NAI—Reforms—Reforms—1933, F. 89/33, kw, p. 7; also telegram no. 1533 from Viceroy to Secy. of State, 24 June 1933 in same file.
167. Ibid., KW, p. 14f.
168. Telegram to Secy. of State (no. 2578) 31 October 1933 para, 6 and 7.
169. Note by W.H. Lewis, 16 April 1934, NAI—Reforms—Reforms—1934, F. 13/34.
170. FBI/C/28/67 Overseas Committee Minutes no. 1346, 25 May 1933; FBI/C/6/13f. 18, BC minutes 12 July 1933.
171. Telegram no. 68 to Secy. of State, 8 March 1933; telegram no. 663 from Secy. of State, 11 March 1933, NAI—Reforms—Reforms—1933, F. 37/33.
172. J. Bhore to L. Kershaw, 26 June 1933 (personal), copy passed on by Kershaw to Alexander Shaw (of the British India Steam Navigation Company) in Runciman Papers (WR 265).

173. A. Shaw to W. Runciman, 13 July 1933 (strictly private), and Runciman to Shaw, 14 July 1933, giving an appointment.

174. B. Chatterji, 'Business and Politics in the 1930s: Lancashire and the Making of the Indo-British Trade Agreement, 1939', *Modern Asian Studies*, vol. XV (1981).

175. Correspondence between John Taylor and Neville Chamberlain in January 1932, quoted in Gupta, *Imperialism and the British Labour Movement*, p. 232.

176. Chatterji, 'Business and Politics'.

177. NAI—Reforms—Reforms—1933, F1 140/I/33, kw, pp. 16–18.

178. Lord Derby to Raymond Streat, 20 March 1934, Derby Papers, Box 37 Folder, 'India correspondence', February 1934–March 1934.

179. Record no. 02 (memo by Earl of Derby and Sir J. Nall) for the Joint Committee on Constitutional Reforms; also proceedings of committee dated 23 July 1934, at pp. 447–57, 597f, in *Parliamentary Papers*, VIII. 1933–4; Derby to J. Nall, 15 February 1934, Derby Papers, Box 37, folder 'India'.

180. Nall to Derby, 19 July 1934; Derby to Nall, 20 July 1934; Derby to Streat, 31 July 1934, Derby Papers, Box 37.

181. Joint Select Committee Draft Report, paras 343–67, *Parliamentary Papers*, VIII, 1933–4. Labour members Attlee and Seymour Cocks tried to delete clauses about the right of the governor-general to reserve bills discriminatory in fact though not in form, but failed. The relevant section in the Government of India Act is clause 12 (e).

182. Cab 27/520, (CI. 32), 42nd meeting, 12 February 1935.

183. Streat to Derby, 10 March 1934, Derby Papers, Box 37.

184. Benthall Papers, Box VII (Diary entry, 25 July 1934, ff 2.4).

185. J. Grigg to Findlater Stewart, 23 July 1934, Grigg Papers, PJGG 2/20/6 (a)–(ii).

186. Benthall Papers, Box VII, Diary entry, 29 August 1934; also see letter quoted in Tomlinson, *Political Economy*, p. 91.

187. There is a lot of evidence in the relevant files of a tussle between Sir George Schuster on the one hand and General Chetwode and General Cassels on the other over this question in the years 1931 to 1934.

188. NAI—Finance—Budget—1937, F. 5. (27) Budget.

189. Cab 16/85 Committee of Imperial Defence: Defence of India Sub-committee D.I.—16th meeting, with enclosed memo no. DI 42.

190. Note on the Chatfield report by General Muspratt, IOR—L/WS/1/165 f. 27.

191. NAI—Industries & Labour—Industries—1932, I-321 (2).

192. Ibid., 345 (2).
193. Ibid., 1935—I-353 (10), 'Mr Brodie's report and memoranda relating to his tour in various provinces'. This 80-page file has not been sufficiently scrutinised by Tomlinson.
194. Ibid., f. 10 (Sir Fazl-i-Husain's note, 8 May 1935).
195. Whether the Niemeyer award should be guided by the need to maintain the different provinces only at their present level of administration (which varied widely from Bombay at the upper end of the scale to Bihar and Orissa at the lower end) was much debated between the officials concerned and Sir Otto Niemeyer in the autumn of 1935; NAI—Finance—17 (60)-f; also see Grigg Papers, PJGG 3/1/9–33.
196. G.D. Birla to Devdas Gandhi, 9 July 1937 (intercepted copy kept in the private office file of the Secy. of State, IOR L/PO/Box 35, ff 102; this document was consulted in 1975 and the filing may have changed since then).
197. Grigg's views, given within quotation marks, acting Viceroy Lord Brabourne to Zetland, 21 September 1938, Brabourne Papers, IOR Mss. Eur. F. 97/65B.
198. James Grigg, *Prejudice and Judgment* (London, 1948), chapter describing Indian experience.
199. Linlithgow to Brabourne, 1 June 1938, Mss Eur. F. 97/87 (ii) ff 42–3, Brabourne Papers, IOR.
200. Grigg's note, 21 September 1938, enclosed with Brabourne to Zetland, 21 September 1938, IOR, Mss. Eur. F. 65 B ff 243–47.
201. Grigg's note, 28 August 1938, ibid., ff 210–12.
202. Zetland to Brabourne, 13 September 1938, ibid., f. 330; ibid f. 235 for Grigg's views as given in note 197.
203. Tomlinson, *Political Economy*, p. 53, and then generalised into a theory about Indo-British partnership by R.J. Moore, *Escape from Empire* (Oxford, 1983), p. 26.
204. Benthall Papers, Box XIX, item 47ff, 154, 186ff (March 1940). There is of course another document in the same box (item 53) which admits that the attitude of Indian industrialists towards the expatriates was 'better than it had been for many years'. This, however, does not disprove the main argument presented here against Moore (and indirectly Tomlinson), as the same document rejects the idea of a negotiation between Assocham and FICCI. The idea of partnership developed only after the debacle of British power in Southeast Asia in 1942. (See the paper of this author on imperial strategy cited in note 16 earlier.)
205. Benthall Papers, Box XIX, item 47f., 157.

THE COURTS OF LAW AND THE
QUIT INDIA MOVEMENT*

I n the course of editing documents on the nationalist movement
in India for the years 1943–4 for a project sponsored by ICHR, I
compiled data on the aftermath of the Quit India Movement, the
steps with which the Raj tried to suppress it and the way Indians fought
back.

One arena where Indians achieved some success was in the lawcourts. The state in India as instituted under the Government of India
Act, 1935 could have been described as a system of 'legal authoritarianism' in which the executive was represented by the viceroy and
his bureaucracy, controlling almost all the levers of power. But it did
provide a space for the criticism of executive action, in three groups of
institutions—(1) the judiciary (the provincial high courts and the federal court at the centre); (2) the central legislative assembly and (3) the
provincial legislative assemblies. To be sure, the provincial legislative
assemblies in all the Congress-ruled provinces had been suspended
and brought under governor's rule. But provinces like Bengal and Punjab
and, for a short period, Orissa, had been outside the purview of Section
93 of the act. Besides, there were institutions like the Calcutta Corporation which continued to function as an elected body throughout the
whole period. These were the arenas where critical observation about
the governor's action could be and were made. As one looks through the
files of the home department of the Government of India one is struck
again and again by the way such critical observations had an impact on

*Chapalakanta Bhattacharya Oration, Federation Hall Society, Calcutta, 1994,
printed in Arun Bose (ed.), *India: Challenges and Responses* (Federation Hall Society,
Calcutta, 1996). The documents referred to in this essay can be found in *Towards
Freedom 1943 and 1944* (Delhi, 1997) edited by the author.

the British bureaucracy, sometimes embarrassing them and sometimes making them slightly self-critical. It is this story that I shall now proceed to narrate.

First of all, let us list the *dramatis personae* of the story. On the British side, at the apex, there was Lord Linlithgow, viceroy (who gave up his post in 1943 when Lord Wavell took over), Sir Reginald Maxwell, home member of the Government of India, Sir Richard Tottenham, additional secretary in the home department. Besides these people who controlled the overall supervision and direction of the police functions of the subcontinent, mention must also be made of some distinguished individuals holding important positions in the judiciary and at the Bar. At the federal court, three names stand out—Sir Maurice Gwyer, Sir Mohammed Zafrullah Khan and Justice Srinivasa Varadachariar. Sir Maurice retired in course of this period and was succeeded by Sir Patrick Spens. Among the justices in the provincial high courts who played an important role in this period, we must remember the names of Justice Vivian Bose in the Nagpur High Court and Justices A.N. Sen, R.C. Mitter and Sir Harold Derbyshire of the Calcutta High Court.

The special legal instruments which the British Raj had created to strengthen the executive to suppress nationalist activities were the following: (1) the Defence of India Act and its various Rules, especially Rules 26 and 129 which allowed the government to arrest a person and detain him without trial; (2) the Special Criminal Courts Ordinance of 1942 (usually known as Ordinance 2 of 1942), which empowered the government to short-circuit the process of criminal justice. Under this ordinance special criminal courts could be set up which would have summary jurisdiction over the suspected offenders. They could be sentenced to imprisonment not exceeding two years, and there was only restricted scope for appeal to the higher courts.

I shall now proceed to enumerate the type of counter-attacks that the government launched on the nationalist movement after August 1942, and show how in course of 1943–4, in the legal arena, nationalists were able to partially thwart the government's attacks.

The story of nationalist insurgency in various pockets of India, like Midnapore, Satara, Balia and many parts of Bihar, is well known. It has to be admitted that as a revolution its success was relatively short-lived and that in course of the next two years the government had managed to reassert its authority in most places. In one of his leaflets sent from his underground base in January 1943, Jayaprakash Narayan admitted as much, saying that the initial momentum of revolutionary anger against the arrest of the Congress leaders the previous August had to a large extent slowed down, though he remained an optimist. Apart from the legal instruments devised by the government, vindictive executive action against the nationalists took many forms—of which I shall discuss three—which created legal complications. First, all symbolic gestures like taking the Independence Pledge on 26 January were to be punished. Second, the government wished to deny grants to Mahatma Gandhi's Village Reconstruction Programme and the institutions created for that purpose (the All India Spinners' Association, the All India Village Industries' Association); these associations were suspected to be cover organisations for supplying money to the rebels of 1942. On that assumption the central government directed all provincial governments to withdraw whatever grants they were giving to branches of these associations. (During the period of Congress rule in various provinces these institutions had started getting government grants on a regular basis.) Third, one type of executive action, which was hotly debated within government circles and on which the central government had ultimately to retreat, was to tamper with the Criminal Procedure Code in the following way. Under normal procedure a person could be kept in police custody for not more than fifteen days at a time, but officials of the Punjab government liked to have the power to keep suspected nationalists for 'scientific interrogation' for an indefinite period in police custody, in order to elicit information from them. The Punjab government claimed that by detaining people in the Lahore Fort under this procedure, they had been able to unravel some of the details of the activities of Subhas Chandra Bose's supporters inside India and they volunteered to provide the expertise to train other provincial governments in this aspect.

The nationalists were able to fight the various methods the government had adopted. The Special Criminal Courts Ordinance 2 of 1942 started being questioned by Indian Judges in minutes of dissent in various provincial courts. In a case heard on 21 April 1943, Justice A.N. Sen of the Calcutta High Court declared Ordinance 2 of 1942 *ultra vires* of the Government of India Act. It was a minority opinion and it did not have any immediate effect. However, the very next day the central government received another setback at the federal court in Delhi. All the justices of the federal court declared, in a case referred to them from Bombay (Keshav Talpade's case) that the Defence of India Rules (DIR) went beyond the rule-making powers of the central government. This started a big exercise by the home department of the Government of India to devise some other ordinance which would enable the purpose of DIR 26 to be fulfilled. Before this exercise was complete, the Federal Court again embarrassed the government by a historic majority judgement on 4 June 1943. In this the two Indian judges gave a verdict (Justice Rowland dissented) declaring Ordinance 2 as *ultra vires* of the Constitution, exactly what Justice A.N. Sen had declared a few months earlier in Calcutta. The Indian Judges were Sir Mohammed Zafrullah Khan and Srinivasa Varadachariar. This embarrassed the government. Many provincial governments were worried as to whether they had legal powers any longer to arrest people as they had been doing till then. Their uncertainty is reflected in a circular sent by the addditional secretary of the home department of Bengal to all district officers asking them to refrain form exercising powers under DIR 26 until further directions. Having done this, the Bengal government wrote some plaintive letters to the centre saying that they were afraid that unless some other ordinance was deployed to counter the effects of the recent judgements, all the detenus in Bengal might be able to secure release, and the government itself would not be able to arrest many people even under Regulation 3 of 1818. In a number of cases the chief commissioner of police in Calcutta suggested that the detenus, held as security prisoners in certain jails in Bengal, might be transferred to Delhi as central government security prisoners. They admitted that they were very doubtful if they could prove cases against the detenus but because of their revolutionary background, the police wanted them kept in detention. Thus they were despatched to Delhi Fort or Lahore Fort. Just four months after the first week of June 1943 the situation was rather difficult for the British Raj; in this period it was suffering a series of reverses in the lawcourts either at the provinces or at the centre and it took some time in trying to devise foolproof measures against these.

An important case which troubled the central government was one involving a labour leader who was also a respected young barrister of Calcutta High Court, Niharendu Dutta Majumdar. He had been released by the high court on a criminal revision appeal, but within a few hours of his acquittal he was rearrested within the premises of the high court under DIR 26. He filed a suit against A.E. Porter, home secretary of the government of Bengal. He won this case, because the majority of the bench—Justice R.C. Mitter and Justice N.A. Khundkar—considered that contempt of court had been committed by the home secretary. The interesting point about this case is the following. On the bench there was also present chief justice Sir Harold Derbyshire. While he did not think that a 'contempt of court' had been committed, he made some observations which were very embarrassing to the central government, especially as they had been made by a British judge holding the eminent position of Chief Justice of Calcutta High Court. Sir Harold remarked that DIR 26 unhappily did not have any provision requiring the government to show cause as to why it had arrested the person concerned; also, the latter was not required to show cause in his defence. A basic principle of natural justice—*audi alteram parten* (hear the other side)—was being violated in all such arrests.

Once the report of the Dutta Majumdar case (generally known in government circles as the 'contempt case') reached New Delhi the home department and the law department got into extensive discussions as to whether government should immediately take some steps by a carefully drafted ordinance to refurbish the image of the government which Sir Harold's remarks had marred. There was a prolonged debate in the home department and the law department from the middle of August till the end of October 1943 on this particular point. The law member of the Government of India at that time was Sir Asoke Ray. Although he had been appointed by Lord Linlithgow himself, Sir Asoke Ray admitted that Sir Harold's observations were correct. It was finally decided that a new ordinance should be passed which would be applicable to those arrested in the future and to all detenus; the reasons why they had been arrested should be given, and they should have the opportunity to make representations against their arrest.

This new ordinance took a long time to get drafted. The panic-stricken Bengal government sent an SOS to the centre asking the latter to hurry up with the new ordinance and issue it before the end of November 1943. A number of *habeas corpus* cases were pending in the Calcutta High Court and the government wanted to arm itself with this ordinance to prevent the detenus from getting the benefit of *habeas corpus* decisions of the high court. However, the central government could not oblige the Bengal governor. Drafting took time and the ordinance was issued only in January 1944: Ordinance 3 of 1944. Incidentally, the military authorities who disliked all these legal difficulties being put in the way of the executive had suggested in August 1943 that martial law be imposed in large parts of the country. To keep them happy, a separate ordinance was issued, also in January 1944, which was directed against the people coming from areas occupied by the Japanese army. The idea of imposing martial law, however, was not taken up because many provincial governments had urged that, since the anniversary of the 'Quit India' resolution has passed without any serious disturbances, there was no need for drastic preventive measures.

It may be asked why the government did not appeal to the Privy Council against the decision of the federal court declaring Ordinance 2 *ultra vires*. Actually it did, and the Privy Council ruled in favour of the government and against the decision of the federal court. But the council's decision was not taken until 6 November 1944. As a result, from June 1943 till November 1944 the central government and the provincial governments were on the defensive and had to work overtime to plug loopholes in the existing rules in order to keep under detention those they had already arrested.

I will now examine how the other executive measures which the central government wished to take against the nationalist movement got into legal entanglements. There are three points to consider. First, the proposed withdrawal of grants from the All India Spinners' Association and the All India Village Industries' Association; second, the punishment of symbolic acts like saluting Congress flags or taking the Independence Pledge; and third, twisting the Criminal Procedure Code for the sake of 'scientific interrogation'. Sir Richard Tottenham believed that the spinners' and industries' associations were functioning as cover organisations to channel funds to the insurgents of the Quit India Movement. He did not believe that Gandhi meant them only to be alternative means of building up national self-respect in the period of emergency. The first setback that Tottenham received in this policy came from a British bureaucrat. Sheehy, the member of the Central Board of Revenue observed on 14 January 1943 that his was a vindictive policy. He pointed out that the Congress had been in office during provincial autonomy before the war, and it might come back to office at some future date. Many people with Congress sympathies were earning their living as members of these associations and it would be unkind and cruel to deprive them of their livelihood by withdrawing of government subsidy or government grants to such associations. A prolonged correspondence took place between the various provincial governments and the centre on this issue. Throughout the Second World War a major contradiction within the British Raj was its desire to win the war with the help of Indian industrial production on the one hand, and its dislike of the Congress, which included many Indian businessmen, on the other. This contradiction in British imperial perception was revealed in the correspondence between the home department and the supply department. The colonial state needed the production from Indian factories and Indian labourers in order to win the war and so the supply department's general policy was that it should not mix business with politics. It argued that Tottenham's policy towards the Village Industries' Association was tantamount to mixing business with politics. Eventually, the decision that was taken as a compromise was the following: that provincial governments should refuse licences to persons who committed overt acts of sabotage. But notwithstanding this compromise the home department found that many provincial governments were evading these instructions. A memorandum by an Indian member of the Indian Civil Service who was then in the labour department in the Government of India— D.L. Majumdar—stated that if the government wished to withdraw licences from people who were getting these under the existing rules, the reasons would have to be given in writing. As soon as this was noted, the home department realised that giving reasons in writing might involve it in a lawsuit by the aggrieved party. We must recall that it was in the months between June 1943 and September 1943 that the government was most sensitive, given the number of legal setbacks it was receiving. D.L. Majumdar's note came on 9 July 1943; this worried the government so much that it decided to shelve Tottenham's favourite plan.

The next point concerns the symbolic gestures of the nationalist movement. On 26 January 1944 at a meeting of the Calcutta Corporation, the mayor, Syed Badrudduja, allowed an adjournment motion moved from the Congress benches in order to enable the members to read the Independence Pledge of the nationalist movement. The British member of the corporation recorded his dissent but the motion was allowed, the corporation took the oath and adjourned for the day. The central government, on reading about this episode, asked the Bengal government for an explanation and demanded that steps be taken against the corporation. The Bengal government sent the file to the legal remembrancer who passed it to the Advocate General Sir S.M. Bose. He argued, in a very lucid memorandum, that there was nothing objectionable in the resolution as it stood because the Cripps Mission also proposed independence for India as the goal at the end of the war. Within the interstices of the administration of the colonial state, there were now enough forces at work which were sympathetic to the nationalist cause and which could undermine the vindictive counter-measures of the Raj.

Finally, I will take up the question of 'scientific interrogation'. This was an idea dear to the Punjab provincial government and its British chief secretary, F.C. Bourne. The Punjab officials argued to the Government of India that only by retaining suspects in police custody for an indefinite period, could an experienced police official extract the maximum information from them about the revolutionary movement. This procedure embodied a way of psychologically penetrating the defence mechanism of the detenu and required patience and time for the police officer to achieve success. So there could be no time limit to the period the prisoner could be kept in police custody. Jail custody was not adequate because regulations of jails prevented this degree of concentrated effort on the part of the police official.

This proposal appealed to Tottenham, Maxwell and the director of the Intelligence Branch, Pilditch. Maxwell thought that this policy should have been adopted much earlier and a lot of useful information could probably have been obtained by this method; Tottenham however wrote that the members of the Congress Working Committee had personalities strong enough to resist such interrogation. However, they authorised Pilditch to persuade the provincial governments to agree to introduce the Punjab system on an all-India basis. At this point difficulties arose within the imperial bureaucracy itself. The redoubtable governor of Uttar Pradesh, Sir Maurice Hallett, who was a former secretary of the home department and a former governor of

Bihar, wrote to Maxwell on 10 September 1943 describing the Punjab proposals as mischievous and ill-conceived, and likely to do a lot of damage to the image of the government. He added that his officials in Uttar Pradesh got good results by applying the Criminal Procedure Code correctly, without going in for so-called 'scientific interrogation'. Besides, there were frequent questions in the central legislative assembly about the detentions in Lahore Fort and Delhi Fort. The government should be in a position to state with confidence that nothing untoward or malafide went on in these forts. Provincial replies to the Punjab proposals were only partially favourable. On 30 October 1943 the Orissa government stated categorically that public opinion would not stand for it. Towards the end of 1943 Tottenham told the Punjab government that the centre was agreeable to the Punjab idea so long as the total period of 'scientific interrogation' did not exceed two months. The central government was drafting an ordinance by which the maximum period of detention was to be four months and the provincial government was to inform the centre after two months of such detention had passed.

This was in January 1944. The Punjab government continued to insist that the provincial governments should be given a free hand to decide the terms of detention in police custody, whether prisoners were arrested under provincial orders or central orders. The Indian joint secretary in the home department, Vishnu Sahay, considered the Punjab proposal to be quite unreasonable.

This happened in early February 1944. Just at that time there was a question in the central legislative assembly about three associates of Subhas Chandra Bose who were detained in Lahore Fort—Sardul Singh Caveeshar, Dwijen Bose and Aurobindo Bose. The Government of India noticed that the Punjab government had not given full details about these prisoners, and asked for more details.

The entire official discussion on the question of scientific interrogation shows that there were limits imposed on the colonial state by its own legal code through clauses of the Criminal Procedure Code and by a few institutions like the legislatures which provided space for interaction between the authoritarian government and the people. This prevented the enforcement of punitive measures by the imperial power in the two years after the 1942 movement.

None of what I have described in any way reduces the characterisation of the colonial state as an authoritarian one. But it does remind us that it was a state different from the totalitarian state that the allied powers were fighting at that time. The survival of juridical liberalism in the interstices of a colonial state is comparable in some ways to the role played by judicial institutions in Czarist Russia at the turn of the century.

IMPERIALISM AND THE LABOUR GOVERNMENT OF 1945–1951*

T he first Labour government to enjoy a working majority, and a massive one, was also a government whose senior ministers had served in the wartime coalition, and had thus become familiar with traditional views about Britain's overseas relations. As Ernest Bevin put it: 'You will have to form a government which is at the centre of a great Empire and commonwealth of Nations, which touches all parts of the world. . . . Revolutions do not change geography, and revolutions do not change geographical need.'[1] In this essay an attempt is made, in the light of recently released archival material, to identify the priorities of the Labour government in its imperial policy and to see to which pressures it was willing to yield and which it resisted.

Previous interpretations have ranged from contemporary hostile verdicts from the extreme Left (like those of R. Palme Dutt or George Padmore) to later judgements which were more sympathetic but which lacked the basis of archival sources (like my own, and those of David Goldsworthy). Dutt in 1949 described British imperial policy as being subservient to the needs of the US and explained away the concession of independence to South Asian countries as a new means of safeguarding British interests.[2] George Padmore, pan-Africanist, ex-communist

*First published in Jay Winter (ed.), *The Working Class in Modern British History: Essays in Honour of Henry Pelling* (Cambridge University Press, 1983).

Unpublished Crown copyright material in the Public Record Office appears by permission of the Controller of Her Majesty's Office. The records up to the end of December 1950 were available for inspection at the time of research. The research on this paper was done while the author was Smuts Visiting Fellow in Commonwealth Studies in Cambridge, 1980–1, and he wishes to thank Cambridge University for the opportunity.

and a future adviser to the independent government of Ghana, conceded the reality of South Asian independence but argued that the Labour party wanted to find new sources of profit in Africa.[3] The Labour party's self-image in the election manifesto of 1950 was complacent. South Asian independence and the adhesion of republican India to the commonwealth were described as 'a bridge of friendship between the people of East and West'. It was claimed that Britain had subsidised colonial development and welfare and laid the economic and social foundations for democratic self-government.[4] Goldsworthy and I, in our different ways, have praised Labour colonial secretaries for their conscientiousness, but we also drew attention to its lack of achievements in the sphere of relations between white settlers and Africans and to periodic gaps in communication between nationalists and the government.[5] I sought to relate these failures to Britain's desire to play the role of a great power and defend the pound sterling as an international currency.[6] A recent study by a historian who served in the Colonial Office during this period argues, on the basis of Colonial Office records and the papers of a senior civil servant with Fabian sympathies, that just at the time when a case could have been made on economic grounds for exploiting Africa further, the trend in the Colonial Office was the reverse. Under Creech Jones and Andrew Cohen, traditional assumptions were revolutionised by planning for self-government in Africa within twenty-five years.[7] However, there is as yet no overview of what weight the colonial reformers' ideas carried within the government's overall assessment of priorities.

I

Before examining Labour's policies concerning particular areas of Asia and Africa, it may be helpful to offer some preliminary remarks on the strategic outlook of the Labour government and on how that outlook was affected by domestic considerations. Labour ministers spent a great deal of time justifying Britain's imperial policy. Such justification was necessary regardless of whether Labour policy was to be the traditional one of maintaining Britain as an imperial power or whether it would be shaped by its electoral pledge of Indian independence and 'the planned progress of our Colonial Dependencies'.[8] On the one hand, criticisms by Labour backbenchers in parliament would have to be met. On the other hand, American misgivings would have to be relieved or deflected. Both the Labour government and the Conservative opposition accepted the need for a close understanding with the US on questions of defence and diplomacy. Considerable uneasiness remained, however, within the Labour government concerning the US attitude to imperial preference and sterling area. Quite early on in the government's life, Bevin, in a cabinet paper, defended British policy as having emanated from 'the last bastion of social democracy', the only real alternative to 'the red tooth and claw of American capitalism and the Communist dictatorship of Soviet Russia'.[9] Similar claims were made in 1948 when the Cold War had intensified and Britain was thinking of a western union (with associated colonial territories) as a viable bloc between the US and the USSR.[10]

The question of the state of the British economy had an important and complex bearing on both the formulation of imperial policy and strategic thinking throughout the period under review. In the course of two meetings of the Cabinet Defence Committee early in 1946, Attlee persuaded his colleagues that only by reducing global military commitments would manpower for domestic reconstruction be released, the balance of payments safeguarded and economic recovery made possible.[11] Imperial status symbols like a large Pacific fleet were to be scaled down, and British troops in India were visualised as short-term liability only, pending the transfer of power.[12] Bevin believed that a British military presence in the Mediterranean and the Middle East was needed both as a barrier against Soviet penetration and as a line of communication to Middle East oil supplies.[13] But when he realised that the presence of British troops was blocking treaty negotiations with Egypt, he supported Attlee's proposal for an alternative line of defence based on the development of British equatorial Africa.[14] What attracted him about this plan was 'that the whole heart and centre of command [would] be on British territory', whereas Egypt was a foreign country and the future of the Palestine mandate was uncertain.[15] East Africa would command the Indian Ocean, and a road across Africa would help 'with the uranium deposits in the Congo'. Furthermore, the defence expenditure would be within the sterling area. These arguments convinced Bevin that a new African strategy 'will modernize the whole character of our defence as well as our trade and bring into the British orbit economically and commercially a great area which is by no means fully developed yet'.[16] But the chiefs of staff quashed the plan of quitting the Mediterranean by suggesting that the Soviet Union would fill the vacuum created by Britain's withdrawal. The question of the defence and economic potential of British tropical Africa was referred to an interdepartmental committee.[17] The committee approved the idea of reinforcing the economic and strategic value of central and east Africa by railway building, but postponed any action on the grounds of cost for the time being.[18]

During the next year, as the cost of defence was periodically criticised by Hugh Dalton, Chancellor of the Exchequer, the basic priorities of containing Soviet influence in Europe and keeping a British presence in the Middle East were constants in the government's policy, and were to influence crucial political decisions in Asia as well as their timing. In South and Southeast Asia the government sought to come to terms with nationalism in order to prevent communist movements from spearheading the post-war colonial discontent. It is a mistake to see this merely as a technique for pursuing traditional imperial purposes by having a client state ruled by a pliant indigenous elite. Such considerations did eventually play some part in Malayan politics,[19] but in India and Burma (and to a lesser extent in Ceylon) the aim was to win the goodwill of representative mass parties, make no preconditions about economic safeguards and ensure assistance in imperial defence.[20]

Military reports indicate that the average British soldier stationed in India in 1945 welcomed the Labour victory in the elections, but expected to be demobilised at the earliest opportunity.[21] The war had transformed the Indian armed forces from a handpicked loyal team of soldiers of the Crown into a large, more politically conscious assembly.[22] By April 1946, senior officials could not guarantee that the forces would stay loyal and united if the Indian National Congress party launched a Civil Disobedience Movement.[23]

The Indian constitution of 1945 (created by a statute of 1935) did not provide for responsible central parliamentary government and erected special safeguards by which the viceroy could protect British business interests. However, Indian political leaders and propertied classes had had an opportunity to infiltrate the administrative and political machinery at the provincial level in the years 1937–9.[24] The Labour government ordered fresh elections to the provincial and central assemblies in 1945; this gave the two dominant Indian parties (the nationalist Congress and the separatist Muslim League) control of different provincial governments. The Labour leadership did not like the strident anti-British nationalist tone of the Congress party during the election campaign, nor were they happy, for military reasons, about the Muslim League's demand for a total division of the country. But Attlee and Morrison learnt to their chagrin that the British authorities in India had no means of convincing the Indian electorate that under the Labour government the Raj was 'the poor man's protector and friend'. A senior provincial governor, who was the viceroy's personal emissary in November 1945, was reported to have said that there was no adequate channel of communication between the government and the people.[25] Doubtless it was this that made Attlee decide to send a high-powered Cabinet Mission early in 1946 to have direct talks with Indian political leaders.

During these talks the Cabinet Mission did not wish to risk the experiment of electing a constituent assembly on universal adult suffrage, even though as late as 1942–3 Cripps and Bevin had thought of appealing to the Indian workers and peasants over the heads of politicians from the propertied classes.[26] Both communist and anti-communist labour leaders in India protested at the inequity of electing a constituent assembly from among legislators who had been themselves elected on a narrow franchise, but the Cabinet Mission ignored their constructive suggestions about how to prepare fresh electoral rolls for universal adult suffrage.[27] Behind this concern for a speedy settlement with existing political parties lay a recognition that any new experiment might cause delay and a drift towards extremist political agitation, either by the Congress socialists or by the Muslim League. British business representatives told Cripps that they feared violent agitation was more likely by the Muslim League.[28]

The need for support from Indian business groups during the war had forced the wartime British administration in India, much against the wishes of Churchill, to agree to debit to Britain military expenditure originating in India. This transformed the subcontinent within six years from a debtor to a creditor country *vis-à-vis* Britain.[29] A recognition of the economic strength of Indian business interests led the

Labour government, despite initial misgivings, to tell expatriate firms in India that it would not press for special safeguards for them in the constitutional talks.[30] The future of British commercial and industrial concerns in India therefore depended on political goodwill.

The federal structure proposed by the Cabinet Mission on 16 May 1946, with a central government controlling only external affairs, defence and communication, gave the British chiefs of staff what they wanted: a large group of provinces in the northwest which would be logistically defensible in a war with the Soviet Union, could be a base for attack on Siberia if necessary and yet would be linked with the industrial and economic heartland of the rest of India.[31] The truncated West Pakistan that eventually emerged after the rejection of the Cabinet Mission plan by the Muslim League and the Congress party had always seemed to the defence authorities to be very much a second best and to be useless for imperial defence purposes unless there was some joint defence agreement within the subcontinent.[32]

In the last twelve months of British rule the options before the government rapidly diminished. On 5 June 1946, the cabinet had refused to set a target date for independence but had also recognised that repression of mass nationalist movements would be unpopular in Britain and would necessitate moving troops from other vital areas.[33] Six months later, the cabinet overruled the objections of Bevin and the chiefs of staff and named a date for the evacuation of British troops and officials.[34] The senior Indian administrative personnel were far more numerous than the British, and their loyalty to the Raj could not be absolutely relied upon.[35] At home, resources were scarce. The ministers preparing the British economic survey for 1947 reported in December 1946, '. . . we feel bound to question whether the country can afford to devote so big a proportion of its manpower to defence at the present time'.[36] In January, A.V. Alexander, minister of defence and a member of the Cabinet Mission to India, reluctantly agreed to a 5 per cent cut in defence expenditure.[37] Two months later, when backbench Labour MPs were successful in having the duration of national service reduced from eighteen months to one year, on economic and moral grounds Field-Marshal Montgomery put it on record that this was done on the assumption that troops would be withdrawn from India, and that the Palestine problem would be solved satisfactorily.[38]

Against this background of reduced defence capability there were devious efforts to secure some insurance for imperial defence from the two successor states. Plans to detach the Indian Ocean islands of Andaman and Nicobar and put them under the Colonial Office foundered on opposition from the Indians which was so implacable as to alarm Viceroy Mountbatten.[39] By bringing forward the date of partition, he succeeded, however, in persuading the Congress, despite its republican orientation, to accept transfer of power on the basis of dominion status and at the cost of partition.[40] But British hopes of general supervision of the defence plans of the two dominions were dashed, first by Mountbatten's failure to secure the governor-generalship of both dominions, and second by the Indo-Pakistani conflict over Kashmir, which started almost immediately after independence.[41]

In Ceylon, defence considerations were paramount. The Soulbury Commission of 1943 on the Ceylon constitution had offered full internal self-government with defence and external affairs under British control. Ceylon was an essential strategic base in the Indian Ocean, and a vital link for the air, cable and wireless communications in the Far East.[42] In the autumn of 1945 the Labour government rejected Ceylonese pressure for dominion status.[43] The Ceylonese leaders finally accepted the Soulbury constitution as an interim measure, but by May 1947, even before elections were held under the new constitution, the pressure of events in India and Burma strengthened their demand for immediate independence within the commonwealth. Even then, though both the governor of Ceylon and Creech Jones recommended meeting this demand, the cabinet hesitated lest such a concession trigger off demands for similar concessions in Malaya and elsewhere.[44] Nevertheless, within a month, after the Ceylonese leader, D. Senanayeke, gave a private assurance that British defence and foreign policy interests would be safeguarded, the cabinet agreed to hold constitutional talks immediately after the Ceylonese elections.[45] A military agreement preceded the granting of dominion status early in 1948. In the words of a junior Labour minister who visited the country for the independence celebrations, power had been transferred to an indigenous elite whose style of politics was reminiscent of the Whig landed gentry of eighteenth-century Britain and who were 'terrified by the Left opposition'. The minister also noted that Ceylonese ministers were vulnerable to attacks from the opposition because a military agreement had been made a precondition of dominion status. He recommended (though it was not acted on) greater reliance on the Ceylonese leaders' goodwill than on the military agreement.[46]

The planners of imperial defence had lost the initiative in the Indian subcontinent but retained it in Ceylon. The financial crisis of August 1947 made them readjust their priorities after a great deal of heart-searching.[47] After October 1947 the army outside Britain remained strongest in Europe and the Middle East, followed by Malaya and the Far East. Naval dispositions were weakened in the Pacific and the Caribbean.[48] In February 1948, 40 per cent of the total overseas military expenditure covered Palestine and Egypt and another 30 per cent covered Malaya, Gibraltar and Malta.[49] The inference was obvious. When funds were tight three things mattered most: a firm stand in Europe as long as the West and the Soviet Union remained deadlocked over the German and Austrian settlement, the protection of imperial communication points, and the protection of areas producing oil, tin and rubber.

II

Labour's colonial and imperial policies after 1945 reflected some of the major political and economic contrasts between the pre-war and post-war periods. Some traditional types of working-class imperialism, noticed before the war, did not recur in the immediate post-war years. Because of shortage of labour in the Lancashire textile industry, one heard little about textile workers being made redundant by the 'sweated' labour of Indian workers.[50] There was no natural demographic pressure for overseas emigration. Ministers were anxious to save manpower, but for reasons of global power politics some ministers approved the principle of encouraging British emigration to Australia and Kenya.[51] Attlee and Bevin hoped that the relatively sparsely populated parts of East and Central Africa would absorb more immigrants from among European displaced persons and provide a home for the Assyrian minority in Iraq.[52] However, there was a reverse flow of migration from the non-white colonial empire to Britain in the post-war period. This aroused misgivings within the party and caused embarrassment to those who believed that the empire–commonwealth was, or should be, evolving in a multiracial direction.[53]

The cost of the Second World War made the orthodox Leninist explanation about the imperialism of finance capital and the export of capital irrelevant. During the war, prospects of a post-war balance of payments deficit made Treasury officials doubt the likelihood of capital exports from Britain.[54] When Britain approached the US for a loan in 1945 and made promises about scaling down sterling balances (which she failed to do in most cases), she became simultaneously a debtor to the richest and some of the poorest countries in the world. Instead of capital, export of goods was necessary to pay off the debt. There was, however, a strong temptation for a weakened Britain to use her powers over the dependent empire both to get essential supplies and to bridge the dollar gap.

At first these temptations did not surface. It was hoped that economic recovery, return to multilateral trade and the convertibility of sterling would come about as expected. As Bevin put it about the proposed International Trades Organisation (ITO), the aim of the 'maximum possible expansion of world trade based upon high and sustained level of employment in every country' was 'in the best interests of the United Kingdom as the world's principal trading nation', and this would promote political stability in all parts of the world.[55] The terms of the American loan of 1945 provoked Aneurin Bevan to talk of the American 'nineteenth century attitude towards international trade', and to suggest (along with Emmanuel Shinwell) building up the sterling area bloc as an alternative to the loan. Alexander adopted what was nearly the Beaverbrook approach to the value of empire trade. Bevin sympathised but, along with the majority of the cabinet agreed with Cripps and Dalton that to refuse to cooperate with the 'first tentative moves towards an international trade agreement' was against the 'declared policy of the Labour Party', and that the sterling area members themselves wished to move away from tight wartime controls.[56] While there were a few 'early day motions' in the House of Commons from backbench Conservative MPs in favour of empire trade as an alternative to an open-door trade policy, very few Labour MPs proposed or signed such motions.[57]

Four years later, in the context of the devaluation crisis of September 1949, Harold Wilson, in a memorandum on Anglo-American economic relations, wrote that the necessary approximate balance in world production and trade which could make multilateralism work had 'never really existed since 1914'.[58] Even with the American loan, Marshall

Aid, and other international financial institutions, recovery had been slow, because the 'pump needed far more priming than [was] thought'.[59] At the mid-point of these four years, in the summer of 1947, the hopes of early success through multilateralism had been shattered with the suspension of convertibility of sterling in August 1947. The expectation of general European recovery through the Marshall Plan was, in August 1947, just beginning to be sketched out by Western European experts.[60] Meanwhile, the Labour government began to have greater (and partly unrealistic) objectives concerning Britain's commonwealth relationship, the sterling area and the colonial empire. Their purpose was to complement and not to displace trade with a recovered Western Europe. The aim was to become as independent as possible of assistance from the US after Marshall Aid came to an end.

As early as January 1947, Bevin had suggested Western European economic cooperation (without prejudicing commonwealth links) as a possible alternative in case the ITO negotiations failed. The rest of the cabinet preferred to await the outcome of the ITO negotiations.[61] As the months rolled by after the fuel crisis of the winter, problems proliferated. The American loan was rapidly exhausted. Domestic production and the export drive did not match up to expectations.[62] The ministry of food received repeated warnings from the Treasury about the level of food imports from the dollar area. It is not surprising to observe, in this atmosphere, a perceptible emphasis on the development of colonial food and raw material supplies.[63] It is clear that the argument that colonial development was a solution to Britain's problems was not merely an afterthought.[64]

There had been no reference to it when the *Economic Survey* for 1947 was being drafted. However, only a month after its publication, Attlee approved a proposal from Creech Jones to set up a colonial development corporation (CDC), on an economic and self-supporting basis, to produce foodstuffs, raw material and manufactures 'where supply to the UK or sale overseas will assist our balance of payments'.[65] The cabinet paper on this stressed that an interdepartmental committee would frame guidelines, so that British supply requirements and the balance of payments of the sterling area as a whole were kept in view.[66] After consulting Bevin, Creech Jones got his Under-Secretary, Ivor Thomas, to put up a memorandum to the cabinet arguing that Britain 'should try to re-establish and indeed improve upon the pre-war position in which exports of primary produce from the colonies to America were among our principal earners of dollars, the colonies in general having a large favourable balance with dollar countries which they spent mainly in the sterling area'.[67]

Cutting across the spectrum of Right and Left, spanning the gap between Bevin and Bevan, there was, from mid-1947 onwards, a quest for salvation by means of the sterling area commonwealth and empire, without, of course, turning one's back on Europe. Bevan's intervention in the cabinet early in August showed a hankering after a closed sterling area bloc.[68] Bevin, in a speech to the Southport Trades Union Congress on 3 September, did some personal kite-flying about a customs union of the commonwealth and empire and persuaded the cabinet to set up a study group on its feasibility.[69] The constant US pressure to eliminate imperial preferences appeared particularly distasteful when William Clayton, the US trade negotiator at Geneva, harped on it in the crisis month of August, with an implication that otherwise Britain might not get Marshall Aid.[70] British resentment at this was shown in refusing to yield on any colonial preferences.[71] Only when the US agreed to relax the legislation requiring the compulsory use of synthetic rubber in American industry and permit a greater use of natural rubber, did the British government, happy at the prospect of more dollars from Malayan rubber, agree to reduce colonial preferences.[72]

Political developments in Malaya and Central Africa were also adversely affected by this preoccupation with the production of dollar-earning commodities like rubber, tin, copper and chromium. As the position in these areas was complicated from the beginning by suspicion and hostility among ethnic groups, the government's options and decisions in these territories are discussed separately below.

The idea of an endeavour by the colonies and the Commonwealth for sterling area development for mutual benefit, and in cooperation with Western Europe, was announced with the enthusiastic support of both parties.[73] It was given a sharp edge by the simultaneous hardening of the Cold War, with the foundation of the Cominform in October 1947, and the communist seizure of power in Czechoslovakia in March 1948. Labour ministers were as opposed to Western Europe becoming 'permanent pensioners on the United States' as they were of allowing

Soviet communism to spread any further.[74] There was general approval in the Labour cabinet of Bevin's strong ideological condemnation of the Soviet Union from a social-democratic standpoint. Most Western European countries, Bevin wrote, had been 'nurtured on civil liberties and on the fundamental human rights'. He added:

Provided we can organize a Western European system . . . it should be possible to develop our own power and influence equal to that of the United States of America and the USSR. We have the material resources in the Colonial Empire, if we develop them, and by giving a spiritual lead now we should be able to carry out our task in a way which will show clearly that we are not subservient to the United States of America or to the Soviet Union.[75]

Colonial development was planned with this aim in mind. Official Labour party policy had earlier justified postponement of self-government for the 'primitive' colonies of Africa on the grounds of their social and economic backwardness, and had recommended a policy of balanced growth.[76] The policy then followed was geared to British requirements. The Economic Policy Committee of the cabinet approved the report of the Plowden Committee which stressed that, for the present, attention should be focused not on the long-range problem of colonial development but on the short-term problem of solving the dollar gap of the sterling area. This could 'require a particular bias to be given to colonial economic development'. Since without sacrificing British standards of consumption, Britain would not be able to provide finance for colonial development, grants would be given only for projects yielding a rapid return.[77] A private letter of Lord Addison on the dollar problem shows his great expectations of getting food and raw material out of 'many hitherto far too neglected parts of the colonial territories'.[78] Lord Listowel, the minister of state for colonies, noted that the House of Lords was not interested in colonial political affairs but in colonial economic development.[79] A year later, Herbert Morrison, worried about Britain's dollar deficit and embarrassed at the idea of asking the US for more direct aid, suggested to Attlee that one way of getting 'the Americans to go on financing the world with dollars as Marshall Aid taper[ed] off' would be to respond urgently to unofficial American feelers on private American dollar investment in the British colonies.[80]

There was awareness at the highest level, periodically prompted by

Colonial Office civil servants, that charges of exploitation must be avoided. While approving of the CDC, Bevin asked Creech Jones to see that it did not become like the old chartered companies, and Shinwell wished to ensure fair working conditions for its employees. Creech Jones assured them that the corporation would have to follow local labour and welfare legislation (much of which had been reformed by the Labour government).[81] On these grounds, he rejected the request of the chairman of the CDC for a completely free hand.[82] Even as the cabinet approved the joint Cripps–Bevin paper for Western European economic cooperation with the colonial territories, it put on record that in opening talks with other European colonial powers 'any suggestions that colonial territories were to be exploited for the benefit of Europe should be avoided'.[83]

At the same time, riots and disturbances broke out in Accra, the capital of the 'model' African colony of the Gold Coast, which shook the British government. Only four months before, the acting governor had warned that 'a fairly vigorous reaction' and a decline of confidence in constitutional progress was likely to happen if, despite higher export prices for cocoa, the purchasing power of the average man stagnated or declined.[84] The Colonial Office had sent a copy of the governor's despatch to certain Treasury officials hoping that it would be 'good for [their] education'.[85] After the disturbances the commission of inquiry under Aiken Watson recommended further constitutional and political progress to counter the frustration of the politically conscious intelligentsia. These recommendations were modified, but generally approved, by an all-African committee of local experts (the Coussey Committee) whose report was ready by the autumn of 1949. In the meanwhile the Cold War made Labour ministers even more sensitive to charges of exploitation.

In the series of memoranda concerning Soviet communism early in 1948, Bevin had stressed the need to reply to Soviet attacks on British colonial policy.[86] He took particular interest (even in administrative details) in the education and accommodation of colonial students in Britain to keep them immune from communist influence.[87] In the context of the Cold War and the events in the Gold Coast, the credibility of British social democracy in the colonial territories could only be sustained if the political process started in February 1947 by Creech

Jones's despatch on local self-government in the African colonies was not only carried through but accelerated.[88]

Attlee noted with concern that there was 'considerable talk in the colonies of "exploitation" of the colonial peoples in order to help Britain out of her difficulties' and that the Soviet Union was making use of this.[89] Shortly afterwards, in October 1948, Creech Jones told the cabinet the views of the unofficial members of the various African delegations who had met for the Africa Conference in London. While they were prepared to reject the exploitation charges, they were afraid that 'when the immediate demand for increased production of certain dollar-earning and dollar-saving commodities became less acute, the local industries would be Left to their fate without protection and without adequate markets'. Creech Jones could offer some security through bulk purchase and long-term contracts, but as regards the demand for more capital and consumer goods imports (against their sterling balances) he could help only if he had the cooperation of those departments of the British government which controlled the supplies.[90]

The basic contradiction between the interests of these other ministries and the political preoccupations of the Colonial Office was again evident at a meeting of the Economic Policy Committee of the cabinet in November 1948. Many members wanted greater central direction from the Colonial Office to local governments on matters such as the greater mobilisation of local resources through taxation. Centralism was opposed on the grounds that it violated 'the fundamental principle of colonial policy to attempt at this stage to treat the colonial governments as subordinate departments of His Majesty's Government'.[91] Similar political arguments made a study group under Harold Wilson, president of the Board of Trade, reject the idea of a customs union of Britain and the colonies. 'Politically it would be suspected in the more advanced Colonies and it would be excessively awkward to leave them out and to have only a partial union.'[92]

The opposition of the Colonial Office to the use of all colonies for the benefit of Britain extended to resisting of American pressure to admit private capital. Creech Jones's official guidelines, drafted in reply to Morrison's suggestions on this, argued that private investors would be welcome as long as they fitted in with colonial development plans, followed local regulations on labour and welfare, and observed a moratorium on the repatriation of capital for ten years.[93] In an undated draft of a speech (written probably in 1949), Creech Jones mentioned that the Americans ought to understand and appreciate that Britain had her own form of the doctrine of 'state rights' in the colonies.[94]

The main injustice perpetrated on some colonies in the name of economic development before they were given self-government stemmed from the structure of the sterling area, and the sterling area dollar pool. The sterling area included the colonial empire, all commonwealth countries except Canada, and a few other countries. Multilateral transactions were permitted within it, and the dollar earnings of the entire area were pooled together. In the period between 1945 and 1950 some countries were persistently in deficit in their balance of payments on current account with the dollar area, whereas others like Malaya, the Rhodesias and Ceylon tended to run a surplus. The slowness of postwar recovery in Europe prevented Britain from meeting the pent-up demand for manufactured goods in the primary producing parts of the sterling area. Even after Marshall Aid, the efforts to narrow the dollar gap between Britain and the US by an export drive, and at the same time to supply South Asia and the colonies with the goods they demanded, caused considerable strain.[95]

In 1946, Hugh Dalton would have been quite happy to scale down the accumulated sterling balances of India and the colonies. Strong arguments from Sir Sidney Caine at the Colonial Office, and equally strong pressure from the Indian side prevented that from happening.[96] From mid-1947 onwards, however, the differential advantage that political independence brought with it was seen in the way that India and Malaya were treated. India was treated more gently (even when she exceeded her agreed dollar quota). Malaya had only a very limited access to dollar imports, despite the fact that she was always earning a dollar surplus.[97] Other colonies like the Gold Coast were in a similar situation. This gentler treatment of the South Asian countries was dictated by economic and political considerations. Attlee considered retention of India within the commonwealth vital for political, economic and strategic reasons at a time when China was becoming communist, and a communist insurgency movement had broken out in Malaya.[98] Any rough treatment of India's sterling balances might have led to the expropriation of British investments in India.[99] Agreeing to India's request for extra food imports from the dollar area in 1947 and 1948 was expected to calm the atmosphere while the question of India's membership of the commonwealth was still uncertain.[100] Though republican India's adhesion to the commonwealth was unaccompanied by any commitment to commonwealth defence, the Labour government considered it a psychological and diplomatic victory.

At the commonwealth finance ministers' conference in July 1949 (hastily summoned to discuss the dollar shortage of the sterling area, and a precursor of the devaluation of sterling the following September) no member state offered to cut its dollar imports by more than the others.[101] Yet before the conference, the colonies had already been instructed by a directive from London to make cuts in their dollar import programme which amounted to an overall cut of 10 per cent in their import programme, throwing their development plans out of gear.[102] Pakistan had brought up the question of help to the less developed dominions, but Creech Jones reminded the conference that the colonies had the same problems as India and Pakistan.[103]

Until the devaluation crisis the ministers had periodically noted that some independent members of the commonwealth were more spendthrift than others, while the colonies as a whole were in surplus.[104] Not until the ministerial conference of July 1949 was a general appeal for economy made, and no institutional means of keeping the sovereign nations of the sterling area under control could be developed. The fact that only some commonwealth countries had prior knowledge of the decision to devalue did not help in that direction.

Harold Wilson wrote of the sterling area dollar pool in September 1949: 'Pooling of dollars by the sterling area may offend United States prejudices, but it represents a rough and ready way of allocating dollars among several major countries according to their needs.'[105] It was certainly rough and ready—rough on the dollar-surplus colonies because the others were only too ready to spend the surplus.

III

Even when allowance is made for the distortions caused in the Labour party's programme for 'planned progress in the colonies' by its wish to maintain the sterling area commonwealth, and even when we recognise the political sagacity shown in the Gold Coast, there remain a number of important areas (Malaya, Central Africa, Kenya and Bechuanaland) where the British government succumbed to the pressure of vested interests whose objectives coincided with its own economic or military aim. All these territories (except Bechuanaland) were ethnically mixed, with the racial groups at different levels of social and political development.

In Malaya and Singapore the prewar British policy of indirect rule through a decentralised administration ensured the survival of the Malayan sultans in most areas.[106] The British community dominated both the bureaucracy and business, though prominent businessmen were also to be found among locally born or immigrant Chinese. By 1945 the indigenous Malay community comprised about 42 per cent of the population. The Malays were relatively indifferent to the rapid collapse of British power under Japanese attack, but the Chinese had resisted the Japanese, and the predominantly Chinese Malayan Communist Party (MCP) had played a part in this.

The wartime coalition cabinet planned to create a unitary state which would include Singapore, with common citizenship for all races and a political structure in which the sultan's powers were to be curtailed and the franchise democratised.[107] This was in line with Labour party policy on Malaya.[108] The Malayan Union constitution, promulgated early in 1946, was, however, in the process of being abandoned by August. Fear of being swamped in their own homeland by a majority of Chinese and Indians led to the rapid emergence of a Malay nationalist party (United Malay National Organisation) with which a new constitutional settlement was negotiated. Its broad outlines were ready by February 1947. Its citizenship laws had a marked pro-Malay bias, and although it was ultimately to be based on an elected legislature, at that time the legislative assembly had a majority of nominated members. Within two months of the inauguration of this constitution in January 1948, the MCP had started an insurrection which did not end during the tenure of the Labour government, nor in that of its successor.[109]

Critical judgements have emphasised Britain's need for Malaya's dollar earnings. They have ranged from a description of the first proposals of early 1946 as annexationist imperialism to an interpretation of the *volte-face* and the pro-Malay bias of the second constitution as a design to curb the increasing powers of the communist-influenced Malayan trade union movement. (The working class was predominantly Chinese and Indian in origin with the Malays comprising only 17.5 per cent of the labour force.)[110] Since the new citizenship laws gave very little scope to the Chinese and were not liberalised until 1952, and since it is accepted that UMNO, though a mass party, was led by Western-educated members of the traditional Malay elite,[111] it can be argued that for the sake of dollars from rubber and tin the Labour government divided and ruled, with nominated representatives of the old British business community and the UMNO leadership as its main collaborators. The official version of the Malayan political troubles of the spring of 1948, in contrast, was that a Soviet-inspired insurrection had brought the Cold War to a turbulent area where the government was trying to proceed with its reforms.

On some points there is now little dispute. The demonetisation of the wartime Japanese currency (designed to hurt Japanese collaborators and also weaken the MCP) actually led to a transfer of real resources to the returning British, and the burden of inflation was borne by the Malayan labouring and salaried classes. It has also been convincingly shown that Malayan reconstruction after the war was hampered because Malaya did not have free access to her dollar earnings.[112] Evidence from the Colonial Office (not used so far) shows, however, that a Machiavellian design to divide and rule for the sake of dollars was *not* decisive during the period of constitution making prior to early 1947.

Concern for efficiency, democracy and modernisation (not dollar earning) was behind the decision to create a Malayan Union with a centralised administration.[113] As the ministers discussed the campaign against the union by the sultans, old pro-sultan retired officials, and UMNO, what they most disliked were the traditionalist pro-sultan appeals, and what they anxiously noted were reports that UMNO had become an umbrella organisation of Malayan nationalism which was as widespread as it was unexpected. They were reluctant to let it become anti-British in the way the Indonesians had become anti-Dutch at that time.[114] When the revised proposals were presented to the cabinet, it was stressed that in nominations to the assembly there should be no mention of interest groups lest it encourage too sectional an approach; special provisions for Malayans in the citizenship rules were justified as they had nowhere else to go, but there should be further consultations with other communities before finalising the rules. In any case, children of citizens would automatically become citizens. 'This will encourage the growth in course of time of an increasing body of men and women irrespective of race or creed, who will regard citizenship as a birthright, and an effective bond of common loyalty will then be created.'[115]

Governor Sir Edward Gent had achieved an understanding with UMNO after much tough bargaining and was reluctant to jeopardise it by further talks with non-Malay elements unless UMNO consented.[116] Two loose-knit associations representing Chinese and Indian communities, some radical Malay groups and pro-communist labour organisations put forward alternative proposals, with an emphasis on citizenship for all residents and constitutional guarantees about a minimum wage.[117] Malcolm MacDonald, the governor-general of Southeast Asia, Creech Jones and Attlee, all advised Gent against giving them an open rebuff lest a communist movement as unexpected as UMNO emerged.[118] However, Gent would not give any respectability to organisations with communist associations.[119] Parliamentary Under-Secretary of State for Colonies Ivor Thomas became concerned, after a visit to Malaya in February 1947, to ensure the unimpeded production of rubber, 'a dollar earning commodity'. He also shared the anti-Chinese and pro-Malay bias of Gent, blamed the estate workers for strikes and frequent wage demands and recommended flogging and banishment as punishments for breaches of law and order.[120]

Creech Jones continued to try for a common citizenship formula throughout 1947 and was anxious that elections should be held as early as possible.[121] An unofficial warning by the economist T.N. Silcock that the local authorities were thinking too much in racial stereotypes impressed him, but his advisers thought that the men on the spot knew best.[122] The result was predictable. When the predominantly Chinese MCP started its insurgency, all classes of the Chinese community were relatively uncooperative towards the counter-insurgency efforts for nearly two years afterwards.[123] In March 1949, commenting on the strain felt by the European settlers, 'on whom the whole rubber and tin economy depended', Creech Jones despaired of getting help from the Chinese community and wondered whether Britain would not be 'faced with a long war of attrition'.[124] Elections could not be held during this period.

Despite efforts to create non-communist trade unions with the help of visits by British trade unionists, the gap between workers' earnings and employers' profits was wide. In 1950, rubber workers had benefited somewhat by an arbitration award by Silcock, but the British tin companies were distributing dividends which, according to the governor, were 'on a dangerously high scale' (between 50 and 60 per cent). He added: 'It must be obvious that success against Communism in Malaya and the continuation of such exploitation on behalf of United Kingdom interests are mutually exclusive.'[125]

After a visit to Malaya in 1950, the secretary of state for colonies, James Griffiths, recognised the need for new political alternatives. He resisted European demands for a public declaration that British rule in Malaya would be maintained for another twenty-five years. He reported: 'Too many of the European population were inclined to hope for a return to the conditions which existed in Malaya before the war. The government would have to make it clear that they had different aims.' These aims included acceleration of the process towards self-government, breaking down the resistance of employers to trade unionism and convincing 'the workers in Malaya that a non-Communist regime offered them greater opportunities for economic and social betterment than any Communist regime'.[126] To have to state these at the end of a five-year period of Labour rule was an implicit admission of failure.

IV

In southern and eastern Africa, apart from the problem of immigrant European and Asian communities (especially in Kenya and the two Rhodesias), there were other obstacles to a progressive policy. The major difficulties were the racial policies of the Union of South Africa and its claim to the High Commission territories of Bechuanaland, Basutoland and Swaziland, the self-governing status enjoyed by settler-dominated Southern Rhodesia and the fact that the external trade of Northern Rhodesia could only be carried on through the south. In the post-war period these problems were aggravated by additional factors. Wartime assistance given by the Union of South Africa to Britain made her unwilling to offend the former on any international issue. It kept a low profile in the India–South Africa dispute at the United Nations (UN) and supported the South African demand for incorporating Southwest Africa into the Union, a demand rejected overwhelmingly at the UN.[127] Despite misgivings at the victory of Dr Malan's Nationalist Party in 1948, a lingering hope remained that the pendulum would swing back, and so Britain tried to avoid offending South Africans whenever possible. In June 1950, some time after having debarred Seretse Khama from the chieftainship of the Bamangwato tribe in Bechuanaland because of his marriage to an Englishwoman, the secretary of state for commonwealth relations noted the universal dislike of mixed marriages among Europeans in South Africa, and added: 'We must also do our utmost to keep the Union solidly in the commonwealth for strategic, economic, and other reasons.'[128]

As we have seen, East and Central Africa as a British power zone had been suggested by Attlee and Bevin in 1946, and the officials had considered it a practical possibility when the economy was developed to defray the cost.[129] The Colonial Office handled the defence of East Africa, Northern Rhodesia and Nyasaland together.[130] In October 1947 the War Office suggested bringing Southern Rhodesia into the defence scheme; Andrew Cohen, head of the Africa section of the Colonial Office, considered it worthwhile, though he had some doubts about the native policy of Southern Rhodesia.[131]

Since 1945, the European settlers in Northern Rhodesia had had an unofficial majority in the local legislature. The wartime need for copper production had strengthened the bargaining power of the European Mineworkers' Union, slowed down the prospect of African advancement in the copper belt, and occasioned the entry of white trade union leaders like Roy Welensky and Brian Goodwin into the political arena.[132] Andrew Cohen believed that recent ex-service immigrants in Southern Rhodesia were less racially prejudiced than the apparently increasing stream of Afrikaner immigrants from the Union of South Africa.[133] On this assumption, and on the information that Sir G. Huggins, the prime minister of Southern Rhodesia, was supported by such British immigrants, Cohen convinced himself that a Southern Rhodesia under Huggins, augmented by more British immigration, would be a useful partner with Northern Rhodesia and Nyasaland in a regional bloc as a counterweight to the Union of South Africa.[134]

This belief in the superior virtues of the post-war British immigrants appears to have been just a personal impression and is belied by the paper on racial prejudice in Britain prepared by the Colonial Office in May 1946. The paper referred to the difficulties in recruiting 'coloured' men in the armed forces and of the 'unfortunate series of racial incidents' in the Royal Air Force since December 1945.[135] When the problem of 'coloured' recruitment in the forces was raised by Creech Jones in the cabinet a year later, the ministers representing the services, with the exception of Philip Noel-Baker (Secretary of State for Air at that time), were reluctant to hasten the pace of recruitment because of rank-and-file prejudice. Anxious to avoid any stigma of colour prejudice, the cabinet asserted the non-racial principle in such a way as to give the authorities discretion in such cases.[136]

Despite occasional prodding from ministers, the desire to reconcile local settler opinion was characteristic of civil servants in Whitehall, including Andrew Cohen. When the formation of trade unions among African railwaymen in Northern Rhodesia was proposed in late 1945, Cohen 'made the reference a guarded one' because it would raise 'political objections . . . particularly in relation to the copper belt'.[137] Nevertheless, British trade union organisers were sent out and by March 1949 more than 50 per cent of the African labour force was unionised.[138] Yet the industrial colour bar could not be breached. Detailed suggestions by the British trade unionist Andrew Dagleish after two visits to the territory were promptly denounced by Roy Welensky.[139] In 1948, Creech Jones, prodded by the Fabian Colonial Bureau, tried without success to find a generally acceptable formula for the implementation of the Dagleish report.[140] Pressure from the Ministry of Supply in Britain for an uninterrupted flow of copper production and the intransigence of the European mineworkers effectively stopped progress.[141] In October 1950 a civil servant in the Colonial Office admitted that progress had been negligible, but displayed characteristic caution in opposing the outspoken parliamentary Under-Secretary of State, J. Dugdale, who had written that effective action on the report would be sufficient to stop Afrikaner immigration into skilled jobs.[142] James Griffiths despaired of governmental action and tried to use international trade union pressure on the European Mineworkers' Union to end the colour bar.[143] Nothing came of this.

In sharp contrast to the accelerated plans for Africanisation of the

civil services in West Africa after the constitutional changes in the Gold
Coast and Nigeria, plans for African education and political advancement in Central Africa were modest, probably because immigrant
communities were already in power.[144] The local governments aimed
'first to educate Africans to fill the more responsible clerical posts' and
assumed that 'many years' would pass before Africans could hold senior
government appointments.[145] African political activity was limited to
local councils, and only two nominated Africans and two Europeans
representing African interests were in the European-dominated legislative council. The proposal to grant Northern Rhodesian Africans
British nationality under the British Nationality Act of 1948 alarmed
the settlers lest some Africans would qualify to vote in the European
constituency. Civil servants, including Andrew Cohen, were prepared
to meet them half-way. Cohen opposed the common electoral roll, fear-
ing a European backlash. Creech Jones had to step in and write: 'If the
seats of Europeans in their small constituencies depend on winning the
goodwill of the few Africans admitted to the franchise, their work in the
Legislative Council would be tempered with some regard to African
development.'[146] His insistence that 'the franchise [was] symbolic of
dignity and equality and racial non-discrimination' prevented official
wavering, and by his personal diplomacy during a visit to Northern
Rhodesia he persuaded the local authorities to ignore the settlers' protests on this issue.[147]

In July 1948, at a meeting at the Colonial Office, the African representative objected when the Northern Rhodesian politicians raised
the question of a Central African Federation.[148] In October 1948,
against the background of the Africa Conference and efforts at colonial
development, Creech Jones wanted some form of regional cooperation
which would safeguard native policy but derive the benefits of a large
unit. 'Our strategic needs in Africa, the importance of more thoroughgoing development, the desirability of certain common services and
regional approach—suggest the need of a closer association of these
territories.'[149] He added, 'I am certain we must not advance an inch if
it involves us in any surrender of African rights.'[150] Cohen agreed and,
against the background of Dr Malan's victory in South Africa, pinned
his faith on Huggins of Southern Rhodesia turning to the North
to form part of a British bloc.[151] This idea of a British bloc was an

argument pressed by the officials in 1950 when maximum pressure was exerted by the settlers for a decision on federation.

In East Africa, the European settlers had managed to increase their representation on the interterritorial council, which provided the mechanism for regional cooperation. In defending this change in the House of commons on grounds of efficiency Creech Jones reassured party experts on colonial affairs by affirming that Britain would have full powers in all matters affecting African interests.[152] In fact the emphasis laid on economic development by the governor of Kenya, Sir Philip Mitchell, who was also the chairman of the interterritorial council, led to a proliferation of technical and developmental officers from overseas without much attempt being made to enlist African participation in the many changes that were taking place.[153] Mitchell's stern paternalism led him to scoff at the sympathy shown by the Watson Commission on the Gold Coast for the frustration of the African intelligentsia. He thought that the Labour government, by speaking about African self-government, had encouraged subversive elements.[154] While Jomo Kenyatta had been allowed to come back to Kenya, Mitchell did not give him much encouragement.[155]

In 1950 all over eastern and southern Africa, critical choices on race relations could no longer be shirked. Three issues called for decision. First, in Bechuanaland there was the question of Seretse Khama's succession to the chieftainship. Second, Southern Rhodesia tried to force the pace for a favourable decision on federation by giving notice to withdraw from the Central African Council, and also by refusing to cooperate in interterritorial projects.[156] Third, in East Africa an extreme statement by some European settlers temporalily united Asians and Africans. The result was the passage in April 1950 of a resolution of no confidence in the Europeans.[157]

Reading through cabinet discussions on the case of Seretse Khama shows that right from the beginning the adverse reaction in South Africa was an important factor. Only at Creech Jones's insistence was an immediate decision to persuade Seretse to give up his title postponed in favour of a judicial inquiry, and it was explicitly recorded that the issue was not to be the merits or demerits of mixed marriages.[158] To the acute embarrassment of the government, the inquiry committee, while accepting the legality and suitability of Seretse, recommended with-holding the title precisely on the political grounds that it would offend South Africa and Southern Rhodesia.[159] The government rejected these arguments but did not want to admit that fact lest it spoil its relations with these countries.[160] When a White Paper giving reasons for keeping the chieftainship in suspension for five years was being drafted, some ministers suggested that suppressing the report of the inquiry com-mittee would be criticised (which it was), and that it would be better to publish it and indicate the government's points of difference. Their suggestion was rejected lest it brought these points into prominence.[161]

Later in the year, apropos of how Britain should vote at the UN over the question of Southwest Africa, James Griffiths and Aneurin Bevan argued that the economic and strategic advantages of British support for South Africa were outweighed by the adverse effects on the British colonial territories. Bevan added that the views of many supporters of the Labour party had to be taken into account. The majority of the cabinet disagreed because South Africa was of great strategic value in 'any struggle against Communism' and because of 'the great value of the military support she seemed likely to promise in the Middle East'.[162] Sir Evelyn Baring, the British high commissioner in South Africa, had noted only a few months earlier: 'So long as the Cold War continues, any UK policy which can be represented as directed against Communism will be certain of the maximum possible collaboration from the South African government . . .'[163] The majority of the Labour cabinet had drifted into a position where fighting the Cold War was an end in itself regardless of the issues for which it was fought.

The paradox was that at the same time as support of South Africa was deemed essential, officials were justifying the Central African federation proposed by the Rhodesian settlers in the fond hope that it would create a counterweight to the Union of South Africa. The brief prepared by Cohen and Lambert in the Colonial Office for the ministers' meeting with Huggins and Welensky in April and May 1950 started by arguing in favour of a 'solid British bloc of territories in Central Africa . . . to resist economic and political pressure from the Union of South Africa'. Transport bottlenecks could be eased by a healthy cooperation between the two territories. The memorandum added that if the British government was itself convinced of the wisdom of the federal idea, then it was 'under no obligation to accept African views'.[164] With this elitist, technocratic, imperial brief before them, Griffiths and Gordon-Walker met Huggins in April and Welensky in May. The Rhodesians asserted that the resources of the territories could only be developed by European capital and entrepreneurship and therefore the Europeans must have firm reassurances of support, especially in view of the progress made towards self-government in West Africa. The British ministers would not budge from their position that African interests would have to be protected, and that further political advance for the Europeans in Northern Rhodesia was contingent on corresponding advance for the Africans.[165] But it is possible that these ministers did not disagree about the importance of European entrepreneurship in Central Africa. Even Creech Jones had written, only some nine months before, 'progress depends very largely on the sound relationship of Europeans with Africans, and the realization of a partnership which will give permanent place to European conceptions of development and enterprise in industry and agriculture'.[166]

A final decision was postponed pending an official fact-finding inquiry about the federation. The civil servants wished to handle the settlers gently.[167] Griffiths would have preferred to emphasise British responsibility to the Africans in the strongest terms, but in announcing the fact-finding committee to the colonies, his language was moderated so as not to offend the Northern Rhodesian settlers.[168]

The embittered relations between Europeans, Asians and Africans in East Africa made Griffiths hold a series of meetings, from May 1950, with the officials and governors concerned. He decided that a public statement of principles was required and got it cleared by the cabinet. The statement, made on 13 December 1950, stressed that everyone, of whatever race, who had made East Africa his home, had a stake in the country and that African social and economic advance should take place in such a way as to enable all communities to live in harmony. The likelihood of Africans reaching the stage of self-government in the near future was ruled out and paternalist control from London was reaffirmed. It was not a statement likely to appeal to Kenyatta and his followers and its main aim was to prevent a South African orientation on the part of the settlers.[169]

V

Preaching racial harmony in the colonies was easier than practising it at home. The Colonial Office and its ministers were anxious for racial harmony in Britain in order to project a more favourable image in the colonies. Yet the natural constituents of the Labour party, the British working class, did not always express full support for a multiracial Britain.

At the ideological level Attlee recognised the importance of multiracialism. In the wartime coalition he had criticized Viceroy Linlithgow for racialist attitudes.[170] He was very pleased at the adhesion of Asian countries to the commonwealth.[171] During his ideological counter-offensive against Soviet propaganda among colonised peoples, Bevin noted a Nigerian official report which said: 'If it should ever become necessary for us to take a line which would be openly unfriendly to the Soviet Union, we should have the greatest difficulty in putting it across.' This would be due to Britain's inability to match the Soviet claim to sponsor racial equality.[172]

In November 1945, C.W. Greenidge, a member of the Fabian Colonial Bureau and secretary of the Anti-slavery and Aborigine Protection Society, asked for legislation against racial discrimination in Britain.[173] Three years later, after having examined the evidence, one senior official (Sir Charles Jefferies) and one minister (Lord Listowel) favoured legislation, especially laws against discriminatory clauses in leases or other tenancy agreements, for their 'good effect on public opinion at home and in the colonies'.[174] Creech Jones doubted its practicality and Listowel was unsure about getting parliamentary time that session.[175]

The complexity of racial problems in Britain was further highlighted in 1948. There was panic among eleven Labour MPs when the ship the *Empire Windrush* brought a number of Jamaican job-seekers to Britain. The MPs (of whom half were trade unionists from working-class districts) wanted a ban on immigration so that Britain could continue to enjoy the absence of interracial conflict, and suggested that colonial development and welfare grants provide for the Jamaicans in their homeland.[176] The reaction of the Economic Policy Committee of the cabinet was also one of panic. Some members suggested that instead of letting them settle in Britain they should be sent to Tanganyika to grow groundnuts![177] As Attlee referred the letter of the MPs to Creech

Jones, he wondered whether there was any organisation behind the immigration.[178] Creech Jones disabused him of that, and took personal care to vet Attlee's reply to the MPs. Attlee finally wrote:

It is traditional that British subjects, whether of dominion or Colonial origin (and of whatever race or colour) should be freely admissible to the United Kingdom. That tradition is not, in my view, to be lightly discarded, particularly at a time when we are importing foreign labour in large numbers. It would be fiercely resented in the colonies themselves, and it would be a great mistake to take any measure which would weaken the goodwill and loyalty of the colonies towards Great Britain.

He added that the policy might, 'however reluctantly', be modified only if 'a great influx of undesirables' occurred, but this would not happen 'except on really compelling evidence' which did not exist then. Furthermore, all the Jamaicans who had come were skilled and were easily absorbed into various occupations.[179] After this, Attlee circulated Creech Jones's memorandum to the cabinet for information and avoided discussion.[180] The prime minister's decision to play down this episode must be seen in the context of contemporary developments. In June 1948 the riots in the Gold Coast were only three months old, the Malayan insurgency had started and British plans for African development were under attack as exploitation. Attlee was also keen to retain India in the commonwealth.

News about labour shortage in Britain attracted many potential immigrants. One stowaway who had landed said, when questioned, that 'he had come in answer to Sir Stafford Cripps' appeal for textile workers'.[181] Some colonial governors made inquiries about openings in Britain for their surplus labour.[182] This resulted in an interdepartmental working party on this problem.[183] The whole question of continuing the policy of free access or repatriating colonials was also discussed by another committee in February 1949, at the request made by some police commissioners to the Home Office.[184] These investigations and discussions brought out two significant trends.

In the first place, there was strong opposition from trade unions to 'coloured' workers. Informal soundings by the National Union of Mineworkers and the National Union of Agricultural Workers revealed this, as did reports from the regional controllers of the Ministry of

Labour.[185] The final report of the committee on the employment of colonial workers stated:

The leaders of the Trade Union movement generally take the line that while they themselves have no objection in principle to the introduction of coloured workers from British territories, the decision whether or not to go on with a recruiting scheme must in every case be Left to the local branch in the area of prospective employment. The local trade union officials usually say that they would help if they could but that the workers in their particular area are not prepared to accept coloured workers into their place of employment.[186]

In the second place, the Colonial Office representatives investigating the rules on stowaways and the repatriation of immigrants successfully upheld the principles of the British Nationality Act of 1948. They rejected the repatriation of the generation born of immigrant parents in Britain, and of able-bodied persons who were not a persistent charge on public funds.[187]

The entire controversy over immigration had overshadowed the original request for legislation against racial discrimination. The Fabian Colonial Bureau revived the issue in February 1949, when Lord Faringdon proposed a private member's bill in the House of Lords. Lord Listowel was willing to seek parliamentary time, but the Lord Chancellor objected on two counts: it was not practicable, and it went against the grain of lawyers to pass legislation merely as a gesture, when there was no public demand for it.[188] In resisting the pressure of backbench MPs over the influx of Jamaicans in 1948, the government had upheld the special role that it had assigned to Britain within the commonwealth. The failure both to press the trade unions to take 'coloured' colleagues and to take steps towards anti-discriminatory legislation (especially in housing) showed, however, that for most members positive steps towards promoting the multiracial ideal took a low priority.

In discussions on immigration during two meetings of the cabinet, held after the general elections of 1950, worries were voiced by a substantial number of ministries. It is not possible to say whether it figured as an election issue at all. That it had introduced a disturbing element for Labour ministers, however, was plain enough. The first cabinet (on 20 March 1950) was told of West Indian complaints about obtaining jobs. Its reaction was to note the 'serious difficulties' that would arise if 'coloured immigration' were to continue.[189] For the next meeting Griffiths produced a memorandum describing his policy of dispersing immigrants from overcrowded areas and helping them to assimilate. He did not question the open-door policy. The memorandum was simply noted, not accepted. The discussion in the cabinet 'turned mainly on the means of preventing any further increase in the coloured population of Britain'. Attlee was asked to review the situation.[190] At the same time, however, the growth of racial prejudice in some commonwealth countries (especially the Union of South Africa) led to a remarkable demonstration by 97 Labour MPs (including 31 trade union MPs), who signed an 'early day motion' on 26 February 1951 in favour of racial equality in the commonwealth.[191] It is quite likely that this partly neutralised the pressure of those who wished to restrict immigration and made Attlee decide that the situation had not changed materially since 1948. At a time when, in the international and commonwealth arena, Britain was trying to live down the Seretse Khama episode and was preaching racial harmony in East and Central Africa, it was impolitic to suggest that Britain could not cope with a multiracial society.

VI

It has been argued that the 'Labour ministry decided that what the British empire needed, even in epilogue or afterthought, was logic'.[192] Logic and consistency are precisely what the Labour government's record do not show. The reasons for this are not the absence of thinking or planning by Labour ministers, especially those in charge of the dependent empire, but the multiple contradictions in Britain's post-war imperial predicament. She aspired to a global role, but she was a debtor country. She thought herself to be the centre of the commonwealth, but the reality was that the commonwealth was a house with many independent mansions. She had made blueprints for planned progress in the colonies, but found her resources severely limited.

Whichever government came to power, these would have been the contradictions in running an empire. For a party with a working-class base, and some degree of commitment to the Fabian gradualist ideology of reform, the burden of reforming the empire proved too much. Where the empire was relinquished gracefully, no problem arose. Where there was a wish to form power blocs and at the same time modernise the 'backward' people, scarcity of resources on the one hand, and the divergent expectations of the party's natural constituents and the elites who ruled the independent commonwealth countries, or who were aspirants after power in the dependent colonies, on the other hand, created potentially explosive situations. Wherever the policy-makers of a reformed empire came in contact with the hard realities of valuable raw materials or exciting prospects of a great power role as the bastion of social democracy against communism, the reforming zeal petered out under pressure from vested interests. It was doubly unfortunate for the reformers that these strategically—or economically—valuable territories would also bristle with political tensions associated with multi-ethnic societies. The imperial role of the Labour government, then, is neither as unselfish as the official manifesto would lead us to believe, nor as single-mindedly Machiavellian as some of its critics have claimed, both then and now.

NOTES

1. Labour Party, *Report of the Annual Conference 1945*, p. 115.
2. R. Palme Dutt, *Britain's Crisis of Empire* (Bombay, 1953), ch. 15.
3. G. Padmore, *Africa, Britain's Third Empire* (London, 1949), pp. 9f, 12.
4. F.W.S. Craig, *British General Election Manifestos, 1900–1974* (London, 1975), p. 159.
5. D. Goldsworthy, *Colonial Issues in British Politics, 1945–1961* (Oxford, 1971), p. 23.
6. P.S. Gupta, *Imperialism and the British Labour Movement, 1914–1964* (London, 1975), pp. 275–348.
7. R. Robinson, 'Andrew Cohen and the Transfer of Power in Tropical Africa', in W.H. Morris-Jones and G. Fischer (eds), *Decolonization and After* (London, 1980), pp. 50, 61–3.
8. Craig, *British General Election Manifestos*, p. 131.
9. DO (46) 40, 13 March 1946, para 6, Cabinet Papers 131/2 (Public Record Office [PRO], London) (hereafter PRO Cab).
10. See note 75 below.
11. DO (46) 1st and 4th meetings, PRO Cab 131/1.
12. DO (46) 5th meeting, 15 February 1946, p. 2, PRO Cab.

13. DO (46) 8th meeting, 18 March 1946, p. 2, PRO Cab.

14. DO (46) 7th meeting, 8 March 1946, p. 10, PRO Cab 131/1; DO (46) 27 for Attlee's views, PRO Cab 131/2.

15. DO (46) 40, annexure, 13 March 1946, PRO Cab 131/2.

16. Ibid., para 15

17. DO (46) 10th meeting, 5 April 1946, PRO Cab 131/1.

18. DO (47) 27, annexure 2, PRO Cab 131/4; also discussion on this on 26 March 1947 in DO (47) 9th meeting, minute 4, PRO Cab 131/5.

19. This is discussed in section III below.

20. The main sources for the Indian developments are the volumes on the transfer of power edited by Nicholas Mansergh. P.N.S. Mansergh and P. Moon, *Transfer of Power* (hereafter *ToP*), 12 vols (1970–80).

21. War Office Papers, 32/12313, para 149 (PRO, London) (hereafter WO).

22. See appreciation of the situation by the Indian Commander-in-Chief Claude Auchinleck, 24 November 1945, *ToP*, VII, document 256; K.S. Himatsinghji to Auchinleck, 19 November 1945, Auchinleck Papers, MUL 1113 (John Rylands Library, Manchester).

23. Note by J.A. Thorne, 5 April 1946, *ToP*, vii, document 60.

24. C. Markovits, 'Indian Business and the Congress Provincial Governments 1937–39', *Modern Asian Studies*, XV (1981), pp. 487–526.

25. 'Talks with Sir Evan Jenkins about the Situation in India, 27 November 1945', Prime Minister's Private Office Papers, 8/58 (PRO, London) (hereafter PREM).

26. Gupta, *Imperialism and the British Labour Movement*, pp. 272ff.

27. *ToP*, VII, documents 87, 120.

28. Ibid., document 85.

29. The evolution of the government's attitudes on the war costs and sterling balances can be seen in *ToP*, II, documents 375, 751, 773, 780. For Churchill's views, Churchill to Linlithgow, 24 September 1942, in *ToP*, III, document 25.

30. *ToP*, VI, documents 169, 186; *ToP*, VII, document 85.

31. *ToP*, VI, documents 86, 105.

32. Ibid., documents 86, 105; also see Auchinleck, 'Military Implications of Pakistan' (Top Secret), 24 April 1947, Auchinleck Papers, MUL 1224.

33. *ToP*, VII, document 455, pp. 817ff. British troops in India were anxious to go home. Auchinleck wrote in his report for the year up to May 1946: 'The morale of British troops remained high ... although service in India continued to be unpopular and questions of release and repatriation were topics of interest to the exclusion of all else,' WO 32/12314.

34. *ToP*, IX, documents 236, 432.

35. On this, see D. Potter, 'Manpower Shortage and the End of Colonialism: The Case of the ICS', *Modern Asian Studies*, VII (1973); T.H. Beaglehole,

'From Rulers to Servants: The ICS and the British Demission of Power in India', *Modern Asian Studies*, XI (1977).

36. CP (47) 20, para 15, PRO Cab 129/16 (hereafter specific cabinet papers are referred to as CP).

37. CM 10 (47) 2, 13 (47) 1, PRO Cab 128/9.

38. Montgomery to Alexander, 9 April 1947; Alexander to Montgomery, 11 April 1947, kept as annexures to CM 35 (47) 5, PRO Cab 128/9.

39. 'India (Misc.)—Andaman & Nicobar Islands', PREM 8/574. This contains all the papers from 27 February to 8 July 1947. See, in particular, Viceroy to Secretary of State, 21 June 1947. Also see Attlee's comments in cabinet, CM 57 (47) 4, 26 June 1947, PRO Cab 128/10.

40. R.J. Moore, 'Mountbatten, India and the Commonwealth', *Journal of Commonwealth and Comparative Politics*, XIX (1981), pp. 12–19.

41. Auchinleck to Geoffrey Scoone, 15 September 1947, Auchinleck Papers, MUL 1259; Mountbatten to Auchinleck, 26 September 1947, Auchinleck Papers, MUL 1260. Two years later, Philip Noel-Baker (Secretary of State for Commonwealth Relations) regretted that the Kashmir dispute had prevented the two countries from playing any part in commonwealth defence plans. A hankering after the former part played by the Indian empire in British strategy is revealed in the following: 'Should they settle their differences they are likely to be the only two members of the commonwealth who are in a position to put reasonably equipped and trained forces into the field at short notice,' 'Defence Burdens and the Commonwealth', 30 December 1949, by Noel-Baker, DO (49) 89, PRO Cab 131/7.

42. This was pointed out by the Chief of Air Staff, Lord Tedder, at a cabinet meeting to discuss the Ceylonese demand for dominion status, CM 44 (47) 2, PRO Cab 128/9.

43. CP (45) 130, 132 and 138, PRO Cab 129/1; CP (45) 244, PRO Cab 129/3; CM 27 (455) 2, 30 (45) 3 and 46 (45) 4, PRO Cab 128/1.

44. CM 44 (47) 2, PRO Cab 128/9.

45. CP (47) 17, PRO Cab 129/19; CM 51 (47) 4, PRO Cab 128/10.

46. The minister was Patrick Gordon-Walker. CP (48) 91, PRO Cab 129/26.

47. CP (47) 221, PRO Cab 129/20; DO (47) 68, paras 15 and 19, PRO Cab 131/4; CM 65 (47) 2, 67 (47) 2 and 78 (47) 3, PRO Cab 128/10.

48. DO (47) 68, para 19, PRO Cab 131/4.

49. CP (48) 61, PRO Cab 129/25.

50. For earlier fears, see Gupta, *Imperialism and the British Labour Movement*, pp. 42–3, 217–20, 236ff; for post-war position, LP (DI) (46) 72, PRO Cab 132/22. This shows that the only 'development area' in Lancashire with an unemployment rate of 5.9 per cent was the mining area of south

Lancashire, not the cotton districts. See also Dalton's remarks at the cabinet on 4 February 1947, CM 16 (47) 2, PRO Cab 128/9.

51. For Australia, the joint paper by Lord Addison and G.A. Isaacs, CP (47) 67, PRO Cab 129/17, and also CM 26 (47) 6, PRO Cab 128/9. For Kenya, Goldsworthy, *Colonial Issues*, p. 141.

52. PREM 8/458; also see CM 78 (46) 7, PRO Cab 128/6. In order to facilitate good relations with Iraq, Bevin was anxious to find a place where this minority (who had fled to Iraq from Asia Minor at the time of the collapse of the Ottoman Empire and the emergence of modern Turkey) could be settled.

53. This is discussed in section V below.

54. 'Overseas Investment Policy, 1932–43', Treasury Papers, 236/173 (PRO, London) (hereafter T).

55. CP (47) 35, 8 January 1947, PRO Cab 129/16.

56. CM 50 (45), PRO Cab 128/4.

57. Only three Labour MPs (Norman Smith, R.R. Stokes and Stanley Evans) supported early day motions of this nature along with Conservative backbenchers in November and December 1945 (data from House of Commons Library).

58. CP (49) 188, para 8, 12 September 1949, PRO Cab 129/36.

59. Ibid., para 6.

60. CP (47) 260, PRO Cab 129/21.

61. CP (47) 35, PRO Cab 129/16; also see cabinet minutes of 28 January 1947, CM 3 (47) 2, PRO Cab 128/9.

62. CP (47) 167, by Dalton, 28 May 1947, PRO Cab 129/19.

63. The Ministry of Food presented its problems at a number of cabinet meetings. CM 30 (47) 5, 33 (47) 5, 39 (47) 5, PRO Cab 128/9; CM 56 (47) 2, PRO Cab 128/10.

64. Gupta, *Imperialism and the British Labour Movement*, pp. 314–15, needs revision in the light of these new pieces of evidence.

65. For the drafts of the *Economic Survey*, CP (47) 19, PRO Cab 129/16; for the Creech Jones–Attlee correspondence on 26 March 1947, PREM 8/457.

66. CP (47) 175, PRO Cab 129/19.

67. CP (47) 242, 23 August 1947, PRO Cab 129/20. Thomas mentioned that Creech Jones had discussed the memo with Bevin before forwarding it.

68. CM 68 (47), afternoon session, 1 August 1947; CM 69 (47) 2, 5 August 1947, PRO Cab 128/10.

69. CM 77 (47) 2, PRO Cab 128/10.

70. CP (47) 245 and 266, PRO Cab 129/21.

71. CM 77 (47) 1 and 79 (47) 5, PRO Cab 128/10.

72. CM 83 (47) 7, PRO Cab 128/10; also see CP (47) 242, PRO Cab 129/ 20 and CM 74 (47), PRO Cab 128/10 for discussions on the sale prospects of Malayan rubber.

73. An early day motion sponsored by the Labour MP R.W.G. Mackey and five other members from all parties on 10 March 1948 was signed by 64 backbench MPs on the first day (37 of them Labour). By 27 April the number of signatures had increased to 170 (of which about 82 were those of Labour MPs) (data from the House of Commons Library).

74. The phrase quoted is from a joint memo by Bevin and Cripps on European economic cooperation, 6 March 1948, CP (48) 75, PRO Cab 129/25.

75. CP (48) 6, 4 January 1948, PRO Cab 129/23. Also see the cabinet minutes on this and related memoranda, CM 2 (48) 5, PRO Cab 128/12.

76. Gupta, *Imperialism and the British Labour Movement*, pp. 276–9.

77. EPC (48) 35, covering note by Plowden, para 9; text of report, para 44, PRO Cab 134/217.

78. Lord Addison to Mackenzie King, 9 April 1948, Addison Papers, Box 137, folder 'Various Personal Letters' (Bodleian Library, Oxford).

79. Memo by Listowel on internal office arrangement (n.d. but from content and provenance some time in 1948), Creech Jones Papers, MSS Brit. Emp. s. 332, ACJ 54/2, fo. 10 (Bodleian Library, Oxford).

80. Herbert Morrison to Attlee, 20 June 1949, PREM 8/977.

81. CM 53 (47) 5, 16 June 1947, PRO Cab 128/10.

82. Minute by Creech Jones, 3 July 1948, Colonial Office Papers, 537/ 3031 (PRO, London) (hereafter CO).

83. CM 20 (48) 2, PRO Cab 128/12.

84. Robert Scott (acting governor) to A. Creech Jones, 30 October 1947, CO 96/795/31312 of 1948.

85. Ibid., marginal comment, signature illegible.

86. CP (48) 7, PRO Cab 129/23.

87. When Bevin heard that the Colonial Office was planning to requisition the Shaftesbury Hotel to accommodate, apart from colonial service trainees, colonial students, he strongly opposed it because it was too near King Street, the headquarters of the British Communist Party. Minute by Creech Jones, n.d., but around July 1948, CO 537/2585, items 10 and 11.

88. Robinson, 'Andrew Cohen and the Transfer of Power in Tropical Africa', pp. 60–7; also see J.W. Cell, 'On the Eve of Decolonization: The Colonial Office Plans for the Transfer of Power in Africa, 1947', *Journal of Imperial and Commonwealth History*, viii (1980), esp. pp. 247–9; on Nigeria, see R.D. Pearce, 'Governors, Nationalists and Constitutions in Nigeria, 1935– 51', *Journal of Imperial and Commonwealth History*, IX (1981), pp. 289– 307.

89. CP (48) 193, para 8, 30 July 1948, PRO Cab 129/29.
90. CP (48) 237, PRO Cab 129/30.
91. EPC (48) 35th meeting, 9 November 1948, minute 4, PRO Cab 134/216. The quotation is at p. 6.
92. EPC (48) 34, PRO Cab 134/217; also see EPC (48) 23rd meeting, minute 2, PRO Cab 134/216.
93. 'Investment of Foreign Capital in the Colonies', EPC (49) 74, 5 July 1949, kw PREM 8/977; also see no. 303, 'Interdepartmental Committee on US Investment in the Sterling Area (November–December 1949)', PRO Cab 130/56.
94. 'Draft to Cabinet of American Aid in Colonial Development', n.d., but sometime in 1949, Creech Jones Paper, ACJ 54/3, fo. 3.
95. Harold Wilson referred to the danger of British solvency being threatened 'by the continuance of unrequited exports on anything like the present scale!', CP (49) 179, para 8, PRO Cab 129/36.
96. In the file on the colonial sterling balances, one Treasury official was impressed by the case for the colonies as presented by Sir Sidney Caine, but Dalton was not. See note on minute by SDW dated 30 July 1946. Dalton added (9 August 1946): 'We must not admit—till a very late stage if at all—that any sterling creditor can make no adjustments,' T 236/51.
97. For Malaya, see M. Rudner, 'Financial Policies in Post-war Malaya: The Fiscal and Monetary Measures of Liberation and Reconstruction', *Journal of Imperial and Commonwealth History*, III (1975), pp. 323–48. For India's tendency to run a deficit, see references in CP (48) 35, para 4 and annex A, PRO Cab 129/24; CP (48) 161 para 11, PRO Cab 129/29; CP (49) 27, para 57, PRO Cab 129/32.
98. CP (49) 58, PRO Cab 129/33; CM 17 (49) 1, PRO Cab 128/15.
99. CP (49) 58, annex, para 18, PRO Cab 129/33.
100. CP (47) 213, PRO Cab 129/20; CM 70 (47) 7, PRO Cab 128/10.
101. Commonwealth Finance Ministers' Conference, EMM (49) 10th meeting, 16 July 1949, p. 53, PREM 8/975.
102. EPC (49) 79, appendix 2, 9 July 1949; Creech Jones's despatch to all colonies, 4 July 1949. All kept in PREM 8/975.
103. EMM (49) meeting on 15 July 1949, at p. 33, PREM 8/975.
104. CM 6 (48) 5, PRO Cab 128/12. During drafting of the economic survey of 1949 it was suggested that the colonial account could be presented separately to show the steady expansion of colonial exports and their contribution to the balance of payments. Cripps thought that to separate the figures 'might have an unfortunate effect on public opinion in the United States'. CM 16 (49) 4, PRO Cab 128/13. Cripps

was evidently afraid of a renewed American attack on imperial preference and a demand for convertibility.

105. CP (49) 108, para 16, PRO Cab 129/36.
106. Gupta, *Imperialism and the British Labour Movement*, pp. 262–3.
107. A.J. Stockwell, 'Colonial Planning during World War II: The Case of Malaya', *Journal of Imperial and Commonwealth History*, II (1974), p. 339.
108. Gupta, *Imperialism and the British Labour Movement*, pp. 262–330.
109. The standard work for the insurgency is A. Short, *The Communist Insurrection in Malaya, 1948–60* (1975).
110. J.D.V. Allen, *The Malayan Union* (New Haven, 1967), p. 19; M.R. Stenson, *Industrial Conflict in Malaya* (1970), pp. 128–32.
111. A.R. Stockwell, 'The Formation and First Years of the United Malay National Organisation (UMNO), 1946–48; *Modern Asian Studies*, XI (1977), pp. 494ff.
112. Rudner, 'Financial Policies in Post-War Malaya', pp. 325–7.
113. C (46) 1st meeting, Colonial Affairs Committee, 7 January 1946, PRO Cab 134/52.
114. Minutes of Governors' Conference, 20 August 1946, CO 537/1596; 'Visit of Capt. Gammans and Col. Rees-Williams to Malaya', CO 537/1594; 'Malayan Policy', CP (46) 439, PRO Cab 129/15; MSS and typed drafts of CP (46) 439 in Creech Jones Papers, ACJ 57/2, item 1; C (46) 3rd meeting, 2 December 1946, PRO Cab 134/52.
115. CP (46) 439, PRO Cab 129/15, annexure, para 7, and covering note by Addison; also see Creech Jones–Edward Gent correspondence from January to September 1946, with the minister insisting that the basic principle of common citizenship must not be flouted. CO 537/1542.
116. Stockwell, 'The Formation and First Years of UMNO', p. 479; also the sources cited in note 114 above.
117. The material is available in CO 537/1567 and CO 537/2148.
118. Governor's Conference, 19 January 1947, CO 537/2165, item 7; Creech Jones to Gent, 4 January 1947, sent with Attlee's approval, CO 537/1567, fo. 14.
119. CO 537/2150, fos 1, 3.
120. CO 537/2175, fo. 1.
121. CP (47) 187, PRO Cab 128/19.
122. CO 537/3670.
123. CP (49) 52, para 8 (d), PRO Cab 129/33; CP (50) 75, paras 6 and 7, PRO Cab 129/39.
124. CP (49) 52 para 9, PRO Cab 129/33.
125. Sir H. Gurney to Creech Jones, 12 January 1950, Creech Jones Papers, ACJ 57/2, item 6.

126. CM 37 (50) 1, 19 June 1950, PRO Cab 128/17.
127. CP (47) 16, annexures E and F, PRO Cab 129/16; CM 1 (47) 4, PRO Cab 128/9.
128. CP (50) 138 para 12, 26 June 1950, PRO Cab 129/40.
129. See note 16 above.
130. CO 537/5348 is a typical file of the joint defence organisation.
131. CO 537/2516.
132. L. Berger, *Labour, Race, and Colonial Rule: The Copperbelt from 1921 to Independence* (Oxford, 1974), pp. 97–9.
133. The average rate of Afrikaner immigration to Northern Rhodesia in the pre-war years of 1937–9 was 45 per cent of all immigrants; in the years 1946–9 it was 49 per cent. CO 537/5896. For Cohen's views on the recent British immigrants, see minute, 12 October 1948, CO 537/3608.
134. Note by Cohen, 11 June 1946, CO 537/1518.
135. CO 537/1224, item 6, pp. 3ff.
136. CM 51 (47) 3, PRO Cab 128/10.
137. Minutes by Orde-Browne, 25 January 1946, and by Cohen, 25 January 1946, CO 537/1510.
138. Berger, *Labour, Race, and Colonial Rule*, pp. 88–92.
139. Ibid., pp. 100–9.
140. Correspondence between Rita Hinden and Creech Jones between 25 May and 30 November 1948, Fabian Colonial Bureau Papers, 25/1, fos. 86–90 (Bodleian Library, Oxford).
141. Berger, *Labour, Race, and Colonial Rule*, p. 114.
142. Minute by Lambert, 9 October 1950 and by J. Dugdale, CO 537/5896.
143. CO 537/5923, item 38, 10 October 1950.
144. CM 30 (50) 6, 11 May 1950, PRO Cab 128/17; CP (50) 171, 17 July 1950, PRO Cab 129/41.
145. CP (50) 171, para 14, PRO Cab 129/41.
146. Note by Creech Jones, n.d., but around August–September 1947, CO 797/164, item 3.
147. CO 797/164, items 6 and 12.
148. Item 38, meeting between Creech Jones and a Northern Rhodesian group, CO 537/3608.
149. Minute by Creech Jones (Top Secret), 8 October 1948, CO 537/3608.
150. Ibid., another minute, n.d.
151. Ibid., minute by Cohen, 12 October 1948.
152. Labour party, International Department, Commonwealth Affairs Sub-committee, meeting on 18 November 1947, and connected papers; Noel-Baker Papers, NBKR 2/70, fos. 7–8 (Churchill College, Cambridge).

153. D.A. Low and A. Smith (eds), *History of East Africa*, 3 vols. (Oxford, 1976), III, pp. 12–15, 53–5, 112–28.

154. P. Mitchell to Creech Jones, 16 September 1948, Creech Jones Papers, ACJ 55/4, item 5; also see his despatch of 30 May 1947, quoted in Cell, 'On the Eve of Decolonization', pp. 252–5.

155. J. Murray-Brown, *Kenyatta* (1972), pp. 227–39.

156. CO 537/5884, items 5, 7, 8, 9, 17, 91.

157. Low and Smith (eds), *History of East Africa*, II, pp. 125–6.

158. CM 47 (49) 8, PRO Cab 128/14.

159. CP (50) 36, PRO Cab 129/38, annexure, 'Report of Judicial Inquiry'.

160. CM 3 (50) 1, PRO Cab 128/17.

161. CM 11 (50) 7, PRO Cab 128/17.

162. CM 62 (50) 4, PRO Cab 128/18.

163. Sir E. Baring to Secretary of State, Commonwealth Relations Office, 24 March 1950, para 28, Board of Trade Papers 11/4441, item 12 (PRO, London).

164. CO 537/5884, item 31.

165. Ibid., item 56 for meeting with Huggins; items 69 and 70 for meetings with Welensky.

166. Creech Jones to Sir A. Vincent, 10 August 1949, Creech Jones Papers, ACJ 7/4, fo. 74.

167. Memo on 'Relations of the Two Rhodesias and Nyasaland', 9 May 1950, by Cohen and Lambert, CO 537/5884.

168. CO 537/5887, item 134, for Griffith's remarks on 20 September 1950, but the special reference to consulting Africans was watered down at the request of the governor of Northern Rhodesia, ibid., item 140.

169. All the relevant papers are in CO 537/5923 and PREM 8/1113; also see CP (50) 270, PRO Cab 129/43; CM 76 (50) 1, PRO Cab 128/18.

170. Gupta, *Imperialism and the British Labour Movement*, p. 269.

171. CM 65 (48) 3, PRO Cab 128/13.

172. CP (48) 7, para 43, PRO Cab 129/23.

173. C.W.G. Greenidge to George Hall, 6 November 1945, CO 537/1224.

174. Minute by Listowel, 9 April 1948, CO 537/2588.

175. Creech Jones minuted on 25 May 1948 that the aim was laudable but education rather than legislation would solve the problem, CO 537/1224.

176. Letter to Attlee, 16 June 1948, from J.D. Murray, C.F. Grey, James Harrison, Frank Mcleavey, R.W.G. Mackay, T. Reid, Louis Tolley, T.J. Brooks, J.R. Leslie, Percy Holman and Meredith P. Titterington, Home Office Papers, 213/244 (PRO, London) (hereafter HO).

177. EPC (48), 23rd meeting, 15 June 1948, PREM 8/827.

178. 'Who Organised this Incursion?' Attlee to Creech Jones, 16 June 1948, PREM 8/827.
179. For the draft reply, HO 213/244; also see A.H. Poynton to T. Hutson, 6 July 1948, in the same file for Creech Jones' role.
180. Note by Attlee, 20 June 1948, PREM 8/827.
181. Memo by Havard, 15 February 1949, HO 213/869.
182. T.I.K. Lloyd to Sir Frank Newton, 11 October 1948, HO 213/716; CO memo on St Helena and on 'Unemployment in the West Indies'.
183. The files of this working party are HO 213/716 and HO 213/868.
184. HO 213/869.
185. HO 213/716, item 3, a ten-page report by the Ministry of Labour.
186. HO 213/868, paras 13–16 of the report.
187. Minutes by W.S. Murrie, 23 June 1949, and by Kenneth Younger, HO 213/870; note by J.E. Thomas of the Colonial Office, 8 October 1949.
188. CO 537/4273.
189. CM 13 (50) 7, PRO Cab 128/17.
190. CM 37 (50) 2, PRO Cab 128/17.
191. Goldsworthy (*Colonial Issues*, pp. 156ff) writes that 106 Labour MPs signed it. An inspection of the House of Commons register showed that 97 signed it on 26 February 1951, and another 15 on 27 February 1951.
192. J. Morris, *Farewell the Trumpets: An Imperial Retreat* (Harmondsworth, 1978), p. 497.

The Army in the
Imperial System

SECTION III

THE ARMY, POLITICS AND CONSTITUTIONAL CHANGE IN INDIA, 1919–1939*

INTRODUCTION

There is a 'Whig interpretation' in British historiography of the coming of independence in South Asia which sees it as a gradual; devolution of authority, going from precedent to precedent, with the intentions of the British government always moving in the same direction, disturbed occasionally by 'unreasonable' extremism on the part of 'die-hards' in Britain and extremist nationalists (terrorist or non-violent) in India. Both are considered basically irrelevant to the unfolding of a story in which the Montagu declaration of 1917 is a starting point, the Irwin declaration of 1929 a natural corollary, the Government of India Act of 1935 the working out of the details to meet the wishes of the heterogeneous peoples of South Asia, and the Cripps proposals of 1942 followed by transfer of power in 1947 the natural culmination. This approach is implicit or explicit in the writings of C.R. Attlee,[1] Percival Spear,[2] S.R. Mehrotra,[3] Peter Robb,[4] and C.H. Philips.[5] Other historians have also shown, in varying degrees, what appears to be an exaggerated enthusiasm for either the 1917 declaration or the inevitability of gradualness.[6] Those who note the bitter controversies in Britain's Conservative party over Indian independence still consider that the matter was settled in favour of independence with the defeat of Churchill's die-hard faction in 1935.[7] Under the influence of this historiography the main questions requiring explanation by the historian are the 'stop-go' character of the Indian nationalist movement, factions in the Congress and the growth and mutation of Muslim communalism and separatism: for the Raj, it is assumed, was trying since

*This paper was read at a seminar in 1982.

1917 to abdicate total power and the problem was really to whom to give it.[8]

Only four British historians appear to have questioned this approach and proceeded from the hypothesis that the aim of the Raj was not to work itself out of business but to find sophisticated and inexpensive ways of looking after its interests. John Darwin has posed the question generally for the empire as a whole,[9] and Tomlinson in his second book admits that Britain did not have any long-term plan of decolonisation but its short-term expedients created situations which brought decolonisation nearer.[10] The limitation of both Tomlinson's works is that he tends to regard the Government of India and Whitehall as two sharply contrasted decision-making authorities. A more perceptive essay than that of Tomlinson's is a paper by his teachers—John Gallagher, and Anil Seal—which frankly admits that the aims of the reforms of 1919 and 1935 were to safeguard imperial interests by concentrating power at the centre.[11]

To test the Whig hypothesis, this exploratory essay takes up a few problems connected with the evolution of the Indian armed forces. The problem is similar to that in the study made of the Indian Civil Service by D. Potter in 1973 and by T.H. Beaglehole in 1977.[12] But while Potter considers the nationalist movement to be of no relevance in his analysis of manpower shortage and decolonisation, my analysis of the Indianisation of the Indian army finds it relevant.

Before going into details, a brief summary of the argument may be stated. The transfer of defence capability to Indian hands was reluctantly conceded, and betrayed racial feeling among some important decision-makers. Even when it was conceded, its implementation was slow and subordinated to imperial security needs. The Government of India Act of 1935 had been intended by its framers to settle the Indian question for a long time to come, and when the success of the Congress in many provinces in 1937–9 appeared to undermine or threaten to undermine British control of defence and foreign affairs, the Government of India looked around for alternative collaborators, well before war actually started. However, the longer the war dragged on, new forces arose which brought about a revolution in the military thinking of the Raj, especially when Auchinleck was commander-in chief. For a time a new strategy to transfer power was contemplated by Wavell and Auchinleck which would be consistent with Britain's military (and, to a lesser extent, economic) interests east of Suez, and there are indications that the Cabinet Mission plan of 16 May took these into account. But by that time both Congress nationalism and Muslim separatism had taken too great a hold on the armed forces for the initiative to remain with the British.

1917–1931

Apropos of the Montford Reforms, Tomlinson and Robb, who have written on defence questions, have stressed the sensitivity of the Government of India to the central legislature, and Tomlinson noticed a discontinuity from past practice in the Government of India's refusal to pay for the use of Indian troops overseas.[13] Robb, after recording the racial prejudices that used to exist about giving commissions to Indians in the armed forces, mentions some central assembly resolutions on the Indianisation of the army as the beginning of a new departure.[14] The actual position on the role of the army, taken by the Government of India and Whitehall, however, suggests less discontinuity.

The use of India as a cheap reservoir of military manpower at the cost of Indian revenues was only an extreme form of imperial exploitation, to which repeated objections had been taken by Government of India in the time of Lord Dufferin, Lord Elgin and Lord Curzon.[15] None of these governors-general were interested in hastening decolonisation, and the arguments were purely financial. A more fundamental question was the ratio of British troops to Indian troops in India, the replacement of British officers by Indian officers and the abandonment of the principle of 'martial races' in recruiting soldiers.[16] On these issues the record of the Raj in the era of the Montford Reforms was characterised by prevarication.

Only three paragraphs of the Montford report dealt with the army, by contrast with a more extended treatment of the other public services. It sidestepped the question of broadening the basis of recruitment for the army as 'a large question in connection with the present proposals', and simply made a general recommendation that race should not be a bar to getting the King's Commission.[17] Probably under the influence of Attlee, the Indian Statutory Commission in 1930 took the Montford report to task for being so vague on these issues.[18] The true nature of the official and semi-official mind between 1918 and 1922 is to be seen in the report of the Army in India Committee (Esher Committee), the controversy over the creation of a European auxiliary force and an Indian territorial force, and the backlash that developed over the so-called Rawlinson report on the Indianisation of the army.

The Esher Committee ignored the question of Indianising the officer corps, and was no doubt facilitated in doing so because, of its two Indian members, one (Sir Umar Hayyat Khan) was as vehemently opposed to it as the other (Sir K.G. Gupta) was in favour of it.[19] No change in the two–one ratio of Indian and British troops was contemplated, and, among other measures designed to attract 'the pick of the Sandhurst cadets' to the Indian army, it was recommended that, notwithstanding the fact that the Indian Medical Service was being recruited more and more from India, British officers' wives and families should be treated by doctors of their own race. It continued to show an implied preference for the traditional catchment area of recruitment for the army ('the rural agricultural population . . . mainly in Northern India') and to ensure the continued loyalty of the classes from which the viceroy's commissioned officers were drawn by recommending liberal educational facilities for their sons, so that they could study at the Prince of Wales College at Dehra Dun and try for an army career.[20]

While the Esher Committee was sitting, Chelmsford was obliged, under strong pressure from the non-official European community in India and some army officers, to create an auxiliary force of Europeans, distinct from a volunteer territorial army for Indians for which the moderate members of the Indian legislature were pressing. The Indian moderates' idea of a mixed territorial force was ignored, for, as one officer put it, the 'ultimate *raison d'être*' of the European auxiliary force was 'the maintenance of British authority in India', while the Indian territorial force was a concession to political aspirations.[21] The auxiliary force became law by September 1920. In its correspondence with Whitehall the Government of India explained that if the regular army was to be ready for frontier or imperial purposes then this force was necessary for internal order.[22]

Later proposals about the Indian territorial force (to be manned by Indians) alarmed Churchill, who thought it 'most inadvisable to encourage any idea that India could develop an army responsible to the Indian legislature'. His misgivings were shared by Worthington-Evans, Secretary of State for War. Both were apprehensive that this would be the thin edge of the wedge by which Indian politicians would cut down the regular army in favour of the territorials. Reassurances had to be given to the effect that the territorial units 'were ... recruited from the loyal elements of the population', that in Madras 70 per cent were Christians, and that in Bombay the Parsee battalions had resisted the 'Gandhi agitators', before the Committee of Imperial Defence would consent to it.[23]

The alarmist prophesies of Churchill (made on 5 July 1922) were irrelevant, because for some time before that Whitehall had indicated, and the Government of India had accepted, that there was going to be no systematic Indianisation of the Indian army. Immediately after the legislative assembly resolutions of March 1921 (which Robb has cited) the Government of India had undertaken an exercise to see the implications of complete Indianisation under a committee headed by Sir John Shea (officiating chief of general staff). The report of this committee (referred to in the British records as the Rawlinson report because it came from Rawlinson, the commander-in-chief in India) had visualised a thirty-year period for complete Indianisation to take place. Its operational recommendations were the establishment of an Indian military college at a very early date (and *pari passu* stopping Indian entry into Sandhurst), and the gradual decrease of the British officers and the Viceroy's Commissioned Officers while Indian officers (holding a commission equivalent to a dominion commission) got trained.[24] When this report came before the subcommittee on Indian military requirements of the cabinet Committee of Imperial Defence, the Chief of the Imperial General Staff, Sir Henry Wilson, said that a considerable section of military opinion would, along with him, oppose the entry of Indians to the Royal College of Artillery at Woolwich, and there were misgivings about the right of entry into Sandhurst. He was unimpressed by the analogy with the Indian Civil Service because, while differences in the personal lifestyles of people from two races need not create problems in civilian occupations, they would do so in the army, where soldiers live in messes.[25] This racial sentiment was going to persist for another decade.

Even if equality of opportunity at Sandhurst was decried and at

Woolwich denied, it was still possible to act on the Shea Committee proposals for an Indian military college. But this idea withered before a broadside from the prime minister, Lloyd George, on 10 February 1922, when he presided over the cabinet committee discussing this scheme. Unimpressed by the argument that the Shea scheme was politically useful in India, that it prevented the chances of European officers serving under Indians, Lloyd George asked Sir Claud Jacob (military member of the Council of India) whether, as a military problem, it was safe to give Indians arms and equipment. Curzon also raised objections. When Jacob said that the Government of India proposals were based on the assumption 'that India should be ultimately handed over to Indians and that the British rule would cease', Lloyd George 'desired Sir Claud, on his return to India, to make it his business to let everybody know that it was the fixed and irrevocable intention of HMG to see that British ascendancy and British rule in India are maintained'. The minutes of this meeting clearly show that the decision pleased Sir Claud.[26] It certainly was no disappointment to Rawlinson, for shortly after he justified his support of the territorial army idea by saying that the latter would draw off 'agitation for early Indianisation of Regular Army'.[27]

Following a suggestion from Curzon at the same meeting (at which, it should be noted, the reformer Liberal E.S. Montagu remained silent after Lloyd George's intervention), the idea of Indianisation was confined to officering eight select units by Indians as and when they earned their commissions. Although this held the field till the breakthrough in 1931, Indian opinion regarded it as a form of segregation.[28]

During 1924, when the advent of a Labour government in Britain made all sections of the Indian members of the legislature close their ranks and press for moves for political change,[29] two Indian members of the Viceroy's Council (Sir Muhammad Shafi and Sir B.K. Sarma) pressed for reconsidering the eight-unit scheme and for a more rapid form of Indianisation. This was evidently a response to the political agitation started in the legislature,[30] for the same members had made no comments when the relevant file had originally come to them in January, except to say that 'the subject [was] of the highest importance' in its relation to the grant of self-government.[31] The European members of the council did not wish to abandon the scheme though some of them realised the need for some change. Malcolm Hailey, one of the shrewdest pro-consuls the Raj had seen, recommended a few moderate steps to the British government, by which the Labour government would not 'come under any political criticism' nor could nationalists continue to argue that the Raj was 'purposely restricting the field of recruitment in order to prove that no candidates [were] coming forward'. He recommended five more places for Indians at Sandhurst (ten were already provided), and scholarships on a liberal scale 'to carry men through both Dehra Dun and Sandhurst'. The social class he was aiming at was, of course, not the elite from which the Saprus, Nehrus or the Sastris came: 'I do believe that in the army specially you need to get men of decent birth, family and surroundings; but there are many such men of the smaller landowning classes who would possibly make better officers than those whose parents are able to provide a more expensive education'.[32] Hotley, C.A. Innes and Basil Blackett all seriously considered the suggestion that, parallel to the regular army, the gradual formation of a dominion army with dominion commission might be desirable. Innes said that 'responsibility for defence is a condition precedent of self-government'.[33] Rawlinson was opposed to the parallel development of the nucleus of a dominion army—'So long as I am Commander-in-Chief I will never sanction its being started'—and he was also sceptical of recommending to Whitehall the opening of places for Indians at Woolwich for the Royal Artillery. He knew of the resentment in the War Office because Indian entrants at Sandhurst entered after a comparatively simple qualifying examination, and for the highly technical science of modern artillery he could not contemplate sending Indian candidates except by open competitive examination.[34] The final recommendation to Whitehall was a compromise: so far as Sandhurst was concerned, the quota was to be increased from 10 to 16 for 1924–5, so that 20 per cent of the commissions in the Indian army would go to Indians; so far as the Royal Artillery and the Royal Air Force were concerned, the Government of India was aware that London did not like Indians being admitted to these branches of the British service, and so it recommended only that Indians should be declared eligible for entry to the colleges at Woolwich and Cranwell on the basis of open competition. The Government of India frankly admitted that in these areas its request was mainly an exercise in public relations: however slight its immediate practical result might be, it would serve to remove what is popularly regarded 'as a racial discrimination against the entry of Indians to certain branches of Army service'.[35]

No action was taken on this letter for the Labour government fell shortly after and the new secretary of state, Birkenhead, had no sympathy with such aspirations. His regime at the India Office, however, saw a thorough discussion at the highest level of the renewed demand put forward by Indian nationalists on this score and showed that both Whitehall and the Government of India (the former more than the latter) were most reluctant to share military secrets with Indians. There were limits to the technique of collaborating.

The occasion for this discussion was the report of the committee under Sir Andrew Skeen, set up in 1925 after the legislative assembly debates of the previous year, the members of which included Motilal Nehru, M.A. Jinnah and others. Although it represented a cross-section of the Indian political elite, the Indian side was united, and so a unanimous report was prepared. Motilal could not remain in the committee till the end because in March 1926, when he led the Swarajist walk-out of the central assembly, he offered his resignation.[36] But in the six months before that he and Jinnah had ensured that divisions on the Indian side would not be allowed to prevent a strong Indian case:

Abdul Qayum with all his communal leanings is at least a gentleman and Major Zorawar Singhji is a fine type of Rajput soldier very well educated and thoroughly independent.... He held a King's Commission and threw it up in disgust. From this alone you can imagine how valuable a colleague he will prove to Jinnah and me.[37]

This unity on the Indian side (in sharp contrast to the divisions in the Esher Committee) made the Skeen Committee proposals rather radical, disturbing the Government of India and horrifying Whitehall. By recommending the abandonment of the eight-unit scheme, increasing the vacancies at Sandhurst to between 20 and 38, and the grant of the King's Commission to Indians, it aimed at introducing racial equality in the officer corps of the army. By fixing a target date of 1933 for creating an Indian military college, providing scholarships for it and for the further training of Viceroy's Commissioned Officers there, it provided both an avenue for upward mobility of the rural classes from which the ordinary soldier was drawn and also a steady enlargement of the Indian officer corps. Eight vacancies for Woolwich and two for Cranwell were designed to create a nucleus of Indianised artillery and air force. On the other hand, the imperial connection was maintained by the continued provision of 20 vacancies at Sandhurst even after the Indian military college came into being and by retaining the British forces' proportion.

What disturbed both the Government of India and the Council of India about these proposals was not the demand for places at Woolwich and Cranwell (to which they were already committed) but the principle of racial equality. To abandon the eight-unit scheme and increase the number of places for Indians at Sandhurst would be prejudicial to British recruitment 'so long as British and Indian officers have to work their way up side by side within a single army, and often within the same regiments'. The Government of India proposed that the setting up of an Indian military college be postponed, the eight-unit scheme be kept with provision to absorb Indian commissioned officers, and the number of vacancies at Sandhurst be reduced, with a special quota for Viceroy's Commissioned Officers. The expanded eight-unit scheme would be similar to the nucleus of a dominion army.[38]

Four sittings of a subcommittee of the Committee of Imperial Defence debated this question from the end of November till the beginning of January. There was no sympathy for the Skeen Committee report and no one questioned Birkenhead's statement that 'the falling off in the number of British candidates of the right class for Commissions in the Indian Army' was due to 'the reluctance of parents to send their sons to serve under Indians and to live with Indians as mess mates'.[39] Sir Claud Jacob, Birkenhead and Churchill all considered that the Government of India proposal was the least objectionable that could be designed, since one could not entirely go back on the Montagu declaration—it would take at least 25 years for Indianisation to come about by this. As Churchill put it (and it was echoed by Birkenhead):

If we were to refuse to accept the proposals of the Government of India the matter would not rest there. As soon as another government came into power they would probably find it expedient to initiate an even more undesirable policy. On the other hand, if we kept the ground fully occupied by this proposal we would be in a good strategical position and could reply with truth for many years to come that we were doing our best to meet Indian susceptibilities.[40]

In the Whig interpretation, Birkenhead and Churchill are usually regarded as Tory die-hards and they are contrasted with more liberal Tories like Samuel Hoare. The minutes of this discussion, both on the phrase 'dominion army' and on the question of admissions to Woolwich and Cranwell, show that on the eve of the agitation in India over the Simon Commission and the Civil Disobedience Movement which followed shortly after there was such a general hostility to surrendering the springs of real power to Indian hands that even phrases were objected to. Birkenhead could not get the committee to accept the phrase 'dominion army' in its observations on the Government of India despatch, even though he assured them that neither dominion status nor dominion army 'would be brought a day nearer by merely being recognised as ultimate goals', and neither was likely to be attained 'in the lifetime of this generation'.[41] In the absence of Birkenhead, the committee was persuaded by the Army Council to postpone Indian admission to Woolwich until the eight-unit scheme proved a success; earlier Hoare had objected to Indians joining the British Air Force as a result of getting admission to Cranwell. Birkenhead needed another meeting with the committee to persuade them to modify this partially. The War Office representative, being assured that the examination would be 'as stiff as possible' and admission would be contingent on future employment prospects in India, agreed to concede the right of admission to Woolwich. So far as Cranwell was concerned, since there was no Indian air force at that time, and since Hoare could not agree 'to anything in the nature of a mixed Air Force', the decision was to make no recommendations about the number to be admitted (which was the demand of the Skeen Committee and the Government of India despatch) but simply to say that Indians would be eligible as soon as a satisfactory scheme for subsequent employment in an Indian air unit was made.[42] This virtually put paid to the early development of an Indian air force.

From this *cul-de-sac* the prospects of Indianisation were rescued by the tempo of the nationalist movement. Without the agitation against the Simon Commission Lord Irwin would not have felt the need to make the announcement about dominion status in October 1929 and about the prospect of a round table conference in London.[43] Without the increased tempo of the Civil Disobedience Movement the Labour government would not have thought it necessary as far as possible to meet the demands of those who came to the First Round Table Conference.[44] The contrast between the Government of India despatch of October 1927 (the Skeen Committee covering note) and the later despatch of September 1930 (dealing with the Simon Commission report) is instructive. The latter was written in the midst of a political crisis. The Simon report itself, though composed by more than one hand, could not but take cognisance of the debate on this question which had gone on since the Shea Committee report, and since some Indians believed that the Skeen Committee report had been rejected. Somewhat disingenuously, the Simon report skirted the history of the Skeen Committee and its aftermath. Probably under the influence of Attlee, it emphasised that if self-government was the goal, the question could not be left to vague generalities, as in the Montford report. Indians should not imagine that difficulties in the way of rapid Indianisation were mentioned for the sake of gloating over them.[45] The Government of India despatch referred all the points of view for discussion at the round table conference.[46] There, in spite of the misgivings of Thomas and Sir George Milne, a unanimous recommendation was made for an Indian military academy and the throwing open of all branches of the forces to Indians.[47] From this decision, theoretically at any rate, there was no going back. Theoretically, then, there is some truth in regarding the opening of the Indian Military Academy at Dehra Dun in December 1932 as an earnest that the British intended to leave India one day.[48]

1932–1939

Even this proposition, however, can be questioned, and the military academy can be interpreted as an agency for creating a new loyalist military elite of collaborators whose training would be less expensive than at Sandhurst. There is a lot of evidence as to how the Conservative elements in London and New Delhi regarded the new military dispensation. One area on which work still needs to be done is an analysis of the social background of the Indian officers who were coming out of Dehra Dun at the rate of 56 a year by 1938, and the criteria for selecting such cadets. It is probable that the bias still went in favour of 'the martial races', following Churchill's preference for 'Indians of the polo playing class, such as the Rajputs', who 'probably made a far better officer than the more nimble minded and quicker developed Bengali'.[49] That at the beginning of the war the catchment area for recruitment was still the traditional areas in the north is suggested by statistics compiled at the time of the Cripps Mission,[50] and that these areas were still regarded by Churchill as most reliable is seen from a letter of his in 1944.[51]

In any case, the framers of the Act of 1935 and the rulers who governed according to the Act did not intend to surrender defence and foreign affairs to Indian hands. Although many sections of Indian opinion had argued before the joint select committee for a time-bound programme for the complete Indianisation of the Indian army, and although Attlee cross-examined Samuel Hoare for an undertaking on this,[52] the report of the joint select committee refused to commit itself on this and, following the White Paper of 1933, simply spoke of the desirability of consultation by the governor-general with his other ministers on matters pertaining to defence.[53]

Expenditure on defence was lower in the 1930s than earlier, but it was still the largest item in the central budget.[54] Even at the height of the Depression, when the Government of India had, in order to balance the budget, done a fair amount of retrenchment, only minimal reductions were made in the army and there were no reductions in the number of British troops. When the Viceroy's Council was divided over securing a saving of Rs 5 crores in the defence budget, the commander-in-chief, Lord Chetwode, argued that 'armed forces alone stood between order and anarchy', and his position was upheld; no reductions of British troops were permitted.[55]

Tomlinson's account of Indian defence expenditure, his treatment of the cost of British troops, and his reference to the Garran tribunal give a misleading impression of the position of India in the imperial system. To talk about India being reintegrated into the imperial system suggests that India went out of it somewhere in the early 1920s.[56] As I have argued earlier, use of Indian troops at India's expense outside India is only an extreme form of imperial domination. As long as the Indian army was officered by Britons, British troops remained in India and Indian revenues had to pay towards the cost of training these British troops by the 'capitation charges', India was part of the imperial system.

The Garran tribunal was set up as a device to cope with the vexed question of 'capitation charges' in the context of the new constitutional settlement proposed after 1931. That the tribunal on this occasion recommended payments *to* India (unlike earlier tribunals in Curzon's time, which had demanded payment *from* India) should not make us ignore some significant points made by the majority of its members. They rejected as arguments the fact of India's capacity to pay, her dependent position, political sentiment in India, and the need for generosity. They also agreed with the War Office view that 'the attempt to weigh in the balance the value of the advantage derived, on one side or the other, from the defence of India by the Empire and the defence of Empire by India' was a barren and impossible task.[57] Essentially, the decision of the Garran tribunal represents a paradox. In a period of economic Depression and political manoeuvrings, Britain had to pay to enjoy her empire. The more the British wished to ignore Indian nationalism and to be free to use India for their imperial foreign and defence policy, the more they had to pay India. Pursuit of power meant the disgorgement of profit—economic imperialism turned upside down.

The architects of the Government of India Act of 1935—of which the viceroy, Lord Linlithgow, was one—had described the Indian National Congress as 'a section of opinion in India with whom the prospect of agreement appeared remote', and placed their faith in 'a body of central opinion' in India which would work the constitution in the way the National government in Britain would have liked.[58] The electoral victories of the Congress in 1937 and its acceptance of office in six provinces was a setback to those aspirations unless the Congress (or part of it) could be made collaborators in terms of the Raj. As yet the All-India Muslim League was without any base in the Muslim-majority provinces, where provincial governments were based on regional cross-communal alliances under Muslim chief ministers. The Congress was also the leading opposition party in the central assembly and it had indicated in its programme for these years that it wanted to hasten the pace of constitutional change, prevent the princely states' representatives coming to the federal assembly simply on the basis of nomination, and expected to be consulted on matters of foreign policy.

By the time the provincial ministries were in office, Britain imperial foreign policy was threatened by Italy's ascendancy in Ethiopia and the possible threat to Egypt and the Suez route, the Azab revolt in Palestine and the need to have the goodwill of the other Arab states in the solution of that crisis, the German menace in Europe, and the Sino-Japanese war in the Far East. Although most supporters of Neville Chamberlain's government approved all the policies of appeasement in 1938 (recognition of Italian conquest in Ethiopia, *anschluss* with Austria, and the occupation of Sudetenland), the Committee of Imperial Defence had discussions and contingency planning for any eventuality.[59] The involvement of the official classes in India in these discussions and their subsequent confidential assessments show that they never gave any serious thought as to whether, with the threatening war-clouds all round, greater consultation with Indians about central responsibility was desirable. On the contrary, long before the outbreak of the war, the Congress had been marked as a major threat to British control at the centre, and the Muslims and the princes had been deemed 'trump cards'. The alienation of the Congress from the Raj in time of war (even an ardent anti-Fascist like Nehru) and the coming together of the Muslim League and the Raj in the twelve months after September 1939 (which is well documented in three recent works by Gopal, Rizvi and Moore[60]) followed inexorably from the assumptions and prejudices of the official classes in both Delhi and London.

The Finance member of the Government of India from 1934 to April 1939 was Sir James Grigg. His autobiography and private papers make it quite clear that he had no sympathy with the Congress at all, had strong imperialist views about the maintenance of British supremacy, of giving no opportunity to the Congress or any other party to whittle down the safeguards, and that he was acutely conscious of the international situation. His view on defence expenditure and the distribution of costs between Delhi and London was expressed in a letter to Lord Trenchard when the latter asked him to develop an air wing in India. Explaining why that was impossible, he argued that owing to excessive cuts in his predecessor's regime, arrears of equipment, etc., heavy demands made for the army and 'any sudden or dramatic increase in Defence expenditure would exasperate political opinion out here a great deal'. Pointing out that the UK did not contribute enough towards the Indian defence budget, considering 'the enormous value to the Empire generally of the existence in India of 60,000 white troops on an active service footing', he suggested that, if the UK contribution were raised from £11/2 million to £5, it would be easier for the UK to control their disposition.[61] In April 1935, with the British defence plans focused to meet the German air menace, this suggestion fell on deaf ears, but by January 1938 the contradictions between imperial needs, on the one hand, and considerations of political management in India, on the other, were so acute that Grigg privately briefed Sir Horace Wilson about the Indian situation as he saw it. The effects of War Minister Hore-Belisha's wage increases for British soldiers generally imposed a corresponding obligation on the Indian budget for the British soldier in India, and this, together with the modernisation plans of the Indian army, could not be met out of revenue unless either the UK helped or Grigg raided the 'Sinking Fund'. The latter course would cause a conflict with the provincial governments because the 'fund' was expected by them to cover their needs and its use to pay more wages to British troops ('an already extravagantly expensive element in the Army in India') might provoke a constitutional crisis and resignations from the provincial ministries for which Grigg was unwilling then to be responsible.[62] Official inter-departmental discussions between March and June 1938 on imperial violence and India's role, along with India's army modernisation schemes, produced the report of the Pownall Committee, and financial appreciations from the Government of India. A point repeatedly emphasised by the Government of India in its papers to this committee was the hostility of Indian, especially Congress, opinion to increases in the defence budget and the use of Indian troops abroad.[63]

In July 1938, when the high-level cabinet Committee on Defence Coordination discussed this issue over three days, this picture of the Congress as being totally indifferent to the menace of Fascism was not entirely true, and was going to be even less true in twelve months' time. To be sure, the Congress president, Subhas Bose, made no secret of his desire to take advantage of the next war to win Indian independence, but ex-president Jawaharlal Nehru had just completed a visit to Britain where he had made known his hostility to Fascism in no uncertain terms and made clear that, if Britain abandoned imperialism, India would support an anti-Fascist war.[64] Even Grigg had admitted in his letter to Horace Wilson that since the Sino-Japanese war aversion to discussing questions of defence was less strong. However, the official classes chose not to explore any new constitutional breakthroughs but the ways and means to assess India's military requirements in terms of imperial needs, and how this could be done without reducing the proportion of British troops in India. Zetland, secretary of state for India, accepted the principle of having an imperial reserve division provided Britain helped finance the modernisation scheme in India. When arguments developed over the latter, with the War Office and the Treasury unwilling to approve a package deal without further inquiry on India's needs and ability to pay, Zetland betrayed the old fear of total Indianisation when he initially opposed sending a committee to India: 'The opportunity would be seized by the advocates of Indianization to point to the high costs of the British establishment, to argue that a wholly Indian army would be much cheaper, and in general to exploit the situation.'[65] Eventually a formula was found by which the Chatfield committee could visit India without it appearing politically provocative .

Admiral Chatfield's political links were with the 'die-hard' wing of the Conservative party (his son-in-law Sir P. Donner had been an official of Churchill's India Defence League), and his report made candid political judgements on the Indian situation from an imperial, anti-Congress, and somewhat pro-Muslim League standpoint.[66] The report warned that even if Congress accepted the federation without demanding the amendment of the Government of India Act of 1935, it would try to whittle down the safeguards; to guard against this, the report added (with emphasis) that the responsibility for the defence of India should rest, through the Government of India and the secretary of state, with the British government and no one else, 'either before or after the coming of the Federation'.[67]

The Chatfield report was ready by February 1939. A very recent work, which is strong on military history but weak on Indian political background, comments that, in making no distinction between Indian and imperial interests in defence, the committee was making 'a bold assumption in view of India's progress towards self-government'.[68] This is a misplaced criticism because, in the mind of the Government of India, India's progress towards self-government had still a long, long way to go and the entire approach towards inviting the Chatfield Committee was guided by the assumption that the Act of 1935 had given the governor-general special powers precisely for situations like this.

The Chatfield report was considered politically so explosive that Secretary of State Marquess of Zetland, while accepting it, suggested to the cabinet that it be kept secret; if the viceroy wished to show it to others, he should do so only to European officials.[69] Linlithgow was also prepared to back the Chatfield report if London would assure him 'support . . . in any measure which he might find it necessary to take in the event of a major crisis'.[70]

Also at the end of February 1939, the commander-in-chief, Lord Cassels, profoundly disturbed at the growing agitation in the princely states and the anti-recruitment campaign in the Punjab, initiated a private discussion between the viceroy, Home Member Maxwell, Finance member Grigg, Laithwaite, Private Secretary to the Viceroy, and himself. These officials were all agreed that far too much latitude had been given to the provincial governments and special powers seldom exercised (Grigg and Cassels being particularly vehement) and that no opportunity should be given for the Congress to stake a claim for central responsibility. With the army's loyalty ensured, it was felt that the Muslims and the princes should be used as two trump cards against the Congress if the latter made a bid for power at the centre when Britain was at war. The entire scenario of the twelve-month period from September 1939 was already sketched out.[71] Linlithgow's remarks on supporting the Chatfield report and riding out any political crisis must be read in the context of this strategy. It was about the same time that Zetland gave Chaudhury Khaliquzzaman some verbal assurances of support about Pakistan.

The involvement of India in the war without Congress support but with the support of other political groups, especially the Muslim League, did not help towards augmenting British power or profit, even if it helped maintain the prestige of a Raj that refused to be hustled into constitutional change under duress. The piling up of the sterling balances in India's favour as a result of the war was a further illustration of the point made earlier—the more Britain tried to keep the empire, the more she had to pay for it.

EPILOGUE

Only in course of the war was the principle of 'martial races' abandoned, and unprecedented expansion took place in the army, navy and air force. By the end of the war official assessments did not rate the threshold of loyalty to the Raj on the part of the two new services very high.[72] The nationalist movement had failed in 1942, but its use of the INA trials was very effective as a form of political mobilisation, and made the commander-in-chief, Auchinleck, realise that almost every middle-class Indian officer was a nationalist. More British officers were now beginning to realise that the racialist policies of an earlier generation had turned most officers (even of Sandhurst vintage) to aspire to serve as officers of free nations.[73] The imperial sunset was inevitable under such circumstances.

NOTES

1. C.R. Attlee, *Empire into Commonwealth* (Oxford, 1961).
2. P. Spear, *Oxford History of Modern India, 1740–1947* (New Delhi, 1976).
3. S.R. Mehrotra, *India and the Commonwealth* (London, 1965).
4. P.J. Robb, *The Government of India and Reform* (Oxford, 1976).
5. C.H. Philips, introduction to H.I. Singh, *Problems and Politics of the British in India, 1885–1898* (Bombay, 1963).
6. Judith M. Brown, 'Imperial Facade: Some Constraints Upon and Contradictions in the British Position in India, 1919–35', *Transactions of the Royal Historical Society*, XXVI (1976), pp. 35–52.
7. D.A. Low, *Lion Rampant* (London, 1973), p. 170.
8. 'Between 1917 and 1940 India advanced steadily towards freedom and it seems inexorably towards division. The process of devolution generated the crisis of Indian unity.' (R.J. Moore, *The Crisis of Indian Unity, 1917–1940* [Oxford, 1974]), p. 317.
9. John Darwin, 'Imperialism in Decline? Tendencies in British Imperial Policy between the Wars', *Historical Journal*, XXIII (1980), pp. 657–80.
10. B.R. Tomlinson, *The Political Economy of the Raj* (London, 1979), p. 151.
11. J. Gallagher and A. Seal, 'Britain and India between the Wars', in C. Baker, G. Johnson and A. Seal (eds), *Power, Profit, and Politics* (Cambridge, 1981), pp. 404–7. Gallagher had characterised the Government of India Act of 1935 as a technique of keeping India under the Raj, in his earlier paper in 'Locality, Province, and the Nation': *Essays on Indian Politics, 1870–1940* (Cambridge, 1973). In this respect he does not fit into the 'Whig' category at all. His critical analysis of the divisions in the ranks of Indian nationalists should not blind Indian historians to the perceptive analysis of the contradictions in British imperialism which he made in this paper published posthumously.

12. D. Potter, 'Manpower Shortage and the End of Colonialism: The Case of the ICS', *Modern Asian Studies*, VII (1973); T.H. Beaglehole, 'From Rulers to Servants: The ICS and the British Demission of Power in India', ibid., XI (1977).

13. B.R. Tomlinson, *Indian National Congress and the Raj* (London, 1976), p. 13. A fuller account of the debate on using Indian troops overseas in the immediate aftermath of the First World War will be found in Keith Jeffrey, 'An English Barrack in the Oriental Seas? India in the Aftermath of the First World War', in Baker, Johnson, and Seal (eds), *Power, Profit, and Politics*, pp. 369–86.

14. Robb, *op.cit.*, pp. 46–50, 279–80.

15. The most thorough discussion is in Werner Simon, *Die Britische Militarpolitik in Indian* (Wiesbaden: Franz Steiner, 1974); also see R.C. on expenditure in India: First Report (c. 8258), Parliamentary Papers (hereafter Parl. Pap.) 1896, XV, and Parl. Pap. 1902, LXX, 515.

16. For a general account of these, Philip Mason, *A Matter of Honour* (London, 1974).

17. *Report on Indian Constitutional Reform* (cd. 9109), Parl. Pap. 1918, VIII, pp. 260–4.

18. See note 44 below.

19. Army in India Committee (Cmd 943), Parl. Pap. 1920, XIV, pp. 79, 103, 105.

20. Ibid., part V, paras 17, 59–60.

21. National Archives of India (hereafter NAI), Army dep., Org. A, November 192 , 2068–79, note by Lt-Col Nevil dated 8 July 1919; also see connected file, NAI, Army, Org., March 1921, Prog. 2462–80.

22. Government of India to Secretary of State, 13 May 1920 (NAI, Army, Org., March 1921; Prog. 2471).

23. PRO, Cab 2/3, Minutes of Committee of Imperial Defence, 158th & 166th meetings, 5 July and 21 July 1922.

24. 'Rates of pay and type of commission to be granted to Indian officers of the Indian Army under a full scheme of Indianization', NAI, Army, Org. B, December 1924, No. 333 and appendix. This gives a summary of the report.

25. Wilson's comments on 12 January 1922 at a meeting of the Indian Military Requirements Sub-Committee of the Committee of Imperial Defence, Cab 16/38 (PRO).

26. Cab 16, IMR, 9th meeting, 10 February 1922.

27. Rawlinson to Lord Cavan (CIGS), 28 June 1922, in Cab 6/4, 127–D.

28. The Simon Commission noted this. See paras 122–5 of the Report of the Indian Statutory Commission.

29. P.S. Gupta, *Imperialism and the British Labour Movement* (London, 1975), pp. 103–8.
30. Their move is mentioned in Reading's order-in-council, which, however, decided against reconsidering the eight-unit scheme, dated 27 June 1924, NAI, Army, Org. B, December 1924, No. 333, pp. 15ff.
31. Note dated 27 January 1924, by B.N. Sarma, in ibid., p. 11.
32. Ibid., dated 22 March 1924.
33. Ibid., dated 22 and 23 January 1924.
34. Ibid., Rawlinson's note, 11 April 1924, and a further note in ibid., appendix p. 9.
35. Government of India, Army Dept. of Secretary of State, 24 July 1924 (No. 33 of 1924), para 4, in ibid.
36. He told his son that his resignation was perhaps a hasty decision (M.L. Nehru to J.L. Nehru, 11 March 1926, in Nehru Memorial Library, MLN-JN XIII).
37. MLN to JLN, 14 September 1925, *loc.cit.*
38. Government of India views, set forth in letters dated 18 July 1927 and 13 October 1927, are in Cab 16/78, IIA 2. The phrase quoted is in Birkenhead's covering letter, 24 November 1927, for the cabinet committee's meeting, ibid.
39. Cab 16/78, IIA, first meeting, 28 November 1927.
40. Ibid., p. 2, and Birkenhead's reference to it at a later meeting on 15 December 1927.
41. Observations on 15 December 1927 and also Birkenhead to Irwin, 12 January 1928 (Halifax Papers).
42. Cab 16/78, IIA 4; also see minutes of meetings of 12 and 15 December 1927.
43. Tomlinson, *Indian National Congress,* p. 16; Gupta, *op.cit.,* pp. 200–3.
44. Benn's memo of 29 October 1930, quoted in Gupta, *op.cit.,* p. 211.
45. Para 111 and 119, 122–6. Also see Attlee, *op.cit.,* p. 34.
46. Proposals for Constitutional Reform, 20 September 1930 (Cmd 3700), Parl. Pap. 1930–1, XXIII, pp. 138–44. That the Government of India Left it to the round table conference, is all the more significant when we note that the view of the prospective commander-in-chief, expressed about three weeks after the Irwin declaration was one of extreme gradualism and against racial equality. In a letter to the former Conservative secretary of state for war, he wrote: 'Nobody supposes for a moment that India can remain as she is for ever in leading strings, but even with the amount of Indianization that has already come about in many of the services, the machinery creaks. . . . Any further experiments in Indianization of the Army must be very gradual in my opinion . . . if we do so in a hurry and

if there is any suggestion of British officers coming under the command of Indians, the supply of British officers for the Indian army will dry up at once, and that will be very serious.' (Philip Chetwode to L. Worthington-Evans, 18 November 1929 (Worthington-Evans Papers, Oxford, Bodleian Ms Eng. Hist. c. 897 ff 142–3).

47. Gupta, *op.cit.*, p. 172.
48. Philip Mason, *op.cit.*, p. 172.
49. The Churchill quotation is from Cab 16/78, 28 November 1927.
50. Mansergh and Moon, *Transfer of Power*, I, doc. no. 246.
51. Quoted in J. Connell, *Auchinleck*, p. 771.
52. Joint Select Committee, mins of ev. qq 6850–2, 6955, 8243, 8245, 8440–8 (in Parl. Pap. 1934, VII); also ibid., vol. VIII, p. 1386.
53. Contrast the White Paper (Cmd 4268), para 23, with Joint Committee report, paras 173ff.
54. Tomlinson, *Political Economy*, p. 155.
55. Cab 16/85, DI 42 and DI 16th meeting, 8 November 1932.
56. Tomlinson, *op.cit.*, pp. 138–9.
57. Cmd 4473, pp. 8–10, 14 (Parl. Pap. 1933–4, IX).
58. Committee on Indian Constitutional Reform, *Report*, p. 25.
59. Brian Bond, *British Military Policy between the two Wars* (Oxford 1980); Gallagher and Seal, *op.cit.*, pp. 411f.
60. S. Gopal, *Jawaharlal Nehru*, vol. I (1975), ch. 16; G. Rizvi, *Linlithgow and India* (London, 1978); R.J. Moore, *Churchill, Cripps and India* (Oxford, 1979), ch. 2, sections i & ii.
61. P.J. Grigg to Lord Trenchard, 22 April 1935 (Grigg Papers).
62. P.J. Grigg to Horace Wilson, 16 January 1938, ibid.
63. Cab 27/653. Also see Brian Bond, *British Military Policy between the Two Wars*.
64. Gopal, *op.cit.*, pp. 233–8; also *Selected Works of Nehru*, vol. IX.
65. Cab 27/653, ID (38), 2nd meeting, 14 July 1938, p. 95.
66. Cab 27/654 ID (38) 10, enclosure, paras 14–17.
67. Ibid., para 19.
68. Bond, *op.cit.*, p. 122.
69. Cab 27/653, Committee on Defence of India, 4th meeting, 20 February 1939.
70. Cab 27/653, 5th meeting, 22 May 1939.
71. Lord Cassels to Viceroy (Most Secret), 20 February 1939, and Proceedings of a meeting held at the Viceroy's House, 26 February 1939 (Grigg Papers).
72. *Transfer of Power*, VII, doc. no. 60.
73. Connell, *Auchinleck*, pp. 948–9.

IMPERIAL STRATEGY AND THE
TRANSFER OF POWER,
1939–1951*

This essay, while trying to do justice to the period 1947–50, will will look at the years from 1939 to 1951. This is required by the question of British imperial strategy in relation to the transfer of power in South Asia. There were elements of continuity as well as significant elements of change in the resources available to the imperial power, in the personnel of the British government and the British Parliament, in the domestic and international priorities of the government in Britain, and consequent shifts in the angle of vision from which the Indian situation was viewed in the critical two years before 15 August 1947.[1] It is necessary to refer to the period till the end of 1951, because in these latter years the former imperial power, though no longer in command of the situation inside the subcontinent, tried to retrieve some of its goals which it had been forced to jettison in the bloody aftermath of August 1947. The motives for wanting to have India in the commonwealth even as a republic, and the hopes and

* This paper was read at a seminar in Delhi in 1984, and published in Amit Kumar Gupta (ed.), *Myth and Reality: The Struggle for Freedom in India, 1945–47* (Delhi, 1987), pp. 1–53.

I consulted the unpublished British sources used in this paper during 1980–1 when I was Smuts Visiting Fellow at Cambridge, and would like to acknowledge the generosity of the Smuts Memorial Fund. Unpublished Crown copyright records, whether in the Public Record Office (hereafter PRO) or the India Office Records (hereafter IOR) reproduced in this paper appear by permission of the Controller of Her Majesty's Stationery Office. I am also grateful for permission to consult and quote from various other private records in Britain, which are acknowledged wherever the first citation from such records occurs in the notes. The records of the Government of India and the papers of General Cariappa have been consulted and quoted from with the permission of the National Archives of India.

achievements of imperial strategy in this area, are a continuation of the issues seriously debated in British circles during 1945–7.

Indians, who have been at the receiving end of major decisions taken in the metropolis, and in particular former residents of western Punjab and East Bengal (and the author is one of them) are often prone to attributing the exact shape of changes that occurred in August 1947 and which affected their families to a well-planned imperial design. This is understandable, but it misses out three very important hypotheses for provincial ministries for which the evidence is very plentiful, and difficult to refute. First, both during the war, and during post-war strategic planning, a very high priority was given by the British War Office and the Indian Commander-in-Chief Claude Auchinleck (with the support of the ex-soldier Viceroy Lord Wavell) for retaining the subcontinent as a single unit in terms of defence organisation and defence potential, whatever be the nature of political devolution in other spheres. Second, the strength of social, religious, and political movements in India had reached such a fever pitch that the imperial masters could take few of their erstwhile allies for granted, and had repeatedly to lower their sights. Third, there were divisions within the British government between foreign minister Ernest Bevin (who had an imperial vision, tinged with a strain of anti-Americanism)[2] and Chancellor of the Exchequer Hugh Dalton, who, along with many others, had a 'little England' vision, and considered overseas military expenditure to be a liability. To reconcile these conflicting aims, in 1946–47 the British government tried to keep all options open, hoping that it would have plenty of room for manoeuvre for its long-term strategic aims. As often happens in life, in trying to do this, particularly when resources are scarce, one ends up having very little option at all.

Strategy has been defined as 'military economy'—the deployment of scarce resources for alternative uses.[3] Ever since the end of the First World War the problem facing any imperially minded British government (and most of them were imperially minded) was how to decide between these alternatives. The advantages of India as a market, field for investment and provider of well-paid civil service and military posts for middle-class Britons had to be balanced against the costs of suppressing mass movements, concessions given to Indians in the services and in business, and of political devolution in the form of provincial autonomy. Leading Conservative politicians (Sir Samuel Hoare and Neville Chamberlain among them) have Left on record their private views that in 1932 their aim in accepting provincial autonomy was to keep control at the centre but divide an all-India anti-imperial front by encouraging greater diversity in the politics of the subcontinent.[4] The fact that the all-India nationalist party (the Congress) failed to win the provincial elections of 1937 in all the provinces, and the important provinces of Punjab and Bengal went to regionally based parties appeared partially to vindicate the strategy. However, on the eve of the outbreak of the war, this constitutional political strategy via constitution making had revealed some inner contradictions. In the Congress-ruled provinces, much to the disappointment of the British authorities, provincial autonomy did not lead to any fragmentation of the all-India, nationalist perspective of the Congress.[5] The rivalry between the Congress right wing and the Left wing also could not be turned to imperial advantage. Finance Member Sir James Grigg considered the Congress right wing to be a greater danger to British economic interests than the left wing.[6] Linlithgow shared the view that Congress was a threat to British commercial interests.[7] The second contradiction lay in the slowness and ultimate failure in getting the princely states to accede to federation. The third, and from the military angle the most important, was the inability of the Indian finances, after meeting the costs of provincial autonomy, to spare any resources for imperial defence or the mechanisation of the Indian armed forces.[8]

In 1939, when the Chatfield Committee had given its report on this last question, it had considered the Muslim leaders to be more responsive than the Hindu leaders to the questions they were raising. They paid scant regard, however, to the issue of rapid Indianisation of the army officer corps.[9] Though the report was considered politically so explosive that Zetland advised that it should not be shown to the Indian members of the Viceroy's Council, Linlithgow was prepared to accept the report in its entirety if he was supported in any firm stand he took against political opposition.[10] In the politics of the eleven months between the outbreak of war and the 'August offer' of 1940, we can see the working out of this mentality of divide and rule in its crudest form. The greatest imperial politician of the period was frank enough to put it on record at a cabinet meeting on 2 February 1940. Arguing against Lord Halifax, Churchill said:

he did not share the anxiety to encourage and promote unity between the Hindu and Muslim communities. Such unity . . . if it were to be brought about, the immediate result would be that the united communities would join in showing us the door. He regarded the Hindu–Muslim feud as the bulwark of British rule in India.[11]

(i) From the Singapore debacle to the end of the war, 1942–1945

The Cripps Mission with its promise of a constituent assembly to decide the constitution of India on the basis of one or more dominions would not have come but for the British naval and military disasters in Southeast Asia. These made Attlee apprehensive that unless a mission was sent with a definite promise of post-war independence India might be lost to the commonwealth. The familiar story of how the mission was sabotaged by Linlithgow and Churchill, and how Wavell, as commander-in-chief, refused to entrust the defence portfolio to an Indian[12] needs no retelling. Even the 'Quit India' movement, remarkable though it was in heroism and self-sacrifice, did not succeed in its immediate objective of driving out the British. However, three important developments, which were connected with the British recovery of their military position, had started undermining the structure of imperial control based on the bureaucracy, a loyal army, and the dominance of the British businessmen during the war. Ideally, from the imperial point of view, the bureaucracy, whether recruited in the UK or India, would loyally serve the interests of the Raj. In practice, the matter was more complex. While in periods of mass upheaval, most of the Indian members of the services would play safe, in the more quiescent periods of political change (1922–9, 1932–9) their role can be shown to have been in support of liberal nationalist points of view, whether it be over fiscal autonomy, reduction of the safeguards for British business interests, or Indianisation of the officer cadre of the armed forces.[13] With the stopping of recruitment of Britons in the UK from 1941, more and more key positions came to be held by people from this stratum.[14] The Viceroy's Council over which Linlithgow and Wavell presided contained spokesmen of Indian business interests. In the former's council, Nalini Ranjan Sarkar helped stiffen the resistance against the scaling down of India's sterling balances, although Churchill would have dearly loved to do it.[15] In the latter's, Sir Ardeshir Dalal became member for planning and development in May 1944, and a British businessman confided in his diary that though this would be 'a popular move with Congress', it was also 'capitulation' to the FICCI, and that 'a brown bloodsucking oligarchy will be worse than a white bureaucracy'.[16] The same commentator had, two years before, realised the weakening position of the expatriate businessman after Britain's military reverses:

. . . Searchers for scapegoats have been making a dead set against the British businessman in the East and blaming him partly for reverses in Malay and Burma. Left wing politicians here hold the field even in the Conservative Party, and British business and British individuals in the East are of no account to them.[17]

During the period of the Cripps Mission, the British business community was split over a speech made by Lord Catto in the House of Lords saying that the 'safeguards' in the Government of India Act (1935) were an anachronism. Under these safeguards the viceroy had special powers to prevent discriminatory legislation against British imports and British expatriate business interests including shipping, and also to prevent any alteration in the rupee-sterling exchange rate if it hurt British interests. Benthall's own position was in favour of some protection but avoidance of the word 'safeguards'—he wrote to his die-hard correspondent that, after the Cripps Mission, 'our community should recognise that these safeguards as we know them, and dominion status do not go together'.[18]

A future governor of the Punjab, Evan Jenkin (whose brother was a senior executive at Calcutta), produced a programme for planned industrialization and hoped that the sterling balances would facilitate the supply of equipment from Britain rather than the US.'He argued that cooperation from Indian business would be forthcoming only if the 'safeguards' were abandoned.[19] The imperial assessment of the Indian business groups early in 1944 came in the context of the publication of the 'Bombay Plan'—an intelligence branch report assumed that left wing socialists belonging to the Congress Socialist Party were increasing in influence in the Congress, and described the relationship between the industrialists who sponsored the 'Bombay Plan' and the Congress as 'a partnership of convenience with no illusion on either side'.[20]

Inch by inch, under pressure, the same party which had put in the 'safeguards' of the 1935 act was forced to reconsider it. Sir John Colville, governor of Bombay, had been a former Conservative MP and a minister in the Board of Trade when that act was passed. Experience as governor made him ask for their repeal.[21] Taking a cue from a legislative assembly resolution by Manu Subedar on 3 March 1945, Dalal promised reconsideration of the 'safeguards' question. Before a team of Indian industrialists visited Britain to meet the Federation of British Industries on 30 May, under Dalal's prompting, Wavell managed to get the Cabinet's India Committee to drop the safeguards issue as a precondition for negotiation despite the opposition of Sir James Grigg, Sir John Simon, and R.A. Butler.[22]

The developments described above were consistent with the post-war imperial strategic plans of Ernest Bevin, the most imperially minded among the Labour members of the coalition cabinet. Now that the controlled British economy was providing full employment to all, and post-war plans of British reconstruction were designed to diminish the importance of the old staples, Indian industrialisation held no fears for either Attlee or Bevin.[23] What Bevin wanted was that this industrialising power should be a partner in commonwealth defence. As early as June 1943, his perception of this role for the subcontinent was set forth in a secret paper for the war cabinet; he wished to develop 'India including Burma up to the Persian Gulf, as an organic defence area in partnership with the British Commonwealth'. With the help of the sterling balances it should be possible, he said, to undertake 'a large industrial development in India to maintain a defensive and highly mechanised force'. The British hold on this partnership would be her sea and air power.[24]

In the Indian armed forces, too, changes were occurring to make it a less reliable instrument of imperial control. Winston Churchill, whose mental image of India had become stereotyped by his recollections as a serving officer towards the end of the nineteenth century, continued to believe that only certain 'martial races' provided efficient and loyal troops. Believing that during 1942 and 1943 the Japanese threat had led to an increase in the number kept under arms, and that most of them were of low quality, he demanded the reduction of numbers by at least half a million in 1944. 'In this process, . . . the greatest care should be taken to improve the quality of the remaining units and to rely as much as possible upon the martial races.'[25]

The martial races theory died a natural death when, in reply to this, Auchinleck blandly replied: 'As a result of maintenance difficulties found necessary to disband six battalions of martial class regiments.' These were 18 Baluch, 15 Sikh, 6 FFR, 16/14 Punjab, 7/6 Punjab.[26] The result of recruitment between November 1941 and September 1942 showed 50.7 per cent recruiting from the pre-war catchment areas, but 49.3 per cent from new groups.[27] Though people from Punjab, the North-West Frontier Province, and Garhwal still accounted for 31.8 per cent, Madras made up 18.4 per cent and the rest were more evenly distributed.

The Royal Indian Navy and the Royal Indian Air Force were recruited on a wider basis, and their loyalty to the Raj could not be relied upon if it came to a crisis. In April 1946 the secretary to the home department was not sure if the three services, especially the last two, would stay loyal, if the Congress launched a mass Civil Disobedience Movement.[28] Another traditional feature of the armed forces was seen by Wavell and Auchinleck, in course of the war, to have given cause for resentment— Indian officers were convinced that they were discriminated against in terms of prospects, pay, and posting.[29] The seniormost Indian officer, and the first Indian to get (in 1942) independent command of a regular unit of the Indian army,[30] Lt.-Col. Cariappa (as he then was), came to be used as a channel for grievance on these questions. Because of his excellent record, his views were seriously considered by Auchinleck.[31] Cariappa, the only Indian member in the committee set up by the government to plan the reorganisation of the army and air force in India, resented the view of the majority that to reach efficiency in a future war the officer cadre of the Indian army, over the next twenty years, should have at least fifty per cent Britons.[32]

The foregoing survey of the relative ascendancy of the Indian element in bureaucracy, business, and the armed forces Left those in Britain and India who wished to postpone the withdrawal of imperial power with two options. One was, as Wavell suggested in late 1944, of creating a coalition government of all parties at the centre, without holding elections (because that would only aggravate communal bitterness) and gradually trying to devolve authority while retaining control of the levers of power. It would involve coming to terms with the Indian capitalist class, but it would ward off both radical demands for the break-up into sovereign states, and a groundswell of popular unrest and a possible swing to the Left.[33] The alternative view, put forward by Amery, was to reject the assumption that 'party leaders [were] providing key to the problems', reframe the Government of India Act to make it more like a presidential system, and win over big business support by making them realise that they were 'not going to get control of the executive by controlling the Congress party's purse strings'.[34] Neither of these options was, however, going to be allowed by the Labour group in the coalition cabinet, which, led by Attlee, and in keeping with the past approach to the question, insisted that fresh elections must determine the relative legitimacy of different parties.[35]

(ii) From the advent of the Labour government to the recall of Wavell, mid-1945 to January 1947

I have discussed elsewhere the global and domestic priorities of the Labour government as revealed by the archival material now available.[36] The first six months of its term of office was taken up with the domestic financial problem of negotiating a loan from the US after the suspension of lend-lease. The terms of this loan, which involved scaling down sterling balances, and a promise to make the pound convertible by mid-1947, made crucial the protection of the British balance of payments and the reduction of overseas commitments wherever possible, if at the same time the welfare state at home was going to be built. Ernest Bevin was a hard-headed social imperialist, and to him areas producing oil, tin, and rubber, (dollar-earning commodities) and the development of Africa for raw materials were more important than the maintenance of a British military presence where it might be a liability rather than an asset. So on 15 February 1946, at a meeting of the cabinet defence committee, Attlee urged the members not to think of expenditure on British troops in India as a long-term liability. In the same meeting Bevin identified the priority areas where troops should not be reduced (in order to help his policy of containing Soviet ambitions) as Greece, Italian colonies, and the Middle East.[37]

The decision to send a Cabinet Mission to India had already been taken sometime before this. One important factor which has not received as much attention as it should, was the fear felt in the British Cabinet that the agitation release to release the INA prisoners, when linked with the forthcoming elections in India, might lead to such a high pitch of anti-British feeling, that post-war cooperation in commonwealth defence and foreign policy might not be forthcoming.

The decision to try the INA prisoners was taken in India, though Auchinleck had expressed his doubts about its wisdom, since every Indian was a nationalist. The senior official who overruled him, wrote:

I agree with you that every Indian, worth anything at all, must be a nationalist. But there is nationalism and nationalism. I am a Scotsman and very 'nationalist-minded'. In fact I am very nearly a Scottish nationalist in the political sense. But that does not make me in any way anti-British. I think that we can support and encourage nationalism in this country, both inside the Army and out of it, without withdrawing the least from our position of condemnation of those who fought for the enemy and took part in sabotage, etc. in 1942 . . . otherwise it seems to me we start down a very slippery slope indeed.[38]

Once the decision was known, it sparked off the inevitable agitation against the trials, and from November 1945 to January 1946, doubts began to assail the civil and military authorities. Benthall considered the trials 'the biggest mistake for many years'.[39] Congress leaders like Bhulabhai Desai, through their private channels, made it known to Auchinleck that they were going to make a major issue of it.[40] That Indian soldiers who had remained 'loyal' did not regard the INA offic-ers or 'jawans' in the same light as the British did was reported to Auchinleck by Governor B.I. Glancy at the end of the year.[41] Cariappa, (who was associated with the court-martial), received a letter from a VCO stationed in Burma that all Indians in Burma whom he had met considered that they owed their life to the INA after the collapse of the British army in Burma and tended to 'worship Subhas Chandra Bose as their living God'.[42] Sarat Chandra Bose urged Cariappa that a national army had to be officered entirely by Indians, and added that 'any scheme which [would] have the effect of converting the British Indian Army into the National Army of India will always have my whole-hearted support'.[43] That senior-most serving Indian officers in the Indian army were making goodwill gestures to radical political leaders was indicated by Cariappa sending Sarat Bose Christmas greetings, and trying, without success, to let him and other public figures inspect conditions at INA detention camps.[44] Cariappa's own inspection of these camps made him argue that after the release of Shah Nawaz, Dhillon and Sehgal, there was no justification for keeping the others in detention.[45] If British rule was to go on for another 20 or 25 years, the position might be different, but since 'India [was] to have her independence in the near future' nothing should be done to embitter relations between serving officers and jawans and the INA persons further.[46]

Meanwhile, at the end of November 1945, reviewing the press campaign against the trials Attlee wondered at the credibility gap between the British government and the population. He was amazed when Sir Evan Jenkins confessed that the entire press was hostile, and that there was no adequate channel of communication between the government and the people. When asked about possible solutions, Jenkins was gloomy. An attempt at revolution was sooner or later inevitable. While the government had plenty of evidence and could arrest the ringleaders 'he doubted if British public opinion would stand for this'. The ministers agreed. Attlee, who had started the discussion, deploring Nehru's speeches glorifying the INA leaders and inflaming the atmosphere 'during the critical months before the elections', ended by suggesting that Nehru and Jinnah be invited to Britain: 'Nehru was an honest but misguided man and if he saw conditions in Germany he might realise what his policy would certainly involve in suffering and destruction for India.'[47]

I have given the reactions of senior Indian army officers and the British ministers in some detail, because while the popular agitation over the INA trials is well recorded, there has not been enough documentation on what dent it made in the imperial mind, and also because these documents are not in the Mansergh-Moon volumes. It certainly does not warrant S. Gopal's judgement that 'there was probably a touch of escapism in Jawaharlal's concentration' on this issue.[48] On the contrary, it was a shrewd political move. It probably led to the sending of the Cabinet Mission. Instead of deciding policy by the well-worn method of despatches and telegrams, sending the mission indicated a wish to reach a settlement before the sands of time ran out.

Measured in terms of imperial necessity, the holding of elections and the resumption of provincial autonomy on the old franchise was a mistake if it was the intention simultaneously to negotiate a transfer of functions at the centre. It would encourage Indian officials at all levels to look towards the indigenous politician for guidance, and, if fairly organised parties captured the provinces, it would limit the Raj's room for manoeuvre regarding the terms on which central control could be abandoned. Seasoned imperialists, who were to be found only among the Conservatives, had understood this all along, and that is why, in 1930–5, they had given priority to provincial autonomy, until a 'safe' centre could emerge. That is why Amery had advised Wavell to think of a presidential style of government.[49] The ideological commitment of the Labour party made it insist on elections, and it suited the interests both of the capitalists supporting the Congress, and of the Muslim League which was anxious to test its political strength eight years after its failure in 1937. G.D. Birla's optimistic account of better chances from a Labour government stressed the emphasis the latter put on elections, and added: 'My own feeling is that we must take charge of the machinery even though we may not be fully satisfied with everything that these people are doing. . . . In fact, without governmental machinery we are all feeling helpless.'[50] The ideological commitment of the Labour party to elections did not extend to the idea of a constituent assembly elected on universal franchise, although, apart from communists, the radical democrats and the widely respected labour leader N.M. Joshi supported it. They showed how, with the use of ration cards, an electoral roll on adult franchise could be prepared without too much delay.[51] The reason for this failure must be attributed to the fact that the dominant parties did not demand it, being anxious not to face the problem of fresh elections on a wider franchise when they had consolidated their gains in the elections early in 1946.

The sending of the Cabinet Mission and the assumption of office had upset the smooth working out of a policy of how to coordinate the work of the provincial police, and the armed forces. It should be borne in mind that resources were limited, and that post-war planning of the Indian army was visualised by the 'general staff branch' to be 'a hardhitting mobile organisation which can also act as a nucleus for rapid expansion in war'. For these reasons, the provinces were expected to increase their police forces and not to call on the army except as the last resort, and to let the army be regrouped 'in areas where they [could] carry out their training in formations preferably of the size of a division'.[52] While home department officials were disturbed at this, a formula was agreed upon, and sent to the provincial governments. Under the Government of India Act of 1935 the elected provincial government had complete control of law and order, with the governors having powers only under Section 93 (and at the centre only the Governor-general in his personal capacity had the powers of superintendence, direction, and control). The future was to show that in a period of intense political bargaining, the majority party in charge of a provincial government would connive at breaches of law and order if it served the interests of that party. (The situation in Bengal and Bihar after August 1946 provides evidence to substantiate this point.)[53]

It was agreed among British military authorities that a common federal centre controlling defence (and therefore foreign affairs and communications) was most advantageous to them, taking global strategy into account. On 12 April 1946, Field Marshal Alanbrooke explained to the cabinet's defence committee with the help of a map that, since the regions claimed for Pakistan controlled the entry points to South Asia on the northwest and the northeast, the division of the present Indian army was wasteful, and Pakistan without any industrial base, would have to depend on 'Hindustan' for military stores. There was the further danger that Sind might identify itself more with Afghanistan and become a conduit for the spread of Russian influence. So the Cabinet Mission's proposed 'scheme' (which was essentially the 16 May plan) was to be supported. Because of Attlee's statement that political settlement required that 'the Mussalman claim to the establishment of Pakistan was accepted in some degree', Alanbrooke proposed that scheme 'B' (the situation that emerged in August 1947) be accepted as very much the second best, provided there was a central defence council.[54] On the eve of the publication of the 16 May plan, Auchinleck, who remained wedded to scheme 'A' until the end of April 1947, produced a six-page memorandum (with map) in which he made additional points in justification of scheme 'A' in terms of commonwealth strategy and the cold war.[55] There is another undated paper entitled 'Strategic Implications of Incorporating Pakistan in the British Commonwealth', with a reference number of the C-in-C's secretariat pertaining to early 1946. Its provenance in the Auchinleck Papers just after his signed paper suggests that this was also written by other officers at the same time.[56] It was probably in response to an earlier note by Abell in the

Viceroy's Council in which, as part of Wavell's 'Breakdown Plan', a kite-flying suggestion was put forward that Britain might withdraw to Pakistan in return for military aid.[57] (We may note in this context that on 9 April 1946, two India Office officials had suggested that if the subcontinent was divided the odds were that the political leadership of India would be neutral in the cold war while the leadership in Pakistan would be pro-West).[58] This other paper of the C-in-C's secretariat argued in favour of leaving Congress-dominated India to its own devices in defence and diplomacy but developing close relations with the dominion of Pakistan (with Punjab having been divided). It justified Britain assuming the responsibility on a number of grounds: the strategic importance to Britain of the Indian Ocean required not only that Britain controlled Ceylon, but also that a hostile power dominated 'Hindustan'; as a buffer state between 'Hindustan' and any potential aggressor like Russia, Pakistan would be useful to Britain and Britain would be able to influence the diplomacy of 'Hindustan'; third, if Nepal remained allied to Britain and if some boundary adjustment could ensure a frontier between Nepal and Pakistan then Britain would have an 'outer arch', a chain of airfields, and Nepali manpower; fourth, Pakistan was one of the few parts of the commonwealth from which the British empire could attack Russian industry in Siberia with modern weapons; fifth, close relations with Pakistan 'would probably have the effect of strengthening our bonds with the remainder of the Moslem world and it might be possible to form a strong Moslem block'. Admitting that Pakistan would be 'a very considerable financial liability to the empire', and both in the short and long run increased expenditure and manpower would be required of the British, the paper thought that these increases would be offset by the British empire being in possession of more modern weapons.[59] Auchinleck considered all these to be unrealistic assumptions and expectations. After making a detailed analysis of commonwealth strategic interests (oil from Persia and Iraq, control of the entrances of the Indian Ocean, air routes across West, South, and East Asia, and control of Ceylon as a port of call and naval air base), he wrote that 'Hindusthan' outside the British Commonwealth might well be tempted 'to give effect to an inevitable urge to conquer and absorb Pakistan and thus restore the unity of India. . . . Russia with her taste for power politics and gangster methods would be likely to take full advantage of any such tendency on the part of Hindusthan. A Russian-influenced Hindusthan might well constitute such a menace to the security of the British Commonwealth as to cause its early dissolution'. He then rejected the hypothesis that a British-controlled Pakistan could influence 'Hindusthan' from a position of strength. Modern warfare required 'depth in the defence', raw material and industrial base. Pakistan would have none of these, and 'Hindusthan' would. Britain would not be able to control an independent 'Hindusthan' and prevent it and its allies from disrupting Britain's sea and air communications. A Pakistan alliance would not help achieve a Muslim block because it would be quite obvious to all the Muslim countries that Britain had ceased to be a power in Asia. The only way for maintaining British communications by sea and air in the Indian Ocean area, so vital to the commonwealth, was 'by keeping in being a United India which [would] be a willing member of that commonwealth, ready to share in its defence to the limit of her resources'.[60]

Auchinleck believed in this so strongly that as late as April 1947 he had made no preparations for the division of the Indian armed forces, and then, as we shall see, let Baldev Singh use that as an argument against Liaqat Ali Khan's demand for two armies.[61] In September 1946 he chose (irrespective of communal consideration), Cariappa and J.N. Chaudhuri for the next course at the Imperial Defence College—the first Indians to be so selected.[62]

The Cabinet Mission plan of 16 May 1946 thus suited the strategic aims of Britain very well. With a central government controlling only external affairs, defence, and communications, it gave the chiefs of staff a large group of provinces in the northwest which would be logistically defensible in a war with the Soviet Union, could be a base for attack on Siberia if necessary and yet would be linked with the industrial and economic heartland of the rest of the subcontinent. Since the central government was bound to be, in the given situation, a coalition of Congress, Muslim League and possibly others, a pro-West tilt in its foreign and defence policy could be reasonably expected. What the mission plan missed out—and this was a surprising omission in terms of its own strategic logic—was any provision for ensuring even partial satisfaction for one community which was a very important element in the Indian army—the Sikhs. As is well known, the Congress acceptance of the mission plan was qualified, with reservations in their own favour.[63]

On 14 June 1946 the cabinet defence committee agreed that, even at the cost of reducing British troops in Italy, Germany or Greece, reinforcements would have to be sent to India if there was a breakdown of law and order, irrespective of whether the Congress or the Muslim League caused it. Ernest Bevin accepted it after a lot of hesitation because he had kept the troops in those parts of Europe to help him in his negotiations at the four-power talks in Paris.[64] Ten days earlier, a full meeting of the British cabinet had refused to set a target date for leaving India, but also recognised that suppression of mass movements would be unpopular in Britain.[65]

Six months later, after communal violence in Calcutta, Noakhali, and Bihar, the government's options had diminished further because its resources were getting scarcer. While it was deciding about Wavell's proposal for naming a target date, and giving its interpretation on the 'grouping' question in the first week of December, it was facing a major fuel crisis, and its American loan was being used up very quickly. The ministerial committee preparing the economic survey for 1947 wrote in December 1946: '. . . we feel bound to question whether the country can afford to devote so big a proportion of its manpower to defence at the present time.'[66] In February 1947 Britain found itself unable to afford the costs of keeping troops in Greece and Turkey and requested the US to take its place; the US obliged by propounding the 'Truman Doctrine'. The empire in the Indian subcontinent was turning out to be more a liability than an asset, except for its long-term usefulness in commonwealth defence because of its geographical location. The declaration of 20 February 1947 giving a terminal date to British rule in India, and the convoluted politics till 15 August over the question of army and defence, have to be seen in this context.

(iii) From January 1947 to 15 August 1947

Before examining the fate of the long-term imperial strategy in these months, I would like to draw attention to a very significant exchange of letters between Ernest Bevin and Prime Minister Attlee in the first two days of the new year. Normally, Attlee Left Bevin with plenty of freedom to formulate his foreign policy (even on issues like the Palestine question on which Labour supporters were sensitive), while, in view of Attlee's experience of India since the Simon Commission, Bevin deferred to him on Indian policy.

Looking at the situation in India in relation to Egypt, Palestine, the Middle East and Persia, Bevin considered 'the defeatist attitude adopted both by the Cabinet' and the viceroy most harmful. He considered Cripps too pro-Congress to give a balanced judgement 'on the importance of the Moslem World', recommended a change of viceroy, and opposed fixing a date. 'I am willing to support a declaration, that we are ready to hand India over as a going concern to established governments. I do not mind, even, using the plural in this sense, if Nehru and Jinnah are not going to agree, but the qualification should be that they can preserve law and order.' He suggested rule by section 93 wherever a provincial ministry resigned, use of the Indian army under strong leadership, and strengthening the British element in the administration by deputation from the forces. Attlee's reply was devastating. He pointed out that while Indian army officers have tremendous cross-communal camaraderie, even they regretfully admitted that large-scale communal strife would split the army; he then made the most telling points of all:

We have always governed India through the Indians. Without the tens of thousands of lesser functionaries we could not carry on. . . . It would be quite impossible if you could find the men for a few hundred British to administer against the active opposition of the whole of the politically minded of the population. . . . If you proposed to govern by main force you would be driven into shootings and the like for which you would find very little support in this country.[67]

One indication of what Bevin called the defeatist attitude of many of his cabinet colleagues is illustrated by the failure of the cabinet to mention the imperial economic stake in India in the first draft of the statement about leaving India by mid-1948, which had been prepared by the cabinet's India–Burma Committee on 23 December 1946. It was E.E. Bridges, a senior civil servant at the Treasury, who afterwards told Attlee that the statement made no reference to British business interests. Eventually, paragraph 14 of Attlee's declaration of 20 February made a reference to them. The Treasury official's comment on the original draft is partly worth quoting, because it illustrates the contrast between constitution making in 1932–4 (when such a mistake would never have been made), and 1946–7, when, in the words of Hugh Dalton, a government wanted to get 'out of a situation which was rapidly becoming quite untenable'.[68] Bridges told Attlee that the draft as it stood could easily alarm British expatriate businessmen in India:

It is by no means clear from the statement that these interests will be permitted to survive the handing over of power to the Indian people. . . . Indeed the whole tenor of the sixth paragraph (about arrangement for repatriation) leaves the impression that the situation is so uncertain or so dangerous that not only persons in the British Services, but civilians may be well advised to leave. . . . India is of course a great market for British goods and its exports to North America have strengthened us in the past and could continue to do so, if favourable commercial arrangements continue.[69]

The assumption in the last sentence was that India would remain in the sterling area, and be part of the sterling area dollar pool. In that case dollar earnings from jute and tea could strengthen Britain's dwindling gold and dollar reserves. Doubts about India remaining in the commonwealth increased after Nehru got the constituent assembly to pass a resolution to establish a sovereign democratic republic.[70] It had three effects: first, it made Attlee decide to tell Mountbatten to talk the Indian leaders out of it and accept transfer of power in a manner consistent with remaining in the commonwealth; second, it made the chiefs of staff (and the government) urge him to spare no pains to retain the joint defence arrangements of scheme 'B'; and third, to detach the Andaman and Nicobar Islands and transfer them to the Colonial Office, on the analogy of the transfer of Aden in the 1935 Act.

The ten weeks from Mountbatten's arrival on 22 March till the announcement of 2 June were characterised by many political manoeuvres and negotiations. The tripartite discussions between Mountbatten, Congress, and the Muslim League have been fairly objectively narrated in a recent work.[71] We shall only recapitulate some landmarks in the negotiations and then examine their bearing on imperial strategic thinking at different levels of the British government.

In the light of Attlee's statement of 20 February the Cabinet Mission plan could be put into effect only if the Muslim League joined the constituent assembly, and a constitution was drafted before June 1948. Since the British government had mentioned a terminal date and also the prospect of more than one successor state, the possibility of the Muslim League joining the constituent assembly was remote. Jinnah had already enlisted British Conservative support for the 'Pakistan' areas being given dominion status, and some princely states had started intrigues for a similar position.[72] In the North-West Frontier Province Sir Olaf Caroe continued to encourage the Muslim League to destabilise the Congress government,[73] and in Punjab the Muslim League succeeded in toppling the coalition government. Governor Glancy had been a firm believer in stressing the *Punjabi* character of his province and discouraging communal politics.[74] His successor, Jenkins, shared this view. Instead of asking the Muslim League to form a government he ruled under Section 93 of the Government of India Act. One element in this decision was the strident demand by Akali leaders that Sikhs should not be put under Muslim 'domination' and if necessary the province should be partitioned.[75] Sardar Patel correctly put it to Mountbatten on 25 April that the 'main result of the statement of 20 February had been a race to capture the different provinces'.[78]

For about two months before Mountbatten's arrival, the Congress point of view had been that the Muslim League had no justification to remain in the interim government since it was continuing to boycott the constituent assembly.[77] The only way administration could be effective while the constitution was being drafted was to let the viceroy become a constitutional governor-general as in the dominions, and give the interim government the powers of a dominion cabinet. There was unofficial support in Congress circles to amend the Government of India Act for a transitional form of dominion government. A proposal along these lines had been drafted by B.N. Rau and V.P. Menon, and reached Pethick-Lawrence by 12 March (hereafter referred to as the Rau–Menon plan).[78] In so far as it indicated willingness of some Congressmen to eschew republicanism and accept dominion status it pleased the British government,[79] but it was not acceptable to many British officials and ministers who argued that it put the Muslim League at the mercy of the Congress.[80]

There emerged between 10 and 14 April the 'Plan Balkan'. This gave all provinces, through a vote by the provincial legislature, the right to choose their own future, and also gave the legislators of Punjab and Bengal the option of dividing their provinces. The provinces could then join the existing constituent assembly or one or more additional constituent assemblies. Until the constitutions were framed there was to be a common governor-general.[81] Nehru opposed it because it opened up the prospect of many partitions, and it was abandoned by the British cabinet on 23 May 1947.[82] Finally came 'Plan Partition', which had been drafted on 13 May, and was accepted by all parties on 2 June.

Since December 1946 Jinnah had been throwing out feelers for a unilateral British award in favour of Pakistan, with the British troops withdrawing to the Pakistan area.[83] By the time Mountbatten started his talks, this prospect of British troops sustaining Pakistan, wrenched as it were from the rest of India without agreement with the Congress, was financially and militarily impossible for Britain. In January, A.V. Alexander had had to accept a 5 per cent cut in defence expenditure. In February, pressure from backbench Labour MPs had ensured that the period of compulsory military service in Britain was reduced to one year only. Field-Marshal Montgomery agreed to it in April only on the understanding that troops would be withdrawn from India.[84] In this situation the interests of imperial strategy could be served only if the successor states did not impose additional military liability, and came into existence by agreement, and helped to meet Britain's commonwealth military obligations. This is why efforts went on to maintain a common centre at least for the purpose of defence.

Within three days of receiving the Rau–Menon plan, Attlee had urged the India Office to explore an early transfer of power to more than one successor state by an interim amendment of the Government of India Act (1935) but retaining a special authority to assume control of the army, which would remain unified.[85] Attlee thus ignored the Congress demand for plenary powers to the interim government, but aimed to retain strategic control of the army. Jinnah and Nehru, in their different ways, had other ideas and indicated that they wanted sovereign control of the army.

In all his meetings with Mountbatten between 5 and 10 April Jinnah reiterated his demand for a sovereign Pakistan and insisted that the only guarantee of sovereignty was a separate army. Liaqat Ali Khan wanted Auchinleck to postpone the reorganisation of the Indian army, so that it did not prejudice the question of partition (Auchinleck had been following the plans of the post-war reorganisation committee which had assumed that there would be an all-India army for the purposes of imperial defence).[86] Confident of support from British Conservatives, Jinnah could ignore Mountbatten's hint that if he failed to agree on the defence question Pakistan's chances of commonwealth membership might diminish.[87]

With Nehru, Mountbatten tried a different technique, trying to get the Congress to disavow the 'republican' clause of the directive principles resolution, and accept dominion status. (The British military authorities' alarm at that has been mentioned earlier.) Efforts were made through Baldev Singh, defence member, and the only Sikh member of the interim government.[88] The Sikhs were a significant part of the Indian army, and they stood to lose if the army was bifurcated, and if the Muslim League claim to the whole of Punjab for Pakistan was accepted. On 14 April Nehru ignored Baldev Singh's plea for remaining in the commonwealth in order not to lose the services of British officers.[89] When on 25 April Baldev Singh supported Auchinleck against Liaqat Ali about maintaining a united army, he got support from the Congress because *unity* was the issue, not commonwealth membership.[90]

A great deal has been written about Mountbatten's attempt to frighten Krishna Menon about Pakistan as a dominion getting the full military support of the commonwealth (and republican India remaining weak) in order to get the Congress to accept dominion status, British control over defence, and partition if necessary.[91] Ultimately, Congress, accepted dominion status, did not make any commitments either on defence or on immediate partition, but reiterated the Rau–Menon plan with the proviso that after the constitution was finalised, provinces or parts of provinces could opt out. This was the substance of the Congress proposals given on 7 May.[92] British interests were satisfied by the acceptance of dominionhood and an all-India army, but those in the British government and the opposition for whom satisfying the Muslim League was essential to British Middle Eastern policy, it seemed as if the League was being handed over to Congress 'dominance'.[93] The implications of 'Plan Balkan' (taken to London on 2 May and revised by the cabinet on 7 May) have to be seen in that light.

'Plan Balkan' has often been interpreted as a sinister move in British imperial interests to fragment the subcontinent into many parts. When we consider its origins, scrutinise the text, and ponder over the short-lived nature of the plan, this hypothesis gets weakened. On the economic plane, the fragmentation proposed was somewhat less than would have been possible under the mission plan, which had Left the centre with only the departments of foreign affairs, defence, and communications. Under the new plan, statutory provisions were made for greater cooperation between the successor authorities. Joint delegations were to discuss matters affecting commerce, customs and excise, income tax, currency and the Reserve Bank, in addition to defence. The delegations were to reach decisions by consensus. This proposal was justified by the argument that in the existing regime the central revenues included customs and excise, the centre collected income tax, and defence costs had to be defrayed out of these.[94]

It is certainly arguable that agreement on these issues by consensus among a number of successor states, under a common governor-general, increased the manoeuvrability of Britain to influence their policies and safeguard imperial commercial interests more than might have been possible otherwise. It is certainly true that the British imperial preference system had been under attack from the US at the preparatory talks on international trade in Geneva (October–November 1946 and again April 1947), and late in March Cripps had found it difficult to get a concerted commonwealth line accepted by the dominions and India. His report on the Geneva talks at the end of April said:

It was also apparent that India might abandon the preferential system in relation to us at an early date, probably in the course of the Geneva negotiation. There is, of course, a good deal of politics behind this, but it is not easy to see any way of persuading the Indians to a different course on purely economic grounds. The head of the Indian delegation was, however, himself anxious to retain some margin of preferences, and we may hope to salvage something.[95]

Had the 'Plan Balkan' been seriously thought up with any intention of helping the commercial lobby, we would have expected pressure to alter the instructions to the Indian delegates or to change the composition of the delegation. Both the finance and the commerce portfolios had been with Muslim League members since October 1946 (Liaqat Ali Khan and Chundrigar). Backstairs hints may have been dropped about the greater willingness of 'Pakistan' to accommodate imperial preference, for it was Jinnah's strategy at this time to argue that his party would be more loyal than the republican Congress to the commonwealth.[96] However, since the division of Punjab and Bengal was an essential part of 'Plan Balkan', and Jinnah was adamantly opposed to it till 2 June, the plan cannot be considered a concerted move between the Muslim League and the British government. Besides, there is no evidence in the records of the Treasury or the Board of Trade dealing with the question of a treaty to protect British commercial interests in the subcontinent that the plan was ever referred to them during the period that it was under consideration (2 May to 23 May).[97]

Given the deadlock over the Cabinet Mission plan, 'Plan Balkan' makes sense as another attempt to maintain an overarching control of the defence of the subcontinent under a common British governor-general. The authorities were trying to steer between the Scylla of the Rau–Menon plan (which would have made Congress all-powerful) and the Charybdis of the Jinnah–Liaqat demand for total division, including that of the army. On 25 April the plan (as prepared by Ismay and V.P. Menon) had been to transfer power to two 'interim governments'; two constituent assemblies could carry on their work, but have a kind of 'super-government' in the shape of a common governor-general, with joint control of defence, external affairs and communications, and parity of representation between the Muslim League and the Congress and its allies in the committee which took decisions on these three subjects.[98] On the same day Patel had told Mountbatten that the 'Congress would not accept any suggestion for a further degree of parity in the present central government'.[99] It is not clear from the text whether he was opposing parity in the *existing* government of which he was a member, or the *new* idea of parity in the joint committee on defence, external affairs, and communications. Mountbatten understood it to mean that Patel 'would never consider parity in the central government'. He commented on 1 May that the Cabinet Mission plan was dead.[100] Next day 'Plan Balkan' was taken to London by Ismay.

'Plan Balkan', then, had no economic significance. There is evidence, however, that this plan was seriously considered in terms of its effects on the armed forces and imperial strategy. On 10 May, the day after Mountbatten had expressed his delight at the news that Congress would accept dominion status, and before he had been told by Nehru of the objections to the plan as it stood, the viceroy visualised that even after the transfer of power the British officers in the Indian army could remain longer than was earlier intended. 'The Indianization programme could go on much more slowly.'[101] On 12 May, before V.P. Menon's 'Plan Partition' had been fully studied in London, the chiefs of staff had discussed the strategic implications of 'Plan Balkan' along with the likelihood of more than two applications for dominionhood.[102] They were told by Attlee that an autonomous Bengal might also emerge, and that feelers had been sent from Travancore for separate commonwealth membership after the lapse of paramountcy. (The India Office had agreements with Travancore for the supply of strategic raw material.)[103] All service chiefs said that while ideally every part of the subcontinent should remain in the commonwealth, the next best course would be the retention of western Pakistan, Travancore, and autonomous Bengal. Field Marshal Montgomery in particular recommended the acceptance of the western part of the subcontinent into the commonwealth as early as possible in order to enable Britain to have bases and airfields there. Ismay argued that Mountbatten objected to having only one part in the commonwealth because in the event of war between 'Hindustan' and Pakistan Britain would incur a liability to defend Pakistan; but the chiefs regarded it as a small risk.[104] How logistic and romantic arguments got mixed up in the military mind is illustrated by the following record of the decision:

There was therefore everything to gain by admitting West Pakistan into the commonwealth. A refusal of an application to this end would amount to ejecting loyal people from the British Commonwealth, and would probably lose us all chances of even getting strategic facilities anywhere in India, and at the same time shatter our reputation in the rest of the Moslem world. From the military point of view such results would be catastrophic.[105]

The British government in London also had in its support of 'Plan Balkan' another argument of military significance. An autonomous Punjab (even more than an autonomous Bengal) might dispel the fears of the Sikhs, because they would no longer be swamped by the Muslim-majority provinces of Baluchistan and the North-West Frontier Province.[106] However, whatever might be the view from London, the communal tension in Punjab in May 1947 made an autonomous Punjab quite unrealistic. As the governor wrote to Mountbatten on 30 April: 'The Sikhs have committed themselves so deeply to the partition of the Punjab that it will be difficult, and perhaps impossible, for them to take a different line.'[107]

From the point of view of imperial strategy, Mountbatten's initial jubilation at the Congress acceptance of dominion status proved to be less well grounded than Mieville's scepticism. On 12 May Nehru told him unambiguously that the role of the joint army councils would be strictly limited to a speedy and equitable division of the human and physical resources of the all-India army.[108] In the privacy of his staff meeting subsequently the viceroy admitted that in view of the Congress attitude the army question 'was going to be the most difficult issue in the transfer of power. . . .'[109] To avoid giving further concessions to the Congress which compromised imperial strategy, Mountbatten took one step even before he reached London for the final drafting of 'Plan Partition'. On 11 May, he rejected the plea that the North-West Frontier Province should be given the option of remaining independent even though the idea of an autonomous Bengal was not given up till nearly three weeks later.[110] The British government also rejected a Congress plea that it should declare that Pakistan should not be allowed to remain in the commonwealth if India eventually Left it.[111]

Even as the Congress leaders accepted 'Plan Partition' they sent signals to Mountbatten not to try their patience by insisting on specific commitments on imperial defence. At the end of May and beginning of June Nehru declared that any attempt to secure foreign bases in the successor states of the subcontinent would be deemed an unfriendly act.[112] In a private letter to Mountbatten on 14 June, Krishna Menon wrote that with the result of the North-West Frontier Province referendum going in favour of Pakistan, the defences of India were Left with Pakistan. If Kashmir for some reason chose to be in Pakistan this strategic position would be further developed. It would be 'tragic' for Indo-British relations if Britain intended to use India's frontier area as the hinterland of imperial strategy in the Middle East, as Ernest Bevin had implied in a speech at Margate.[113]

The most effective counterattack of the Congress leaders was to scotch the plans to detach the Andaman and Nicobar Islands from India, plans which had reached such an advanced stage in London as to be put in the shape of a special clause in the first draft print of the India Independence Bill prepared for the cabinet. As early as October 1943, Lt.-General G.N. Molesworth, who was in charge of military planning at the India Office, had written to Auchinleck saying that the islands might be needed as a military base for a long time after the war, and that it was also quite likely that they would not revert back to India.[114] These ideas were resurrected when Attlee made his declaration of 20 February 1947. The chiefs of staff needed the islands as an important link in the chain of commonwealth defences, and the Colonial Office was asked to examine how they could take over the administration in that area.[115] A.V. Alexander reiterated the military point of view in the final round of discussions that Mountbatten had in London before his broadcast of 2 June.[116] One Indian newspaper (*The Times of India*, 9 June 1947) liked these plans. Another, with Congress links (*The Hindustan Times*, 11 June), commented on them editorially in such a manner that the viceroy on 13 June cabled the secretary of state stating his inability to raise the question with the Indian leaders.[117] The defence minister still insisted on a guarantee that these islands (and if possible the Laccadive islands also) would be available for imperial defence.[118] Mountbatten cabled back on 21 June to say that to confront the leaders with the draft bill with the clause on the Andaman and Nicobars 'would severely damage our future relations with India', and urged the 'complete exclusion . . . of any reference' to the islands. London still wanted a clause to the effect that the islands should be governed by a chief commissioner until an agreement was reached about their future disposal. Whether inspired by this or not, Jinnah claimed the islands because they were on the line of sea communications between the two wings of Pakistan. He asked that his claim should be conveyed not only to the government but also to Churchill, which was duly done.[119]

All this was of no avail. Constitutionally the British position was very weak, although some officials thought that the separation of Aden from India under the Government of India Act of 1935 provided a parallel. The major difference between 1935 and 1947 was that in the former case the decisions had been taken exclusively by the British Parliament, regardless of Indian opinion, whereas on this occasion the whole thrust of negotiations had been to secure a tripartite agreement. To keep the Congress in the dark about British intentions regarding these islands and then to spring a surprise at the eleventh hour was to head for an open rupture. Nehru, after all, had not yet shed his misgivings about British views on 'balkanisation', because the first clarification he sought from W.S. Morris-Jones, when the latter met him, was about the future of the princely states.[120]

With the advantage of hindsight we can say that the failure to secure Congress–Muslim League agreement about the states of Hyderabad and Kashmir made the task of securing Indo-Pak cooperation in the commonwealth defence very difficult. Mountbatten himself admitted on 11 July that he should have paid attention to the states question earlier.[121] He may not have seen the urgency of the question because in late June he was still assuming that he would be asked to be the governor-general by both dominions. (How completely he had taken this for granted is indicated by his loss of composure at finding out that Jinnah wished to be the governor-general of Pakistan.)[122] After 4 July, as the governor general-designate for India alone, Mountbatten had to ensure that his credibility with the Congress leaders was not impaired by any further false step. Although Hyderabad was making a bid for independent status within the commonwealth (with the support of Conservative lawyer-politician Sir Walter Monckton),[123] and the Maharaja of Kashmir was postponing a decision,[124] Mountbatten in his speech to representatives of the princely states on 25 July urged them to sign treaties of accession to one or other of the two successor dominions. The secretary of state criticised him for not leaving them the option to remain free, but the viceroy replied:

The Indian dominion, consisting nearly of 3/4 of India, and with its immense resources and its important strategic position in the Indian Ocean, is a dominion which we cannot afford to estrange for the sake of the so-called independence of the states. I have no doubt that you will agree with me that we should leave no stone unturned to convince the Indian dominion that although we had to agree to the plan of partition we had no intention to leave it balkanised or to weaken it both internally and externally.[125]

This letter was written a week before the transfer of power in the subcontinent. By that time the prospects of using the successor dominions as willing partners in commonwealth defence were beset with more difficulties than had appeared to Mountbatten on 9 May. Not only was there to be no common governor-general, but the division of the armed forces was also complete. On 30 June 1947 Auchinleck had told Cariappa, the seniormost Indian officer, to get the views of officers 'on the question of the defence problems of a politically divided India'. Any hope that Auchinleck had of keeping the officer corps out of the partition process was dashed when Cariappa reported: 'Officers representing Pakistan collectively said that "one army" for India as a whole was desirable but was not practicable in the present circumstances. They, therefore, expressed their inability to associate themselves in putting up this representation.'[126]

Otherwise the procedure for the division of military resources appeared to have been worked out relatively smoothly.[127] There was still to be a joint defence council to supervise transitional arrangements, a Supreme Headquarters staff of which Auchinleck was to be the chief, and the commanders-in-chief of India and Pakistan were going to be British officers—Sir R. Lockhart and Douglas Gracey respectively. Pakistan continued to have the services of 736 British officers at various levels for at least the next two years, including the three heads of the armed services and three provincial governors. India had far fewer, but Mountbatten was governor-general and the three service chiefs were British. Military cooperation after 15 August now depended on the extent to which the forces were free from communal tension, the extent to which there was a willingness to solve the problems of Kashmir and Hyderabad through negotiations, and the extent to which Britain succeeded in convincing both India and Pakistan that it was not partial, and that all had a common stake in commonwealth defence. As we shall see, on all these points circumstances were adverse to Britain.

(iv) Independence and after

I shall now consider how India and Pakistan figured in the shifting priorities of British commonwealth strategy till the defeat of the Labour government in 1951. India's continued membership of the commonwealth even after it became a republic was accepted, with strategic considerations playing only a slightly less important part than the economic and the psychological. With the advantage of hindsight we can see, which the decision-makers could not, that throughout this period there were some long-term economic constraints on Britain's ability to play a global imperial role.

That Britain would have serious problems with the balance of payments had been foreshadowed in the *Economic Survey* published in February 1947.[128] This journal had made an impassioned appeal for austerity at home and an all-out export drive. Long-term plans to produce dollar-earning goods in the areas under the Colonial Office had also been started.[129] In the short run, however, the foreign holders of sterling began to have doubts about the strength of the English currency as compared to that of the dollar. When, on 15 July 1947, pursuant to the Anglo-American loan agreement of December 1945, sterling was made convertible, there was a rush to convert it into dollars. This led to a major balance of payments crisis and convertibility had to be suspended by the end of August.[130] From then onwards, as long as sterling remained an inconvertible currency (and yet had the status of an international currency given to it by the Bretton Woods agreement), there were certain latent tensions between the UK and the US. These were overcome only by the diplomatic solidarity required by the cold war. On the American side, resentment at the continued existence of imperial preference led occasionally to crude attempts to make Britain reduce them.[131] The US was also resentful of the arrangement by which the dollar earnings of all sterling area members were pooled. By this the surpluses of the colonial empire and Ceylon were spent, in effect, by Britain and the old dominions, India and Pakistan.[132]

Imperial preference and the sterling area were visualised by British policy-makers as the means of making Britain and the commonwealth less dependent on the US in the long run.[133] There was a wide measure of bipartisan support for this viewpoint when it got linked, early in 1948, with the idea of a union of the states of Western Europe.[134] However, within the area, Britain had no power to strengthen the monetary and commercial cooperation beyond what the sovereign dominions would agree to. On 3 September 1947 Bevin publicly aired the view about creating a customs union of the commonwealth and empire, but when the cabinet met to discuss it later in the month, they noted that Bevin's speech 'had an unfavourable reception in Canada, South Africa, and India', while Australia and New Zealand had been non-committal.[135] A study group on the more limited aim of a customs union of Britain and the areas under the Colonial Office decided against it because, *inter alia*, it would be politically suspect in the more advanced colonies.[136]

On the question of letting India retain the sterling balances, there had been divisions in Britain since 1942, cutting across party lines. Churchill had wanted them scaled down, and so had Hugh Dalton, the Labour Chancellor of the Exchequer.[137] On the other hand, both

Amery and Bevin had argued that these would enable the subcontinent to place long-term orders for British manufacturers, and provide the latter with a secure market.[138] Three weeks before the transfer of power, when Britain was faced with a balance of payments crisis, and India with an acute shortage of foreign exchange, Mountbatten had warned the secretary of state that 'any repudiation of the debts and any suggestion that India [was] not entitled to the money would have the worst possible effects'.[139] Hugh Dalton, while releasing a large part of the money immediately needed by India, gave a note stating that Britain was not 'committed to recognise the total without further cancellation or adjustment'.[140] However, as the next years were to show, the balances would not be scaled down, only the mode of payment rescheduled.

After the suspension of convertibility in August 1947 this huge debt, from a macro-economic point of view, was a liability for Britain in so far as it diverted production for export away from the dollar area. When another balance of payments crisis hit Britain in June 1949 and, after talks in Washington, led to the devaluation of the pound three months later, the dilemma was evident in discussions. On 14 June 1949 Harold Wilson, as president of the Board of Trade, invited some businessmen, including N. Kipping, president of the Federation of British Industries, to a meeting and urged them to give priority to exports to the dollar area. When he was asked what existing orders the manufacturers were expected to sacrifice in order to switch production towards the North American market he '[was] not prepared to say that we should sacrifice India or Pakistan or anywhere else to make more room for Canada and the USA'.[141] Sir Percy Hannon, a Birmingham-based manufacturer with a lifelong commitment to the British Commonwealth Union, agreed with Kipping that 'priority schemes' interfered with existing channels of trade, because in his firm he had 'a series of contracts relating to India which offer[ed] a wholesome outlook for expanding trade'; there were similar prospects in Australia, New Zealand and South Africa.[142] What suited many individual manufacturers did not suit a Labour government. Its members were anxious at that time that its social welfare expenditure should not be cut, nor real wages reduced simply to convince the US administration that British exports were competitive.[143] Scaling down the sterling balances of India and Pakistan was another possibility. Wilson hinted at that in a background paper prepared for the cabinet on the eve of the Anglo-American talks on Britain's crisis. He wrote that Britain's solvency was threatened 'by the continuance of unrequited exports on anything like the present scale'.[144]

When the cabinet considered Wilson's paper on 29 August 1949, it agreed on the need to enlist US support to deal with Britain's overseas sterling balances. It recognised that there was no prospect of the US giving extra dollar aid and thereby reducing the burden which these balances imposed on the British balance of payments. It also put on record that it was 'politically inexpedient to bring any undue pressure to bear on India or Pakistan to accept the cancellation of their sterling balances'. It was desirable, however, to tell the US government how, by running down the balances, Britain had contributed 'to measures of economic reconstruction which the US would otherwise have been called upon to finance'.[145] The entire debate within the government on the crisis of sterling from June 1949 till September 1949 (when devaluation was resorted to) highlighted the difficulties of being a great power allied with, but trying partly to be independent of, the US, and also playing a role in South Asia. As long as this was considered important it was not possible to scale down the balances, for that would offend both India and Pakistan. It was also not possible to treat the Pakistan and Indian balances differentially because of the fears that British investments in India would be expropriated.[146]

It is within these economic parameters that British strategic assessments after August 1947 can be judged. When 'Plan Balkan' had been discussed the chiefs of staff had indicated very clearly their preference for western Pakistan as a dominion partner of proven loyalty in commonwealth defence, to strengthen the British position in the Middle East. On the other hand Mountbatten's despatch of 8 August to Listowell had stressed the need for tactful handling of India because it was very important to keep it as a permanent member of the commonwealth. The pro-Pakistan and pro-India lobbies continued to influence policy formulation in a period of unprecedented stress in the subcontinent and diminished the capability of Britain to influence the course of events.

Almost from the morrow of independence mass migration of refugees between Pakistan and India had followed communal riots of unspeakable ferocity. Within ten weeks of the transfer of power the two dominions were at war over Kashmir, triggered off by the Pakistan-inspired incursion by tribals into that state on 22 October. Neither development, in their timing or scale, had been anticipated by the British government, and in the absence of a common British governor-general, no guidance could be given to British officers on how to conduct themselves under the dominion governments. The steps taken by each successor-state to cope with the crisis (in terms of their own self-interest) hardened attitudes on both sides (and that of some British officers). Thereby the prospects of cooperation between the two armies receded further. Yet at the highest level the British government went on hoping that the Kashmir question would be resolved and that if India could be persuaded to remain in the commonwealth, cooperation of both dominions in commonwealth defence would eventually materialise.

The outgoing commander-in-chief, Claude Auchinleck, remained, in his capacity as the chief of Supreme Headquarters, the chairman of the Armed Forces Reconstitution Committee, with five other members— the secretaries of the defence departments of India and Pakistan, and three deputy chiefs of the army, navy, and air force respectively. (Each deputy chief had been the seniormost serving British officer before the transfer of power.) Auchinleck expected that they would have ample time to carry out the delicate task of partitioning the army, especially the mixed units (i.e. battalions containing two companies of Punjabi Muslims, one of Sikhs and one of Hindus), that the exchange of individual officers and men of the administrative services of the old army would be a gradual process, and that for some time there would be no need to have separate training establishments like military academies, artillery schools, etc. because most of these were located in India, and Pakistan was starting from scratch. Auchinleck also expected 'to retain control of the complicated problem of movement by rail between the two dominions, in accordance with [his] responsibility for the general supervision of partition'. Of the 8400-odd British officers serving with the Indian army on 15 August, about 2700 initially volunteered to continue, during reconstitution under Auchinleck's control for a maximum period of one year, terminable by three months' notice. Auchinleck overruled the wish of the defence department of the Indian government that British officers serving in India should be definitely and finally allotted to India on 15 August and not be transferable. He kept them on a single list under the Supreme Headquarters.[147]

The ferocity of communal rioting had not been anticipated by either the British, Indian, or Pakistani authorities. As Ismay reported to the British chief of staff on 8 October:

As recently as the first week in August, the Hindu officers at G.H.Q. Delhi had given a large farewell party to their Moslem brother officers, in the course of which speeches had been made testifying to their comradeship of the past, and swearing eternal blood brotherhood for the future between the armies of India and Pakistan. It was difficult to believe that within the space of three weeks, the ingrained mutual trust of a lifetime—indeed of many lifetlmes— would be dissipated. But this, alas, was what happened.[148]

On 15 September 1947 Auchinleck wrote to the military adviser at the Commonwealth Relations Office, that

. . . the idea that the coming of Partition and the grant of dominion autonomy would cause communal feeling to die down has proved entirely false. . . . There is no doubt now, I fear, that the Army has become infected with the communal virus, and it has become so hot in those establishments like schools of instructions which are still joint, that we are taking steps to separate Pakistani trainees in such schools from the Indian trainees . . [149]

An Indian corroboration of this state of tension among all ranks of the armies of the subcontinent was provided by Major-General Cariappa in a talk given to Indian officers towards the end of September in which he asked them to control communal passions, both among their soldiers and among themselves:

Quite a few of the men you command who may hail from the disturbed areas may have lost their all and with it in their minds are likely to have developed a quite natural feeling of bitterness and retaliation. However natural this feeling may be from a psychological point of view, it is imperative that you and I as officers . . . take every possible step to see that their feelings of retribution and retaliation do not get the better of them. . . . Many cases of growing unfriendly relationship between young officers of our Army and those of Pakistan Army still in India awaiting move ex-India have been reported. If true, this is most unbecoming of us as officers whether those of India or of Pakistan. We have lived, worked, played and fought together for years before this division of the Armed forces was decided. . . . Please stop this.[150]

Instead of presiding over a relatively peaceful division of the armed forces, in which British officers would be listened to by their former subordinates, these officers found themselves in a situation where, in the words of Auchinleck, 'their old loyalty to and faith in their regiments and their men [were] being rapidly destroyed by the march of events'.[151] In both the Indian and the Pakistani part of Punjab, he wrote in another report, 'the morale of the British officers now serving there [was] lower than . . . ever before. . . .'[152] Till 28 October open conflict between Pakistan and India had not broken out over Kashmir, but organised rioting by displaced communities, breakdown of all intelligence network, spread of rumours on both sides—all created an atmosphere of deep suspicion between the two countries. Auchinleck, being based in Delhi in charge of Supreme Headquarters, saw the riots against Muslims in Delhi, and not against Hindus and Sikhs in western Punjab. He was particularly critical of the Indian government's failure to round up Sikh political extremists, who according to him, had 'taken the major part' in the riots in east Punjab 'under some central direction'.[153] He later alleged that the Maharajah of Faridkot was behind a move to create a Sikh state with Simla as its capital, and that there was a plan afoot to send the troops of the Sikh states and Sikh units of the Indian army to march to Lahore and retake it along with the rich lands of Montgomery and Lyallpur.[154] Two days before that an allegation about a Sikh invasion of the canal colonies of west Punjab had been made by Jinnah in course of a request to Sir Archibald Carter for massive military aid from Britain (or other commonwealth countries).[155] A similar allegation against the same community, with a plea for UN observers to tour east and west Punjab was made by Liaqat Ali Khan shortly before 29 September.[156]

The Indian government came to the conclusion that Auchinleck was taking a very one-sided view of the question, and in the Armed Forces' Reconstitution Committee, taking a pro-Pakistani point of view. (Auchinleck himself admitted that because of the irregular attendance of the defence secretary of Pakistan in this committee he had taken it upon himself on a number of occasions 'to suggest or present the case for Pakistan'.)[157] In the letter in which Lord Mountbatten reluctantly asked for Auchinleck's resignation and the end of the Supreme Head-quarters, he wrote: 'One of the most balanced and level headed Ministers complained recently that you seemed to regard yourself as the champion of Pakistan's interest; such is the reward of strict impartiality.'[158] The Indian distrust of Supreme Headquarters was paralleled by a desire to be as little dependent on British military personnel as possible. Auchinleck noted that when considering the question of the future employment of British officers, the Indian government was 'showing an ever-increasing if natural tendency to bypass or ignore Rob Lockhart and his British staff officers and to take backstairs advice from Cariappa etc'.[159]

The British strategic position at the beginning of October, then, was least helpful for the purpose for which Mountbatten had originally been sent out to India. Pakistan was demanding more of Britain than she could give in return. Within British military circles in the subcontinent, there was a distinct bias in favour of Pakistan. With the abolition of the Supreme Headquarters the terms of service of British officers volunteering to serve in either of the two dominions had to be renegotiated. It was found 'that the great majority of British officers had indicated a strong preference for service in Pakistan'.[160] On the other hand the arguments for wishing to make commonwealth membership attractive to India from a long-term strategic point of view still held good. So, while the British cabinet continued to get a pro-Pakistan brief from some of the officials in the Commonwealth Relations Office, the need for neutrality and appreciation of Nehru's standpoint was repeatedly stressed by Lord Ismay and Lord Mountbatten, and supported in the cabinet by Cripps and Attlee. Ismay, in his written and oral statement to the cabinet and the chief of staff early in October, considered the curbing of Hindu communalists and the survival of the government of India with Nehru at its head a necessary precondition for peace in the subcontinent: 'Pandit Nehru had, since the transfer of power, shown statesmanship of a high order and moral and physical courage in a marked degree.'[161]

By mid-October 1947, the terms of service of British officers staying on in the two dominions after 1 January 1948 were renegotiated. Pakistan made a request for between 700 and 1000 British officers, giving the defence of the northwest frontier as a major argument.[162] The cabinet was disturbed to note that not only was the Pakistani request much greater than that of India but the number of British officers who had volunteered to serve in Pakistan was significantly in excess of those volunteering for India. They 'feared that Indian opinion would find in this confirmation for the longstanding belief that British officers in the Indian forces were pro-Muslim in outlook'. They asked the War Office to find suitable volunteers for service in India up to the limited number for which the Indian government was likely to ask.[163] The terms offered by Pakistan were also attractive, including exemption from local jurisdiction. The Indian terms stopped short of that, arguing, correctly, that it was derogatory to dominion status. The majority of the cabinet committee, including even the imperially minded Minister of Defence A. V. Alexander, saw the force of the argument. Only Secretary of State for War Emmanuel Shinwell (who had travelled a long way since he was a red firebrand on Clydeside) spoke up for them. He believed that 'in the event of anti-European feeling developing, British officers might be sentenced by Indian courts to long periods of imprisonment. . . .' This argument got short shrift when the eminent lawyer Lord Jowitt, the Lord Chancellor, said that 'in his view the general administration of justice in India by Indians could be regarded as definitely good'. Attlee, Alexander, Cripps— all agreed that the plea for extraterritorial jurisdiction 'would . . . establish a colour bar incompatible with the conception of dominion status'.[164]

While making this gesture to India the cabinet was unwilling to forego the chances of a large number of British officers remaining in Pakistan. So it decided to inform the latter that while Pakistan was free to modify its terms in line with the Indian ones, such modification might adversely affect the 'number and quality of the volunteers for service with the Army of Pakistan . . . and that they might be well advised to leave their terms unaltered'.[165] A large contingent of British officers in Pakistan to support Britain's traditional northwest frontier policy was desirable. It was equally desirable to secure India's partnership in commonwealth defence.

(v) Imperial priorities in the subcontinent

The request by Jinnah on 3 October for military aid against the alleged threat of invasion by India was repeated at the same cabinet committee,[166] but Attlee rejected it with the argument that he was convinced after talking to Lord Mountbatten that the Indian government did not want the destruction of Pakistan.[167] By the time the cabinet committee met, the Pakistan-inspired tribal invasion of Kashmir had occurred on 22 October, followed by Kashmir's accession to India on the 27th and the airlift of Indian troops on the 28th. At a meeting with Jinnah on 1 November Jinnah had rejected Mountbatten's suggestion of a plebiscite under the auspices of the UN (something Pakistan later was to insist on) in return for help in securing the tribesmen's withdrawal.[168] The fighting in Kashmir went on until the cease-fire on 1 January 1949, but a mutually agreed-upon settlement on Kashmir between India and Pakistan has not been achieved to this day. British attempts to enlist both countries in the defence plans of the commonwealth foundered on the icy rocks of Kashmir, but the efforts went on till 1951.

In mid-December 1947, Sir George Cunningham, one of the architects of partition who was serving in Pakistan as the governor of the North-West Frontier Province, reflected on Indo-Pak tension. In a letter to a former viceroy he wrote that Mountbatten should have foreseen clashes between Muslims and Sikhs in the Punjab once partition had been decided on. The trouble was 'enormously aggravated by the speed with which everything was done'. 'Another cause of friction which . . . ought to have been cleared out of the way—*pace* the old Political Department—was the states'. Hyderabad should have gone to India, Kashmir to Pakistan. 'Indeed, I doubt if there were any really borderline cases, even Junagadh. . . . If only the Kashmir business had not arisen we would, I think, have been in fairly smooth water now.'[169] The bland acceptance of the two-nation theory which this letter reflected was of course in tune with the mental make-up of the British strategists who visualised Pakistan's usefulness to the commonwealth not just because of its location near the Soviet border, but also because of its being part of a cluster of Muslim states in West Asia.[170] Mountbatten's original suggestion to Nehru was to refer the Kashmir question in general terms to the Security Council. This proposal (which Nehru rejected) was essentially an attempt to get help from the Security Council to make up for his own tardiness in settling the question of the princely states before 15 August. In suggesting to Gandhi a possible partition of Kashmir (which Gandhi rejected) Mountbatten was again trying to get for Pakistan a stake in Kashmir, to salvage some of his original mandate.[171] British officers seconded to Pakistan identified themselves with that country sufficiently strongly to ignore the stand-down order. It was a revelation to Attlee in September 1949 that in January 1948 General Gracey, and again in October 1948 General Cawthorn had reported that the order might not be obeyed. The Commonwealth Relations Office had told the officers that such action would be punishable under the Army Act, but, writing in August 1949, Patrick Gordon-Walker

(Under-Secretary for Commonwealth Relations) was dubious about the effectiveness of such warning 'if India invaded Pakistan' and having to obey the order 'put the officers themselves and their families and also other members of the British community in danger of violence'. He added 'it might well be exceedingly difficult to take strong disciplinary measures against them if they disobeyed orders in such circumstances'.[172]

The Indian government limited the reference to the Security Council to the issue of Pakistani aggression. Nehru felt that by aiding Sheikh Abdullah's government against the raiders, secular ideals were being vindicated.[173] Henceforth no Indian minister or civil servant would agree to be equated with Pakistan so far as Kashmir was concerned. Nehru's promise of a plebiscite was conditional on the restoration of peace. That implied the evacuation of Pakistani forces and tribals from Kashmir and the strengthening of the government of Sheikh Abdullah. No Pakistani leader would concede the legality of Kashmir's accession to India, the legitimacy of Sheikh Abdullah's government or the demand that the invading troops be evacuated. To do so would weaken his case.

Therefore in 1948, while fighting went on in Kashmir, the long-term aim of keeping both countries in the commonwealth made the British government walk a diplomatic tightrope. It did not endear itself to either country, and it hoped that if a cease-fire could be effected quickly, followed by UN mediation, the foundations for Indo-Pak cooperation for commonwealth defence could be laid.

India had taken offence at the proceedings of the first meeting of the Security Council in February, where the British had supported moves to generalise the issue to cover disputes between India and Pakistan, and to give the Pakistan government and the tribals an equal stake in the issue.[174] The cabinet committee was disturbed at India's reaction. Philip Noel-Baker, the secretary of state for commonwealth relations, defended his role at its meeting. It was nevertheless noted that 'there seemed to be some ground for thinking that the Security Council would have been well advised to pay greater attention to the Indian case before proceeding to explore means for securing a comprehensive settlement of the Kashmir problem'. Also, since the appeal to the Council 'had been made on Lord Mountbatten's suggestion . . . it was now being said in India that His Majesty's Government had been responsible for the Council's unsympathetic attitude towards the Indian case'. An alternative suggestion sent by Mountbatten that India and Pakistan should settle by direct negotiation (with Patrick Gordon-Walker, Under-Secretary of state for commonwealth relations, acting as a mediator) was rejected. 'If the negotiations failed, the British Government would be held responsible, and this might have dangerous and embarrassing consequences. An offer of mediation in the sense suggested by Lord Mountbatten would indeed impose on His Majesty's Government a degree of responsibility which it had, so far, been their policy to avoid.'[175]

On 8 April, when the Kashmir issue again came before the Council, the cabinet committee suggested amendments to the draft resolution to recognise that 'the Government of India had an effective veto on the entry of Pakistan troops into Kashmir'.[176] Even this modest tilt to the Indian point of view 'profoundly disquieted' the Pakistani prime minister. He complained that the 'UK delegation had not only shifted their ground on the Kashmir issue by accepting Indian arguments regarding the presence of Indian troops in Kashmir and retention of Sheikh Abdullah as head of the administration, but were also actively pressing their new point of view on other delegations to the detriment of Pakistan'. He added that 'public opinion in Pakistan was coming more and more to the view that Pakistan had gained nothing by being in the commonwealth and would lose nothing by leaving it'.[177] Even the minimum arms and ammunition necessary for defence had not been received. The Pakistani high commissioner complained to Bevin that this delay was because Britain was 'subordinating Pakistan interests to those of India with the object of keeping the latter within the commonwealth'. Bevin put in a word for speedier arms deliveries at the cabinet committee meeting.[178]

The same cabinet committee expressed its concern that the UK delegation at the Security Council had been unable to include in the draft a passage which had read: 'Pakistan should take all possible steps to secure the withdrawal of intruders, to prevent their further entry and to deny help to those now fighting in the state.' It recorded: 'The effect of this omission was to create the impression, not only that the Security Council had ignored the original complaint of the Government of India, but that the document was in effect a condemnation of the latter's actions in Kashmir. This impression was confirmed by the fact that the greater part of the Resolution was concerned with suggestions for action by India rather than by Pakistan.'[179] British avowals notwith-standing, Indian officials held Britain responsible for this outcome.[180] In a sense they were right, for the cabinet committee had authorised the UK delegation to vote for the Chinese draft 'even in the event of failure to secure agreement'.[181]

India's distrust of the British attitude made her step up military action in Kashmir, ignore Mountbatten's suggestion that Sheikh Abdullah be dropped from the Kashmir administration even if temporarily, and nominate Czechoslovakia as a member of the UN commission.[182] The irritation of both India and Pakistan at what they considered Britain's lack of sympathy was reflected in the refusal of both prime ministers to reply formally to a memorandum given to them in April 1948 by the chiefs of staff of the UK. This had suggested tripartite talks on how the successor states could undertake some commitments of commonwealth defence.[183]

The pro-Pakistan lobby was assisted in its task because Bevin, the foreign secretary, was keen to contain the spread of communism and also believed that British links with a Muslim dominion would help in fostering British influence in West Asia. On 8 January 1948 Bevin pre-sented a paper to the cabinet on Soviet policy along with another on the extinction of human rights in Eastern Europe, and urged that Western European powers (along with their colonies) should come together as a bloc against the Soviet Union, without being overdependent on the US.[184] On Kashmir, the allegedly Left-wing character of Sheikh Abdullah's government was used to suggest that it was not fully dependable. In December 1947 a US diplomat in India was told by a UK High Commission official that Abdullah was Left-wing and Bakshi Ghulam Mohammad an 'almost openly avowed Communist'.[185] In September 1948 an intelligence report sent by the UK High Commission said that the communists in Kashmir 'led by the deputy Prime Minister and two other Ministers as well as Communists in India and Pakistan [were] working for the establishment of Kashmir as an independent state'.[186] In October 1948 Bevin confided to Hugh Dalton that Pakistan was important in his strategy of organising the 'middle of the planet', which included West Asia. 'He has told Liaqat that Pakistan ought to take the lead in organising the Arab States.'[187]

The pro-Pakistan lobby did not succeed in ensuring governmental backing for the Razakar aims in Hyderabad, although there was a fair deal of unofficial Pakistani support, as well as support from influential circles in the Conservative opposition in Britain. On 8 July 1948 the cabinet committee took up Indian complaints about British airmen using British aircraft for gun-running, and 'it was generally agreed that all possible efforts should be made to persuade or compel the Corporation and any British subject participating in the traffic to withdraw from it. It had been alleged that Air Vice Marshal Bennett was concerned in the matter and . . . should the Secretary of State . . . obtain more conclusive evidence of this, he might consider sending a personal communication to Air Vice Marshal Bennett in suitable terms.'[188] The UK High Commissioner in India reported that the speech of Attlee in the parliamentary debate on Hyderabad on 30 July 'made a good impression' on members of the Indian cabinet in contrast to that of Churchill.[189] At no stage during the run-up to the entry of the Indian forces into Hyderabad was it suggested that Britain had any advantage in supporting the Nizam's claim to independence or appeal to the Security Council. Attlee minuted 'yes' in the margin of a note by Noel-Baker where it was said that 'having regard to our very delicate relations on the one hand with India and on the other hand with the Arab States, who may be expected to feel sympathy with Hyderabad, the United Kingdom Delegation should take as little active part as possible at UNO in discussion of the situation. They should, however, avoid committing us to the recognition of Hyderabad as a sovereign independent state in any solution proposed.'[190] At Nehru's suggestion Krishna Menon sent Attlee confidential information found in the Hyderabad records after the police action, showing how the Razakars had sent large sums of money to banks in Karachi and London to further their interests.[191] Although Conservative military officers like Lord Ismay were very angry at India's action,[192] Menon was pleased that Attlee understood the Indian point of view.[193] British intelligence reported that the growth of communist insurrection in Telangana was one motive for India's intervention when it happened,[194] and this doubtless played a part in quietening the pro-Pakistan elements in the CRO.

On Kashmir the position was different, given the assumptions of Bevin's foreign policy. Reports about the presence of communist or pro-communist elements in Abdullah's government, and expectations from Pakistan that it would lead the Arab states, made it important that Pakistani troops should have a foothold in Kashmir. The formula that Bevin suggested to Nehru in the autumn when the latter went to Europe was an immediate cease-fire, no insistence on the withdrawal of the Pakistani forces from Kashmir at that stage, and a tripartite agreement between the UNCIP, India and Pakistan on arrangements for a fair plebiscite. Bevin considered it significant that Nehru had not rejected the suggestions 'outright' but agreed 'to consider these proposals'.[195] To make this package acceptable to India the CRO noted: 'If India stipulated for the prior withdrawal of Pakistani troops from Kashmir, they could be told that the ceasefire is a purely military solution for a military situation which in no way prejudges political claims.'[196]

At five meetings of the cabinet committee, held between 3 November and 10 December, it was anxiously debated whether Britain should take the initiative at the Security Council then in session in Paris till 15 December to mobilise international opinion for an immediate cease-fire. They were aware that Britain had little time to work out a common policy with the US or with other powers to force the issue to a successful conclusion before mid-December.[197] They were nevertheless anxious, in conversation with the US administration, 'to emphasize the significance of the Kashmir issue in the wider setting of recent developments in the Far East'.[198] On 17 November the Pakistani prime minister complained about a massive Indian build-up in Kashmir along a broad front, and threatened to retaliate in a big way.[199] The committee asked Attlee to assure Liaqat that he was trying 'to secure the halting of any offensive that may be taking place' and urging him not to 'precipitate any action on his part' until these measures had been tried out. To Nehru, Attlee referred the assurances given at the time of the commonwealth conference in October that neither side wished 'to settle the fate of Kashmir by military force'.[200] By 10 December it was clear that a coordinated move with the other powers in the Security Council would have to wait till the first week of January, but this might have made Pakistan take precipitate action 'in view of the deterioration of their military position'. The shadow of communist advance in Asia lay heavily over the ministers. The committee's further discussion focused on 'the increasing gravity of the situation in the Far East generally; the Communist advance in China was a direct menace to the whole of Asia; and even in Burma there had been substantial Communist progress during recent weeks. Against this background the continuing tension between India and Pakistan over Kashmir was indefensible.' Cripps agreed to write a personal letter to Nehru making these points.[201]

The Cripps–Nehru exchange on this is not available, but two near-contemporary British official sources state that a combination of Pakistani military action and British diplomatic pressure brought about the ceasefire on 1 January 1949, making India throw away its military advantage. A note dated 18 July 1949 from the CRO for Attlee stated: 'The bombardment of the Indian lines of communication by the Pakistan artillery in December 1948 (and our threat that in default of a ceasefire we would see that the Security Council debated the matter) were the most important factors in India's decision to agree to a cease-fire last Christmas.'[202] Much earlier, in the third week of January the UK High Commissioner in India had told Sir William Strang, the permanent under-secretary of state for foreign affairs that 'he had waited for an approach from Nehru and then, but only then had advised that there should be no military solution but that the Indian government should make a gesture in the direction of a political solution. He thought his advice, reinforced by the steadiness and wisdom of the Indian Commander-in-Chief [General Bucher] had borne fruit.'[203] (The high commissioner had told his government five weeks earlier that Cariappa was going to take over as Indian commander-in-chief from General Bucher on 15 January 1949; and he was known to favour an aggressive policy in Kashmir; also, that British 'knowledge of Indian plans [would] be much less precise' after Cariappa took over.)[204]

The changing balance of power between communist and non-communist forces in Asia, which had made the British look for an early cease-fire in Kashmir even before Pakistani troops had withdrawn, also made them decide to accept India in the commonwealth virtually on India's terms, giving up all the wrangling about the legal and constitutional position of the Crown which had characterised their treatment of the subject in 1948. On 28 October 1948 Attlee told the cabinet 'that he was anxious to keep India within the commonwealth if a constitutional basis could be formed which would be acceptable to the Constituent Assembly'.[205] The old dominions, when consulted in mid-September, had said that a republican India was acceptable in the commonwealth only if it accepted the king's jurisdiction for external relations.[206] By the beginning of November they had not shifted from their position. Besides, Nehru's suggestion for a common commonwealth citizenship had disturbed them; the Labour prime minister of Australia opposed it, reflecting the views of his constituents, although Philip Noel-Baker did present the Indian case.[207] When Attlee met them again on 15 December he said: 'India clearly wished to maintain a close association with the commonwealth, and there were very great advantages for all commonwealth countries in preserving that association, particularly at the present time'. He had specially in mind 'the communist threat to Southeast Asia and the difficulties which would arise, so long as the Kashmir dispute was unsettled, if Pakistan remained a member of the commonwealth and India severed all connections with it'. Since Nehru had made 'great efforts' to preserve India's links with the commonwealth, he should not be rebuffed.[208]

Malcolm MacDonald, commissioner-general for British Colonies in Southeast Asia, told Sir William Strang during the latter's tour in January 1949 of the importance of strengthening nationalism against communism in Asia and thought that 'it would . . . be a serious blow to our prestige and influence if India entirely Left the commonwealth'.[209]

Sir William had already been given the impression during his talks in India that both the prime minister and senior civil servants were firmly anti-communist and strongly nationalist. At a private meeting with Nehru, where the latter 'chose the topics himself', Nehru 'spoke first of communism. The results of communism in Russia must in the long run be evil because the means are evil. He said this in spite of the intellectual attraction which Marxism has for him. . . . He added, incidentally, that he thought that communism, in whatever country it might appear, would in the long run be overlaid and transformed by the national character, which must prevail in the end.' The British diplomat also described his conversations with the secretary to the home department H.V.R. Iyengar as 'one of [his] most interesting talks. . . .' Iyengar also spoke first about communism. He said: 'The Communists are hostile to the Congress Party. . . . Suppression alone . . . is no cure for communism. There are 12,000 troops acting against the Communists in Hyderabad, but at the same time remedial economic measures are being taken. Like Pandit Nehru, he wondered whether some such combination should not be tried in Malaya.'[210] These conversations must have persuaded the ministers and officials in Whitehall (except those with a strong attachment to Pakistan because of earlier experience in the subcontinent) that while India did not share the Western powers' perception of communism as a military threat, the elites who ruled India were firm in their nationalism and anti-communism.

An interdepartmental meeting of senior civil servants on 17 February discussed the pros and cons of India remaining in the commonwealth, despite a change in her constitutional status, and came to the conclusion that the balance of advantage lay in retaining her as a full member of the commonwealth. The economic departments (Board of Trade and the Treasury) were unanimous, the Colonial Office and the Foreign Office somewhat divided. Each department had produced detailed working papers. The Board of Trade concluded by noting that 'the interests we [Britain] had at stake were greater than she [India] had'.[211] The Treasury considered that membership of the sterling area was more important than commonwealth membership, and the Egyptian precedent showed that the two did not have to be coterminous. Because of its hard currency deficit and other reasons India had an interest in staying in the area, but the UK (which owed large sterling balances to India) also had an interest in keeping it in the commonwealth. In the words of the department itself:

It cannot be said that the commonwealth connection contains any obligation to refrain from discriminatory measures in the internal economic field if this is justified on grounds of national economic necessity. Nevertheless, to retain India in the commonwealth seems to provide the best hope of maintaining friendly economic relations and fair treatment for United Kingdom subjects in India.[212]

Towards the end of the paper it stated:

. . . leaving aside the political factors involved, the question resolves itself into a balancing of the large demands which India might make, because of her economic instability . . . against the adverse effects which India's departure from the commonwealth and the Sterling Area might have on our financial and commercial position in Southeast Asia. Above all, India and her possible demands need careful handling on a strictly empirical basis. If we can ensure this then it is in our interest to keep her within the commonwealth and the Sterling Area.[213]

The Colonial Office would have preferred that India retain its allegiance to the Crown, but since that was out of the question, it recommended commonwealth membership as a republic. Its effects would be least destabilising on the nationalist movements in the colonies, especially in those with a large Indian population. 'In Malaya . . . the moderating influence which Nehru has so far exercised upon the Indian community would be continued and the Indian Congress would probably continue to cooperate with Government.' Besides, 'should India remain a member of the commonwealth, despite non-allegiance, this would impose a certain restraint upon Nehru's more active anticolonial activities, although his fundamental attitude in this matter would not be affected'.[214] Should India become a foreign state 'the example of her secession would be fully exploited by the more extreme nationalist elements'.[215] The Foreign Office memorandum was emphatic that if India left the commonwealth without at least a treaty relationship with the UK, it would be most damaging to UK interests. However, opinion was divided between having a republican India within the commonwealth and having a treaty with it. The argument of those who only favoured a treaty relationship was 'that the presence within the commonwealth of a large nation publicly pledged to neutrality in case of world war would be a weakness rather than a strength', and that 'commonwealth membership [was] a privilege which must be paid for'.[216] The argument in favour of retaining India in the commonwealth was that 'failing the steadying influence of commonwealth membership, it might be that India would display greater intransigence in her handling of international affairs. . . .'[217] The interdepartmental meeting considered that the Foreign Office paper had exaggerated India's commitment to total neutrality and noted that the appreciation sent by the Ministry of Defence (which is not available) had treated India and Pakistan as one single unit.[218]

In the light of all these considerations, on 3 March Attlee recommended to his cabinet that if a mutually acceptable formula could be found to accommodate the British monarchy in the new scheme of things, a republican India should be accepted in the commonwealth: 'The threat of Communist encroachment in Southeast Asia was very real and, from the political angle as well as from the strategic and economic angles, there were very great advantages in retaining India within the commonwealth'.[219] As it is well known, at the Commonwealth Prime Ministers' Conference in April 1949 a formula was found by which republican India was accepted as a full member of the commonwealth, by the expedient of its recognition of the king as the symbol of the free association of independent states. A British Foreign Office paper of 1950 records that India's decision 'was taken on the explicit understanding that it did not involve the assumption by India of any military obligation, expressed or implied, to the other members of the commonwealth'.[220] When Attlee reported the results of the commonwealth conference to the cabinet, some ministers grumbled at the absence of any reference to a common defence policy in the final communique. It was pointed out to them that since the Statute of Westminster even the older dominions never openly accepted the obligation to have a common defence policy.[221] Die-hard Conservatives like Lord Salisbury and Lord Swinton (the latter led the Conservative opposition in the House of Lords) were very annoyed that India had thrown off allegiance to the king without giving any *quid pro quo* in defence policy. They were ready to move a resolution in the House of Lords protesting against this (which would have embarrassed the government) when they learnt, to *their* discomfiture, that Attlee had cleared the matter with Churchill beforehand.[222]

The underlying British motive was that, with the cease-fire in Kashmir, a political solution to the dispute might emerge. Meanwhile membership of the commonwealth should be made attractive enough to India, so that, eventually in a crisis, both India and Pakistan would be pro-West. Noel-Baker's report to the cabinet defence committee at the end of 1949 admitted that no contribution by either country should be expected towards the defence of the commonwealth until the Kashmir dispute had been settled. But he added: 'Should they settle their differences they are likely to be the only two members of the commonwealth who are in a position to put reasonably equipped and trained forces into the field at short notice.'[223] Auchinleck, who was planning to visit India in a private capacity as director of Grindlay's in the winter of 1949, wrote to Cariappa, 'I and your many friends in this country wish with all our hearts that some solution could be found to this Kashmir affair. . . . But it is a matter which only you yourselves can settle.'[224]

From Pakistan's point of view Britain had been overgenerous to India at the commonwealth conference. In late June 1949 Liaqat Ali Khan told the UK high commissioner that while touring West Punjab, the North-West Frontier Province and the 'Azad Kashmir' territory, he found a 'common assumption that a commonwealth which could apparently diminish the status of His Majesty the King in order to placate India would not hesitate to sacrifice Pakistan to India, were this demanded by Delhi'. He demanded a British guarantee for the security of Pakistan if India attacked and also an assurance that British officers would not have to obey the stand-down order.[225] The UK high commissioner supported this because it seemed to him 'unfortunate that Pakistan should drift away from the British connection, with incalculable consequences both here and in the Middle East, simply because other countries of the commonwealth are unwilling to accept the hypothesis of an Indian attack upon the territorial integrity of Pakistan. . . .'[226] Attlee had a meeting with Bevin and the secretary of state for commonwealth relations on 2 July. A paper, produced doubtless at their request by the CRO on 18 July, reflected the tussle within the department between the more pro-Pakistan and less pro-Pakistan elements. The paper argued that Britain should take a more active part in the Kashmir dispute and persuade the Indian government to abandon the valley. 'No settlement could be lasting which Left India with the Muslim majority of the Valley, with control over Pakistan's water supplies and with an indefensible frontier'.[227] That Bevin had not been fully successful in enlisting American support for military aid to Pakistan was revealed in another passage: 'They regard the problem as our baby, created by the untidy state in which we Left the position of the Indian States on the transfer of power'.[228] While recognising that pressure on India might make her leave the commonwealth the paper said:

It may be felt that if we have to choose between India or Pakistan leaving the commonwealth, India is the more valuable member, because of her greater size, population and industrial resources. On the other hand, account must be taken of the influence of Pakistan in the Middle East, her importance as a source of raw materials, the greater virility of the Punjabi Mussalman and likelihood that, if we come down on her side against India, she would probably prove a more loyal member of the commonwealth than India is ever likely to be.[229]

Having weighed various types of guarantees that could be given to Pakistan against India, and concluding that most of them, being directed against India, would annoy (and might prompt her to leave the commonwealth), it was suggested that a Middle East pact might be the least inoffensive and least burdensome to Britain:

There is a proposal already under preliminary consideration for the establishment of such a Pact, on the lines of the Atlantic Pact, directed in practice, although not necessarily overtly, against Russian aggression, and covering the area between Greece and Persia. It might be possible to extend this to cover Afghanistan and Pakistan. Such a pact could be drafted in such a way as to cover Pakistan against an Indian attack without expressly saying so. It would also share our obligations under the Pact with the United States and the other participants. It would however take time to negotiate, and Britain could not raise the matter with the USA until the Atlantic Pact was ratified by them.[230]

Despite the bias in the CRO paper, the ministers were not going to align totally with Pakistan. Gordon-Walker minuted, 'I have told the High Commissioners that in my view there can be no question of a military guarantee to Pakistan in any form. . . . In so far as Pakistan has been temporarily offended by the London Declaration, this represents our firm and decided policy and we could do nothing about it.' But, he added that 'since Britain could not count with certainty on all [its] officers obeying a Stand-Down order . . . it would be wise to make a virtue of necessity' and permit a one-sided stand-down. That might 'indeed be the only thing that would keep Pakistan firmly in the commonwealth'.[231] Attlee would not even go that far. He agreed that there should be no military guarantee, that keeping India in the commonwealth was Britain's decided policy, strongly opposed a one-sided stand-down, and wanted the officers to be told that this was a breach of their service rules. A political solution of the Kashmir problem was necessary: 'I do not believe that anything effective can be done to improve relations with Pakistan until the Kashmir situation is cleared up.'[232] Both ministers were silent on a Middle East pact.

Over a year later, in September 1950, when Pakistan broached the possibility of defence talks with Britain, it was told that Britain could not change its position on the question of guaranteeing Pakistan's frontiers with India.[233] In the intervening period the devaluation of sterling had brought home to Britain her limited capabilities for playing an independent world role. Though Nehru's publicly aired position on non-alignment was not to the taste of the Anglo-American alliance, British diplomats noted a number of developments which were favourable to British interests. There was 'precision and determination' in India's 'handling of the Communist menace in India'. 'This [was] largely due to the personality of Sardar Patel, but on this issue he enjoyed the full support of Pandit Nehru . . .' reported the British high commissioner.[234] He also praised Nehru for defusing the danger of a war with Pakistan during the East Pakistan riots in April 1950, and Patel for standing by Nehru against the Hindu communalists.[235] On Kashmir he thought it a 'significant step forward that at long last the possibility of a solution by partition with a plebiscite has been officially proposed'. India's rejection of Owen Dixon's proposals did not necessarily mean that the Security Council should wash its hands off the matter. Patel was believed to be interested only in Jammu.[236] India's support of the UN resolution on North Korean aggression was welcomed, but its misgivings about the US policy in the Far East was understood.[237]

Reflecting on the place of India in British foreign policy a Foreign Office memorandum, prepared at the end of 1950 for a proposed commonwealth prime ministers' conference, said:

At the moment, however, it is fair to say that India has *not* yet turned decisively to the west; and freedom of action in world affairs remains the basic principle of India's external relations. The result is that India is at present unlikely to agree to consider defence discussions with the United Kingdom or any other member of the commonwealth. On the other hand. . . . India retains a number of high ranking British officers in important administrative posts in her armed forces, and continues to look to the United Kingdom as her source of supply for arms and equipment and for the higher training of her officers. Contacts of this kind, together with an increasing awareness of the danger from Communist expansion may help to bring India closer to the United Kingdom in the defence field; and our ultimate aim must certainly be to achieve as close an understanding as is possible with India with a view to ensuring that in the event of a world war she would take an active part on our side.[238]

It also recorded that while Pakistan had been rather more ready than India 'to show that her sympathies lie with the West', it had demanded a guarantee of Pakistan's frontiers against attack by India as a precondition of entering into defence discussions with Britain. This is a condition which is unacceptable to the United Kingdom Government and there the matter officially rests'.[239]

(vi) Retrospect

If one has to sum up the imperial strategy of the political and economic elites of Britain with regard to the Indian subcontinent in the late 1940s in a few words, one would call it a study in failure, failure in the pursuit of multiple illusions. One illusion was that the political leadership in the subcontinent would be willing to sacrifice their long-term aims for the sake of Britain's imperial defence strategy. A devolution of authority in the subcontinent which would nevertheless maintain the integrity of the all-India armed forces was an ideal which required either that more political parties like the Unionist Party of Punjab successfully emerged on the scene, or that elections were dispensed with and the government settled down to ruling and managing the transition from a war economy to a peace economy by the bureaucracy and army alone. The first alternative was very unlikely, considering that the Unionist Party itself had lost ground in the Punjab.[240] The second alternative would have met with stiff resistance from all political parties. Beyond a point even the Muslim League was not a party of 'collaborators', and it proved this by its adamant attitude over having its own independent army for Pakistan. Having once hoisted the flag of Pakistan in 1940, the Muslim League would not run it down for the sake of the Cabinet Mission plan. The Congress supported dominion status (with a British governor-general to start with) only when it appeared a speedy way of achieving effective power, but it made no commitments on imperial defence. Conservative viceroys and secretaries of state always instinctively sensed that this would happen—which is why Linlithgow opposed the Cripps Mission, Amery wanted a 'presidential' type of constitution, and Wavell opposed Attlee's demand for general elections.

The second illusion was that unless the Muslim League was supported, British policy in the Middle East would be irretrievably weakened. The preceding account has shown that in the four years after 1947 Pakistan was more a supplicant to Britain than an assistant. By unilaterally launching a war in Kashmir it showed where its priorities lay, and these were certainly not the protection of British bases in the Persian Gulf and elsewhere in West Asia. Professor W. Roger Louis's monumental work on the decline of British power in the Middle East from 1945 to 1951 shows that Pakistan did not figure at all as an aid to British diplomacy.[241] Admittedly, if the Raj had ridden roughshod over the apprehensions of Muslim-majority areas where the Congress had no base, the resultant grievance might have marred Britain's image with many Arab states. Yet attempts could have been made to allay those apprehensions along the lines that Punjab governor Glancy once suggested,[242] and by remembering that the Pathans of the North-West Frontier Province, who had voted a Congress ministry to power, were also Muslims and had enlisted for the army during the Second World War.

The constitutional proposals of 16 May, which provided for a common centre in defence and foreign affairs but otherwise gave away the powers of constitution making to elected representatives meeting in three groups, were a compromise between the imperial vision of Bevin and the chiefs of staff, and the desire of Cripps and Attlee to concede as much as possible to the leading Indian parties—to the Congress a constituent assembly, and to the Muslim League two groups of provinces corresponding to the Pakistan resolution of 1940. By equating the satisfaction of Muslim interests with the satisfaction of the Muslim League it gave the Muslim League an importance which weakened Britain's own manoeuvrability, and prevented it from winning the support of the Sikhs, who were no less important for the all-India army than the allegedly more virile 'Punjabi Mussalman'. A policy along the lines of that version of 'Plan Balkan' as was drafted by the India Office on 2 May 1947,[243] could have been put forward a year earlier as an alternative to the 16 May plan, and this might have given the imperial power some room for manoeuvre before the communal riots made it very difficult for the government to enforce its will. Though it is idle to speculate whether this would have succeeded, it was the only card the government could have played with some chance of success, because provincial autonomy was an argument the Congress itself started using against the compulsory grouping proposals of the 16 May plan.[244]

The third illusion was the notion that a strategic presence in the subcontinent was worth more than the substantial economic links Britain still had in India. Compared to Malayan tin and rubber and Middle Eastern petroleum, the products of the subcontinent were of less consequence as dollar-earners, but the goodwill of the Indian business groups (and of the political and economic elites dependent on them) was more valuable than any strategic base Britain could get in the subcontinent to play an independent anti-communist role in world affairs. The discussions on India's membership of the commonwealth (and the sterling area) brought this out clearly.

The final illusion was of course the illusion of world power, or rather the hope of recovering it. To many inhabitants of southern Asia the image of Britain as a world power had faded away on 10 December 1941 in the smoky haze of the ships the Japanese bombed, the *Prince of Wales* and the *Repulse*. Yet the dogged determination with which Britain achieved the reconquest of Burma and Malaya with the help of the Indian army made officers like Auchinleck and Mountbatten, and politicians like Attlee and Bevin continue to believe that military links between a successor state and Britain would endure, that British personnel would be available for the transition from war to peace, and from colonial status to dominion status. The harshness of the terms of the American loan of 1945 should have sounded a warning, the 'bleak winter' of 1946–7 another. Yet even as the *Economic Survey* of 1947 proclaimed Britain's dire economic straits to the world, Attlee was hoping that somehow Mountbatten would be able to maintain imperial unity on defence at the centre. It became impossible to achieve that once the promise to leave by a specified date was given to more than one successor state. Things fell apart, the centre could not hold, anarchy was let loose in such a way that it required the highest degree of statesmanship to restore order and sanity and build new states. Such statesmen were not lacking either in India or Pakistan, but the shadow of the cold war fell between them. There is a lesson in it for us today.

NOTES

1. A general overview of the imperial vision of the Attlee government is provided in P.S. Gupta, 'Imperialism and the Labour Government of 1945–51', in this volume. One may also refer to my earlier work (written before the cabinet papers of this period were released), *Imperialism and the British Labour movement, 1914–1964* (London, 1975).

Hereafter these two works are cited as Gupta (1983) and Gupta (1975) respectively.

2. Gupta (1975), p. 306 (quotation from Dalton's diaries); Gupta (1983), p. 191 (quotations from a joint Cripps–Bevin paper and another by Bevin alone).

3. M.E. Yapp, *Strategies of British India* (Oxford, 1980), p. 19.

4. Intervention of Sir Samuel Hoare in the Cabinet Committee on India on 18 October 1932 (Cab 27/520, CI [32] 12th meeting [PRO]); Neville Chamberlain to Hilda Chamberlain, 6 December 1931 (Birmingham University Library, Chamberlain collection, NC 18/1/764—by courtesy of the Birmingham University Library).

5. A recurring theme in the quarterly appreciation of the Indian political situation presented to the British cabinet is the control exercised by the Congress Working Committee over the provincial Congress ministries. The appreciation of 19 August 1938, for example, criticised the Congress Working Committee and Gandhi in particular for 'overweening interference of the High Command in provincial affairs, or its denial of constitutional relations between the Governor and Ministers, or its imputation of motives to the Governor' (Cab 24/278 CP 192 [38], pp. 3f).

6. Grigg's views, given within quotation marks in a letter from Lord Brabourne (acting viceroy) to Lord Zetland, 21 September 1938 (Brabourne Papers, IOR Mss Eur. P 97/65B).

7. Benthall's report of talks with Linlithgow, 1 March 1940 (Benthall Diary, 1940, ff 38–9, Benthall Papers, Box VII, Cambridge University South Asia Archives, quoted by permission of Sir Paul Benthall and the South Asia Archives.

8. J. Gallagher and A. Seal, 'Britain and India between the Wars', *Modern Asian Studies,* XV, July 1981, pp. 413f. A fuller account is provided in my article 'Federalism and Provincial Autonomy as Devices of Imperial Control' in this volume.

9. Cab 27/654 ID (38) 10, enclosure, para 13 for the pro-Muslim slant, para 150 for its cursory treatment of the question of Indianisation.

10. The Chatfield report had laid down, in para 19 that the defence of India, even after the federation of the princely states, should remain the exclusive responsibility of the viceroy in his personal capacity, and the British Parliament, and no departure from this was to be allowed. For this reason Zetland advised keeping it secret from the Indian members of the Viceroy's Council (Cab 27/653, Committee on Defence of India, 4th meeting, 20 February 1939 [PRO]). For Linlithgow's willingness to stand firm, ibid., 5th meeting, 22 May 1939.

11. Quoted in R.J. Moore, *Churchill, Cripps, and India* (Oxford, 1979), p. 28.

12. Moore, *op.cit., passim*; Gupta (1975), pp. 269–73.

13. Anybody who has taken the trouble to go through the files of the Reforms Office, Commerce Department, or the Industry and Labour Department of the Government of India will find ample evidence of this in the notings of Indian officials. Among them were V.P. Menon, B.N. Rau, B. Rama Rau, G.S. Bajpai, S. Lall. Their approach was always to prepare the file on a topic in such a manner as to highlight the most liberal interpretation that could be put on any British constitutional pronouncement.

14. D. Potter, 'Manpower Shortage and the End of Colonialism: The Case of the Indian Civil Service', *Modern Asian Studies,* vol. VII, no. 1, pp. 48–73.

15. P.N.S. Mansergh and E.W.R. Lumby (eds), *India: The Transfer of Power* (hereafter *ToP*), vol. I (London, 1970), doc., 753 para 3 for Churchill's views; also doc. 769; later volumes edited by Mansergh and Moon. The role of N.R. Sarkar is to be found in *ToP*, vol. III, doc. 10.

16. Diary of Sir Edward Benthall, diary entry 28 May 1944 (Benthall Papers, Box VII, f 58).

17. Edward Benthall to Sir G. Scoone, 26 April 1942 (Benthall Papers, Box XVII, item 22, f 78).

18. Chapman Mortimer to Benthall, 5 March 1942 (ibid., item 14); Benthall to Mortimer, 26 April 1942 (ibid., item 21).

19. Memo by Jenkins, 13 July 1943 (*ToP*, IV, doc. 36).

20. *ToP*, IV, doc. 404.

21. *ToP*, V, doc. 409.

22. The records of the Federation of British Industries has a confidential note by Dalal criticising the 'safeguards' as a hindrance to Indo-British collaboration in the file 'Visit of Indian Industrialists May 1945' (FBI/S/Waller/106/3–FBI records, Modern Records Centre, University of Warwick, Coventry, by kind permission of the University). The Indian team included J.R.D. Tata, G.D. Birla, N.R. Sarkar, Mir Laik Ali, etc. and their advisers included Sir Jehangir Ghandy, P.S. Lokanathan, B.C. Ghosh, etc. The arguments between the viceroy and different sections of the British coalition cabinet can be followed from the published records in *ToP*, V, doc. nos. 434, 438, 444, 447, 449.

23. For earlier fears, see Gupta (1975), pp. 63, 216–20; for the changed outlook of Attlee and Bevin, ibid., pp. 281–2.

24. 'First draft of a paper for the war cabinet, Secret. Dictated by the Minister, 21 June 1943' (Bevin Papers, BEVN 2/4 ff 35–9, at Churchill College, Cambridge, by kind permission of the librarian, Churchill College).

25. 'India: army reduction and size', minute dated 17 January 1944 from Prime Minister to Chief of Staff, kept in COS (44) 51 (0) dated 20 January 1944 in the War Office records (WO/32/10841 (PRO).

26. Ibid.

27. WO 32/4406, appendix 23 (PRO) and L/WS/1/136 ff 46, 51 (IOR).

28. See minute by Thorne, 5 April 1946 (*ToP,* VII, doc. 60); also see the appreciation by the commander-in-chief (hereafter C-in-C) of the internal situation, 24 November 1945, para 6 (ibid., doc. 256).

29. For the anxieties of Wavell and Auchinleck on this count, see *ToP* V, doc. 11.

30. For Cariappa's promotion, a congratulatory letter from ex-C-in-C W. Birdwood to Cariappa, 20 July 1942 (Cariappa Collection, File 'Letters from foreigners, 1925–52'—National Archives of India [hereafter NAI] Lt-General Candeth (retd) told the author that in his opinion Birdwood was the only C-in-C in the interwar period with a real interest in Indianisation.

31. 'Bannu' to Cariappa, 29 November 1943 (Cariappa Collection, 'Correspondence with military officials living abroad'); Cariappa to Auchinleck, 22 August 1945 (Cariappa Collection, File 'Pamphlets, Notes etc', serial no. 2 NAI).

32. *Reorganisation of the Army and Air Forces in India: Report of a Committee set up by His Excellency the Commander-in-Chief in India,* vol. I, Text (New Delhi, 1945), para 44 at p. 15. (A copy of this secret report is in the Cariappa Collection, NAI.) There are many pencilled marginal notes by Cariappa in this personal copy of the report, including a defiant 'NO' against the point mentioned in the text, but it is not possible to say when these notes were made. He is a signatory without dissent to this report (he was the only Indian member) and such dissent on technical matters that he did record are given in certain footnotes. His more critical pencilled comments are on racial and political issues, on which he evidently preferred to be discreet when he signed the report. Brigadier J. Enoch Powell (later to become a controversial Conservative MP in Britain) was a member of this committee, and is reported to have claimed the authorship of the text of the report. See Roy Lewis, *Enoch Powell* (London, 1979), p. 18; also see Andrew Roth, *Enoch Powell: Tory Tribune* (London, 1970), pp. 45–6.

33. Wavell to Amery, 20 September 1944, and 22 October 1944 (*ToP,* V, docs 19 and 61); also see Feroz Noon to Wavell, 19 September 1944 (ibid., doc. 18).

34. Amery to Wavell, 7 December 1944 (*ToP,* V, doc. 144); also see Wavell's reply of 20 December 1944 (*loc.cit.,* doc. 156), rejecting Amery's view and saying that Amery had based his argument on Sir Reginald Coupland's

latest book, which had hardly been noticed in India and which the nationalists treated with contempt.

35. For the Attlee–Wavell differences on this see *ToP,* VI, docs 33 and 92. (There is a brief summary of the respective positions in the author's review article of all the *ToP* volumes in *Indian and Foreign Review,* XXI, no. 20, p. 13.) For the Labour party's ideological commitment to elections, see Gupta (1975), p. 38.

36. Gupta (1983), pp. 181–87; also see Gupta (1975), chs IX and X.

37. Cab 131/1 DO (46) 20, meeting of 15 February 1945 (PRO).

38. Signature illegible to Auchinleck, 14 July 1945 (Auchinleck Papers, MUL 1094, John Rylands Library, Manchester. I am grateful to the librarian for permission to consult these papers).

39. Benthall's diary entry, 26 November 1945 (Benthall Papers, Box VII, f 100). Cambridge South Asia Archives.

40. Col. H.S. Himatsinghji to Auchinleck, 19 November 1945, reporting a talk with Bhulabhai Desai (Auchinleck Papers, MUL 1113). Enclosed with this is a letter from a young British officer, Major C.M. Cockin to Himatsinghji, 19 November 1945, where he observes; 'this is causing a wider and wider breach between Britain and India at a time when it is virtually necessary that there should be on both sides confidence and goodwill' (MUL 1114).

41. Glancy to Auchinleck, 29 December 1945, 'Brief survey of typical reactions to the INA recorded in the Punjab' (Auchinleck Papers, MUL 1125).

42. IO Jemadar B.I. Ganapathy to Cariappa, 28 November 1945 (Cariappa Collection, File 'Correspondence with Army Officers, 1920–25', serial no. 57, NAI). General Cariappa marked all the passages in this letter pertaining to the INA.

43. Sarat Bose to Cariappa, 16 December 1945 (Cariappa Collection, File 'General Cariappa's correspondence with different individuals relating to Army affairs', NAI).

44. Sarat Bose to Cariappa, 29 December 1945, 7 February 1945 (enclosing Philip Mason's letter to Bose rejecting his request 4 February 1946), and 28 February 1946 (Cariappa Collection, File 'General Cariappa's correspondence with Military Officials', NAI).

45. Cariappa to Lt.-General Sir R.S. Deedes (Adjutant-General), 30 January 1946 (ibid.)

46. Cariappa to Deedes (Personal & Confidential), 2 February 1946, ibid. A significant passage after the portion quoted in the text runs: 'When the British leave India, Indians now serving under them in the Indian Army will remain in India. The supporters of today's "INA" will be the rulers of India tomorrow and I feel that nothing should be done now which may

lead to giving only the 2nd place to the Indian officers and men of today's Indian army in the National armed forces of tomorrow.'

47. Talks with Sir Evan Jenkins about situation in India (1945) 8, on 27 November 1945 at Chequers, the Prime Minister's official country residence (PREM 8/58, PRO).

48. S. Gopal, *Jawaharlal Nehru: A Biography*, vol. I, (Delhi, 1976), p. 307.

49. See note 34 above.

50. G.D. Birla to Sardar Patel, 14 September 1945, in G.M. Nandurkar (ed.), *Sardar Patel's Letters, Mostly Unknown*, Birth Centenary, vol. IV (Ahmedabad, 1977), p. 173.

51. *ToP,* VII docs 87, 120.

52. Minutes by Philip Mason, 31 October 1945 and Major-Gen. Bruce, 12 October 1945 in 'Post-war role of the Indian Army and the Police Force vis-à-vis the internal security of India' (Home—Police—1945—File 174/ 32/45 [Secret], NAI).

53. Although Jawaharlal Nehru was the leading member of the interim government from September 1946, he found himself helpless to do anything about the killings in Bengal, where the Muslim League ministry was in power, whereas he had some effect in curbing the communal frenzy unleashed against Muslims in Bihar, where a Congress ministry was in power. Even there he found plenty to criticise in the role of individual Congress workers. See. S. Gopal (ed.), *Selected Works of Jawaharlal Nehru*, 2 series, vol. I (New Delhi, 1984), pp. 26, 52, 55, 63, 65, 69.

54. For 'scheme A' and 'scheme B' of the Cabinet Mission and Attlee's reply see *ToP,* VII, docs 86 and 105. For the discussions in the cabinet's defence committee (which are not reproduced in the *ToP* volumes), see Cab 131/1, DO (46), 11th meeting, item 3 (PRO).

55. 'A note on the strategic implication of the inclusion of Pakistan in the British Commonwealth' (with attached map), dated 11 May 1946 by Auchinleck (copies sent to Wavell, General Mayne, and Lt.-Gen. A. Smith), Auchinleck Papers, MUL 1152).

56. 'Strategic implications of incorporating Pakistan in British Commonwealth' (undated, but the provenance of the document suggests that it was written shortly before 11 May 1946); it is marked 'C-in-C's secretariat, GOS Committee, GOS (46) 750, revised JPD (46) 8 Auchinleck Papers, MUL 1953.

57. *ToP,* VII, doc. 295. Abell's note is undated but it was discussed by the Cabinet Mission on 16 May 1946.

58. *ToP,* VII, doc. 78.

59. As in note 56.

60. As in note 55.

61. See note 86 below.

62. Auchinleck to Cariappa, 28 September 1946 (Cariappa Collection, File 'Correspondence with Army Officers, 1920–1950', serial no 78, NAI).

63. The Punjab governor Glancy had been opposed to any settlement that made the Sikh community feel that they were put under the domination of the Muslim League. He had opposed the Cripps Mission scheme of provincial option on this ground. He reiterated his view that the Punjabi rather than the communal character of his province must be stressed and the theory of Pakistan deflated (*ToP,* I, docs 236 and 248; *ToP*, VI, docs 29 and 39). The available evidence suggests that the British authorities were so obsessed with the need to placate the Muslim League in order to establish credibility as a friend of Middle Eastern Muslim states that they ignored Sikh aspirations. It was only in the context of 'Plan Balkan' in May 1947 that the British secretary of state suggested that an autonomous Punjab (within the commonwealth) might allay the misgivings of the Sikhs (*ToP*, X, doc. 475).

64. *ToP*, VII, doc. 527.

65. *ToP*, VII, doc. 455, cabinet meeting of 5 June 1946, pp. 817–19.

66. Cab 129/16 CP (470 20 para 15 (PRO).

67. *ToP*, IX, docs 236 and 243. Section 93 read as follows: 'The Governor may (with the governor-general's concurrence) by proclamation exercise in case of the breakdown of the constitution in the province, like functions to that of the governor-general subject to control by Parliament for a maximum of three years.'

68. Gupta (1975) p. 298.

69. Bridges' minute, 23 December 1946, for the Prime Minister (PREM 8/541, PRO).

70. Field-Marshal Montgomery at once refused to invite officers of the Indian army to the staff exercises in Britain, lest secret strategic plans of the Anglo-American alliance were leaked (Montgomery to Auchinleck, 30 January 1947, Auchinleck Papers, MUL 1213). Pethick-Lawrence confirmed the ban a couple of months later (Pethick-Lawrence to Attlee, 31 March 1947, *ToP*, X, doc. 3).

71. R.J. Moore, *Escape from Empire: The Attlee Government and the Indian Problem* (Oxford, 1983), ch. 4.

72. R.J. Moore, 'Jinnah and the Pakistan Demand', *Modern Asian Studies,* XVII (1983), p. 557.

73. *ToP*, X, docs 1, 12.

74. See note 63 above; also, Jenkins' minute, 29 March 1947 (*ToP*, X, doc. 32).

75. Some of the key documents on the Sikh demand for partition are the following: *ToP*, IX, docs 13, 32, 57, 109 with its enclosure.

76. Ibid., doc. 216 at p. 425.

77. Jawaharlal Nehru and others to Lord Wavell, 5 February 1947 (*ToP,* IX, doc. 350).
78. *ToP,* IX, doc. 524 (Memo for Pethick-Lawrence, 12 March 1947).
79. Ibid., no 529, especially p. 939.
80. Cf. Ismay's attitude, as quoted in R.J. Moore, *Escape* (1983), p. 279. This particular extract is of course with reference to Mountbatten's advocacy of the Congress proposals of 8 May, but the same reaction was evident earlier.
81. *ToP,* X, doc. 273, p. 826, dated 1 May 1947, finalised by Christie.
82. Ibid., docs 406, 521. The term 'Plan Partition' had been taken from Professor Moore's work.
83. When in Britain in the first week of December 1946, Jinnah sent out these feelers, not just to Conservative politicians. The Liberal elder statesman Lord Samuel was also approached by him. See 'Notes of conversation with Jinnah, 4 December 1946' by Lord Samuel (Samuel Papers, A/153 [XII], item 43, f 66, House of Lords Record Office, by kind permission of the heirs of Lord Samuel and the archivist, House of Lords).
84. Gupta (1983), p. 103 (the original sources are cited there in notes 37,48.
85. *ToP,* IX, doc. 529, minute 5 dated 13 March 1947.
86. *ToP,* X, doc. 64, 92, 94, 203.
87. Ibid., doc. 229, Viceroy–Jinnah interview, 26 April 1947; see Jinnah's reference to support from Churchill at p. 452f.
88. *ToP,* X, doc. 161.
89. Gopal, *Jawaharlal Nehru,* vol. I, p. 353.
90. *ToP,* X, doc. 215, 221.
91. R.J. Moore, *Escape* (1983), pp. 251–3.
92. Ibid., pp. 266–7.
93. Ibid., p. 279.
94. These are to be found in an India Office plan prepared in London (*ToP,* X, doc. 289, p. 576 paras 7–10). Of course, 'Plan Balkan' as drafted in Mountbatten's secretariat did not go into such details but gave only a general reference to the importance of joint consultation on common subjects such as defence (ibid., doc. 260 Appendix C).
95. 'British Commonwealth discussions, London 1947', note by Sir Stafford Cripps, 22 April 1947, for the Overseas Economic Policy Committee of the cabinet, Cab 134/541 OEP (47), 16, p. 6.
96. As in note 72.
97. The following files, pertaining to India's sterling balances and trade with India, which have been inspected, do not have any references to 'Plan Balkan'—T 236/148–51. Also see CO 537/2969 (all in PRO).
98. *ToP,* X, doc. 222 dated 25 April 1947.

99. Ibid., doc. 216, meeting on 25 April 1947 at 3 p.m.

100. Ibid., doc. 264, meeting on 1 May 1947 at 10 a.m. The quotation is at p. 511.

101. Viceroy's staff meeting on 10 May, ibid., doc. 381 at p. 730.

102. *ToP,* X, doc. 416, meeting on 12 May at 11.30 a.m. well before there was even a hint of any shift of opinion in New Delhi. (Ismay got a brief message about Nehru's adverse reaction on 13 May at 8 a.m., and the fuller details of that reached India Office on 14 May at 2.20 a.m.)

103. The relevant files of the Prime Minister's Office are PREM 8/547 and 581. As late as the middle of June (if not even later) the possibility of Travancore staying out was taken seriously by some officials in Britain. The Colonial Office, for example, which dealt with Ceylon, got a cable from Ceylon (dated 18 June 1947) asking whether since Travancore was likely to be free Ceylon should proceed to have a separate commercial treaty with it. The way the Colonial Office posed the problem to the India Office showed that the options were kept open—'only question is whether it would be premature and politically embarrassing for the Ceylon government to approach many of the Indian states'. (W.A. Morris to H.A.F. Rumbold, 1 July 1947 (CO 537/2969, item 2; item 1 gives the cablegram from Ceylon (PRO).

104. As in note 102; the views of Montgomery and Ismay are towards the end of the minutes of the meeting.

105. As in note 102, last paragraph.

106. Listowell made the point about the Sikhs in a letter to Mountbatten, 17 May 1947 (*ToP,* X, doc. 475 at p. 887).

107. *ToP,* X, doc. 263 (Jenkins to Mountbatten, 30 April 1947).

108. Ibid., doc. 405, item 2 at p. 766.

109. *ToP,* X, doc. 414, item 2 at p. 781.

110. For the viceroy's categorical rejection of independence for the North-West Frontier Province see *ToP,* X, doc. 415, India and Burma Committee meeting, paper IB (47) 66, dated 12 May 1947, item A. For the more flexible approach to Bengal, see Mountbatten's telegram to Ismay, 13 May 1947 (*ToP,* X, doc. 429, para 4 a at p. 807), where he wrote: 'I am seeing Suhrawardy on Wednesday, May 14, and will tell him that I cannot make provision in the plan for Bengal remaining independent; but that there is nothing in the plan to prevent the Bengal Legislative Assembly passing a resolution for independence which I would treat on its merits.' That Mountbatten was interested in retaining a united autonomous Bengal, provided its sponsors dropped the idea of calling it a 'socialist republic', is seen in Mountbatten to Burrows, 16 May 1947 (*ToP,* doc. 462). As late as 31 May the viceroy and the

British government kept on hoping that an autonomous Bengal might emerge (*ToP,* XI, docs 1 and 2).

111. Mountbatten to Mieville, 21 May 1947 (*ToP,* XI, doc. 496).

112. *ToP,* XI, doc. 6 (India and Burma Committee meeting noted Nehru's interview with Norman Cliff).

113. *ToP,* XI, doc. 201.

114. Lt-Gen. G.N. Molesworth's weekly letter to Auchinleck, 14 October 1943 (Molesworth Papers, GNM 136, at the National Army Museum, London, by courtesy of the Director of the Museum).

115. 'India (Misc.) 1947 Andaman & Nicobar Islands' (PREM 8/574) has the relevant documents. For the request to the Colonial Office, see A. Creech Jones (Secy. of State for Colonies) to Listowell, 14 June 1947, where the Colonial Office was willing to take on the responsibility provided the Treasury gave a grant-in-aid (ibid.).

116. *ToP,* X, doc. 553, minute 5 at p. 1017.

117. Viceroy to Secy. of State, 13 June 1947 (PREM 8/574).

118. IB (47) 31st meeting, 17 June 1947 (ibid.).

119. Viceroy to Secy. of State, 5 July 1947, and note by Ismay, 8 July 1947 (ibid.).

120. W.S. Morris-Jones, 'The Transfer of Power, 1947: A View from the Sidelines', *Modern Asian Studies,* XVI (1982), p. 5. Denied the opportunity in India, the British government made the retention of a naval base at Trincomalee a precondition for granting dominion status to Ceylon (Gupta, 1983, p. 104). Later, when in 1956 the Bandaranaike government in Ceylon insisted on the removal of that obligation, Britain started developing an alternative Indian Ocean strategy based on the Australian air base on the Cocos islands, and a proposed new airfield on the island of Gan, 400 miles southwest of Ceylon. In November 1965, another Labour government proclaimed a new colony called the British Indian Ocean territory, grouping a number of small islands of the empire of which Diego Garcia was important. In the seventies close Anglo-American cooperation developed on that island (C.J. Bartlett, *The Long Retreat: A Short History of British Defence Policy, 1945–70* [London, 1972], pp. 127, 209, 227).

121. *ToP,* XII, doc. 65, para 34 (p. 99).

122. *ToP,* XI, doc. 506, especially para 31 at pp. 899f.

123. Morris-Jones, *op.cit.,* pp. 8f.

124. *ToP,* X, docs 108, 319 (para 5), 369 (para 30); *ToP,* XII, docs. 4 and 280 (dated 29 July 1947).

125. *ToP,* XII, doc. 317 and 383 (para 10).

126. Cariappa to Auchinleck (Confidential), 15 July 1947 (Cariappa Collection, 'Letters from the officers of Army Headquarters', serial no. 7).

127. *ToP,* XI, doc. 506, para 2 (Viceroy's personal report, 4 July 1947).

128. Gupta (1975), pp. 313f.

129. Gupta (1983), pp. 189–90.

130. S. Pollard, *The Development of the British Economy,* 1914–67 (London, 1969 edn), p. 360.

131. Gupta (1983), p. 190 for the role of the US trade negotiator at Geneva.

132. Ibid., pp. 194–5.

133. Ibid., pp. 187–195.

134. Ibid., pp. 190–191.

135. Cab 128/10 CM 77 (47) 2, dated 25 September 1947.

136. Gupta (1983), p. 194

137. The sterling balances story can be traced in *ToP,* II, docs 375, 379, 751, 773, 780; *ToP,* III, doc. 25, Dalton's views in T 236/51 (PRO). See also note 96 on p. 212 above.

138. For Amery's views, his letter to Wavell, 24–25 February 1944 (*ToP,* IV, doc. 399). For Bevin's views the document cited at note 24 above.

139. Viceroy to Secy. of State, 24 July 1947 (kept in PREM 8/544).

140. Dalton's cabinet paper CP (47) 213 dated 5 August 1947 (also in PREM 8/544).

141. N. Kipping to P. Hannon, 17 June 1949 (Hannon Papers, Box 46, File I ff. 46 f—House of Lords Record Office, Beaverbrook Collection, by kind permission of the Keeper of the Records).

142. Hannon to Kipping, 24 June 1949 (ibid.).

143. Gupta (1975), pp. 307–8.

144. Cab 129/36 CP (49) 179, para 8.

145. Cab 128/16 CM 54 (49) 5.

146. During the interdepartmental discussions in Whitehall in February 1949 on the desirability, from Britain's point of view, of having India in the commonwealth, the memorandum of the Treasury observed, *inter alia*: 'Outright expropriation has been mentioned as the Government of India's natural remedy for any attempt to repudiate the Indian sterling balances and might be provoked by measures in the financial field such as the blocking of India's sterling balances to a degree unacceptable to her' (Cab 130/45 Gen 276/2 'The financial consequence of a change in India's constitutional position: memo, by the Treasury, 16 February 1949', para 6).

147. This discussion is based on an eleven-page report to the Commonwealth Affairs Committee of the British cabinet by Auchinleck sent towards the

end of September 1947 (Cab 134/54 CA [47] 6 enclosure 'Situation in India and Pakistan: Report by the Supreme Commander Sir Claude Auchinleck'). The words given in quotes in the text are at p. 5.

148. Lord Ismay's report to the British chiefs of staff, 8 October 1947 COS (47) 116, p. 1 (also kept as annexure to Cab 134/54 C.A. [47] 6).

149. Auchinleck to Gen. Sir Geoffrey Scoones (Private & personal), 15 September 1947 (Auchinleck Papers, MUL 1259, John Rylands Library, Manchester).

150. Script of 'General talk to Indian Officers of the Indian Army by Major-Gen. K.M. Cariappa, September 1947 (Cariappa Collection, File 'Pamphlets, Notes etc.', serial no. 3 [NAI]).

151. As in note 147, p. 9.

152. 'Pt. II, *For the personal information* of the Prime Minister, the Chief of Naval Staff, the Chief of the Imperial General Staff, the Chief of Air Staff only' (italics in the original), p. 3 (PREM 8/587 dated 28 September 1947).

153. Ibid.

154. Auchinleck to Sir Geoffrey Scoones (Top secret & personal), 5 October 1947, postscript, at p. 5 (Auchinleck Papers, MUL 1263).

155. 'Note by Sir A. Carter of conversations . . . in Karachi . . . 1st to 3rd October 1947', p. 2. This note is kept as an annex to a memo by Philip Noel-Baker, Secy. of State for Commonwealth Relations, dated 8 November 1947, for the Commonwealth Affairs Committee of the cabinet, entitled 'The policy of financial assistance to Pakistan' (Cab 134/54 CA [47] 13).

156. Referred to in a letter from Mountbatten to Gandhi, 29 September 1947 (copy kept in PREM 8/586, 'Letters between Gandhi and Mountbatten: copies sent to Prime Minister').

157. As in note 147, p. 3 under the section headed Joint Defence Council.

158. Mountbatten to Auchinleck 26 September 1947 (strictly personal) (Auchinleck Papers, MUL 1260).

159. Auchinleck to Geoffrey Scoones, 5 October 1947 (Top secret & personal), p. 2, para 4 (ibid., MUL 1263). Two Indian corroborations of this come from the following: (i) a note by Cariappa, as Deputy Chief of General Staff, dated 7 October 1947, goes as follows: 'In a free India, governed entirely by the people of India, it is hard to expect 100 per cent loyalty to the government from non-nationals who may be serving in the Armed Forces of the country. . . . From reports in the press and from comments expressed by the people of the country, including some highly placed government officials, it is regrettable to see that there is a feeling in India that British officers cannot be expected to serve in the Indian Army with

the same degree of enthusiasm and sincerity as they have done in the past.' The note goes on to say that this opinion has to be recognised and agreed to, and Indians should be at the helm completely. Specific areas of command (staff college, various training centres) should still be British, and 25 per cent instructional staff should be British officers. This would release Indian officers to hold executive commands. (Cariappa Collection, File 'Pamphlet, notes etc.', serial no. 4; NAI) (ii) letter from a Brigadier to Cariappa commenting on the above: 'I am not in favour, under any circumstances, to retain any British Officers in staff appointments at Army Headquarters and Commands, because it would be wrong in principle and in addition it was not the unanimous decision of the Indians at the conference that you held' (Brigadier Hira Lal Atal to Cariappa, 15 October 1947, ibid., serial no. 5).

160. Cab 134/54 CA (47) 3rd meeting (31 October 1947) item 1, p. 2.
161. Cab 134/54 CA (47) 6, enclosure, p. 5. It is also available as COS (47) 116.
162. As in note 160, p. 1.
163. Ibid., p. 2.
164. Cab 134/54 CA (47) 4th meeting (14 November 1947), item 1.
165. Ibid.
166. For the request by Jinnah, see 'Note by Sir A. Carter', dated 8 October 1947, given as an appendix to Noel-Baker's memo dated 8 November 1947 (Cab 134/54 CA [47] 13); other relevant memoranda by Noel-Baker between 8 October and 8 November are Cab 134/54 C.A. (47) 8, 12, 13, 14.
167. Cab 134/54 CA (47) 4th meeting, 14 November 1947, item 2, p. 4.
168. Sisir Gupta, *Kashmir, A Study in Indo-Pak Relations* (New Delhi, 1966), p. 129, also Lord Birdwood, *Two Nations and Kashmir* (London, 1950), p. 63.
169. Sir George Cunningham to Lord Halifax, 17 December 1947 (Hickleton Mss A 2.278.16. 54.3, at the Borthwick Institute of Historical Research, York, by kind permission of the owners of the copyright and the archivist).
170. See note 105 above.
171. Gopal, *Jawaharlal Nehru: A Biography,* vol. II, *op.cit.,* pp. 20–2.
172. PREM 8/1219, minute no. G.1/49 by P.C. Gordon-Walker for prime minister, dated 22 August 1949, para 4.
173. Ibid., p. 22.
174. Ibid., p. 23.
175. Cab 130/37 Gen 223 (India, ad hoc committee) 1st meeting, 18 February 1948. (This ad hoc committee, whose minutes are kept in this classification at the PRO, sat from 18 February to 10 December 1948 to discuss

Kashmir—and occasionally Hyderabad—and had Attlee, Bevin, Cripps, Noel-Baker and A.V. Alexander as regular members; the officials always present were Archibald Carter, M.E. Denning, with S.E.V. Luke acting as the secretary).

176. Cab 130/37 Gen 223/3rd meeting.

177. UK High Commissioner in Pakistan to Commonwealth Relations Office (hereafter, CRO), no. 356, 13 April 1948 (kept as annexure to Cab 130/37 Gen 223/4th meeting [PRO]).

178. Cab 130/37 Gen 223/4th meeting 15 April 1948, item 2.

179. Ibid., item 1.

180. UK High Commissioner in India to CRO, no. 939, 13 April 1948, reporting a talk with H.V.R. Iyengar (kept as annexure to Cab 130/37 Gen 223/4th meeting, 15 April 1948).

181. As in note 176, p. 4.

182. Gopal, *Jawaharlal Nehru: A Biography*, p. 29.

183. This is mentioned in paras 53 and 54 of a confidential British Foreign Office appreciation prepared in December 1950 for the Commonwealth Prime Ministers' Conference 1950 (Cab 130/64 Gen 338 [1].

184. Cab 128/12 CM (48) 2, item 5. The papers were CP (47) 313 and CP (48) 7.

185. M.S. Venkataramani, *The American Role in Pakistan*, 1947–58 (New Delhi, 1982), pp. 40–1.

186. 'Communism in India and Pakistan'. CRO fortnightly summary, no. 8 for second half of September 1948 (CO 537/2725).

187. Hugh Dalton's diary, entry for 15 October 1948 (Dalton Papers, London School of Economics, by courtesy of the librarian, LSE).

188. Cab 13/037 Gen 223/5th meeting, item 1 (9 July 1948).

189. Terence Shone (UK high commissioner) to P. Noel-Baker, no. 116, 12 August 1948 (PREM 8/818 at PRO).

190. Noel-Baker's minute for Attlee no. 61/48, 9 September 1947, para 4 (b) in PREM 8/318.

191. Enclosure, V.K. Krishna Menon to Attlee, 21 October 1948, in PREM 8/806.

192. Lord Ismay to Attlee, 21 September 1948, in PREM 8/818.

193. V.K. Krishna Menon to Attlee (secret), 20 September 1948, ibid.

194. CO 537/2725, 'Monthly appreciation of the General Situation in India' by the UK high commission, no. 9 for September 1948, dated 27 October 1948, has a passage as follows: 'When speaking of the need of liquidating the Communists in Hyderabad, a prominent Indian official recently stated, "We are not going to have another Burma there".'

195. Cab 130/37, Gen 223/7th meeting, 3 November 1948.

196. Ibid., annexure.

197. Cab 13/37 Gen 223/7th to 11th meeting inclusive. The lack of coordination with the US or other European powers was admitted at the 8th meeting (p.2), and even more fully in a paper by Noel-Baker, 9 December 1948, kept as Cab 130/37 Gen 223/2, annexure, para 2 (iv) & (v).

198. Ibid., 8th meeting (7 November 1948). At this time the Chinese communist forces had got the upper hand over the Kuo-min-Tang in the civil war in China. In course of November 1948 all of Manchuria came under the Chinese communists. Peking was besieged and surrendered in January 1949. From the 'liberated' areas the Chinese communist forces were converging towards Nanking, which also surrendered in January.

199. Ibid., 9th meeting (17 November 1948).

200. Ibid., annexure (telegram dated 18 November 1948).

201. Ibid., 11th meeting (10 December 1948).

202. 'Memorandum on relations between Indian and Pakistan, 18 July 1949', by HAF (Pol. 2443/49), p. 3f. kept as enclosure in PREM 8/1219 (PRO).

203. 'Report by Sir William Strang, on his visit to New Delhi, 16–20 January 1949' (Cab 129/33 CP (49) 67, para 15.

204. Cab 13/37 Gen 223/2, annexure to memo by Noel-Baker, 9 December 1948, para 3 (v).

205. Cab 128/14 CM (48) 67, 28 October 1948, minute 3 (confidential annexure).

206. Cab 129/30 CR (48) 5, 14 September 1948 (Report by the Cabinet Secretary Sir Norman Brook, para 3).

207. Cab 129/31 CP (48) 286, annexures A and B (Record of discussions, 17 November 1948).

208. Cab 129/31 CP (48) 309, annexure 1f. (Record of discussions 15 December 1948).

209. As in note 203, para 67.

210. Ibid., paras 18, 32.

211. Cab 130/45 Gen 276/3.

212. Cab 130/45 Gen 276/2, para 7.

213. Ibid., para 17.

214. Cab 130/45 Gen 276/1, pp. 2–3.

215. Ibid., p. 5.

216. Cab 130/45 Gen 276/1, paras 6, 8.

217. Ibid., para 13.

218. Cab 130/45 Gen 276/1st meeting, pp. 1–2.

219. Cab 128/15 CM 17 (49) 1, 3 March 1949.

220. Cab 134/64 Gen 388/1, para 54.

221. Cab 123/15 CM 29 (49) 1, dated 27 April 1949.
222. For Swinton's views, see Swinton Papers at Churchill College, Cambridge, SWIN III/3/1 'India's foreign policy, 1949'. In another file (SWIN III/3/2) the correspondence between 28 March and end of April 1949 showing the effort to move a resolution in the House of Lords is to be found. Lord Salisbury wrote to Swinton, 'So far as I can see, India's continued association with the commonwealth does not help us in any way. . . . She will not agree to any co-ordinated foreign policy. She is definitely hostile to our colonial policy. She reserves the right to stab us in the back at any moment at the United Nations on these and other aspects' (Salisbury to Swinton, 22 April 1949 [SWIN 174/4/2]).
223. Cab 131/7 DO (49) 89, 'Defence burdens and the Commonwealth', memo by Noel-Baker, 30 December 1949.
224. Auchinleck to Cariappa, 25 September 1949 (Cariappa Collection, File 'Correspondence with military officials living abroad', NAI).
225. L.B. Grafftey-Smith (UK high commissioner to Pakistan) to P. Noel-Baker, 24 June 1949, paras 1, 2 (PREM 8/1219).
226. Ibid., para 7.
227. Note by Attlee, 2 July 1949 on minute of Noel-Baker, 1 July 1949; memo by H.A.F. Rumbold, 18 July 1949, para 2 (all in PREM 8/1219).
228. Memo by Rumbold (as in previous note), para 4.
229. Ibid., para 6.
230. Ibid., para 9 (iii).
231. Gordon-Walker's memo for Attlee, 29 July 1949, paras 5, 6 (PREM 8/1219).
232. Attlee's notings on Gordon-Walker's memo, 29 July 1919, ibid.
233. 'Top Secret. Record of conversation between Mr Ghulam Mohammad and the Secy. of State for Commonwealth Relations on 27 September 1950 by P.C. Gordon-Walker, ibid.
234. 'India: Review of events from June to September 1950', by UK High Commissioner in India for the CRO, 27 October 1950, para 16 (CO 537/5668).
235. 'India: Review of events in first quarter of 1950', by UK high commissioner for the CRO, 21 April 1950, para 6, ibid.
236. As in note 234, para 31.
237. 'India: the Indian attitude on the Korean question', by Frank Roberts (UK high commission) for Sir P. Liesching, 5 August 1950, ibid.
238. Cab 130/64 Gen 338/1 (Commonwealth Prime Ministers' Conference 1950), para 55.
239. Ibid., para 57.

240. I.A. Talbot, 'The Growth of the Muslim League in the Punjab, 1937–46', *Journal of Commonwealth and Comparative Politics*, XX (1982); Prem Chowdhury, *Punjab Politics: The Role of Sir Chhotu Ram* (Delhi, 1984), pp. 322–7.

241. W. Roger Louis, *The British Empire in the Middle East, 1945–51* (Oxford, 1948).

242. See above, the documents cited in note 63.

243. *ToP*, X. doc. 289, p. 576, paras 7–10.

244. Statement of the Congress Working Committee on the declaration of 6 December 1947, as in S. Gopal (ed.), *Selected Works of Jawaharlal Nehru*, vol. I (New Delhi, 1984), p. 29 para 3.

N.B. This paper was read at the Nehru Memorial Museum and Library in February 1984 and went to the press sometime thereafter. The author was, therefore, unable to see the publications of Dr Anita Inder Singh in the following three articles: 'Decolonisation in India: The Statement of 20 February 1947'. *The International History Review* (May 1984); 'Keeping India in the Commonwealth: British Political and Military Aims, 1947–49', *Journal of Contemporary History* (1985); 'Post-Imperial British Attitudes to India: The Military Aspect, 1947–51', *The Round Table* (1985).

INDIA IN COMMONWEALTH
DEFENCE, 1947–1956

T his essay looks at the complex interaction between Britain, the older dominions and India in terms of their perceptions of their respective defence needs. India's admittance to the commonwealth in 1949 has been the subject of much discussion by scholars because of her republican status. A neglected area, however, is the ambivalent approach of Britain and the older dominions to cooperation on commonwealth defence and on the issue of whether the admission of the republic was consistent with this.

On 9 May 1947 Lord Mountbatten, the viceroy, told his staff that the willingness of the Congress and the Muslim League to accept transfer of power on the basis of dominion status and partition was of great importance to the strategists of commonwealth defence.[1] The underlying assumption that the commonwealth was a single unit for defence purposes might have appeared strange to those who knew that the Statute of Westminster had virtually given each dominion complete freedom in its external policy, including defence. Old habits die hard, however, as Phillip Darby points out:

At the end of the Second World War the theory of commonwealth defence still rested on the decision of the Imperial Conference of 1926. According to this decision, general defence, meaning the defence of the Empire's lines of communication, was the responsibility of the UK and was to be carried out by the Royal Navy, assisted by such forces as the dominions could provide. Local defence was the responsibility of each dominion and the function of their respective land forces, while the UK assumed responsibility for the local defence of the colonies.[2]

The notion of commonwealth military interdependence was deeply ingrained in the minds of the military elite and Conservative politicians

in Britain. Some cabinet members even regretted that republican India
had been admitted to the commonwealth without any conditions about
strategic defence burdens. A British Foreign Office memorandum,
written in late 1950, records that India's entry into the commonwealth
was 'taken on the explicit understanding that it did not involve the
assumption by India of any military obligation, expressed or implied, to
the other members of the commonwealth'.[3] In the light of this evidence
we might ask if India had a role in commonwealth defence at all.

There are three major areas for discussion. First, the degree to which
the commonwealth defence perspectives of India, the older dominions
and Britain became bipolarised by the cold war, and the impact of the
US on the relationship between Britain and other members of the
commonwealth, and India in particular. A second area concerns India's
own quest for security, which sometimes clashed with British notions
of imperial defence, most markedly in the case of Pakistan. However,
on occasions and on some issues, there was a proximity between the
Indian and the British position. The third area is India's role as a non-
aligned nation. While India's non-aligned position prevented Britain
from getting any military support in imperial combat operations, in
the course of time, as the cold war heated up in Asia, India was found by
its commonwealth partners to be useful as a mediator in some crises.

The development of east-west tension in Europe and the Middle
East modified the geopolitical strategic priorities of Britain and each
of the older dominions. Defence needs would be more Eurocentric or
centred on the North Atlantic for Britain or Canada, whereas they would
focus on the Pacific and Southeast Asia for the Australasian dominions.
A recurrent question in British defence planning discussions was, given
her limited resources, how far Britain should commit her armed forces
to the cold war in Europe at the expense of providing military security
for the colonial empire in Africa and Asia. Britain still had a valuable
colony in Malaya, where a communist-led insurgency started in the
spring of 1948, as well as in her trading outpost in Hong Kong which
was threatened by advancing Chinese communist forces in May 1949.
Clearly Britain's defence strategy had to take Southeast Asia and parts
of the Pacific region into account.[4]

India's preoccupation in the first years after independence was with
consolidating national unity. This involved her in armed conflict with

Pakistan over Kashmir. Under these circumstances, and given the disturbing evidence that British officials and military personnel were partisan to Pakistan, India was hardly likely to be interested in sharing the global defence concerns of Britain.[5] Both India and Pakistan, engrossed in the war over Kashmir, showed relative indifference to such issues as commonwealth defence, as seen when their prime ministers failed to give a formal reply to a memorandum from the British chiefs of staff on the defence of the commonwealth.[6] Australia and New Zealand agreed to some rudimentary form of institutionalised defence cooperation to 'protect' imperial interests in Malaya. The ANZAM arrangement of 1947 made provision for a commonwealth strategic reserve in Malaya.[7]

Nehru's position on such defence arrangements was slightly ambivalent. He made it 'perfectly clear that both in Burma and in Malaya [there was] no question of Indian troops functioning', when it was suggested that the Indian population in those countries might need protection in the Burmese civil war. But he permitted the friendly government in Burma to buy arms from India, just as he had not objected to the British recruiting Gurkhas in the war against communist rebels in Malaya.[8] These were deviations from Nehru's own guidelines on foreign policy enunciated in September 1948: 'We have repeatedly stated that India should not ally herself with any of the power blocs. This policy fits in with our basic principles and is at the same time beneficial even from the narrow opportunist point of view.'[9]

One explanation for this ambivalence lies in Nehru's concern that the communist parties of India and Southeast Asia had, according to the Indian intelligence service, under Soviet and East European influence, used a youth conference in Calcutta in 1948 to spread the idea of violent revolutionary action against the post-colonial states in India and neighbouring countries.[10] As long as the Communist Party of India (CPI) remained committed to this form of struggle (it was formally called off in 1950), Britain hoped that Nehru would respond favourably to her perception of the communist 'threat' in Asia. That did not happen. While Nehru privately sympathised with Britain's difficulties in Malaya, he insisted in a letter to Sir Stafford Cripps that a military posture was unsuitable for eradicating incipient communist revolts, and that programmes for economic and social betterment took priority.[11] He reiterated this on many occasions to British and commonwealth civil servants and statesmen, including Lord Strang of the Foreign Office on his visit to India and Southeast Asia to assess Britain's strategy, and at the Commonwealth Prime Ministers' Conference in 1948.[12]

Here it is useful to reflect on a question at the heart of any analysis of interstate cooperation on military security. Alliances and treaties diminish a nation's freedom of manoeuvre in defence and external affairs.[13] Newly liberated nations, like India, were anxious to demonstrate this in the position they took on defence and foreign affairs.[14] On the other hand, supporters of an alliance with the US (Australia and New Zealand in 1951 through the ANZUS Pact, and Canada through the North Atlantic Treaty Organization [NATO]), argued that in the unsettled international situation after 1945 interdependence in questions of foreign affairs and defence was a *sine qua non* for the security of nation-states. Britain had Great Power status but not the resources to support it, as the American loan agreement of December 1945 had made painfully clear. Behind the anachronistic assumptions about commonwealth defence there lay a desire to assert British national independence against the dictates of the US. Many of the feelers thrown out by Ernest Bevin as foreign secretary were symptomatic of a wish to play an independent role in Western Europe against Soviet communism with the support of the commonwealth and colonial territories.[15] This aspect of Bevin's outlook gave a pro-Pakistan bias to his assessment of the Kashmir question and thus did not bring him any closer to understanding the Indian side.

Members of the commonwealth had varying perceptions of strategic requirements, but it is essential to remember that dominating their assessments of defence capability was the towering presence of the US. The emergence of the US as the superpower on whom Britain was financially and militarily dependent through the Marshall aid of 1947 and NATO from 1948 undermined traditional notions of an integrated commonwealth defence strategy. This was exemplified in the conclusion of the ANZUS in 1951, whereby the US was seen by the Australasian dominions as providing greater security for their defence in the Pacific region than Britain, which was pointedly excluded from the treaty and also from the preliminary discussions.

A few months before India became independent, Britain begged the US to undertake the military defence of Greece and Turkey, of which

Britain herself was no longer capable. Historians consider this episode significant for two reasons: it indicated Britain's abdication of superpower status in the confrontation with the Soviet Union and, second, the response of the US to the British request was expressed in the open-ended cold war rhetoric of the Truman Doctrine.

The rationale of non-alignment was an Indocentric appreciation of India's security needs, given India's geographical position. Those countries, old or newly independent, which readily got absorbed into the military alliances in the late 1940s, subordinated their national interest to those of the alliance: 'the primary reference point to assess the implications and result of any developments [was] its impact on the US–USSR relationship'.[16] 'Containment' of the Soviet Union was the cardinal principle of cold war strategists, whether in the US or Britain, but there were differences in the emphasis on regional priorities. For Britain the Middle East was of greater importance than the rise of communism in China, whereas for the US the latter phenomenon appeared a major disaster. Neither the US nor its ANZUS partners recognised Red China. In West Asia the logic of the Truman Doctrine forced the US to work out the blueprint of a Middle East defence pact, which would include countries from Turkey to Pakistan.

During the final discussions on the division of the subcontinent, the British chiefs of staff had emphasised the value of West Pakistan in their scheme of commonwealth defence.[17] From Britain's point of view, West Asia had traditionally been strategically useful because of the Suez Canal, the 'lifeline' of the empire. One should not forget that this utility was shared by Australia and New Zealand. In the context of the cold war and Bevin's wish to create a space for independent British diplomatic and military initiatives, the traditional imperial commitment to West Asia acquired a new aspect. The British Foreign office suggested to the US that the government of the Indian part of Kashmir was permeated with communist sympathisers. Such suggestions were no doubt designed to prepare the US administration for the diplomatic initiative by which Bevin intended, with Pakistan's help, to organise the 'middle of the planet' (West Asia) and swing it towards the British Commonwealth bloc.[18] Indo-Pakistani tension over Kashmir created a problem for Britain which was trying to identify a common cause on which the defence of Pakistan, India, and Britain could be based.[19] An

Indo-Pakistan rapprochement over Kashmir would release far greater numbers of 'reasonably-equipped and trained forces ... at short notice' for commonwealth defence than could be provided by any other dominion—so ran the wishful thinking in the British Cabinet Defence Committee.[20] Pakistan's desire for a British military guarantee against India, to which the Labour government would not agree, could not be reconciled with the long-term British aim of shifting Indian diplomatic orientation from non-alignment to a more openly pro-Western stance. Towards the end of 1949 Britain was hopeful that the US might solve Britain's predicament by incorporating Pakistan within the framework of a Middle East pact, in which the US had shown some interest. In this way a convergence between American global cold war strategy and the West Asian strategic desiderata of Britain was likely to materialise.[21]

A wide gap existed, therefore, between the way Britain perceived its geopolitical defence requirements and the way the Indian government looked at its problems of security. Nevertheless, it is interesting to note that in February 1950 Nehru recorded that if any world crisis occurred India could not take a pro-Soviet or an anti-West position:

If there is a world war, there is no possibility of India lining up with the Soviet Union whatever else she may do. It is obvious that our relations with the US as with the UK in political and economic matters are far closer than with other countries. We have practically no such relations with the Soviet.[22]

Towards the end of the same year (after the Korean War had started and communist China had sent its troops to Tibet) the evaluation of the British Foreign Office on Indian defence policy and diplomacy more or less confirmed what Nehru had noted earlier in the year:

At the moment, however, it is fair to say that India has not yet turned decisively to the west; and freedom of action in world affairs remains the basic principle of India's external relations. The result is that India is at present unlikely to agree to consider defence discussions with the United Kingdom or any other member of the commonwealth. On the other hand. ... India retains a number of high-ranking British officers in important administrative posts in her armed forces, and continues to look to the United Kingdom as her source of supply for arms and equipment and for the higher training of her officers.

Contacts of this kind, together with an increasing awareness of the danger from Communist expansion may help to bring India closer to the United

Kingdom in the defence field; and our ultimate aim must certainly be to achieve as close an understanding as is possible with India with a view to ensuring that in the event of a world war she would take an active part on our side.[23]

From mid-1950, the Korean War and developments in Tibet brought about a qualitative change in how Britain, India, and the older dominions approached intra-commonwealth defence problems and the cold war. The cold war was no longer cold in the north-eastern corner of Asia. Throughout 1950–1, especially after the UN forces crossed the 38th parallel, there was apprehension that the crisis would escalate into a major war with China, and that nuclear weapons would be used. Almost from the start the US enlarged the scope of the Korean crisis by providing naval protection to the Kuomintang regime in Taiwan, an action which might have made communist China believe that war was imminent, a war in which the US would use places like Taiwan as part of its strategy.[24] The Korean crisis brought to light latent differences in the American, British and Indian approaches to the maintenance of security in Asia. Britain undertook an additional and economically burdensome programme of rearmament with an eye to her own position in the balance of power in Europe. The reorientation in British strategic thinking was marked by an increased reliance on nuclear options and readjustments of its overseas forces as between the Far East and West Asia.[25] The entry of Chinese communist forces into Tibet in 1950 brought India uncomfortably close to a situation where the simple notion of the territorial defence of the northern frontier could be subsumed in the bipolar ideological confrontation of the cold war. It was especially awkward for Nehru who had launched peace initiatives to end the Korean War a few months earlier (initiatives which irritated the US).

The latter half of 1950 showed up the strength and weaknesses of the way India had visualised her role in maintaining peace, especially among the Asian nations. India endorsed the UN resolution on aggression by North Korea but refused to send Indian troops as combatants, an indication that she would maintain a non-aligned stance even when the international community got involved in a war in which the partiality of each side to the ideological power blocs was obvious. Such non-alignment could be interpreted as a form of isolationism. India had no interest in committing scarce resources to what was, in effect, a war between two superpowers by proxy. However, the initiatives for peace and an early cease-fire which India undertook by direct appeals to the heads of state of each superpower showed a more constructive side of non-alignment. The mediatory role that India sought to play between communist China and the Western powers, when the former threatened to intervene in Korea as General MacArthur's forces approached the Yalu river, illustrated the new role that a non-aligned power in the commonwealth could play.

Almost within three months of the outbreak of the Korean War and the launching of peace initiatives by India, the latter was unexpectedly confronted with the Chinese incursion into Tibet. Not only did this disturb and irritate Indian statesmen (who felt let down by the Indian Embassy in Peking), but it weakened India's position in international fora as she went on pressing for China's admission to the UN, and opposing the American proposal to brand China as the aggressor in Korea. Since India considered Tibet an autonomous territory within an overarching Chinese suzerainty, a point not accepted by China, the diplomatic interchanges and the memoranda after the invasion were characterised on both sides by a note of acerbity.[26] Neither Britain nor the Australasian dominions regarded China's occupation of Tibet as an immediate threat to their security, though a case could be made out that it *was* one to India. The later disputes over the Sino-Indian border, with China's maps claiming territories that India regarded as hers, bear this out. By the mid-1950s Nehru told Michael Brecher that any Chinese infiltration into India's Himalayan border states would be a hostile act and that his policy towards China (after her occupation of Tibet) was not based on unqualified trust.[27]

The US, from its cold war perspective, saw China in Tibet as a threat. She sought to use the alarm felt by Indian diplomatic circles to offer military assistance, an offer which was studiously ignored. The Indian government deemed it unwise to be stampeded into a relationship of military obligation to the US since, until the Tibetan crisis, the American government had been so lukewarm in its support. Such an obligation would only have reduced India's room for manoeuvre in diplomacy and made it a puppet in the cold war.[28] During the Korean War it became evident that there was a powerful lobby in the US which wanted to enlarge the scope of American-supported military action to roll back the tide of social revolution in China. British and Indian diplomacy was running on almost parallel lines to resist the machinations of this lobby.[29] Both countries were among the first to recognise communist China. India did not choose to criticise Britain for her counter-insurgency activities in Malaya, in contrast to India's sharp reaction to the Dutch attempt to reconquer Indonesia in late 1948. The mediatory role that India was willing to play (as during the Korean cease-fire talks and during the discussion on the repatriation of prisoners of war) was increasingly appreciated in Britain, regardless of which party was in power. Britain had taken on additional rearmament burdens at the request of the US for its NATO commitments in Europe, but it was clear that she had no desire to 'contain' communist China. Instead, India's membership of the commonwealth provided an opportunity for Britain to avail herself of India's mediatory role when another crisis occurred in Southeast Asia.

The granting of American military aid to Pakistan, when the latter joined the Baghdad Pact (later known as CENTO), blighted the prospects of a settlement of the Kashmir question, on which the Pakistan's prime minister, Mohammed Ali, had reached an understanding with Nehru.[30] As noted earlier, Britain had avoided any official commitment to help Pakistan against India, and had been trying to do it by proxy, by suggesting that Pakistan would be a valuable member of the Baghdad Pact. Ironically, this convoluted diplomacy was counter-productive; instead of softening the tension between two commonwealth countries, it put an end to any settlement of the major source of tension between them.

Krishna Menon attended the Geneva Conference on Indo-China (26 April–20 July 1954) with Nehru's approval because the conference concerned the ending of colonialism.[31] Moreover, the international scenario in Southeast Asia in the first four months of 1954 gave considerable cause for alarm to non-aligned powers like India, which aimed to reduce the risks of war in Asia as colonialism retreated and social revolution became consolidated. At the time of the Korean armistice, in July 1953, the French foreign minister, Georges Bidault, had suggested an international conference to end hostilities in Indo-China. At the end of the Four-Power Conference in Berlin in February 1954 it was announced that the interested countries, including China, would meet in Geneva in April. Meanwhile the Viet-Minh guerrillas moved from success to success, culminating in the fall of the French bastion of Dien-Bien-Phu on 7 May.[32] The US was so anxious to negotiate from a position of strength that it tried to mobilise its West European allies for concerted aero-naval (and probably military) operations against the Viet-Minh. Since the Australasian dominions were already bound to the US under the ANZUS treaty, Britain was apprehensive that questions affecting the defence of commonwealth territories in Southeast Asia would be decided by the US. This was shown in the British complaint that the southern dominions were being kept better informed than Britain about changing US strategy in Indo-China.[33]

The timing of the US hydrogen bomb test (1 March 1954) and its possible implications disturbed Churchill and Nehru. The British cabinet papers suggest a widening divergence between Britain and the US on Indo-China, which persisted even through the Geneva Conference. Britain was opposed to any military intervention before talks had been tried, and she was alarmed at the suggestion that nuclear weapons might be used, especially as it was based on the bland assumption by the US government that the Soviet Union had not yet reached the stage of being able to retaliate. The cabinet talked Churchill out of a proposed visit to Eisenhower to discuss the bomb, so as to avoid the impression that the weapon would be used to force a settlement.[34] This evidence of very real Anglo-American divergences over military action in Indo-China suggests that Nehru was mistaken in thinking that American pressure had made Churchill reject India's request for a commonwealth prime ministers' conference to discuss nuclear tests.[35] A more likely explanation was that the British wished to keep their independent nuclear deterrent which they had tested in October 1952. From Churchill's point of view, a conference in April would have revealed the cracks in commonwealth solidarity in the Anglo-American 'special relationship' and Britain's declining leverage with the southern dominions since the conclusion of ANZUS.

Along with the widening divergence between Britain and the US on Indo-China, there developed a convergence between Indian and British perceptions of how the crisis should be handled. Nehru, in order to make a public stand against what he saw as America's effort to force the issue in Indo-China, went, in April, to a conference of South Asian prime ministers (those of Burma, Ceylon, India and Pakistan) held in Colombo. He secured a unanimous resolution to be used as a guideline for the Geneva Conference.[36] Meanwhile, Eden refused to be associated with Dulles's efforts to organise a meeting of the ambassadors of Britain, Australia, New Zealand, France, Thailand, and the Philippines to discuss collective security in Southeast Asia. He thought this would provoke the members of the Colombo Conference, and would detract from the vital and more immediate task of making the Geneva Conference a success. Thus Nehru's stand at the Colombo Conference had obviously made an impression. Eden added, for good measure, that nobody in Britain took Siam and the Philippines seriously as representatives of Asian opinion.

The Geneva Conference succeeded in ending French colonial rule, restoring peace, and creating an international control commission to supervise developments in Laos. India was a member of this commission along with Canada and Poland. Britain and the commonwealth had accepted India's mediatory role in the crisis; she was no longer seen simply as a provider of military manpower, but as a state which could effectively resolve problems in intra-commonwealth relationships created by the cold war and by the stand of the US. One country which benefited from India's role at Geneva was China. Chou En-lai stopped at Delhi on his way back from Geneva, complimented India on her diplomacy, and praised the commonwealth connection. Objectively speaking, he was correct. It was the institution of the commonwealth that enabled India to express her reaction to the changing international situation in Asia and Africa. Association with the commonwealth had so far not been a liability to India in terms of national security and self-interest.

The Indo-British understanding about Southeast Asian security had been very marked at Geneva. But there were unstated hypotheses in Britain's strategic thinking, about the positions she and the US were going to take, hypotheses of which India had no knowledge. India was under the impression that only the US was obstructing a thaw in the cold war, and Nehru retained a 'basic goodwill for Britain and the Eden government'.[37] Eden had been attracted by the idea of a Southeast Asian treaty organisation, when it was first broached by the US in April 1954, especially when it carried the prospect of US support for the British colonial war in Malaya and for the British control of Hong Kong.[38] Once the Geneva Conference was concluded, he responded to American initiatives to create such a collective security agreement, though he must have been aware that neither Eisenhower nor Dulles was happy about the Geneva Agreement. The US wanted the proposed South East Asia Treaty Organization (SEATO) agreement to apply to Laos and Cambodia as well, although these territories had been effectively neutralised by the Geneva Accord. Britain was informed that the Chinese had misgivings on this score, but since Britain had deliberately deceived China on this point during the Geneva talks, she finally agreed to the US position that the SEATO agreement, as drawn up at Manila on 8 September 1954, should also include the defence of these two territories.[39] There was only one indication that Britain was concerned to retain the goodwill of India, the leading state among the Colombo powers. This was contained in a Foreign Office note that if SEATO's aims were spelt out as a defence arrangement against communism it would be difficult for India and Burma to join it. Eden had hopes, which proved to be vain, of including these countries as a counterweight to Siam and the Philippines, which he regarded as satellites of the US. The cabinet was prepared to retain the reference to communism, if the US insisted on it.

By the end of 1954 the Indian diplomatic moves against American bellicosity, so successful at Geneva, had failed to deflect Britain from a position that can only be described as subservience to the US in defending traditional imperial interests. India's reply to SEATO was to organise the Afro-Asian Conference at Bandung. One of the beneficiaries of this meeting was China, whose foreign minister established a personal rapport with the leaders of a number of countries including Pakistan. As a gesture of solidarity by the ex-colonial world it merited attention on the part of the Big Four of the UN, although its resolutions and communiques had no clout in terms of international law. After Bandung, the tension of the cold war seemed to have decreased in Europe, and India could justifiably claim to have played a part in this. Nehru visited the Soviet Union in June 1955, encouraged the Soviet premier to take an attitude of positive cooperation at the forthcoming Geneva Summit of the heads of state, and then went on to Britain to convey his impressions of the thaw in Russia. There was a general expectation of better relations in Europe in 1955, though the same could not be said about East Asia, where the US continued her sabre-rattling against China from Taiwan. Before the Geneva Conference the Soviet Union had projected a less Stalinist image to the West in the Austrian Peace Treaty and the resumption of diplomatic relations with Yugoslavia in May 1955. The visit to India by Bulganin and Khrushchev in 1955–6 and their speeches denouncing British imperialism irritated Conservative opinion in Britain, but the cabinet did not cancel the invitation already extended to the Soviet leaders to visit Britain.

At about this time Nehru was increasingly alienated from the US, and the Soviet Union was approached for assistance in economic development and even for defence equipment. None of this implied giving up non-alignment or any surrender of India's economic independence to the Soviet Union. From the point of view of Britain, the purchase of defence equipment was disturbing, and Mountbatten was asked to intercede with Nehru to postpone decisions on this.[40] While the commonwealth connection had advantages, and gave India a forum for voicing her views on international issues, it diminished the area of her freedom in defence planning.

The Suez crisis came as a rude shock to India's belief in the need for commonwealth consultation in international matters concerning more than one of the member states. The pillars of Indian foreign policy which Nehru assumed had been accepted and appreciated by the West— anti-colonialism, respect for national sovereignty, respect for the UN Charter—were violently shaken as a result of the collusive Anglo-French secret diplomacy, which was concerned with the Israeli attack on Egypt in October 1956. Nehru was able to save the commonwealth connection for India because the blame could be focused, just as it was in Britain, on one person—the British prime minister. The knowledge that Mountbatten was opposed to the operation and had thought of resigning; that the Labour party leaders and veterans like Pethick-Lawrence and Noel-Baker spoke out against it must have strengthened Nehru's determination not to change course. India would not be dislodged from the unique diplomatic alignment Nehru had built out of two overlapping communities in the post-war world—the commonwealth and the non-aligned nations.[41]

NOTES

1. R.J. Moore, *Escape from Empire* (Oxford, 1983), p. 269.
2. Darby, Phillip, *British Defence Policy East of Suez, 1947–68* (London, 1973), pp. 27–8.
3. Cab 134/64 Gen 388/1, para 54.
4. C.J. Bartlett, *The Long Retreat* (London, 1972), chapter 2.
5. P.S. Gupta, 'Imperial Strategy and the Transfer of Power' in this volume.
6. Cab 130/64. Gen 338 (1).
7. Darby, *British Defence Policy*, p. 29.
8. Quoted in S. Gopal, *Jawaharlal Nehru*, vol. 2 (Delhi, 1979), p. 167.
9. J.L. Nehru, *Selected Works* (hereafter *JLNSW*), second series, vol. VII, p. 611.
10. *JLNSW*, second series, vol. VIII, p. 361.
11. *JLNSW*, second series, vol. VIII, pp. 335–6.
12. *JLNSW*, second series, vol. VII, p. 276ff.
13. For a good theoretical discussion on this point, see F.A. Beer, (ed.), *Alliances: Latent War Communities in Contemporary World* (New York, 1970).
14. *JLNSW*, second series, vol. VII, pp. 611–12.
15. P.S. Gupta 'Imperialism and the Labour Governments, 1945–51' in this volume.
16. K. Subrahmanyam, 'Evolution of Indian Defence Policy, 1947–64', in B.N. Pande, (ed.), *A Centenary History of the Indian National Congress*, vol. IV (Delhi, 1989), p. 538.
17. N. Mansergh and P. Moon, (eds), *Transfer of Power*, vol. 10, doc. no. 416.
18. Gupta, 'Imperial Strategy'.
19. Ibid.
20. Note by Philip Noel-Baker, 30/12/49. DO (49) 89, Cab 131/7.
21. Gupta, 'Imperial Strategy', n. 230.
22. Gopal, *Nehru*, vol. 2, p. 64.
23. Gupta, 'Imperial Strategy'.
24. Gopal, *Nehru*, p. 108.
25. Bartlett, *The Long Retreat*, pp. 60–8.
26. Gopal, *Nehru*, p. 176.
27. L.J. Kavic, *India's Quest for Security: Defence Policies 1947–65* (California, 1967), chapter 3.
28. Subrahmanyam, 'Evolution of Indian Defence Policy', pp. 539–40.
29. P.S. Gupta, *Imperialism and the British Labour Movement* (London, 1975), p. 291.
30. Gopal, *Nehru*, pp. 181–9.
31. M. Brecher, *India and World Politics* (Oxford, 1968), p. 44.

32. G. Warner, 'La Grande-Bretagne et la crise de Dien-Bien-Phu. L'echec de l'action unifiée', in D. Artaud and L. Kaplan, (eds), *Dien-Bien-Phu* (Lyon, 1989), p. 161.
33. Warner, 'La Grande-Bretagne' p. 182.
34. G. Warner 'De Geneve a Manille: la Grande-Bretagne, l'Indo-Chine et L'OTASE' in D. Artaud and L. Kaplan, *Dien-Bien-Phu*, p. 239.
35. Gopal, *Nehru*, p. 191.
36. Ibid.
37. Ibid., p. 274.
38. Warner, 'La Grande-Bretagne et la crise de Dien-Bien-Phu', p. 180.
39. Ibid., pp. 155–8, and p. 260, note 61.
40. Gopal, *Nehru*, p. 274.

Labour History

SECTION IV

NOTES ON THE ORIGIN AND STRUCTURE OF THE INDUSTRIAL LABOUR FORCE IN INDIA, 1880–1920*

The purpose of this essay is to suggest some lines of enquiry on Indian labour history in the light of work already done and sources readily available. In the period between the 1880s and 1920s an industrial labour force had begun to emerge in India, and was going to play a significant role in the social and political history of the country in subsequent decades.[1] If we examine the problems of labour supply, wage payments, factory discipline and labour protest for these years, we might build some hypotheses on the composition of the industrial labour force and its possible social and political roles.

I

Measured against the industrialisation of India in recent years, industrial growth between 1880 and 1905 might appear insignificant. Yet in both absolute and relative terms there was considerable growth in cotton textiles, jute mills and coal mines. The number of workers in cotton mills increased from 39,537 in 1879–80 to 196,369 in 1904–5, in jute mills from 27,494 to 133,162, and in coal mines from 14,804 to 92,740.[2] Attention must also be paid to the growth in the number of factories which needed skilled labour, such as iron and brass foundries, whose number increased from 38 in 1893 to 89 in 1904.[3]

By the end of the 1880s Calcutta, Kanpur, Ahmedabad and Bombay had assumed some of the characteristics of industrial towns. In the countrywide distribution of factories employing more than 100 persons, Calcutta and its suburbs, Hooghly, Howrah and 24-Parganas had 76

*Published in R.S. Sharma (ed.), *Indian Society: Historical Probings: Essays in Memory of D.D. Kosambi* (New Delhi, 1974) establishments in 1888.[4] In the same period Kanpur had seven such factories, of which four employed more than 1000. Bombay had the largest number; an estimate carried out in 1885 put the figure at 98.[5] Data on the number of smaller establishments for Bombay city for 1890 show the existence of 52 factories employing between 20 and 100 persons.[6] Similar data for Calcutta and its suburbs prove the existence of many small workshops using steam machinery for casting metals and processing raw materials, food and drink.[7] Some of these smaller establishments in both cities and provinces were of course seasonal industries, such as cotton ginning and pressing, jute pressing and sugar refining, where the rhythm of activity could fit in with the rhythm of agricultural labour in the countryside.[8] In the present essay we shall be concerned mainly with the labour force of industrial establishments which operated all the year round.

From what regions and castes, and under what motivation did the original workforce at these urban centres come? Reliable statistical data on the caste distribution of the industrial labour force are fully available only from the census of 1921. The evidence given before the Factory Commission of 1890 cannot provide definitive quantified data, but does produce enough qualitative data for some preliminary hypotheses. In the factories in and around Calcutta, 20 witnesses from among workers gave evidence: almost all of them were landless–17 were Bengalis, and the castes represented were the Tanti (weaver), Kaibarta (peasant and fisherman), Bagdi (labourer), Muchi (cobbler), Sankari (bangle-maker) and Bairagi (a religious sect).[9] It is worth noting that three of these—Kaibarta, Bagdi and Muchi—were sufficiently low down in the social hierarchy to be given the status of 'depressed classes' in 1921.[10] The female labouring population invariably comprised widows: as one witness put it, 'As a rule Bengali women never come to work in the mills unless they are widows in bad circumstances',[11] a testimony repeatedly corroborated by others. This sample of 20 witnesses may not be quite representative of the labour force, yet it shows that at that time the ethnic composition was predominantly Bengali. By 1929 the Royal Commission on Labour was commenting on the predominantly non-local character of factory labour in Calcutta; Bengalis comprised less than a quarter of jute-mill workers, most of whom came from western Bihar and eastern Uttar Pradesh.[12] There must, therefore, have been a definite shift in the recruitment pattern of the factories. This is suggested by other authorities as well. Buchanan discovered that in one jute mill in Calcutta 80 per cent of the employees in 1896 were Bengalis, whereas in 1926 the proportion was only 25 per cent.[13] The shift had probably occurred by 1905, when about two-thirds of the labour force in Bengal were immigrants.[14] The explanation usually given for this transition—apart from generalisations about the Bengali aversion to manual labour—is that immigrants from Uttar Pradesh and Bihar were available at lower wages, rather like the Irish immigrants in the factory towns of early-nineteenth-century England.[15] But the process needs to be more fully documented and alternative hypotheses tested.

The main industrial city in the upper Ganga valley, Kanpur, always recruited its labour from the densely populated neighbouring districts. This was true for 1890, and corroborated by the Royal Commission of 1929.[16] In the early years the local factories were almost entirely cotton or jute mills, with the notable exception of the big leather manufactory of Cooper Allen & Company. In these the labour came from three sources. Prompted mainly by financial necessity, the Koeris handloom weaver provided labour for most of the weaving mills. There is a case of a Koeri who had sent his son to a jute mill to get extra income while he himself plied his craft for a few more years, until he too gave it up and followed his son to the factory.[17] The second source consisted of tenants evicted by landlords. The post-1858 land settlement in Awadh (the Oudh Rent Act of 1868) had strengthened the *taluqdars'* powers of eviction, which was only partially modified by the subsequent legislation of 1886.[18] Reluctantly, many erstwhile agriculturists—some of them Brahmins—were forced to seek factory employment. Of the five workmen interviewed, who were from agricultural families, two were Brahmins who had been evicted, one a Kshatriya similarly situated, and two (one Ahir and one Kurmi) came from families that still lived on land but were unable to find enough work or income from this source alone.[19] The role of the factories in taking 'a part of the population of the land' was appreciatively commented upon by the magistrate of Kanpur in 1888.[20] The third source was peculiar to one industry (Cooper Allen's army boot factory), but illustrates the more general point of the caste origins of certain types of industrial labour. The Chamar (cobbler) caste appears to have formed a major part of the factory's labour force.[21]

In the second decade of the twentieth–century the labour force in Uttar Pradesh still retained certain early features. The unfavourable land man ratio prompted steady migration of the landless or partially landless castes to other provinces. Commitment to industry was not uniformly strong among lower castes. Castes accustomed to cultivating the soil, such as the Kurmi, Lodhi and Jat, tended to prefer semi-agricultural industries such as tea cultivation or manufacturing of sugar. Other castes—the Kahar, Ahir and Chamar—willingly took to spinning and weaving, the Chamars having become unable to find sufficient employment similar to their traditional crafts in leather factories.[22]

A similar process of adaptation by castes plying traditional handicrafts in comparable factory jobs occurred in Ahmedabad. An important manufacturer wrote in 1890: 'The hands employed in the weaving department in Ahmedabad are generally those who themselves or their fathers [sic] were handloom weavers', adding that these people had been suffering under the competition of Lancashire until the local textile industry provided alternative jobs.[23] Ahmedabad also got a fair amount of its unskilled labour from a local landless low caste, the Wagri, who traditionally lived by begging.[24] There was no change in this reliance on the local supply of labour over the next 40 years: in 1929, 65 per cent of the labour force still came from the Ahmedabad district or Baroda.[25]

The overpopulated agricultural district of Ratnagiri in the Konkan region and, less so, the districts of Kolhapur, Poona and Ahmadnagar in the Deccan contributed the bulk of labour to the city of Bombay during the whole period. From the earliest days we notice the migration of Muslim handloom weavers from the Uttar Pradesh and Delhi regions to Bombay in quest of jobs in mills as weavers, as a result of which by 1921 the weaving departments tended to have a large proportion of Muslim workmen. Otherwise, there does not appear to have been any marked predominance of certain castes in the labour force. Certainly, the 'untouchables' did not provide the original labour force for the Bombay textile industry.[26] Rural overpopulation provided the main impulse for a cross-section of castes to migrate to the town. Any serious analysis of why certain castes tended to migrate must not only ascertain the *jati* hierarchy but also locate the 'dominant caste' in that region. Perhaps the migrant factory labourers came from castes which lacked prospects of upward mobility in the given pattern of dominance in their villages.

From what has already been said about the regional and caste origins of the industrial workers in some cities, a few hypotheses emerge regarding the motivation behind the quest for employment. In discussing these we shall also touch on the scarcity of labour that was alleged to have been a feature of industrial recruitment in the years before 1914.[27] Calcutta, Kanpur, Ahmedabad and Bombay got their supply of labour without difficulty, thanks to the pressure of population on the land and the diminishing opportunities for handicraftsmen. A rural landless class had existed even before the establishment of British rule;[28] even where they had some rights of cultivation the income was seldom adequate. In some regions such as Ahmedabad, castes like the Wagri had traditionally suffered this lot. Elsewhere, as in Uttar Pradesh, British tenancy legislation left many tenants with no option but to go into the factory. Whether there was or was not 'deindustrialisation' under the impact of foreign competition is still a matter of controversy among economic historians.[29] The evidence, however, suggests that in some places (namely, Ahmedabad, Bombay and Calcutta) handloom weavers were saved from destitution by the opportunities provided by textile-weaving industries. It is possible that the traditional craft castes shifted to analogous factory occupation because of the attraction of higher and regular wages, rather than of the whiplash of technological unemployment. The migration of some handicraftsmen to factories in Kanpur was no doubt of this sort. Thus it was suggested that employment in the mills 'is well-paid and popular and has undoubtedly raised the wages of labour all round in the neighbourhood of Cawnpore'.[30] Even where the difference between the income of a common coolie and that of a mill-hand was not substantial, factory labourers had the attraction of regular payment.[31]

In his detailed study of the cotton textile labourers in Bombay city M.D. Morris made out a good case against the oft-repeated allegation of a shortage of labour supply before 1920.[32] He interpreted the tendency of wages to remain at the same level over a period of time (except for the years of the plague) as evidence for the existence of a pool of potential recruits. He corroborated this by qualitative evidence from contemporary sources. In addition, he argued that the relatively little use made by the Bombay mills of female labour (contrast Lancashire) suggests an abundance of adult male labour supply.[33] A similar inference may be drawn from the widespread practice of giving *baksheesh* to the jobber

to secure employment.[34] This is corroborated by evidence for the 1880s
for places as far from each other as Broach and Surat in the west, Kanpur
in the north, and Calcutta in the east. The magistrates of Broach and
Surat testified to 'the competition for places at the mills'.[35] Practically
all the witnesses from Kanpur and Calcutta called before the Factory
Commission of 1890 admitted that it would be easy to fill their vacancies.
In the light of these facts, whether a labour shortage existed at all should
be considered afresh.

In the early days of the construction of railways, roads and other
public works, especially in parts of Central India, labour had to be
recruited on a contract basis from a long distance. Plantations in Assam
relied on indentured recruitment from outside the province from an
early date.[36] The steel town of Jamshedpur got its labour from a cross-
section of many provinces, because it was started in a thinly populated
forest area.[37] In recruiting labour in the coal-mining industry in Bengal
and Bihar up to the First World War, colliery owners had to use the
zamindari method of recruitment by which the Santhal tribesmen were
attracted by offers of plots of land.[38] A reasonable hypothesis would
be that labour migration followed a well-observed pattern of moving
in stages of relatively short-distance migration from village to small
town in the first instance, and from there to the big industrial towns in
the second. Reluctance to venture into the uncertainties of construction
work or plantation labour in a distant region undoubtedly limited the
area of mobility. Apart from this, the migrant labourer had no inhibitions
on moving in quest of better economic opportunities. Even in the
plantations, by the end of the 1870s, there had begun the 'free migration'
of labourers (that is, without reference to the Bengal Labour Districts
Emigration Act of 1873). The Government of India recognised this
by passing the Inland Emigration Act in 1882, which permitted free
recruitment of labour.[39] In the coalfields the non-*zamindari* system of
recruitment by contract started at the turn of the century, became more
popular and successful after the First World War, and gave the Bengal
and Bihar coalfields a fairly stable source of skilled labour from the
migrants of Uttar Pradesh.[40]

Did the notion of labour scarcity arise because of a temporary difficulty
faced by some industries in the first four or five years of the twentieth
century, and persist in the minds of managers and entrepreneurs for

reasons so far unexplained? Morris has shown that while the plague in 1896–7 did create a shortage of labour in Bombay, its effects wore off within a couple of years and there was no complaint of scarcity of labour later.[41] Yet we have evidence that between 1902 and 1904 Kanpur suffered more severely from the plague, which persisted up to 1908.[42] Labour shortage affected Bengal too. In course of discussing the desirability of preventing children under nine years being brought inside the factory, a government despatch stated: 'The Special Inspector of Factories . . . draws attention to the fact that mills are at present shorthanded; and states that, if children are altogether denied admission not only will hardship be entailed on the parents, but that the industry will also be affected adversely, because much female labour will thereby be lost to it.'[43] Two years later a similar complaint of labour shortage was made by the commissioner of the Nagpur division in the Central Provinces. He said: 'Famines and plague epidemics have been followed by a most marked increase in the demand for labour, a demand which cannot be regarded as ephemeral . . . already there is springing up the beginning of a demand for labour-saving appliances. At the moment the Empress Mills . . . are short by 500 hands, and are anxious to employ a further 1,000 hands in an extension of their factories.'[44]

Obviously, we need to examine more closely the effects of plague and famine in different parts of the country and assess the demographic implications for labour supply. It is quite possible that the vacuum created by plague in the labour requirements of Indian industries was quickly filled by migration so far as the big cities and densely populated areas were concerned, whereas in places in the interior, such as the Central Provinces, the process took longer.

The notion of labour scarcity may have implied a scarcity of skilled hands. This has not been adequately examined. Morris was primarily concerned to show the existence of a surplus pool of raw labour. He has, however, stated that he finds no evidence for the allegation of a shortage of skilled labour as far as the Bombay textile industry is concerned.[45] Since the textiles produced in Bombay were of a relatively coarse quality not requiring a high degree of skill (except a few types of work), this is plausible. In other industries there might have been certain processes for which there was a persistent need to train a cadre of skilled artisans. The increase in the number of iron and brass foundries, the growth of the railway workshops, and the starting of the iron and steel factory at Jamshedpur, all point to the growing need for some skilled operatives. Even the simpler industries and workshops using steam power (cotton presses, jute presses, bone-crushing mills, etc.) needed a few men each to run the engine-room. The 1921 census in Bengal and Bihar gives us data on the relative proportions of skilled and unskilled labour among different castes in various industries, but hardly any studies have been made to show how and when certain castes or groups of people became the principal, if not the only, source of skilled labour in different industries. More research at the level of individual firms and industries is needed. One point worth examining is to see whether the traditional craftsmen who turned to analogous factory work managed to have a head-start over migrant agricultural labour in learning these skills. The evidence is conflicting. In Bombay the weaving section had tended to become a closed shop of Muslim weavers and a few Hindu workers from upper castes.[46] On the other hand in the iron foundries, machinery and engineering works in Bengal in 1921 the Kamars and Lohars (the blacksmith castes) were 'unexpectedly few'. Muslim Sheikhs, Hindu Kaibartas, Chamars and Muchis made up the skilled grades.[47]

II

The Royal Commission on Labour repeatedly affirmed in its report of 1929 that the Indian worker remained only partially committed to industrial life; half his attention was on the village from where he had come. A high degree of labour turnover and absenteeism was cited as evidence of this. The management came to terms with this by keeping more men on the rolls than was necessary, and preferring to make men work for longer hours at a slow pace than for shorter hours with their noses to the grindstone. Thus for nearly 40 years of its existence the industrial labour force appears to have only partially accepted the discipline of an industrial society. This picture of the past is accepted by Charles Myers in his study of industrial relations in post-1945 India.[48]

It is wise not to take these statements completely at face value. Although evidence for 1888 shows that even efficient and well-managed factories such as the Empress Mills at Nagpur found it necessary to keep 2450 persons on the muster-roll, the average attendance did not exceed 2200, and the latter figure included 200 workers as substitutes for still others on authorised leave.[49] In the same year the inspector of factories for Bombay reported that though official holidays were very few, 'all the hands . . . take holidays on their own account when it suits them. On an average, a hand does not work more than 300 days in the year, and can get leave pretty much as he likes.'[50] This need not necessarily imply the pull of the village, but can be interpreted as one form of labour protest against the drudgery and monotony of industrial work. Absenteeism has often played a similar role in developed industrial societies. The evidence of workers from Calcutta and Kanpur before the Factory Commission of 1890 does not, by and large, suggest prolonged holidays spent in native villages. Only one of the 20 witnesses examined had land and cattle in his Orissa village to which he returned periodically. Two others, who had some land or a cow, lived near their place of work and did not need to go on long leave. The rest had little to attract them to their village, where they seldom went.[51] The minutes of the Textile Factory Labour Committee of 1907 contains the deposition of a number of former factory workers in Bombay who for one reason or another had given up factory work. Even these did not take leave frequently when in service.[52]

Morris has tried to examine all the available data on labour turnover and absenteeism in Bombay. He rightly points out: 'High labour turnover in individual mills, which is all that observers could identify, must not be correlated automatically with a return to the countryside. High labour turnover in individual mills is clearly compatible with low rates of departure from the industry.'[53] His general conclusion is that although there might have been a lot of intra-industry mobility, the number of workers permanently attached to the industry increased over the period.[54] Absenteeism, too, appears to have been overstated.

Indications of a high labour turnover and absenteeism cannot, then, be automatically equated with a propensity to return to the villages. It may be consistent with the acceptance of industrial life. The other line of argument regarding the reluctant submission by Indian workers to the rhythm of factory work refers to the slackness of discipline within the factory. In 1888 Inspector W. Drew reported: 'For a mill with the same number of spindles quite twice as many hands are employed in

Bombay as in England. . . . On an average about 9 per cent at a time are taking their meals or resting.'[55]

A jute mill manager near Calcutta with six years' experience of supervising nearly 4000 persons wrote:

At home I have seen a squad doffing to 18 frames; out here they never have more than 10 to 12 frames. We have really about three times the number on a squad we have at home. This holds good throughout the works, as we have over double the number at work always than what is allowed at home: for instance, a boy will look after one roving here, while at home a boy looks after two. A woman will look after one drawing, while at home I have seen a woman looking after three and never less than two of the same size that are here. A full-bodied man will only look after one loom.[56]

Finally, in 1907 the Factory Labour Committee commented: 'No legislation can alter the nature and ingrained habits of Indian workers. They have been in the habit of leaving their work at odd and uncertain periods throughout the nominal working hours.'[57]

From the above it would not be correct to infer that the ingrained reluctance of the Indian factory hand forced the management to accept this remarkably lax pattern of work regulation. The policy of the management could have been a cause rather than a consequence of the workers' laxity. When we see evidence such as that of a Madras factory manager complaining that over the years the workers' skills had improved, but application had not,[58] we should ask whether the management was willing or able to sell products containing a high input of skill and prepared to give high rates for skilled work. This hypothesis has been tested by Morris for Bombay. Employees there seldom took steps to shorten hours and increase efficiency to provide the minimum facilities for food and other necessities at the place of work, and consequently the workers developed their own style of work. With Bombay managing agents being paid a commission for every pound of output, with labour being paid by piece-work, with labour costs being only a small proportion of total costs, and with the product not needing great supervisory skill, it is not surprising that very little was done by the management to promote labour efficiency and create a disciplined labour force.[59] Research along these lines to test how far and for what reasons factory discipline remained loose is suggested for the jute and coal industries.

III

From the preceding discussion on the source of industrial labour and the extent to which it was accepting industrial society it would appear that we can talk of some categories of urban industrial workers as becoming a distinctly industrial proletariat, with little nostalgic attachment to the land. The questions that now arise relate to the way in which this working class got differentiated into groups according to economic, social and political pressures and to the types of organised protest against the injustice of the industrial society that arose.

In Europe and the US craft unionism was the earliest type of trade unionism. Skilled workmen doing similar operations in different industries or in different firms in the same industry in different parts of the country tended to form countrywide associations to maintain a standard rate of wages and an agreed limit to the hours of work. Such craft unions emerged in all industries which were prospering as a result of industrial growth and which were dependent on the services of the skilled grades. It did not matter whether the industries were mechanised or not, as long as they were growing industries. Successful craft unions existed in the building trades, metal and engineering industries, certain grades of cotton textiles and others.

In India similar skilled labour was needed in several industries that had grown in the period before 1920. Payment by piece-work in the textile trades being widespread, the differential between the wages of the slightly skilled and the unskilled was 70 per cent as early as 1888.[60] Yet there is not much evidence of craft unionism. From the beginning Indian trade unions have been organised on the basis of firms or industries. This may have been owing largely to the fact that, by the 1920s, when trade unions were given legal recognition, political parties and philanthropists were giving a lead to the workers, and therefore tended to take a view of trade unionism wider than one covering only the skilled worker. Still, since craft unionism tends to be the natural form of self-organisation by skilled workers, we need to think more about the reasons for its non-appearance. Research could be done on caste associations in different crafts to see whether any of them tried to take on the functions of a craft union. Investigating the Bihar and Bengal data in the light of the census of 1911, Broughton came to the conclusion that the caste councils fixed trade holidays, prevented rivalry for the same client between two craftsmen, and could outcaste recalcitrants. He adds: 'These are, however, at best negative functions. There is no attempt to improve conditions of working or to regulate wages or hours. Further, there is no organisation to weld together members of different castes who follow the same occupation.'[61] In Uttar Pradesh there was an institution comparable to a local craft union that united different castes in the pursuit of economic aims. 'The Rajs (brick masons) of Meerut are not a real caste, but an occupational group recruited from many castes (Chamar, Khatik, Muslim, etc.). They have a system of apprenticeship. . . . The members of the guild remain members of their own castes as regards social matters.'[62] Historians and anthropologists should find out whether similar associations existed in other parts of the country.

The essence of trade unionism in its economic aspects is job control against newcomers, craft unions being the 'closed shop' of the skilled worker. In Indian industries efforts at job control by workers appear to have been made in these years through the media of caste loyalties. The recruitment of mill-hands was done by a jobber (*mistry* or *muqaddam*), who tended to get people from his native region or community. As an overseer of piece-workers, he had an incentive to maintain the output of his department and to encourage workers to develop skills. It was not easy to organise craft unions that cut across the barriers of caste and reduced the dominance of the jobber. So, elements of craft unionism combined with regional and communal loyalties led to the dominance of the skilled occupations in different industries by castes and communities which had been sufficiently numerous and intelligent to carve out niches for themselves.

From the census of 1921 in Bengal and Bihar it has been possible to show the relatively greater preponderance of certain castes in some skilled jobs in some industry.[63] The same caste might be in a relatively weak position in some industry and strong in another, so far as skilled jobs were concerned. The explanation lies in the early history of recruitment in the industry, in which more research should be done. In the coal-mining industry in Bengal the Santhals comprised 36.1 per cent of the total labour force and 14.3 per cent of the skilled and 38.3 per cent of the unskilled respectively; the Bauris comprised 21.4

per cent of the labour force and were almost equally divided between the skilled (23.7 per cent) and the unskilled (21.3 per cent). Muslim workers comprised only 3.4 per cent of the total labour force, but accounted for 10.2 per cent of the skilled grades and only 2.9 per cent of the unskilled grades. In the jute industry, Muslims were in more than proportionate control of the skilled grades; they were 28.6 per cent of the labour force, 37.7 per cent of the skilled grades and 21.2 per cent of the unskilled grades. On the other hand the Chamar caste, which formed 10.3 per cent of the labour force, controlled only 5.5 per cent of the skilled grades and filled 13.9 per cent of the unskilled grades. In two other industries, where skill was at a premium, a similar more than proportionate hold of the Muslim community is noticed. In iron foundries they constituted 18 per cent of the labour force, but 25.1 per cent of the skilled grades and 14.1 per cent of the unskilled grades. Contrast the Chamars again, who accounted for 9.3 per cent of the labour force, but 4.5 per cent of the skilled and 11.8 per cent of the unskilled grades. Two Hindu castes had a slightly more than proportionate control over the skilled grades. The Chasi (cultivating) Kaibartas and Jalia (fishermen) Kaibartas were each 3.1 per cent of the labour force respectively; both, however, controlled between 6.5 and 6.8 per cent of the skilled grades and filled only 1.3 to 1.4 per cent of the unskilled grades. In the machinery and engineering works the Chasi Kaibartas were stronger, being 11.1 per cent of the labour force, but 16 per cent of the skilled and 3.4 per cent of the unskilled grades. Here the Muslims were practically in the same proportion to the total labour force, skilled and unskilled grades.

In Bihar the Muslims were in a relatively strong position in the skilled grades of the iron and steel as well as the machinery and engineering industries. In the former they comprised 12.6 per cent of the total labour force, but controlled 21 per cent of the skilled jobs and only 7.3 per cent of the unskilled grades. In the latter they formed 18.5 per cent of the labour force, but 25.9 per cent of the skilled grades and only 12.5 per cent of the unskilled. No other caste approached them in strength in the engineering industries, but in the iron and steel works Rajputs and Brahmins (mainly from outside Bihar) had more than a proportionate share of skilled jobs. The Rajputs formed 6 per cent of the total labour force, 10.9 per cent of the skilled labour, and 2.9 per cent of the unskilled labour; the Brahmins formed 4.5 per cent, 9.7 per cent and 1.1 per cent respectively of the three categories.

The census of 1911 does not give data comparable in all respects to that of 1921. Nevertheless, research both on the census figures as well as on the records of individual industries is needed to test how far the caste-wise distribution of skilled jobs changed in course of time, how far it was the outcome of informal job control exercised by the workers, even without formal trade unions, and how far it was the result of management policies.

IV

It remains now to discuss strikes or, to use a more generalised term, 'labour protests'. In writing labour history it is a mistake to study it simply as a series of protest movements. Some modern labour economists have even suggested that in the story of the growth of an industrial labour force it is not so much protest that is the central theme as the response of the body of workers to the technical needs of a particular industry, to the 'web of rules' at the place of work and to the prospects or lack of these that a market economy holds out to them. Protest movements tend to be numerous at an early stage of industrialisation and are more often against industrialism as such than against the policies of individual employers. In later stages, industrial labour develops—with or without the assistance of other agencies such as the government, management or political parties—subtler forms of asserting its demands.[64] Without going all the way with this school of thought we would suggest that studies of the protest elements in the Indian labour movement should be preceded by careful research into the way industrial labour has been structured in different parts of the country. Only then would one be able to ask precise questions regarding protest movements and classify them for subtler analysis.

Studies of strikes should seek to distinguish between the economic and political elements in them, and some instances of rioting can be more fruitfully studied as having functional similarities with strikes. To take the last point first, in the early stages of industrialisation it was difficult to organise effective strikes by peaceful picketing because the sense of class solidarity had not yet broken the barriers of regional or caste loyalties. So, aggrieved workers often found it necessary to resort to machine-wrecking, physical violence against employers and blacklegs, or the destruction of industrial products. Moral questions apart, there was a method in this madness, the rationale of which has been shown by Hobsbawm in his discussion of the Luddites in England.[65] In India many of the early strikes saw such scenes of violence, and there must be many episodes described officially as riots, of which a partial explanation might be the discontent of industrial labour.

Economic strikes, pure and simple, probably became less common in the 1920s and 1930s with the increased participation by political parties in the labour movement. In the pre-1918 period we have instances of purely industrial grievances sparking off a strike. We should try to distinguish between those caused by technological factors such as the speeding up of the pace of work or lengthening the hours at the same rate of pay (as happened with the strikes over the introduction of electric lighting in Bombay between 1905 and 1908)[66] and those which were simply responses to the rising cost of living (as happened in the last years of the First World War).[67] Measured against precise questions, the behaviour pattern of different groups of workers before, during and after a strike will become intelligible.

It would also become easier to understand the extent to which outside political leadership exercised any permanent influence on the responses of industrial workers. In the period before 1914 the most notable political strike was that over Tilak's arrest in June 1908. The published sources suggest that since December 1907 Tilak had built up a following among mill-hands, and commanded special influence over jobbers and head jobbers—who were urged by him to give a moral lead to mill-hands. The strike protesting against his arrest was undoubtedly an index of his personal popularity.[68] What needs to be examined is the relationship between the strikes of 1905 and 1907, which were primarily economic in character,[69] and the strike over Tilak's arrest in 1908, which was political. Did the same rank-and-file leadership take initiative in all these strikes? Did the nationalist organisation manage to maintain any permanent hold over workers in important textile mills?

Tilak worked through the jobbers with primarily a political end in view. The political leaders of the trade union movement in the 1920s were to be critical of the way jobbers were hindering the development of a stable workforce and often playing the employers' game. The shift in emphasis was evidently owing to the fact that whereas Tilak's campaign among the factory workers had a limited agitational aim, trade union leaders of a later generation wanted to build up enduring bases within the working class. By that time, however, different industries had created hierarchies of skilled workmen, various degrees of workforce commitment, and different caste and community compositions in the labour force. The interaction of outside political leadership with these was complex. The history of the labour movement in the 1920s and 1930s will have to start by analysing these complexities.

NOTES

1. In 1892 the total number of factory hands was 316,715; in 1918–19 it rose to 1,292,700, R.K. Das, *Factory Labour in India* (Berlin, 1923), pp. 16, 19.
2. Government of India, *Financial and Commercial Statistics of British India* (Calcutta, 1906), pp. 361, 377, 384.
3. Ibid., p. 399; also see Government of India, *Financial and Commercial Statistics of British India, 1893* (Calcutta, 1893), pp. 402–3.
4. P. Nolan, Secy. to the Govt. of Bengal, General Dept, to Secy., Home Dept, Govt. of India, 10 November 1988 (NAI, Legislative, April 1891, no. 94).
5. For Kanpur, see W.F. Wells to Secy., Govt. of North West Province and Oudh, 21 September 1888, appendix (NAI, Legislative, April 1891, no. 135). For Bombay, see 'Extract from the Proceedings of the Govt. of Bombay in the General Department, no. 375, 4 February 1885' (NAI, Legislative, April 1891, no. 228).
6. H.W.I. Bagnell, Inspector of Factories, to Acting Under-Secy., Govt. of Bombay, 27 February 1890 (NAI, Legislative, April 1891, appendix. A 39, pp. 2–30).
7. Government of India, *Financial and Commercial Statistics of British India, 1893*, pp. 387–418.
8. See Magistrate of 24-Parganahs to Commissioner, Presidency Division, 29 February 1888 (West Bengal Govt. Archives (hereafter WBGA)— General Misc., August 1889, File 107/15–17); K.G. Gupta to Commissioner, Presidency Division, 13 August 1892 (WBGA—General Misc. December 1892, 2A/8, nos. 1–2).
9. Proceedings of the Factory Commission, 27–30 October 1890, at Calcutta (NAI, Home-Judicial, March 1891, nos. 33–7).

10. *Census of India, 1921*, V, *Bengal, pt. 1* (Calcutta, 1923), p. 365.

11. Proceedings of the 22nd meeting of the Factory Commission, 1890 (NAI, Home-Judicial, March 1891, no. 33), p. 135.

12. Royal Commission on Labour in India (hereafter RCL), *Report* (1931), p. 11.

13. D.A. Buchanan, *Development of Capitalist Enterprise in India* (New York, 1934), p. 296.

14. Foley, *Report on Labour in Bengal* (1906), as quoted in R.K. Das, *Factory Labour in India*, p. 24.

15. G.M. Broughton, *Labour in Indian Industries* (London, 1924), p. 74.

16. RCL, *Report*, pp. 9f.

17. Evidence of Rajab, Proceedings of the 21st meeting of the Factory Commission, 24 October 1890, Cawnpore (NAI, Home-Judicial, March 1891, no. 32), p. 131.

18. T.R. Metcalf, *Aftermath of Revolt: India, 1857–70* (Princeton, 1965), pp. 195–7.

19. Evidence of Sheo Shankar, Sheo Audhar, Ramdeen, Bhola and Durga, Proceedings of the Factory Commission, 1890, at Cawnpore (NAI, Home-Judicial, March 1891, nos. 30–2).

20. H.D. Moule to Secy., Govt. of the North West Province and Oudh, 26 December 1888 (NAI, Legislative, April 1891, no. 137).

21. Proceedings of the Factory Commission, 1890 (NAI, Home-Judicial, March 1891, nos. 30–2).

22. Broughton, *op.cit.*, p. 58.

23. R. Chotalal to Secy., Govt. of India, Home Dept, 12 December 1890 (NAI, Legislative, April 1891, no. 351), p. 240.

24. Ibid., p. 238.

25. RCL, *Report*, pp. 9f.

26. M.D. Morris, *Emergence of an Industrial Labour Force in India: A Study of the Bombay Cotton Mills, 1854–1947* (Bombay, 1965), p. 74.

27. RCL, *Report, passim*; A.R. Burnett-Hurst, 'Suggestions for Labour Legislation in India', *Indian Journal of Economics*, III (1920–2), 497.

28. D. Kumar, *Land and Caste in South India* (Cambridge, 1965).

29. D. Thorner and A. Thorner, *Land and Labour in India* (Bombay, 1962), ch. VI *passim*; articles by M.D. Morris, B. Chandra and T. Raychaudhuri in *Indian Economic and Social History Review*, V, no. 1 (1968).

30. H.D. Moule to Secy., Govt. of North West Province and Oudh, 26 December 1888 (NAI, Legislative, April 1891, no. 137).

31. H.E.M. James, Collector of Ahmedabad, to Commissioner, Northern Division, 28 July 1888 (NAI, Legislative, April 1891, no. 119); also see NAI, Commerce & Industry—Factories, July 1907, nos. 2–14. (The file

has evidence of workers who had Left factory work but acknowledged its value as giving more regular employment than agriculture.)

32. Morris, *Emergence of an Industrial Labour Force,* pp. 44–71.
33. Ibid., p. 69.
34. Ibid., p. 135, no. 18.
35. NAI, Legislative, April 1891, nos. 121–2.
36. R.K. Das, *Plantation Labour in India* (Calcutta, 1931), *passim.*
37. RCL, *Report,* pp. 9f.
38. B.R. Seth, *Labour in the Indian Coal Industry* (Bombay, 1940), pp. 24, 43ff.
39. R.K. Das, *History of Indian Labour Legislation* (Calcutta, 1941), pp. 16–20.
40. Seth, *op.cit.,* pp. 27f.
41. Morris, *op.cit.,* pp. 55–6.
42. V.B. Karnik, *Strikes in India* (Bombay, 1967), pp. 29–31.
43. A. Earle, Secy. to Govt. of Bengal, to Secy., Govt. of India, 2 February 1904 (NAI, Commerce & Industry—Factories, May 1905, no. 6).
44. R. Craddock to Secy. to the Chief Commissioner, Central Provinces, 13 July 1906 (NAI, Commerce & Industry—Factories, January 1907, no. 24).
45. Morris, *op.cit.,* p. 130.
46. Ibid., p. 79.
47. *Census of India 1921,* V, *Bengal,* pt. I, *Report,* pp. 406f.
48. C.A. Myers, *Industrial Relations in India* (Bombay, 1958), pp. 75–85.
49. NAI, Legislative, April 1891, no. 106, p. 2.
50. W. Drew to Under-Secy., Govt. of Bombay, 10 July 1888 (NAI, Legislative, April 1891, no. 117).
51. NAI, Home-Judicial, March 1891, nos. 33–7.
52. NAI, Commerce & Industry—Factories, July 1907, nos. 2–14.
53. *Op.cit.,* p. 87.
54. Ibid., pp. 88–91.
55. NAI, Legislative, April 1891, no. 117.
56. R. Keddie to Magistrate, 24-Parganahs, 15 February 1890 (WBGA, General, Misc., April 1890, File 92, nos. 27–8).
57. *Report of the Factory Labour Committee, 1907,* p. 12 (NAI, Commerce & Industry—Factories, July 1907, no. 14, enclosure 1).
58. Das, *Factory Labour in India,* p. 100.
59. Morris, *op.cit.,* p. 117.
60. H.E.M. James, Collector of Ahmedabad to Commissioner, Northern Division, 28 July 1888 (NAI, Legislative, April 1891, no. 119).
61. Broughton, *op.cit.,* p. 45.

62. Ibid., p. 61.
63. The percentages have been worked out from the basic data in the following volumes of the *Census of India 1921*; for Bengal, V, pt. II, table XXII, pts. IV–V; for Bihar, VII, pt. II, table XXII, pts. IV–V.
64. C. Kerr. J.T. Dunlop, F.H. Harbison and C.M. Myers, *Industrialism and Industrial Man* (Harvard, 1960), *passim*.
65. E.J. Hobsbawm, *Labouring Men* (London, 1964), chapter on 'Machine Breakers'.
66. Morris, *op.cit.*, p. 164; Karnik, *Strikes in India*, pp. 32f.
67. Karnik, *op.cit.*, pp. 60–2.
68. Government of Bombay, *Source Material for a History of the Freedom Movement in India*, II (Bombay, 1958), pp. 252–75.
69. Morris, *op.cit.*, pp. 164f, 179.

BRITISH RAILWAY LABOUR'S LOBBY, 1870–1900*

The history of legislation in favour of railwaymen's conditions between 1870 and 1900 in Britain helps clarify certain as pects of the genesis of nineteenth-century social reforms. It also has a bearing on the gradual decline of the Liberal Party as a factor in working-class politics.[1] O. MacDonagh, in his provocative writings, has tended to belittle the role of utilitarian ideas and to emphasise administrative experience sometimes influenced by a humanitarian Christian conscience.[2] Jennifer Hart and H. Parris criticise his views, although Parris's approach in his book on government control over the railways is analogous to MacDonagh's.[3] He argues that between 1840 and 1867 a great deal of *de facto* control was steadily extended over the railways by the Board of Trade. This can be explained sufficiently with reference to departmental administrative knowledge.[4] Up to a point his treatment carries conviction, but not so much when, surveying the extension of legislation after 1867, he says that 'the contrast is less pro-

*First published in Barun De and others (eds), *Essays in Honour of Professor S.C. Sarkar* (Delhi, 1976).

This is based on part of my doctoral thesis entitled 'History of the Amalgamated Society of Railway Servants, 1871–1915' (Oxford, D. Phil., 1960), with subsequent revision. To the general secretary of the National Union of Railwaymen of Britain I am grateful for allowing me to inspect their records and for permitting publication. I am also grateful for permission to consult and quote from material in their possession to the British Railways Board Historical Record Office, the Controller of HM Stationery Office for unpublished Crown copyright material at the Public Record Office, London, and to Mr C.E. Gladstone for the Gladstone Papers at the British Museum.

The following abbreviations have been used: ASRS (Amalgamated Society of Railway Servants), RCA (Railway Companies' Association), *RR* (*Railway Review*), *RSG* (*Railway Service Gazette*), NER (North Eastern Railway).

found than at first appears'.[5] Precedents of an earlier period probably explain the further public safety measures taken by the government after 1870, but do not explain why nearly all useful railway labour laws were bunched together in the 1890s and after. On the other hand the official history of the National Union of Railwaymen[6] has exaggerated the role of the Amalgamated Society of Railway Servants (ASRS) in promoting public safety.[7] It has not answered crucial questions on the timing of reforms and the relative responsibility of officials, politicians and union leaders. In a few places the picture has been distorted by a slight bias against the railway companies and the Board of Trade.

By 1873, when the ASRS was maintaining a precarious existence and was beset with organisational problems, government control over the railways had certain well-defined characteristics. Before 1867, despite the absence for over twenty years of public general acts significantly extending the powers of the Board of Trade, the latter had enlarged its powers of intervention 'by developing a system of delegated . . . legislation, administrative tribunals, appeal to the minister, and quasilegislation'.[8] Though the Royal Commission on railways in 1865 had recommended against any further legal extension of its powers, between 1867 and 1873 three new acts required the companies to provide accurate returns of accounts and statistics, compulsory reports of accidents affecting public safety, and annual returns on the installation of safety devices like the interlocking of points and signals.[9] A fourth act set up the administrative tribunal of the railway commission as a machinery in reserve to adjudicate on rates and fares if necessary.[10]

Though these acts followed hard on one another, most of them did not mark any new departure in government policy.[11] Only the Railway and Canal Traffic Act of 1873, arising out of the amalgamation scare of the previous years, marked in theory something of an advance over 'Cardwell's Act' of 1854.[12] All were only in the interests of the trading community and the travelling public. Even in these spheres there was a deep-seated reluctance to transfer responsibility to the government and officials continued to rely on the 'voluntary cooperation of the companies' as far as possible.[13] There is little evidence of government concern for the welfare of railway servants in this period, although a few instances could be found in the 1840s.[14] Mid-Victorian England would not accept the legal regulation of the hours of adult male labour

and enlightened middle-class opinion preferred to let collective bargaining decide union rates and the normal day. By 1875, having passed
two laws safeguarding the trade unions' legal position, the government
absolved itself from direct involvement in industrial conciliation.[15]

Against this background we have to examine how by 1900 certain
acts of parliament dealing wholly or partly with railway labour questions
got passed, how far this was exclusively the work of the lobby of the
ASRS, and what developments in electoral and party politics reciprocally
influenced the union's efforts.

I

In the period before 1886 the union's lobbying limped along behind
public opinion, sporadically assisted by a few humanitarian parliamentarians. A Royal Commission on railway accidents had been set
up by Disraeli's government in June 1874. This was in response to
the persistent criticisms of Earl de la Warr, a Conservative member of
the House of Lords, who had read the reports of accidents publicised in
the previous months by Michael Bass, the patron of the ASRS.[16] Since
1871 Bass had used the occasions when the railway laws cited above
were discussed in parliament to press for measures in the interests of
public safety.[17]

The commission's terms of reference concerned public safety in
general. As the evidence provided by the secretary of the ASRS added
little to what some Board of Trade inspectors had already stated, his
plea for giving compulsory enforcement powers to the Board of Trade
cut no ice with the commission.[18] The report reviewed the technical
progress made in safety devices and recommended that the companies
should provide regular returns of relevant safety devices. The precedent
already established by the Act of 1873 requiring returns of signalling
equipment was to be extended to brakes,[19] which was done by an act in
1878.[20] This fitted in with the departmental techniques of using moral
pressure, and explicitly rejected extending Board of Trade jurisdiction
over railway servants' problems of safety and hours of work.[21]

The poor performance of the union before the commission was
symptomatic of organisational weaknesses that had repeatedly affected
the union in the 1870s, culminating in the rapid dwindling in member-

ship between 1879 and 1882.[22] The economic Depression had contributed to it and slowed down the revival of the union in the mid-1880s. The Depression, however, increased the pressure by the trading community on the Board of Trade to regulate railway rates and fares.[23] Being obliged to balance the competing claims of the traders, the companies, and a very small trade union, the Board of Trade understandably ignored the latter. From the public-safety angle the board found little to complain of in the 1880s, for most of the companies had been steadily introducing the continuous brakes and better signalling methods which its inspectors had been urging since the 1860s.[24] Because safe methods of coupling vehicles did not concern public safety, departmental prodding on this was limited, and technical problems had not been solved. The union's secretary Edward Harford publicised some experimental devices which were useful curtain-raisers to a legislative effort in 1886.[25] But the general disregard of the Board of Trade official was typified by the remark, 'Oh, I know Mr Harford, he wants the government to take charge of the railways.'[26]

Yet, after the extension of the county franchise in 1884, a significant Liberal–Labour platform emerged on railwaymen's questions. After Michael Bass's death in 1884, the only regular parliamentary link of the union was its president P.S. MacIver, Liberal MP for Plymouth, who lost his seat in 1885. He searched for a constituency with many railwaymen and was eventually adopted at Doncaster in April 1889, with prospects of success, for the union then had 180 members at Doncaster and 107 members at Mexborough.[27] Meanwhile the union had found an ally in F.A. Channing, the radical MP for East Northamptonshire since 1885, and also in W.S.B. McLaren, the radical who won Crewe after electoral reform had made it less of a pocket borough of the London and North-Western Railway.[28] The president of the Board of Trade in Gladstone's short-lived third cabinet was A.J. Mundella, a friend of trade unionism in general, who had known Edward Harford since 1873 when the latter was a union organiser at Sheffield, the minister's constituency.[29] So the ASRS got parliamentary time for a second reading of Channing's private bill on safe railway working on 19 May 1886, in spite of the absorption of parliament with Gladstone's Irish measures since April, and Mundella's own preoccupation since March with the Railway and Canal Traffic Bill dealing with rates and fares. In introducing the

government bill Mundella had made a commendatory reference to
Channing's bill.[30] The companies had launched a powerful campaign
against the government bill, though how much general support they
got is debatable.[31] Despite their objections Channing's bill got a second
reading, Mundella supporting its main ideas and then suggesting reference to a committee, 'where the railway servants and the Directors can
be heard'.[32] Not all the five nominees of the companies could get on to
this committee, while labour was represented by John Wilson and Ben
Pickard.[33] Hardly had the committee met when the home rule crisis
came to a head and parliament was prorogued. A big political crisis
rather than the pressure of the companies sealed the fate of the bill.[34]

In the new parliament, Earl de la Warr secured the publication of
a special statement of the long hours worked in March 1888,[35] and
Channing and Mundella tried to raise the question in the House of
Commons, but the Conservative–Unionist government went on stalling.
This was perhaps because there were fifty-three railway directors on
government benches, including the president of the Board of Trade,
Sir Michael Hicks-Beach.[36] A thin-attended house heard Channing
and Mundella speak in favour of increasing the board's powers on
railway labour problems and Hicks-Beach reply with the long-standing
departmental view that this would lead to divided responsibility.[37] A
promise of legislation given in this debate was redeemed more than a
year later, only after the Armagh train accident had focused attention
on the existence of passenger trains still without continuous brakes.
Under the regulation of the Railways Act of 16 July 1889 the Board of
Trade had powers to enforce railway companies to adopt continuous
brakes, the block-signalling system and safe couplings and to produce
periodic returns of long hours worked.[38] But within a week, under pressure
from the companies' association, Hicks-Beach wished to withdraw the
clause on safe couplings.[39] In spite of an effort by the Lib–Lab and
radical MPs to put the railwaymen's case before the minister on 23 July,
the companies succeeded within a couple of days not only in eliminating
the clauses on couplings but also in making the compulsory adoption
of continuous brakes applicable to passenger trains only.[40] Thus, by
linking its parliamentary campaign since 1870 to the question of public
safety, the ASRS failed to achieve any alterations in the really dangerous
aspects of railway work, aspects which went on undetected in shunting

yards, on the permanent-way, and while operating goods wagons. What was achieved for public safety owed little to the union's work.

II

Nevertheless, even if the year 1889 had produced a law of only limited value, it marked the beginning of a new period in the union's history when, with a steadily increasing membership it got two laws passed within a decade. Once, with Liberal help, the Railway Regulation Act was passed in 1893, the union acquired a right to be consulted by the Board of Trade, thus breaching the traditional wall of indifference. The earlier years of this decade showed that up to a point the Liberal–Labour alliance was mutually advantageous. Already in October 1889 in a by-election at the railway junction of Peterborough, the radical A.C. Morton, campaigning on a trade union platform, had got solid support at the polling booths 'in the quarters in which the Great Northern and Midland Railway men live' and had surprised poll-forecasters by defeating the favourite Conservative candidate R. Purvis.[41] Subsequently he supported Channing on railway labour questions. About a year later, before Gladstone's Newcastle programme was announced, Channing suggested to Francis Schnadhorst, secretary of the National Liberal Federation, the adoption of a genuinely collectivist programme. Though that was ignored he and many other radicals campaigned on that plank.[42]

The Scottish railway strike of the winter of 1890–1 enabled Channing for the first time to have a full house listening to him on railwaymen's conditions on 23 January 1891 and to get five Conservative and Unionist members to vote with the entire Liberal opposition and the Irish nationalists in support of his motion.[43] The Railway Companies' Association (RCA) had hoped that some Liberals would speak against Channing,[44] but prominent railway directors in the Liberal Party like M. MacInnes, Sir Joseph Pease and R.A. Ellison were absent during the debate, and from the Liberal front bench Sir William Harcourt intervened to criticise the attitude of the companies to trade unions and asked Channing not to withdraw his motion.

The select committee which was the follow-up to this debate took evidence during 1891 and 1892 and produced two reports—a majority report by Sir Michael Hicks-Beach strictly confining itself to questions of public safety and a minority report written by Channing which demanded that the state should provide 'just conditions of labour' for railwaymen.[45] With the exception of Liberal railway directors all Liberal members of the committee signed Channing's report. With the Scottish strike a fading memory in the public mind and with divided counsel coming from the select committee, the ASRS might have failed to campaign effectively. However, in April 1892 a 'breach of privilege' motion against two Conservative railway directors for victimising stationmaster Hood for his evidence before the committee renewed public interest,[46] which was maintained with the publication of the two reports five weeks before the general election. Meanwhile Channing had sent a pre-publication copy of his minority report to Gladstone, adding, 'The Railwaymen are a splendid class. . . . I am quite sure that a broad and generous and sympathetic attitude of the Liberal Party towards them will not be thrown away politically.'[47]

In some constituencies the railwaymen's vote was quite an important factor, for the ASRS had mounted an effective campaign since February, instructing its branch secretaries to send copies of a centrally prepared questionnaire to their local parliamentary candidates.[48] The replies were published in full in the *Railway Review* every week until 15 July. Most of the 185 replies answered each point of the questionnaire fairly fully.[49] Early in June the division list of Channing's motion of January 1891 was reprinted and when parliament was dissolved his minority report was serialised and also issued as a pamphlet.[50]

Though a general Liberal swing occurred all over the country, in certain constituencies this particular agitation was a contributory factor. In Durham city the sitting Conservative member T. Milvain, who had signed the majority report of Hicks-Beach, saw his electoral majority of 274 transformed into a Liberal majority of 75. Both parties attributed the Liberal victory to what the Conservative press bitterly called 'the trumped-up railway grievance, and the audacious untruths of Mr Channing', which had made the railwaymen act 'as the serfs of Harford, the secretary and monarch of their union'.[51] In Doncaster the union's one-time president MacIver had resigned the Liberal candidature because of ill-health,[52] but the next Liberal candidate, C.J. Fleming, had wisely nursed the steadily growing ASRS branch in 1890 by supporting rallies in favour of its national programme.[53] His favourable replies to the election questionnaire were contrasted with those of the sitting unionist MP, W.H. Fitzwilliam.[54] In course of the campaign both sides realised that the Irish question was less important than the labour question in this mining constituency, and that marginal groups like the railwaymen mattered. Belated efforts by Fitzwilliam to canvass railwaymen's support were ignored by the ASRS branch, which actively campaigned for Fleming, and the latter, in a higher total poll, transformed his opponent's majority of 213 into a majority of 279 in his favour.[55] In the London constituency of West Islington, which stretched around King's Cross station, the railwaymen campaigned for the Liberal T. Lough who won the seat from the Conservatives.[56] Elsewhere, at the railway junction of Reading, the metropolitan railway and dock centre of Deptford, and the NER centre at York the campaigns showed the ASRS as an important factor.[57] Doubtless drawing a lesson from this, Sir Albert Rollitt, Conservative MP for South Islington and a signatory to the majority report, and whose neighbouring constituency had been won by T. Lough, shifted his position. In his address to the union's annual general meeting in October 1892 he supported legal enactment and the following year became a co-sponsor of Channing's private bill.[58]

The Railway Regulation Act of 1893, while mainly a child of this campaign, was partly due to new attitudes of new men at the Board of Trade. This legislation cannot simply be dismissed as having made a weak bill 'weaker after its passage through parliament' or the act dismissed as having become a dead letter.[59] Mundella, once again at the Board of Trade, considered the select committee's report to mean 'that increased powers be given to the Board of Trade to prevent the overworking of Railway Servants, that is, working too long hours at the *risk of their health and lives,* and the public safety'.[60] It was no doubt at his advice, and at a time when the opponent of state interference, Permanent Secretary Sir H. Calcraft, was absent, that the department asked many companies for returns of overtime from August 1892 onwards.[61] By the end of the year one inspector commented, 'In none of these cases does the explanation given for overtime appear to me to be satisfactory',[62] and Gladstone thought of introducing legislation on this question before Christmas.[63] The government bill, introduced in February 1893, empowering the Board of Trade to call for schedules of

hours and order their revision, displeased the ASRS on three counts—
the absence of specified standards of hours, intervals of rest, and Sunday
relief, the absence of the right of trade unionists to bring complaints to
the Board of Trade, and the absence of a special legal limit for signalmen.[64] Consultation between the union leaders, Channing and Mundella,
ensured at the committee stage satisfaction on Sunday relief, intervals
of rest, and trade union right of complaint. The continued absence of
defined standards of hours mattered less, for in its implementation
certain standards were laid down.[65] The only serious failure concerned
the provision for signalmen partly because it was a recently formulated demand that had not been part of the union's campaigning plank
and partly because Board of Trade officials felt that this would mean
state management of all signal boxes.[66]

It now remained to be seen if government interference would extend
beyond the exigencies of public safety. It also remained to be seen whether
the railwaymen's interests would continue to be linked with the fortunes
of the Liberal Party.

III

As far as the Liberal Party was concerned, Edward Harford secured
adoption as the Liberal candidate for Northampton in the summer of
1894 in spite of the opposition of a middle-class rival.[67] This contrasted
with the normal practice of Liberal caucuses[68] and strengthened the
Lib–Lab elements in their belief that 'direct labour representation
has nothing to gain by wantonly ignoring, much less repudiating, the
political party willing to cooperate with us for a common object'.[69]
Railwaymen who voted Conservative had been annoyed at Harford's
candidature and so were the ILP-ers and together they got a general
resolution on independence passed by the annual meeting of the union
in 1894.[70] But in 1895, as Harford's election campaign came very near
to success, the ILP-ers realised that they were not strong enough to
oppose or challenge workable Lib–Lab compromises that promised
to pay dividends.[71] Nevertheless the general results of the election of
1895 showed that the tired and divided Liberal government of the
post-Gladstonian period had become barren of new ideas on social
questions.[72]

Meanwhile the Board of Trade expanded its activities. Mundella took the initiative, despite the explicit objection of his predecessor Hicks-Beach, in creating two subinspectorships in the Board of Trade to be filled by workingmen with experience of railway work. An old ASRS member was appointed to one of them. While returns of accidents to railwaymen had been coming in as part of general returns since 1872, in 1894 for the first time a departmental committee formulated the precise methods of finding out the nature of such accidents.[73]

Harford used his rights to lodge complaints about long hours under the Act of 1893 quite often and was struck by the 'great change' for the better in the officials' attitude, especially that of F.J.S. Hopwood, assistant secretary to the railway department, who was willing to extend the area of its operation.[74] Even a supporter of the legal eight-hour day agreed five years later, writing, 'The Board has manipulated the Act in a way far beyond the most sanguine expectations.'[75] Between July 1893 and July 1895 all instances of inordinately excessive hours were abolished and the twelve-hour booked day became the maximum on British railways. Even after the change of government in July 1895, the Board of Trade ignored suggestions by railway companies that the act be ignored since public safety was no longer endangered.[76] The new minister C.T. Ritchie, talking to a deputation of signalmen, was willing to abolish twelve-hour days generally but was doubtful of the political practicability of fresh legislation so soon. The alternative policy was to refer companies persisting in twelve-hour workloads to the Railway and Canal Commission under the provision of the existing act.[77] Since this went against the spirit of give and take with which Hopwood had been negotiating with the companies, it involved the risk of retaliatory wage reductions by the latter, something that had been avoided so far.[78]

As the Act of 1893 appeared to have reached its operational limits, union opinion (including that of Harford) swung in favour of a legal eight-hour bill, with guaranteed week's pay, discarding earlier ambiguities on this question, and Channing took charge of it.[79] Despite this shift towards greater collectivism, the Lib–Lab pragmatists who ran the union did not make, or feel it necessary to make, a general reappraisal of their position *vis-à-vis* the state. To the historian it is clear that the Liberal government, acting under pressure from traders on the one hand and railwaymen on the other, left a legacy of rather contradictory laws—

the Hours of Labour Act which involved the companies in expense and the amended Rates and Charges Act which froze their sources of additional revenue.[80] In the absence of union recognition by the companies a joint rates and wages policy could not be worked out. Despite the passing of a resolution on nationalisation in 1894, no serious thought was given to this as a practicable alternative.[81] Acting under pressure from well-organised grades Harford shelved the eight-hour bill and concentrated on national wages and hours movements in 1896–7. The partial success of some of these and the greater fiasco of an all-grades movement underlined that however well disposed to the ASRS individual Board of Trade officials might be, the department regarded its role as an industrial conciliator in the railway industry as limited, despite the recent enlargement of its labour and railway departments.[82]

After 1897 union members more frequently advocated collectivist measures—railway nationalisation, the legal eight-hour day, and the amendment of the Conciliation Act of 1896 in favour of compulsory arbitration,[83] but their new leaders like Richard Bell were concerned more with achieving what was possible by cooperation with the Board of Trade than with agitating for immediately impracticable demands. Having impressed Sir Courteney Boyle and Francis Hopwood with the hard realities of a railway trade unionist's life,[84] he enlisted their help both for industrial conciliation and for safety legislation. Industrial conciliation did not get very far in the face of employers' hostility culminating in the Taff Vale dispute, but safety legislation made progress.[85]

IV

Improved methods of accident inspection had made the Board of Trade realise the need for safety devices for shunters. After an official visit to the US in the summer of 1898 Hopwood proposed legislation to introduce automatic couplers within a time-limit, if only to stimulate invention and prevent dilatoriness.[86] Having seen him when he was preparing this note, Bell spent a month lobbying in the department and parliament so as to make Ritchie openly commit himself to initiate a bill in February 1899.[87] When the bill was set down for second reading in March, the railway companies, startled into action by this latest development, prepared for a strong counteroffensive.[88] They persuaded Ritchie to postpone the second reading from 6 to 27 March, joined forces with private wagon-owners, and wanted the bill referred to an expert committee of railway engineers instead of to a select committee, if it could not be withdrawn altogether. Signed letters on their behalf appeared in *The Times* and the chairman of the Great Eastern Railway, Lord Claud Hamilton, resigned from the presidency of the North Kensington Conservative Association.[89] When they met Ritchie on 15 March two colliery wagon-owners had taken up a similar attitude. Sir Alfred Hickman (Conservative MP for Wolverhampton West) wavered between his loyalty to fellow industrialists and regard for his party's electoral prospects in working-class districts. A.G. Barnes, who came from a Unionist family, bluntly threatened to withdraw political support.[90]

But Ritchie reacted sharply to this type of blackmail and declared himself as deeply impressed by the departmental officials' views on the need for state action. Though he was prepared to drop the coupling clauses to satisfy colliery owners—who found the cost prohibitive— the railway directors did not care for his two alternative proposals, a truncated bill or a Royal Commission with wide terms of reference.[91] Further pressure led to the postponement of the bill by another fortnight, but the ASRS, acting on a hint from Ritchie, tried to secure official Liberal Party support to strengthen his hand.[92] The newly elected Liberal leader Sir Henry Campbell-Bannerman had recently alluded to Ritchie's difficulties with the remark 'a parliamentary seat in the hand is worth any number of shunters' lives in the bush'.[93] The union leaders, on Sir Charles Dilke's advice, approached Tom Ellis, the Liberal chief whip.

The time was hardly propitious for expecting solid Liberal support because the party was split over foreign and colonial policy, and ever since Harcourt's resignation in December 1898 it had been preoccupied with the succession question.[94] The railwaymen's friend Channing had for a while toyed with supporting a Harcourt comeback but eventually seconded Sir Joseph Pease's proposal to elect Campbell-Bannerman.[95] Since Pease was one of seventeen railway directors in parliament the new leader could hardly afford to annoy them at this critical moment.[96] In any case the unexpected death of Tom Ellis, personally known to the ASRS leadership and Liberal chief whip, reduced the chances of getting official Liberal support.[97] Even though seventy radical MPs led by Sir Charles Dilke pledged to support the original bill if Ritchie would press it, the latter, after a talk with Richard Bell, decided to appoint a Royal Commission to inquire into all types of accidents involving railwaymen, and to include a union member in it.[98]

Appointed within five weeks, the commission had as its chairman Lord James of Hereford, who knew railway labour problems, having arbitrated in the North Eastern Railway dispute of 1897, when Richard Bell had been the men's advocate.[99] Though the RCA was suspicious of the whole inquiry the two railway directors on the commission were open to new ideas.[100] The evidence of union members and Board of Trade inspectors was very well presented. A unanimous report, published in January 1900, declared that like mining and merchant-shipping the work of goods guards, brakemen, shunters and permanent-waymen should be classified as dangerous trades. It firmly supported state interference, because the railways possessed special statutory privileges. The Board of Trade was to get powers 'for the inspection and regulation of the work done by Shunters, Goods Guards, Brakesmen, and Platelayers' and to define a dangerous practice and to order the companies to adopt general or specific safety rules.[101]

The first draft of a government bill, introduced four weeks later, met 'the requirements of railwaymen generally' if it was 'allowed to pass in its present form'.[102] Six clauses unequivocally increased the powers of the Board of Trade regarding accident affecting all classes of railwaymen. State inspection of railways in the interests of railwaymen's safety was enacted for the first time, twenty-two years after a similar act for factories and workshops. The board could now make rules to force the companies to stop any type of work deemed dangerous by the inspectors, and the right of companies to appeal against such draft rules to the Railway and Canal Commission was hedged about by restrictions to prevent misuse. Other clauses allowed companies to raise fresh capital to introduce government-sponsored safety devices.[103]

Bell, who had been lobbying vigorously and getting branch secretaries to do so ever since January, saw his labours rewarded when the concerted efforts of the companies to whittle down these extensive powers given to the Board of Trade were frustrated. This was largely due to Ritchie's firmness, and the support given by Conservatives like R. Purvis, who had won Peterborough from Morton in 1895 and deemed it electorally wise to champion railwaymen's causes.[104] Besides, traditional pro-Labour radicals like Channing, Dilke and Maddison helped. All efforts at the committee stage by railway director parliamentarians to circumscribe the scope of the act as regards inspection provisions, grades of railwaymen covered, or the type of safety devices desired, failed, sometimes by only one vote.[105] Further efforts at the report stage to give the companies a universal and unlimited right of appeal against decisions of the Board of Trade were checked by the alert interventions of Lib–Labs like Fenwick and Maddison.[106] In the House of Lords the bill was introduced by Lord James of Hereford, who lived up to Bell's description of him as the 'one friend who [could] be relied upon'.[107] Having firmly rejected a private suggestion from the RCA for an unlimited right of appeal against the Board of Trade, he steered the bill through safely.[108]

V

The preceding account shows that apropos of what Jennifer Hart has called the 'Tory' interpretation of the origins of the welfare state,[109] while the trade union movement cannot claim the whole credit for safety legislation on railways in general, the timing of the extensions of government's powers in railwaymen's interests was causally linked with trade union agitation. The way the Board of Trade came round to accepting responsibility for railwaymen by the mid-1890s had the same element of empirical administrative adjustment which Parris noticed for an earlier period. The utilitarian notion of marginal collectivism in the interests of society can also be detected in Channing's minority report of 1891 and Lord James's report of 1900. But the evidence of the records and reports at the Board of Trade suggest that Sir Courteney Boyle and Francis Hopwood were guided more by what was administratively possible within a given tradition rather than by any theories of what the state should do. Yet mere experience would have led nowhere had there not been a steady pressure from the ASRS. As long as the union was weak, appeals to the humanitarian Christian conscience of Victorian England fell on deaf ears. Michael Bass and the Earl de la Warr had little success in the 1870s and 1880s, nor was the solitary example of church assembly support anything more than an ineffective pious wish.[110] It was only after electoral reforms in 1884 and mainly after the ASRS was well organised and well versed in techniques of parliamentary pressure that it made headway.

Despite the extension of its powers by the Act of 1900 the Board of Trade remained relatively ineffective in matters of wages and hours and industrial conciliation. Since the ASRS at this time was not a tightly disciplined centralised union with a strongly collectivist outlook, it did not agitate for nationalisation as a solution.[111] Local pressures and the desire for union recognition alternately dictated its strategy in this period. So further increases in government powers were sought mainly in the field of compulsory arbitration which, Richard Bell hoped, would discipline both recalcitrant companies and militant local activists.[112]

The experience of lobbying before the Act of 1900 had different political lessons for different groups of railwaymen. When in April 1899 the union struggled in vain to prevent the postponement of the first bill and to secure official Liberal Party support, the ILP-ers in the union and outside it argued that an independent party of even ten working men would have pushed the bill through by virtue of its strategic position.[113] This strengthened their efforts within the union to unite the socialists and the trade unionists, which was symbolised by the resolution on labour representation at the Trades Union Congress in 1899 and the formation of the Labour Representation Committee (LRC). But others like Bell saw no reason to doubt the effectiveness of a large radical-labour group teaming up with men like Dilke, who had done a great deal for the passage of the Act of 1900. Having been adopted as a trade union candidate in Derby in September 1899[114] with a tacit understanding with the Liberals, he expected, if elected, to continue the railway labour lobby in association with Liberals. Since all working-class members in the parliament of 1900–5, with the exception of Keir Hardie, were Lib–Lab by temperament, and since cooperation between radical members and trade unionists appeared to work,[115] for some time the ASRS could be swayed against its socialists by Bell, its newly elected parliamentary representative, who was a member of the LRC but a Liberal at heart.[116] Only after the LRC had triumphed in the election of 1906 and organised itself as the Labour Party (including railwaymen like Walter Hudson and George Wardle), with Bell getting isolated by his arrogance, did the Labour Party become the union's main political ally.

NOTES

1. J. Hart, 'Nineteenth Century Social Reform: A Tory Interpretation of History', *Past and Present,* 31 (July 1965), pp. 39–61; H.J. Hanham, 'Liberal Organisations for Working Men, 1860–1914', *Bulletin of the Society for the Study of Labour History,* 7 (Autumn 1963), pp. 5–9; Peter Stansky, *Ambitions and Strategies* (Oxford, 1964); H. Pelling, *Popular Politics and Society in Late Victorian Britain* (London, 1968), ch. VI, *passim.*

2. O. MacDonagh, 'The Nineteenth Century Revolution in Government: A Reappraisal', *Historical Journal,* I (1958), pp. 52–67; O. MacDonagh, *A Pattern of Government Growth* (London, 1961), pp. 17, 58, 346–50; G.R. Kitson-Clark, *Making of Victorian England* (London, 1962), pp. 19, 192, 284.

3. Hart, *op.cit.*; H. Parris, 'The Nineteenth Century Revolution in Government', *Historical Journal,* III (1960), pp. 17–57; H. Parris, *Government and the Railways in Nineteenth Century Britain* (London, 1965).

4. Parris, *op.cit.,* p. 210; also see ch. V, VI, *passim.*

5. Ibid., p. 212.

6. P.S. Bagwell, *The Railwaymen* (London, 1963). Also see my paper, 'Railway Trade Unionism in Britain, 1880–1900', *Economic History Review,* April 1966. Despite my criticism of inadequacies in Bagwell's work made in this essay, I remain personally grateful to him for letting me continue my work on the union records after he was appointed the official historian in 1959.

7. See the exaggerated claim, 'In so far as the ASRS was successful in its advocacy, it benefited not only the railwaymen but also the travelling public' (ibid., p. 99).

8. Parris, *op.cit.,* p. 210.

9. C.I. Savage, *An Economic History of Transport* (London, 1959), p. 66; Parris, *op.cit.,* p. 217. The acts were (i) Regulation of Railways Act, 1868 (31 & 32 Vict c 119), (ii) Regulation of Railways Act, 1871 (34 & 35 Vict c 78), (iii) Railway Regulation (Return of Signal Arrangements) Act, 1873 (36 & 37 Vict c 76).

10. Railway and Canal Traffic Act, 1873 (36 & 37 Vict c 48).

11. Of the three requiring statistical returns, the first was the product of the Royal Commission on Railways of 1865, the other two of public alarm at railway accidents in 1870–2 and in line with the limited degrees of control the Board of Trade had already been exercising (Parris, *op.cit.,* pp. 182–200).

12. Savage, *op.cit.,* pp. 67–9; Parris, *op.cit.,* p. 221.

13. Parris, *op.cit.,* p. 217.

14. Ibid., pp. 125, 128.

15. I.G. Sharp, *Industrial Conciliation and Arbitration in Great Britain* (London, 1950), pp. 289f.

16. *RSG*, 21 March 1874, p. 5; *The Times*, 25 March 1875, p. 6; *The Times*, 28 April 1874, p. 6.

17. See, for example, *Parliamentary Debates*, 3rd S, CCV, 34–9; ibid., CCVII, 699f.

18. *Royal Commission on Railway Accidents*, min of ev. Q. 1126ff (*Parliamentary Papers* (henceforth *Parl Pap.*, 1877, XLVIII).

19. *RC on Railway Accidents*, Report, p. 21 (*Parl Pap*), 1877, XIVXI.

20. Railway Returns (Continuous Brakes) Act, 1878 (41 & 42 Vict c 20).

21. *RC on Railway Accidents*, Report, p. 26.

22. Bagwell, *op.cit.*, pp. 72–88, for some details of this decline.

23. J.H. Clapham, *Economic History of Modern Britain*, vol. II (Cambridge, 1932), pp. 196f.

24. From parliamentary returns we find that while in 1880 only 12 per cent of engines and 7 per cent of vehicles complied with the official requirements regarding brakes, by 1886 the proportion had gone up to 52 per cent for both types, and by 1880 to 75 per cent of engines and 72 per cent of vehicles. In 1884 95 per cent of the tracks in Britain were fitted with the block-signalling system (*Parl Pap*, 1886, LXXIX). These had been initiated in the 1860s (Parris, *op.cit.*, pp. 182–200).

25. *RR*, 16 October 1884, p. 4; *RR*, 9 October 1885, p. 7; ASRS, *Annual Report*, 1886, pp. 3–5.

26. Harford said this to the annual meeting of the union in 1886 (*RR*, 8 October 1886, p. 5).

27. After he was defeated the union decided to find him a constituency dominated by railwaymen to secure his re-election (ASRS, *EC Minutes*, February 1886, p. 3). For the Doncaster adoption, see *Doncaster Reporter*, 20 March 1889, p. 8; ibid., 3 April 1889, p. 8; *Doncaster Gazette*, 22 March 1889, p. 6; ASRS, *EC Minutes*, May 1889, pp. 1f. Doncaster was then held by a unionist.

28. For Channing, see F.A. Channing, *Memories of Midland Politics* (London, 1918), p. 37; for McLaren, see W.H. Chaloner, *The Social and Economic Development of Crewe*, 1780–1923 (Manchester, 1959), p. 159.

29. For Harford's early connections, see report of an executive committee meeting of the union, *RSG*, 17 January 1874, p. 10; also see recollections of another Sheffield member, W.D. Dancey ('Judex'), in *RR*, 8 July 1898, p. 5. Unfortunately the Mundella Papers at Sheffield University Library (which I was permitted to consult) do not contain any written correspondence between union members and Mundella. See, however, W.H.G. Armytage, *A.J. Mundella* (1951), p. 254, for evidence of contacts in 1886.

30. *Parl Pap*, 1886, V, bill no. 97 for Channing's bill; ibid., bill no. 138 for the Railway and Canal Traffic Bill. For Mundella's commendatory reference, see *Parl Deb*, 3rd S, CCCIII, 564, 585.

31. P.M. Williams, 'Public Opinion and the Railway Rates Question in 1886', *English Historical Review*, LXVII (1952), pp. 50–63; for an earlier view of the strength of the railway lobby on this question, Armytage, *op.cit.*, pp. 246–56.

32. *Parl Deb*, 3rd S, CCCV, 1462; six days earlier the RCA had decided to ask Mundella to stop the second reading, and, should he refuse, to mobilise all the railway director MPs to press for opposing the second reading (RCA, *Minute no. 270* dated 13 May 1886, p. 3f). During the debate, however, while railway directors gave a thinly veiled criticism of the policy of increasing the powers of the Board of Trade over management questions, the main speaker against Channing was the distinguished Quaker Sir Joseph Pease, who was agreeable to referring the bill to a committee. After Mundella's intervention, railway opposition did not persist in trying to stop the second reading.

33. The companies had nominated J.W. Pease, J.C. Bolton, Edward Watkin, Jackson and H.W. Tyler, of whom the first two, as well as another director. D.R. Plunket (of the L & NW) were on the committee (RCA, *Minute no. 271*, 27 May 1886, p. 2; *Parl Deb*, 3rd S, CCCVI, 783, 1112–13).

34. Contrast Bagwell, p. 105, whose brief statement seems a *post hoc ergo propter hoc* fallacy. The committee was finally constituted on 4 June, and the division on the home rule question was on 8 June. Any organised lobby that the companies may have had in mind was hardly started before the end of parliament. Except in so far as the split within the Liberals was partly aggravated by disaffected railway directors (on which, however, see Williams, *loc.cit.*, pp. 54f), the failure of Channing's bill was due to an unfortunate coincidence of circumstances.

35. *RR*, 7 October 1887, p. 5; *Parl Pap*, 1988, LXXXIX, 437.

36. All statements on the strength of the railway lobby are based on relevant volumes of Dod's *Parliamentary Companion* and Bradshaw's *Railway Manual.*

37. *Parl Deb*, 3rd S, CCCXXV, 1667–1707. Just over forty members were present as a check to see if there was a quorum revealed.

38. *Parl Pap*, 1889, VII, bill no. 333.

39. RCA, *Minute no. 311*, dated 17 July 1889, p. 6, for decision to lobby the Board of Trade on the 'coupling' question. On 23 July Hicks-Beach asked for a postponement of the second reading because of 'very large and persistent opposition' to the coupling proposals (*Parl Deb*, 3rd S, CCCXXXVIII, 1174f).

40. *RR*, 26 July 1889, p. 352, for the labour lobby. RCA Minute no 312

dated 25 July 1889, shows that they pressed for further alterations and Hicks-Beach let their solicitors discuss details with those who drafted of the bill. The final version was introduced as a new bill (*Parl Pap*, 1889, VII, bill no 360).

41. *The Times*, 9 October 1889, p. 10; also see *Peterborough Advertiser*, 12 October 1889, p. 4.
42. Channing, *Memories* (1918), pp. 115, 117.
43. *Parl Deb*, 3rd S, CCCXLIX, 904–1007; the notice of the motion had been given before the Scottish dispute had reached an acute stage (*RR*, 5 December 1890, editorial) but the strike ensured a full house. Three Conservative members and one Scottish Unionist member spoke in support of Channing, namely Stafford Northcote (Exeter), A.A. Baumann (Camberwell), E.H. Llewellyn (Somerset N) and T.R. Buchanan (Edinburgh West).
44. RCA, *Minute no. 319*, dated 23 January 1891, p. 3.
45. *SC on Railway Servant (Hours of Labour) Report* (hereafter *Hours 1892 Report*), p. 11, *Parl Pap*, 1892, XVI, 123.
46. *Parl Deb*, 4th S, III, 883–963; *The Times*, 8 April 1892, p. 9.
47. Channing to Gladstone, 28 May 1892, BM Add Mss 44514 f 309.
48. ASRS, *EC Minutes*, February 1892, pp. 3f, 17.
49. The reactions of the candidates and the members elected are tabulated in Table IV of my thesis (p. 155) of which the following is a summary (Source: *RR*, 15 April 1892 to 15 July 1892; Dod's *Parliamentary Companion*, 1892, pt II: Bradshaw's *Railway Manual*, 1892):

(A) *Candidates' replies*

	Lib	Con	Total	(Railway directors)
10-hour day and six-day week by law	68	20	88	(3)
Channing's report with right of trade union complaints and Board of Trade enforcement	31	12	43	(4)
Majority report with limited powers with the Board of Trade	4	20	24	(2)
Opposed to legislation or hostile and evasive	4	25	30	(5)

(B) *Replies of those who were eventually elected*

	Lib	Con and Unionists	Total
10-hour day and six-day week by law	32	4	36
Channing's report	20	9	29
Majority report	3	12	15
Uncertain, hostile or evasive	5	17	22

50. *RR*, 3 June 1892, p. 3; *RR*, 24 June 8192, p. 4; F.A. Channing, *Overwork on Railway and the Remedy* (London, 1892).

51. *Durham County Advertiser*, 8 July 1892, p. 15; also see *Durham Chronicle*, 1 July 1892, p. 8; ibid., 8 July 1892, p. 6.

52. *RR*, 18 April 1890, p. 181.

53. *RR*, 15 August 1890, p. 386.

54. *RR*, 17 June 1892, p. 5. The Fitzwilliam family had traditional influence here among the agricultural votes (H. Pelling, *Social Geography of British Elections 1885–1910*, London, 1967, p. 236).

55. *Doncaster Chronicle*, 8 July 1892, pp. 5, 7; ibid., 15 July 1892, p. 5; *Doncaster Gazette*, 15 July 1892, p. 6, and also previous issues. In contrast to the countrywide swing against Conservatives, there was no proportionate swing in Doncaster. There the Conservatives in fact increased their share of the total poll from 48.6 to 48.8 per cent (Pelling, *op.cit.*, p. 231, Table 22). So the turnout of railwaymen at the polling booths might have been a crucial factor in securing Fleming's return in spite of the improved Conservative performance.

56. *Daily Chronicle*, 30 June 1892, p. 6; ibid., 4 July 1892, p. 6.

57. In Reading, to the jubilation of the *RR* the sitting Conservative MP, C.T. Murdoch, a director of the Great Western Railway, lost to the Liberal G.W. Palmer, who had campaigned among the railwaymen by pledging support to Channing's report (*Reading Observer*, 2 July 1892); *RR*, 8 July 1892, p. 1; in Deptford and York, while there was no clear gain for one party as in the other places cited, this issue figured prominently (*Daily Chronicle*, 4 July 1892, p. 5; ibid., 5 July 1892, p. 8; *Yorkshire Herald*, 24 June 1892, p. 5; ibid., 25 June 1892, p. 7; 28 June 1892, p. 5; 29 June 1892, p. 5; 2 July 1892, p. 5).

58. *Hours 1892 Report*, p. li; *RR*, 7 October, pp. 4f.

59. Bagwell, *op.cit.*, p. 169.

60. Mundella to Gladstone, 9 June 1892 (BM Add Mss 44258 f 274). My emphasis.

61. PRO MT 6/618 file 8317 of 1892 and all other files attached to it show

that, as recommended by the majority report, schedules of long hours and the reasons for them were being asked of a number of leading companies. Sir H. Calcraft had testified against state control before the select committee on hours of labour (*op.cit.*, min of ev, q 4196, *Parl Pap*, 1892, XVI) but had gone frequently on leave after Mundella took over the Board of Trade (Mundella to Gladstone, 4 May 1893, and same to same, 8 May 1893, BM Add Mss 44258ff, 314, 316). Bagwell (pp. 168f) erroneously assumes that a reluctant Board of Trade had to be forced to do something.

62. PRO MT 6/618 file 10429 of 1892, memo by Marindin dated 24 December 1892. In January, commenting on a revised schedule sent by the North British Railway, Marindin wrote, 'Taken all round this return shows an improvement, but I cannot call it by any means satisfactory' (memo dated 19 January 1893, MT 6/618, file 677 of 1893).

63. BM Add Mss 44648 ff 36, 83, 84 (Gladstone's cabinet memoranda).

64. ASRS, *EC Minute*, 21–25 February 1893, pp. 4f, 25.

65. That the act (56 & 57 Vict c 29) was a definite improvement on the government bill and was nearer what the union wanted is evident from a comparison with the ASRS-sponsored Channing's bill (*Parl Pap*, 1893–4, III, bill no. 53) with the government bill (*Parl Pap*, 1893–4, VII, bill no. 165) and the final act. For standards laid down by the Board of Trade, see *Report by the Board of Trade . . . under the Railway Regulation Act 1893* (hereafter *Hours Act Reports*). . . . July 1894, p. 16, dealing with signalmen (*Parl Pap*, 1894, LXXV). But the board's standards were not as rigorous as the union wanted.

66. See Mundella's remark, *Parl Deb*, 4th S, XI, 1373–80.

67. The full story of Harford's Northampton candidature will be found in my thesis (*op.cit.*, pp. 331–7).

68. In the same month as the Northampton Liberals adopted Harford, the Sheffield Liberals refused to have a well-known local working-class leader as their candidate for the Attercliffe by-election. H. Pelling, *Origin of the Labour Party* (London, 1954 edn), pp. 173f.

69. ASRS, *Annual Report* 1895, p. 8.

70. See my thesis, pp. 334–5.

71. Though Harford in his campaign had openly disavowed socialism and paraded his radicalism (*Northampton Daily Reporter*, 15 January 1895, p. 4) an ILP-er ASRS member was allowed to write an article in the ILP official organ advocating his election (*Labour Leader*, 6 April 1895, p. 10). This was significant because the general policy of the ILP in this election was to discourage workingmen from voting for non-socialist candidates.

72. Stansky, *op.cit.*, pp. 167–80.
73. For Hicks-Beach's views, *Hours 1892 Report*, p. ix. For the appointment of subinspectors, *Parl Deb*, 4th S, XXIV, 1419f, ASRS, *EC Minutes*, June 1894, p. 1; ASRS, *Annual Report* 1894, pp. 2f. For the departmental committee, see *Railway Accidents Returns Committee Report*, pp. 3–5, (*Parl Pap*, 1895, LXXXVI, 37).
74. ASRS, *Annual Report* 1894, p. 2; ibid., 1895, p. 2.
75. *RR*, 7 October 1898, p. 1. (This was an editorial comment by George Wardle, ILP member.)
76. *Hours Act Report*, July 1895, p. 26 (*Parl Pap*, 1895, LXXXVI); also see *RR*, 1 November 1895, p. 4 (main editorial discussing attitudes of railway officials).
77. ASRS, *Signalmens' Hours of Duty: Verbatim Report of an Interview with. . . . C.T. Ritchie* (London, 1896), pp. 11ff; also see *RK*, 21 February 1896, p. 5.
78. *Hours Act Report*, July 1895, p. 26, where Hopwood discussed this.
79. ASRS, *EC Minutes*, March 1896, pp. 2f, 42; branch reactions in each issue of the *RR* from 8 May to 12 June 1896 (they appear on pp. 2f of each number); ASRS, *EC Minutes*, June 1896, p. 7. Earlier ambiguities arose from having committed the union to a programme in 1888 which sought to augment earnings for trainmen by giving overtime at a daily rate. These could have been avoided by substituting a wages claim for different grades instead of this demand for daily overtime. But the multigrade character of the union bedevilled the emergence of a satisfactory wages policy. These are discussed in P.S. Gupta, 'Railway Trade Unionism in Britain, c. 1880–1900', *Economic History Review*, 2s., XIX(April 1966), pp. 129–31, 139f.
80. J.H. Clapham, *Economic History of Modern Britain*, III (Cambridge, 1938), pp. 358–61.
81. E. Eldon Barry, *Nationalisation in British Politics: The Historical Background* (London, 1965), p. 96.
82. Gupta, *op.cit.*, pp. 146f. Though the goods guards dismissed by the L&NW had been reinstead by an appeal for Board of Trade mediation under the Conciliation Act of 1896, the board did not wish to support the ASRS in its strategy of winning recognition on the L&NW (cf. Hopwood's memo in March 1897: 'the L&NW is making concessions in its own way and I suggest we should let matters rest'. (PRO MT 6/978 file 3241 of 1897). Later in the year, apropos Bell's invoking of the Conciliation Act to secure support for the all-grades movement, Courteney Boyle was only prepared to work for 'obtaining a friendly meeting between the *several* companies and *their own man*' (MT 6/808 file 18809 of 1897, his italics).

83. Resolutions in favour of these were passed at the annual meeting of 1898 (*RR*, 7 October 1898, p. 13; *RR*, 14 October 1898, pp. 9, 10). In this year we have evidence of branches responding favourably to the propaganda of the Railway Nationalisation League (*RR*, 17 June 1898, p. 3; *RR*, 24 June 1898, p. 4; *RR*, 16 September 1898, p. 3) but there was no sustained campaign afterwards. After Bell became an MP in 1900 he discouraged members from proposing eight-hour bills at the annual meetings and many delegates responded (*RR*, 16 October 1903, pp. 3, 7; *RR*, 14 October 1904, p. 11).

84. This he did by bringing some victimised railwaymen to the Board of Trade on 7 February 1899 after a year's campaign on their behalf. Both Hopwood and Boyle were prepared to write a polite letter of admonition to the companies but Ritchie vetoed it (PRP MT 6/911 file 1454 of 1899).

85. Once when Hopwood averted a strike by getting Bell recognised by the manager of the small Port Talbot Railway in South Wales in October 1899 he earned Ritchie's approval (PRO MT 6/911 file 13437 of 1899 and attached files). But the Great Eastern Railway dispute, occurring a month before the Taff Vale dispute, showed that when a company was determined to ignore ASRS-sponsored deputations the board was unable to help and put pressure on the union to retreat (PRO MT 6/966 files 9450 and 9313 of 1900). Against such a background Bell and some other trade unionists were agreeable to Ritchie's suggestions for an extension of the Conciliation Act (1896), but the employers' parliamentary council opposed it (ASRS, *Annual Report 1899*, pp. 18–20: also see H.Clegg, A. Fox, and A.F. Thompson, *A History of British Trade Unions since 1889*, vol. I (Oxford, 1964), p. 265.

86. *Parl Pap*, 1899, LXXXV, 695.

87. Bell had seen Hopwood on 24 November and 18 December 1898. For the campaign, see issues of *RR* in February 1899 and ASRS, *EC Minutes*, March 1899, pp. 10ff.

88. RCA, *Minute no. 366* dated 22 February 1899, pp. 6f; *Minute no. 367* dated 2 March 1899, *passim*; *Minute no. 368* dated 8 March 1899 *passim*; ASRS, *EC Minutes*, March 1899, pp. 11f.

89. *The Times*, 7 March 1899, p. 11; *The Times*, 16 March 1899, p. 12.

90. *Regulation of Railway Bill. . . . Deputation from the Mining Association of Great Britain* (1899), pp. 18f, 29 (kept with RCA, *Minute no. 370*).

91. Ibid., pp. 30–44; RCA, *Minute no. 370* dated 17 March 1899, pp. 1ff.

92. *RR*, 31 March 1899, p. 8; *RR*, 7 April 1899, p. 5.

93. *The Times*, 23 March 1899, p. 10.

94. Stansky, *Ambitions and Strategies*, pp. 270–92.

95. Ibid., pp. 288, 292.
96. Liberals like Pease and Sir James Joicey would be affected by the bill because both were railway directors and Joicey was also a colliery-owner.
97. *RR*, 21 April 1899, p. 1.
98. *RR*, 21 April 1899, p. 1; 28 April 1899, p. 5; ASRS, *EC Minutes*, June 1899, pp. 2f; *Parl Deb*, 4th S, LXX, 695f.
99. North Eastern Railway, *Wages Arbitration and Award of Lord James of Hereford* (York, 1897).
100. See the minutes of the RCA for July and August 1899 (RCA, *Minutes nos* 380–5).
101. RC on *Accidents to Railway Servants, Report, passim* (*Parl Pap*, 1900, XXVII).
102. ASRS, *EC Minutes*, March 1900, p. 23.
103. *Railways (Prevention of Accidents) Bill* (*Parl Pap*, 1900, IV, bill no. 78).
104. In 1898 Purvis had interceded with Ritchie over the question of the victimisation of railway trade unionists, saying, '(sc. Peterborough) is a constituency containing very many Railwaymen and I am of course anxious to oblige them as far as I can' (R. Purvis to C.T. Ritchie, 7 October 1898, PRO MT 6/911 file 11973 of 1898). Also see note 41 above.
105. *Report from the Standing Committee . . . on the Railways* (*Prevention of Accidents) Bill . . . passim* (*Parl Pap*, 1900, VII, 279).
106. RCA, *Minute no. 397* dated 24 May 1900, p. 3; *Parl Deb*, 4th S, LXXXIII, 1608–23.
107. ASRS, *EC Minutes*, June 1900, pp. 2f.
108. RCA, *Minute no. 400* dated 3 July 1900, pp. 2f; *Parl Deb*, 4th S, LXXXV, 1441. It received the royal assent on 30 July 1900 (63 & 64 Vict c 27).
109. J. Hart, 'Nineteenth Century Social Reform', *loc.cit.*
110. *RR*, 11 October 1889, pp. 482f.
111. But the nationalisation agitation was making slow progress among the public (Eldon Barry, *op.cit.*, pp. 98ff). Only after a seven-year gap did the union's annual meeting reaffirm nationalisation unanimously in 1905, the initiator hinting at workers' participation by saying, 'the mode of managing State institutions required altering. . . . They should have practical men to control the railways . . .' (*RR*, 13 October 1905, p. 10). On the power structure of the cited earlier union, see my article in *Economic History Review*, 1966.
112. See Bell's plea which the union endorsed in 1900 and reaffirmed in 1901 by supporting his compulsory arbitration bill (ASRS, *Annual Report 1900*, p. 5; ASRS, *Decisions of the Annual Meeting 1900*, p. 13; ASRS, *Annual Report 1901*, pp. 6f; *RR*, 11 October 1910, pp. 9f, 12).
113. *Labour Leader*, 15 April 1899, p. 113; also see George Wardle's editorial comment, *RR*, 26 May 1899, p. 1.

114. *RR*, 1 September 1899, p. 1; *RR*, 15 September 1899, p. 1.

115. Clegg, Fox, and Thompson, *op.cit.*, pp. 364–72.

116. For Bell's Liberal links which made the LRC tighten its constitution see F. Bealey and H. Pelling, *Labour and Politics, 1900–06* (London, 1958), pp. 139–42, 193–7. When Ramsay MacDonald went to see the ASRS executive regarding Bell's conduct he found that Bell's propaganda since 1900 had had some effect. Appealing to the long-term ideal of a strong labour group, he said, 'Do let me beg of you not merely to regard your own special trade interests.' The lib–lab G. Beadon replied, 'We have come to deal with the facts of the day, not with what might happen in six years' time' (ASRS, *EC Minutes*, March 1904, pp. 97f). The union did not make Bell sign the LRC constitution (ASRS, *Decisions of the Annual General Meeting* 1904, p. 7).

BRITISH LABOUR AND THE
INDIAN LEFT 1919–1939*

The purpose of this essay is to analyse the interaction between the British Labour movement and the Indian labour and socialist movements between 1919 and 1939. How did different leaders and institutions of the two movements regard one another? What did they expect of one another, and how far were these expectations fulfilled? A full-length study of the attitudes of the British Labour Party to the question of Indian independence has already been done by Dr Fischer, a French scholar.[1] He has touched on the party's attitude to Indian labour,[2] but has not attempted to analyse the ebb and flow of mutual understanding and cooperation in the course of these twenty years. Besides, his concern is mainly with the Labour Party, whereas the present study aims to cover the British Trade Unions Congress as well as the Independent Labour Party (ILP), both of which were important elements in the British Labour movement. The communist parties of Britain and India fall outside the scope of this inquiry, but due weight has been given to the effects of their policies.

* Published in B.R. Nanda (ed.), *Socialism in India* (Delhi, 1972).

   I am grateful to Shrimati Indira Gandhi and the Nehru Memorial Museum and Library for permission to consult and quote from the correspondence of Jawaharlal Nehru. Thanks are due to the Nehru Memorial Museum and Library also for permission to use the files of the All-India Congress Committee, the papers of N.M. Joshi, and the newspaper files at their library. I would like to thank the National Archives of India and the West Bengal Government Archives for permission to consult their records. The following abbreviations have been used in the notes: NAI—National Archives of India; WBGA—West Bengal Government Archives; ILP—Independent Labour Party; NMJP—N.M. Joshi papers kept in the Nehru Memorial Library; JLNP—Jawaharlal Nehru Papers kept in the Nehru Memorial Library; AICC—Files of the All-India Congress Committee kept in the Nehru Memorial Library).

The First World War had created divisions inside the British Labour movement, divisions between the anti-war ILP and the pro-war majority, including all the trade unions and many Fabians. Wartime economic problems had created a militant left wing trade union movement in Glasgow and other places on the Clyde. In politics many of these trade unionists were attracted to Marxism, and joined either the ILP or the British Socialist Party, a left wing party unaffiliated to the Labour Party. Many non-socialist Liberals with a genuinely internationalist outlook (like E.D. Morel, and Charles Trevelyan) had joined the ILP after the war, as a result of which, at the beginning of our period, the ILP was a coalition of radical socialists as well as democratic pacifists, their unity welded together by the shared experience of persecution for their beliefs during the war.[3]

A bird's-eye view of the traditional attitudes of these groups to the British empire and the ideal of international cooperation would help us understand their approach to the social and political problems of India. The ILP had always been strongly anti-imperialist politically, and its view of international economic relations was based on Cobdenite principles of free trade. Over the question of tariff reform and an Imperial Customs Union suggested by the Conservative supporters of Joseph Chamberlain, the ILP and the rest of the Labour Party had followed the Liberals in opposing it.[4] Yet the anti-imperialist ILP-er did not visualise a dissolution of the political links of the empire, but rather its transformation into a commonwealth of equal sovereign states. This stemmed partly from the idea of socialist international cooperation, and partly from a belief in socialist trusteeship of underdeveloped colonial lands—a belief to be found even in the writings of the noted anti-imperialist J.A. Hobson.[5] Some Fabians, with their neo-Benthamite preference for efficient administration and their belief in the efficacy of permeating the existing political parties and the existing civil service with their ideas, took socialist trusteeship one stage further, and contemplated as their goal a prolonged period of modernisation under enlightened colonial administration.[6] On India, all the British socialists in the pre-war era took a stand in favour, not so much of granting self-government, as of improvement in administrative standards in the interests of the people, and of gradual progress towards self-government.[7] Greater emphasis on administrative improvement as opposed to the grant of self-government was characteristic, naturally, of the Fabians. In the pre-war days some cooperation had developed between Indian leaders and British Labourites, between H.M. Hyndman and Dadabhai Naoroji, and Keir Hardie and Gokhale and Bipin Chandra Pal.[8]

The Bolshevik revolution in Russia in 1917, the conclusion of a separate peace by Russia with Germany in 1918, and the founding of the Third International (Comintern) in March 1919 evoked somewhat different responses from different sections of the British Labour movement. The entire movement was united in opposing allied intervention in Russia (their most dramatic gesture being the dock and shipping strike of August 1920 to stop arms going to the Poles), and also for recognising the Soviet Union, but sharp differences arose over the policy of the Comintern and the emergence of a Communist Party in Britain.[9] When the Comintern eventually developed its own strategy of political action in India and the rest of the colonial world, the policies of different socialist groups in Britain towards Indian problems was bound to be affected by the way they looked at communist tactics and policy.

II

Among the different organisations in Britain in 1919, working for political change in India, only two had obvious connections with the Labour movement—the London section of the Indian Home Rule League founded by Mrs Besant in 1916 to lobby the government for constitutional reforms,[10] and the Workers' Welfare League of India founded in 1916 for work among Indian seamen in London.[11] Thanks to Mrs Besant's personal contacts through Theosophism, the former organisation had enlisted the active cooperation of three Theosophist Labourites—David Graham Pole, George Lansbury, and John Scurr. The last two were also anti-war ILP-ers, and in course of 1917–18 their speeches aroused a fair measure of interest in Indian self-government in ILP branches and local trades councils all over South Wales and Yorkshire, and also in some big industrial towns elsewhere.[12] A prominent Indian expatriate leader of the Workers' Welfare League, Shapurji Saklatvala, was also a member of the Home Rule League;[13] since the Bolshevik revolution he had been fired with a zeal to convert the ILP—of which he had been a member since 1909–actively to support

Bolshevism, and he devoted all his spare time to lecturing to ILP branches on Bolshevism and allied topics.[14] In the beginning of 1919 his policy was to urge the pro-Indian ILP-ers to persuade moderate Indian nationalists to be more socialistic in their political and economic programmes. To the resolution of John Scurr at the annual conference of the ILP in April 1918 asking for a 'measure granting self-government to the Indian people', Saklatvala moved a supplementary pleading for 'immediate legislation to improve the hours, wages, and general conditions of workers, and an open advocacy of the nationalisation of lands, railways, mines, and other large and important industries'. Both resolutions were carried.[15]

It is quite possible that the resolution on India which the Labour and Socialist International (Second International) adopted at its first post-war meeting in Berne in February 1919, was influenced by the policy adopted by the ILP the previous April at Saklatvala's suggestion, because it was sponsored by the Labour Party delegation, which included a strong ILP contingent. This resolution, in addition to criticising the 'capitalistic and imperialistic policy in India' and the Rowlatt Act, and supporting the efforts of 'the Indian population to claim . . . the establishment of democratic governments', demanded 'direct representation' of Indian working classes in the legislative councils. It added, 'As the extreme poverty and misery of the Indian working class is the consequence of the exploitation of Indian labour by the great Indian and English landowners and capitalists, which yearly exposes millions to death by famine and disease, the conference is of the opinion that the land and soil, railways and mines of India should be socialised.'[16]

In linking up the question of political change in India with the plea for social and economic reconstruction of a radical nature, Saklatvala was trying to link up the left wing of the British Labour movement with that of the Indian nationalist movement. To paraphrase his own words in April 1918, 'His imagination carried him to the time when the Independent Labour Party might have ten million members' in India.[17] In keeping with the same policy, five left wing British trade unionists had petitioned the secretary of state in January 1919 on behalf of the Workers' Welfare League of India, protesting against inadequate safeguards for the labouring classes in the reform bill and attributing it to the 'non-inclusion of the representatives of organised

British labour in committees which have been appointed and are now working in India.' They opposed transferring to the provinces questions affecting industrial labour, especially as the provincial assemblies were to be on a narrow franchise, argued for keeping the question with the central government, and ended with a plea that 'British labour representatives . . . should continue to exercise the privilege of recommending to those responsible for Indian affairs in parliament the needs and rights of their Indian fellow-workers'.[18]

While the signatories to this memorial were all near-Marxists, such an approach could equally be consistent with a Fabian policy of prolonged tutelage under progressive governments in Britain. Philip Snowden and Ramsay Macdonald, although members both of the ILP and the Home Rule League, did regard themselves as trustees for the Indian masses. When Austen Chamberlain had raised Indian cotton duties against Britain early in 1917, the opposition of Liberals and the Lancashire trade union MP, Tom Shaw, was to be expected, but Philip Snowden puzzled his Indian admirers by his opposition, until he explained his position: as long as India did not become a dominion with fiscal autonomy, the British labour representatives have to protect the unrepresented Indian masses 'against the rise in price of a necessity of life'.[19]

Notwithstanding these differences in approach, the British Labour Party was united in 1919 in supporting the Constitutional Reform Bill (which included fiscal autonomy). As Colonel Josiah Wedgwood, a new recruit to the ILP and a friend of Indian nationalists said, 'India is as much entitled to make her own tariffs as Canada, or any other community within the Empire'.[20] What all of them were concerned about was simultaneously to secure clauses in favour of the wage-earning and agricultural classes' franchise, especially as British and Indian capitalist interests had got special privileges in the new constitution.[21] Their plea for a direct working-class franchise was so strongly stressed when the bill returned from the committee stage[22] that Montagu, the secretary of state, felt obliged to urge the viceroy, in the despatch enclosing the act, to see 'what can be done to allay the apprehensions' of Labour members on this matter.[23] The provincial bureaucracies were unenthusiastic about the extension of the working-class vote in places like Calcutta and Bombay, one official commenting, 'This is a wild-cat franchise which, at the instance, I understand, of the Labour Party at home we are asked to provide.'[24] The matter was shelved.

The effective liaison between Indian nationalists and British Labour in 1919 was Mrs Besant's Home Rule League, which occupied at this time a centrist position between the Indian Liberals under Srinivasa Sastri and those Congressmen under Gandhi who later launched the non-cooperation movement.[25] Whatever the future might hold, at this time the Home Rule League and its trade union connections appeared dangerously radical to the Government of India, as was evident from the furore over nominating the first Indian trade union representative to the International Labour Conference at Washington.[26] B.P. Wadia, a follower of Besant who since 1918 had organised Madras textile workers in the Madras Labour Union, spent the summer of 1919 in Britain giving evidence on behalf of the Home Rule League before the Parliamentary Committee on the Montford Reform Bill, and spoke at the annual conference of the British Trade Union Congress (TUC). The British TUC undertook to help financially and with expert advice the growing trade union movement in India and presented Wadia with their gold badge.[27] Faced with the suggestion from certain Indian unions in favour of Wadia representing Indian labour at the Washington conference, the Government of India hesitated, as one official considered him 'an extremist in politics'[28] and another 'an advertising politician'.[29] Montagu preferred Wadia, in view of his standing with the British TUC, and warned the Indian government that any spurious government-nominated labour leader ran the risk of having his credentials challenged in Washington.[30] The government ultimately nominated N.M. Joshi (a fellow worker of Srinivasa Sastri and the late G.K. Gokhale in the Servants of India Society), but Montagu insisted, against the viceroy's wish, on Wadia being also sent in an advisory capacity, doubtless in deference to the British Labour movement.[31]

The wider significance of the episode was threefold. It helped to bring the All-India Trade Union Congress (AITUC) into being the following year, so that future delegates to the International Labour Organisation (ILO) could be authorised by some co-ordinating body of trade unions in India. It illustrated the growing interest in the political and economic destinies of Indian labour on the part of the British TUC. It also showed, however, that whatever the political sympathies of Indian trade union leaders, any international association was liable to be interpreted as a political act. The last phenomenon was to affect Indo-British labour relations throughout the period under review.

In the immediate aftermath of the foundation of the AITUC, it was kept somewhat insulated from the controversies of nationalist politics, partly because by the end of 1920 Mrs Besant and the Indian Liberals held practically identical views in favour of a critical acceptance of the Montford Reforms.[32] So non-political trade unionists like N.M. Joshi, and R.R. Bakhale could cooperate with Wadia, J. Baptista, B. Shiva Rao and others in building up a trade union movement and using the machinery of the new constitution to further its prospects. In this task, until the middle of 1922, a fairly united support was given by different wings of the British Labour movement. The London Home Rule League dissolved itself in October 1920, saying, 'We feel it will be best in future to work through the Labour Party, especially as our chairman, Mr George Lansbury, is on its executive committee.'[33] The Workers' Welfare League became the British representative of the AITUC,[34] thus maintaining a link between the Indian labour leaders and left wing British trade unionists, some of whom soon joined the Communist Party.[35]

Near-communist, ILP-er, or moderate Fabian, all Labourites deplored the non-cooperation movement and the boycott of British goods, though for slightly different reasons. To Josiah Wedgwood, who was not a socialist, opposition to the idea of self-government within the empire might make the Congress–Labour Party cooperation 'more difficult, if not impossible'.[36] Members of the Workers Welfare League, 'at considerable cost to their popularity [in Britain] steadfastly differentiated between the international solidarity of Labour and the non-cooperation movement as a temporary political weapon in India against the imperialist exploiter'.[37] One of their members, J. Potter-Wilson, justified the case for trade union legislation in India on the grounds that the rise in Indian workers' standards of living would expand markets for British goods and reduce competition between Indian and British industries.[38] Left wing trade union leaders could indeed be won for radical change in India only by underplaying non-cooperation and emphasising the areas of cooperation between progressive forces in Britain and India. Not surprisingly, in February 1922 the National

Joint Council of Labour (a representative cross-section of the trade union and Labour Party leadership which at this time included left-wingers like Robert Smillie, A. Pugh, and C.T. Cramp) passed a resolution criticising both the Government of India and the non-cooperators. The latter were mistaken in not using the parliamentary institutions granted so far, and the former were criticised for political repression and urged to grant an amnesty, have talks with Indian leaders, and set a dateline for dominion status.[39] While this resolution was ignored by the people to whom it was addressed, the Labour movement had meanwhile set in motion one line of development—legal security of trade unions in India.

When at the end of 1920 the judgement of the Madras High Court in *Buckingham Mills Co. v. B.R. Wadia* raised legal obstacles in the way of trade union work, the effort of N.M. Joshi in the legislative council was supplemented by lobbying in Britain.[40] The Parliamentary Committee of the Trade Union Congress, accompanied by Potter-Wilson of the Workers' Welfare League, urged the secretary of state on 22 March 1921 to grant trade unions in India the same immunity from prosecution as British trade unions enjoyed apropos the tortious acts of its agents.[41] As they were insistent on ensuring that any future legislation should provide genuine legal safeguards, Montagu urged the Government of India to think seriously on such legislation and also to let him have the draft bill.[42] The Government of India took time over it; two years passed eliciting opinion of local governments, and then anxiety about preventing strikes in public utility services delayed further action.[43] Only when, early in March 1924, within six weeks of assuming office, Lord Olivier, the secretary of state in the first Labour government, telegraphed the Indian government to hurry up with the proposal, did the machine start moving again.[44] One civil servant commented wryly, 'I rather anticipated this enquiry when the Labour government came into power at home.'[45]

The TUC delegation to Montagu had a pro-communist spokesman on behalf of India, but they did not all think alike on Indian problems. Where trade union questions were not involved, J.H. Thomas of the railwaymen's union was inclined to believe in government propaganda.[46] Early in 1920 he had discussed with Rushbrook Williams, the government's publicity officer, how to ensure 'that the Labour Party should derive its information concerning India from authentic rather than from tainted sources'. The publicity officer had failed to get official sanction to get a labour delegation 'of the right type', 'neither cranks nor notoriety hunters', brought out to India at government expense.[47] He had, however, been unofficially permitted to try out 'if something [could] not be done with the Members of Parliament who [were] coming out to attend the Congress [of 1920]'.[48] This process of gradual persuasion of very moderate labour leaders into an acceptance of the government's case started sharpening the divisions inside the British Labour movement on the policy best suited for India. Communist–Labour tensions also contributed to this. By 1928 fairly clear-cut alignments had developed between British and Indian leaders, disturbing the pattern of cooperation that had worked so far.

III

In April 1921 Saklatvala Left the ILP to join the Communist Party along with Potter-Wilson, Ellen Wilkinson and others.[49] The majority of the ILP, being unable for justifiable reasons to accept the twenty-one conditions of the second Comintern Congress but also being reluctant to accept Ramsay Macdonald's recommendation to join the Second International, had joined the Vienna Union. The latter tried in vain during 1922 to see if cooperation between the three internationals could be brought about on a permanent basis. When these failed the ILP, along with the Vienna Union, rejoined the Second International in 1923, but from the end of 1925 the ILP tried, once again in vain, to renew negotiations between the two internationals.[50]

The position of British communists (including Saklatvala) became ambivalent *vis-à-vis* the other groups in the British Labour movement after 1921. The directives of the Comintern to communists in Western Europe and Britain, it has been rightly remarked, contained within them a 'latent incompatibility ... between a policy of peaceful infiltration on the national plane and a policy of frontal attack on the international plane'.[51] By indiscriminately blaming non-communist trade union leaders whenever a strike failed, the British communists lost ground in the Labour Party, and the charge of subservience to Moscow killed their plea for affiliation to the Labour Party.[52] Saklatvala, who was returned to parliament as a Labour MP in 1922 lost his Labour Whip after this. While he continued to be in parliament till 1929, except for the year 1924, he carried weight only with the extreme left wing of the parliamentary Labour Party, and occasionally on Indian questions got support from people like Wedgwood or T. Wheatley. While he himself was very critical of Indian Liberals,[53] Srinivasa Sastri's first impression of him was that of 'an able, sincere, and patriotic man'.[54]

Communist–Labour rivalry in helping Indian labour was somewhat masked in 1924–6 because of the increasingly left wing trend inside the General Council of the Trades Union till the General Strike of 1926.[55] Leaders of the type of Ernest Bevin, Walter Citrine, and A. Pugh (who was also a member of the Workers' Welfare League)[56] were at this time class-conscious trade unionists in favour of a militant policy, and further to their left stood George Hicks, Alonzo Swales, and A.A. Purcell. Purcell had visited Russia in May 1920, had supported Lenin's idea of a new trade union international, and joined the Communist Party at its foundation.[57] He probably left the Communist Party in the early 1920s, to save his links with the Labour Party, and to keep his parliamentary seat.[58] Nevertheless he worked for unity between the two internationals, inviting Tomsky to the Hull Trade Union Congress over which he presided, setting up the Anglo-Russian trade union committee, and trying to persuade the International Federation of Trade Unions (IFTU) and the Red International of Labour Unions (RILU) to come together.[59]

The first Labour government widened the gulf between moderate Labourites and Indian nationalists. Even a moderate like Annie Besant was disappointed at Olivier, instead of Wedgwood, being the secretary of state.[60] In spite of the pressure of the ILP, the cabinet ignored the Swarajists' request for an immediate conference between the government and representative Indian opinion for further constitutional change.[61] The appointment of the Reforms Inquiry Committee satisfied few people. The moderate Liberal, Srinivasa Sastri, while lobbying in Britain, was disappointed to note that the cabinet 'had no big plan for India' and only wished 'to tide over the difficulty somehow'. He found Olivier weak, and Chelmsford 'dead against advance'.[62]

If a Liberal felt disappointed, it is not surprising that Swarajist leaders readily believed the Labour government to be as imperialist as its predecessor. Motilal Nehru refused to serve on the Reforms Inquiry Committee,[63] and in Bengal C.R. Das successfully wrecked the system of diarchy, embittering the Liberal governor Lord Lytton.[64] Wedded as they were to the idea of gradual constitutional evolution, the Labour cabinet sympathised with Lytton's condemnation of the Swaraj Party's tactics, and supported the official request for promulgating the Bengal Ordinance. Sydney Webb, who was a party to it, thought that they had taken care not to penalise expressions of opinion and only to punish violence,[65] but nevertheless the ordinances tarnished the image of the government in the eyes of most nationalists.[66] They were too much even for Srinivasa Sastri, who refused support to the renewed efforts at lobbying the Labour Party by the ever-hopeful Mrs Besant.[67]

Left wing critics of the government's policy, headed by Lansbury, had also tried to stop the persecution of communists in India, just as they had tried to smooth the difficulties in the Anglo-Soviet negotiations which had followed the recognition of the USSR in February 1924.[68] They were successful in the latter, but not in the former, because the government was sensitive to charges from Conservative benches of permitting revolutionary violence in India. Apropos of the Kanpur Conspiracy Case against communists, which tried M.N. Roy *in absentia,* Lansbury and James Maxton tried to get a British lawyer to argue that 'apart [from] actual breaches of law Indians have same legal right [of] forming working Communist parties as British subjects have in all dominions'.[69] These were as unsuccessful as M.N. Roy's application to Ramsay Macdonald for an amnesty so that he could return to India.[70]

Roy tried from abroad to persuade his Indian contacts to prevent N.M. Joshi from affiliating the AITUC to the IFTU at its conference in April 1924.[71] He cleverly emphasised the chinks in the armour of British trade union leaders—Tom Shaw's support of the excise duty on Indian cotton, the discriminatory attitude of Havelock Wilson and Harry Gosling to Indian seamen, and so on. His criticism of the British TUC was unfair, for not only was it not subservient to the Labour government, but it was a useful lobby for the AITUC, supplementing the efforts of the Workers' Welfare League.[72] On 25 July 1924, a delegation of leading trade unionists consisting of Purcell, Swales, Hicks, Cramp, Lansbury, Robert Smillie and four others met Lord Oliver. The delegation (the left wing character of which was obvious) discussed a whole range of labour questions, ranging from miners' hours and plantation labour to trade union legislation, and asked the government to conduct an inquiry into the economic conditions of labour in India.[73]

The next four years saw attempts at trade union cooperation between the two countries, which were partially successful but also bedevilled by continuing differences between the Labour Party leadership and radical Indian nationalists on the one hand, and on the other by communist–Labour relations.

In February 1925 the Dundee jute workers sent money to Joshi to help organise jute workers in India,[74] and in the following June their secretary, with Saklatvala's assistance, got in touch with Joshi in London, because he was 'arranging to go out to India to help the jute workers there, and to find out ways and means of continued cooperation'.[75] H.W. Lee, the lifelong associate of H.M. Hyndman in all his agitations, including those on behalf of India,[76] was then working at the TUC headquarters, and 'wanted to maintain as much interest as possible in Indian labour affairs'.[77] His suggestions for sending a top-level delegation of the General Council of the TUC proved futile because time and money could not be spared. To his alternative suggestion 'that two or three trade union organisers should come over and spend, say, six months among the Indian workers',[78] Joshi was agreeable. 'It is a very good idea', he wrote, and added: 'As they will not know any of our languages they will not be able to do much work themselves. But they will be able to teach methods of organisation to those who are already doing some work here. You can therefore take up the suggestion and see if it could be carried out.'[79]

Similar suggestions were made by the ILP in its special report on India published in March 1926 by a committee under the chairmanship of Fenner Brockway, and the research assistance of the Indian ILP-er T.P. Sinha.[80] Founding a trade union college 'in the East with its centre in India' was suggested as a task for the IFTU and the Labour and Socialist International, pending which 'it might be possible to make special arrangements for Indians to attend our Labour colleges, and for a British trade unionist of judgment and experience to go to India, for a time, in an advisory capacity'.[81] These suggestions never materialised, for the British TUC was caught up in the crisis of the General Strike soon after. Nevertheless, Joshi used his personal contacts to get copies of rules and regulations of various British unions (in the textile and railway industry for example), their journals, and details of labour legislation—all of which he hoped to use as possible models for work in India.[82]

During the first year of the Anglo-Russian coordination committee, the British communists, much against the wish of M.N. Roy, had tried to concentrate the direction of colonial work in their hands.[83] Receiving reports from Percy Gladding (a communist member of the Amalgamated Engineering Union who had visited India and spoken at the AITUC early in 1925) that the number of communists in India was negligible, they decided, against Roy's wish, to influence the AITUC, first through contacts with N.M. Joshi, Chaman Lall and T.C. Goswami during their visit to Britain in June and July 1925.[84] They had already made the Workers' Welfare League a communist-controlled unit.[85] The Indian leaders were thus able to include among their contacts not only the British TUC and the Indian committee of the Parliamentary Labour Party, but also communist front organisations like the Workers' International Relief, the National Minority Movement and communist leaders like C.P. Dutt.[86] Except for a very short-lived stand taken in favour of these organisations by Chaman Lall in the winter of 1925–6,[87] hardly any conversion to the communist theory of trade union work took place—the Indian leaders remained, in Leninist terms, attached to 'economism'.

Non-communist British friends of Joshi were, however, worried about communist infiltration. H.W. Lee wrote repeatedly to Joshi about this, inquiring first about the effects of Gladding's speech to the TUC,[88] later about reports of efforts to 'Bolshevise' the Indian trade union movement, and of the possible affiliation of the AITUC to the RILU. Pointing out that talks between the IFTU and RILU were still going on, he added that the talks would succeed only if the Russian trade union movement became 'more independent of the Communist Party than it [had] been hitherto'.[89] When the trade unions are more powerful', he wrote,

it will be for them to consider the political action they shall take, but at present, I should imagine, strong political policies would be rather disruptive than anything else. Certainly anything in the way of affiliation with the Red Trade Union International would be a false move from the point of view of the progress of the Indian Trade Unions.[90]

Joshi did not take seriously Lee's fears about communist infiltration: 'I do not see here any effort on the part of the Communists to Bolshevise the Indian Trade Union Movement. As a matter of fact there are very few communists in India. Even these very few people who call themselves communists are, in my judgement, not real communists. They are nationalists before everything else.'[91] As regards international affiliation, he had, in the previous year, had talks with the left wing British leaders most active in the efforts to achieve international trade union unity,[92] but he did not encourage any suggestion of unilateral affiliation to the RILU.[93] Joshi privately was inclined in favour of the IFTU, but asked Lee's opinion on the wisdom of affiliation.[94] Lee, while preferring the IFTU, wondered 'whether the issue might not raise divisions in your ranks just when every effort and attention [was needed] to consolidate and extend.'[95]

The general secretary of the British TUC, Walter Citrine, in reply to an official query from Joshi regarding affiliation, consulted Purcell and others informally and suggested, in March 1926, that 'it will be well for the All Indian Trade Union Congress to affiliate at once to the International Federation of Trade Unions at Amsterdam'.[96] Possibly they felt that this would strengthen their hands in their negotiations with the Soviet trade union. It also fitted in with the suggestions of the ILP that the IFTU should help the Indian labour movement. Joshi, however, had realised that the Indian 'trade union movement [was] likely to be divided over this question'.[97] He knew that Saklatvala's preference for the RILU was likely to influence some of his colleagues, and Saklatvala's Workers' Welfare League had recently been reappointed as the official agent of the AITUC in Britain.[98] 'If I find that our movement is likely to be divided I shall avoid decision. Of course, we cannot consider this question till next December or January', wrote Joshi privately to Lee,[99] and officially he simply told Citrine to wait until the following January.[100]

Politically, Joshi at this time had become a member of the ILP.[101] The AITUC office thus was made familiar with the creative socialist thought which the ILP through its journals and pamphlets was putting about.[102] Nevertheless, he did not wish to break with Saklatvala, partly in order not to divide the AITUC, and partly out of genuine regard for him. H.S.L. Polak, at the behest of Gillies of the international department of the British TUC, had written that to retain the Workers' Welfare League as the official agent of the AITUC in Britain was 'a very grave practical mistake as that body [had] not any influence with the Labour Party, and [was] usually associated with 'left wing' activities of an objectionable kind'.[103] Joshi had replied, 'I am avoiding raising this question for the fear that it will unnecessarily create complications here. As I am in direct contact with the Secretary of the General Council of the British Trade Union Congress there is no practical harm done by the Workers' Welfare League continuing as our agent in name.'[104]

The position in the Indian trade union movement, Joshi knew, was different from that in Britain. In Britain, the aftermath of the General Strike had been characterised by vituperation against all leaders of the TUC on the part of the Soviet and British communist parties, so much so that it convinced people like Bevin and Citrine that it was futile to continue the work of Anglo-Soviet trade union cooperation.[105] In India Saklatvala, during his visit in the first half of 1927, played a generally constructive role at the AITUC session in April,[106] although he naturally took every opportunity to push the communist ideology. Joshi, when he asked Lee privately whether Saklatvala would be acceptable as a fraternal delegate to the Edinburgh TUC, pointed out, 'He being a member of Parliament, Indians are naturally proud of him.'[107] When Lee vehemently protested, that it would create a wrong impression,[108] Joshi dropped the idea. He commented, 'I fully appreciate the attitude of the British Trade Union movement towards the Communists. As the Communists here in India have not started the trouble which they have created in Europe our people here do not fully appreciate your position.'[109]

A year after the General Strike, the Edinburgh TUC in September 1927 authorised A.A. Purcell and J. Hallsworth to visit India on their behalf and present a report. They attended the Kanpur Trades Union Congress in November 1927, toured India and produced a useful report.[110] Neither in his speech to the conference nor in his report did Purcell speak the language of Fabian trusteeship, but attempted a Marxian socialist analysis of the need for cooperation. Criticising the distorted imperial history on which working-class children were brought up in British schools, he made out a case that Indian and British workers' interests were identical, because to a large extent their enemies were the same—British capitalist and financial interests in both countries.[111] In his joint report with Hallsworth he urged British trade unionists to accept the inevitability of Indian industrialisation, approved the rapid growth of the Indian trade unions, and stressed the need of the British trade union movement to assist it, both on the grounds of altruism and self-interest.[112]

By April 1928, when this report came out, there was less and less prospect of a united British Labour movement assisting the Indian labour movement. At the TUC of September 1928 Citrine obtained a clear mandate to conduct a full inquiry into the disruptive role of communists in the British trade union movement.[113] By that time in India communist trade union workers, with the help of a few British communist trade unionists like Ben Bradley, had built up a powerful group in the AITUC, and on international questions they followed RILU. In these circumstances no one heeded the plea of Purcell, who had been disappointed in his efforts at international trade union unity, that the task of helping trade unionism in India was so urgent that it could not 'wait upon the caprice of various International units each wondering what its advantage [was] likely to be and then moving swiftly or slowly as [suited] the individual case'.[114]

IV

On the political plane, too, by 1928, the distance between radical nationalists and many British Labourites had grown wider than it had been even five years before. The Indian labour delegation to the Commonwealth Labour Conference in July 1926 included Diwan Chaman Lall, N.M. Joshi, and the Swarajist leader T.C. Goswami. Probably because Purcell presided over one session, the Indian leaders were able to get adopted an unscheduled resolution approving the grant of 'immediate self-government' to India in that session.[115] This was followed by the British TUC of September 1925 passing a resolution recommending the freedom of India and criticising British imperialism in Marxist terms.[116] Both these resolutions were anathema to Fabian gradualists like Lord Oliver, who thought that only 'immediate anarchy' would follow if 'the cement of British control' was replaced by 'immediate self-government'.[117]

In Britain in June and July 1925, Goswami and Chaman Lall had tried to 'repudiate the idea which had obtained some credence in England that [the Swarajists] were afraid of democracy and . . . favoured the establishment of an Indian oligarchy'.[118] This belief, however, died hard. Graham Pole, after a visit to India in the winter of 1925–6, gave some evidence to sustain this belief in an article he wrote for *Lansbury's Labour Weekly*.[119] The charge was to some extent justified, because the Swarajists really had very little base among the working class or the peasantry, and their efforts at organising labour agitations had been almost at the level of political stunts.[120] From this analysis, however, people like Oswald Mosley and Graham Pole mistakenly drew the conclusion that Indian nationalist sentiments could be ignored and that efforts should be made to develop political movements like an Indian Fabian society or an Indian Labour party.[121] Fenner Brockway's approach was different. Speaking on the main resolution on India in April 1925 he had rejoiced in 'the steps being taken to form an Indian Labour Party under the leadership of Mr Lajpat Rai, who was himself a member of the ILP',[122] but he had not visualised the new party as an alternative to nationalism but a supplement. His resolution had fully endorsed C.R. Das's last political initiative and had urged the immediate appointment of a commission to revise the constitution.[123]

Hardly any progress was made with the Indian Labour Party. Lajpat Rai and N.M. Joshi knew that a party formed purely on the platform of labour interests would invite the charge that it was dividing the national movement in the interests of foreign capitalists.[124] Although the AITUC in January 1926 decided to elicit opinions on the advisability of forming a Labour party, the real difficulties were pointed out by N.M. Joshi to Brockway: 'Very few workers have votes.'[125] Saklatvala had urged Joshi not to let the labour movement be split from the national movement, in particular, from the Swaraj Party, and also asked him publicly to repudiate Graham Pole's charges against it.[126] Joshi refused to dispute in public with Graham Pole, especially as he 'did not believe that either the Swaraj Party or any other political party in India [cared] very much for Indian Labour'.[127] Privately, later in the year, he reminded Graham Pole that, however laudable, efforts to start a Labour party or a Fabian society in India were 'extremely small, spasmodic, and the result [was] transient'. In order that British Labour should not have any illusions on this he added, 'What makes me apprehensive is the desire of these people to send calls to England and about matters which are scarcely heard of in India. These methods of disproportionate advertisement give a false idea to people in England of the movements [in] India which I am anxious to avoid.'[128]

The efforts of Graham Pole and his colleagues of the commonwealth of India group in 1925–6 had been unrewarding both in England and in India—in England because they failed to get the sponsorship of the Labour front bench for their constitution,[129] and in India because their efforts to create parties in their own image were regarded with either hostility or scepticism by Indian leaders. Only the ILP, which had by the end of 1925 come under the left wing leadership of men of the stamp of Brockway and Maxton,[130] understood that the only way the British Left could have a progressive influence on Indian affairs was by supporting both the cause of national independence and the emancipation of the toiling masses. The Empire Policy Committee of the ILP had not visualised the break-up of the commonwealth,[131] but on India, on the advice of the special committee under Brockway, the ILP passed a resolution implicitly endorsing the demand for Purna Swaraj: 'The ILP recognises the full right of the Indian people to self-government and self-determination. Should they elect to belong to the British group of Nations, it must be on the basis of equality and freedom.'[132]

The report of the ILP's Special Committee on India was in many ways a masterly analysis of the Indian political and economic situation. By emphasising that the Montford Constitution denied India the 'rudiments of self-government', and was based on a franchise of privilege, and by asking the government to 'respond to the proposal of the Legislative Assembly' for a 'Convention to submit a scheme of Indian self-government for immediate adoption', it firmly placed itself in opposition to the gradualists of the Labour Party leadership.[133] The report also made proposals for working-class and peasant enfranchisement, for giving 'immediate effect . . . to the Universal and compulsory educational Acts passed by Provincial Councils', for getting the Royal Commission on Agriculture widen its terms of reference 'to include the root question of land tenure'[134]—all with the hope that the labouring classes would be able to keep their end up in a free India.

Towards the end of 1925, paralleling Purcell's efforts at international trade union unity and against the wishes of the Labour Party, the ILP authorised Fenner Brockway, its representative on the Second International executive, to persuade the Second International to negotiate with the Comintern.[135] Brockway failed in this,[136] but succeeded in getting the Zurich Congress of the Second International to accept the policy of the ILP of helping colonial workers with the assistance of the IFTU. To quote Brockway's own words, 'The reception of these proposals by the Executive was encouraging, but months passed and little was done.'[137] Meanwhile, the communists seized the initiative by organising the League Against Imperialism in February 1927.

The League Against Imperialism was started under Comintern auspices with communists like Willy Munzenberg in key positions in the secretariat at a time when Comintern policy was to direct communist movements in colonial lands to support the nationalist movement.[138] Jawaharlal Nehru attended its first meeting in Brussels in February 1927, was tremendously impressed by it, and got the Indian National Congress to become affiliated to it.[139] While he was aware that the League had many communist members, he doubted the possibility of communist domination because the delegates were 'by no means purely Communist'.[140] In the case he made out to the Congress for affiliating to it, he rebutted two possible arguments that could be used against it. The socialist character of the League ought not to be a handicap; while nationalism took precedence in colonial countries over all other sentiments', he agreed with Western socialists that 'such . . . nationalism . . . might derive its strength from and work specially for the masses, the peasants and the other workers'. Second, the danger of Russian foreign policy utilising 'the League to further their own ends' was not very great. 'The presence of Lansbury as chairman and some others in the executive committee shows that it is not a one-sided affair.'[141] Nehru was impressed by Lansbury's speech urging nationalists to become socialists and asked the AICC to circulate it.[142] He was equally appreciative of the stand taken against British imperialism in China by the British delegation which included ILP-ers like Fenner Brockway, Ellen Wilkinson, and Lansbury himself.[143]

Nehru could not, however, appreciate the hesitation felt by these ILP-ers on the possibility of getting the ILP or the Labour Party to directly affiliate to the League Against Imperialism, although he heard that the ILP leaders had braved the displeasure of the Second International in coming to the congress.[144] Not being familiar with the rather bitter history of Communist–Labour cooperation till 1927, nor understanding how the communist 'fraction' in a 'front organisation' was always able to manipulate it to their own ends, he wrote, 'The executive committee of the League has, I believe, a majority of non-Communists and there is no reason why they should be led by the nose by the minority.'[145] He understood by February 1930[146] that the League was basically subservient to the Comintern but in the intervening three years he used the League (including its British branch under Reginald Bridgman) as the main channel of communication to the British Left. This created awkward problems for people like Lansbury, Brockway, and James Maxton—all of whom, while supporting the anti-colonial aims of the League, gradually had to withdraw from active participation in it because of pressures from the Second International or the Labour Party. (Lansbury Left late in 1927, Brockway retired from the executive of the League in 1928, and Maxton, who succeeded Brockway as the ILP representative, was forced out by the communists in late summer of 1929, in pursuance of the sectarian policy enunciated at the sixth Comintern congress.[147])

Eight months after the first congress of the League Against Imperialism, the Labour Party conference unanimously carried a resolution moved by Lansbury recommending Dominion Home Rule in India.[148] Yet within a month the rapport between Indian nationalism and the Labour Party was broken. Against the wishes of Lansbury, Ellen Wilkinson, T. Wheatley, Wedgwood and other ILP-ers, Ramsay Macdonald agreed to let two Labour members (Clement Attlee and Vernon Hartshorn) participate in the Simon Commission.[149] Fenner Brockway, who visited Indian in the winter of 1927–8, was not only impressed by Jawaharlal's socialist leanings but also by the social revolutionary justification given by Jawaharlal for the demand for 'Purna Swaraj'.[150] On his return he tried to get the parliamentary Labour Party to withdraw the Labour members from the Simon Commission, without much success.[151] In sharp contrast to July 1925, the Commonwealth Labour Conference of July 1928 saw a walk-out by the Indian trade union delegation when they were not allowed to table a resolution criticising the Simon Commission. Most Labour Party leaders felt that the interests of Indian workers were not being served by bringing a prestige question of nationalist politics in this forum—a view which all Indian labour leaders (including moderates like R.R. Bakhale) resented.[152] After this episode, at a meeting organised by the British branch of the League Against Imperialism, Srinivasa Iyengar of the Indian National Congress was very caustic about Labour Party politicians, who could be at the same time 'a member of the ILP, also a member of the Labour Party, Liberal in certain tendencies and co-operating with the Tories'. 'Great causes', he added, 'could never be won by such divided allegiance.'[153] Brockway, who had sat on the platform as Iyengar made these remarks, tried in the following October at the Labour Party conference to criticise the party executive for its Indian policy, but was defeated.[154] Ramsay Macdonald somewhat pompously criticised Indian nationalists who, in his opinion, 'were much less inclined to favour the Indian bottom dog than they themselves were or their own representatives in India were'.[155]

How deeply the two movements had become distrustful of the *bona fides* of each other, by 1928, was also illustrated, tragically, by Lala Lajpat Rai in the last months of his life. A friend of Keir Hardie and Josiah Wedgwood, a member of the ILP, Lala Lajpat Rai for some time past had been getting bitterly disillusioned with the Labour Party.[156] In the winter of 1927–8, he wrote scathing articles entitled, 'English Socialism a huge mockery' and 'Labour Party under Imperialistic Macdonald'.[157] About a month before his death, just before returning to Punjab to demonstrate against the Simon Commission (during which he was badly injured by the police), Lala Lajpat Rai told Jawaharlal Nehru 'that we should expect nothing from the British Labour Party'.[158]

It is no wonder that the tenure of the second Labour government was characterised by a militant and uncompromising temper among left wing nationalists in India. It affected the labour movement as well as the wider political movement.

Two decisions of the Indian government, taken before British Labour's electoral victory in May 1929, split the Indian labour movement—the Meerut conspiracy case, and the appointment of the Royal Commission to enquire into Indian labour conditions. Between April and July 1929, on behalf of Jawaharlal, who was president of the AITUC at that time, Reginald Bridgman of the League Against Imperialism lobbied to get official support for the Meerut prisoners from the general council of the TUC. The response was not encouraging.[159] Citrine, the secretary of the TUC, was then finalising his report on communist infiltration (which he submitted to the Belfast TUC the following September), and he was convinced that the League Against Imperialism was a communist organisation controlled from Moscow.[160] Jawaharlal was irritated at Citrine's indifference, and wrongly suspected N.M. Joshi of poisoning the British TUC against the Meerut prisoners.[161] He later withdrew this accusation that Joshi had been working behind his back,[162] but there remained a difference in out-look between them. Joshi wrote to him: 'It is true that I do not take your view regarding the Meerut case, but I have not concealed that fact from you. . . . But I am sure that I gave you no ground to expect active support in this matter. . . . I am very doubtful that even with my active support the right-wingers in the Trade Union Congress General Council would have done anything in this matter.'[163]

As the Royal Commission on Labour was a culmination of the efforts of the AITUC since 1924 to get a comprehensive inquiry started on Indian labour, people like Joshi, Bakhale, Chaman Lall, V.V. Giri, Shiva Rao and others were willing to participate in it. The communist members of the AITUC executive wrote from behind prison bars advocating boycott,[164] and their view was shared by left wing nationalists because, in the words of Subhas Bose, 'boycott was then in the air'.[165] At the Nagpur session of the AITUC in December 1929 Jawaharlal decisively tipped the scale in favour of a boycott. Already in September he had publicly denounced the Labour Commission.[166] There was just a chance that after Lord Irwin's declaration on dominion status on 31 October, he might have reconsidered his decision to refuse cooperation with the British government, because he did sign the Delhi manifesto. This was, however, a reluctant acquiescence.[167] In his speech to the Nagpur session of the AITUC he questioned the sincerity of the Labour government and said, 'Indeed the time has come when we should make it perfectly clear that we cannot cooperate with any such Commission or with the British Government that appoints them.'[168]

During these critical months from May to December 1929, Jawaharlal appears to have been in touch mainly with Reginald Bridgman of the League Against Imperialism and not directly with Left Labour MPs like Fenner Brockway or James Maxton.[169] Before taking the plunge

into civil disobedience at the Lahore session of the National Congress
he was unable or unwilling to coordinate efforts at wringing the maximum concessions from the British government by allying with the left-
ist ILP-ers, quite a number of whom had been returned to parliament.[170]
Yet the latter were anxious to help. Fenner Brockway repeatedly lobbied
Wedgwood Benn for declaring a general amnesty (including the Meerut
prisoners), and Benn was inclined to go part of the way with him in
late October and November.[171] Brockway's main contact with India at
this time was the weekly publication of the Servants of India Society, for
which he wrote the *London Letter.* It is not known whether Jawaharlal
and the 'Congress Left' took any notice of the accounts of Brockway's
efforts that were published in the *Servant of India* between October
and December, although in one of them there was a personal appeal to
Jawaharlal.[172] Without any positive response from the Indian radicals,
and with positive hostility coming from Indian official circles, and
only half-hearted cooperation from Benn,[173] Brockway's efforts were
doomed. Yet, after the Civil Disobedience Movement had started, the
ILP's attitude was different from the general disapproval with which
the non-cooperation movement had been greeted in British labour
circles ten years before. ILP left-wingers repeatedly criticised the
Macdonald government for repression in India and wrote books explaining the Indian point of view.[174] They organised, under ILP auspices, a
special India weekend in ILP branches in August 1930.[175] One of them,
Reginald Reynolds, started the Friends of India Society to carry on
propaganda to justify the Civil Disobedience Movement, and to urge
that without Congress participation the round table conference would
be worthless.[176]

The image of the Congress as a left wing organisation was projected
in Britain only by the ILP in 1930–1. Alone of all British parties the
ILP took notice of and welcomed the left wing resolutions passed at
the Karachi congress.[177] The communists had by their sectarian policy
isolated themselves both from the Congress Left as well as from the
British Labour Left. There was no love lost between the ILP and the
British Communist Party. All the same, unlike Walter Citrine,[178] the
ILP did not allow its dislike of communist policy to deflect itself from
the task of continuing to agitate for the release of the Meerut prisoners.[179]

The only group of Indian leaders who cooperated hopefully with
the Labour government were liberals like Sapru or Srinivasa Sastri and

Labour leaders like N.M. Joshi and B. Shiva Rao who had seceded from the AITUC to form the ITUF in December 1929. They used the forum of the British Commonwealth Labour Conference in July 1930 to get support from the British TUC, so that special safeguards and electoral arrangements for labour could be considered in the constitutional talks at the round table conference.[180] They were very disappointed at the rejection of universal suffrage at the First Round Table Conference and said so.[181] Macdonald does not appear to have made any special efforts to meet their point of view, although he had repeatedly claimed to be more concerned for the Indian masses than the Indian nationalists.[182]

V

The eight years from the fall of the Labour government in August 1931 to the outbreak of war in September 1939 saw a gradual renewal of contacts and mutual understanding between sections of the British Left and the Indian Left. The process was on both sides influenced by new forces.

In India, in the early 1930s senior political leaders were in jail and the government ruled through ordinances. Moderate congressmen and Gandhi were at a loss for political initiative and tried, through personal contacts, to influence opinion abroad.[183] At first the communists remained in self-imposed isolation, while the Roy-ist and the Congress socialists aimed, in their own different ways, to link up the socialist and labour movements with the movement for national independence. The AITUC under Roy-ist influence was indifferent to the question of international affiliation and somewhat prejudiced against the ILO.[184] The leaders of the ITUF united with the railwaymen's union to create the NTUF but remained suspicious not only of communists but also of Roy-ists and rejected the 'Platform of Unity' drafted by M.N. Roy.[185] The government of India recognised only the NTUF for purposes of representation at the ILO.

In Britain, Macdonald's defection not only shook the Labour Party out of excessive complacence but led to the emergence of Lansbury as the leader of the party for the next few years. Some other pro-Indian Labour politicians and journalists like Brockway and Reginald Reynolds broke with the Labour Party when the ILP disaffiliated from the former, taking some of its members with it.[186] In course of the 1930s the ILP became a dissident Marxist party, sharply critical of Stalinist Russia as well as the social democratic parties of the West for their alleged compromises with capitalism and imperialism.[187] More realistic left wing Labour intellectuals like G.D.H. Cole started the New Fabian Research Bureau (NFRB) to give the Labour Party an armoury of socialist ideas.[188] As the danger of war grew by the mid-1930s, many left wing Labour Party members tried to unite all Left forces for a radical policy at home and abroad, first by means of the Socialist League (sponsored by Stafford Cripps) and later by advocating the Popular Front and supporting the work of the Left Book Club. Apart from Cripps, the leading role inside the Labour Party executive in these moves was played by Harold Laski, Ellen Wilkinson, and D.N. Pritt. Other Labour Party leaders remained suspicious of communist–Labour cooperation, which was reinforced by the purges carried out by Stalin in Russia.[189]

Ever since Britain introduced Imperial Preference in 1931 and extended it to the dominions and the colonies by 1933, trade within the empire increased at the expense of trade with countries outside the empire.[190] The Conservative Party welcomed the increasing interdependence of the empire-commonwealth, but the economic crisis of the early 1930s made even some left wing Labour leaders think in terms of maintaining the integrity of the empire-commonwealth for the purposes of socialist planning.[191] In a world with a tendency towards autarchic combinations, and in a Britain faced with unemployment and hunger marches, such a view could easily encourage, as one Labour MP pointed out, a British variety of national socialism.[192] Fortunately, economic recovery had started by the mid- and late 1930s. It was based, as we now know, on a domestic boom in the building industry and the growth of new industrial products oriented to a high-wage economy. These growing sectors of the British economy were not dependent on the trade of the tropical colonies.[193] So there was little justification for the apprehensions of Sir Stafford Cripps that the British working class was fattening on imperial exploitation, and that this might be an obstacle to the progress towards Indian independence.[194] It explains also why hard-headed trade union leaders like Ernest Bevin, who were prepared to accept capitalism at home,[195] nevertheless became committed to granting India dominion status by the end of the decade, and personally lobbied for it in Churchill's war cabinet.[196]

In the various constitutional discussions prior to the enactment of the Government of India Act of 1935, the Labour Party leadership showed itself to be more aware of nationalist sentiments and more purposefully determined to fight for provisions specifically in the interests of the Indian working classes and peasantry than Macdonald had done in the first and second round table conferences. In 1928, despite the universal boycott of the Simon Commission, Labour members had remained in the commission, but in 1932, when the Indian Liberals refused to participate in the constitutional talks any more, the Labour Party also refused to attend the Third Round Table Conference.[197]

In commending the Royal Commission on Labour for the successful completion of its work 'in the midst of the difficulties and struggles of the last two years', the Labour Party showed that it continued to believe that for 'the Indian wage-earners the Party [had] a special responsibility'.[198] However, this did not lead it any more to encourage bureaucratic tutelage in opposition to nationalist forces. At the time of the publication of the White Paper of 1933, and again in the opening paragraphs of Attlee's draft minority report on the Indian Constitution in the joint select committee in June 1934, the Labour front bench asserted that the constitution should aim to establish India 'at the earliest possible moment as an equal partner with the other members of the British Commonwealth of Nations', and suggested steps which could expedite the process.[199] Attlee appreciated the achievements of British rule in India, and 'the devotion' of British officials in 'their tasks as servants of India', and made constitutional provisions 'for the living forces of Indian nationalism to be harnessed to the great tasks which confront any government in India'.[200] But he was concerned about the danger of putting 'the Indian rural population and the urban wage-earners at the mercy of a politically dominant section in the possession of economic power', especially as 'the Hindoo social system [was] based on inequality'.[201] His solution was to recommend in the constitution not only the abolition of special representation of landlords, university men, and commercial bodies, but also the increase of labour representation to a minimum of 10 per cent of the total number of seats as recommended by the NTUF. In addition, adult suffrage was suggested for Labour constituencies in the large industrial cities, immediately; and within ten years the provinces were to have universal adult suffrage.[202] During discussion in the select committee, the four Labour members pressed to the vote these points, as well as the suggestion to abolish the second chambers.[203] Considering that Attlee had signed the report of the Simon Commission with hardly any reservations, these efforts of his were a step forward and a denial of a bi-partisan approach on Indian policy.

The leader of the Labour Party, George Lansbury, was less inclined than Attlee to stress the positive achievements of British rule. In a book expounding his political ideas he wrote, in the same year as Attlee's draft report, 'These benefits of British rule are benefits paid for in hard cash, and well paid too. This tribute is almost entirely spent outside India. . . . Whatever the Press may say, we do not in fact make India rich and contented.'[204] Among Labour intellectuals who were influential in the NFRB there were, in the early 1930s, cross-currents of opinion. J.M. Keynes regarded the Indian White Paper as being, 'broadly speaking, the utmost progress which [could] be made at this stage', and criticised Kingsley Martin for his readiness 'to inflame, rather than pacify Indian grievances against it'.[205] Harold Laski, on the contrary, having participated in all the round table conferences as an unofficial adviser to Lord Sankey, had shifted from the view that India 'really [was] not fit to govern itself',[206] to sympathetic understanding of the nationalist psychology, and a personal rapport with Gandhi.[207] After working with Sankey in 1932, he concluded that Sankey's draft bill was so 'cluttered up with all kinds of checks and balances' that it would 'reproduce the worst features of the worst modern Constitutions'.[208]

Laski and Lansbury were closely associated with V.K. Krishna Menon. Menon was the pupil of the former and the publisher of the latter's books.[209] Thanks to Menon's efforts in the India League and the encouragement given to the League by Jawaharlal Nehru, the non-communist Labour Left was able to re-establish contact with the Congress and the Congress Left in the early 1930s. Menon had come to Britain in the late 1920s after having worked in Madras with Mrs Besant. He had therefore a link with the commonwealth of India League associated with Graham Pole and H.S.L. Polak. In the early 1930s Menon transformed it into the India League with a new commitment to Purna Swaraj.[210] As a result the League lost the support of some people like Polak,[211] but radical Labour MPs began to give Menon active support. Members of its various committees included Brockway, Purcell, George Hicks, Lansbury, H.N. Brailsford, Wilfred Wellock, J.F. Horrabin—names which had been associated with the more radical moves by Labour leaders in the 1920s.[212] Among those who started taking an active interest in India now were Bertrand Russell, Horace Alexander, and Dorothy Woodman, the last named providing a link with Kingsley Martin, editor of the increasingly influential journal *New Statesman and Nation*.[213] To these people Menon distributed Congress propaganda material, defeating government censorship. The chief of the intelligence branch commented wryly:

We do all we can to prevent such information as is published in Congress bulletins reaching England, but the energetic editor of the *Information Bulletin*, Menon . . . is quite cunning in arranging post boxes in England . . . a certain amount of this kind of propaganda reaches Mr Lansbury, and we have so far refrained from tapping the correspondence of the Leader of the Opposition of the House of Commons.[214]

Till 1934, the India League agitated in Britain against the repressive ordinances and, on constitutional questions, to secure radical amendments to the Government of India Bill and to get support for the idea of an Indian constituent assembly to frame India's future constitution. The most important achievement was to organise a tour of India by three British Labour politicians (of whom two were ex-MPs)—Ellen Wilkinson, Leonard Matters, and Monica Whateley. In June and July 1932 Pandit Madan Mohan Malaviya discussed details of the tour with C.F. Andrews and Horrabin, and gave £500 towards its expenses.[215] The delegates were not allowed to see the leaders who were in jail,[216] but were able to study the political and labour movement in different parts of the country.[217] The Indian government was so worried about the possible effects of this trip on British public opinion that the under-secretary of state for India urged them, before they left Britain, to keep 'in close touch with officials', and promised 'to write to prominent people, outside Congress circles, whom it would be worth their while to meet'.[218] Later, in India, the government ruefully noted that despite the best efforts of the officials, the delegates were spending much of their time listening to the Congress and other left wing points of view.[219] When their report came out in March 1934, with an introduction by Bertrand Russell,[220] it was banned in India, because, according to the chief of Intelligence, 'The book as written contains more Congress propaganda than any volume seen by me.' He admitted, however, that 'very many of the allegations are or may be true'.[221]

The book highlighted the suppression of political and civil rights in India, and warned the Labour Party against being led to underestimate the strength of nationalism through an overdose of the official point of view.[222] Having met all shades of Indian labour opinion, the delegates were able to appreciate both the non-communist Left who dominated the AITUC in 1932, as well as the NFTU under N.M. Joshi.[223] They emphasised the fact that all trade union movements in India had a political colour—'indeed, in modern India no live movement can escape it'.[224] This conclusion must have helped to disabuse some British Labour leaders of the belief that the NTUF contained the only genuine trade unionists. The delegates also added that the communists 'appeared to be in hostility to the Indian National Congress and to the labour organisations'.[225]

This picture of the Indian labour movement probably explains why from March 1933 the British Labour movement launched a high-level agitation to get the Meerut prisoners released at once. The National Joint Council of Labour cooperated with a committee, set up by Leonard Matters, for the release of the prisoners. Unlike 1929, Citrine, Bevin, Morrison, and Attlee unanimously agreed with leftists like Swales, Grenfell, and Lansbury that 'at a time when it [was] more important than ever that the difference between British and Indian opinion should be reconciled . . . no wiser step could be taken by the government . . . than to grant all these men their unconditional freedom'.[226] This belated gesture was successful. Thereafter, while the British TUC kept in touch with the NTUF through the IFTU, to which both were afiliated,[227] it did not interfere in the efforts towards reuniting the Indian labour movement. These efforts were to succeed in 1938, on the condition that the united Indian movement, while participating in the ILO, would not affiliate to any of the rival trade union internationals.[228]

The report of the India League delegation had been published three months before Attlee submitted his minority report to the joint select committee. It may have exerted some influence on him. The Congress proposal of a constituent assembly was put across early in 1934 in the Labour press by Horace Alexander,[229] and by George Lansbury in his book *My England*.[230] The parliamentary Labour Party decided, after the rejection of Attlee's draft report by the joint select committee, not to raise the Indian proposal for a constituent assembly in parliament but to press for other radical amendments during the second reading.[231]

Even if these amendments were defeated, however, they would vote for the bill at the third reading, because otherwise the extreme right wing Conservatives under Churchill, who wanted no constitutional change at all, would win.[232] This approach did not satisfy Labour's Indian lobby. They were more successful the following year, after the Government of India Act had been passed, at the party conference in October 1935. This conference accepted a resolution from the floor— 'the freely elected representatives of the Indian people shall formulate a settlement of the problems of India, in the interests of the Indian masses'. Though the mover of the resolution had criticised Attlee's draft report of the previous year, Attlee, on behalf of the national executive did not oppose the resolution, possibly because the Government of India Act was quite the reverse, in letter and spirit, of his draft.[233]

A typical representative of the younger generation of promising Labour politicians, Anthony Greenwood, said, in the course of a speech on the above-mentioned resolution, 'In India we have got growing up a virile and determined socialist movement. One-third of the members of the Congress party today are convinced socialists and members of the Congress Socialist Party.'[234] This appreciation of the Congress as a potentially left wing organisation was enormously increased by Jawaharlal's visits to Britain in the course of the next four months. Thanks to contacts suggested by Ellen Wilkinson, C.F. Andrews and Horace Alexander,[235] he was able to meet Leonard Woolf (secretary of the Colonial Subcommittee of the Labour Party),[236] Sir Stafford Cripps, Harold Laski, George Catlin,[237] and other members of the Labour Left, some of them left wing Fabians, others semi-Marxists. Nehru was able to convince all of them, unlike the Swarajist leaders eleven years earlier, that the only way to help the Indian masses was to support the Congress and other Left forces. In the 1920s British socialists had had doubts about the working-class and agrarian base of the national movement, and their rationalism had rebelled against Gandhi's philosophy. (It is not surprising that those close to Gandhi in British Labour circles were mainly Quakers and Pacifists.) These doubts about the difficulties of combining the grant of self-determination with the promotion of socialism in the colonies recurred as late as 1937 in Attlee's book, *The Labour Party in Perspective*.[238] Nehru's *Autobiography*, published shortly after his visit, dispelled these doubts for many people. Ellen Wilkinson wrote to him, 'The ignorance of even good "lefts" on India is abysmal. I think . . . your socialist summing up will give a great impetus to the interests of the socialists in England.' She particularly appreciated his criticism of Gandhi's policy on the agrarian question in India.[239] To a wider socialist reading public Brailsford wrote of the book, 'Here is a man who is one of us, by his culture, his humanity, and his scientific vision. He aims at doing what Englishmen in India have boasted that they did but could not do. He is struggling to bring the social organisation that reflects this culture of ours to a very backward people. But we are the obstacle.'[240] The judgement of these two people about the likely impact of the book was further confirmed when Reginald Reynolds, requesting a foreword from Jawaharlal for his book *The White Sahibs in India* (1937), wrote, 'Your stock is very high over here just now—the *Autobiography* and your personal visits having done incalculable service to the Indian cause at this end.'[241]

Nehru appreciated the work done by the ILP-ers associated with Reynolds' 'Friends of India' group. Nevertheless, his visit convinced him that the most effective organisation was the India League, because it had 'some prominent men in it like Harold Laski' and as a result 'it [was] definitely socialistic in outlook [and] of the three it [was] the only really political organisation'.[242] About Menon he wrote, 'I met him for the first time. He is very able and energetic and is highly thought of in intellectual, journalistic, and left wing Labour circles. He has the virtues and failings of the intellectual. I was very favourably impressed by him.'[243]

Menon was able in 1936 to involve Sir Stafford Cripps' Socialist League effectively on the Indian constitutional problem. The League passed a long resolution on India, in which it urged that the next Labour government should seek 'an agreement with Indian opinion through the Congress and the organisation of workers and peasants as to the time of summoning and the methods of conducting the Constituent Assembly'.[244] Cripps urged the delegates to help the India League in its efforts. Menon also noted that 'the official Labour party [appeared] to have become a little more receptive to what [was] happening in India' and he explained 'in a general way . . . in their official organ the main trend of Indian development . . .'[245] Unlike the late 1920s, when Nehru's British contacts were mainly through the League Against Imperialism (which was effectively controlled by communists), his British allies were now active members of the Left of the Labour Party itself. A year after the success of the Congress in the election of 1937, Horace Alexander wrote a pamphlet about the Congress governments for the New Fabian Research Bureau.[246]

What were the ideological effects of these renewed contacts with the British Labour movement on the Indian non-communist Left? Indian socialists mostly thought in Marxist terms, as their writings, bibliographical preferences, and lectures indicate. Acharya Narendra Deva was avowedly Marxist and his differences with communists arose over their extraterritorial loyalty and their claim that they alone were the correct interpreters of Marxism.[247] Lecture topics suggested by Jayaprakash Narayan to Ram Manohar Lohia abound in phrases like 'Development of Socialist thought culminating in Marx and Lenin', 'Fascism and the decay of capitalism', and on world politics Palme Dutt's book *World Politics* was recommended.[248] Only a few leaders of the Congress Socialist Party show a greater influence of British democratic socialist tradition in their intellectual evolution, and the influence of the writings of Laski, Cole, Tawney, or J.A. Hobson. These were Asoka Mehta, B.P. Sinha (of Bihar), and M.R. Masani.[249]

Given the political realities in India—the absence in the mid-1930s of constitutional instruments of mass democracy which could be used for social change—the attraction of revolutionary Marxism (and even its Leninist variant) was natural. Subhas Bose criticised the Congress Socialist Party for not being sufficiently revolutionary, because they supported the proposal for a constituent assembly, whereas Lenin had dissolved the constituent assembly after the Bolshevik revolution.[250] The renewed contacts with the British Left were being made with people like Laski, Cripps, Ellen Wilkinson and others, who were at that time either supporting the Popular Front and/or organising the Left Book Club. Thus the contacts strengthened rather than weakened the Marxist trend in Indian socialism. The books of the Left Book Club were banned in India, but copies were secretly circulated.[251] Only shortage of funds made Jawaharlal unable to follow up an idea of simultaneously having published some of these titles in India by Indian publishers, in the freer atmosphere of the Congress regimes after 1937.[252] The only person who appears to have thought of the New Fabian Research Bureau as a model for serious socio-economic studies to aid the Congress governments was V.K.R.V. Rao.[253]

In Britain, Marxists who dissented from the Comintern were mainly to be found in the ILP, now fast dwindling in membership and influence.[254] On Stalin's purges and on some aspects of the Spanish Civil War they had perceived the truth,[255] whereas Labour Party supporters of the Left Book Club tended to evade these uncomfortable facts.[256] The ILP went further. It rejected the idea of an alliance of imperialist powers with the Soviet Union within the framework of the League of Nations, because that would strengthen the ruling classes and weaken the colonial liberation movements by tying them to the great power interests of Britain, France, and the Soviet Union.[257] They were able, as a result, to get the support of some colonial leftists, like the Ceylonese 'Trotskyites' and Jomo Kenyatta.

Among the Indian Left there was a fair degree of indifference to the diplomatic strategies of the popular front in Britain. The general approach of Subhas Bose to the prospects of a war in Europe, and the amendments to foreign policy resolutions of the AICC proposed by the Congress socialists, indicate this. At Fenner Brockway's request M.R. Masani had sent Kamaladevi Chattopadhyaya to represent the Congress Socialist Party at the 'International Congress against War and Imperialism', organised under the auspices of the 'Fourth International'.[258] (At the same time Krishna Menon, on behalf of the Congress had supported Romain Rolland's committee against war and Fascism, which had the support of the Popular Front socialists and communists.[259])

The Soviet purges disturbed Indian socialists too, and we have on record Masani, Yusuf Meherally and Kamaladevi Chattopadhyaya discussing with Jawaharlal the possibility of the growth of 'narrow nationalism' in Russia.[260] Lohia still considered that 'Soviet Russia [was] the only great power which [had] definitely discarded imperialism . . . and [was] reconstructing society in the interests of workers and peasants'. Yet he admitted to John Dewey that his vindication of Trotsky against Stalin's charges was correct and that these made 'it all the more imperative that without for a moment forgetting that Soviet Russia [was] the only great non-imperialist and non-Capitalist power we should make strenuous efforts to help bring about the rule of normal law.'[261]

Indian socialist reactions to the Soviet purges made Krishna Menon write an anxious letter to Nehru about the possible spread of Trotskyite views in India. Nehru replied that 'there [was] no such thing here', but also expressed forcefully misgivings about the purge trials.[262] A few months later, when Nehru visited Britain, Menon was in charge of his itinerary,[263] and Nehru spoke at successful demonstrations on Spain, and on 'Peace and Empire' along with most of the Labour Left and some communists.[264] ILP-ers like Brockway, Reginald Reynolds and others complained that they hardly had an opportunity of meeting Nehru, and that communist pressure had prevented the ILP being represented at the welcome meeting for Nehru.[265] Brockway felt, with a lot of justification, that the claims of the ILP as a fighter for India were being neglected, and told Nehru, 'I want to warn you very earnestly against the clever intrigue which is going on to capture you for the Communist Party.'[266]

Possibly, without sharing the communist viewpoint, Nehru and Menon considered that their most important task was to harness the growing volume of Labour Party opinion in favour of a popular front and alliance with the Soviet Union also to the cause of the anti-imperialist movement in India. Therefore getting involved in ILP communist controversies could weaken the larger purposes.[267] In the same letter to Menon in which Nehru had been critical of the Moscow trials, he had ended the letter with the words 'They are more or less academic questions which do not affect our actions.'[268] A logical expectation from the alliance that Nehru was encouraging and Menon was trying to forge between the India League and the Popular Front Labourites was that in the event of war between Britain and the Fascist powers, the Popular Front (while supporting the British), would agitate for Indian freedom. The Indian Left would reciprocate by helping an anti-Fascist Britain in the war effort.[269] The events of September 1939 upset the whole strategy. With the British communists not supporting the war because of the Soviet–German pact, the popular front idea in Britain was weakened. With the British government refusing to listen to the Congress request for a statement of war aims as it affected India, the prospects of the Indian Left supporting Britain receded. Kingsley Martin campaigned vehemently through his journal in September and October 1939 for a forward-looking policy on the part of Britain,[270] but by and large, British Labour forgot India for the time being. Meanwhile the Indian Left was getting psychologically prepared to fight Britain even when she was at war with Fascism. The seeds of the Quit India Movement and the Indian National Army were sown. Thus, in the short run, the strategy of the India League had failed. In the long run, however, the fact that the third Labour government, unlike its predecessors, recognised Indian independence, showed that the strategy of sustained work inside the Labour Party, carrying on and radicalising the tradition started by Mrs Besant had worked.

VI

Most of the Indian non-communist labour and socialist leaders studied here were more influenced by the Russian revolution and by varieties of Marxist thought than by the models provided by the experience of the British Labour movement. This was not because they were enamoured of Bolshevik theory and practice, or of the Comintern. Nationalism inoculated them against the latter, and their organisational methods were in fact more characteristic of mass democratic institutions than of a conspiratorial vanguard organised under 'democratic centralism'. What really prevented the British Labour movement and these Indian leaders from being on the same wavelength were the assumptions which guided the actions of the Labour Party leaders between 1921 and 1931. The belief in progress towards independence only by stages, the assumption that the timing of constitutional changes should be guided entirely by the exigencies of the British parliamentary situation, the acceptance of a bi-partisan approach in many fields of foreign and colonial policy,[271]—all these, however justified in the context of British politics, projected an image of benevolent patronage which no self-respecting Indian nationalist could accept. The record of the first Labour government and the support given by the Labour Party to the Simon Commission strengthened this impression.

Many members at the policy-making level in the Labour Party took their duties as trustees for the Indian masses seriously. The sincerity of people like Graham Pole, H.S.L. Polak, Lord Olivier, Wedgwood Benn, or Clement Attlee need not be questioned. The role of trustees, however, was to be played by making steady empirical adjustments within the framework of the existing imperial bureaucracy. To be sure, the two ex-ICS officers who were advisers to the Labour Party—Sir John Maynard, an expert on the agrarian problem, and G.T. Garratt, the historian[272]—were of a different cast of mind from the average Indian civilian. Yet because of their specialist knowledge of Indian social injustices they were unable to give unequivocal support to all aspects of the Congress agitation, especially in the 1920s.[273]

To Indian nationalists, the bureaucracy was simply bolstering up a great deal of Indian social privilege and British capitalist strength, and so the gradualist approach of the Labour Party policy-makers did not appeal to most of them. They were attracted to those British Labour leaders who had some Marxist or semi-Marxist tendencies, people who made a connection, however crudely, between the misery of the Indian masses and the fact of imperial rule. In the 1920s these were people like George Lansbury, Fenner Brockway, and A.A. Purcell. In the late 1930s intellectual mentors were to be found among the writers of the Left Book Club.

In this situation, in the 1920s, cooperation with communists did not appear reprehensible or dangerous to Indian leaders, especially as the only Indian MP in the House of Commons was the communist Saklatvala. Pro-Indian British Labour leaders (again with the exception of Brockway and Purcell) would have preferred this not to happen, and instead they hoped to create replicas of the Fabian Society or the British Labour Party on Indian soil. In the heyday of Annie Besant's Home Rule movement this might have been possible. As the paths of the Labour Party leadership and the Indian National Congress diverged in the 1920s, the chances became thinner.

The British Labour influence was not successful in trade union organisation and legislation. Despite the split of 1929 and despite the challenge of Royist and communist leadership, the NTUF maintained its position in the 1930s. The personal integrity of N.M. Joshi and their life-long devotion to the cause of labour enabled them to win the respect of even those who found their political positions too moderate.

NOTES

1. G. Fischer, *Le parti travailliste et la decolonisation de l'Inde* (Paris, 1966). Dr Fischer has not used the archival sources available in India, and, even with regard to British sources, has more or less concentrated on published sources. Besides, his approach is that of an analytical political scientist and not that of a historian. Consequently, having taken the twenty-five years 1914–1949 as one unit, and analysed ideas in terms only of their subject matter and divorced from their time context, he

has failed to bring out the ebb and flow of mutual understanding, which I have attempted in these pages.

2. Ibid., pp. 268–80.

3. There is a huge literature on the subject matter of this paragraph. The books most useful for the conclusions of this paragraph are as follows: B.C. Roberts, *The Trade Union Congress, 1868–1922* (London, 1958); A.M. McBriar, *Fabian Socialism and English Politics, 1884–1918* (Cambridge, 1962); H. Pelling, *The British Communist Party* (London, 1958); L.J. Macfarlane, *The British Communist Party, Its Orgin and Development until 1922* (London, 1966); R.E. Dowse, *Left in the Centre: The Independent Labour Party, 1893–1940* (London, 1966); C. Tsuzuki, *H.M. Hyndman and British Socialism* (Oxford, 1961); F. Brockway, *Inside the Left* (London, 1942); A.J.P. Marwick, 'The Independent Labour Party, 1918–32' (unpublished B. Litt. thesis, Oxford, 1960, microfilm copy available in Delhi University Library).

4. Dowse, *Left in the Centre*, p. 11; the Fabians were split on the tariff question and took a pragmatic viewpoint (McBriar, *Fabian Socialism and English Politics, 1884–1918*, pp. 131–4). Ramsay Macdonald had criticised the Australian Labour Party for supporting the idea of an imperial tariff (G. Fischer, n. 1, p. 80, n. 45).

5. In fairness to J.A. Hobson, although arguments to justify trusteeship could be found in part II, ch. iv of his famous classic, the general trend of the argument of his book was a refutation of the claims of trusteeship made by contemporary imperialists (J.A. Hobson, *Imperialism—A Study*, London, 1938 edn, pp. 230–84.)

6. McBriar, n. 4, pp. 125–30.

7. After a visit to India in the first decade of this century Ramsay Macdonald wrote, 'Thus for many a long year British sovereignty will be necessary for India. . . . Britain is the nurse of India' (R. Macdonald, *The Awakening of India*, London, 1910, p. 301.) Also see Fischer, n. 1, pp. 38–42.

8. On Hyndman and Naoroji, see C. Tsuzuki, *H.M. Hyndman and British Socialism*, pp. 23, 48, 76, 127, and R.P. Masani, *Dadabhai Naoroji* (New Delhi, 1960), pp. 82–5, 110f. On Tilak, see S. Wolpert, *Tilak and Gokhale* (California, 1962), p. 227. On Bipin Chandra Pal, ILP, *Annual Report* 1910, p. 83, for the speech by Pal at the ILP annual conference.

9. The best volume on this is Stephen R. Graubard, *British Labour and the Russian Revolution* (Harvard, 1956). See, in particular, pp. 104–16, 291ff.

10. Arthur H. Nethercot, *The Last Four Lives of Annie Besant* (London, 1963), p. 220.

11. The actual date of the foundation of the Workers' Welfare League is 1916, but the efforts had been on since 1911 (S. Saklatvala, 'India in the

Labour World', *Labour Monthly,* November 1921). Other organisations on India were the British Committee of the Indian National Congress (rather too moderate), 'Britain and India', and students' associations. Some idea of all these organisations and their political roles will be found in the perceptive contemporary despatches sent by Sant Nihal Singh for Mrs Besant's paper, the *Commonweal.* See, in particular, Sant Nihal Singh, 'When the Deputation Arrives in London', *Commonweal,* 25 April 1919 and 2 May 1919, pp. 258f, 278–80.

12. Note by P. Quinn, Superintendent of Police of the search on the offices of the Home Rule for India League on 7 November 1917 (NAI, Home-Pol., May 1918, A36–54, proc. no. 50, enclosure); also see NAI, Home-Pol., May 1918, A158–161.

13. The minute book of the Home Rule League, discovered and noted by the British police during their search in November 1917, mentions among names of leading members 'Mr. Saklatarals'. This most probably is a misprint for Saklatvala. His relations with the Home Rule Leaguers at this time were good for they were all members of the ILP. His references to the League in his *Labour Monthly* article of November 1921 are complimentary (n. 11, p. 449).

14. Intelligence report in the UK on search of Saklatvala's house, 18 October 1920 (NAI Home-Pol., January 1921, Part B 306–7), gives full details of these activities). Also see A.J.P. Marwick, 'The Independent Labour Party, 1918–32', pp. 97–100, 113–16.

15. Labour Party, *Report of the Annual Conference held at Leicester,* April 1918 (London, 1918), pp. 80–1.

16. Labour Party, *Annual Report* 1919, p. 229.

17. ILP, n. 15, p. 81.

18. NAI, Home-Pol., April 1919, Part B 92.

19. *Commonweal,* 20 April 1917, p. 297.

20. Sant Nihal Singh, 'An interview with Col. Josiah Wedgwood, M.P.', *Commonweal,* 2 May 1919, p. 275. Wedgwood had joined the Home Rule League and written a preface to the English edition of Lajpat Rai's book, *Young India,* which was published by the London Home Rule League in 1917. (NAI, Home-Pol., May 1918, A36–54, proc. no. 54).

21. Wedgwood said, 'India wants no Manchester slums, and exploitation. Indian capitalists are as dangerous as British' (*Commonweal,* 2 May 1919, p. 275). During the cotton duties controversy of 1917, H.N. Brailsford, the distinguished Labour journalist, urged Indian nationalists not to regard a concession given to Bombay capitalists by the Conservative supporter of Imperial Preference, Austen Chamberlain, as something which was in the long-term interests of the Indian masses. In his opinion there was a danger of a docile Indian capitalist class being created by modest tariff

concessions within Imperial Preference, and this class would be an obstacle to national independence (H.N. Brailsford, 'The Affairs of the West: Lancashire v. Bombay', *Commonweal*, 4 May 1917).

22. UK *Parliamentary Debates* (Commons), 5th Series, vol. 122, Col. 474.

23. Despatch from the Secretary of State to the Government of India, 25 December 1919, para 7 (NAI, Reforms Office-General, April 1920, A133–7, proc. no. 133.)

24. Note by H. Wheeler, 12 January 1920 in the keep-withs of the following file: WBGA, Appointments dept. April 1920, A3–10 (file 6R-2).

25. Nethercot, n. 10, pp. 290–8; S.R. Mehrotra, *India and the Commonwealth* (London, 1965), pp. 110–12. Srinivasa Sastri, who had founded the Liberal federation when Mrs Besant elected to remain in the Congress, commented on her change of front on Montagu's reforms proposals by saying, 'That woman is mad, I tell you' (Srinivasa Sastri to Tej Bahadur Sapru, 5 March 1919) (NAI, Srinivasa Sastri Papers, Correspondence [1] no. 306).

26. All the documents on this are in the following file: NAI, Commerce & Industry-Factories, February 1920, A1–75.

27. Telegram from Montagu to Chelmsford (private), 15 September 1919, (NAI, Commerce & Industry-Factories, February 1920, A1–75, keep-withs, p. 29).

28. Note by C.G. Freke, 11 September 1919, in ibid., p. 23

29. Note by G.S. Barnes, 15 September 1919, in ibid., p. 29.

30. Secretary of State to Viceroy, 13 September 1919 (NAI, Commerce & Industry-Factories, February 1920, A1–75, proc. no. 61).

31. NAI, Commerce & Industry-Factories, February 1920, A1–75, proc. nos. 68–71, and keep-with, p. 31.

32. Nethercot, n. 10, p. 303.

33. George Lansbury to Mrs Besant, 27 October 1920, quoted in K. Dwarkadas, *India's Fight for Freedom, 1913–1937: An Eye-Witness Story* (Bombay, 1966), p. 135. (Dwarkadas was able to draw on Graham Pole's papers as well as his personal contacts with many of the leading personalities. Therefore, if one discounts an anti-Gandhi bias in the book, his book can yield a lot of useful and correct information.)

34. D. Petrie, *Communism in India, 1924–1927* (Simla, Home Dept. confidential report, 1927), p. 278.

35. J. Potter-Wilson, secretary of the Workers' Welfare League, was one of the ILP dissidents who joined the Communist Party.

36. Mehrotra, n. 25, p. 117.

37. Saklatvala, 'India in the Labour World', *Labour Monthly*, November 1921, p. 450.

38. See Potter-Wilson's remarks at the TUC deputation to Montagu on 22

March 1921, in Minutes of Proceedings at a deputation from the Trade Union Congress Parliamentary Committee to the Secretary of State for India . . . 22 March 1921 (NAI, Industries & Labour, October 1921, A1–7, proc. no. 3 [enclosure]).

39. Labour Party, *Annual Report*, 1922, p. 37.

40. N.M. Joshi raised the matter in the legislative assembly on 1 March 1921.

41. NAI, Industries & Labour, October 1921, A1–7, proc. no. 3 (enclosure).

42. Telegram from Secretary of State to the Viceroy, No. 2010, 14 April 1921 (NAI, Industries & Labour, October 1921, A1–7, proc. no. 1).

43. See note by A.H. Ley, 5 November 1923, in keep-withs of NAI, Industries & Labour-Labour, 1924, file L-925 (coll. 21); also note by A.C. Chatterjee, 13 March 1924, in the keep-withs of the same file.

44. Telegram from the Secretary of State to the Government of India, No. 754, 6 March 1924, was terse and to the point: 'Your secretary's letter L. 925 of 28 September 1921. Trade Union legislation. May I expect to receive proposal shortly'? (NAI, Industry & Labour-Labour, 1924, files 925 [coll. 21] Series No. 101).

45. Note by A.H. Ley, 10 March 1924, in the keep-withs of the file mentioned in the previous note, p. 29.

46. Thomas had reacted sharply to a suggestion from Montagu on 22 March 1921 that the British TUC should help the Indian government 'in getting the Trade Unions on to the right lines'. (NAI, Industries-Labour, October 1921, A1–7, proc. no. 3 [enclosure]).

47. L.F. Rushbrook Williams, 'Memorandum on the education of public opinion in Britain in matters relating to India, 29 July 1920' (NAI, Home-Pol., November 1920, A212 [enclosure]).

48. Note by Rushbrook Williams, 9 October 1920 in the keep-withs (p. 6) of the file mentioned in the previous note; also see note of E.H.F., 3 November 1920 in the keep-withs (p. 4) of NAI, Home-Pol., February 1921, A360–4. The Labour MPs at the Congress session of 1920 were Ben Spoor, Holford Knight, and Col. Josiah Wedgwood.

49. Marwick, 'Independent Labour Party', pp. 108ff. Ellen Wilkinson came back to the ILP soon after.

50. Dowse, n. 3, pp. 51–9; Marwick, n. 49, pp. 112, 219–21.

51. E.H. Carr, *The Bolshevik Revolution*, 1917–23 (London, 1953), vol. III, p. 207.

52. Graubard, n. 9, ch. vii, viii, *passim*, and pp. 146–8, 152, and 164–82 in particular.

53. 'Jamnadas, Dwarkadas, Sir Ali Imam, Sir Sankaran Nair, Right Honourable Srinivasa Sastri, S.R. Bomanji . . . none of them has ever given any assistance, either organizing or financial, to the workers' and peasants'

movement in India, and . . . they are all of them determined opponents of any real move towards working-class freedom' (Saklatvala to N.M. Joshi, 10 March 1926, NMJP file 8, p. 277).

54. Srinivasa Sastri to Vaman Rao, 16 July 1924 (NAI, Srinivasa Sastri Papers-Correspondence [1] Series No. 405).

55. For a general account, see J. Lovell and B.C. Roberts, *A Short History of the TUC* (London, 1968), pp. 72–86; Lord Citrine, *Men and Work: an Autobiography* (London, 1964), pp. 73–215; and A. Bullock, *Life and Times of Ernest Bevin,* vol. I (*Trade Union Leader*) (London, 1960), pp. 260–84.

56. He was one of the signatories to the memorial sent by the Workers' Welfare League to Montagu in January 1919 (*vide* note 18 above); his name recurs as a member of its council for 1924 in the printed circular of the League (Circular of the League, June 1924, NMJP, file 5, p. 33).

57. Carr, n. 51, p. 206; H. Pelling, The *British Communist Party* (London, 1958), p. 9; James Klugmann, *History of the Communist Party of Great Britain,* vol. I, 1919–1924 (London, 1968), p. 79.

58. Dr Henry Pelling, in a letter to me (17 May 1969) has suggested the early 1920s as the date when Purcell might have left the Communist Party for the sake of his parliamentary career.

59. Citrine, n. 55, pp. 89–93; for a general account of these efforts at Anglo-Russian Trade Union cooperation, see Lewis L. Lorwin, *The International Labour Movement* (New York, 1953), pp. 97–109. Purcell was also active in other attempts at communist–Labour cooperation for a Left wing policy in Britain, *vide* Macfarlane, *The British Communist Party,* pp. 142–4.

60. Nethercot, n. 10, p. 340.

61. ILP, *Annual Report* 1924, pp. 68f; ILP, *Annual Report* 1925, pp. 15, 68; Mehrotra, n. 25, pp. 128f; B.R. Nanda, *The Nehrus, Motilal and Jawaharlal* (London, 1962), pp. 227–32.

62. Sastri to Patwardhan, 22 May 1924, quoted in T.N. Jagadisan, (ed.), *Letters of Srinivasa Sastri* (Bombay, 1965), pp. 134f.

63. Srinivasa Sastri to Vaman Rao, 5 June 1924 (NAI, Srinivasa Sastri Papers, Correspondence [i] Ser. No. 401).

64. J.H. Broomfield, *Elite Conflict in a Plural Society: Twentieth Century Bengal* (Berkeley and Los Angeles, 1968), pp. 187–91, 244–57.

65. Sidney Webb, 'The First Labour Government', *Political Quarterly,* vol. XXXII (January–March 1961), pp. 23–4. (This note on the Labour cabinet was written by Webb shortly after the fall of the government, while the issues were fresh in his mind. It was published, years after his death, in 1961.)

66. Subhas Bose, *The Indian Struggle, 1920–42* (Bombay, 1964 edn), pp. 107ff. Lest Bose's verdict be considered biased, attention is also drawn to the remarks of a member of the British ILP, who toured India on the eve of the second Labour government and came to the same conclusion (V.H. Rutherford, *Modern India: Its Problems and Their Solution*, London, 1928, pp. 260f).

67. Srinivasa Sastri to Annie Besant, 4 November 1924, quoted in Jagadisan, *Letters of Srinivasa Sastri*, pp. 140f.

68. Marwick, n. 3, p. 172 (The mediatory role was played by E.D. Morel, G. Lansbury, A.A. Purcell).

69. Telegram from Lansbury, Maxton and Macmanus to the government of the Uttar Pradesh, enclosed in a letter from the Uttar Pradesh government to the Indian government, 28 March 1924. (NAI, Home-Pol., 1924, file 261, Ser. No. 78.)

70. M.N. Roy to J.R. Macdonald, 21 February 1924 (copy in NAI, Home-Pol., 1924, File 111); in this effort Rajni Palme Dutt was helping him (cf. R. Palme Dutt to M.N. Roy, 6 March 1924, intercepted by the government, in NAI, Home-Pol., 1924, file 176.)

71. M.N. Roy to the Editor, *Bombay Chronicle*, date indecipherable from the postmark on the envelope, but from internal evidence and provenance most probably February or March 1924. Intercepted copy, kept in NAI, Home-Pol. *Secret*, 1924, Part B, file 72.)

72. Circular of the Workers' Welfare League, June 1924 (kept in NMJP file 5, p. 33).

73. Labour Party, *Annual Report* 1924, p. 58f.

74. Sime to N.M. Joshi, 5 February 1925. (NMJP file 8, p. 315.)

75. Saklatvala to N.M. Joshi, undated but internal evidence points to its being written not more than a week before 19 June 1925 (NMJP file 7, p. 223).

76. H.W. Lee, who was in his late fifties at this time, had, since the 1890s acted as secretary to the Social Democratic Federation, its successor Social Democratic Party, and *its* successor the British Socialist Party. In the split in the British Socialist Party over the war of 1914–18, he had sided with Hyndman and Left the organisation. (On this and other information on him, see Tsuzuki, n. 3.)

77. H.W. Lee to N.M. Joshi, 29 January 1926. (NMJP file 8, p. 319); see also an earlier letter referring to his work with Hyndman for India, Lee to Joshi, 29 July 1925 (NMJP file 7, p. 81.)

78. Lee to Joshi, 22 March 1926 (NMJP file 8, p. 293); also see Lee to Joshi, 29 January 1926 (NMJP File No. 8, p. 319).

79. Joshi to Lee, 9 April 1926 (NMJP file 8, p. 301).

80. 'India today and the duty of British Socialists towards it', in ILP, *Report of the Annual Conference*, April 1926 (London, 1926), pp. 9, 53–5. Tarini Prasad Sinha was at this time working in the ILP office and was closely associated with Fenner Brockway. He assisted Jawaharlal Nehru when the latter went to Brussels for the Oppressed Peoples' Conference, and later helped Brockway in his campaign on behalf of the Meerut prisoners. His subsequent history is not known. (Information derived partly from AICC Foreign Department files, N.M. Joshi Papers, file 8, and a letter from Lord Brockway to myself, dated 1 February 1969.)

81. Ibid., p. 55.

82. N.M. Joshi to H.W. Lee, 24 September 1926 (NMJP file 8); N.M. Joshi to M. Brothers, 22 May 1927 (NMJP file 9, p. 49); N.M. Joshi to H.S.L. Polak, 15 April 1927 (NMJP file 9, p. 95.)

83. Report by R.W. Robson on a Colonial Conference held at Amsterdam, 11–12 July 1925, pp. 80–3. (This was document No. 42 among the communist papers seized by the British government by a raid on the offices of the Communist Party of Great Britain), reproduced in *Parliamentary Papers* 1926 (Cmd. 2682), XXIII, pp. 686ff.

84. Ibid., pp. 84–6.

85. CPGB, Report of Colonial Activities, p. 99 (Document No. 46 in *Parliamentary Papers* 1926, Cmd. 2682, XXIII, p. 701ff).

86. Helen Crawford to N.M. Joshi, 19 June 1925 (NMJP, file 7, p. 217); C.P. Dutt to N.M. Joshi, 21 July 1925 (NMJP file 7, p. 75); Harry Pollitt to N.M. Joshi, 5 October 1925 (NMJP file 7, p. 47).

87. D. Petrie, *Communism in India, 1924–1927* (Simla, Home Department confidential report 1927), p. 167.

88. Lee to Joshi, 15 July 1925 (NMJP file 7, p. 171).

89. Lee to Joshi, 7 January 1926 (NMJP file 8, p. 367).

90. Lee to Joshi, 29 January 1926 (NMJP file 8, p. 319).

91. Joshi to Lee, 25 February 1926 (NMJP file 8, p. 323).

92. R. Page Arnot to N.M. Joshi, 19 June 1925 (NMJP file 7, p. 215).

93. 'There is absolutely no talk of affiliation with the Red International', wrote Joshi to Lee, 25 February 1926 (NMJP file 8, p. 323).

94. Ibid.

95. Lee to Joshi, 2 March 1926 (NMJP file 8, p. 29).

96. Walter M. Citrine to N.M. Joshi, 11 March 1926 (NMJP file 8, p. 267).

97. Joshi to Lee, 9 April 1926 (NMJP file 8, p. 301).

98. Ibid.; also see Saklatvala to Joshi, 4 February 1926 (NMJP file 8, p. 317).

99. Joshi to Lee, 9 April 1926 (NMJP file 8, p. 301).

100. Joshi to Citrine, 9 April 1926 (NMJP file 8, p. 269).

101. N.M. Joshi to Fenner Brockway, 15 April 1926 (NMJP file 8, p. 263); Tarini P. Sinha to N.M. Joshi, 17 July 1926 (NMJP file 8, p. 157); John Paton to N.M. Joshi, 21 July 1926 (NMJP file 8, p. 153); N.M. Joshi to Tarini P. Sinha, 22 October 1926 (NMJP file 8).

102. Dowse, n. 3, pp. 122f, 130–6.

103. H.S.L. Polak to N.M. Joshi, 1 July 1926 (NMJP file 8, p. 105). Polak, who was a friend of Mahatma Gandhi from his South Africa days, was at this time closely associated with the moderate Labour Party members who supported Mrs Besant's Commonwealth of India League. He was also on the advisory committee of the Labour Party on colonial affairs, of which Leonard Woolf was secretary. Leonard Woolf, *Downhill All the Way* (third volume of the autobiography), London, 1967, p. 223.

104. Joshi to Polak, 16 July 1926 (NMJP file 8).

105. Bullock, n. 55, pp. 384f; Citrine, n. 55, pp. 92f.

106. *Indian Quarterly Register,* January–June 1927, vol. I, pp. 436f.

107. Joshi to Lee, 29 April 1927 (NMJP file 9, p. 81).

108. Lee to Joshi, 18 May 1927 (NMJP file 9, p. 55).

109. Joshi to Lee, 3 June 1927 (NMJP file 9, p. 31).

110. A.A. Purcell and J. Hallsworth, *Report on Labour Conditions in India* (London, TUC General Council, 1928).

111. *Indian Quarterly Register,* July–December 1927, vol. II, pp. 112f.

112. Purcell and Hallsworth, n. 110, pp. 42f.

113. Lovell and Roberts, n. 55, p. 106.

114. Purcell and Hallsworth, n. 110, p. 43.

115. Labour Party, *Annual Report* 1925, p. 59; *Indian Quarterly Register,* July–December 1925, vol. II.

116. Quoted in the appendix of B. Shiva Rao and D. Graham Pole, *Problem of India* (London, 1926), p. 95.

117. Lord Olivier in his preface to Shiva Rao and Graham Pole (note 116 above), pp. 3f.

118. Speech by T.C. Goswami at a meeting in Essex Hall, London, 22 July 1925 (*Indian Quarterly Register,* July–December, 1925, vol. II, p. 152 [c]).

119. D. Graham Pole, 'Mr Gandhi's Fall', *Lansbury's Labour Weekly,* 6 March 1926, p. 12 (cutting kept in NMJP file 8).

120. Broomfield, n. 64, pp. 214–19, on the Chandpur strike; N.M. Joshi to F.J. Ginwalla, 22 July 1924 (NMJP file 2, p. 71); Joshi to Saklatvala, 9 April 1926 (NMJP file 8, p. 279).

121. *Indian Quarterly Register,* January–June 1925, vol. I, p. 19; ibid., January–June 1926, vol. I, p. 9; L.P. Sinha, *The Left Wing in India, 1919–1947* (Muzaffarpur 1965), pp. 198–9.

122. ILP, *Report of the Annual Conference 1925* (London, 1925), p. 161. These remarks were greeted with applause from the delegates.
123. Ibid., p. 159.
124. Fischer, *Le parti travaillists*, p. 283.
125. Joshi to Brockway, 15 April 1926 (NMJP file 8, p. 263).
126. Saklatvala to Joshi, 10 March 1926 (NMJP file 8, p. 277).
127. Joshi to Saklatvala, 9 April 1926 (NMJP file 8, p. 279).
128. Joshi to Graham Pole, 22 October 1926 (NMJP file 8, p. 1).
129. The list of sponsors of the Commonwealth of the India Bill of 11 December 1925 does not include any Labour front benchers. Some were active members of the ILP Empire Committee, namely, H. Snell, Haden Guest, John Scurr, and, of course, Col. Wedgwood, *Parliamentary Papers* (Commons), 1924–5, I, pp. 499–556. Also see Nethercot, n. 10, p. 360. When a similar bill was reintroduced on 11 February 1927, there was hardly any change in terms of the absence of front bench support, (*Parliamentary Papers* [Commons], 1927, I, pp. 249–306).
130. Dowse, n. 3, pp. 124ff; Marwick, n. 3, pp. 237–64.
131. Marwick, n. 3, p. 208.
132. ILP, *Report of the Annual Conference* 1926, pp. 53f.
133. Ibid.
134. Ibid., pp. 54–5.
135. Marwick, n. 3, pp. 219–21.
136. Labour Party, *Annual Report* 1926, pp. 28f.
137. Brockway, n. 3, p. 167.
138. R.N. Carew Hunt, 'Willi Munzenberg', in D. Footman, (ed)., *International Communism*, St Antony's Papers, no. IX (London, 1960), pp. 76f; J. Degras, (ed.), *The Communist International: Documents* (London, 1960), vol. II, pp. 354, 529; AICC, Foreign Department (Correspondence, 1926–7), File G 21 (TL No. 79).
139. Report on the International Congress Against Imperialism held at Brussels. . . . Submitted by Jawaharlal Nehru to the Working Committee of the Indian National Congress, 20 February 1927 (AICC file G 29, 1927, Part II, TL No. 82–A, pp. 80–114). Later references are to the pages of this manuscript.
140. Ibid., pp. 9f.
141. Ibid., pp. 16, 18f.
142. J. Nehru to Rangaswamy, 16 March 1927 (AICC file G 29, Part II (TL 82-A, 1927, p. 68). The speeches of Lansbury and Harry Pollitt which Nehru commended, are in AICC file G 29, Part I (TL No. 82-A), 1927, pp. 27ff, 38ff.
143. J. Nehru to Rangaswamy, 16 March 1927 (AICC file G 29, Part I, pp. 116ff).

144. 'Report on the International Congress Against Imperialism held at Brussels . . . submitted by Jawaharlal Nehru to the Working Committee of the Indian National Congress, 20 February 1927', p. 9 (AICC file G 29, Part I).

145. Nehru to Rangaswamy, 7 March 1927, enclosing a 'Note for the Working Committee' (AICC file G 29 (TL No. 82–A), 1927, Part II, p. 6.

146. AICC file FD-1 (TL No. 175-D), 1929–30, Document No. 17.

147. Brockway, n. 3, p. 168; for Maxton's exit, see Marwick's thesis, which has used Maxton–Chattopadhyaya-Bridgman correspondence, n. 3, p. 277.

148. Labour Party, *Annual Report* 1927, pp. 255–9.

149. *Indian Quarterly Register,* July–December 1927, pp. 92–8.

150. F. Brockway, *The Indian Crisis* (London, 1930), p. 114, describes his discussion with Nehru on 'Purna Swaraj' early in 1927 before Nehru Left Europe; also see Brockway, n. 3, ch. 18, *passim.*

151. F. Brockway to J. Nehru, 11 May 1928 (AICC file 28 (TL No. 88–M, 1928).

152. Labour Party, *Annual Report* 1928, pp. 308f, 311f; for a fuller account, including statements given by the Indian delegates who walked out, see *Indian Quarterly Register,* July–December 1928, vol. II, pp. 293–5. A fortnight later, at the Third Congress of the Labour and Socialist International, Diwan Chaman Lall and R.R. Bakhale sought to elicit support for a resolution critical of the policy of the Labour Party on the Simon Commission, and were strongly supported by the ILP left-winger John Paton. But opposition from the official delegates of the Labour Party led to a compromise resolution being passed (*Indian Quarterly Register,* n. 149, pp. 285f).

153. *Indian Quarterly Register,* n. 149, p. 280.

154. Labour Party, *Annual Report* 1928, pp. 171f.

155. Ibid., p. 173.

156. See the recollections of his friend, Wilfred Wellock, Labour MP, in the Lajpat Rai memorial number of the *People,* 13 April 1929, p. 29.

157. These, published in the *Tribune* (Punjab) of 11 and 14 December, 1927, have been reprinted in V.C. Joshi, (ed.), *Lala Lajpat Rai: Writings and Speeches* (Delhi, 1966), vol. II, pp. 366–8.

158. J. Nehru, *An Autobiography* (London, 1936), p. 176.

159. Leaflet, 'War on Indian Workers', May 1929 AICC Misc. 12 (TL 144), 1929. Nehru–Bridgman correspondence in AICC FD 23 (TL 175 R), 1929–30, pp. 47–139.

160. Lovell and Roberts, n. 55, p. 112.

161. J. Nehru to R.R. Bakhale, 24 September 1929, AICC Misc. 16 (TL 159), 1929, p. 34.

162. J. Nehru to Bakhale, 4 October 1929, AICC Misc. 16 (TL 159), 1929, p. 11.

163. N.M. Joshi to J. Nehru, 11 October 1929, AICC FD 1 (ii), Part II (TL 143), 1929, p. 130.

164. See their letter to the Assistant Secretary, AITUC, 20 September 1929, AICC Misc. 16 (TL 159), 1929.

165. S.C. Bose, *Indian Struggle* (Bombay, 1964), p. 166.

166. J. Nehru, 'Statement on the Whitley Commission', 20 September 1929, AICC Misc. 16 (TL 159), 1929, p. 40.

167. J. Nehru to Mahatma Gandhi, 4 November 1929, in J. Nehru, *A Bunch of Old Letters* (New York, 1960 edn), pp. 76–8.

168. Report of the Nagpur session of the AITUC, *Indian Quarterly Register*, July–December 1929, p. 427.

169. There are no letters either in his file of personal correspondence or in the AICC files, between him and Brockway or Maxton, whereas there are quite a few with Reginald Bridgman.

170. These included Brockway, J.F. Horrabin, Fred Longden, Ellen Wilkinson, James Maxton, John Scurr, Josiah Wedgwood, Wilfred Wellock, M. Brothers, D.R. Grenfell, Jennie Lee. Besides, there were more moderate but genuine friends of Indian nationalism like George Lansbury, Pethick-Lawrence, Graham Pole and the Rev. James Barr.

171. Brockway, n. 3, pp. 202–4. The correspondence between Wedgwood Benn and the Indian government on Brockway's suggestion is in NAI, Home-Pol., 1929, file 299. Also see an earlier account by Brockway in his *Indian Crisis*, pp. 130–3.

172. Brockway, 'The Declaration and the Conference' (London Letter), *Servant of India*, 21 November 1929, contains the personal appeal to Jawaharlal. It was written on 30 October, after a talk with Benn, but reached India by mail three weeks later. To some extent Brockway's efforts were frustrated due to the time lag between his letters and their publication. On 27 November 1929 he wrote privately to S.G. Vaze about the parliamentary resolution on India that he was going to move with Benn's permission, but the long article in which he expounded the theme of his resolution was published only on 19 December 1929, too late to have any effect. Brockway to Editor, S.G. Vaze, 27 November 1929 (NAI, Srinivasa Sastri Papers—Correspondence [i] Ser. No. 534); *Servant of India*, 19 December 1929.

173. See the references to note 171; also see Wedgwood Benn to Lord Irwin (private and personal), 24 December 1929 (NAI, Home-Pol., 1930, file 11/19).

174. On one occasion Brockway was disciplined by the Speaker for insisting on moving a resolution on arrests in India. He wrote *The Indian Crisis*

in 1930. An ex-ILP journalist H.N. Brailsford visited India later in the year and wrote *Rebel India* (1931).

175. ILP, *Annual Report* 1931, pp. 19f.

176. Notes and documents on the 'Friend of India' Society, London, by the Intelligence branch (NAI, Home-Pol., 1931, file 117).

177. ILP, *Annual Report* 1931, pp. 124f. The Labour Party conference of October 1930 saw a drawn battle between the resolution of Kenworthy approving the Labour government calling the round table conference, and the amendment by the ILP left wing critical of the government and calling for release of prisoners. The left wing leader A.J. Cook got the 'previous question' carried but both resolution and amendment were shelved. Brockway wrote, 'I think this meant that whilst the Party is not prepared to censure its own government, it is uneasy about the policy being pursued and is not in the mood to give it whole-hearted endorsement' (Labour Party, *Annual Report* 1930, pp. 216–20; Brockway, 'The Labour Party and India', *Servant of India,* 30 October 1930, p. 526).

178. Walter Citrine did inquire about the Meerut prisoners early in 1930 but was easily convinced by the official view on the procedure adopted to try the accused (NAI, Home-Pol., 1930, file 108).

179. ILP, *Annual Report* 1931, p. 117. Brockway said that the Meerut trial was 'as disgraceful as the Dreyfus and Sacco and Vanzetti trials'. He tried, unsuccessfully, to raise the matter at the Labour Party conference in October 1931 (Labour Party, *Annual Report* 1931, pp. 168ff).

180. Labour Party, *Annual Report* 1930, p. 308, gives the names of participants but no details. I am grateful to Shri B. Shiva Rao, who was one of them, for telling me his recollections of the details (interview with Shri B. Shiva Rao by P.S. Gupta, 23 December 1968).

181. Indian Round Table Conference, *Proceedings, November 1930—January 1931* (Cmd. 3778) (London, 1931), p. 433.

182. Macdonald, in his concluding speech, ignored the points raised by Joshi and Shiva Rao.

183. *Vide* 'Record of the Home members', interview with H.S.L. Polak of the India Conciliation Group, 18 March 1933 (NAI, Home-Pol., 1933, file 79).

184. See the article of the Royist Labour leader V.B. Karnik, 'A clean reply to Mr Bakhale', *The Mahratta,* 14 May 1933, p. 11 (kept in NMJP file 4, second folder); I am also indebted to Shri Rajani Mukherjee, who was organising secretary of the AITUC then, and is now an official of the Hind Mazdoor Sabha (interview on 6 July 1969).

185. R.R. Bakhale, 'Trade Union Unity', *Servant of India,* 4 May 1933, pp.

209f. The authorship of the *Platform of Unity* is attested by Shri Rajani Mukherjee, who was actively associated with M.N. Roy (interview on 6 July 1969), and is hinted at by Karnik, n. 184.

186. Dowse, n. 3, pp. 179–84.

187. Ibid., ch. 13, *passim.*

188. M. Cole, *The Story of Fabian Socialism* (London, 1961), pp. 226–30.

189. G.D.H. Cole, *A History of the Labour Party from 1914* (London, 1948), ch. IX, *passim;* C. Cooke, *The Life of Sir Richard Stafford Cripps* (London, 1957, ch. X, *passim;* Kingsley Martin, *Harold Laski* (London, 1953), pp. 102–12; D.N. Pritt, *Autobiography: From Right to Left* (London, 1965), pp. 97–104.

190. A.K. Kahn, *Great Britain in the World Economy* (London, 1946), p. 244.

191. Ben Tillett, in his presidential address to the Belfast TUC of September 1929, had visualised the British Commonwealth being organised as an economic unit comparable to the US (Lovell and Roberts, n. 55, p. 111). In 1930 Ernest Bevin further developed the idea of a Commonwealth Economic bloc (Bullock, n. 55, vol. I, pp. 440–6). George Lansbury, in explaining Labour's colonial policy, suggested reorganising the British empire the way the Soviet Union had reorganised the Tsarist colonies (G. Lansbury, *My England,* London, 1934, pp. 166f).

192. John Parker, 'Socialism and the Problem of Nationalism', in G.E.G. Catlin, (ed.), *New Trends in Socialism* (London, 1935), pp. 222–5.

193. H.W. Richardson, *Economic Recovery in Britain, 1932–1939* (London, 1967), *passim.*

194. Sir Stafford Cripps, 'The British Working-class and Indian Independence', *Congress Socialist,* 11 January 1936, pp. 7f.

195. On Ernest Bevin's evolution, see the perceptive comments of E.J. Hobsbawm, in his *Labouring Men* (London, 1964), pp. 339f.

196. Bullock, *Life and Times of Ernest Bevin,* vol. II, *Minister of Labour* (London, 1967), pp. 205–7.

197. Labour Party, *Annual Report* 1933, p. 73. For the reasons why the Liberals withdrew, see Dwarkadas, n. 33, p. 432.

198. Labour Party, *Annual Report* 1931, p. 84.

199. *Joint Committee on Constitutional Reform,* session 1933–4, vol. I (Part II, Proceedings, London, 1934), para 3.

200. Ibid., paras 11, 19.

201. Ibid., para 12.

202. Ibid., paras 36, 37.

203. Ibid., paras 335, 347, 351.

204. G. Lansbury, *My England* (London, 1934), p. 171.

205. J.M. Keynes to Kingsley Martin, 23 April 1933, quoted in full in K. Martin, *Editor: A Volume of Autobiography, 1931–1945* (London, 1968), p. 42. This must have been caused by the editorial approval given to a long letter a fortnight before from an 'Indian', sharply criticising the White Paper (*New Statesman and Nation,* 8 April 1933, pp. 442–3).

206. Laski to Justice Holmes, 15 June 1930, quoted in M. de W. Howe, (ed.), *Holmes-Laski Letters* (London, 1953), vol. II, p. 1261.

207. Ibid., pp. 1264, 1301, 1332, 1335–6. On 3 December 1931 Gandhi had a serious discussion with Labour Party intellectuals at the flat of J.F. Horrabin, M.P. At the end of it, Harold Laski, at Gandhi's request, summed up the various points of view (Woolf, *Downhill All The Way,* pp. 228–30).

208. Laski to Holmes, 12 July 1932, in Howe, n. 206, p. 1396.

209. T.J.S. George, *Krishna Menon: A Biography* (London, 1964), p. 52. George Lansbury's *My England* (London, 1934) was part of a series which Menon was editing for the publishers Selwyn and Blount.

210. George, n. 209, pp. 53–7.

211. Ibid., also see the home department's dossier on Polak (NAI, Home-Pol., 1936, file 137).

212. The names are taken from the printed notepaper of the India League of 1932, used in a letter from Menon to H.G. Haig, 10 October 1932 (NAI, Home-Pol., file 40/XII, p. 105).

213. Martin, *Editor,* pp. 157–62, for the work of Dorothy Woodman in the Union of Democratic Control, and the links of the UDC with the India League.

214. Note by H.W. Williamson (DIB), 14 March 1933 on a PUC on the India League's work (NAI, Home-Pol., 1933, file 30/2).

215. Telegram from Malaviya to Horrabin, 15 July 1932 (intercepted copy in NAI, Home-Pol., 1932, file 40/XII, p. 26); also Andrews to Malaviya, 22 July 1932 (NAI, Home-Pol., 1932, file 40/XII, p. 45) and Horrabin to Malaviya, 2 August 1932 (NAI, Home-Pol., 1932, file 40/XII, p. 41).

216. R. Peel to M.G. Hallett, 5 August 1932, No. Pt J(S) 805/32 (NAI, Home-Pol., file 40/XII, pp. 49f).

217. NAI, Home-Pol., file 40/XII, *passim.*

218. Peel to Hallett, 5 August 1932, n. 216.

219. See, for example, H.S. Turnam to M.G. Hallett, 17 October 1932 (DO No. 1088, PSD) (NAI, Home-Pol., file 40/XII, pp. 134f); note by C.H. Everett, Superintendent of Police, CID, 25 October 1932 (ibid., p. 191). The Law Member, Sir B.L. Mitter, tried to argue a very pro-government and anti-Gandhi case to Ellen Wilkinson, giving the moderate Liberal point of view, and felt pleased with himself for 'the opportunity

of dealing a few direct blows at popular delusions' (Note by Sir B.L. Mitter, 30 October 1932, ibid., p. 167a).

220. India League, *Condition of India* (London, 1934).

221. Note by H. Williamson, 23 March 1934, in NAI, Home-Pol., 1934, file 35/3, pp. 4–7.

222. India League, n. 220, pp. 45, 47f, 102, 118ff.

223. Ibid., pp. 433–42.

224. Ibid., p. 441.

225. Ibid., p. 436.

226. Labour Party, *Annual Report* 1933, p. 19.

227. Ibid., p. 146 (Lansbury's statement); National Trade Union Federation, Circular No. 1 (11 October 1933), issued by R.R. Bakhale (NMJP file 3, p. 6); interview with Shri B. Shiva Rao, 23 December 1968.

228. V.B. Karnik, *Indian Trade Unions: A Survey* (2nd revised edn, Bombay, 1966), p. 80.

229. H. Alexander, 'India', *New Statesman and Nation,* 14 April 1934, p. 540.

230. G. Lansbury, *My England* (1934), pp. 172f.

231. Labour Party, *Annual Report* 1935, pp. 84f.

232. *Servant of India,* 29 November 1934, pp. 557f, 565, and ibid., 6 December 1934, pp. 573, 597.

233. Labour Party, *Annual Report* 1935, pp. 84–6, 240ff.

234. Ibid., p. 241.

235. Ellen Wilkinson to J. Nehru, 5 November 1935 (JLNP, Correspondence, Wilkinson file, No. 1); C.F. Andrews to J. Nehru, 3 November 1935 (JLNP, Correspondence, Andrews file); J. Nehru to H. Alexander, 17 January 1936 (Nehru Library, Horace Alexander Papers, Accession 73, p. 37).

236. Woolf, n. 103, pp. 230–2.

237. Vera Brittain (Mrs Catlin), *Envoy Extraordinary* (London, 1965), p. 12.

238. C. Attlee, *The Labour Party in Perspective* (London, 1937), pp. 228–9, 239–40, 245–6. Dr Ram Manohar Lohia took offence at Attlee's book and implied that Attlee should have openly recognised the fact that the Congress was a socialist organisation (R.M. Lohia, 'Indian Problem Misunderstood', *AICC Foreign Department Newsletter,* No. 26, 30 September 1937, AICC, FD 11 KW (ii) TL 716-H, 1936, p. 25.

239. Ellen Wilkinson to J. Nehru, 22 March 1936, in J. Nehru, *A Bunch of Old Letters,* p. 177.

240. *New Statesman and Nation,* 9 May 1936, p. 730.

241. Reginald Reynolds to J. Nehru, 23 June 1936 (JLNP, Correspondence, Reynolds file, pp. 7f).

242. J. Nehru to Rajendra Prasad, 20 November 1935 (intercepted copy of

letter, the original of which was passed on, in NAI, Home-Pol., 1936, file 1/2).

243. Ibid.

244. Intercepted copy in NAI, Home-Pol., 1936, file 32/8.

245. V.K. Krishna Menon to J. Nehru, 5 June 1936 (intercepted copy passed on, NAI, Home-Pol., 1936, file 32/8).

246. John Parker, MP to the Secretary, AICC, file FD 40.1, 1936 (TL No. 970 F).

247. For a general account, see Hari Kishore Singh, 'Rise and secession of the Congress Socialist Party of India, 1934–48', in Raghavan Iyer, (ed.), *South Asian Affairs*, No. 1 (St Antony's Papers No. 8), London, 1960, *passim*. Also see Acharya Narendra Deva, 'Problems of Socialist Unity', 9 April 1938, reprinted in his *Socialism and the National Revolution* (Bombay, 1946), p. 116.

248. Jayaprakash Narayan to Ram Manohar Lohia, 13 February 1937, AICC, Misc. Category file, 21 (TL 660), 1936–8, pp. 461–3; Jayaprakash Narayan to Ram Manohar Lohia, undated (probably early 1937). AICC FD 40, 1 (TL 970 F), 1936.

249. Hari Kishore Singh, n. 247, pp. 129f; B.P. Sinha, 'Why am I a Congress Socialist', *Congress Socialist*, 10 March 1935, pp. 5f; articles by Asoka Mehta in *Congress Socialist*, vol. I, No. 10 (February 1935) and ibid., 8 August 1936.

250. Subhas Bose, 'Congress Socialist Party' (first published 15 March 1935), reprinted in Bose, *The Indian Struggle*, p. 384.

251. Home Political files show that the government, instead of directly banning them, resorted to their prohibition under the Sea Customs Act. Jawaharlal Nehru got copies through private channels (J. Nehru to Sasadhar Sinha, letters in 1936, JLNP Sasadhar Sinha file). In our own family, in the 1930s, copies of the Left Book Club edition of Sidney and Beatrice Webb's *Soviet Communism*, and John Strachey's *Theory and Practice of Socialism* were acquired (P.S.G.). There is evidence of many such unofficial pipelines.

252. Discussion between J.L. Nehru and Victor Gollancz about proposal to start an Indian Left Book Club to publish in India 'Left Literature', in NAI, Home-Pol., 1938, file 41/13).

253. 'Are you thinking of any Economic Research Bureau, something on the lines of the New Fabian Research Bureau'? wrote Dr Rao to Nehru. (V.K.R.V. Rao to J. Nehru, 9 July 1937, JLNP Correspondence, V.K.R.V. Rao file pp. 12f). There may have been other socialists influenced by Fabian models, but in the AICC and Nehru Correspondence this is the only example of a conscious imitation of the Fabian technique.

254. Dowse, n. 3, pp. 193, 202.

255. H. Pelling, *The British Communist Party* (1958), p. 104; Fenner Brockway's report on his journey to Spain and the experience of the POUM, June 1937 (AICC FD 7 (TL 906-E), 1936–8); George Orwell, *Homage to Catalonia* (London, 1938), *passim*.

256. Kingsley Martin did not publish Orwell's reports. See his justification of this action in *Editor* (London, 1968), pp. 215f. In fairness, it must be said that the *New Statesman and Nation* took a critical line on the purges, while advocating an anti-Fascist alliance with the USSR. But the Left Book Club did appear to be a little too pro-Soviet and pro-communist. (See controversy in the *New Statesman and Nation*, 10 April 1937, p. 587 [letter by Allen Skinner]; ibid., 17 April 1937, pp. 632f; ibid., 24 April 1937, pp. 672f, ibid., 1 May 1937, p. 712, ibid., 8 May 1937, p. 768.

257. F. Brockway to M.R. Masani, 25 May 1936 (copy sent to J. Nehru, JLNP, Correspondence, Brockway file, No. 4); F. Brockway to J. Nehru, 20 June 1938 (ibid., No. 8).

258. Brockway to Masani, 25 May 1936 (n. 257); *Congress Socialist*, 29 August 1936, p. 4. T.J.S. George, in his book *Krishna Menon*, mistakenly says that the Brussels Congress of the International Bureau of Revolutionary Socialist Unity was 'Communist-inspired' (n. 209, p. 109). It was Trotskyite. The official Comintern line was to support the other Congress organised by Romain Rolland and others (see note 259).

259. J. Nehru to F. Brockway, 21 June 1936 (JLNP, Correspondence, Brockway file No. 7); George, n. 209, p. 109. Harry Pollitt, on behalf of the British Communist Party, and following the line of the Seventh Congress of the Comintern, attended this Congress (*New Statesman and Nation*, 19 September 1936, p. 386 [letter from Harry Pollitt]; also see Critic's (Kingsley Martin) comments on the moderation of the Congress and the communists' reluctance to take an extreme stand in the interests of unity (ibid., 12 September 1936, p. 343).

260. Mohan Kumaramangalam to J. Nehru, 17 October 1937 (JLNP, Kumaramangalam file) refers to a conversation between himself, Nehru, Masani, Meherally, and Kamaladevi on this.

261. Ram Manohar Lohia to John Dewey, 26 March 1938. AICC FD 7 (TL No. 906 E), 1936–8.

262. J. Nehru to V.K. Krishna Menon, 11 November 1937 (JLNP, Correspondence, Menon file, No. 1). The letter from Menon to Nehru is not available, but from Nehru's reply its purport can be inferred. Also see a letter Menon wrote to Masani, probably about this time, deploring the 'Trotskyite streak' and the 'campaign to isolate Russia' (George, n. 209, p. 92).

263. 'My programme in England is being fixed up by Krishna Menon in consultation with others', J. Nehru to Agatha Harrison, 28 April 1938 (JLNP Correspondence, Agatha Harrison file).

264. The Peace and Empire rally was on 15–16 July 1938. Speakers were Nehru, Cripps, Ellen Wilkinson, Paul Robeson, Wilfred Roberts, MP, Reginald Soresmen, MP, etc. The rally on Spain was at Trafalgar Square on 17 July 1938 with a large number of speakers ranging from the Young Liberals' representative to Communists like J.B.S. Haldane (AICC, Misc. 31 [TL 1067-P], 1938).

265. Réynolds to Nehru, 21 June 1938; 30 June 1938; 31 July 1938 (JLNP, Correspondence, Reynolds file). The letters show that had Nehru been able to spare time to see Reynolds, he would have had an opportunity to meet George Padmore, the African leader, George Orwell, and others.

266. Brockway to Nehru, 6 August 1938 (JLNP, Correspondence, Brockway file, No. 13).

267. Menon had begun to feel the dwindling significance of the ILP in 1936. He wrote, 'The internal war between Trotskyites and Stalinists to capture this shade of a once-militant socialist movement is pathetic' (*Congress Socialist,* 25 April 1936, p. 25).

268. Nehru to Menon, 11 November 1937 (n. 262).

269. India League propaganda was careful to combine agitation for complete independence with a pledge to 'have the closest contacts . . . with all progressive countries, including England, if she has shed her imperialism'. (India League, *Indian National Congress—Foreign Policy Resolutions and Views,* March 1937), p. 10, kept in AICC Misc. 31 (TL 1067-P), part 2, 1938).

270. *New Statesman and Nation,* 30 September 1939, pp. 448–9. He suggested bringing national leaders into the Viceroy's Council and making Nehru 'Premier in fact if not in name'. Also see ibid., 14 October 1939, p. 510. When finally Linlithgow gave an indefinite reply to the Congress, he wrote, 'The Viceroy's reply . . . has missed an opportunity that comes only once in a generation' (ibid., 21 October 1939, p. 537).

271. Fischer, n. 1, pp. 323–30, for a useful summing-up of these ideas.

272. Woolf, n. 103, p. 223.

273. See G.T. Garratt, *An Indian Commentary* (London, 1928), pp. 150f, 155. The second edition of the book (1930) was more sympathetic to the Congress.

Culture and the Raj

SECTION V

MUSIC AND COMMUNALISM
IN BENGAL*

In disseminating social and political awareness among a predominantly illiterate population music and drama play a much more important role than the written word. This essay highlights the works of some songsters of Bengal, and examines their role in the politics of communalism there.[1]

Music was an integral part of the folk literature of rural Bengal; the lifestyle of ordinary people, Hindus and Muslims alike, was characterised by various musical forms, whether for religious services, or as rhythmic accompaniment during work. Over the centuries many different styles of folk-songs evolved, each with their regional, occupational, and devotional specificities. One characteristic of these singing traditions was that the words and music reflected in many cases the vitality of a syncretic tradition among the followers of Islam in Bengal.[2] Islam had reached Bengal in the thirteenth century; the area had been ruled by independent Muslim rulers during the sultanate period before being absorbed within the Mughal empire, and the census of 1872 categorised nearly half the total population of Bengal as Muslims. During this long period of the assimilation of the Islamic faith by a rural folk whose earlier devotional moorings had been mainly Buddhist or Hindu, a composite culture developed in the countryside, characterised by the intermingling of Vaishnav and Sufi traditions, by the smooth assimilation of Arabo-Persian words in the Bengali language, and the contribution to Bengali ballads by both Muslim and Hindu writers.[3] Itinerant mendicant devotees developed the *baul* style of music—a style

*First published in P. Mehta, N. Gupta and Rajivlochan (eds) *Society, Religion and the State: Identity Crises in Indian History* (Indo-British Historical Society, Madras, 1996).

in which Hindu and Muslim mystics expressed their religious experience—which passed into the common currency of folk melodies by
the oral tradition of the *guru–shishya parampara*.[4] Bengalis are tempera-
mentally emotional; their social and personal aspirators get translated
effortlessly into musical notes.

In the cultural history of nineteenth-century Bengal, we notice
certain discontinuities which can be traced to the colonial impact. In
the urban centres of Calcutta and the lower Hooghly basin, the patrons
of literature, music, and the fine arts were the English-educated professional and landowning classes (beneficiaries of the 'permanent settlement' who mainly lived as absentee landowners in the metropolis). Some
of the great composers of lyrics and patriotic songs like Rabindranath
Tagore (1861–1941), Atul Prosad Sen (1871–1934), and Dwijendra
Lal Roy (1863–1913) belonged to this social stratum. They grew up
in an atmosphere where they could imbibe the influence of north
Indian classical music as well as Western music. They were also influenced—in greater or lesser degree—by the first institutionalised association devoted to the propagation of a nationalist ideology through
meetings, fetes, essay competitions and songs, the Hindu Mela (founded
in 1867). The songs composed by people involved in the Hindu Mela—
which included Rabindranath Tagore's elder brothers, Dwijendranath
and Satyendranath Tagore—were suffused with an ideology of nationalism in which Hinduism and Bharatvarsha were synonymous and the
ancient Indian myths and legends were the main source of inspiration.[5]
The first crop of nationalist songs thus developed in an urban milieu
of Hindu *bhadralok* who were beneficiaries of the colonial state but
whose sense of indignity at the behaviour of the European bureaucracy
had made them express their nationalist identity in these patriotic songs.
The Russian Tsarevich was surprised to hear from an Indian Sanskrit
scholar, who described how these songs were aimed at 'the inculcation
and the development of the national spirit of the Hindu race', that the
British government had not prohibited such hymns.[6]

The other discontinuity in the cultural history of nineteenth-century
Bengal is in the Islamic syncretic tradition. This tradition was deeply
embedded in rural Bengal where the peasantry was predominantly
Muslim. The Wahabi and Faraizi movements provided an ideology for
peasant resistance to the inequities of the permanent settlement and

the oppression of the colonial state. These ideologies supported armed rebellion against the Raj, and their *mullahs* advocated the 'purification' of the religious practices of Bengali Muslims by eliminating all signs of syncretism.[7]

If at the levels of cultural mediation the anti-landlord and anti-colonial movements described above contributed towards an erosion of Islamic syncretism, these movements were not confined exclusively to Muslims. Many Hindu *ryots* took part in the agrarian rebellion led by the Wahabi rebel Titu Mir, which was as much against British indigo planters as against Bengali zamindars.[8]

There is no anthology, at least to my knowledge, of folk-songs or ballads that commemorated peasant resistance to the exploitative machine of the permanent settlement. If any such compilation were made it would enable us to examine whether the idioms and images used in these songs retained traces of the old syncretic tradition and reflected cross-communal cooperation in the peasant struggle. However, in the general lifestyle of rural folk in districts with a Muslim majority in East Bengal, the effect of the Wahabi and Faraizi movements appears to have been to discourage music and singing, though it could not eliminate the human yearning for music. As the great Muslim poet Jasim-ud-din, who has written superb poems about Bengal rural life, writes in his autobiography about his childhood in Faridpur district in East Bengal (now in Bangladesh):

Faridpur district was the scene of the Faraizi movement. Here prosperous Muslim families would not only refrain from having any musical performances in their houses, but also ostracize those Muslims who practised singing or playing musical instruments. However, the hunger for music is an eternal human craving; therefore, notwithstanding many insults and indignities the Muslims would satisfy this hunger by listening to music during Hindu religious festivities.[9]

As we shall see, in the twentieth century, when the swadeshi movement produced a rich harvest of popular political songs, and when the mechanical reproduction of audio material became possible through the gramophone and the radio, contributions to Bengal's musical wealth came from Muslim as well as Hindu musicians. In the western part of the province—in the Burdwan division—where the tradition of Hindu religious music was overlaid with the Vaishnav movement associated with Shri Chaitanya, there seems to have been less of the phenomenon which Jasim-ud-din describes. Nazrul Islam (1898–1976) who was born in a poor village family in Burdwan district, spent part of his childhood composing and singing songs for a wandering troupe of singers and actors who entertained villagers by depicting Hindu religious legends. He holds a pre-eminent place in the story of the efforts to communicate through music the ideal of a nationalism rising above religious differences. But before analysing his work a brief assessment of the musical legacy of the swadeshi movement is necessary as a background.

The swadeshi movement in Bengal refers to the agitation against the partition of Bengal. The movement produced a remarkable output of patriotic songs by many authors, and music was one of the major techniques of mass contact.[10] However, the appeal of the agitation to Muslims in general was limited.[11] While one cannot deny the involvement of some Muslim leaders and their followers, and the composition of patriotic songs by Muslim writers (like Ismail Husain Shirazi), most of the songs and plays had not shed Hindu imagery and historical allusions to the 'glories' of ancient Indian civilisation.[12] The revolutionary secret societies excluded Muslims from membership,[13] even when some young Muslim boys wanted to join them.[14] Nevertheless, in this period we do come across popular songs, one of which appeals to Ram and Rahim to unite in the common cause. Its authorship is attributed to an anonymous member of the Mymensingh Suhrid Samiti,[15] though some scholars think it was written by Mukunda Das, an itinerant minstrel whose influence reached out to stir the Muslim masses.[16]

The swadeshi movement and the imperial policy of the first decade of the twentieth century (introduction of communal electorates in the wake of the Morley–Minto reforms) were to create a gulf between the religious, cultural and political aspirations of Bengali Muslims and Bengali Hindus which, according to one historian was going to be 'unbridgeable'.[17] Without necessarily taking such a teleological view, we have to concede that henceforward the anti-imperialist forces in Bengal could not, at all critical conjunctures of social and political crisis, avoid thinking in terms of the relative gains and losses that would accrue to each community from any new political development. Thus, the annulment of the partition of Bengal (1912) was unpopular with Bengali Muslims, especially in East Bengal.[18] The politically conscious among them were further incensed by the fact that during the First World War (1914–18), Britain was opposed to Turkey, which was allied to Germany. In such circumstances they made common cause with Bengal Congress members for a Hindu–Muslim alliance to demand constitutional concessions from the government, which eventually bore fruit as the Montford Reforms of 1919. However, the lesser demographic weightage given to Bengali Muslim electorate in the Lucknow Pact (1916) embittered Bengali Muslim opinion, which was by no means mollified by Montagu's indifference to their views.[19]

It is a testimony to the power of words and ideas that notwithstanding the low rate of participation of Bengali Muslims in the swadeshi movement, many songs of that period left an abiding impression on the minds of musically inclined as well as politically sensitive Bengali Muslim poets and composers. To give just three examples: at the time of the Khilafat movement, a song writer called Abdul Matin wrote two pieces the words, rhythm and tunes of which imitate two swadeshi songs written respectively by Rabindranath Tagore and D.L. Roy. The song by Tagore ran thus (the opening two lines):

Banglar mati, Banglar jal
Banglar vayu, Banglar phal
Punya houk, punya houk, punya houk
Hey Bhagwan ['The soil of Bengal, its water, air and fruit, grant their well-being, O Lord']

Substituting '*Turki*' for Bangla, Abdul Matin wrote (third and fourth lines):

Turkeer mati, Turkeer jal,
Turkeer vayu, Turkeer phal
Punya houk, punya houk, punya houk
hey khodawand [The soil of Turkey, its water, air and fruit, grant their well-being, O Lord.][20]

The song by D.L. Roy (an extract given below with a translation by his son, the great singer Dilip Kumar Roy) was saturated with Bengali regional patriotism, selective use of history and myth-making about ancient Bengal when Buddhism and Hinduism were the dominant religions. Yet so great was the emotive power generated by this song, on everybody's lips during the swadeshi period, that Abdul Matin's song about the Khilafat movement and pan-Islamism clothed itself in the style of D.L. Roy's song, despite its Hindu bias.[21]

The first lines of Roy's song and the refrain (sung in chorus) are given below (his son's English translation is in the footnote):[22]

Banga amar, janani amar, dhatri amar
amar desh
Keno go Ma tor shushkha nayan
Keno go Ma tor rukkha kesh . . .
Kisheyr dukkha, kisheyr doinya,
kisher lajja, kisheyr klesh
Sapta koti milito kanthey dakey jakhon
amar desh

The first two and last two lines of Abdul Matin's song show his indebtedness to D.L. Roy's verse:[23]

Kisheyr dukkha, kisheyr doinya,
Kisheyr lajja, kisheyr bhoy
Challis koti bhatri miliya gahibo
Jokhon dharmeyr jai . . .
Swadhin Islam, swadhin Moslem, Manav
swadhin satata roy,
Kisheyr dukkha, kisheyr doinya, kisheyr
lajja, kisheyr bhoy.

The third example of how the tune of swadeshi songs with Hindu imagery was internalised by a Muslim song writer is from Nazrul Islam, about whom I will have a lot to say in the remainder of the essay. D.L. Roy had composed a song about Mother India (Janani Bharatvarsha), with a rapid, rousing tempo. It treated the topography of the subcontinent in a deified anthropomorphic manner, using the symbolism of the Hindu mother goddess, with repeated use of adjectives like Jagattarini (World Saviour—one of the names of Durga) and Jagatdhatri (World Mother) in association with Bharatvarsha. In one of Nazrul's earliest songs, called 'Bodhan' (inspired by a poem of Hafiz), the tune was the same as in the above-mentioned song of D.L. Roy.[24]

It is necessary at this point to give a brief biographical sketch of that unique personality—Nazrul Islam—who is central to any discussion on music, patriotism and communalism in Bengal. Nazrul Islam was born in May 1899 in a poor Muslim home in village Churulia in the Asansol subdivision of Burdwan district in Bengal.[25] Having lost his father at the age of eight, he passed the lower primary examination from the village *maktab* two years later, and taught in the same place for a year to support himself. A restless boy, with superabundant *joie de vivre*, and a good singing voice, he was introduced to a local itinerant folk band of musicians called the *Leto dal*, through an uncle who belonged to it. These groups used to move from village to village giving song and verse performances, often drawing on the Ramayana, the Mahabharata and other puranic lore of the Hindus. Nazrul, who had already been in the company of the sufis and fakirs in the neighbourhood, thus acquired a syncretic approach to religious questions, an experience which enabled him, in later years, to communicate with the people of both Hindu and Muslim communities with perfect ease. *Leto* performances were seasonal and the income generated was dependent on the prosperity of the villagers. In the event, this.could not provide him a steady livelihood. He was a domestic servant in the house of a railway guard for a while, and then worked in a baker's shop. A Muslim police inspector, impressed by the boy's flute playing and general intelligence, sent him to his own village in East Bengal in Mymensingh, to study without having to pay any tuition fee. After a year Nazrul returned to his native Asansol. He obtained a free studentship, a stipend of Rs 7 per month, and free board and lodging at the Muslim hostel. When he chose to, he could do very well in studies, and earned a double promotion from Class VIII to Class X. While in Class X, he left formal studies in enlist in the 49th Bengali regiment that was created in 1917 for promoting the war effort in west Asia. For two years (1917–19)—till the regiment was disbanded—Nazrul was an army NCO rising from the ranks to become a havildar. He had postings in Naushera (North-West Frontier Province) and Karachi. His songs made him popular in the army barracks. He learnt Persian and Persian poetry from a Punjabi Maulvi and was influenced by Hafiz.

Nazrul's poems started appearing in a literary journal started by some young members of the Bengali Muslim intelligentsia, among whom was the future communist leader Muzaffar Ahmad who remained a life-long friend. One of Nazrul's school friends, Sailajananda Mukhopadhyay had started his literary career in Calcutta. With their help he began a career as a journalist and writer just after demobilisation in March 1920.

Nazrul's poems and songs at once made him popular among both communities, the tone of rebellion fitting in with the atmosphere of the Non-cooperation and Khilafat Movements, in which he himself took part. He was jailed for a year in January 1923 for writing an allegedly seditious poem.[26] Two of his earliest collections of songs (*Bhangar Gan* and *Visher Banshi*) were banned by the government in 1924. In April of that year he married a Hindu girl with whom he had fallen in love while staying in Tripura district in East Bengal for two to three months for political and journalistic work. The relatively mild opposition that this courtship had aroused among the menfolk of his wife's family was counterbalanced by the profound affection for Nazrul shown by her mother and aunt.

In terms of political involvement and musical output, Nazrul's life can be divided into two phases—the first until 1930 when his four-year-old son Bulbul died, the second, in its aftermath. In the first phase he was intensely involved in politics, first with the Non-cooperation Movement, and then with the more left wing Labour Swarajya Party of Bengal. In the second phase a religious trend is visible, which drew both on Hindu and Islamic traditions, and such political songs as he composed were contemplative, melancholy and more influenced by classical *ragas* than the songs of the early 1920s. He was widely popular as the composer and singer of devotional songs to the goddess Kali, and of songs about Islam, the Muslim religious festivals, and Prophet Mohammed. A crippling neurological illness extinguished his creative output in 1942. He lived on till 1976—the governments of both West Bengal and East Pakistan (later Bangladesh) awarding him a pension in these declining years.

Nazrul's creative years spanned a complicated phase of the Bengali-speaking people's political history. The nineteenth century opened with mass movements associated with Non-cooperation and Khilafat and saw the ascendancy of C.R. Das in Bengal's nationalist politics. This period had also, unfortunately, been preceded by communal riots between Hindus and Muslims in Calcutta in September 1918. On this occasion, the actual pattern of conflict was between poorer sections of Calcutta's urban populace and the rich Marwari mercantile community, although religious idioms and symbols were used by both sides. Inter-community relations were not permanently embittered by this, but it was a warning.[27] The future was to show how far the leaders of the political elite and their second-rung cadres would heed the warning, as they settled down to confront the Raj in the years of dyarchy.

The efforts of C.R. Das in the early 1920s to regroup nationalists in the Swaraj Party after the failure of the Non-cooperation and Khilafat Movements are well known. There was no leader of his stature after his death. Factionalism became characteristic of Congress politics in Bengal. Protest movements among different sections of society—workers, the student community, the lower middle class which contained a sizeable number of ex-terrorists—could not be coordinated and given a steady anti-imperialist aim.[28] Among the Hindu *bhadralok* class there was a recrudescence of the Hindutva sentiments of the swadeshi period, a sentiment which found literary expression in the writings of Sarat Chandra Chattopadhyay.[29]

Music could and did play the role of a morale-boosting tonic in these difficult times. Until the 1930s the wireless did not come into vogue as a medium for disseminating songs, but in the 1920s the Gramophone Company of India had started producing records for the mass market. Since this was a British-owned monopoly (with the trade mark HMV), it was careful about recording songs which the government might consider seditious. In the 1920s, sixty-nine of Tagore's songs were recorded.[30] Of these the number of patriotic songs must have been a very small proportion; from a publication of the HMV we find that between 1910 and 1938 only eight out of the fifty-eight patriotic songs of Tagore were recorded.[31] Although Nazrul started working on an ad hoc basis for the Gramophone Company from 1929, and in 1935 was appointed their exclusive 'composer' on a regular basis, the company preferred to record his love songs and devotional songs. The great political songs for which he became famous in the 1920s were not recorded then, and one of his greatest choral songs 'Helmsman, beware' was recorded only two months before independence.[32] On the other hand, indigenous entrepreneurs like the Hindustan Record Company did release more patriotic songs of the swadeshi period, songs by Atul Prasad Sen, Rabindranath Tagore's '*Jana Gana Mana Adhinayaka*', Bankim Chattopadhyay's '*Vande Mataram*'. Some of these songs—though not all—were saturated with the Hindu imagery of the swadeshi period, resulting in a renewed churning of the Hindutva sentiments in a period when Bengal politics was bedevilled by communalism.

Many of these creative artists had not consciously aimed to treat Muslims as outside the national mainstream. The same writer, while writing one song would extol Indian pluralism, the concept of 'unity in diversity', but while writing another praising Bharatmata, would take the entire imagery from Hindu mythology. A record of Atul Prasad Sen, issued by the Hindustan Record Company in the 1930s, had on one side the hymn 'Utha go Bharat-Lakshmi' (Arise, India, who's like goddess Lakshmi) and on the other a didactic choral anthem for young people, one of the lines of which is:

Many languages, many faiths, many styles of dress. But see, amidst diversity a great unity. On seeing the awakening of a great nation in India the people of the world will be astonished . . .[33]

In the early 1920s, before the death of C.R. Das, and even for a couple of years after that, Nazrul Islam was very much in demand as a composer and singer for political movements of the nationalists, peasants and industrial workers. The popularity of the songs he composed can be gauged by the following. In February 1926 at the second session of the All Bengal Praja (*Ryots*) Conference in Krishna Nagar, Nadia he wrote a song for industrial workers. Its first stanza reads:

Orey dhangsha pather yatri dal
Dhar hathori, tol kandhey shabol
Amra hater sukhey gorechi Bhai
Payer sukhey bhangbo bal
Dhar hathori, tol kandhey, shabol.[34]

It travelled by word of mouth, and three years later, during the first general strike in Calcutta by the jute mill workers, the pickets were singing this song, recalled one participant in the strike.[35]

Nazrul's involvement in song-writing for the nationalist movement started with a song written for the Non-cooperation and Khilafat movement. In a period of Hindu–Muslim fraternisation, its simultaneous use of words like 'Vidhi' (which in Bengali is used to mean God as well as Law) and 'Khuda' in the first two lines is noteworthy. That humanism was the guiding principle of this nationalism (and not what different religious books stated) comes out in the last two stanzas where Gandhiji is put in the same tradition as Christ, Buddha, Mohammad, Krishna, and Rama:

* * *

Punthir Vidhan jak purey jak,
Vidhir vidhan satya hok
Khudar upar khudkari tor
Manbey ne ar sarbalok

* * *

Chinechhilen Khrista, Buddha
Krishna, Mohammad O Ram
Tai Manush jader korto ghrina
Tader bukey dilen sthan
Gandhi abar gan shey gan[36]

In the context of Hindu–Muslim relations, this song, written by a Muslim poet, had a special message for that stratum of the Bengali Muslim population which had moved away from the syncretic tradition to embrace the *Tariq-i-Muhammadi* movement. The very first line, with its disparaging reference to the laws in the holy books, and the general affirmation of humanism bear testimony to this. Later on, Nazrul had repeatedly to take a stand against the narrow-mindedness of the communal ideologies of both communities.

When C.R. Das was in prison in December 1921, at the personal request of his wife Basanti Devi, Nazrul wrote a song whose rapid tempo and frequent movement from low notes to high notes was in keeping with the theme of the song: that all prison doors will be broken open, in the same way that things come crashing down when Shiva dances his dance of destruction at the end of one *yuga* and the beginning of another.[37] The familiarity with which this young Muslim poet could use imagery from Hindu mythology was characteristic of him—no Hindu poet of Bengal in this period was equally at home in Islamic tradition. Hindu political detenus remained immersed in their Hindu nationalism—perhaps they sang the above-mentioned song with great gusto because it had a Hindu mythological allusion. Their hostile reaction to C.R. Das's statesmanlike political gesture of the Bengal Pact brought out the narrowness of their social and political horizons. Nazrul sensed that, and in a comic song portrayed the fragility of elite-level political 'pacts' as solutions of the communal problem. The sense of the first few stanzas is given below, which is followed by the profoundly tragic statement in the last stanza.[38]

The *shikha* (tuft of hair of the Hindu Pandit) is tied firmly to the beard (of the Maulvi)
Is the knot firm enough? Never mind.
As one pulls forward, the other pulls back
The pulling in opposite directions would make the knot firm

* * *

(Last stanza)

Sa-rara-rar shahasha uthilo adurey horir horra,
Shambhu chhutilo bamboo tuliya, chhoku mian nilo chhorra

* * *

Masjid paney chhutilen Mian, Mandir paney Hindu
Akashey uthilo chira-jiyaasa, karun chandra bindu

Which translates as

Suddenly, nearby, noises of Holi playing,
Shambhu ran with his stick,
Chhoku Mian brandished his dagger
The Mian ran to the Masjid, the Hindu ran to the temple
And like a sorrowful eternal question mark,
The crescent moon rose in the sky.

The answer to this question, in Nazrul Islam's mind, lay in the cross-communal solidarity of workers and peasants. The Labour Swaraj Party brought out a peasants and workers' magazine called *Langol* ('The Plough'). In December 1925 Nazrul wrote a sequence of poems called *Samyavadi*, on themes like equality, god, man, sin, woman, thieves and robbers, the prostitute, *raja* and *praja* (king and subject), *samya* (equality), coolie, *mazdoor* (worker). All of them attacked the conventional notions of right and wrong in a society with class differences and private property.[39] In the same spirit he wrote the opening songs for the labour conference the following February, which I have already referred to. He also wrote, for a peasants' conference held a little later, an opening song where he used imagery that would be understood by peasants of both communities. In one stanza he referred to Ram and Sita (the latter being symbolic of the plough which yields a harvest of corn, which Ravana, the imperialist predator, is snatching away). In the very next stanza, he wrote:

O brothers, we martyrs in the Mecca of the fields, we sacrifice our lives
And Satan robs the crop born of that blood.[40]

In the original Bengali he used the phrase 'Korbani dei jaan' (sacrifice our lives)—a Persianised style of Bengali, which he knew would be understood by the Muslim peasant audience.[41]

Such messages about the need for a united stand against imperialism on the issue of economic exploitation take time to percolate down to the consciousness of the masses. Hardly had this peasants' conference ended, when from April onwards, the political scene in Calcutta and the lower Hooghly basin was clouded by bitter communal riots and a backlash of Hindu *bhadralok* reaction. A historian has written about the Calcutta riots, which occurred in three phases between 2 April and 25 July, 'The scale of the disturbances was . . . unmatched in the history of Calcutta, or indeed of Bengal itself.'[42]

The intelligence reports of the government in May said that in the mofussil the situation was getting better: 'Excitement is chiefly attributed to outside influence, especially the Calcutta Press. The people are generally disposed to do their best to preserve peace.'[43] This corroborates the recollections of Nazrul's intimate friend, the communist leader Muzaffar Ahmad, who wrote,

In April Hindu–Muslim riots started in Calcutta. Nazrul was in regular touch with Calcutta (he was living then in Krishnanagar, three hours by train from Calcutta). He had never seen such a riot in his life. So this riot disturbed him so very much that it came out in his contemporary writings. . . . It was very fortunate that it did not spread to the villages or to any other town. He was still in the army, posted outside Bengal, when riots occurred in Calcutta in 1918.

Muzaffar Ahmad's recollection is wrong at this point, for riots did occur in Pabna Dacca (see n. 42).

But living in Calcutta we felt that the citizens of this place have become either ultra-Muslim or ultra-Hindu. The weekly and daily newspapers were spreading the poison of communalism every day.[44]

The Bengal Provisional Conference (that is, the annual meeting of the Bengal Provincial Congress Committee) was scheduled to take place in Krishnanagar at the end of May 1926 and, as usual, especially because he was locally available, Nazrul Islam was asked to compose and sing the opening song. Thus came about 'Helmsman, Beware': of its six stanzas of four lines each, preceded by a two-line opening stanza to be sung in chorus, I am quoting three, and providing a translation by Basudha Chakrabarty

Chorus

Durgama giri, kantar maru, dustara parabar
Langhitey hobey ratri nishithey, yatrira hoshiar
Asahay jati dubichhey moria, janey na santaran
Kandari, aji dekhibo tomar matri mukti pan
Hindu na ora Muslim? Oi jiggashey kon jan
Kandari, balo dubichhey manush, santan mor mar

* * *

Fansheer monchey geye gelo jara jeebaner jayagan
Ashi alakhye daraeychhe tara dibey kon balidan
Aji pariksha jatir othoba jaterey koribe tran
Dulitechhey tori, phulitechhey jal, kandari hoshiar

Chorus

Pilgrims, beware! You have to cross at dead of night,
Mountains hard to climb, dense wilderness and boundless, difficult seas!

* * *

The helpless nation is about to drown, knowing not how to swim
Captain! Now is the hour of test for your vow to free the Mother
Who is he that asks, 'What are they, Hindu or Muslim?'
Captain, say it's man who drowns—my Mother's offspring

* * *

Those who on the gallows' floor sang the song of triumph of life
Are here unseen and stand by
What sacrifice will you make unto them?

The test today is, whom you deliver—the Nation, or a Community?
The boat lurches, the ocean swells—Helmsman, beware![45]

The song remains a favourite in the repertoire of Bengali patriotic songs.[46] However, it fell on the deaf ears of the ex-revolutionaries who had come to the conference determined to annul the Bengal Pact. They made it impossible for the president, Birendra Nath Shashmal, who was uneasy about the cult of physical exercise and violence practised by these people, to conduct the meeting. The meeting took its fatal decision under the effete chairmanship of J.M. Sen Gupta.[47]

Bengal politics now started getting polarised more sharply along communal lines—a polarisation which was noticed throughout the next two decades, culminating in the partition of the state in August 1947. In the remaining part of this essay I shall highlight the efforts that were made, through the medium of music, to bridge the gap.

In August 1926, the renowned Bengali novelist Sarat Chandra Chattopadhyay wrote apropos of the communal problem,

Hindustan is the country of the Hindus, and so the responsibility of liberating it from bondage is for Hindus alone. The Muslims have turned their faces towards Turkey and Arabia—their minds are not focused on this country . . . . There is no need to worry about the number of Muslims in the population. In this world numbers do not indicate the ultimate truth. There is a greater truth which dismisses any calculation based on a head-count.'[48]

At the same time as this fifty-year-old popular writer wrote this offensive, anti-democratic piece, 27-year old Nazrul Islam published a song in the left wing newspaper *Ganavani*, whose words and tune blended beautifully with each other, and was deeply moving.[49] It runs as follows:

*Ek Brinte Duti Kusum**
'Two Flowers on the Same Stalk'

We are two flowers on the
same stalk—Hindus and Muslims
The Muslim is the apple of her
eyes, the Hindu is her soul.
The same sun and moon swing
in the lap of the same mother-sky.
The same blood flows beneath
the heart, the same is the
bond of affection for both:
We are two flowers on the
same stalk—Hindus and Muslims
We breathe the air, drink the
water of the same country.

The same flowers and fruits
blossom in the heart of the same mother
We get final rest in the soil
of the same country—some of
us in graves, others in the burning *ghat*.
We call the mother in the
same language, we sing to the same tune:
We are two flowers on the
same stalk—Hindus and Muslims.
In the darkness of night we
fail to recognise each other
and strike at each other,
When it is morning again, we
shall know each other as brothers,
Then we shall embrace each
other and shed tears.
We shall seek pardon of each other,
And then this our Hindustan
will smile out of pride:
we are two flowers on the
same stalk—Hindus and Muslims.

(Kazi Nazrul Islam, *The Rebel and Other Poems*, translated by Basudha Chakrabarty, Sahitya Akademi, New Delhi, 1874, pp. 97–8).

Sarat Chandra Chattopadhyay's remarks about the extra-Indian consciousness of the Muslim community was a reference to the effects of the Faraizi movement on Bengali Muslim consciousness, which has been referred to already. Nazrul Islam's song, quoted above, affirmed that the Bengali Muslims were rooted in the soil of Bengal. To wean the student community away from a futile nostalgia for the days of Mughal glory, in one of his songs, composed specially as the opening song for the Muslim literary conference in March 1928, he inserted certain stanzas, which are quoted below. This song, meant to be a marching song for youth, has been widely popular.[50]

March on, march!
The drum resounds in the sky above,
the earth below is all agog,
You the corps of youth of the scarlet dawn—
March on, march on!

We shall knock at the door of dawn
and usher in the bright red morning.
We shall put an end to the murky night
and to obstacles as big as the mountains.
We shall sing the song of the ever new
and shall liven up the cremation ground of thousands.
We shall impart new life and fresh strength in arms.

Above, thunder rolls out the command:
You soldiers pledged to martyrdom,
muster, march out in all directions
and open up the chamber of sleep!
Long ago you lost the royal status,
Yet the wanderer still longs for the past
and sings and sheds tears.
Let the throne of bygone empires be forgotten.

Awake, you insensible one!
Note how countries like Persia, Rome,
Greece, Russia and so many of them went under.
Yet they have all awakened again.
You weaklings, awake, arise!
We shall build a new Taj Mahal out of dust and soil!
March on, march on, march on!

(Basudha Chakravarty, pp. 92–3)

The Muslim literary conference was part of a progressive intellectual movement among a section of the Muslim intelligentsia in Dhaka University, called 'Buddhir Mukti' (emancipation of the intellect). It is in their journal *Shikha* that this song was first published.[51]

Unfortunately, the early 1930s during which the slow-moving machinery of the imperial administration eventually produced a constitution (the Act of 1935) for provincial autonomy, also saw communal riots in Dhaka and its neighbouring districts, and again in Calcutta. Against this background the secular approach of the 'Buddhir Mukti' group did not make much headway. Instead the political space came to be dominated by the Krishak-Praja Party of A.K. Fazlul Haq, which became the dominant party in the first two cabinets under provincial autonomy after 1937. The old songs of Nazrul about the peasantry were sung in the rallies of this party, and so were songs on purely

Islamic themes. The old taboo against music imposed by the *mullahs* had been broken, but music had emerged for the Muslim masses not in its old syncretic role, but in the role of a medium emphasising the community's separate identity.[53] The coming of provincial autonomy with separate electorates and a statutory majority for Muslims in the provincial legislature created a favourable background for the simultaneous affirmation of Bengali patriotism and the glorification of Bengal's last independent Nawab, Siraj-ud-daulah.[54]

Attempts to bridge the communal divide through music occurred as crisis-management exercises. In the context of riots in Dhaka in 1941, the government enlisted the services of Abbas-ud-din, whom it had appointed as 'recording expert to the Government of Bengal', in the Department of Information. Abbas-ud-din sang a duet on communal amity with Mrinal Kanti Ghosh which was recorded, with a statement by Nazrul Islam on the other side of the disc.[55] However, except for a song written for a play on the Bengal famine of 1943 (*Navanna*, by Bijon Bhattacharya) by the IPTA (Indian Progressive Theatre Association),[56] we do not see any evidence of songs which remind the people, in the spirit of Nazrul's 'Helmsman, beware', 'Who is it who asks, "What are they, Hindu or Muslim? Captain, say it is *man* who drowns—my mother's offspring".'

And they all drowned in the bloody twelve months from August 1946 to August 1947.

NOTES

1. There are a number of books in Bengali of political songs. A useful analytical survey, with good photographs, may be found in Geeta Chattopadhyay, *Swadeshi Gan* (Delhi, 1983).

2. On this theme, refer to the outstanding work by Asim Roy, *The Islamic Syncretistic Tradition in Bengal* (Princeton, 1983).

3. Md. Enamul Haq, *Manisha Manjusha*, vol. 1 (Dhaka, 1975), pp. 43–55; Sukumar Sen, *Islam Bangla Sahitya* (Burdwan, 1951), D.C. Sen, *Banga-Bhasha O Sahitya* (Calcutta, 8th edn, 1950), chs 6–9. Another important work is by Rabindranath Tagore's colleague in Visva-Bharati, Acharya Kshiti Mohan Sen; see his *Bharatey Hindu Musalmaner Yukta Sadhana* (Calcutta, 1950). Also see A. N. Chatterjee, *Sir Krishna Chaitanya: A Historical Study on Gaudiya Vaishnavism* (New Delhi, 1983), pp. 47–7, 82–3.

4. On baul songs, and their place in the context of the development of devotional *bhajans* and *kirtans*, see Kshiti Mohan Sen, *Vedottar Sangeet*, (Calcutta, 1984), pp. 156–66. The word 'Baul' is comparable to the Hindustani 'Baura' (as in 'Baiju Baura') and refers to groups of devout people who broke loose from the restrictive atmosphere of ritualised religion, and expressed their faith in devotional songs. Also see the same author's *Banglar Baul*, pp. 48ff. This was the 'Leela' lecture of Calcutta University, 1949 (reprint, 1993).

5. An English translation of these songs sung at the Hindu-Mela was published from Lahore. D. Gangopadhyay, *Indian National Songs and Lyrics* (Lahore, 1883).

6. Chattopadhyay, n. 1, p. 13.

7. Rafiuddin Ahmad, *The Bengal Muslims 1871–1906: A Quest for Identity* (New Delhi, 1981), ch. II.

8. Q. Ahmad, *Wahabi Movement in India* (Calcutta, 1966), pp. 88–95; Rashid al Faruqi, *Muslim Manas: Sanghat O Pratikriya* (Dhaka, 1989), p. 18.

9. Jasim-ud-Din, *Jibon Kotha* [Autobiography] (Dhaka, 1964), p. 142. The phrase 'insults and indignities' can be understood in the context of this quotation, where the author refers to an incident when the local *zamindar*, in whose house the puja ceremony was taking place, hit the Muslims with a stick to drive them out of the house, and no one protested.

10. Sumit Sarkar, *The Swadeshi Movement in Bengal* (New Delhi, 1973), pp. 289ff.

11. Ibid., pp. 462ff, 441.

12. Ibid., pp. 306–14.

13. Ibid., p. 313.

14. Jasim-Ud-Din, n. 9, p. 235.

15. Sarkar, n. 10, p. 295. The text of the song is at ibid., n. 163. Its music is available in a rendering by Sabitabrata Datta in an HMV cassette (No. HTCS 02B 2666 Stereo Side A No. 4).

16. On Mukunda Das, see Sarkar, *op.cit.*, pp. 301–3. Dr Chatterjee (n. 1) attributes the song to Das, but she is likely to be wrong, because the Gramophone Company describes the words and tune as 'traditional'.

17. Ahmed, n. 7, p. 179; also see ch. IV, *passim*.

18. Abul Mansoor Ahmad, *Amar Dekha Rajnitir Ponchash Bachhor* (Dhaka, 1975), pp. 29–30.

19. J.H. Broomfield, *Elite Conflict in a Plural Society: Twentieth Century Bengal* (Bombay, 1968), pp. 113–22.

20. The song by Tagore is song No. 20 in his *Geeta-bitan*, vol. 1. The Khilafat song about Turkey is taken from Chattopadhyay, n. 1, p. 257.

21. An analysis of the biases of Roy's song is to be found in my 'Music and Political Consciousness (regional, pan-Indian and communal): A Critical Study of D.L. Roy and Nazrul Islam' (Nehru Memorial Museum and Library, Occasional Papers in History and Society, Second Series, XV), pp. 10–13.

22. The English version (by Dilip Kumar Roy) of these lines:

> O my Bengal! O my mother!
> O my nursery, nurse and home!
> Why dishevelled are thy locks
> and dim thine eyes with tears of gloom
>
> ***
>
> There is no sorrow and there's no shame
> no coward truce with tyrant fate,
> when seventy million voices
> sing thy name inviolate.

N.B. Seventy million refers to the population of Bengal.

23. Taken from Chattopadhyay, n. 1, p. 256. There is no sorrow, no want,/ No shame, no fear/When four hundred million brethren/Chant the victory of religion./May Islam be forever independent,/All Muslims and all of mankind,/There is no sorrow, no want, no shame, no fear.

24. When the song was published in his song book entitled *Visher Banshi*, under the title it was mentioned that the tune should be the same as that of D.L. Roy's above-mentioned song. The book *Visher Banshi* was, incidentally, banned by the government. The text of the song is republished in Abdul Kader, (ed.), *Nazrul Rachanabali* (Dhaka, 1967), vol. I, p. 73.

25. This paragraph on his life is a shorter version of my occasional paper, cited in note 21 above, pp. 40–1. In English a short life is available in Gopal Haldar, *Kazi Nazrul Islam* (New Delhi, 1973). Also see Buddhadeva Bose, *An Acre of Green Grass* (Calcutta, 1946), ch. 4. A picture of his boyhood and adolescence is given in the account by a friend, the novelist Shailajanand Mukhopadhyay, *Keu bhole, Keu na bhole*. Another reliable source is in the communist leader Muzaffar Ahmad's *Kazi Nazrul Islam: Smritikatha* (Dhaka, 1987).

26. During this prison sentence, when along with other detenus, he went on a hunger strike in protest against ill-treatment by the prison authorities, Rabindranath Tagore sent him a telegram 'Give up hunger strike, our literature claims you'. Tagore also dedicated his latest collection of songs (*Vasant*) to him, making his fellow prisoners envious, and the jail authorities astonished.

27. Suranjan Das, *Communal Riots in Bengal, 1905–1947* (Delhi, 1991), pp. 58–74.

28. Tanika Sarkar, *Bengal, 1928–34: The Politics of Protest* (Delhi, 1987), pp. 11–75.

29. Rajat Ray, *Social Unrest and Political Conflict in Bengal* (Delhi, 1984), p. 361.

30. Information supplied by the HMV Company in Calcutta in June 1988.

31. HMV, *Sharada-Arghya* (Calcutta, 1988) esp. pp. 11, 18, 60.

32. Issued in April 1947, HMV (No. N. 27666), sung by Satya Choudhury. I knew the text as a powerful poem, but heard it as a song on 15 August 1947 when this was being played over the public address system in the streets of Calcutta. For further details on the significance of this song, see below.

33. '*Nana bhasha, nana math*'. The record was in my father's collection in my childhood (1930s).

34. The text of the whole song, along with the musical notations, is in Nazrul Islam, *Sangeetanjali*, Part II (ed., Nitai Chatak, Calcutta, 1970), p. 12. The stanza quoted means:

    Oh trekkers on the road towards destruction
    Hold fast the hammer, lift the spade to your shoulder.
    We have built happily with our hands,
    We shall gladly kick them with our feet to break
    Hold fast the hammer, lift the spade to your shoulders.'

35. T. Sarkar, n. 28. Sarkar has not mentioned that the song was one of Nazrul's compositions, probably because her source did not say so.

36. A translation of these stanzas is given here (my translation)

    Let the laws of the Holy Books be burnt
    Let the truth of God prevail
    Your claim to interpret the word of God
    Will no longer be accepted by people
    ***
    Christ, Buddha, Krishna, Mohammad and Ram
    All knew the worth of humanity
    So those who were despised by other men
    Found a place in their arms.
    And again Gandhi is singing the same song.

37. '*Kabar eyi loha kapat*'. A cassette with this song is available in '*Swadeshi Yuger Gan*' (HMV Cassette No. STHVS 24029).

38. There is, unfortunately, no recording available, nor have I been able to

locate its musical notations. However, in Nazrul's *Selected Poems: Sanchita*, (Calcutta, 8th edn, 1952, p. 257) it is listed as a song. Other Nazrul specialists refer to it as a song; it reads well as a poem too. The song was written in 1923, just after the Swaraj Party's conference in Sirajganj, Pabna, where the pact was announced.

39. The *Samyavadi* sequence of poems is available in English in the proceedings of the Meerut Conspiracy Case, 1929, among 'English translations of Bengali exhibits'.

40. '*Uthorey chashi jagat bashi*'. This is taken from Kazi Nazrul Islam, *The Rebel and Other Poems*, translated by Basudha Chakravarty (New Delhi, 1974), pp. 63–4.

41. Like the Hindi–Urdu controversy in Uttar Pradesh, the use of words of Arabo-Persian origin had political overtones in Bengal. On this, see my Occasional Paper, n. 21, pp. 34–9.

42. Das, n. 27, pp. 75–6 for fuller details on the background and course of the riots in Calcutta, and its repercussions in Pabna and Dacca in East Bengal.

43. Home-Poll, 1926, file 112/IV (NAI).

44. Muzaffar Ahmad, *Kazi Nazrul Islam: Smriti-Katha* (Dhaka, 1987), pp. 293–4 (my translation).

45. Basudha Chakrabarty, (no. 40), pp. 65–6.

46. A number of recordings exist, HMV cassette Nos. HTC 02B 2533 and SPHOS 23026. It was first issued by HMV in a 78 rpm record (N27666).

47. Muzaffar Ahmad, n. 44, pp. 299–300.

48. Sarat C. Chattopadhyay, *Sarat Rachanabali* (Centenary edn, vol. III). (Calcutta, 1981), p. 475.

49. No commercial recording exists. The West Bengal government has popularised this song. The musical score is in Kazi Aniruddha Islam, *Sunirvachita Nazrul Swaralipi* (Calcutta, 1975), Part I, p. 4.

50. HMV cassette No. SPHOS 23026.

51. On this movement, see Kazi Abdul Wodood, *Shashwata Banga* (Calcutta, 1951), preface.

52. Das, n. 27, ch. IV, *passim*.

53. Abbas-ud-din Ahmad, *Amar Shilpi Jeebaner Katha* (Dhaka, 3rd edn, 1991), pp. 62–9.

54. Ibid., pp. 69f.

55. Ibid., p. 84.

56. The song by a Muslim Fakir at the end of Scene II, Act. IV in B. Bhattacharya, *Navanna* (Calcutta, 1944).

RADIO AND THE RAJ*

T he beginnings of broadcasting in Britain and India were almost contemporaneous, but while in Britain progress was relatively smooth, in India the advent of this new medium, and its reception by the government and the public had a chequered history. There is a problem here to be explained because monopolistic control of information strengthens the authority of those in power, and one would expect a colonial state to make the most of this device. In the 1920s the Indian scene was characterised by social unrest and political agitation. Europe showed that the broadcasting medium could be used by Fascist Italy to manufacture an illusion of political consensus and by the Soviet Union to broadcast revolutionary messages through the length and breadth of the former Tsarist empire. In Britain itself radio came to the aid of the ruling circles during the nine-day General Strike in May 1926.[1]

*S.G. Deuskar Lectures on Indian History and Culture delivered at the Centre for Studies in Social Sciences, Calcutta, in 1993, and published in 1995.

I am grateful to the following for permission to consult original sources in their possession, and to publish extracts from those in which they hold the copyright. The BBC Written Archives Centre, at Caversham, Reading, UK for extracts from memoranda and letters written by members of the BBC staff, from the letters of Sir John Reith, letters written to him by Lionel Fielden, and from the diary of Sir John Reith; for providing photocopies of reports on the defunct Indian Broadcasting Company sent to Reith by Eric Dunstan; the Archives of the House of Lords Record Office, Westminster, London for extracts from the letters written to Viscount Samuel; Public Record Office, London for Crown copyright records from the prime minister's private office and extracts quoted with permission of Her Majesty's Stationery Office; India Office Records and Library, British Library London for extracts from Crown copyright records of the India Office, with permission of Her Majesty's Stationery Office; and Tamil Nadu State Archives, Madras for extracts from the records of the Madras government.

In India, however, the key decision-makers on media policy did not show the same concern for developing broadcasting as had been shown in Britain between 1920 and 1926. In Britain, in 1920, several radio companies were licensed to make experimental transmissions, with the Marconi company becoming the pace-setter in making innovation. In October 1922 Marconi, Metropolitan-Vickers, General Electric Company and three others formed a consortium called the British Broadcasting Company, and by the beginning of the following year it was functioning, under licence from the post master general,[2] with an energetic young man called John Reith as its general manager.

The extraordinary personality of Reith enabled him to get together a band of radio enthusiasts, make such successful experiments both on the technical side and on programme development that by the end of 1924 more than one million receiving licences had been issued. The staff increased from a nucleus of only four people on 31 December 1922 to 465 exactly two years later. When the company faced financial problems two years later, Reith took the initiative in influencing the government to set up a committee (the Crawford Committee) on how to solve them. The committee reported in favour of converting the organisation from a private company into a public corporation established by Royal Charter. At the end of 1926 the old company was dissolved, the shareholders repaid at par, and the British Broadcasting Corporation (BBC) started functioning on 1 January 1927, with the recently knighted Sir John Reith as its director-general. He had a staff of 773 and a clientele of 2.5 million licensees.[3]

By contrast, in India, although a private company was registered in September 1926, and began broadcasting from Bombay in August 1927, the government's interest in and support to the media was far behind the alacrity shown in Britain. The private company had extended its operations to Calcutta but faced serious financial problems and had to go into liquidation. After prolonged discussion and hesitation the government took over the assets of the old company and, almost nine years after the BBC started functioning as a public corporation, started All India Radio (AIR) with Lionel Fielden, a person seconded from the BBC, taking charge in August 1935. This was under the constitution and political structure of the Government of India Act (1935), quite different from the imperial control available to the Raj under the Montford

Reforms. The AIR was denied the status of a corporation but remained a department of the central government. On his Indian experience Fielden commented, twenty years after leaving India in 1940:

Four years of hard labour had produced 14 transmitters and a competent staff and in four years the 400 million people of India had bought exactly 85,000 wireless sets. It was the biggest flop of all time.[4]

The actual number of licences at the end of 1932 had been 8557, which had risen to 92,782 at the end of 1939.[5] So Fielden's figures were not wide off the mark. His sense of disappointment in failing to create an institution analogous to the BBC was genuine, and its causes lay buried in the hesitant start of this medium in the 1920s. It is this background to which I will devote this essay.

Although there were enthusiasts for the radio among the ruling elite in India, there were a fair number of sceptics. Specific personality factors also affected its development in the early years. Wireless as a technique for communication had been used by different government departments—civil and military—for over two decades (with the Marconi Radio Telegraph Company being a principal supplier of technology).[6] However, the problem arose about its specific application and dissemination of the spoken word. Birkenhead, as secretary of state, got interested in the development of radio, especially after its usefulness to the government was proved during the General Strike,[7] but the despatch on broadcasting which he had asked for in July 1926 was sent to him only on 28 April 1927. While Viceroy Lord Irwin was agreed on 'its potential value' and offered to keep his mind open 'to all such instruments of communication and publicity'[8] the matter was left to be dealt with by officials, and there is no evidence of the viceroy taking any personal interest in the matter, not even commenting, in his private correspondence, that he had inaugurated the Bombay and Calcutta stations of the Indian Broadcasting Company.

There was a specific reason for the slow progress in the development of radio during the tenure of Irwin's predecessor, Lord Reading, who was viceroy from 1921 to 1925. Ten years before, when the latter (as Rufus Isaacs, Bar-at-Law) had been Lord Chancellor in Asquith's Liberal cabinet, he had unwittingly got involved in a scandal about pushing the shares of the Marconi Radio Telegraph Company, of which his younger brother Godfrey Isaacs was joint director. It had caused him great strain, and his biographer writes, 'He never referred to it again. He seemed determined to blot out of his memory so harrowing an ordeal.'[9]

During Reading's viceroyalty therefore, no official initiative was taken to sponsor broadcasting under government auspices, but private enterprise was given its head. An enterprising pair of Parsee entrepreneurs—R.M. Chinoy and Sultan Chinoy—floated a company in 1923 called the Indian Radio Telegraph Company; they secured, for use in India, the technology of the Marconi Company, and started constructing transmitters at Poona in 1925.[10] An oblique reference to the Marconi scandal was made by Commerce Member Sir A.C. Chatterjee on the file that dealt with the application of Chinoy, when he insisted that there should be a six-month period for calling of tenders and that the successful company should provide training to Indians in this new technique.[11] The company was formally registered on 25 July 1924.[12]

During Reading's viceroyalty hardly any more active interest was shown by the government in the development of this medium. The BBC's manager John Reith approached the India Office with offers of help, but was told to write to the Government of India directly.[13] Reith's letter to the India Office had advocated the advantages of centralised broadcasting in India, following the pattern that was developing in Britain.

The erection of broadcasting stations would provide a connecting link between all parts of the Indian empire, bringing even the most outlying districts into close touch with the principal cities.[14]

Coincidentally, about the same time as Reith was lobbying the India Office, R.W. Nicholson, director of wireless, Government of India, put up a memorandum for department discussion on what government policy should be if and when broadcasting developed under private enterprise. The upshot of this discussion was a letter to the provincial governments embodying the central government's provisional conclusion. It clearly opposed centralised control and government ownership. The operative sentences were:

It might be possible perhaps for Government themselves . . . to retain the monopoly of providing broadcasting services in India. . . . But any such solution is undesirable and . . . it is clearly best that the development of broadcasting services in the country should be entrusted to private enterprise under suitable regulation and control.[15]

It delegated the power to grant licences to set up broadcasting stations—'only one licensee for each specified area'—to the provincial governments. In that context it commented:

The government of India have considered an alternative proposal that only one company should be licensed for the whole of India, with a monopoly of establishing stations in any area desired. Such a solution . . . would follow the practice in the United Kingdom. The Government of India, however, are provisionally of the opinion that in such a vast country as India, and in the existing state of development of the science and practice of broadcasting in this country the grant of such an extensive monopoly would be unnecessary and unduly restrictive.[16]

Many other points were made in this letter, until the question was re-opened in July 1926 and discussed at length by officials for a year and a half, following the inquiry from Birkenhead mentioned earlier.

Four important issues recur again and again in these discussions. It is useful at this stage to elucidate the divergent imperial perceptions under these four heads. First, there was a reluctance to invest public funds in what was as yet an untried commercial venture, a reluctance reinforced by a somewhat doctrinaire objection to the creation of a public sector in pioneering industries. Such objections were frequently voiced by finance members like Sir Basil Blackett and Commerce Member Charles Innes.[17] The post-war policy of reducing government expenditure—which the Retrenchment Committee was symptomatic of—pervaded most decision-making on policies. Second, under the reformed constitution, with the provinces enjoying partial autonomy under the system of dyarchy, and the constitution due for review in 1929, the future relationship of the central government and the provincial governments within the imperial system was not clear to the Governor-General in Council. Those who wished to retain for an indefinite future the overarching control of the Raj over Indian affairs found themselves in a dilemma under the new constitution. Central control in many departments of state would strengthen imperial ties, but already an institution like the central legislative assembly was proving to be a forum for focusing anti-imperial sentiments. On the other hand, while some form of limited provincial autonomy would divert political energies towards local and parochial issues, there was no guarantee that pockets of 'sedition' would not emerge in the provincial context. This dilemma became even more acute in the eight years after the Simon Commission was instituted in 1927, especially after the commission recommended full provincial autonomy but not transfer of responsibility at the centre.[18] A small minority of Liberal imperialists welcomed the growth of a pan-Indian national consciousness, hoping it would not become hostile to the maintenance of the British connection.[19] The majority of the official hierarchy, however, had sensed the strong nationalist sentiment dominating the Congress after the advent of Gandhi, and were placing their hopes on provincialising political aspirations in India. It was in keeping with this approach that broadcasting policy was Left to provincial discretion. In the early 1920s radio-minded European expatriates had set up local radio clubs and district officers concerned with rural development like F.L. Brayne of Punjab were using the new medium in Gurgaon district.[20]

This brings me to the third point. The utility of broadcasting as a supplementary aid to the departments of education, health and land was recognised, provided receiving sets or public address systems could be arranged in the rural districts. The early years of broadcasting under private enterprise had an urban bias, which was unavoidable because the owners of radio sets were townspeople, but this made many officials look askance at this medium and made them worry about its potential as a politically subversive factor.

Political information was the fourth issue which worried the official hierarchy. Throughout the discussion on broadcasting the question of censorship cast its shadow over the development of broadcasting. In the initial stages the Raj was not so paranoiac about political discussions as it later showed itself to be. In the letter sent out to the provinces on 19 March 1924, referred to earlier, it stated:

It would be. . . . undesirable to prohibit the broadcasting of political matter, such as speeches by leading politicians, which may, indeed, be of great educative value and the banning of political matter broadcast by others would reduce the value of political and propaganda matter broadcast by Government. . . . At the same time there is obviously some danger of the use of broadcasting for

the propagation of matter which is either of a seditious character, or which
otherwise offends against the law.[21]

The Indian Radio Telegraph Company—in which the Marconi
Company held two-thirds of the issued capital—was instrumental in
promoting a new company called the Indian Broadcasting Company
(registered on 1 July 1926) with an authorised capital of Rs 15 lakh.
Shares worth Rs 6 lakh were issued by the middle of 1927, of which
a major Indian shareholder was Raja Saheb Dhanrajgirji Narsingirji,
whose holdings were almost the same as those of the Radio Telegraph
Company.[22] The Chinoy brothers—as the sole agents of Marconi's
technology—were the moving spirit behind floating the new company,
but they had empanelled on their board of directors some distinguished
businessmen of Bombay.[23] They secured the services of a former
employee of the BBC, Eric Dunstan, who arrived in India at the very
end of December 1926, just when the BBC was being converted into
a public corporation.[24]

Under its terms of agreement with the Government of India—
which were concluded on 13 September 1926—the company undertook
to be and remain a genuine Indian company, install and work within
nine months, efficient broadcasting stations at Bombay and Calcutta,
expand the service, if commercially practicable, and allow any bona
fide importer of wireless apparatus to be a member of the company.
In return, the government gave it a five-year monopoly and promised
to pay it 80 per cent of all licence fees received on account of wireless
stations in British India (excluding Burma) from the date the broadcasting
service was started.[25]

From January 1927 till March 1928 the development of broadcasting
can be traced at two levels. At one level, we observe the birth-pangs of
a new company and the fortunes of its stations in Bombay and Calcutta,
with the BBC advising Eric Dunstan to try and transform the Indian
organisation into a public corporation on the BBC model. At another
level we notice sharply divided opinions in the higher levels of officialdom
about the usefulness of the medium and the advisability of financial support
from the government.

Although the company had been registered at the beginning of July
1926, and Dunstan had been given to understand that the sites for the
transmitters in Bombay and Calcutta had been acquired with all legal

formalities completed, he found on his arrival that this was not so. Only by the middle of March 1927 was he able to report a breakthrough in this area, but warned about the slow-moving wheels of both business and government. His own director, deputed to settle problems involving the firm and any public authority, could spare only a few hours each week to attend to this problem.[26] Another problem, which became acute by September 1927, was finance. Even before that, he was commenting that the company was undercapitalised. As he put it,

£42,000 was a dangerously small sum to start on especially when the estimates—to which I suppose one must always add 25 per cent—show a capital expenditure of £21,000 and running expenses at the rate of nearly £28,000 a year for the two stations. No provision was apparently taken into consideration of the running expenses of those months which must precede actual broadcasting, or for such heavy items as staff passages to India.

On the revenue account Dunstan noted that till they were 'actually "on the air" firms had hung back with their orders for wireless sets', but he was optimistic about a steady income from the 10 per cent royalty on all wireless apparatus imported into India which the government had permitted it to receive.[27] The target date for starting the service in Bombay was the month of August, because the towers 'were only shipped from England on the 2nd of April', and the prospective date for constructing the plant was the beginning of June.[28]

During this gestation period of the company the government records show scepticism, and a tendency to dampen the enthusiasm of P.J. Edmunds, director of wireless. A terse comment by Sir Bhupendra Nath Mitra, (member of the Viceroy's Council) on the memorandum prepared by Edmunds and his superiors for despatch to Birkenhead illustrates this:

I am, however, afraid that it will be years before there is any material development of broadcasting among the masses in India.[29]

Edmunds had suggested that if India wanted to make broadcasting as well developed as in Britain the government should 'take a much more active part'. This was shot down by his superior, who described it as the 'personal opinion' of the director of wireless. He also postponed drawing the attention of provincial governments to the ways in which broadcasting could be popularised in the villages and schools until the newly established company actually went on the air.[30] Edmunds persisted in his efforts to persuade the government to take a more active interest: 'The part played by wireless in England during the recent strike has established the importance of broadcasting.'[31] He repeated the same point a month later when the draft despatch to Birkenhead was circulating among members of the council. At this point his enthusiasm and his wish that the central government should give a lead to the provinces about how to make broadcasting popular received a cold douche from the home department. Home Member Sir Harry Haig noted, 'So much stress is laid on the advantages to government from the spread of broadcasting that the undoubted dangers and the necessity for a very careful guidance of the movement receive perhaps hardly sufficient prominence.'[32]

From now on, this note set the tone for all official discussions till an interdepartmental meeting took place the following August. The only concession that the nascent broadcasting business received was a reduction of the customs duty on wireless apparatus to 2.5 per cent.[33] The utility of broadcasting as a means of spreading education and as an aid to propagating the government point of view among the rural population was mentioned in the despatch to Birkenhead, but the thrust of the letter was to stress the heavy expenditure involved in developing wireless stations and towards the end to repeat Harry Haig's point:

. . . the spread of broadcasting carries also dangerous possibilities, and it will be necessary to guard against its possible misuse for propaganda inimical to government interests and the spread of misleading or unreliable information.[34]

Censorship—especially the censorship of political information or opinion—figured a lot in the official discussion. Both the purpose and agent of censorship was the matter of dispute. Those who did not like the growth of pan-Indian nationalism reacted peevishly when an advocate of broadcasting, Professor John Coatman (director of public information) praised it 'as one of the strongest of all the agencies working to create a feeling of common interest and common nationality among the different peoples of this country'.[35] Other officials side-stepped this point and preferred to discuss what should be censored and by whom. It was finally decided—at the insistence of Haig and McWatters—that all news broadcasts should be based on agency reports of the Associated

Press (in whom the government had faith), that nothing would be permitted which offended against public morals or was seditious or would arouse racial, religious or communal animosity. On political matters the liberalism of the letter of 19 May 1924 was still retained:

It is necessary to see that there is no undue bias in favour of any particular point of view, and that the government gets its due share of publicity. The object should be to keep the balance even.

Each provincial government was to select a censoring officer, who was expected to work in close cooperation with the company.[36] The needs of imperial control were ensured by McWatters insisting that the centre 'must keep the general control of any wireless censorship . . .' and that, under central guidelines the power of the provincial governments 'must clearly be a delegated power'.[37]

All these policy discussions had been prompted by the Indian Broadcasting Company informing the central government on 25 April 1927 that they would like the viceroy to inaugurate the Bombay station in late August.[38] Cautionary rather than constructive policy characterised the interdepartmental committee which met on 8 August. Inconclusive discussions took place on how to develop educational broadcasting in the rural areas or its extension to *pardanashin* women 'by means of wires joined to the public broadcast receivers'. These questions were referred to the provincial governments, who were also expected to find the money for these purposes: 'No share of the cost of the broadcast transmitters should be borne by the Government of India.' An equally cavalier attitude was displayed to all local voluntary efforts to develop socially useful broadcasting services (F.L. Brayne's plans in Gurgaon district, plans of the Madras Corporation). These were discouraged 'as they would interfere with the general scheme'. What the committee was categorical about was the exclusion of political information. Sir Denys Bray, of the foreign and political department, swung the committee to 'prohibit entirely all political matters of a controversial character' and to propose, 'that with the exception of the Viceroy and of the Governors of provinces no one should be allowed to deliver a speech by means of the broadcasting service'.[39]

Although Edmunds in one of his memoranda had stated that 'to prohibit all political discussion [would] undoubtedly detract very considerably from the value and popularity of broadcasting',[40] he was probably too junior in the official hierarchy to protest effectively against Sir Denys Bray's approach.[41]

The company found, within a month of starting the Bombay station, that its financial position was not very satisfactory. It is best stated in the words of Dunstan, who wrote a detailed letter to Reith:

Briefly, our expenditure on the two stations is at the rate of Rs 35,000 a month and our income is at the moment negligible and in the future difficult to estimate. . . . I sincerely hope we shall realise a definite error has been made in trying to start on so small a capital and correct that error by a further issue on which we can carry on with great care and economy until we reach a position of profit making. To cut down our programmes at this stage would, in my opinion, be absolutely fatal and only delay our demise which is inevitable if we do not act quickly. . . . Neither our capital cost nor our running expenses appreciably exceed the original estimates but, as I have already said, certain items were not considered. I don't believe we shall have any difficulty in getting the money, there is already a demand for our shares and the I.R.T. Co. [Indian Radio Telegraph Company] have been selling at par.[42]

The question of government assistance naturally came up for consideration. Earlier in the year, when the despatch to Birkenhead was taking shape, the eventual control of the media by the government was suggested as a possibility at some future date.[43] At that time Dunstan's reaction was unfavourable because, as he put it to Reith, '. . . Government institutions are suspect and broadcasting as a Government concern will never attain that penetration which it might under private direction'.[44]

At the end of September, under different circumstances he was less indifferent to the idea of government involvement. The directors of his company were hoping that the government would pick up a substantial part of a fresh capital issue.[45] This was similar to an idea that Edmunds had earlier put to the interdepartmental committee, suggesting that the government should purchase 50 per cent of the shares in the company; broadcasting would have become, to use present-day jargon, a 'joint sector'. The committee had noted the suggestion but, characteristically, taken no decision.[46]

The company was to be disappointed. Early in the new year Dunstan reported,

Our appeal for some financial assistance in these early lean days after three months of havering has been turned down in these words, 'it is against the policy of the Government of India to give any financial assistance whatever to the Indian Broadcasting Company'.[47]

The other difficulties that the company was facing—where vigilance on the part of the government would have helped it—was the slack administration of the collection of licence fees and, more important, the collection of the 10 per cent royalty on all imported wireless apparatus.[48]

In 1928, as Sir John Reith received these reports about the problems of broadcasting in India, he tried two lines of approach to solve them. One was to make the British radio industry interested in the Indian market. The other was to try and create a public corporation in India for broadcasting on the BBC model, with a distinguished non-official Indian as its chairman. Both approaches failed, but they are worth mentioning and reflecting upon.

Reith wrote a series of letters to a large number of British companies asking them to take up shares in the Indian company. The companies approached were Standard Telephone Cables, Metro-Vickers Electricals, Mullard Radio Valve Company, Chloride Electrical Storage Company, and British Thompson Houston Company.[49] The last-named replied that in a matter of imperial importance the government should take the initiative, not a 'mere manufacturing company' like them.[50] Sir Hugo Hirst, a leading manufacturer and a prominent figure in the Federation of British Industries, could not advise his company on commercial reasons to put up capital, but if all the other manufacturers were willing, would contribute 'from a national and patriotic point of view.'[51] Chloride Electricals wrote saying that though it was outside their area, they would have been willing to contribute if it had been combined with an energetic and successful campaign for radio equipment, but their inquiries had shown that India at that time did not provide suitable prospects for radio development.[52]

This reaction on the part of British manufacturers is puzzling at first sight, for one would expect that, with the British home market depressed because of the deflationary policy pursued by the Treasury, the 'new' industries which were going to replace the old staples like Lancashire cotton textiles would look for markets in the empire. However, the businessmen needed a reasonable degree of certainty, and the atmosphere in India in 1928 was anti-British, with the agitation against the Simon Commission in full swing.

The attempt to create a public corporation in India on the BBC model did not get off the ground, and remained a blueprint within the BBC archives. On the basis of the information received from Dunstan by mid-February, the senior officials of the corporation thought that the Indian company was failing because its programmes were 'European type' (which would elicit, at the utmost, 35,000 licence holders), and what was needed was a public corporation, which would oversee programmes aimed at the indigenous population. This board was to have:

four elements: (1) nationally respected Indians representing all the chief religions, parties and geographical areas; (2) if inevitably a government representative, preferably a senior high-grade Indian; (3) a high-class business man with accountant's training from England as business manager; (4) the remainder of the board representative of the radio interests.[53]

The other details in this blueprint are of no great significance, except a remark which showed that the BBC had realised the degree of alienation of the Indian people from the government: 'If the government handles broadcasting direct, the native population will largely boycott it . . .'[54]

The BBC plans were stillborn, while in India the company survived on a shoestring budget for another year, after which it folded up. Public pressure made the provincial governments of Bengal and Bombay take over the radio stations and run a skeleton service. In 1930, when the Civil Disobedience Movement was in full swing the central government had an Indian sympathetic to the question of broadcasting in the person of Sir Joseph Bhore, as member in charge of industry and labour, who promised that the Calcutta and Bombay stations would be under their local station directors and have a local advisory committee to guide them.[55]

Nevertheless, the immediate future of broadcasting in India was very bleak, especially in the context of the world economic crisis, and the deflationary policy followed by the finance department of the Government of India. The Federation of British Industries heard alarmist rumours that the Bombay and Calcutta radio stations might be sold to foreign (probably American) concerns; it lobbied the India Office in the winter of 1931–2 and was told that because of representations from many quarters the Government of India was reconsidering the matter and might drop the idea. There was still hope for the radio stations.[56]

II

Various factors contributed to the revival of an interest in broadcasting in government circles in the early 1930s, otherwise even the 'lame duck' stations of Bombay and Calcutta would have closed down under the retrenchment policy pursued after the economic crisis of 1931.[57] Marching orders were given to the respective station directors of Bombay and Calcutta on 12 October 1931 with the suggestion that the assets of these places 'be sold outright for what they would fetch'.[58]

Dealers of broadcasting equipment in Bombay and Calcutta argued for the decision to be reconsidered, substantiating that the government was getting 'a considerably greater resource from Broadcasting in the shape of customs revenue and otherwise'.[59] The government increased the customs duty on imported broadcasting equipment in the next budget with the intention of reversing the earlier decision, so that it could be argued that the general taxpayer was not being burdened with the costs of a service catering only to the urban listeners of two metropolitan cities.[60]

So much for the first-aid being given to the patient. There were other developments which made the government realise that it could not afford to abandon a potent weapon which would otherwise be used by its opponents, both inside and outside the country.

During the continued civil disobedience in August 1932 the station director of the Bombay station reported that on three days he heard an unidentified station on about 400 metres broadcasting Congress propaganda in English, Marathi and Hindi, urging the boycott of British goods and Britishers.[61]

The other threat to the empire was Radio Moscow. The Intelligence Bureau reported on 16 March 1932 that though its English language broadcasts were mainly 'for European consumption' describing conditions in Russia in the most favourable light, radio amateurs in India were picking them up and responding to the general invitation from Radio Moscow to write to them about the broadcasts. Williamson, the Director of the Director of the Intelligence Bureau (DIB), commented a year later:

The only danger to India from Russian broadcasting lies in the fact that communists in the USSR find by this means an opportunity of establishing direct contact with Indians in India. As to the future we shall have to watch for the establishment of the proposed station near Novo Sibirisk, especially if the Moscow and Leningrad universities for Eastern Studies turn out men capable of broadcasting in Indian dialects.[62]

Finally, the standing committee of the central legislative assembly recommended that the Indian State Broadcasting Service, as it was now called, should not be wound up.

Lord Lothian, visiting India as a member of the Franchise Committee in 1932, made inquiries from Marconi's representative about the technical feasibility of a hand-operated generator that could activate a wireless receiving set. He was in touch with Sir John Reith, and reawakened interest within the BBC about broadcasting possibilities in India.[63] The BBC's loss of interest in India since the liquidation of the old company ws reflected in its official organ *World Radio*, where a diagram of countries with wireless connections did not mention India at all—the DIB found this 'insulting to India'.[64]

In London, in October 1933, the lobbying was continued among opinion-formers on India (the East India Association) by C.F. Strickland, an ex-Punjab official with experience of work in the cooperative movement, on the following lines. Speaking on the theme 'Broadcasting in the Indian village', he stressed the importance of enlightening an untried class of rural voters who will have responsibility thrown on them under the proposed constitution (enacted later in 1935); he praised Lord Lothian's efforts, and said,

the most closely comparable example is that of Soviet Russia . . . geographically, economically, and culturally India bears a resemblance in many respects to Soviet Russia. The Indian area is vast, the standard of living low, illiteracy widespread, and the culture of the rural population takes the form of folklore, religious story, and familiar songs. . . . The influence of the juvenile schools is slow to be felt, and the diligent preaching of reformers, official or unofficial, is still too seldom heard in each village, to produce a widespread or permanent effect.

Strickland went on to examine the financial aspects of the subject, emphasising the feasibility of his ideas. He concluded with a preference for a separate transmitter for the rural programme on a wavelength different from the urban.[65]

Strickland's paper was circulated both in Britain and in Delhi (it was filed in the Home-Political series). The cumulative effect of these pressures made the Indian government ask the imperial authorities in February 1934 for approval of a proposal to reactivate the Indian State Broadcasting Service which would involve the erection of a transmitting centre at Delhi, whose aim would be to reach the large Urdu- and Hindustani-speaking areas around it, possibly to cover the area from Lahore to Allahabad.[66] This initiated a ten-month-long tripartite discussion between the Government of India, India Office and the BBC. During this period Sir John Reith and the BBC took a more active part than either the India Office or the Government of India, which was preoccupied with suppressing the Civil Disobedience Movement and passing the Government of India Bill, the chief characteristic of which was provincial autonomy and an enlarged electorate. A BBC official reported, after spending forty minutes with Sir Findlater Stewart, permanent under-secretary at the India Office,

I think he is frankly apprehensive as to the future, because he fears that whatever new constitution is given to India it is conceivable that unless some measures are taken pretty soon broadcasting may get into wrong hands and may be made an instrument of government.[67]

Within the BBC, which he had joined as a news editor, John Coatman continued his passionate advocacy for broadcasting as a means to promote all-India unity. He prepared memoranda for Reith, with a request to approach the viceroy directly.[68] During this period, Viceroy Lord Willingdon, in course of a visit to London, got persuaded by Reith about the importance of broadcasting, and on his return wrote and asked him to send an expert on a five-year contract. He asked for 'the very best man available', and said something more which worried the senior bureaucrats in India.

He will not have an easy task, but he will have a wonderful field to work in. He will need great tact, and a complete sympathy with the Indian point of view and with Indian aesthetic standards. He will be brought into contact with all conditions of people in far greater variety than he meets in England, and will have to have the right word for each for them. [69]

The home department officials of the Government of India, who regarded themselves as the ultimate authority in matters of imperial security, and looked at other departments like industries and labour *de haut en bas* had not been consulted about Willingdon's letter to Reith. Director of Public Information I.M. Stephens wrote a 'Private and Confidential' letter to his opposite number in the India Office, commenting on the second sentence of the paragraph just quoted,

There is nothing to indicate also the extreme desirability of his being a man whose political views are not of a kind which, under Indian conditions, would render him troublesome to those whose official business it is to deal with such matters. This, to my mind, is a point of the utmost importance, and I confess that the quoted sentence in the Viceroy's letter, standing as it does alone, scares me. . . . Five or six years ago, I had some friends among the younger members of the BBC staff. . . . My general recollection is that the tone of the junior staff was politically advanced. The man we need as our Controller of Broadcasting is someone with an adaptable mind, who is capable of feeling at home in India and being keenly interested in her problems, but we definitely want to avoid a man with 'a complete sympathy with the Indian point of view' as I fear this phrase might be interpreted in the BBC offices. Personally, I would prefer what might be described as 'a concealed die-hard'.[70]

There were many discussions, formal and informal, between the India Office and the BBC, not just about the proposed Delhi station. The BBC records show that they were finding the Indian suggestions somewhat amateurish—the notion that a 20 kh. station at Delhi could be the nucleus of an All-India chain—and gradually the Indian High Commission came around to recognising that some of their expectations were unrealistic. The BBC in return accepted the India Office argument that the radio had to be a branch of a government department (industries and labour), and that there was no possibility of an autonomous corporation on the BBC model.[71] On another point—central–provincial relations regarding control of the radio—prolonged disputes had taken place between the two sides. The retired Indian civil servants had become very hostile to the idea of all-India unity and pinned their hopes on the provincialisation of the Indian polity. They argued against Coatman's memorandum which the BBC had put up.[72] At one point Reith, inspired by a book on Cecil Rhodes which he had been reading, had to intervene personally and persuade Samuel Hoare (secretary of state) that broadcasting should be under overall central control.[73] Another source of disappointment to some BBC officials was that the call for tenders for building the transmitters of the Delhi station was not to be limited to British firms.[74] This was the result of the concessions that the Indian business classes had been able to extract during the round table conference on the question of stores purchase.[75]

By December 1934, the central government in Delhi had got enough clarification of what it was possible to do within the parameters of the impending constitutional settlement, and was able to tell all provincial governments about their plan of action. Out of central revenues the Delhi broadcasting station would be set up and, hopefully, by October 1935 it would supply programmes in Urdu and English 'to an area which will include Lahore on the north-west and Allahabad on the south-east'. Afterwards, as funds became available, other stations would be erected and improvements would be carried out in the two existing stations at Calcutta and Bombay. A new branch of broadcasting under the department of industries and labour would be organised with the help of an expert from the BBC, and its task would be to investigate the best possible locations for other broadcasting stations, and advise on overall development of broadcasting and connected policy issues. While the central revenues would determine the rate at which broadcasting could be rapidly developed, provincial governments were encouraged to accelerate the pace of development by contributing 'a part of the extra recurring expenditure involved, particularly that portion of it required for the programme staff of the new station'. However the centre undertook to meet the initial capital cost of installation and the recurring costs of their technical upkeep for all proposed radio stations. These financial questions needed reiterating, because one of the points that the architects of the Government of India Act (1935) had to give a lot of thought to was the allocation of finance between the centre and provinces.[76]

Having thus reassured the provincial governments on the financial side the centre indicated the type of programmes that they hoped to start.

They will consist chiefly of matter intended for entertainment—music, sketches, news bulletins, running commentaries on interesting events, addresses of a non-controversial nature and so forth. The programmes, apart from such European element as may be found to be in demand, will be in the literary languages of the area served, and it will be the policy of the Government of India to seek the close cooperation of the local government in determining their nature.[77]

The second half of the 1930s were uneasy years for the British empire, with foreign powers using their overseas propaganda machine via broadcasting to undermine its image. The main trouble-spots were west Asia (Palestine and the independent Arab states of Egypt and Iraq), apart from the omnipresent broadcasting from the Soviet Union. The military authorities that periodically listened to these broadcasts commented, in April 1935, that Moscow Radio programmes 'did not appear to be dangerous, and were mostly confined to the glorification of the Soviets'.[78] Home Secretary Maurice Hallett had raised the question about foreign anti-British propaganda, and was answered by a level-headed observation from E.M. Jenkins, one of the few British civil servants who did not show a paranoiac attitude on this topic. He agreed that the gradual extension of good Indian programmes as a counter-attraction would eliminate whatever 'danger' there was from foreign broadcasts being picked up.[79]

The department of broadcasting and its British controller-general Lionel Fielden experienced a great many pin-pricks from officials of the type who headed the home department in the late 1930s—Secretary Maurice Hallett and Home Member H. Craik. The BBC compiled a file consisting of the various *cris-de-coeur* from Fielden to Sir John Reith, from which the following extracts are self-explanatory:

My only real difficulties are with the Home Department. Both Hallett (Secretary) and Craik (Home Dept. Member of Governor-General Executive Council) hate broadcasting with bitter, unreasoning old-fashioned hatred . . . (28 January 1936).

I quarrel frightfully on paper with all the Secretaries and Deputy Secretaries and I don't see how I can do anything else. Noyce is more and more a broken reed . . . none of the other except the Deputy Secretary Jenkins . . . are any use of at all (1 April 1936).[80]

There is plenty of material to write at length on the problems of adjustment which the new controller, although he was an old Etonian from a wealthy background, had with the British officials in Delhi. Since my purpose is not biographical, I will focus on two questions dear to Fielden's heart, and historically significant—the possibility of political broadcasts (following the BBC precedent) and the degree of censorship of broadcast talks, especially book reviews.

Just after Fielden arrived, E.M. Jenkins, deputy secretary in the department of industries and labour, had prolonged discussions with the home department (with both the secretary and the director of public Information), and worked out certain ground rules on both the points. The news service should be under an editor,

who should be given a free hand as though he were Editor of a reputed newspaper. . . . Talks may be on (i) News Subjects (ii) on 'political' subjects (the term 'political' being used in a very wide sense) and (iii) miscellaneous subjects. Government Servants would be permitted to talk about their work, and on . . . the 'miscellaneous group', but talks by Government Servants about their work must be subject to a very careful departmental scrutiny and must not include propaganda matter. . . . There should be a fairly close censorship of talks especially in the 'political' group with the object of keeping off the more violent controversies and of keeping discussions within reasonable bounds. The political parties as such should not be permitted to make use of the service. This is a corollary to Governments undertaking not to use the service for political purposes.[81]

This was not exciting enough for Fielden, who noticed at once that Congress was a popular party. He was on terms of personal friendship with Asaf Ali, and wrote to Reith saying:

. . . we ought to follow English practice and have a balanced series of political talks. After a year in this country, I would say quite definitely that conditions are not so different as people (especially ICS) like to imagine.[82]

Fielden's strictures on the die-hard ICS mentality—which equated expression of political opinion with sedition—did not go entirely unheeded in London. The architects of the Government of India Act of 1935 had intended the new constitution, with 'provincial autonomy' and separate electorates, to deflect the energies of politically conscious Indians from all-India nationalism towards provincial politics, and thereby accentuate the cracks in the nationalist front. That political broadcasts could aid the divisive purposes of imperialism was fully understood by a Conservative politician in London, though not by a seasoned bureaucrat in New Delhi. On the eve of the elections to the provincial assemblies in 1937 Home Member Maurice Hallett banned political broadcasts. Disagreeing with him, the Conservative under-secretary of state for India, R.A. Butler, minuted,

I can see the force of the arguments in Mr. Hallett's letter to Mr. Fielden but would have thought it possible for one leader from each main political or communal group in a Province to use the wireless in much the same way as our political leaders do here. . . . The theory that they might 'disseminate sedition' seems to show a misapprehension of the objects of the new Constitution which, among others, are to encourage Indians to blackguard each other (as we do in politics at home) and not us as a nation.[83]

Butler's views, which reflected the ministerial view of Indian politics, remained on official record, but the authorities in Britain allowed the 'man on the spot' to take decisions, and so Hallett's ruling guided the Government of India's policy on political broadcasts, much to the annoyance of Lionel Fielden. In his private correspondence with an elder statesman of the Liberal Party he expressed his irritation quite sharply.[84]

The question of the censorship of foreign political broadcasts had, as we have seen, worried the Intelligence Bureau. Political developments in West Asia (Arab–Jewish relations in Palestine), and the Italian aggression in Ethiopia had weakened Britain's international position. Anxious officials inquired whether Soviet broadcasts aimed at a population following Islam could be picked up in Cairo or Delhi, and if so, whether they should be jammed. The director of the Intelligence Bureau, Williamson, had, by now, understood the limited financial resources of a Liberal empire, which was no match for a totalitarian regime. He commented,

Personally, I doubt whether anything could be done. The transmitting station [for counter-propaganda] has, I think, in the nature of things to be almost all-powerful. At the present time it is as painful to listen to the Nazis boosting themselves from Berlin, as it is to hear the Communists of Moscow singing their own praises.[85]

A few years later, in April 1938, when Fielden had been in charge for three years, we get an amusing piece of evidence of AIR being told off for broadcasting anti-Soviet propaganda. The furore arose over the Delhi station wanting to review Leon Trotsky's *The Revolution Betrayed* and Eugene Lyons's *Assignment in Utopia*. The home department commented that the script 'might rightly be considered a hostile act by the Russian government', and telegraphed to have the talk cancelled. In the post-mortem on the episode, the mind of the external affairs branch of the Indian government was revealed. The talk was,

unsuitable as an item in the programme of a broadcasting station controlled and financed by the government of India, since it could justifiably be regarded by the Soviet government as officially inspired propaganda against Stalin and his system. It must however be recognised that the talk does not publish any new facts, but merely quotes (without much obvious bias) from books which have been published and are probably being widely read. Had it therefore appeared in a privately owned and controlled journal or review, I do not think that the Soviet government or the Government of India could have taken any exception to it.[86]

At the level of high policy it reflected the uncertainty in the minds of government officials on whether to treat the USSR as a foe or a possible ally. I have not seen any reference to this episode in the India Office Records and cannot say whether it reflected a local view or an imperial perspective. Whatever might be the case, it enabled Fielden to argue that if the home department wished to scrutinise routine activities like book reviews then they themselves should be saddled with the nitty-gritty job of reading book reviews. The senior ICS officers should not expect the station directors to exercise the preliminary task of censoring. One official suspected what was probably nearer the truth:

My impression is that CB [Controller of Broadcasting] is being deliberately obtuse about this as a protest against any censorship by government at all, and in order to give him frequent opportunities of continuing to write letters asking for the system to be changed.[87]

Fielden's line was that since the script was going to be read by the home department anyway, it was a waste of time for the station directors to scrutinise the book reviews. Finally, however, the Government of India managed to have its cake and eat it too by arguing, in a cleverly worded letter drafted by Sir Satyen Roy, that while the CB was not obliged to send all scripts of book reviews it had to send 'books on live political controversies or current affairs'.[88]

Fielden left India in 1940. His post was taken by his deputy A.S. Bokhari, whom Fielden had recruited from Punjab University. By that time war had started, in the initial stages of which Britain had suffered serious reverses. On the use of the radio during wartime we have valuable evidence not only from the national and provincial archives, but from the BBC as well. The latter sent an official, Brander, to do a survey of Indian response to the BBC's wartime broadcasts. Brander's reports, *inter alia*, also provide an insight into the way AIR functioned, and provide a version against which the six-monthly reports prepared in the home department by Sir Satyen Roy can be checked.

Wartime developments can be divided into two parts, till the outbreak of the Quit India Movement, and the period after that. It was evident in the first period that the British Raj was ill-prepared to face the propaganda onslaught of a well-organised totalitarian regime, and that the colonial subjects were more inclined to believe the propaganda of the other side than of their imperial masters. In the first-ever listener research which the AIR conducted in May 1940 in five major Indian cities, covering 13,507 listeners, it found out that more Indians were using the radio for news, and for news hostile to Britain. This was opaquely reported by the department of communication in the following officialese:

Listeners were somewhat reluctant to indicate to what extent they were attracted by foreign broadcast propaganda but the evidence elicited was enough to show that German broadcasts in English and Hindustani are widely listened to although the belief in their truthfulness varies.[89]

A more candid and honest appraisal had been made some months earlier by Lionel Fielden in some of his letters to F.W. Ogilvie, who had succeeded Reith as the director-general of the BBC. Towards the end of 1939, he called a conference of all the station directors and 'asked them to carry out a certain amount of elementary mass observation in order to try and discover what rumours were current'. On the basis of reports he wrote,

The general feeling . . . is that in every strata of society, and throughout India, there is what one might call a mild anti-British feeling which at present amounts to not much more than a certain amusement at British embarrassments and a tendency to regard British news and British newspapers as suspect.

The Hindustani news bulletin from Berlin was 'widely listened to', and regarded 'as more truthful than the English version'. One of his handicaps in launching a counter-propaganda was the crippling legacy of the Indian government's earlier financial policy:

As you know, the Government of India has spent very little on building stations and we cannot claim an all-India coverage such as Berlin undoubtedly has.[90]

A week later he returned to the superiority of German over British propaganda.

We are a long way away, we are short of material and the general feeling in the country is none too good. The Germans bang away continuously and their Hindustani service has a very large audience indeed. Their propaganda may be crude but it is swallowed by the masses like a patent medicine advertisement.[91]

The question of jamming enemy broadcasts was considered but given up. An officer of the Southern Command had asked the provincial government of Madras to propose jamming enemy broadcasts as a general policy to the central government. The chief engineer pointed out the practical difficulties—'with our communications and interests strung out all over the world, we stand to lose more than we gain by creating chaos in the air'.[92]

Yet the repeated successes of Germany by May 1940 made the government concerned about how, without resorting to jamming, it could prevent Indians from listening to Nazi broadcasts. The Maharaja of Jodhpur reported that 'at 8 p.m. every day practically every owner of a wireless receiving set in the city tuned into the broadcast from Berlin and . . . there was a marked tendency to believe the German rather than the British news'.[93]

The central government suggested a policy of penalising private licence holders if they allowed people in the neighbourhood to listen to German broadcasts, while they were free, in the privacy of their home, to hear what they liked. The Madras government's view, as endorsed by the governor, is reflected in the following note:

a complete prohibition on listening would be a good thing if it could be enforced completely. But without a huge Gestapo organisation that would be impossible.[94]

From 1 June 1940, the central government prohibited holders of commercial receiver licensees from publicly disseminating broadcasts by the Axis Powers.[95]

Why Indian listeners continued to show such *schadenfreude* about British reverses even after Japan entered the war was investigated by Brander. He found that the credibility of the BBC broadcasts overseas of war news was low, because these often showed

. . . ignorance of small points of sensibility to Indians. Again and again little things slipped in, e.g., in a recent reference in a talk [broadcast] to Australia to the Black Hole of Calcutta, which has now disappeared from the history books here . . . as a discredited atrocity story. Had we no one going through all out scripts to point out where the toes were we were treading on?

It was in the talks directed to countries like Australia and New Zealand (part of the Eastern Transmission) that such *faux pas* were made. Indians preferred 'to listen to these other transmissions because then, speaking to our own people, we may be saying what we really think'. An Indian Brigadier

referred to 'insult to Asiatic people', and instanced Curtin's recruiting speech, 'We are fighting to obtain a White Australia'. . . . It was used by the Japs for field broadcasts and had a direct effect on our Indian troops.[96]

The Indian director-general of the AIR, A.S. Bokhari, told Brander, 'Don't forget that British prestige in this country has never been lower.'[97] A couple of months after this remark, the Congress launched the Quit India Movement. Brander's report to his superiors showed the sense of helplessness which the Raj felt on the propaganda front:

Congress has an organisation that will cover all India, suiting the lie to the audience everywhere; and we have radio almost completely undeveloped. Nor does radio seem to be used in a planned way; a speech will be put on, usually without anything like sufficient publicity; or reported; but real propaganda planning is not very evident to the ordinary observer, I am told by the ordinary observer.[98]

The radical elements in the Congress—a group with affiliation to the Congress Socialist Party and led by Ram Manohar Lohia—started their own underground broadcasts on a clandestine transmitter in Bombay from 27 August till they were detected by the police on 12 November 1942. It broadcast regularly in English and Hindustani giving reports of insurgent activities in different parts of the country from the North-West Frontier Province to Bengal, and also of police and military brutalities. The themes repeated time and again in these broadcasts were that the villages should adopt a policy of self-sufficiency and refuse to sell to middlemen, and stop working on the railways and the factories as these only helped the British military machine.[99]

Even after the success of the Raj in containing the Quit India Move-ment by police and military action, and even after the Allied Powers began to register victories, not much enthusiasm was noticed by

Brander among Indian listeners for the Allied victories, because they felt that these would mean a continuation of alien domination. As he put it,

> The crazy state of things is that we now have the Indian audience because we have the victories. They are listening to our bulletins; but these victory bulletins bring many of them no joy, for they see no helpful future for India in our victories.[100]

A counter-attraction till the monsoon of 1944 was the broadcasts on behalf of the Indian National Army coming from the Japanese occupied areas in Southeast Asia.[101]

One reason why, after 1943, the AIR could not operate with optimum efficiency as a propaganda machine for the Raj, lay in its pre-war history as a financially starved government department. It was admitted by a British ICS officer in January 1945 that only in 1944 were the staff of the AIR converted into a permanent service; till then, 'the members of its staff [were] in theory liable to have their services terminated on a month's notice, and with no claim to pension or provident fund at the end of their service, however long it lasted'.[102] Apart from the temporary nature of the work, the starting salary of a programme assistant was only Rs 175 per month, and his function, which required a lot of *savoir-faire*, was made to approximate more that of a clerk.[103] With the end of the war, and the dismantling of wartime emergency regulations, the AIR reverted back to its pre-war functions of providing cultural entertainment and broadcasting news and carefully avoiding taking sides in politics. As we have seen, in the 1930s, the government had opposed giving political parties any slot in broadcasting time, even during election campaigns.[104] At that time a British official, E.M. Jenkins, had stressed the need for the government to put a self-denying ordinance on itself, to make the ban on political party broadcasts palatable to the central legislative assembly.[105] After the war, this policy made the Raj hoist with its own petard. The same Jenkins (now Sir Evan) was reporting, on behalf of Viceroy Lord Wavell, to Prime Minister Attlee in November 1945. Attlee asked him why the AIR could not counter the strident nationalist speeches of Nehru, and the communal propaganda of Jinnah, and go on to tell the Indian people that the Labour government meant well, and was the poor man's friend. Jenkins replied that the Indian government had been following the BBC's policy of political neutrality, as he understood it, and to try out Attlee's suggestion at that stage in the history of the Raj was no longer possible or credible.[106]

The Raj thus failed to make use of broadcasting medium to its own advantage, the nationalists were also not able to use the official medium. By an ironic twist of fate the last laugh was with the creator of Pakistan. On that momentous evening on 2 June 1947, when the political leaders were allowed to broadcast after Mountbatten spoke over the air giving the details of partition and the transfer of power, Jinnah devoted the last two paragraphs of his speech to appeal to the Muslims of the North-West Frontier Province to vote to join Pakistan in the proposed referendum.[107] Sardar Patel, as Member for information and broadcasting in the interim government, registered a strong protest, but the damage had been done.[108]

Radio failed to achieve the political purpose its liberal imperialist supporters expected it to, because of the multiple contradictions within that imperial system as it functioned in India. Too many vested interests and practices were working at cross-purposes. Except in wartime, throughout the period under review, a tight-fisted attitude to public expenditure, prompted by the financial needs of the city of London, left very little resources for the media, whether it was a private enterprise or under a government department. A second contradiction lay in the ambivalence of the imperial administration about the division of functions between the centre and the provinces. As an instrument of indoctrination a centralised control, carefully developed over the years, might have enabled the Raj to make its propaganda machine more efficient and sophisticated. However, faced with the challenge of all-India nationalism, the imperial masters preferred to encourage provincial particularism, thereby slowing down the development of the media. The third contradiction lay in the expectation that what a totalitarian regime with an official ideology can achieve with the help of the radio was possible for the British Raj. The Raj did provide a political space for the presentation of non-official viewpoints. Yet the Pavlovian reflexes of the home department whenever political questions were mentioned restricted the scope to introduce variety and spice in the radio programmes. It prevented the development of healthy conventions by which political broadcasts could be regulated. In the absence of such a tradition, it is not surprising that Jinnah could spring an unpleasant surprise on his opponents.

NOTES

1. Asa Briggs, *The BBC: First Fifty Years* (Oxford, 1985), pp. 94–101.
2. Briggs, *op.cit.*, pp. 27–57.
3. Ibid., appendix, showing the landmarks in the development of the organisation.
4. L. Fielden, *The Natural Bent* (London, 1960), p. 204.
5. Seth Drucquer, *Broadcasting* (Oxford pamphlets on Indian Affairs, no. 27, Bombay, 1945), p. 31.
6. There was a director of Wireless in the Post & Telegraph department, and an interdepartmental body called the Indian Wireless Board, which met periodically to discuss policy questions which affected more than one department, under the chairmanship of the Director-General, Posts & Telegraph. Some indication of the issues discussed are to be found in Home-Poll—1922—file 902 & file 902/II.
7. Birkenhead to Irwin, 15 July 1926 (Halifax Papers, microfilm in NMML reel 1).
8. Irwin to Birkenhead, 5 August 1926 (ibid.).
9. H. Montgomery Hyde, *Lord Reading* (New York, 1967), pp. 122–61. The quotation is at p. 161.
10. Sultan Chinoy's own account is to be found in S. Chinoy, *Pioneering in Indian Business* (Bombay, 1962), pp. 53–58.
11. On 27 June 1923 A.C. Chatterjee minuted, 'We do not conceal from ourselves the fact that our company will almost certainly be an offshoot of the Marconi Company and have throughout been anxious to avoid all difficulties with regard to patents and royalties, and have adequately safeguarded ourselves in this respect in our proposed arrangements.' (NAI—Industries & Labour—Telegraph branch—November 1924—file no. 56 [PT 23]).
12. *Times of India*, 26 July 1924. (press-cutting kept in the file mentioned in the previous note at kw, pp. 4–5). Chinoy's memoirs (n. 10 above) say that the company was registered in 1923, but the records show that the actual date of registration was 25 July 1924.
13. Minutes of BBC board meeting, 13 March 1924, item 2 (f); J. Reith to Viceroy of India, 19 March 1924, enclosing his correspondence with the India Office between 13 and 17 March 1924 (BBC Written Archives E1/897/1).
14. J. Reith to Secretary of State of India, 13 March 1924 (ibid.).
15. A.H. Ley, Secretary, Dept. of Industries and Labour, to all local governments and administrations, no. 153–PT, 19 May 1924, para 2 (NAI—Industry & Labour—Telegraphs—1924—file 56 [PT 23]).
16. Ibid., para 3, section 1 (note).

17. See their attitudes in some other cases in the early 1920s, described in P.S. Gupta, 'State and Business in India in the Age of Discriminatory Protection' in this book.

18. I have discussed this point at length in 'Federalism and Provincial Autonomy as Devices of Imperial Control' in this book.

19. British politicians like Lord Lothian, Clement Attlee, J.R. MacDonald would fall in this category. Indian Liberals like Srinivasa Sastri and Tej Bahadur Sapru had a good rapport with them.

20. The British expatriates who were interested, as part of their professional duties, in making use of broadcasting, were C.F. Strickland, F.L. Brayne, ICS, H.H. Peterson, secretary, YMCA at Lahore, and Colonel H.R. Hardinge, a non-official businessman the source is BBC archives E896/1. f. 21–2. ('Indian Vernacular Broadcasting Scheme').

21. Para 5 of the letter cited in n. 15 above.

22. These facts are taken from two memoranda prepared by P.J. Edmunds, Director of Wireless. One on 17 July was about the radio policy of the Government of India; the other was put up on 5 August 1927, as a background paper for an interdepartmental meeting on broadcasting policy at Simla on 8 August 1927 (NAI—Industries & Industries—PT branch—1927—f. no. 60-T[1] and 60-T[3]).

23. The directors were, apart from the Chinoy brothers and P.J. Edmunds (nominee of the Government of India, ex-officio, as Director of Wireless) the following: C.N. Wadia, Sir N.N. Wadia, Raja Saheb Dhanrajgirji Narsingirji, R.D. England, F.E. Rosher, and Sir Ibrahim Rahimtoola (taken from the statutory report of the company, kept with the Dunstan-Reith correspondence in the BBC archives, BBC Written Archives E1/897/2).

24. E. Dunstan to J. Reith, 5 January 1927 (BBC Written Archives E1/897/2).

25. P.J. Edmunds' memo, 17 August 1926, paragraph no. 3 (NAI—Industty & Labour—P & T branch—1927—f. 60-T[3]). The date of the conclusion of the agreement is given in another note by Edmund, 5 January 1927 (NAI—Industry & Labour—Telegraph—1927—f. 60-T[9]).

26. Dunstan to Reith, 10 March 1972. This Director was C.N. Wadia. 'He can only be seen between 11 and 12 on certain mornings—never on Race Days, Wednesdays and Saturday's (BBC Written Archives E1/897/2).

27. Dunstan to Reith, probably July or August 1927, because only the second page was allowed to be xeroxed by the BBC from Reith's private archives, the date could not be checked. Internal evidence suggests that it was written about the time the Bombay station was inaugurated (BBC E1/897/1).

28. Dunstan to Reith, 'Good Friday', 1927 (BBC E1/897/2).

29. Note by B.N. Mitra, 28 August 1926 on the file 'Present position of

Broadcasting and its future development in India'. This file was created to consider how to prepare a despatch to the Secretary of State regarding broadcasting (NAI—Industries & Industries—P & T branch—1927—file 60-T[3]).

30. Para 8 of Edmunds' memo, 17 August 1926, and the observation of A.H. Ley, Secretary, 25 August 1926, thereon (ibid.).

31. Edmunds' note, 5 January 1927 at the end of the keepwiths in the file entitled 'Proposal to set up advisory boards' (NAI—Industry & Industry—Telegraphs—1927—60-T(9).

32. Edmunds' note, 3 February 1927; Haig's minute 15 February 1927, endorsed by Muddiman (NAI—Industry & Labour—Telegraphs—1927—file no. 60-T[3], keepwiths, pp. 9s–10).

33. Governor-General-in-Council to Secretary of State of India, 28 April 1927 (Despatch no. 2-Telegraphs), para 6 (NAI—Industries & Labour—P & T branch—1927—no. 60-T[3]).

34. Ibid., para 7. Examination of the papers leading up to the final text of the despatch shows that it was a compromise document, in which the positive points about broadcasting were taken from supporters like P.J. Edmunds and John Coatman, and the negative and 'undesirable' aspects from officials connected with the Home Department like J. Crerar and H. Haig.

35. Coatman's note, 31 March 1927, (NAI—Industry & Labour—Telegraph branch—1927—file 60-T[4] keepwiths f. 15).

36. Haig's note, 2 June 1927 (ibid., f. 19).

37. McWatter's note, 2 June 1927 (ibid.)

38. Note by Edmunds, 6 May 1927 (ibid., f. 6).

39. 'Minutes of an informal conference of representatives of Govt. of India . . . 8 August 1927' (NAI—Industries & Labour—P & T branch—1927—file 6-0 60-T[3]).

40. Edmunds' memorandum, 1 July 1927, para 9 (NAI—Industry & Labour—P & T branch—1927—f. no. 60-T[1]).

41. J. Coatman, Director of Information, was to have attended, but could not come. Only Haig showed up for the Home Department. The other heavy-weight departments which sent senior officials were Army, Foreign and Political, and Finance.

42. E. Dunstan to J. Reith, 30 September 1927 (BBC Written Archives E1/897/2).

43. Paras 8 and 9 of the document cited in n. 33 above.

44. Dunstan to Reith, 28 April 1927 (BBC E1/897/2).

45. Same to same. 8 October 1927 (ibid.).

46. Para 8 of the document cited in n. 39.

47. Dunstan to Reith, 21 January 1928 (BBC E1/897/3). No information

corroborating this is available in the files of the telegraph branch of the Industry & Labour Department in the National Archives of India. It is possible that the matter was dealt with by some other department or at some other level.

48. Ibid.

49. All the correspondence is in BBC Written Archives E1/897/3 file 3 (Indian Broadcasting).

50. Reply on 25 May 1928 (*loc.cit.*).

51. Hugo Hirst to J. Reith, 22 May 1928 (*loc.cit.*).

52. Reply on 30 May 1928 (*loc.cit.*).

53. 'Internal circulating memo' marked 'Very urgent' on 'Indian Broadcasting', 7 March 1928 (BBC E1/897/3).

54. Ibid.

55. Report of the speech of J.R. Stapleton, Station Director, Calcutta in August 1930 (English translation from the Bengali version printed in *Betar Jagat*, vol. I, no. 24, 15 August 1930).

56. Federation of British Industries, Executive Committee Minutes, 9 December 1931 and 10 February 1932 (University of Warwick, Business History Archives, FBI/c/613, ff. 30, 33, 47).

57. That there was a possibility of this happening is seen from the following observation of T. Ryan, Jt. Secretary of the Industries & Labour Dept. Telegraph branch on 4 September 1931.
'I have every reason to expect that the Retrenchment Committee will advocate the cessation of government broadcasting. . . .' On 7 October, the same person noted, '. . . the Government of India have just decided definitely to close down the State Broadcasting Service . . .'
(NAI—Home Poll—1932—file 21/6/Poll-note pgs., pp. 27, 30).

58. T. Ryan to the Director of the two stations, 12 October 1931 (*loc.cit.*, f. 7).

59. Note by Ryan on this deputation, 21 October 1931 (*loc.cit.*, pp. 32–3).

60. Note by Ryan, 5 March 1932 (*loc.cit.*, p. 39).

61. Home-Poll-1932-file 21/12.

62. Foreign Political—External—1933—file 269 (X). Note by J.W. Cowgill, 16 March 1932 (Appx. to notes, *loc.cit.*) and by H.L. Williamson, 18-5-1933 (note p. 11).

63. Lothian to Reith, 5 February 1932 (Edinburgh, Scottish Record Office, GD40/17/159 ff. 8–10).

64. As in note 62 (*loc.cit.*, p. 7).

65. Offprint of 'Broadcasting in Indian Village' by C.F. Strickland, kept in Home Poll—1934—f. 119/1/34-Poll.

66. D.G. Mitchell (Industries & Labour) to Secretary of State, 28 February

1934 (IOR)-L/P & J/7/754 file 955 of 1934 annexed to P & J 4102 of 1934).

67. Memo by C.A.H., 19 June 1993, on 'Broadcasting in India' (BBC Archives E1/896/2).

68. J. Coatman to J. Reith (Holograph), 28 July 1934 enclosing a memo, J. Reith to Findlater Stewart, 30 July 1934 (BBC E1/896/1).

69. Willingdon to Reith, 7 September 1934 (BBC Archives E1/896/2; also available in NAI: Home Poll—1934—file 119/1/31-Poll).

70. I.M. Stephens to H. MacGregor, 17 September 1934 (copy in BBC Archives E1/896/2.) Stephens' opening sentence confessed that he was writing an 'indiscreet' letter which he did not wish to be circulated in the India Office. But since he had ended with a suggestion that someone should 'put in an appropriate word on the subject to Sir John Reith', Mac-Gregor passed a copy to him. Stephens recorded his thoughts, however, on the file in India, for the Home Secretary, Maurice Hallett (Mitchell to Hallett (D.O.G. 82) 18 September 1934, enclosing all the DO correspondence between Sir Findlater Stewart of the India Office and F. Noyce of the Viceroy's Council (Home-Poll—1934—f. 119/1/34-Poll. pp. 22–3).

71. Report of meeting at the India Office, 18 October 1934 (BBC Archives E1/896/2).

72. See the marginal comments of A.G. Clow, a former Secretary, Department of Industry & Labour, on the memorandum of Coatman cited in note 68 above. Also see 'Memo of interview with A.G. Clow and Greaves', 21 September 1934 (BBC E1/896/2).

73. The Diaries of John Reith, vol. 4, folio 50, entries for 5 July 1934 and 30 July 1934. The latter entry shows the India Office admitted that broadcasting had never been discussed in the Viceroy's Executive Council.

74. 'It is unfortunate that the call for tenders is not to be restricted to British firms'—comment by the ACE to the Controller (A), 30 October 1934, giving his opinion on a letter to the BBC from the Stores Department, Indian High Commission (BBC Archives E1/896/2).

75. P.S. Gupta, 'State and Business in India', in this book.

76. P.S. Gupta, 'Federalism and Provincial Autonomy', in this book.

77. D.G. Mitchell, Secretary, Industries & Labour, to all local governments, 15 December 1934 (copy endorsed to Home Department Home-Poll—1934—f. 119/1/34-Poll).

78. Note by Major M.O.3. 'I' 26 April (Home-Poll—1935—file 52/1-35f. p. 7).

79. Observation of E.M. Jenkins, in the same file as in note 72 on behalf of the Industries & Labour Department, 9 April 1935, p. 5.

80. BBC E1/896/3.

81. E.M. Jenkins' note of 13 January 1936 (Home-Public—1936—f. no. 106/36-Pub.).
82. BBC E1/896/3.
83. R.A.B.'s minute, 21 October 1936 on the letter from M. Hallett dated 5 August 1936 (IOR, L/P & J/7/754, P & J file 4174 of 1936, annexed to P & J 4102/34).
84. L. Fielden to Viscount Samuel, 19 February 1938 (Samuel Papers, A/106, H.L. R.O., item 10).
85. Note by Williamson, 1 April 1935 (NAI, Home-Poll—1935—f. 52/1/35).
86. Notes by J.A. Thorne, 25 April 1938 and H.M. Metcalfe, 28 April 1938 (NAI Home-Poll—1938—f. 52/5/38)
87. Note by J.A. Mackowen, 16 July 1938 (NAI, Home-Poll—1938—f. 52/10/38).
88. Note by S.N. Roy, 3 January 1939 (NAI, Home—Public—1939—f. 103/39).
89. Report by S.N. Roy for the second quarter of the calendar year 1940, 26 August 1940 (NAI Home-Poll) (1)—1940—no. 62-1/40).
90. L. Fielden to F.W. Ogilvie, 5 December 1939 (BBC Archives El/1896/3).
91. Same to same, 14 December 1939 (ibid.).
92. D.N. Strathan (D-G, Inf.) to Chief Secretary, Madras, 10 June 1940 enclosing Goyder's note (Tamil Nadu Archives SF 1231 [a] dated 21 August 1940).
93. A.C. Lothian (Rajputana Agency) to C.G. Herbert, (Govt. Rep.), 2 December 1940 (NAI—Home-Poll (I)—1940—file 60/2 [40] Int)
94. Memo, 3 July 1940, kept in the file as in note no. 85.
95. Para 5 (e) of the document cited in no. 82.
96. J.H. Davenport's summary of Brander's letter of 12 May 1942. (Davenport to E.S.D., 15 June 1942. BBC Archives E1/880).
97. Ibid.
98. Davenport to E.S.D., 31 August 1942, quoting a report from Brander received on that day (BBC E1/880).
99. S. Sengupta and G. Chatterjee, *Secret Congress Broadcasts and Storming Railway Tracks* (New Delhi, 1988), pp. 35–109.
100. Brander's report, 11 January 1943 (BBC E1/880).
101. Details are to be found in the fortnightly reports from Bihar, Orissa and Punjab between February and April 1944. (NAI—Home-Poll (I)—1944—files 18/2/44, 18/3/44, 18/4/44).
102. Seth Drucquer, *Broadcasting*, (Oxford pamphlets on Indian Affairs, no. 27, Bombay, Oxford University Press, India 1945), p. 22.
103. Ibid., p. 22.

104. See note 21 above.
105. Notes by E.M. Jenkins, 13 January 1936 and 7 February 1936 (NAI, Home-Public—1936—file 106/36 kw, pp. 17–18).
106. Memo in the British Prime Minister's Secretariat entitled 'Talks with Sir Evan Jenkins about situation in India (1945) on 27 November 1945' (PRO-PREM 8/58).
107. *Transfer of Power*, vol. XI, document no. 47 at p. 98.
108. Ibid., document no. 51 at pp. 102–3.

THE QUALITY OF LIFE AND
INDIAN SCHOLARSHIP*

The purpose of this essay is to examine the forces that have shaped the world of Indian scholarship in the recent past and the present day. Doing full justice to the title would require superhuman knowledge in many branches of learning, careful research at a number of academic centres all over India, and the production of a two-volume work instead of an essay. Nevertheless, within a narrower frame of reference, one can hazard a few hypotheses and conclusions about the state of Indian scholarship as long as it is remembered that the data is based on limited surveys in limited areas, and that the definitive work remains to be written.

The narrower terms of reference are to examine the institutional framework of higher learning in India in the last hundred years and consider in what ways the structure of society and the pattern of government influenced this institutional frame, affecting, for better or worse, the development of various academic disciplines.

In spite of what extreme nationalists might like to believe, the state of scholarship was at a low ebb in the traditional seats of Arabic–Persian or Sanskritic studies in India in the early nineteenth century. It needed Macaulay's Minute of Education (1835), Sir Charles Wood's Education despatch (1854), and the establishment of the older colleges and universities to lay the foundations of higher learning in India. The first graduate was produced in 1858. While the history of some of the older colleges goes back to the period before the revolt of 1857,[1] most of them started giving an academic diet of some richness only after they shed their schoolteaching functions and were reorganised to endow

* Presented at a seminar in Delhi in 1966.

degrees up to the graduate, and in some cases the postgraduate, stage. As these took place around the 1860s, and as postgraduate specialisation did not get going until the late 1870s at the earliest, any assessment of the quality of academic values has to take the generation that came of age in the 1860s as the starting point. Since the greater part of this renaissance took the shape of an attempt to assimilate Western standards into the traditional frame of values in the Indian mind, we would not be far wrong of we concentrate on the territories known as British India, and, for the sake of convenience, those within the academic radius of the two oldest universities—Calcutta and Bombay.

II

It is a mistake to assume, as some have, that the relative poverty of Indian universities in the field of scholarship is due to the British policy of developing an educational system designed to produce clerks and minor bureaucrats.[2] The demand for higher education originally came from Christian missionaries and far-sighted Indians, and the early courses concentrated on mathematics and logic, political thought and poetry, philosophy and physics. As one writer has pointed out, if the aim had been to produce clerks, stress would have been laid on secretarial training of one sort or another—precis-writing, simple accounting and office manuals.[3] British policy was based on the 'filtration' theory, which is why they, on the whole, neglected primary education and concentrated on collegiate and higher education: if a rigorous academic grounding was given to a selected elite, eventually the desire for learning and the acquisition of skills in various specialisations would filter down to other branches of society. The syllabi of the older universities can be criticised for a strong linguistic and classical bias and for paying relatively less attention to the experimental sciences. As Britain was not the country where, in the late nineteenth century, fundamental developments in mathematics were taking place, the courses in mathematics up to the degree stage were more oriented towards learning a range of sophisticated methods of calculation and measurement than towards providing the foundation for a way of thought that would benefit the development of basic sciences and philosophical inquiry.[4] The absence of a technological base prevented the simultaneous growth of interest in scientific studies.

The only professional schools that developed fairly early were law and medicine. Medical training, however, had for a long time a strong clinical bias, which perhaps explains the slowness of the development of first-rate research by Indians even in this field.

The questions before us are: How far did these early efforts achieve their aims of creating reasonably strong centres of study and research from which scholarly works would blossom, and which would set the pace for further and sustained development in other centres? How far did the political and social problems of the era before independence prevent even the development of such strong centres? To what extent has the fast-changing Indian society since the Second World War helped or hindered the development and maintenance of high standards of scholarship? In pursuing these queries we might also get some clue to three of the commonest failings of Indian academic standards and Indian scholarly writings. The bulk of our work has been imitative rather than creative; our universities have been, at their best, disseminators of knowledge rather than the creators of new lines of thinking in various disciplines. Standards of teaching as well as research have put a high premium on memory work, the accumulation of data with somewhat rudimentary classification, rather than on the development of judgement and the capacity for sustained argument. In some of the social studies the scholar has been a willing member of an intellectual colony, aping the modes and norms of thinking either in Britain or, if he was a rebel and yet wanted a personal identification with an international movement of thought, in communist Russia.

Until the second decade of the twentieth century, higher learning including postgraduate instruction was given primarily in the old colleges set up in Calcutta, Bombay and Madras and in their neighbourhoods. By that time roughly three generations of intelligentsia had been produced among the communities living in those areas, and these had become familiar, through the medium of English, with some of the specialised disciplines in the humanities and sciences. But this process was not accompanied by any significant development of some of these colleges into powerhouses for the generation of scholarly research. This was due, first, to the fact that the concept of a research-oriented graduate school was Germanic and unfamiliar to the British educationists with their Oxford or Cambridge penchant for stressing a rigorous course of liberal education ending in a first degree. Even there, Oxbridge standards varied. Oxbridge, in these years, was most rigorous in the courses of instruction in the basic sciences and the classics, so that a person could follow it up by further research on his own, but in the school of history for example (founded in Oxford in 1872 and in Cambridge in 1873) 'the aim . . . was to give the students . . . a fund of general knowledge of history', and the 'process of acquiring that knowledge was held to be of educational value as a mental training, and the knowledge itself of practical utility for political life and other purposes'.[5] However, Sir Charles Firth admitted that, 'no serious attempt was made to train men systematically, so that they might be capable of adding to knowledge. In this respect the historical teaching given in our universities fell far behind the scientific teaching given in them during the same period.'[6] In the second place, the experience of recruitment of teachers for government colleges revealed that the bulk of the teachers recruited from Britain in this period were ideally suited to be sixth-form masters in British public schools or junior tutors in colleges, but not many were even potentially research-minded specialists who would inspire their brightest students to develop into scholars.[7] Until the 1880s even the most advanced degree, like the MA in Calcutta University, was not sufficiently specialised to encourage research in a specific branch of a discipline and only around the end of that decade was the system rectified. European teachers with a specialist bent of mind did not stay long in this environment for fear of getting rusty.[8] Those that remained, or those who came subsequently, found their abilities on the one hand and the pattern of undergraduate teaching on the other, conformed closely to sixth-form teaching in British public schools, with the aim of producing gentlemen with a taste for liberal education, but not specialists who would go far in their disciplines.[9] How many of the Europeans came from a sense of devotion to duty to government service awaits further research. But the somewhat cynical comments of C.H. Tawney, after forty years of experience in India, may not be out of place in this context. In one of his official notes he wrote:

I suppose that men enter the Educational Service mainly for two reasons, they wish to be married or they wish to be in a position to support mothers and sisters, who may have fallen into pecuniary difficulties owing to the sudden death of a father. Men with high degrees might, under these circumstances, be attracted by an increase in the basic pay of Rs 700/-, whereas Rs 500/- . . . would have little charm for them.[10]

Even the good man found himself burdened with either too many administrative duties—and with his academic post being interchangeable, for promotion's sake, with an administrative post,[11]—or with a heavy teaching load without any facilities for research. Sir Patrick Geddes, describing Sir Jagadish Chandra Bose's early years at Presidency College, Calcutta, writes:

The departmental view was that the teaching of classes was the whole duty of a professor, and that research must therefore involve neglect of his proper functions: even this in spite of his giving, with characteristic thoroughness and pride, twenty-six hours of weekly lectures and demonstrations in the college, although the average performed by his colleagues was much less.[12]

While the best Europeans could not be brought into the service, the best Indians were discouraged from joining the profession by a series of accidental or intentional measures of the government. Ever since 1881 the salary of Indians in the graded education service had been two-thirds that of the Europeans appointed there, making one Indian teacher of mathematics complain: 'I was educated in England and at the University of Cambridge. In the Mathematical tripos of 1866 I was placed in the second class. My degree therefore is as good as that of several gentlemen who are now holding graded appointments.'[13]

But while English teachers were quite keen, in this generation, to encourage equality of pay and status with their Indian colleagues,[14] the administrative routine of the finance department precluded any intelligent policy in this regard. The left hand of Gladstonian cheese-paring finance dissipated much of the spirit of intellectual tolerance and cooperation which its right hand had nourished.[15] After 1896 the creation of the imperial service and the provincial service, and the *de facto* exclusion of Indians from the imperial service further diminished the attraction of the teaching profession for the brightest Indian graduate. A few exceptionally brilliant men like the mathematician R.P. Paranjpye did well in Cambridge, refused the offer of an appointment in the Indian Education Service and served the Deccan Education Society in Fergusson College,[16] but by and large it seems true to say that only a small fraction of the very best Indian students were coming to teaching whether in government service or outside. This was true of the 1880s; it became truer on the eve of the First World War. Most Indian teachers (with the exception of R.P. Paranjpye) shared Sir Jagadish Bose's view, given before the Islington Commission: 'Unfortunately, on account of there being no opening for men of genius in the Educational Service, distinguished men were driven to the profession of Law.'[17] Even those who had learnt science switched over to law or competed for the civil service. The few governmental agencies needing technical personnel excluded Indians from the higher posts.[18] Of course it requires investigation as to whether this was due to racial prejudice and an unconscious belief that no matter how hard he tried the Indian was unlikely to do well in science, or based on an objective assessment of the abilities of Indians in each department. The truth probably lies in between—the net result being the continued neglect of scientific studies by the brightest Indians.

As a result, Indians who joined the teaching profession came from the category of 'reasonably good' or 'average' students. They were ideally suited for the diffusion of knowledge, and, against the background of increasing demand for popular education, their work in starting private educational societies and institutions was admirable.[19] But at the turn of the century it remained true that the old colleges had failed to be centres for the creation of knowledge, and the universities were only examining bodies.[20] One of the founders of a private college of some repute, Ananda Mohan Bose, admitted that his college was not equipped to do advanced graduate work and for the enhancement of standards he suggested the transformation of Presidency College, Calcutta, into a teaching university, thus creating at least one strong centre.[21] But this was not followed up.

Yet scholarly research did develop, in spite of the absence of institutional facilities, thanks to the effect of Western education on three generations, in the field of Indian classical studies and related branches of Indology. R.G. Bhandarkar made his name in the last quarter of the nineteenth century. Mahendra Lal Sircar's Indian Association for the Cultivation of Science was at least a promise of earnestness and endeavour in this field, which was to be redeemed thirty years later by the work of C.V. Raman there. But the institutional handicaps in the form of the hierarchical structure of government colleges and differential pay scales for Europeans and Indians persisted. The latter had not been much of a grievance in the 1880s, but with the bifurcation of the services it bedevilled the development of a corporate intellectual community in the colleges. As Sir Patrick Geddes remarked in 1920, after many years of work in India,

it is to this unfortunate system that the lower general level of individual studies and of original productivity, in comparison with the staffs of other universities in the world . . . is plainly not a little due. In the Civil Service, at the Bar, or on the Bench, Europeans and Indians must and can work together; yet in every university and its colleges, where unity of working is the daily necessity, and should be far easier of attainment, they are practically segregated into two distinct racial camps, and this with deterioration of the one and Depression of the other. . . . If real efficiency of higher education, with corporate spirit and active intellectual life, are to be adequately realised in India, this system will have not only to be abandoned in its working but transformed in its spirit . . .[22]

We must remember that the years 1900 to 1918 were marked by increasing nationalist resentment against the pro-consuls of Lord Curzon and his type, and that these were the years when E.M. Forster paid his visit to India getting an impression of racial arrogance later portrayed in his *Passage to India*.

These political developments also vitiated a constructive development of scholarly centres in the form of centralising postgraduate teaching and research in the universities like Calcutta, Bombay or Madras. Lord Curzon's desire to exorcise 'the monstrous and maleficent spirit of cram' from Indian universities failed to work as all leaders of Indian opinion, rightly or wrongly, suspected him of ulterior political motives.[23] In Calcutta, the ten years of Sir Ashutosh Mukherjee's vice-chancellorship produced mixed blessings. There was a contradiction between his policy of developing research of a high standard and bringing in people from all over India, and his willingness to lower the standards of the Entrance, FA, and BA (Pass) examinations to encourage the emergence of a graduate in every home.[24] By insisting on rigorous standards of admission to BA (Hons) and MA courses Sir Ashutosh certainly tried to prevent dilution of standards at the higher level. But for a number of reasons which are not clear, Calcutta University failed to get financial assistance from the government in sufficiently large quantities to put the postgraduate centres on a secure base.[25] By the time the postgraduate departments were founded in Calcutta University after 1917 the assets were the existence of a number of chairs and endowments and professors brought from all over India. But the liabilities were considerable: lower rungs in the academic ladder were too few to encourage young scholars and the dead weight of administering school education continued. In some of the relatively less developed disciplines like history or Indian languages, no intelligent policy was evolved of developing curricula in such a manner that successive age-groups got trained in sophisticated methods of thinking, so as to be able to do research later. Sir Ashutosh also laid perhaps an undue stress on the production of research output in quantitative terms.[26] A writer who had been in a position to know about the academic atmosphere of Calcutta in the 1920s has written that the privately financed colleges—which were by now many in number—remained largely untouched by whatever wind of scholarly research was blowing through the university portals.[27]

Bombay University was more successful in ensuring quality control by refusing affiliation to colleges much more than Calcutta did, by endowments from wealthy business communities, and by not divorcing the old colleges from participating in the university teaching work. Bombay question papers show a lesser degree of deterioration in standards, for the examinations mentioned earlier, than Calcutta in this period.[28] But cosmopolitan and business-oriented Bombay lacked Calcutta's sense of being rooted in an indigenous tradition. Notwithstanding other distressing features of Bengali parochialism, this was one of the sources of strength of Calcutta University in the 1920s and 1930s. A none-too-friendly critic wrote around 1940: '[Calcutta University] has done good work of recent years in advanced teaching and research; and if its control of education in the high schools and colleges has been educationally, politically, and economically detrimental, this is by no means the view of the people of Bengal.'[29] The social prestige of the teacher and the scholar remained very high in Calcutta in these years, and in the mofussil towns the local college was the nerve-centre of whatever cultural activity there was.[30]

Nevertheless, there was very little sustained development of scholarship and improved methods of graduate training in a number of disciplines at these two places. Many scientists went on working in Calcutta Science College, and the Bombay School of Economics and

Sociology produced useful empirical studies in the field of economics. But sociology appears to have stagnated in Bombay. All through the 1920s and 1930s Bombay and Calcutta remained affiliating institutions, thus burdening their teachers with the unavoidable and tempting distractions of paid administrative work. After 1937 the number of affiliations to colleges shot up even in Bombay, suggesting that it might be causally connected with the lowering of the franchise and the formation of responsible ministries after the Government of India Act of 1935.[31]

III

The 1920s and 1930s were years full of unfulfilled promises. The creation of a number of teaching universities like Lucknow (1920), Aligarh (1920), and Dacca (1922) were aimed at closely coordinating rigorous training with the pursuance of research. Some could not make the best use of their men, having been created in areas lacking an already developed academic tradition. All were rather poorly equipped in library resources, and in the end they remained centres for the diffusion of knowledge only, producing occasional researchers here and there. With the coming of provincial autonomy and the transfer of education to the provinces there was no longer the racial divide that put a bar to Indian prospects of promotion, but the old status symbols persisted in government colleges.[32] (The stamp of Oxford and Cambridge was valued not for the academic discipline provided there, but for snobbish reasons, which explains why, for every single first-rate product of those universities, there were more than one enjoying similar pay and status whose academic worth was much lower.[33]) More unfortunate, in most places the salaries at both college and university levels remained pegged to the scales of the old provincial services, thus still discouraging the brightest Indians from joining the profession. Fuller research is needed to bring out the difficulties of recruitment, the problems of promotion, the absence of library and other facilities, etc., that plagued different provinces in different ways, and research is also needed to make an objective assessment of how far communal politics bedevilled educational improvement in places like Bengal, Uttar Pradesh, or Punjab. But it can perhaps be said without exaggeration that, in the context of niggardliness of resources and the political and social problems of the 1920s and the 1930s, the multiplication of university centres dissipated resources rather than enabled any one area to develop into a really first-rate all-round centre of learning.[34] Even departments which made some contributions contained a load of substandard equipment, human and material.

The nature and quality of Indian scholarly output in this period, in three disciplines (history, economics and Bengali language) indicate that even where there was a flow of work it was a narrow stream which showed a disconcerting tendency to dry up frequently on account of the institutional factors mentioned earlier.

A lot of antiquarian work had already developed in the field of Indian history (ancient and medieval). The renewed self-awareness of different communities in different parts of India had led to an interest in India's past and a particular interest in the histories of their own areas and communities. Standards of scrupulous analysis of evidence and objectivity had been set from the time of R.G. Bhandarkar in ancient Indian history,[35] and in the field of medieval Indian history from around the time of Sir Jadunath Sarkar. But in medieval Indian history Indian scholarship remained strictly in the field of military, diplomatic and dynastic histories, following the fashion of some British historians of the late nineteenth century. The more rigorous aspects of the disciplines of British historical scholarship at the beginning of the century lay in the field of constitutional and administrative history (economic history was as yet in its infancy), but the generation of Jadunath Sarkar was not touched by it at all. With the formation of postgraduate centres there did develop research in the field of administrative history of an analytical character (*vide* the work of Professor R.P. Tripathi at Allahabad), but the bulk of the historical writing continued to be dynastic and military histories. In Allahabad a bright constellation of men like Sir Shafaat Ahmad Khan, Dr R.P. Tripathi, Dr Beni Prasad, and Dr Tara Chand produced a distinct school of writing on medieval Indian history. But the uneven development of different departments in the social studies in any particular university prevented a highly desirable cross-fertilisation from related disciplines. (Yet in Britain the school of jurisprudence had helped the school of history and produced Maitland, Vinogradoff, and others, and just when postgraduate centres were developing in

India, at the London School of Economics the foundations were being laid of a school of economic history, drawing on talents in both disciplines.) Whether in Calcutta, or Allahabad, the research institutes in Poona or farther south, training and research soon fell into a rut of narrative political history writings. Everywhere the intellectual assumptions of British Whig historians (who were then becoming absolute in Britain), together with some of the preoccupations of the nationalist and communal movements, introduced assumptions and biases in the study of the history of India, which sometimes vitiated the soundness of their analysis.[36]

But nationalist preoccupations led to a healthy interest in doing empirical research in economics and economic history to find out the causes of India's poverty, to follow up the spare-time researches of an earlier generation of administrators and politicians like Dadabhai Naoroji and Romesh Chunder Dutt. Apart from Bombay and Calcutta schools new voluntary centres like the Gokhale Institute at Poona started in 1930. Nevertheless, most of the works, while useful additions to knowledge, were rather pedestrian in their range and scope. Very few Indian economists went into the field of research in economic theory, indicating that either the brightest intellects among economics graduates were not coming in sufficient numbers to teaching—which was partly true—or that those that did come were too burdened with teaching loads in different papers to be allowed to specialise. Research themes, in this context, tended to be chosen from easier options.[37]

Scholarship in the field of Bengali literature took the understandable form, in the initial stages, of a series of monographs in philology and literary history and textual criticism.[38] These were valuable contributions to knowledge. But subsequent research under the mentors who produced these works followed the same pattern, and as the vein of literary history was worked for some time it began to yield diminishing returns. New standards of literary criticism, which would combine textual rigour with novel critical insights, were rare. Tagore's literary criticism was a highly subjective personal response; other professional critics drew on the Sanskrit texts or on some nineteenth-century English critic. The Bengali literary world did not produce an F.R. Leavis. Some Marxists introduced a new angle but only a very few of them did the job seriously.

The poets and writers of the 1930s, associated with papers like *Kallol,*
Parichaya, and others included men of considerable critical insights
but apart from producing occasional long review articles they did not
do much in this field. How far the fact that the medium of instruction
was English even at the school stage, and that social prestige and prospects
were linked with mastery of that language prevented Bengali intelligentsia
from taking more than a dilettante interest in serious Bengali writing, is
a big problem that requires further investigation.[39]

In the field of the sciences, too, the 1920s and 1930s produced the
first generation of men taught by the postgraduate science faculties in
Calcutta, Allahabad, Bombay, and Lahore, but so far as the basic sciences
went, not all of them were uniformly strong. Those boasting reasonably
strong departments in a particular branch attracted people from all
over India, of whom a fortunate few acquired further training abroad.
In India, struggling hard for the minimum facilities, some gave up the
effort to keep abreast when the odds were so heavily against them. Many
mathematicians and statisticians were rescued from utter frustration
and stagnation by the creation of the Indian Statistical Institute. But most
of such institutions founded by voluntary efforts in these years suffered
from poverty and sometimes from too close a personal identification
with the founding father, which was not always beneficial for further
academic growth.[40]

IV

On the eve of the Second World War, some of the urban academic centres could boast of having reasonably good institutes for the diffusion
of a fixed body of learning, a few schools of research of a pedestrian
sort in a few disciplines, and a very small number of scholars trying hard
to be in step with the world movement of knowledge. Economic changes
that started from 1940, and the rapid political changes after 1945 played
havoc with the development of academic disciplines. Unplanned uncoordinated quantitative inflation of centres of higher education led to
a general lowering of standards all round.

The filtration theory had rested on the assumption that there would
develop certain institutes of advanced study which would compare with
the best in the world and which would set standards for others to follow.

The preceding account has shown that few approaching this ideal existed in 1947; those that could have made some claim rested on weak foundations. Instead of strengthening these foundations the new leaders of India, under various pressures and assumptions, pursued policies which dissipated resources and which aggravated the damage done to the academic profession by the ravages of inflation and partition. Leaders of independent India were aware of the importance of developing higher learning and encouraging scholarship, especially in the basic sciences, but in implementation their record is, on the whole, one of failure.

Governmental thinking continued, for fourteen years, which is more than half a generation, to be influenced by certain obnoxious value systems of the bureaucracy of the British Raj when these were fast becoming irrelevant and injurious to the academic community. Salaries may have been standardised between universities but they were not upgraded until 1961, while ever since 1947 the expansion of governmental functions created more well-paid jobs in increasing numbers for routine administrative duties. There was an exodus from colleges and universities in the decade immediately after independence—the two special recruitments to the services undertaken in the late 1940s and the mid-1950s assisting the process. As brighter men did not join the profession in the same period, unless they were highly idealistic, the proportion of substandard staff increased. At the same time, with the coming of mass democracy and the incessant competition of party leaders to satisfy emerging social groups with the loaves and fishes of office, non-academic considerations played a part in government policy towards universities in some provinces, as for example in parts of Uttar Pradesh and Madras. This snapped whatever academic traditions some of these places had tried to build up, and the good men who felt pushed into a corner migrated to newer university centres or old ones under new leadership like Baroda (1948), Delhi (now under Sir Maurice Gwyer), and Aligarh (under Dr Zakir Hussain). Very soon, in the field of sciences, they were to migrate abroad.

While independence did release a lot of bottled-up energy among the intelligentsia, many men of the younger generation with an academic bent who did not leave the profession or wanted to join it found that while opportunities were not lacking abroad, some of the opportunities provided by the Indian government were misconceived. Scientific research institutes set up with a lot of investment in building, etc. were divorced from teaching work and organised in a hierarchical manner. By the beginning of the 1960s there were serious doubts among leading scientists as to whether this had been wise. In October 1963 Professor D.S. Kothari said: 'The experience of more than a century . . . has clearly shown that teaching and research flourish best in combination: in isolation they both wither . . . Every endeavour should be made . . . to raise the proportion of small and modest laboratories doing big work to big laboratories doing small work.'[41]

The hierarchic pattern of values persisted in maintaining pay differentials between the scales of schoolteachers and college and university teachers, regardless of the fact that each of these functions have their intrinsic worth and should be rated in order to get the right men. A genuine scholar specialising in a particular field in a university department does not mind if schoolteachers are paid as much as he is as long as people who are really fit to be good schoolteachers are not, *faute de mieux*, appointed to do specialised work at the postgraduate level. With the expansion of the number of universities in the late 1950s, and before the revision of pay scales began to have any effect on the profession, the combined influences of political pressure, increase in the number of substandard staff, and the alternative attraction at home and abroad led to the fossilisation of old centres which lost their men to new places. As yet there has been little net addition to the intrinsic quality of scholarship in India.

Of course, since research has become fashionable and the universities are in the grip of 'Ph.Ditis' there has been, in the midst of a great deal of pedestrian and a lot of third-rate work, some useful research of a very high order—indicating that the talented Indian academic, given a minimum degree of facility, can grow in intellectual stature. Economics, under the stimulus of planning and developing, has been drawing more and more talented men. Science and technology are doing so on a larger scale, but, as mentioned earlier, the best work apparently is being produced abroad. In the other disciplines, except for individual departments here and there (like medieval Indian history at Aligarh), there has not been any all-round advancement. In the absence of improved techniques of secondary education, the pool of creative talent has remained fixed in proportion to the number being educated, but there has been a shift in the preference pattern of the bright student from law, language and history to the sciences and economics. So in the former group of disciplines there has been a dearth of talent to follow up and develop the lines of inquiry which an older genxeration of scholars, for all their limitations, had opened up.

V

Looking at Indian academic standards and scholarly values today, we have to confess that to a large extent quality has been sacrificed to quantitative inflation and non-academic pressures. Democratic countries which have successfully combined the maintenance and enhancement of standards with the expansion of the number receiving higher education have done so only because, prior to the emergence of mass democracy, certain academic centres had been able to develop their own traditions and values on a stable foundation. In India, scholarly research in fields other than classical studies started only at the beginning of the twentieth century and got institutionalised only in the 1910s with the development of postgraduate centres. The development of a large number of universities in the 1920s made a heavy demand on the relatively small band of Indian scholars. Some of the older universities in these years gave opportunities to individual scholars and a few departments to grow in academic stature, but the institutions remained burdened with the administration of a wide area of affiliated colleges, and did not have enough resources. Some of the new centres were failures. Political issues, as in 1900–6, bedevilled an objective assessment of the problems of the universities—nationalists and bureaucrats, Hindu communalists and Muslim Leaguers playing their parts. Each extension of the franchise generated pressure to increase institutions of higher learning, which became overwhelming after 1947.

On top of the arrested development of the 1920s and 1930s came the convulsions of wartime inflation, riots and partition. New avenues drained away talented men. Foundations, never firm, were severely shaken, precisely when there was an urgent need to give immediate first-aid to existing centres of learning and not develop grandiose schemes. By now a generation is about to enter the university portals, none who were born before 1947. Will these hungry sheep be properly fed? Most likely their diet will be barely nutritious and their degree a debased currency. Yet fifteen years of economic development have opened up exciting possibilities of tapping the best talents among both the cosmopolitan English-speaking elite as well as the educated vernacular-speaking groups in the states. But as long as genuinely strong centres of learning are not developed by fighting whatever vested interests stand in the way, Indian intellectuals will include a few brilliant scholars, a large number of dilettantes, and far too many charlatans.

NOTES

1. Hindu College was founded in 1817 in Calcutta, Elphinstone Institution in Bombay in 1824.
2. Margaret L. Cormack, *She Who Rides a Peacock* (Bombay, 1961), p. 31.
3. Humayun Kabir, *Education in New India* (1956), p. 98.
4. I am indebted for this information to Dr Sukhamoy Chakravarti, Sir Shankar Lal Professor of Mathematical Economics, Delhi University.
5. Sir Charles Firth, 'Historical Research and University Teaching', *Report of Proceedings of the Second Congress of the Universities of the British Empire* (1921), p. 348.
6. Ibid.
7. The main sources for this and other statements on the government education services are, unless otherwise stated, the minutes of evidence of (1) the Royal Commission on Public Services in India, 1886–7 (Aitchison Commission), Education Appendix and (2) Royal Commission on Public Services in India, 1913 (Islington Commission), Education Appendix (*C.* 7908).
8. This is the burden of the evidence of a number of well-qualified European teachers before the Aitchison Commission.
9. See evidence of G. Wathen before the Islington Commission.
10. C.H. Tawney to the Officiating Secretary of the Government of Bengal, 9 May 1892 (letter no. 3757), (reprinted in *Selections from the Educational Records*, p. 36).
11. This is the burden of the evidence of W.H. Sharp, Director of Public Instruction (DPI) Bombay before the Islington Commission in 1913. Minutes of Evidence, Q. 84, 340, p. 208.
12. Patrick Geddes, *Life and Work of Sir Jagadish C. Bose* (London, 1920), p. 41.
13. G.V. Kurkare to the Principal, Elphinstone College, Bombay, 25 April 1883 (NAI, Home Education, July 1883, no. 49, p. 4.)

14. See the note of W. Wordsworth, Principal, Elphinstone College, in forwarding the letter cited in the previous note to the DPI Bombay (same file as above).

15. The origin of the two-thirds pay, which started in the education service in 1881, can be traced in a letter of Lord Ripon, as President of the Council, to the Secretary of State for India, 6 December 1880. In asking for more posts to employ natives, he suggested, for reasons of economy which would have appealed to a cabinet headed by Gladstone, that the two-thirds scale of pay would suffice, 'it being extravagant to pay Native Professors in their own country at the rate which is required to secure University Graduates of European birth' (Govt. of India, Department of Finance and Commerce, Letter no. 404 of 1880, dated 6 December 1880).

16. Government of Bombay, *Review of Education in Bombay States*, 1855–1955 (Poona, 1958), p. 259.

17. Islington Commission, Education Appendix (*c.* 7908), Minutes of evidence, Q. 83, 635.

18. Evidence of Prafulla Chandra Ray before the Islington Commission, *op.cit.*, p. 140.

19. The New English School was founded in Poona in 1880 and the Deccan Educational Society in 1884.

20. Sir Goorodas Banerji admitted, in his convocation address to Calcutta University in 1890, that so far little contribution had been made to the advancement of knowledge (A.N. Basu ed., *Sir Goorodas Centenary Commemoration Volume* Calcutta, 1948, p. 36).

21. See his evidence before the Aitchison Commission in 1887.

22. Geddes, *op.cit.*, pp. 34f. Also see evidence of C.F. Andrews before the Islington Commission.

23. University of Calcutta, *Hundred Years of the University of Calcutta* (Calcutta, 1957), pp. 163ff.

24. This is based on a survey of Calcutta University question papers for these examinations in English, logic, and history for the years 1899 and 1925 and a few ones in between. Also see the admission of an admirer of Sir Ashutosh in Dineshchandra Sen, *Ashutosh-Smriti-katha* (in Bengali) (Calcutta, 1936), pp. 94–9.

25. *Hundred Years of the University of Calcutta*, pp. 190, 195ff.

26. This is based on Dineshchandra Sen, *op.cit.*, and conversations with a large number of university teachers who recall those days, some of whom stayed in Calcutta and liked it, and some of whom went to other universities.

27. Anath Nath Basu, *University Education in India, Past and Present,* (Calcutta, 1944), p. 70.

28. Based on a comparison of Bombay papers of the late 1890s and the mid-1920s.

29. J. Cunningham's chapter on 'Education', in L.S.S. O'Malley (ed.), *Modern India and the West* (Oxford, 1941), p. 174.

30. Interview with Professor Apurba Kumar Chandra, IES (Retd), who had taught in mofussil colleges as well as at Calcutta (4 January 1966). Supplemented by information from professional men who had worked or had been taught at these colleges.

31. See graph facing page 265 in *Review of Education in Bombay State— 1855–1955* (Poona, 1958).

32. Private information from former members of the Education Service and others.

33. It is said by Professor Chandra that he saw a letter from Sir Michael Sadler to Sir Philip Hartog (then vice-chancellor of Dacca University) in which the former had written that he would prefer appointing a man from Oxford who had gone through the course of an Honours School and got a 4th class than someone who had done only a D.Phil. there and specialised narrowly (interview on 4 January 1966). If this can be verified from the Hartog Papers it does indicate an exaggerated view of the Oxford Honours Schools, which the author of this paper has been through.

34. Discussion with a number of senior teachers of science has elicited the admission that while Professor M.N. Saha's work in Allahabad was very good for that place, and Dr. J.C. Ghosh and Professor S.N. Bose enriched Dacca, Calcutta would have grown more in scientific studies had their talents been pooled with those of Sir C.V. Raman, Dr J.N. Mukherjee, Professor D.M. Bose and others who stayed in Calcutta.

35. I am indebted for this information to specialists in ancient Indian history.

36. This is based partly on my own reading and recollections of history curricula of student days and discussions with fellow history teachers.

37. Private information from a number of economist friends spanning two generations. Also see Bhabatosh Datta, 'Indian Universities and Economic Research', *Journal of University Education*, vol. I, no. 1 (1962), pp. 33ff.

38. Two of the founding fathers of the school of Bengali literature made their names in literary history and the collection of texts, namely, Dinesh-chandra Sen, who wrote *Vanga—Sahitya Parichaya* (Calcutta, 1914) and *Vaishnava Literature of Medieval Bengal* (1917) among his main works; Sushil Kumar De, who wrote *Bengali Literature in the Nineteenth Century* (Calcutta, 1919). These were followed by a second stream of scholarship of the same sort like Suniti Kumar Chatterji's pioneering *Origins and*

Development of the Bengali Language (Calcutta, 1926) and Sukumar Sen's *History of Brajabuli Literature* (Calcutta, 1935).

39. It was not until 1940 that the medium of instruction and examination up to the school-leaving stage was changed to the vernacular.
40. Information obtained from conversations with senior and younger university men in these disciplines.
41. D.S. Kothari, *Science and the Universities* (Calcutta, Indian Science Congress Association, Fifteenth session proceedings, 1963), pp. 11, 13.

PARTHA SARATHI GUPTA: LIST OF WRITINGS (OTHER THAN BOOK REVIEWS)

1951 'Can Intelligent Students Today Afford to be Good Students?', *Presidency College Patrika*

1960 'The History of the Amalgamated Society of Railway Servants, 1871–1913', D.Phil. thesis, University of Oxford

1961 'The Modern Period', Symposium on the Historian and National Integration, Indian History Congress, Delhi

1965 'Concepts and Interpretations of Modern European History', J.C. Webster (ed.), *Study of History and College History Teaching*

1965 'India—the British Period, 1757–1947', Ministry of Commerce, Government of India

1966 'The Quality of Life and Indian Scholarship', Delhi

1966 'Railway Trade Unionism in Britain, 1880–1990', *Economic History Review*, 25, XIX

1967 'The Scope and Methods of British Labour History, Indian Institute of Advanced Study, Shimla

1968 'The Social Roots of Political radicalism in Britain in the Early and Middle Victorian Era', *Proceedings of Seminar on Non-Indian History*, Allahabad

1969 'Napoleon III: An Essay in Historiography', Department of History, Delhi University

1971 'British Labour and the Indian Left, 1919–39', B.R. Nanda (ed.), *Socialism in India*, Delhi

1971 'Secularism and the Indian National Movement', Shimla

1972 'The Perennial Quest', *Illustrated Weekly*, Bombay, 2 January

1973 'The British Raj and the Communal Question, September, 1939–January 1940', *Indian History Congress Proceedings*

1974 'Notes on the Origin and Structuring of an Industrial Labour Force in India 1880–1920', R.S. Sharma (ed.), *Indian Society: Historical Probings: Essays in Memory of D.D. Kosambi*

1975   'Post-War Germany: Confrontation to Coexistence', Max Mueller Bhawan Seminar, Delhi

1975   *Imperialism and the British Labour Movement 1914–64*, London

1976   'The Zionist Lobby in the British Labour Party', *Indian History Congress Proceedings*

1976   'The Decline and Fall of the British Empire', *Indian History Congress Proceedings*, Sectional Presidential Address

1977   'Indo-British Relations One Year after Independence', *Indian Historical Records Commission Proceedings*

1978   'The Theory and History of Economic Imperialism: Reflections on British Imperialism, 1895–1914', Indo-GDR Seminar, Berlin

1979   Edited, *Britain Ka Itihas*, Delhi

1982   'The Army, Politics and Constitutional Change in India 1919–39', GDR Seminar, Delhi University

1983   Edited, *Europe Ka Itihas*, Delhi

1983   Edited, *Adhunik Paschim Ka Uday*, Delhi

1983   'Imperialism and the Labour Governments of 1945–51', J.M. Winter (ed.), *The Working Class in Modern British History*, Cambridge

1983   'An Association Recreated', special issue on the Commonwealth, *Economic Times*, Delhi, 19 November

1983   'British Strategic and Economic Priorities during the Negotiations for the Transfer of Power in South Asia 1945–47', *Bangladesh Historical Studies*, VII

1984   'From Dependency to Freedom', *Indian and Foreign Review*, vol. 21, nos. 20 and 21

1987   'State and Business in India and the Age of Discriminating Protection', D. Tripathi (ed.), *State and Business in India*, Delhi

1987   'Imperial Strategy and the Transfer of Power 1939–51', A.K. Gupta (ed.), *Myth and Reality—The Struggle for Freedom in India*, Delhi

1988   'Music and Political Consciousness (Regional, Pan-Indian, Communal): A Critical Study of D.L. Roy and Nazrul Islam', Nehru Memorial Library Occasional Papers, 2nds, XV

1988   'Recent Western Historiography on Capitalist Imperialism', Indo-Soviet Seminar on Colonialism and Capitalism, Delhi

1989   'The Mixed Economy System: The UK Labour Party's Experience', B.L. Agarwal (ed.), *Alternative Economic Structures*, Shimla

1989   'Historiography of the French Revolution', Indo-French Seminar, Delhi

1989   'Federalism and Provincial Autonomy and Devices of Imperial Control', Aparna Basu (ed.), *Imperialism, Nationalism and Regionalism in Canadian and Modern Indian History*, Delhi

1990   'From Ethiopia to Singapore-Equivocation in British Strategy in India', *Storia e Dossier*, Anno V, no. 43, Rome

1992   'India in Commonwealth Defence, 1947–56, Seminar on 'India, the first ten years', Texas

1992   'The "New World"—Historians' Perspectives', Colloquium on 'Meeting of Cultures, 1492–1992', Delhi

1992   'How the Raj Perceived the Threat from the INA during the War', Delhi

1993   'E.P. Thompson 1924–93', *Indian History Congress Proceedings*

1994   'Three Studies in Western European Democratic Socialism 1960–70' (Britain, France, Netherlands), study prepared for ICSSR/IDPAD

1995   *Radio and the Raj, 1921–47*, S.G. Deuskar Lectures on Indian History and Culture, Calcutta

1996   'Music and Communalism in Bengal', *Indo-British Review*, Madras

1996   'British Onslaught in the Aftermath of the August Movement and the Battle in the Law Courts Against It', Federation Hall Society, *India: Challenges and Responses*, Calcutta

1997   Edited, *Towards Freedom, 1943 and 1944*, 3 vols, Delhi

1998   Script for 'Vande Mataram—The History of the Song', Akashvani, 15 August 1998

1998   *Identity—Formation and Nation-states*, Presidential Address, Indian History Congress

1999   'Of Shared Days with Amartya', *India International Centre Quarterly*, Spring Issue

1999   'March of Nationalism', *India International Centre Quarterly*, Monsoon Issue

1999   'Paradoxes of Partition', Delhi

2000   'Who Divided the Bengalees?', Amrik Singh (ed.), *The Partition in Retrospect*, Delhi

INDEX